LEADERSHIP EDUCATION 100

TRADITIONS, WELLNESS, AND FOUNDATIONS OF CITIZENSHIP

Excerpts taken from:

AGS Life Skills Health Student Text

Civics: Government and Economics in Action, Student Edition
by James E. Davis, Phyllis Fernlund, and Peter Woll

PEARSON

Cover photos appear courtesy of:

© 14ktgold/Fotolia.com; Michael Wetzel/US Air Force JROTC; © Rfsole/Fotolia.com; © Michael Flippo/
Fotolia.com

Excerpts taken from:

AGS Life Skills Health Student Text
Copyright © 2006 by Pearson Education, Inc.
Published by Pearson AGS Globe
Saint Paul, MN 55126

Civics: Government and Economics in Action, Student Edition
by James E. Davis, Phyllis Fernlund, and Peter Woll
Copyright © 2009 by Pearson Education, Inc.
Published by Prentice Hall
Upper Saddle River, New Jersey 07458

Pearson Learning Solutions, 501 Boylston Street, Suite 900, Boston, MA 02116
A Pearson Education Company
www.pearsoned.com

Printed in the United States of America

1 2 3 4 5 6 7 8 9 10 V057 19 18 17 16 15

000200010271747073

JH/KE

ISBN 10: 1-256-96280-5
ISBN 13: 978-1-256-96280-9

Contents

Contents

LESSON 3 The Constitution of the United States 436

LESSON 4 Interpreting the Bill of Rights and Other Amendments 474

LESSON 5 US National Government 500

Preface

Leadership Education 100: Traditions, Wellness, and Foundations of Citizenship is the first component of Junior Reserve Officers Training Corps (JROTC) leadership education. It is intended for students who are entering the JROTC program and beginning their high school studies. This textbook, and the course it has been designed for, will help prepare you for success as a member of JROTC and a high school student.

You will be introduced to the history, organization, mission, goals, and objectives of JROTC for the Air Force, Army, Navy, Marine Corps, and Coast Guard. You will learn how the military uniform embodies a tradition of proper grooming and uniform wear for today's male and female cadets. You'll look at key military customs and courtesies, and learn how to project the positive attitude and discipline expected of cadets and leaders by examining the principles and practice of ethics, values, and morals.

You'll also learn study skills and note taking, as tools for academic success. You will learn how to be emotionally, mentally, and physically healthy. Avoiding and preventing violence in today's society will also be covered, including how to recognize types of bullying and how to be an advocate for preventing violence. You will learn about healthy living, physical fitness, and making safe, drug-free, and responsible decisions. By examining the negative effects of air and water pollution, you'll learn what you can do to keep our environment safe.

You will be introduced to civics and our national government, including a historical understanding of the American flag and other important national symbols. You will learn how the Constitution protects our rights and freedom as American citizens.

All chapters and lessons contain full-color diagrams and other visual information. Each lesson includes a "Quick Write" exercise at the start of each lesson. A "Learn About" box tells you what you should take away from the lesson. A vocabulary list ensures that students will understand the terms they encounter throughout the text.

At selected points in each lesson, "Keys to Leadership" and other learning aids highlight useful information, including stories from people who have been successful applying these keys. Each lesson is followed by "Checkpoints" to allow cadets to review what they have learned. An "Applying Your Learning" section at each lesson's end presents one or more discussion questions to further reinforce what students have learned.

The text has five chapters, each divided into multiple lessons.

Chapter 1: Introduction to JROTC Programs explains the purpose and structure of the nation's JROTC programs. In this chapter, you will discuss the history and current organization of each JROTC program, including the lines of responsibility and authority. You will learn about the military uniform, including how to properly wear the uniform and meet the appearance and grooming standards expected of a cadet.

You'll also learn to recognize the different US military ranks and grades. You'll learn military customs and courtesies such as saluting, many based on historic practices, which distinguish the JROTC as an important part of our nation's traditions.

Through understanding JROTC as an environment that builds leadership and good citizenship through respect for others, you'll learn how to project a positive attitude and self-discipline. You will consider how to apply ethical and moral concepts, including those of the military services and various cultures. The chapter's final lesson will help build your social skills through proper behavior, personal hygiene, and grooming. You'll learn how to plan and participate in military functions, especially Military Balls, Dining-Ins, and Dining-Outs.

Chapter 2: Personal Behavior focuses on success in school, personal life, and community. You'll learn effective methods for taking notes and studying. You'll also learn to manage stress in school and elsewhere by recognizing its main causes, positive versus negative stress, and stress' effects on the body. Stress-handling strategies, including time management, can make you more productive in all aspects of your life. The chapter then covers how to make positive decisions on your behavior through goal setting and effective communications—important for success and leadership in today's high-tech environment.

You will find out how to recognize emotional problems, and how to seek professional mental health care for yourself and others. You'll then learn about factors that contribute to teen violence in our society, from bullying and cyberbullying to gangs and drug use. You'll identify ways to deal with violence in schools and elsewhere, including ways of preventing bullying, rape, and other sexual violence.

Chapter 3: Be Health Smart first examines your body systems by identifying the key components of the human body. You will explore the functions of the skeletal, muscular, circulatory and respiratory systems, as well as those of the nervous, digestive, and waste systems. Applying this knowledge, you'll learn how to make healthful dietary decisions. You will then consider the importance of physical fitness and the benefits of an active lifestyle. You will also consider how body image, eating, and physical activity affect health. To reduce risks of physical injury during exercise, you will identify safety concerns for participating in sports, and consider the risks of performance-enhancing drugs (PEDs).

This chapter also covers first aid for treating yourself or others in a medical emergency. You'll learn how to recognize and treat common emergencies, from sprains, choking, and shock to heat-related illnesses. You'll also learn how cardiopulmonary resuscitation (CPR) and the Automated External Defibrillator (AED) can save lives.

Chapter 4: Making Safe, Drug-Free Decisions focuses on staying mentally and physically fit by avoiding illegal drugs. Understanding how medicines differ from drugs will help you see how substances can be used for good or harm. You will compare drug misuse with drug abuse, and learn the effects and dangers of popular drugs. Cadets will study the history of tobacco, the harmful substances it contains, and its terrible costs to society. You'll learn how to avoid tobacco use, and proven ways to quit the habit.

You'll also study alcohol's effects, and why it can harmful. You'll consider why some teens drink alcohol, examining how what teens may say can be different from the truth about drinking. Finally, you'll learn refusal techniques to overcome peer pressure to drink, and review the healthy alternatives to drinking alcohol.

The chapter's final lesson considers how the environment relates to your health. You'll study different types of pollution, including air, water, land, and other forms. You'll examine aspects of the greenhouse effect, and learn about methods of preventing and reducing pollution, including laws and community actions, as well as things you can do individually to make the environment healthier.

Chapter 5: Foundations of United States Citizenship opens with a history of the American flag, and discusses the courtesies rendered to the flag, the National Anthem, the Pledge of Allegiance, and the American's Creed. You'll learn about the Great Seal of the United States and the military services' seals. You will consider the role of civics in society and the need for effective government. You will study the nature of citizenship and how the naturalization process grants this lifelong privilege to those who were not born citizens. The lesson will then cover the duties and responsibilities of citizenship.

You will then learn about the fundamental document of our government, the United States Constitution, by studying its parts and what they mean. You will also cover the process of amending the Constitution and be able to explain how the Constitution is interpreted. You will look at each amendment to identify ways the Bill of Rights and other amendments to the Constitution protect the rights of all Americans, in all possible situations.

The final lesson of this chapter covers the three branches of the national government. By analyzing the functions of the legislative, executive, and judicial branches, you will understand the concept of checks and balances. By looking at the political system in operation in the House of Representatives and the Senate, you will be able to see how Congress works to meet the nation's needs and interests.

At the end of the textbook, you will find a glossary defining all the vocabulary words and telling you which page each term appears on. You'll also find an index organized by subject at the end of the text, as well as a list of references.

This textbook will increase your awareness of the knowledge, skills, and attitudes you'll need to succeed in your high school career and beyond. Here at the beginning of your high school career, recognize that you are one of our nation's most treasured assets: a citizen of character and a future leader. Through applying the knowledge and skills you will learn as a student and cadet over the next four years, you'll make the future a brighter one for you, your friends, your community, and your nation. Every one of us involved in the production of this book wishes you the best throughout your time in high school, and in JROTC.

LEADERSHIP EDUCATION 100

http://www.pearsoncustom.com/us/af_le100/

Contact Your Instructor for Website Login Information

Acknowledgments

The AFJROTC mission is to develop citizens of character dedicated to serving their nation and communities. This new edition of *Leadership Education 100: Traditions, Wellness, and Foundations of Citizenship* was developed to meet the needs of students beginning their high school studies and their roles as JROTC cadets. Revision of this textbook is based in part on suggestions from JROTC instructors, who are responsible for implementing this curriculum.

The Jeanne M. Holm Center for Officer Accessions and Citizen Development (Holm Center) Curriculum Directorate team involved in the production effort was under the direction of Dr. Charles Nath III, EdD, Director of Curriculum for the Holm Center at Maxwell Air Force Base, Alabama and Ms. Vickie Helms, MEd, Chief, AFJROTC Curriculum. Special thanks to Ms. Linda Sackie, MACI, instructional systems specialist, who was the primary Air Force editor and reviewer for the LE 100 instructor guide and companion website. A special acknowledgment goes to Mr. Michael Wetzel, MEd, an instructional systems specialist and Academic Credit Liaison for the Holm Center Curriculum, who was the primary Air Force contributor, researcher, editor, and reviewer for the LE 100 textbook. We commend Michael for his persistent efforts, commitment, and thorough review in producing the best academic materials possible for JROTC cadets worldwide.

We are deeply indebted to Master Sergeant Larry Smith, USAF (Ret), Lieutenant Colonel Gary Essray, USAF (Ret), and the cadets of AFJROTC unit AL-951, Prattville High School, Prattville, Alabama; Master Sergeant William Poe, USAF (Ret), and the cadets of AFJROTC unit WV-20021, Jefferson High School, Shenandoah, West Virginia. Because of their support and contributions, this revision will benefit all JROTC programs.

We would also like to express our gratitude to the Pearson publishing team, including Jacquelyn Hodgman and Rich Gomes for project and production management; Mia Saunders, of Gamut+Hue, for design and art direction; John Seely and Seth Morgan for digital media coordination; and Abe Chang and Kathryn Bass for account management. Thanks also to the Deerpath authoring team, led by Dr. W. Dees Stallings, PhD and principal writer-researcher Bill Noxon, for all their hard work on this textbook revision. Our appreciation also goes to Erin Kelmereit, chief developer of the Instructor Guide.

All the people identified above came together on this project and combined their efforts to form one great team, providing 21st-century learning materials to all our schools. We believe this curriculum will continue the precedent of providing world-class curriculum materials. Our goal is to create materials that provide a solid foundation for educating future members of society to be productive and responsible citizens.

CHAPTER 1

© 14ktgold/Fotolia.com

Introduction to JROTC Programs

Chapter Outline

"Ask not what your country can do for you—ask what you can do for your country."

President John F. Kennedy

LESSON 1

Organization of the JROTC

Quick Write

Describe two things that you have done that have helped you become a better citizen, and have helped prepare you for success in life and service to others.

Learn About

- the history of the nation's Junior ROTC programs
- the organization of Junior ROTC programs
- the lines of responsibility and authority in Junior ROTC programs

"Being involved in AFJROTC made high school so much fun and enjoyable for me. It's interesting to look back at myself in 9th grade and see how much I've changed, grown, and developed after graduating—all because of joining JROTC."

Lindsey Clem, freshman Air Force ROTC cadet at West Virginia University

Reflections of a Recent AFJROTC Cadet

JOINING AFJROTC my freshman year in high school was one of the best decisions I've made in my lifetime. I had experiences and made friends that will last a lifetime. I had the best instructors I could have ever asked for, and the unit became a second family to me pretty quickly.

AFJROTC helped me get out of my comfort zone, become a leader, and open my eyes to new things. Throughout those four years, I experienced things that I never would have experienced on my own, and I'm so glad I got the opportunities that I did.

AFJROTC and my instructors are one reason I'm the person that I am today. I learned so many skills that I have used repeatedly since graduating and moving out into the real world. AFJROTC helped me learn how to hold myself to a higher standard than most people. If I could go back, there wouldn't be one thing that I would do differently.

Being involved in AFJROTC made high school so much fun and enjoyable for me. It's interesting to look back at myself in 9th grade and see how much I've changed, grown, and developed after graduating—all because of joining JROTC. I became someone my family was proud of. I love the person that I am, and AFJROTC taught me to always strive to be better than the person you were yesterday.

I'm now a freshman Air Force ROTC cadet at West Virginia University Detachment 915, majoring in Criminology. Because of my major, I didn't get a scholarship right out of high school. However, taking AFROTC as an elective at college and working towards an in-college AFROTC scholarship is a great way to go.

On one of my first days in AFROTC at college, they sat us down and said "Look at the person to your right and look at the person to your left. These people will more than likely become your best friends over the course of the next four to five years." When I heard that, my mind automatically went back to high school because my best friends were people I was in AFJROTC with.

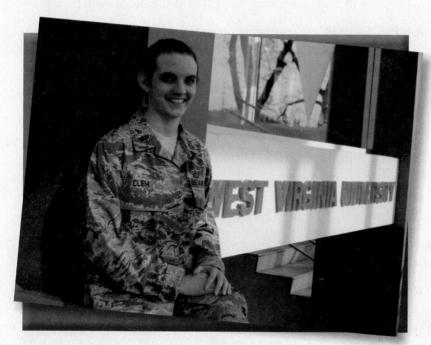

Lindsey Clem is a recent Air Force JROTC cadet, now attending West Virginia University.
Courtesy of Lindsey Clem

Vocabulary

- organization
- organizational chart

The History of the Nation's Junior ROTC Programs

As a cadet in the Junior Reserve Officer Training Corps (JROTC), you are part of an honored national tradition. You are among those valued young people who are being prepared to be tomorrow's leaders. By joining JROTC, you will gain tremendous insight into a citizenship program that will give you a unique educational experience. It will also make you aware of your rights, duties, and privileges as a citizen.

Through JROTC, you will develop self-discipline and self-confidence. The leadership skills you learn will allow you to meet the challenges of adulthood successfully. Your instructors will be experienced retired officers or enlisted personnel from the Air Force, Army, Navy, Marine Corps, and Coast Guard.

Today's JROTC has evolved and grown over almost 200 years. As the timeline shows, the concept of building citizenship, character, and service to our nation and communities evolved first at colleges, and then at high schools, into today's JROTC programs.

Important Events in the Growth of the Junior ROTC

1820 ***Norwich, Vermont*****. First purely technical and military school** in the United States for training students in citizen soldiery, named the American Literary, Scientific, and Military Academy. Today, it is known as Norwich University. The school still combines military and civilian studies to produce educated citizens.

Founder: Army Captain Alden Partridge.

Goal: To educate students in both academic subjects and the art of war.

1911 ***Cheyenne, Wyoming*****. First JROTC program**, established as a merger of high school education with noncompulsory military training.

Founder: Army Lieutenant Edgar R. Steevers, first to organize a JROTC program, who believed that military training could help create better citizens.

Goal: To teach young men the advantages of a strong body and a clean mind, self-control and restraint, and civic duties and responsibilities.

1916 **The US Army formally adopts JROTC** in response to the National Defense Act of 1916.

Goal: To authorize a junior course for non-college military schools, high schools, and non-preparatory schools.

1917 ***Leavenworth, Kansas*****. The first officially established JROTC unit** under the 1916 National Defense Act is organized at Leavenworth High School.

1964 **The Reserve Officer Training Corps Vitalization Act** allows JROTC to be expanded to all branches of the military.

Goal: To direct the secretaries of each military branch to establish and maintain JROTC units at public and private secondary schools across the nation.

The 1964 ROTC Vitalization Act set the national criteria for schools to begin JROTC programs. It established goals and policies based on earlier successes at individual schools. It focused especially on building good citizenship. The basic requirement was that schools applying for a JROTC program had to agree to provide at least three years of military-supported instruction. For a program to be approved, the law required a minimum enrollment of 100 physically fit students, or 10 percent of the student body, whichever was less.

Since then, the military services have applied some of their own criteria to meet the needs of different high schools and their students. Generally, schools interested in a JROTC program must apply and meet criteria set by each military service. Schools are chosen to ensure fair and equitable coverage nationwide. Students must be US citizens and enrolled in the ninth grade or higher. The law also authorizes the services to provide equipment and uniforms.

The Organization of Junior ROTC Programs

All JROTC programs develop cadets' citizenship, character, leadership traits, and responsibility. Cadets participate in community service, drill and ceremonies, and traditional educational programs. They have uniform inspections. They study military history and customs, and take part in fitness training. Today, more than 3,000 high schools nationwide and overseas offer Air Force, Army, Navy, Marine Corps, and Coast Guard JROTC classes. All JROTC instructors are certified by their training commands. They serve as teachers and mentors to the young cadets.

While in the program, you will learn a wide range of life skills for success in school, work, and family. You will participate in social events, drill competition, field trips, and other special activities. You will wear the uniform as directed by your service instructor. Most importantly, you will learn to be a productive and valued citizen in your community.

JROTC Programs—By Service

Below are summaries of the individual JROTC programs. Each program offers an academically sound curriculum combined with extracurricular activities suited to the culture of each service.

Air Force JROTC (AFJROTC)

Mission. To develop citizens of character dedicated to serving their nation and communities.

History. The AFJROTC began in 1966 with just 20 units. It has since grown to almost 900 units worldwide. More than 120,000 cadets are now enrolled in the program, taught and mentored by some 1,900 instructors.

Courtesy of the US Air Force Junior ROTC

In the beginning, only young men were allowed as cadets. However, that changed in 1972 when young women were allowed to enroll in the program. Since then, the number of women in AFJROTC has increased dramatically, from 9 percent to over 40 percent of the cadet corps.

Objectives. The objectives of the AFJROTC are to:

- Educate and prepare high school cadets in citizenship and life skills
- Promote community service
- Instill a sense of responsibility
- Develop character and self-discipline through education and instruction in air and space fundamentals—supporting the Air Force's core values of "Integrity First, Service Before Self, and Excellence in All We Do"

The overall goals of AFJROTC are to instill the values of citizenship, service to the United States, personal responsibility, and a sense of accomplishment.

Curriculum. The AFJROTC's curriculum is a three- or four-year program offered to high school students in grades 9–12. The curriculum includes aerospace science, leadership education, and wellness components.

While focusing on the practice of good citizenship and service to the community and nation, AFJROTC cadets can attend the most advanced courses in aerospace science in high schools today. Subjects include aviation history, the science of flight, and exploring space. Also covered are development of aerospace power, aerospace vehicles, rocketry, space programs, space technology, and the aerospace industry.

Leadership education includes Air Force heritage and traditions, military customs and courtesies, civics and citizenship, and the principles of management.

Students also cover a wide variety of practical subjects. These include study skills, personal responsibility, communication, individual and group behavior, and management. Health and fitness courses include first aid, wellness, and principles for healthy living. Lessons in personal financial literacy, college and career planning, and human relations help prepare cadets for life after high school.

Instructors. All AFJROTC instructors are retired Air Force commissioned and noncommissioned officers (NCOs). They serve as full-time employees of the host school. The Senior Aerospace Science Instructor (SASI) both teaches and has overall responsibility for the AFJROTC program at a school. The Aerospace Science Instructor (ASI) works for the SASI and teaches leadership education, for the most part. Both are trained in the latest instructional techniques and technologies through the AFJROTC Initial Instructor Course. The SASI and ASI supervise, teach, mentor, coach, and motivate cadets in all their courses and other activities.

Army JROTC (AJROTC)

Mission. To motivate young people to be better citizens.

Courtesy of the US Army Junior ROTC

History. The AJROTC came into being in 1916. Six units in high schools started operating with military equipment loaned from the federal government. Active duty soldiers were instructors. In 1964, the ROTC Vitalization Act opened JROTC up to the other services and replaced most of the active duty instructors with retirees who work for and are cost-shared by the schools.

AJROTC has evolved over the years into a character and leadership development program. It emphasizes citizenship, personal responsibility, lifelong learning, and individual success. AJROTC today has programs in 1,731 schools. Units are in every state in the nation and in American schools overseas. Cadet numbers have grown to 300,000. A minimum of 100 cadets, or 10 percent of the school's students in grades 9–12, are organized into a chain of command that makes up an AJROTC unit.

Objectives. The AJROTC program is designed to:

- Promote citizenship
- Develop leadership
- Develop critical and creative thinking skills
- Improve communications skills
- Improve health and physical fitness
- Strengthen positive self-motivation
- Provide a global awareness, including a historical perspective of military service
- Facilitate high school graduation

AJROTC cadets train to work as team members with common goals. The program encourages students to seek higher learning and to pursue careers in science, technology, engineering, and math.

Curriculum. The AJROTC core curriculum is divided into six major units: citizenship; leadership theory and application; foundation for success; wellness, fitness, and first aid; geography, map skills, and environmental awareness; and civics. These courses help prepare young men and women for adulthood and supplement what they learn in their regular high school classes.

In addition, students develop work and personal finance skills, and learn how to be strong writers and communicators.

The AJROTC curriculum is based on national standards, including performance-based, learner-centered education. Every classroom is equipped with leading edge technologies to teach, assess, and report student progress. Teachers are trained to use the technologies to develop students' academic, social, and emotional skills.

AJROTC learning extends beyond the classroom to include opportunities to solve problems that matter to cadets in their school, community, or society at large. Each lesson typically requires cadets to:

- Make a decision
- Perform a skill
- Solve a problem
- Create a product

Instructors. There are approximately 4,000 instructors in AJROTC classrooms. Two instructors, usually one retired officer and one noncommissioned officer, teach the curriculum. The Senior Army Instructor (SAI) is the officer in charge of the AJROTC Program. An NCO serves as the Army Instructor (AI). The SAI and/or AI supervise, mentor, coach, and motivate cadets in all their activities. Besides having state-of-the-art instructional techniques, AJROTC instructors serve as role models for maturing teenagers.

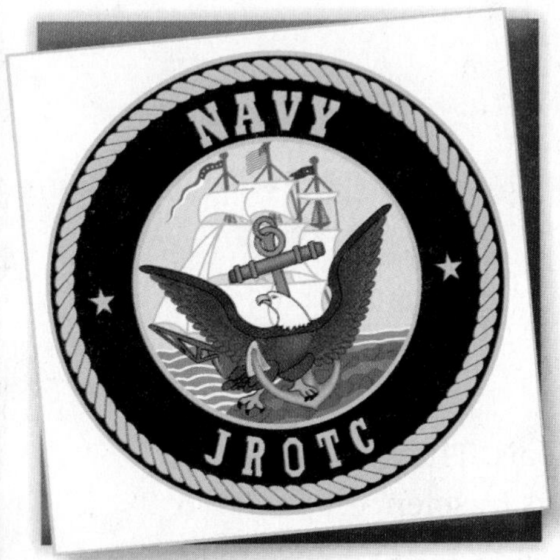

Courtesy of the US Navy Junior ROTC

Navy JROTC (NJROTC)

Mission. To instill in students the value of citizenship, service to the nation, personal responsibility, and a sense of accomplishment.

History. The Navy's first JROTC programs began in 1966. There are now almost 600 programs nationwide. There are more than 89,000 students enrolled, about 40 percent of them women. The NJROTC program is directed by the Naval Service Training Command, Citizenship Development Department, headquartered at Naval Air Station (NAS) Pensacola, Florida.

Objectives. The NJROTC seeks to:

- Promote patriotism
- Develop informed and responsible citizens
- Promote habits of orderliness and precision
- Develop a high degree of personal honor, self-reliance, individual discipline, and leadership

- Promote an understanding of the basic elements of and need for national security
- Develop respect for and an understanding of the need for authority in a democratic society
- Promote community service
- Provide incentives to live healthy and drug free
- Develop leadership potential
- Provide an alternative to destructive behavior and activities, such as gang involvement
- Promote high school completion
- Promote continuing education
- Provide information on the military services as a possible career

NJROTC emphasizes staying in school, graduating, and becoming responsible citizens. Cadets are urged to consider higher education, and to take part in community service. Other goals include promoting patriotism and understanding the need for national security.

Curriculum. The NJROTC's curriculum emphasizes developing citizenship and leadership. Leadership courses include theory and practice. An NJROTC unit is run by the cadets as a leadership laboratory where cadets rotate positions of leadership to accomplish a mission as a team.

There are Navy-specific courses in maritime heritage and naval history, as well as a look into military and international law, the significance of sea power, and fundamentals of naval operations. Cadets learn basic seamanship, navigation, shipboard organization, and weapons systems. They learn about the sciences that affect the naval service. These include meteorology, oceanography, astronomy, fundamentals of flight, radar, sound propagation in water, and electronics.

Cadets participate throughout the year in many hours of community service. There are also air rifle, academic, athletic, drill, and orienteering competitions. Cadets visit naval bases and engage in other activities. They also practice marksmanship and train in physical fitness. They also conduct close order drill, color guard, and parade ceremonies during school and community events.

Instructors. The almost 1,300 instructors in NJROTC are retired officers and NCOs. They come from the Navy, Marine Corps, and Coast Guard. The officer who is the head of a high school NJROTC program is called the Senior Naval Science Instructor (SNSI). They are assisted by Naval Science Instructors (NSIs) who are normally senior enlisted first class or chief petty officers (E-6 through E-9) or their equivalents in the Marine Corps. They assist the SNSI in carrying out all facets of the program.

Courtesy of the US Marine Corps Junior ROTC

Marine Corps JROTC (MCJROTC)

Mission. The MCJROTC Program's intent is to develop character in high school students—allowing them to become informed citizens prepared to willingly accept their responsibilities as citizens. The program stresses the learning of leadership skills that will enhance the lives of the young adults who participate.

History. The Marine Corps JROTC program began in 1964 after the ROTC Revitalization Act was signed into law.

Objectives. The Marine Corps Junior ROTC program develops:

- Informed and responsible citizens
- Leadership skills
- Strong moral character

The program also promotes an understanding of the need for national security. It instills a sense of pride and personal discipline. It also emphasizes respect for authority.

Curriculum. The MJROTC curriculum covers five categories. They include:

- Leadership
- Citizenship
- Personal growth
- Public service and careers
- General military subjects

Cadet character development focuses on discipline, loyalty, and a sense of responsibility.

The curriculum progresses by year, with cadets being introduced first to leadership and citizenship. They also learn techniques of personal growth and responsibility. There is an introduction to military structure and tradition.

Cadets later move into the study of general military subjects, including marksmanship and land navigation using maps and compasses.

As cadets advance, they apply their leadership training in positions of increased authority and responsibility. They also learn skills for life beyond high school, including personal finances.

Senior cadets conduct formations and inspections, as well as supervise training events with younger cadets. Seniors also conduct research projects.

Instructors. Retired Marine officers serve as Senior Marine Instructors (SMIs). Retired NCOs serve as Marine Instructors. The senior instructors serve as regular faculty members. They have the same responsibilities as department heads. Marine Instructors are also faculty members. They work for the Senior Marine Instructor. They work with the SMI, other school officials, and faculty members. Both work with community leaders and parents to keep making improvements in the program.

US Coast Guard Junior Leadership Program (USCGJLP)

History and Mission. The US Coast Guard is the newest of the programs, and is modeled after those of the other military services. The US Coast Guard JLP operates out of two high schools in Florida and North Carolina. They are overseen by the Office of Inclusion and Diversity at the US Coast Guard Academy in New London, Connecticut.

Courtesy of the US Coast Guard

The first US Coast Guard JLP was created in 1989. It is located at the Maritime and Science Technology Academy (MAST) in Miami, Florida. MAST has about 500 students. Of those, about 160 students are enrolled in the US Coast Guard JLP program. MAST is competitive, focusing on academic success, career preparation, and appreciation of the sea and the environment. MAST started as a trade school, but has become a nationally recognized high school.

The newest US Coast Guard JLP unit is in Camden County, North Carolina. It was created in 2010. The Camden County High School Junior Leadership Program (JLP) lasts two semesters; each participating student takes JLP classes for one semester per school year. During their off semesters, students participate in physical training, drill, and other program-related activities.

Objectives and Curriculum. Both programs' objectives include instruction and experiences that develop leadership, teamwork, personal responsibility, self-confidence, and devotion to school, community, and country. Through living by the Coast Guard's core values of Honor, Respect, and Devotion to Duty, cadets learn how to be better students and citizens who proudly represent Coast Guard traditions while serving their school and community. The JLP programs also focus on science, technology, engineering, and math (STEM). Cadets are engaged in rich and rigorous 21st-century learning that helps prepare them for success in college and careers, and encourages the pursuit of advanced STEM careers.

JROTC and Community Service

All JROTC programs encourage cadets to get involved in their local communities. As a cadet, you will become better informed and helpful as a citizen. Your unit will perform as a team. You will be asked to help coordinate and participate in activities from car washes to candy sales for your unit. You may organize Jog-A-Thons and paper drives. Some JROTC units donate aluminum cans for recycling programs. Proceeds from these fund-raisers benefit the respective units.

Cadets also volunteer their time to support local non-profit groups like the March of Dimes and the Muscular Dystrophy Association. Many join with Adopt-a-Highway Programs and the Special Olympics. Cadets have worked to clean and refurbish cemeteries. They rebuild parks and sponsor little league teams. They also work with the physically and mentally impaired, and assist veterans and the elderly.

keys to LEADERSHIP

No matter which JROTC program you participate in, it will be steeped in tradition and service to your local community and the nation. By participating, you will gain valuable leadership and life skills. You will develop character traits and citizenship that will serve you well in your adult life.

Your unit may find itself involved in building and cleaning projects, food drives, and acquiring toys for toddlers. You may help the Salvation Army deliver holiday gifts and food baskets to the needy. You may assist flood relief victims. You may also participate in Adopt-a-Family activities and community tree planting.

One unit organized a volunteer team to help a paralyzed boy walk again by assisting with his physical therapy. Another unit worked with Multiple Sclerosis Swimming Therapy Sessions. Yet another unit helped distribute clothing and food for homeless Native Americans.

Cadets are encouraged to get involved in their local communities by volunteering.

JROTC cadets also tutor fellow students. They provide color guards for community functions and high school sporting events. They also host and participate in summer leadership encampments and other activities.

The Lines of Responsibility and Authority in Junior ROTC Programs

An **organization** is *two or more people combining their efforts to do a job*. In the US Armed Forces, hundreds of thousands of men and women combine their efforts to carry out a mission essential to national security. They are able to do their jobs because they are organized to keep our nation safe.

Every Junior ROTC unit is organized to carry out its own specific mission. The main jobs for individual cadets are normally shown on an **organizational chart**. This is *a graphic description of positions and lines of authority and responsibility in an organization or unit*. Written job descriptions explain duties in the unit in detail, while the charts provide a quick view of the parts of the unit.

In Figures 1.1 through 1.5, you can see how the various military services organize their JROTC units.

You should notice that when organizing any operation, it is necessary to do three things:

1. Identify skills needed.
2. Set up a working structure.
3. Assign available resources within the structure to carry out the mission successfully.

Organizational Structures and Charts

As you review the displayed sample JROTC programs, note some of the differences between each of the services. This will give you a basic understanding of how each of the Armed Forces would conduct its portion of our nation's security mission. A JROTC unit's organization normally reflects that which exists within its parent military service.

The senior JROTC instructors are responsible for the overall function and management of units. They appoint cadets for the top command and staff positions within their units. The various staff positions closely mirror those found in the staffs of their respective services.

While building your individual knowledge and skills as a 21st-century citizen and future leader, you also develop as a member of a team supporting the community's and nation's needs. Recognizing yourself as part of this team will make you a more successful cadet and citizen.

- Cadet Wing Cmdr (CWg/CC)
  - Vice Cmdr (CV), Special Asst (CCA), Safety (SE), History (HO), Cmd CMSgt (CCC), Exec (CCE), Chaplain (HC), Comptroller (FM), History (HO), Plans (XP)
  - Cadet Ops Gp (COG/CC)
    - Operations Spt Sq (COSS/CC)
      - Current Operations (OSO)
      - Plans (OSX) (*optional*)
    - Operations Sq (COS/CC)
      - A (Flt/CC)
      - B (Flt/CC)
      - C (Flt/CC)
    - Operations (COS/CC) (if needed)
      - D (Flt/CC)
      - B (Flt/CC)
      - C (Flt/CC)
  - Cadet Spt Gp (CSG/CC)
    - Mission Spt Sq (CMSS/CC) (if needed)
      - Mission (Spt Flt/DPS)
      - Personnel (DPM)
      - Pub Affairs (DPA) (*optional*)
      - Comptroller (DPF) (*optional*)
    - Services Sq (CSV/CC)
      - Special Projects (SP)
      - Physical Fitness (PT)
      - Color Guard (CG)
  - Cadet Logistics Gp (CLG/CC)
    - Logistics Spt Sq (CLGL/CC)
    - Supply Sq (CLGS/CC)

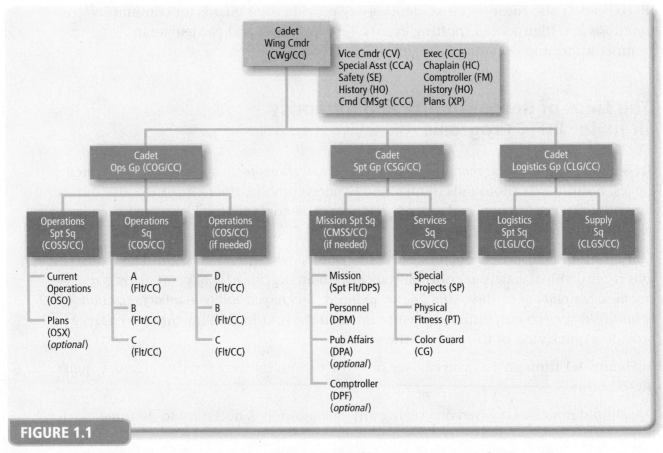

FIGURE 1.1

US Air Force JROTC Organizational Chart for a Typical Cadet Wing (251 or more cadets)

Courtesy of the US Air Force JROTC

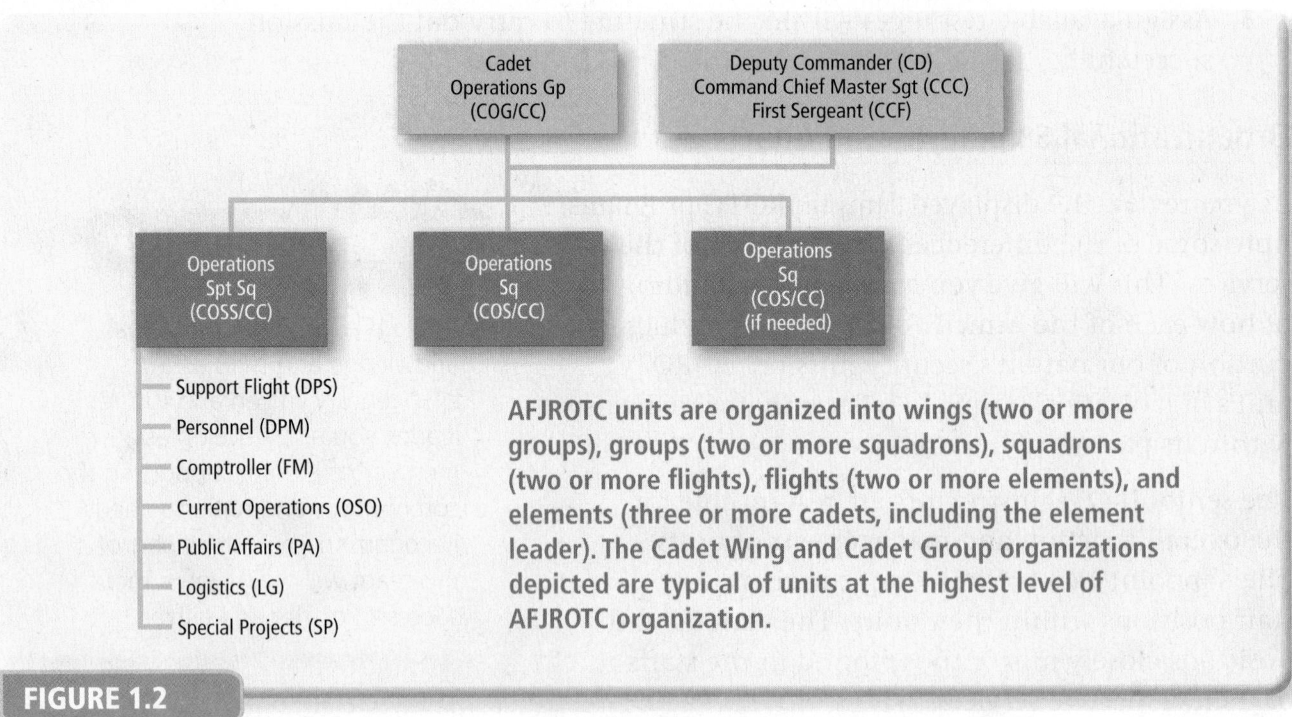

FIGURE 1.2

US Air Force JROTC Organizational Chart for a Typical Cadet Group (250 or fewer cadets)

Courtesy of the US Air Force JROTC

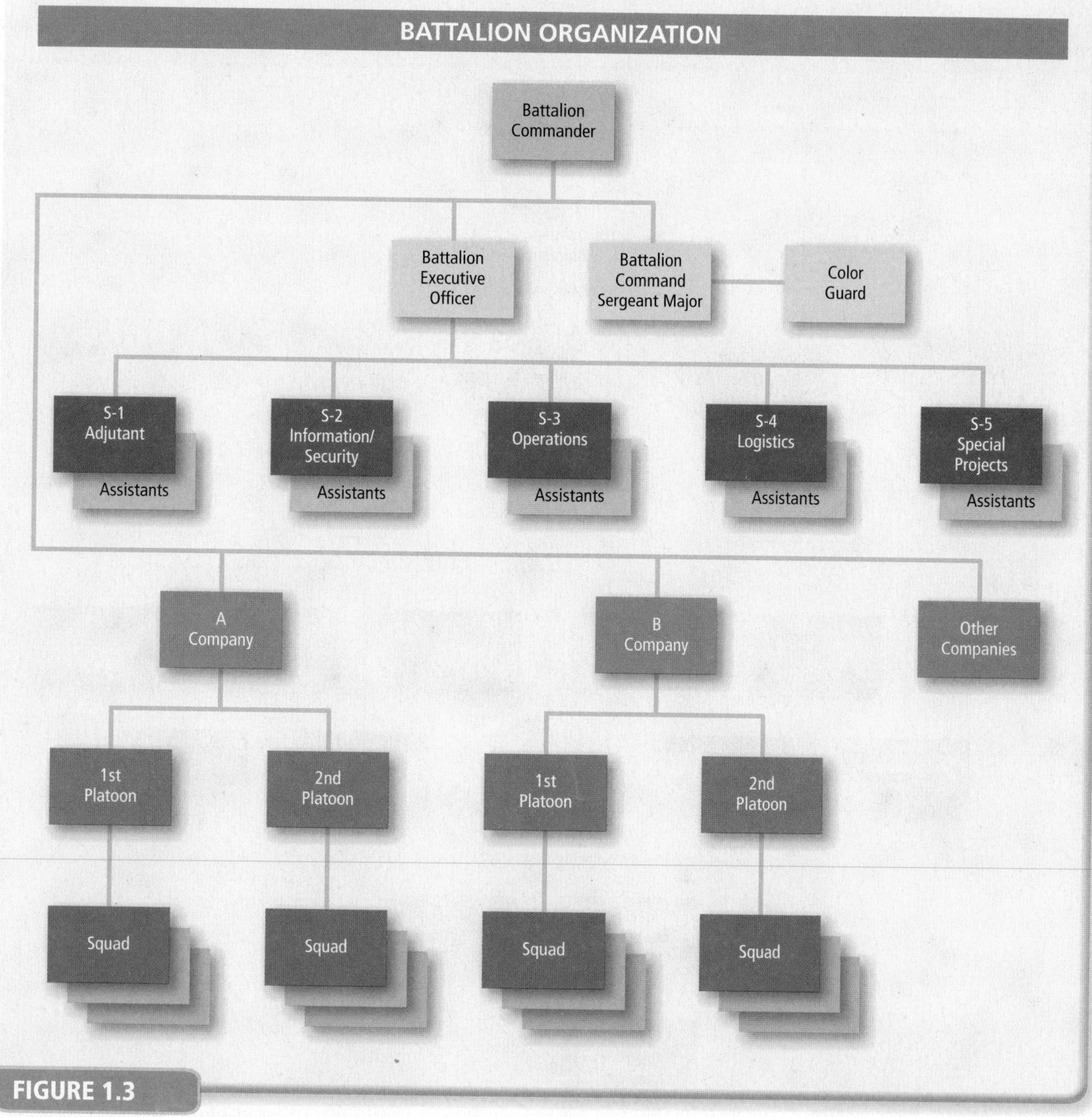

FIGURE 1.3

US Army JROTC Organizational Chart

Courtesy of US Army JROTC

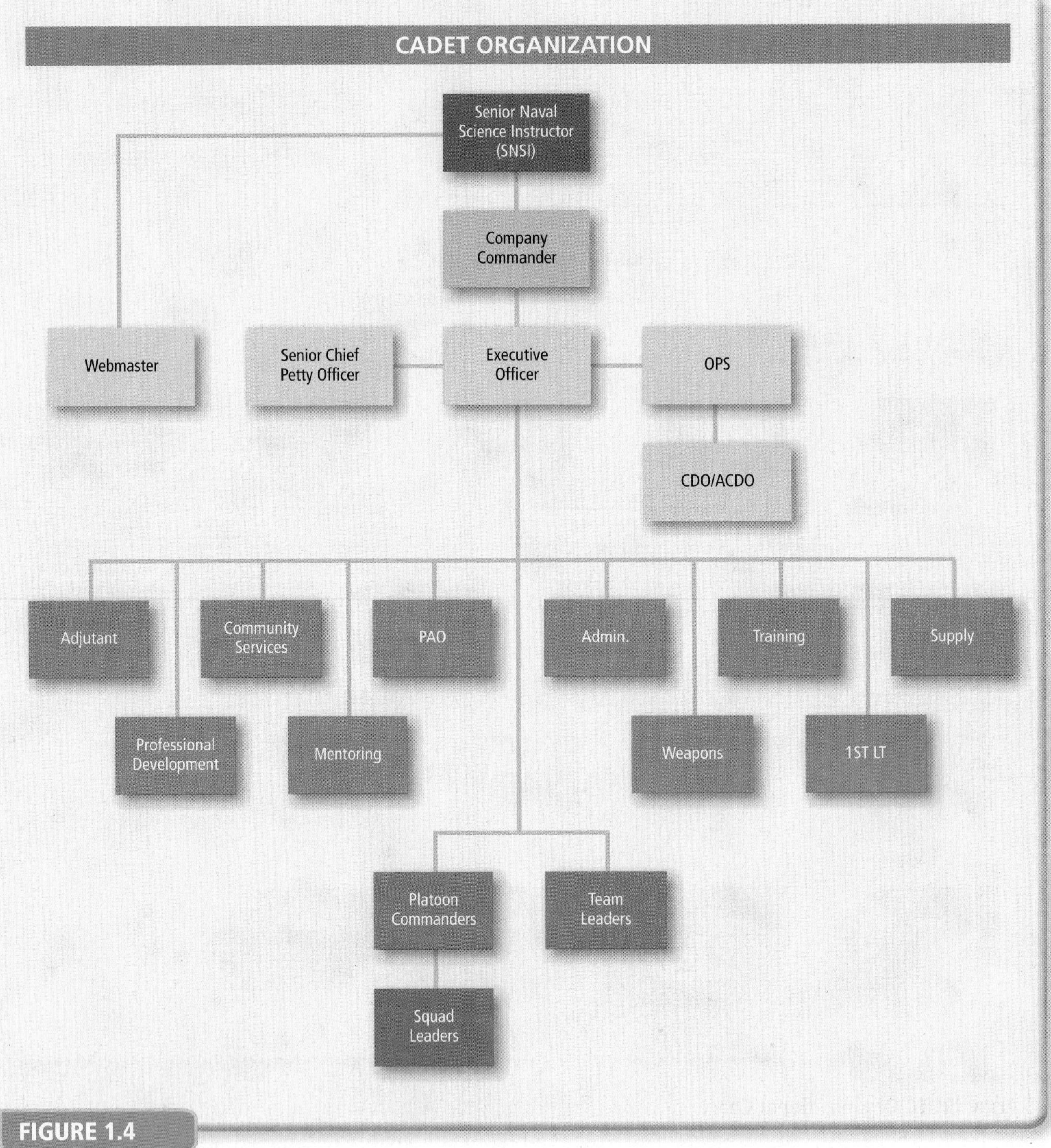

FIGURE 1.4

US Navy JROTC Organizational Chart

Courtesy of US Navy JROTC

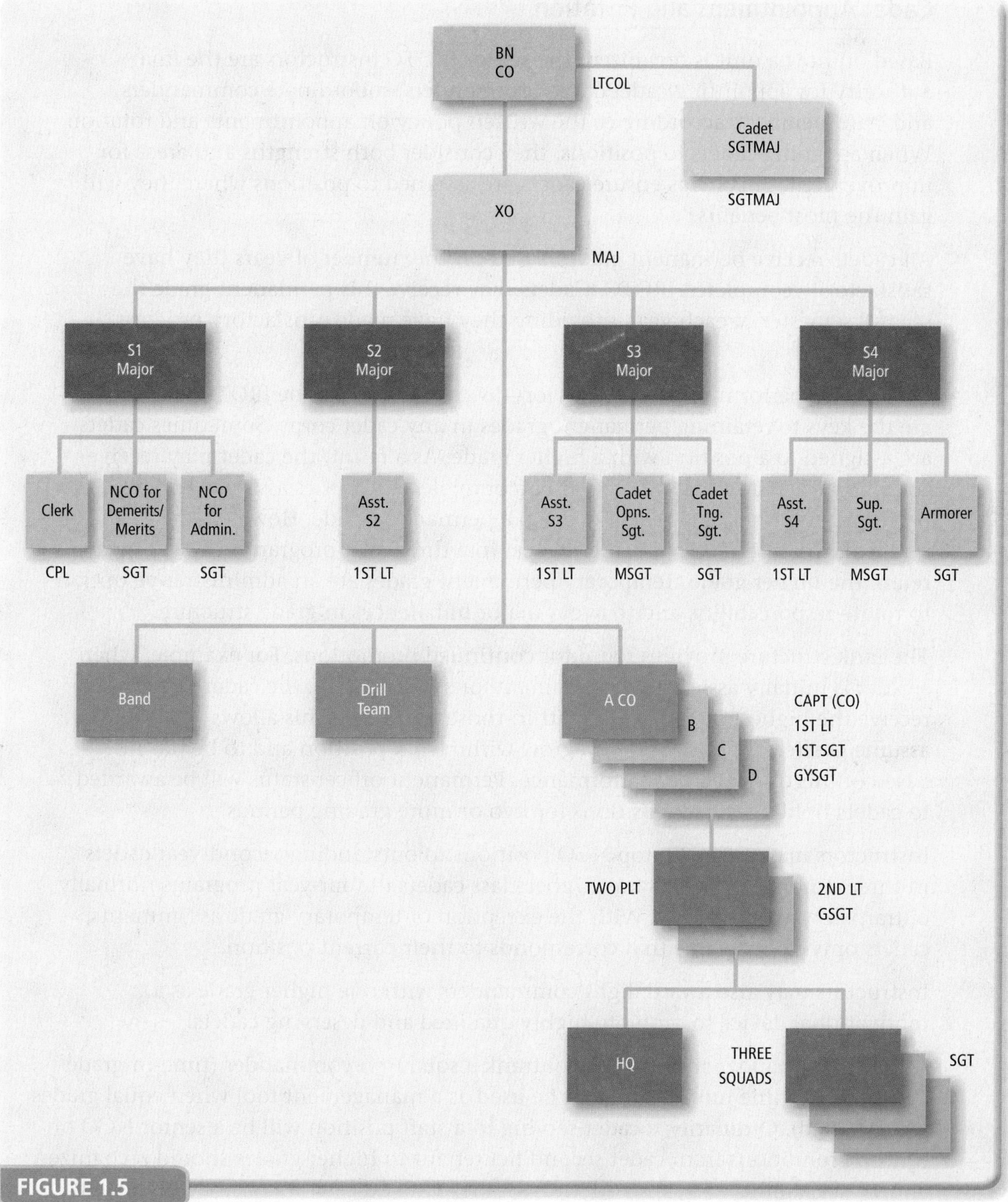

FIGURE 1.5

US Marine Corps JROTC Organizational Chart

Courtesy of US Marine Corps JROTC

Cadet Appointment and Rotation

Based on how a unit is organized, the senior JROTC instructors are the final authority for appointing cadet corps commanders, subordinate commanders, and staff members, according to the written policy on appointments and rotation. When assigning cadets to positions, they consider both strengths and areas for improvement. This helps ensure cadets are assigned to positions where they will gain the most benefits.

All cadets receive permanent grades based on the number of years they have satisfactorily completed JROTC. Cadets may receive this permanent grade the second semester of each year, providing they have made satisfactory progress that year.

Satisfactory performance and behavior—as determined by the JROTC instructors—are the keys to retaining permanent grades in any cadet corps. Sometimes cadets are assigned to a position with a higher grade. As a result, the cadet may receive a temporary grade. Once the cadet has completed the duties assigned to that position, his or her grade may revert to a permanent grade. However, if the cadet is a graduating senior or third-year cadet in a three-year program, the cadet may retain the higher grade. Temporary permanent grades are an administrative option to rotate responsibility, and to avoid major imbalances in grade structure.

The rank structure provides room for continued promotions. For example, when a cadet is initially assigned to a command or staff position, the cadet does not receive the highest rank possible within those positions. This allows the cadet to assume greater responsibility and grow within that position and to be promoted based on his or her actual performance. Permanent officer status will be awarded to cadets holding officer positions for two or more grading periods.

Instructors may authorize top NCO positions to outstanding second-year cadets in three- to four-year programs. Upper class cadets in four-year programs normally outrank lower class cadets. With the exception of temporary grade assignments, cadets only hold a grade that corresponds to their current position.

Instructors may also award flight commanders with one higher grade as a motivational device to promote highly qualified and deserving cadets.

A flight commander should never outrank a squadron commander (time-in-grade or promotion line numbers should be used as a management tool when equal grades are involved). Ordinarily, a cadet serving in a staff position will be a senior NCO or officer. Promotions from cadet second lieutenant to higher grades should recognize and reward ability and effort. AFJROTC cadet rank descriptions will be discussed in the next lesson.

Lesson 1 Review

Using complete sentences, answer the following questions on a sheet of paper.

1. Who was Lieutenant Edgar R. Steevers, and what did he do?
2. What did the ROTC Vitalization Act of 1964 authorize?
3. What are the four things common to all JROTC programs related to cadets' development?
4. Based on your reading, what are three main objectives of your Junior ROTC program? (*Note*: Cadets should answer for their chosen JROTC program.)
5. Who is responsible for the overall function and management of a Junior ROTC unit?
6. What are three things needed when organizing any JROTC operation?
7. What are the two keys to retaining permanent grades in any cadet corps?
8. When assigning cadets to staff positions, what should the instructor consider?

APPLYING YOUR LEARNING

9. Describe why cadets who are appointed as Flight Commanders should not hold a rank higher than a Squadron Commander.

LESSON 2

The Military Uniform and Appearance Standards

Quick Write

List the first three things you think of when you see a person in a uniform.

Learn About

- uniform wear and history
- uniform wear, restrictions, and standards
- uniforms used within special teams
- cadet appearance and grooming standards
- military pay grades and rank insignia

"Everybody can be great, because anybody can serve."

Dr. Martin Luther King, Jr., civil rights leader

Uniform Wear and History

People wear uniforms to show they belong to an organization. Members of sports teams, marching bands, and people in a variety of jobs—from the ambulance driver and the doctor to the termite inspector and the airline pilot—wear distinctive garb to show they are part of a team, a profession, or an organization.

When we see someone in uniform, we identify that person with an organization and its reason for being—its mission. The ambulance driver and the doctor represent health care; the termite inspector makes us think of pest control; the airline pilot signifies travel by air.

Every organization has standards, or *widely recognized and expected levels of value or measurement* that we expect from people in uniform, whether they are involved in sports, medicine, or transport. We expect our doctor to treat our ills competently, and the airline pilot to get us to our destination on time and safely.

As a cadet, your uniform represents standards and values that have evolved over many centuries.

Uniform Wear

What is the first image that flashes into your mind when you think of someone in the military? Like most people, you probably pictured a person in uniform. The military uniform is more than just clothes. It is the public symbol of the nation's defense forces. It represents a long and honorable tradition of devotion to duty in the service of one's country. Therefore, the uniform should be worn proudly and—equally important—it should be worn properly.

How you wear the uniform reflects upon the nation's military—the Air Force, Army, Navy, Marines, and Coast Guard. As a Junior ROTC (JROTC) cadet, you will often be in the public eye. This means that you and your fellow cadets must maintain a high standard of dress and personal appearance while wearing the uniform. The key elements are neatness, cleanliness, safety, and military image.

Vocabulary

- standards
- uniform
- citizenship
- bulk
- insignia

History of the Military Uniform

The English word *uniform* comes from a combination of two Latin words, *unus* and *forma*, which means "one form." The word uniform means *a distinctive mode of dress*. In ancient times, the Roman togas provided a unique dress code. The toga is a loose outer garment worn by Romans appearing in public to show their status as citizens. Citizenship is *the status of a person loyal to a nation, entitled to its rights and protection, while also assuming some responsibilities for service to the nation.*

The toga came in several styles. The *toga candida* was a white garment worn only by candidates for public office. The *toga palmata* was a fancy toga worn to ceremonial affairs. The *toga praetexta*, a white toga with a purple border, was worn only by emperors. The *toga sordida* was worn by mourners. Those who were not citizens typically wore a shorter garment, the *tunic*.

The toga, worn here by a Roman, served as a badge of coveted Roman citizenship.

Military dress in ancient times acquired a certain degree of sameness, but in a much different sense from modern military uniforms. In Greece, Athenian and Spartan soldiers dressed according to their position in military formations during the Peloponnesian War in the 5th century B.C. The Greek heavy infantryman wore a helmet, breastplate, and armor covering his legs below the knee. He also carried a shield and sword. The light-foot soldier wore no armor and carried a lighter shield and a spear. These were military uniforms in the sense that all soldiers looked alike. To this extent, therefore, we assign the origin of the military uniform to an early date in Western civilization.

In ancient Greece, uniforms varied based on a soldier's position in military formations.

Copyright © Morphart/Fotolia.com

During the 15th and 16th centuries in Europe, national armies, wearing standardized uniforms, came into being. In the 17th century, during the Great Rebellion in England (1642–1646), the English Parliament decided to raise and support an army. The English uniform was red, with different colored facings for different regiments. These regiments were named by their facing's colors: blue, red, orange, etc.

The uniform styles were really just a version of civilian dress. The uniform had an ample coat, waistcoat, knickers, stockings, and shoes or, in the case of cavalry, boots. Colors and standards were used to identify units. Wealthy leaders dressed the troops who served under them in distinctive and colorful uniforms.

Early European uniform style and civilian dress.

Copyright © Erica Guilane-Nachez/Fotolia.com

From this start, the military uniform evolved. During this gradual process, uniforms ranged from very ornamented to very drab. Some claim that the more colorful the uniform, the more uncomfortable the soldier. High, tight collars, tight trousers, and boots that restricted knee action looked fancy, but they weren't good in action.

Uniform Wear, Restrictions, and Standards

JROTC cadets generally wear the same uniform—the standard Air Force, Army, Navy, Marine Corps, or Coast Guard service uniform—as that worn by their parent military service. Cadets are expected to honor the uniform—to wear it properly and with pride. The uniform is an important and distinctive aspect of JROTC. Whenever you wear the uniform—during indoor and outdoor training periods, at cadet social functions, and during base visits—you represent the corps. How you wear the uniform exposes you to praise or criticism from fellow cadets, fellow students, and society at large.

Restrictions

Certain restrictions apply to wearing the military uniform. For example, cadets may *not* wear the uniform while hitchhiking, in student demonstrations, for crowd control, political events, or for any other inappropriate activity. (However, JROTC cadets may wear the uniform while acting as ushers, parking lot attendants, runners, etc., at the discretion of the instructor staff.)

Federal law bars military personnel from engaging in any form of public political activity—such as attending rallies and political speeches or passing out political flyers—while in uniform. In addition, military personnel are prohibited from publicly supporting a particular candidate, party, or political issue when it is clear to others that they are members of the US military. The intent of the law is to avoid the perception that any military official supports one political cause, candidate, or party over another.

The role of the military requires absolute obedience to direction from elected civilian leaders, so public perception regarding the allegiance of military members is critical.

Nevertheless, members of the military are also citizens who are actively encouraged to vote and participate in the processes of the governing of a democratic nation. They are allowed to place political bumper stickers on their own vehicles and/or signs on their private property. They can participate in political events as long as they are *not* in uniform and do *not* identify themselves as military members. Since JROTC cadets wear a form of the US Air Force, Army, Navy, Marine Corps, or Coast Guard uniform, they should also follow this standard while in uniform.

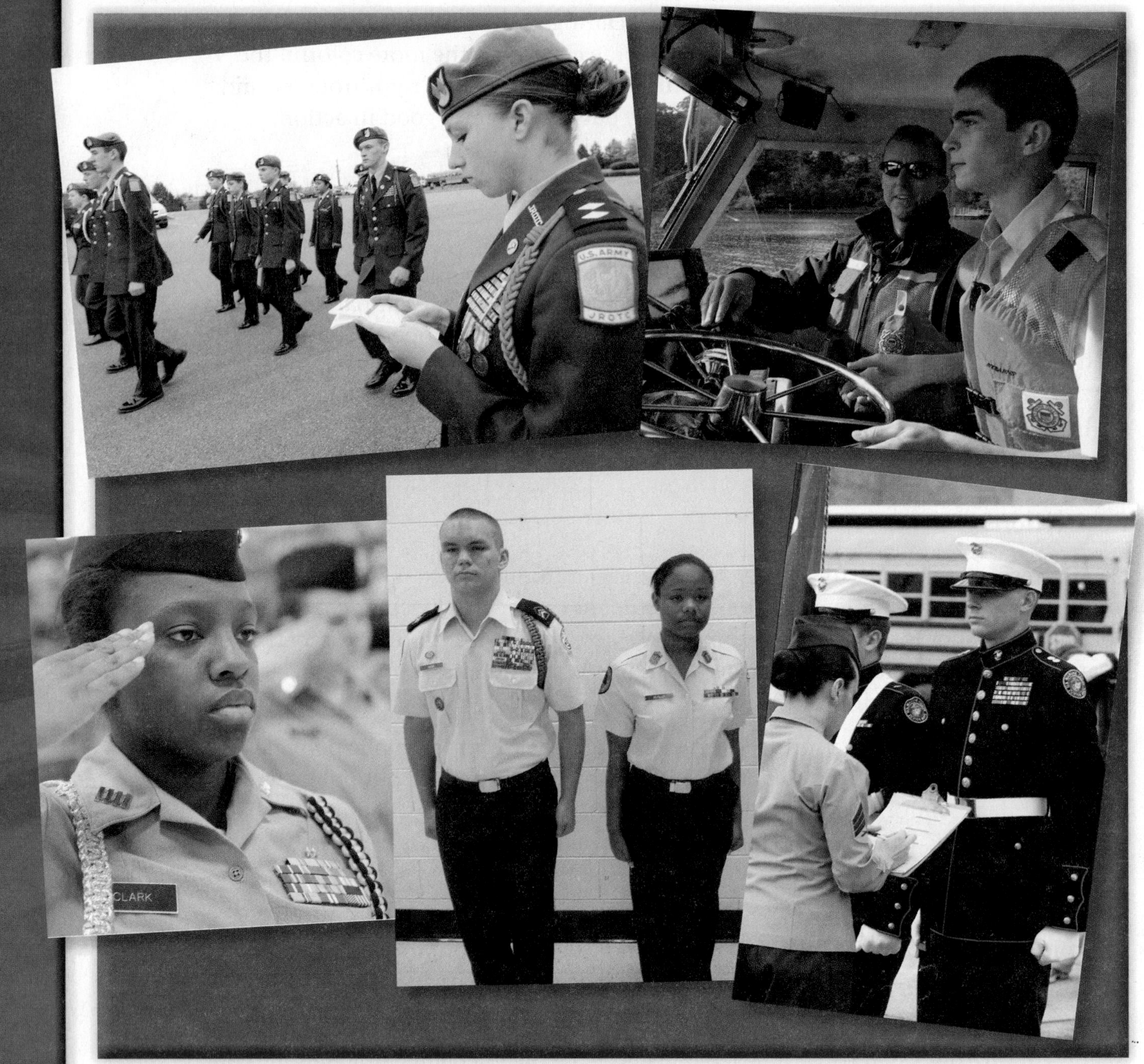

Cadets in standard service uniforms.

Clockwise, from top left: Courtesy of US Air Force photo/Greg L. Davis/Defense Video & Imagery Distribution System; Chief Petty Officer Rudy Patten/Defense Video & Imagery Distribution System; US Air Force photo/Greg L. Davis/Defense Video & Imagery Distribution System; Michael Wetzel/US Air Force JROTC; Lance Cpl. Nana Dannsaappiah/Defense Video & Imagery Distribution System

Federal laws also forbid those in military uniform from participating in other public demonstrations where it might be implied that the military service supports a particular cause. Engaging in an activity that might imply endorsement by one of the services of a commercial interest or engaging in private employment while in uniform is also banned.

In addition, no item of the JROTC uniform may be worn by members of groups that sponsor a JROTC program. Cadet auxiliary societies, for example, may not create a special uniform that includes any item of the JROTC uniform. This includes school faculty, parent support groups, and sponsors other than JROTC instructors.

Dos and Don'ts for Wearing the Various Service Uniforms

Here are a few general dos and don'ts about wearing the JROTC uniform.

Dos

- Wear the standard service uniform properly and with pride.
- Wear the uniform on the day established by the instructor staff.
- Wear the uniform at other times specified by the instructor staff.
- Wear the uniform when you fly on military aircraft.
- Wear the uniform when you participate in a color guard or on a drill team.
- Keep your shoes polished and shined, including the heels and edges of soles.
- Make sure your shoes are appropriate for the activity as specified by each service JROTC unit. Safety is the major concern.
- Ensure that badges, insignia, belt buckles, and other metallic devices are clean and free of scratches and corrosion.
- Keep ribbons clean and replace them when they become worn, frayed, or faded.
- If your JROTC unit is at a military academy, wear the distinctive uniform required by the school for special occasions or ceremonies.

Don'ts

- Do not wear the uniform with other clothing.
- Do not lend your uniform to anyone who is not a member of the JROTC program.
- Do not allow articles such as wallets, pencils, pens, watch/wallet chains, checkbooks, handkerchiefs, and combs to be visible. You may allow parts of pens and pencils to be exposed when you carry them in the left shirt pocket or pen pocket of the Airman Battle Uniform (ABU).
- Do not wear earphones or headphones while in uniform, unless required.
- Do not carry pagers or cell phones, unless required. (If required, they must be clipped to the waistband or purse or be carried in the left hand when not in use.)

Uniform Standards

All JROTC programs have the same general uniform standards. Most JROTC units have published information on the cadet uniform and how to wear it, based on directives, handbooks, instructions, or regulations issued by a particular service. In this section, we explain the uniform standards that apply to Air Force Junior ROTC (AFJROTC) cadets.

For the AFJROTC, the standards for the uniform are in three instructions: AFI 36-2903, *Dress and Personal Appearance of Air Force Personnel*; Air Force Junior ROTC Instruction (AFJROTCI) 36-2001, *Air Force Junior ROTC Operations*; and the *AFJROTC Operational Supplement*. These three publications provide complete details on fitting standards and wearing instructions for the uniform and personal grooming requirements for AFJROTC cadets. The *AFJROTC Operational Supplement* and AFJROTCI 36-2001 include diagrams of uniforms for both female and male cadets. AFJROTC cadets can find all three of these publications online at the AFJROTC website. You can download or copy them for unit use.

It is your responsibility to maintain all uniform items in a clean and orderly condition during the school year and when you turn your uniform in. Just as the person on active duty, you are also obligated to wear the uniform properly and proudly. In doing so, you uphold the dignity of the Air Force, Army, Navy, Marine Corps, or Coast Guard, your unit, your fellow cadets, and yourself.

With practice and attention to detail, all the dos and don'ts about the proper wear and care of the uniform and personal appearance will become almost automatic. You should be proud of the uniform and the way it looks. A smart appearance is important, not only in drill practice, but also in performing various school activities and attending military functions.

Male and female Air Force cadets in standard service dress uniforms.

Courtesy of Michael Wetzel/US Air Force JROTC

Standard Cadet Uniform

The AFJROTC male service dress uniform consists of the dark blue service coat and trousers, light blue long sleeve shirt, and dark blue tie. The female service dress uniform consists of the dark blue service coat with slacks or skirt, light blue blouse, and tie tab. In both cases, the coat will be form fitted, meaning that it must not be tight in the shoulders, chest, and underarms. The sleeve length should extend to one-quarter inch from the heel of the thumb when the arms are hanging naturally at the sides. The bottom of the coat should extend 3 to $3^1/_2$ inches below the top of the thigh.

The trousers for males must be trim-fitted with no bunching at the waist or bagging at the seat. Slacks for female cadets should fit naturally over the hips, with no bunching, sagging, or bagging at the seat. The trousers or slacks should rest on the top of the shoe with a slight break in the crease. The backs of the trousers or slacks should be seven-eighths inch longer than the front. The proper length of the trousers or slacks can be determined while standing at attention.

The cadet uniform identifies you as a future leader in your community and the nation. By being active in your unit's community projects and other activities, you'll find that it will open doors to new opportunities, new friends, and new self-confidence.

Uniforms Used Within Special Teams

With the appropriate approval, color guards, honor guards, sabre teams, and drill teams may wear additional uniform items or wear distinctive, yet conservative, uniform of military style. Greater latitude will be permitted in the design of open competition drill team uniforms where the intent is to allow maximum flexibility and freedom of movement in executing complex drill routines; however, these uniforms must reflect the proper military image. Units using this style of uniform may be expected to have their regulation uniform or a second, more conservative military style uniform for the inspection and regulation drill requirements found in most drill meets. Ascots are authorized for wear at the discretion of the instructor staff.

Except for shoulder cords, these items or uniforms are worn only when performing as a member of a specialized group. AFJROTCI 36-2001 provides procedures for obtaining and controlling cadet uniforms.

If your uniform does not fit properly, talk to your instructor staff. Do not wait until someone else calls attention to it. Check the appearance of your uniform in a mirror. Remember that how you look influences others.

Cadet Appearance and Grooming Standards

When you wear the uniform, you are responsible for presenting a neat, clean, and professional military image. Appearance and grooming standards help cadets present the image of disciplined individuals who can be relied upon to do the job they are called on to do. A professional military image has no room for the extreme, the unusual, or the faddish. The standards for wearing the uniform consist of four elements: neatness, cleanliness, safety, and military image. The first three are absolute, objective criteria for the efficiency, health, and well-being of the force. The fourth standard, military image, is also a very important aspect of military appearance. People, both military and civilian, draw conclusions as to the military effectiveness of the Air Force by how they perceive those in uniform.

The uniform standards in AFI 36-2903 are influenced to some extent by military tradition, and they reflect the image the Air Force desires to project to the civilian community. The basic concept of the Air Force uniform is a plain but distinctive dress, with an absolute minimum number of badges, insignia, and devices authorized for wear.

Additional Uniform and Appearance Rules

Here are some additional guidelines about uniform and appearance.

Jewelry

While in uniform, you may wear a wristwatch and rings, but no more than three rings total for both hands at any one time. You may wear one wrist bracelet if it is neat and conservative; however, ankle bracelets are not allowed. Furthermore, the bracelet must not detract from the military image, must not be wider than $^1/_2$ inch, may be gold or silver, and must not subject anyone to potential injury. Bracelets supporting a cause, philosophy, individual, or group are not allowed. You may not wear ornaments on your head or around your neck that are visible while in uniform.

Female cadets in uniform may wear earrings if the earrings are conservative and kept within sensible limits. For example, you may wear one small spherical (diamond, gold, white pearl, or silver) pierced or clip earring on each earlobe. The earring worn in each earlobe must match. Earrings should fit tightly without extending below the earlobes, unless they are clip earrings.

Male cadets in uniform may not wear earrings.

Eyeglasses or Sunglasses

If you wear glasses, they must not have any ornaments on the frames or lenses. Eyeglass lenses that are conservative, clear, slightly tinted, or have photosensitive lenses may be worn in uniform while indoors or while in military formation. When outdoors and in uniform, sunglasses and eyeglasses must have lenses and frames that are conservative; faddish or mirrored lenses are prohibited. Sunglasses are not allowed while in a military formation. Neither eyeglasses nor sunglasses can be worn around the neck or on top of the head while in uniform.

Tattoos or Brands

Whether you are in or out of uniform, tattoos or brands anywhere on the body are not allowed if they are obscene or if they advocate sexual, racial, ethnic, or religious discrimination. Tattoos or brands that might harm good order and discipline or bring discredit upon the Air Force are also barred, whether you are in or out of uniform. Excessive tattoos or brands, even though they do not violate the prohibitions in the above paragraph, will not be exposed or visible (including visible through the uniform) while in uniform. Excessive is defined as any tattoo or brands that exceed one-quarter of the exposed body part, and those above the collarbone and readily visible when wearing an open collar uniform.

Body Piercing and Other Attachments to Body Parts

Cadets in uniform are not allowed to attach or display objects, articles, jewelry, or ornamentation to or through the ear (except as mentioned previously), nose, tongue, or any exposed body part (including anything that might be visible through the uniform).

Specific Female Cadet Guidelines

Here are some specific guidelines for female cadets.

Hair

Hair will end above the bottom of the collar edge and any side of an invisible line drawn parallel to the ground. Your hairstyle must be conservative—no extreme or faddish styles are allowed. Hair color must complement the cadet's skin tone and result in natural, human hair colors such as brown, blonde, brunette, natural red, black, or gray. It should also look professional and allow you to wear uniform headgear in the proper manner, so your hair must not be too full or too high on the head. Bangs will not touch either eyebrow while in uniform. In addition, your hairstyle shouldn't need many grooming aids. If you use pins, combs, barrettes, or similar items, they must be plain, similar in color to your hair, and modest in size. Wigs or hairpieces must also conform to these guidelines.

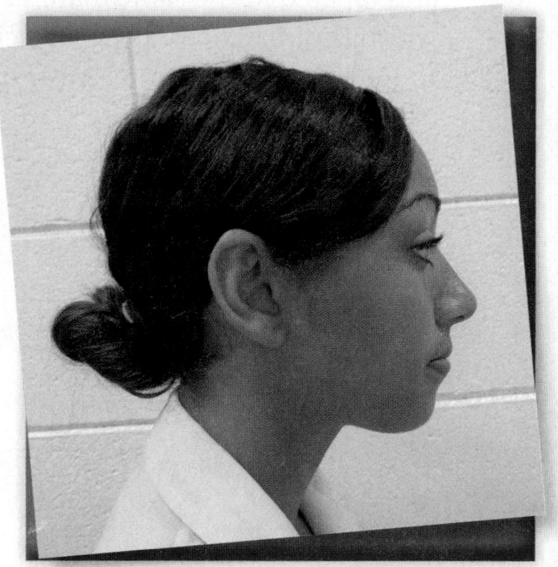

An example of a proper hair style for a female cadet in uniform.

Courtesy of Michael Wetzel/US Air Force JROTC

Skirts

The length of your skirt may not vary beyond the top and bottom of the kneecap. Your skirt should fit smoothly, hang naturally, and not excessively tight. You must wear hosiery with the skirt. Choose a sheer nylon in a neutral, dark brown, black, off-black, or dark blue shade that complements the uniform and your skin tone.

Specific Male Cadet Guidelines

Here are some specific guidelines for male cadets.

Hair

Keep your hair clean, neat, and trimmed. It must not contain large amounts of grooming aids such as greasy creams, oils, and sprays that remain visible in the hair. When your hair is groomed, it should not touch your ears or eyebrows, and only the closely cut or shaved hair on the back of your neck should touch the collar. Your hair should not exceed 1 and ¼ inch in bulk regardless of the length. **Bulk** is *the distance that the hair projects from the scalp when groomed* (as opposed to length of the hair).

The bulk and length of your hair must not interfere with wearing any Air Force headgear properly, and it must not protrude below the front band of the headgear. Your hair must have a tapered appearance on both sides and back, both with and without headgear. A tapered appearance means that, when viewed from any angle, the outline of the hair on the side and back will generally match the shape of the head, curving inward to the end point.

Your hair may not contain or have attached to it any visible foreign items. If you dye your hair, it must look natural. You may not dye your hair an unusual color or one that contrasts with your natural coloring. You may have sideburns if they are neatly trimmed and tapered in the same manner as your haircut. Sideburns must be straight and of even width (not flared) and end in a clean-shaven horizontal line. They may not extend below the lowest part of the outer ear opening. No extreme or faddish hairstyles are allowed.

A close-up of accouterments placed on a male cadet uniform.
Courtesy of Michael Wetzel/US Air Force JROTC

Military Pay Grades and Rank Insignia

Members of the Air Force perform duties that reflect their skill and pay grade. This also applies to AFJROTC cadets. The higher the rank or grade, the more responsibility cadets are given. In turn, cadets are expected to perform their duties in accordance with this increased responsibility.

An **insignia** is *a badge or mark of office or honor.* Rank insignia identify the rank of each member of the armed forces. In each of the armed forces, the pay grade system is broken down into two categories: officer grades and enlisted grades. Below, we will first review the Air Force pay grade system and follow with the Air Force JROTC rank insignia. (See Figures 1.6 and 1.7 for military officer and enlisted grade system.)

US Military Insignia of Grade

Officers

Figure 1.6 shows the military pay grade abbreviation for each commissioned officer title. The subdued insignia worn on the ABU is made of cloth. Gold appears as brown and silver appears as dark blue.

Proper methods of address when speaking to officers are:

- "Lieutenant" for a second lieutenant and a first lieutenant.
- "Colonel" for either a lieutenant colonel or a colonel.
- "General" for all general officers.

Use full titles for official written correspondence.

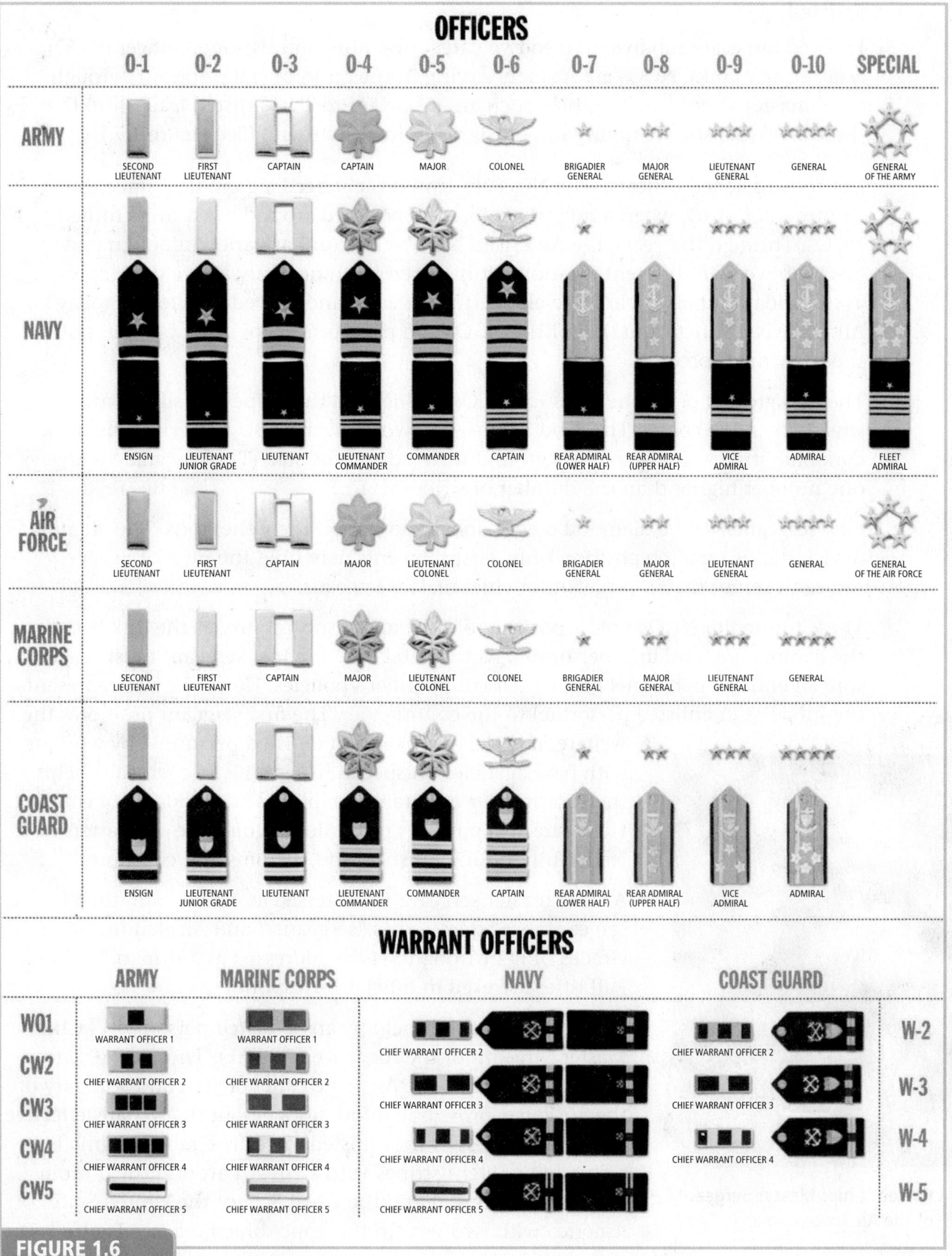

FIGURE 1.6

US Military Officer Grades and Ranks

Enlisted

Enlisted ranks are subdivided into two categories: noncommissioned officer (NCO) and Airman ranks. NCOs are Airmen serving in the ranks of staff sergeant through chief master sergeant. NCOs play such an important role in enlisted leadership that there are five distinct military rank insignia to identify them. (See Figure 1.7.)

Noncommissioned Officers. The NCO chevron has changed a great deal since the Continental Army, when a brightly colored ribbon tied around the arm identified NCOs. Through the years, the American NCO's chevron has varied in design and has been worn in different locations. It has been worn not only above the elbow, as it is today, but also below the elbow. The inverted and curved chevron of today's Air Force is distinct from that of the NCOs and petty officers of other branches of the US Armed Forces.

The background of AF chevrons for NCOs is blue, and the stripes are silver with a silver star in the center. The subdued insignia worn on the ABU uniform consists of dark blue stripes on a green background with a dark blue star. (The pay grade is always one number higher than the number of stripes worn.)

First sergeants wear a diamond device above the star on their chevrons. The diamond device stands for a job position only. First sergeants may hold the rank of master sergeant, senior master sergeant, or chief master sergeant.

These top senior NCOs hold a position of trust and responsibility as the link between the commander and unit personnel. As this vital link, the first sergeant must make sure all enlisted personnel know their commander's policies. He or she also represents the interests of enlisted personnel to the commander. The first sergeant promotes the welfare, morale, and health of enlisted personnel by working with base agencies on special issues. The first sergeant helps the commander maintain discipline and standards of conduct. He or she also provides professional guidance on matters of leadership, military justice, and customs and courtesies.

Current Chief Master Sergeant of the Air Force, James A. Cody.
Courtesy of the US Air Force

A chief master sergeant is addressed as "chief." All other sergeants are addressed as "sergeant," and Airmen in the Grades of E-1 through E-4 are addressed as "Airman." Full titles are used in official correspondence.

The highest position held by any enlisted personnel is Chief Master Sergeant of the Air Force (CMSAF). The CMSAF acts as personal advisor to the Air Force Chief of Staff and Secretary of the Air Force, providing information about the welfare, effective use, and progress of the enlisted force. The rank insignia is a chevron of eight stripes with a wreath around the bottom and sides of the star and the Great Seal of the United States of America with two stars in the upper blue field (see Figure 1.7).

FIGURE 1.7

US Military Enlisted Grades and Ranks

The CMSAF position was created to add prestige to the NCO Corps. Air Force Chief of Staff General John P. McConnell announced the creation of this position on October 24, 1966. The first CMSAF was CMSgt Paul W. Airey. He was awarded the unique insignia with the wreath around the star in April 1967. Over the next decade, support for the office grew among both the senior Air Force leadership and the enlisted force. The creation of this office, as well as the appointment of command chief master sergeants and the granting of more responsibility to all senior NCOs, represented the Air Force's concrete recognition of the professionalism of its enlisted force, especially its NCOs.

Airmen. There are four Airman ranks:

1. Airman basic (AB)
2. Airman (Amn)
3. Airman first class (A1C)
4. Senior Airman (SrA)

An Airman basic (AB) doesn't wear any rank insignia. An Airman's rank insignia is a chevron of one silver stripe with a silver star in the middle. An AIC rank insignia is a chevron of two silver stripes with a silver star in the middle. The senior Airman rank insignia is a chevron of three silver stripes with a silver star in the middle. Pay grades for Airmen are: AB (E-1), Amn (E-2), A1C (E-3), and SrA (E-4). (See Figure 1.7 for Airmen military pay grade and rank insignia.)

A close-up of accouterments placed on a female cadet uniform.

Courtesy of Michael Wetzel/US Air Force JROTC

Air Force JROTC Rank Insignia

Figure 1.8 shows Air Force JROTC cadet rank insignia. Please see your *AFJROTC Operational Supplement* for the insignias of the other military branches.

Officers

Table 1.1 describes the rank insignia for each cadet officer title. Rank insignia for military officers are very different from rank insignia for cadet officers.

Enlisted

A comparison of military insignia (Figure 1.7) and Air Force JROTC cadet rank insignia (Figure 1.8) shows only slight differences between enlisted ranks. The star inside the chevron for active duty personnel is replaced with a torch for cadets, and the chevron is pointed at the bottom. Cadets, like active duty personnel, may wear other insignia and badges, when authorized. Table 1.2 describes the rank insignia for each cadet enlisted title. Figure 1.9 shows other insignia (badges) for Air Force JROTC cadets. For current US Air Force Occupational and Duty Badges please refer to AFI 36-2903.

AIR FORCE JROTC INSIGNIA

CADET OFFICER RANK

SECOND LIEUTENANT

FIRST LIEUTENANT

CAPTAIN

MAJOR

LIEUTENANT COLONEL

COLONEL

CADET AIRMEN RANK

(NO RANK INSIGNIA)

AIRMAN BASIC

AIRMAN

AIRMAN FIRST CLASS

SENIOR AIRMAN

STAFF SERGEANT

TECHNICAL SERGEANT

MASTER SERGEANT

SENIOR MASTER SERGEANT

CHIEF MASTER SERGEANT

FIGURE 1.8

Air Force JROTC Cadet Rank Insignia

Courtesy of US Air Force JROTC

Table 1.1 Cadet Officer Rank Insignia

Title	Rank Insignia
Cadet Second Lieutenant (c/2d Lt)	Chevron of 1 inverted stripe
Cadet First Lieutenant (c/1st Lt)	Chevron of 2 inverted stripes
Cadet Captain (c/Capt)	Chevron of 3 inverted stripes
Cadet Major (c/Maj)	Chevron of 1 double-wide inverted stripe
Cadet Lieutenant Colonel (c/Lt Col)	Chevron of 2 inverted stripes; 1 double-wide, 1 regular
Cadet Colonel (c/Col)	Chevron of 3 inverted stripes; 1 double-wide, 2 regular

Table 1.2 Cadet Enlisted Rank Insignia

Title	Rank Insignia
Cadet Airman Basic (c/AB)	None
Cadet Airman (c/Amn)	Pointed chevron of 1 stripe, with torch in the middle
Cadet Airman First Class (c/A1C)	Pointed chevron of 2 stripes, with torch in the middle
Cadet Senior Airman (c/SrA)	Pointed chevron of 3 stripes, with torch in the middle
Cadet Staff Sergeant (c/SSgt)	Pointed chevron of 4 stripes, with torch in the middle
Cadet Technical Sergeant (c/TSgt)	Pointed chevron of 5 stripes, with torch in the middle
Cadet Master Sergeant (c/MSgt)	Pointed chevron of 6 stripes, with 1 stripe inverted above the torch in the middle
Cadet Senior Master Sergeant (c/SMSgt)	Pointed chevron of 7 stripes, with 2 stripes inverted above the torch in the middle
Cadet Chief Master Sergeant (c/CMSgt)	Pointed chevron of 8 stripes, with 3 stripes inverted above the torch in the middle

AIR FORCE JROTC BADGES

OFFICER'S FLIGHT CAP AND BERET INSIGNIA

OFFICER'S SERVICE CAP

DISTINGUISHED AFJROTC CADET BADGE

GROUND SCHOOL BADGE

FLIGHT SOLO BADGE

FLIGHT CERTIFICATE BADGE

MODEL ROCKETRY BADGE

AWARENESS PRESENTATION TEAM BADGE

AEF ACADEMIC EXCELLENCE BADGE

ACADEMY OF MODEL AERONAUTICS BADGE

KITTY HAWK AIR SOCIETY BADGE

SHOULDER TABS

MARKSMANSHIP BADGE

EXPERT MARKSMANSHIP BADGE

FIGURE 1.9

US Air Force JROTC Badges

Courtesy of US Air Force JROTC

Ribbons

All ribbons should be in proper order based upon the AFJROTC ribbon chart located in the *AFJROTC Operational Supplement*. If a ribbon is awarded more than once, oak leaf clusters will be used to signify each additional award unless directed otherwise.

Order of Precedence. The lowest ribbon will be worn at the lowest left position, and the highest ribbon will be worn at the top right. Refer to the ribbon chart located in the LE 100 Companion Website for order of precedence and guidance for wearing ribbons.

The AFJROTC Patch

The ***yellow*** **arrow**, a timeless design that doesn't limit itself to airplanes or a particular period, is a stylized aircraft. The arrow points to the future, and depicts high technology, supporting the goal of aerospace education and careers in aerospace. Some active-duty units have adopted this design from AFJROTC.

The longstanding tradition of the **lamp**, which represents knowledge, lit with red flame, signifies that knowledge prevents one from traveling life's journeys in ignorance.

The ***colors*** of the emblem are secondary to the symbolism of the emblem. The colors of the Air Force, ultramarine blue and Air Force yellow, should appear in the design.

Courtesy of US Air Force JROTC

- The ***blue*** represents "the sky," which is the primary theatre of Air Force operation.
- The Air Force ***yellow*** represents "the sun" and the excellence required of Air Force personnel.
- The ***white*** represents daylight, innocence, perfection, purity, truth, and wisdom.
- The ***red*** color represents the blood of life, boldness, courage, hardiness, liberty, magnanimity, passion, patriotism, sentiment, strength, valor, and zeal.

The **disc shape** is used because the AFJROTC organization is not a group or higher organization authorized its own flag. Flag-bearing organizations display their coat of arms on a modified heater-shaped shield.

Lesson 2 Review

Using complete sentences, answer the following questions on a sheet of paper.

1. Why do people wear uniforms?
2. List two professions that you would associate with wearing a uniform.
3. What does wearing the military uniform represent?
4. What did Romans wear to indicate they were candidates for public office?
5. List two things that helped identify military units in the 17th century.
6. List three activities in which wearing the military uniform is not allowed.
7. List two activities where the military uniform is allowed to be worn.
8. How is a cell phone properly carried while in uniform?
9. Describe the special teams uniform.
10. If you wear a bracelet, what restrictions apply while in uniform?
11. When are sunglasses allowed to be worn?
12. Provide two examples of what natural hair coloring should look like.
13. If a ribbon is awarded more than once, what device is attached to the ribbon to indicate this?
14. What is the highest position held by any enlisted personnel in the US Air Force?
15. When wearing ribbons on your uniform, what is the order of precedence?
16. On the AFJROTC patch, what does the lamp represent?

APPLYING YOUR LEARNING

17. Review appearance and grooming standards from this lesson. Explain three standards you think are most important.

LESSON 3

Customs and Courtesies for Junior ROTC

Quick Write

Jot down three customs in your everyday life—based on friendships, family, sports, or community activities—that you think are important. Why are they important?

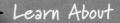

Learn About

- customs and courtesies
- historic customs and courtesies
- proper methods to demonstrate recognition and respect
- military time

"If a man be gracious and courteous to strangers, it shows he is a citizen of the world."

Francis Bacon, English philosopher and scientist

Customs and Courtesies

One of the most important things you will learn in life is taught in this first chapter. It is a series of traditional military customs and courtesies. You will learn to use these as you talk and act among the people inside your Junior ROTC unit. These customs and courtesies will also help you build confidence in yourself as you deal with all kinds of people as you grow toward adulthood.

What is a custom? A courtesy? Why are they different? Why are they important independently?

The *American Heritage Dictionary of the English Language* defines custom as *a traditional practice or usual way of doing something followed by a social group or people; a habitual practice of a person; or, the tradition or body of such practices.*

Although we often use the term, we rarely think about how customs affect our lives.

Consider clothing. By custom, you can wear certain types of clothing for some occasions but not for others. Shorts or jeans might be just right for a backyard cookout, but considered unsuitable for a formal dinner. Custom dictates some functions require you to be dressed more formally than others. People who mock an established custom—by wearing shorts to a formal dinner, for example—show an indifference to or lack of consideration for the standards and feelings of other members of a group or society.

Every group involved in a common undertaking observes customs. Customs vary from family to family, region to region, and country to country. For example, families celebrate major holidays differently. How do you greet other people?

Many people in Asian countries bow, rather than shake hands, when they meet someone. Religious customs also differ widely around the world. Even in your town or neighborhood, you will find different practices in worship.

Even professions have customs. Doctors and lawyers, for example, have a custom to respect the privacy of their patients or clients. If doctors gossip about their patients, they will lose them. If a lawyer violates the privacy of a client, the lawyer's reputation and practice will suffer. In addition, professionals who betray their patients' or clients' confidentiality may be sued or discredited.

Customs, then, are like unwritten laws. People obey customs because they help us get along with others. People cannot create their own customs and expect others to follow them. As a member of a JROTC program, you will inherit many customs. Some customs began with the Army or the Navy; others started when the Air Force became a separate military branch. All of these customs serve as keys to proper behavior in both military and civilian life. Paying attention to these customs will help you adjust to your JROTC unit. The carryover into civilian life will be almost automatic, and will greatly benefit you in your future career path and social life.

Let's now discuss courtesy. In general, the act of **courtesy** is an individual act of *polite behavior or gesture; a willingness or generosity to provide what is needed (to a person or group)*. In the military, a courtesy is an expression of consideration or respect for others. Military customs and courtesies go beyond basic politeness. They help build morale and discipline. **Morale** is *a mental and emotional state of enthusiasm, confidence, and loyalty in team members and followers*.

Customs and courtesies also contribute to an **esprit de corps**. This is *a common spirit of enthusiasm and devotion to a cause among the members of a group*. Military customs teach us about how to pay **allegiance**, or *loyalty or obligation to a person, nation, leader, or cause*. Customs and courtesies also remind us of the sacrifice required by all who have served or currently serve in the military.

Vocabulary

- custom
- courtesy
- morale
- esprit de corps
- allegiance
- board
- RHIP
- title
- taboo
- court-martial
- military time
- Greenwich Mean Time (GMT)

"To be humble to superiors is duty, to equals, courtesy, to inferiors, nobleness."

—Benjamin Franklin

Military customs and courtesies can also help with mission success. They ensure a consistent respect for the chain of command. They build a base for self-discipline that is needed in times of crisis.

The customs and courtesies surrounding traditional ceremonies allow us to honor properly those who have served well and faithfully. The custom of mass formation helps develop units that act together in their efforts to execute movements, render honors, preserve tradition, and stimulate esprit de corps.

Historic Customs and Courtesies

Many customs and courtesies have a long history as part of people's behavior.

Position of Honor

We learn, as part of military courtesy, to walk or sit to the left of individuals of higher rank or position. This custom began centuries ago when men still fought with swords. Because most men were right handed, the heaviest fighting occurred on the right. The shield was carried on the left arm, and the left side became defensive. Men and units were proud of their fighting ability; they considered the right of a battle line to be a post of honor. When an officer walks on your right, he or she is symbolically filling the position of honor.

Cadets showing position of honor.
Courtesy of Michael Wetzel/US Air Force JROTC

Hand Salute

The hand salute is another example of a military custom that began long ago. In fact, it is so old that its origin is uncertain. Some say it began in later Roman times (1 A.D. to 500 A.D.). Others trace the beginnings of the hand salute to the Middle Ages. Knights wore suits of armor, which included a helmet and a visor. When two knights on horseback met, they would raise their visors to expose their faces. If the knights recognized one another as allies, they would leave their visors up and drop their hands. This was always done with the right hand, since the left hand held the horse's reins.

The salute changed when European free men who served as soldiers began carrying their own weapons. When these soldiers met, they would raise their right hands to show that they held no weapons and that the meeting was friendly. This practice gradually became a way of showing respect. In early American history, the custom sometimes involved removing the hat. By 1820, this was modified to touching the hat. You may have even seen this practice repeated often in old western movies. Cowboys, for example, greeted each other in this way. They would tip their hats to those in authority, like a local sheriff, or to prominent men and women of wealth or position in society. Since then, the hand salute has become the one used today.

Though it varies in form across the globe, the hand salute says, "I greet you." It is also customary to greet another member of the military with words when you meet face-to-face. When you salute an officer, say "Good morning (afternoon or evening) sir/ma'am," depending on the time of day. By returning the salute you say, "I return your greeting."

The salute signals that you recognize and respect your comrades in the honorable profession of arms. A sloppy salute, on the other hand, shows a lack of confidence or respect. People may think that you do not understand the meaning of the salute or that you are not proud of the unit.

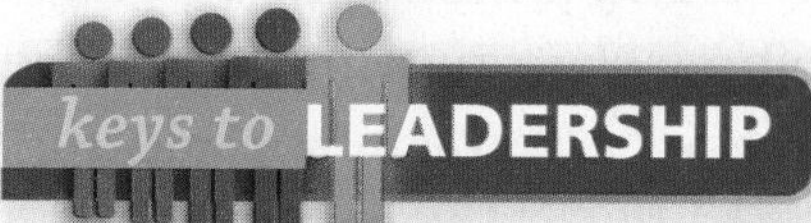

You should salute your fellow cadets and officers with pride in a friendly, cheerful, and willing manner.

In addition, when you honor the Colors you show respect for your country with a firm, confident hand salute.

How you salute tells a lot about your attitude as a cadet. If you salute proudly and smartly, it shows your personal pride and your pride in the unit. It shows that you have confidence in your abilities as a cadet.

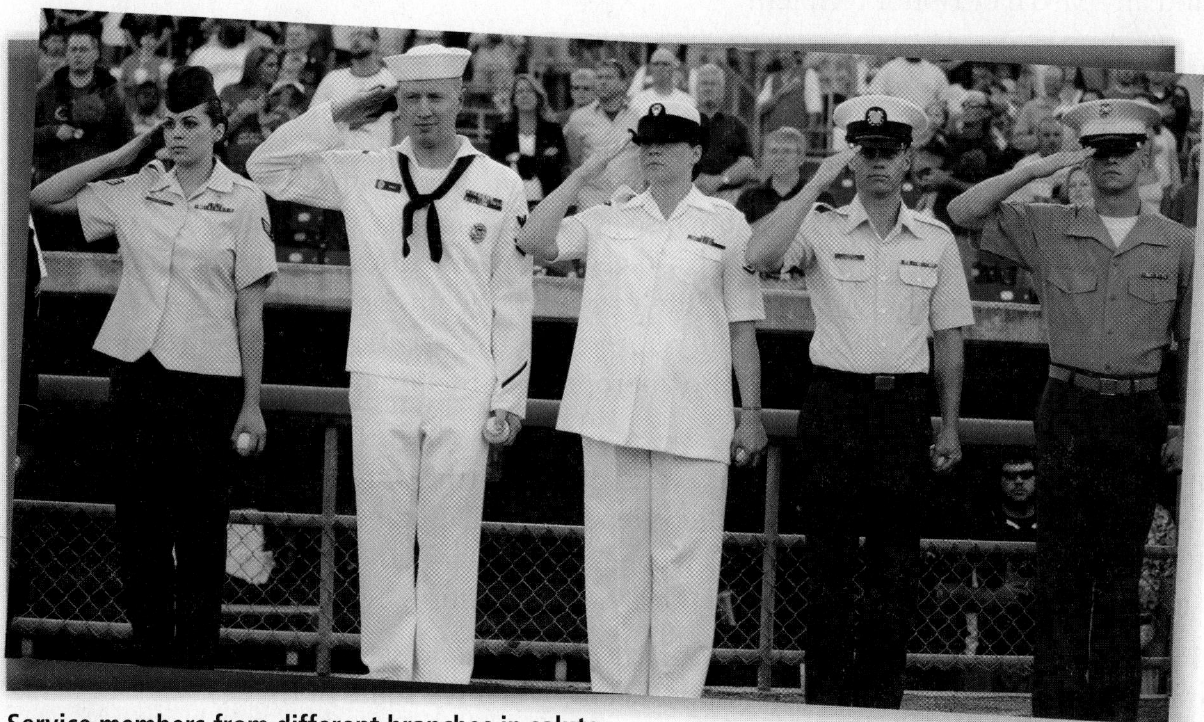

Service members from different branches in salute.

Courtesy of Senior Airman Kayla Newman/Defense Video & Imagery Distribution System

How to Salute

To execute the hand salute (see previous photo), raise your right hand smartly so the tip of your forefinger touches the lower part of your headgear just to the right of your right eye. When you are not wearing headgear, your forefinger should just touch your right eyebrow. If you are wearing glasses, touch the tip of the right forefinger to that point on the glasses where the frame meets the right edge of the eyebrow. Your arm, shoulder to elbow, should be parallel to the ground at a natural angle (about 115 degrees forward) from your body. Your thumb and fingers should be extended and joined with a straight line between the tip of your middle finger and your elbow. Your posture should be erect and alert; head and eyes should be turned toward the person you are saluting, unless you are in formation. Be careful not to tilt your head toward your hand; bring your hand all the way up. Drop the salute smartly. Move your hand smoothly to your side in one motion without slapping your side. Never have anything in your mouth or your right hand when saluting.

You must be in one of the following positions before rendering the salute: standing at attention or marching at attention. A junior member should begin the salute in time for a higher-ranking officer to return it before passing the junior member. Remember, when you are returning a salute, turn your head and eyes toward the officer and salute.

Whom to Salute

Salute the President of the United States, all commissioned and warrant officers of the United States Armed Forces, and officers of friendly foreign nations. You should also salute the Secretary of Defense, the secretaries of the US military service branches, and any Medal of Honor recipient.

When to Salute

Members of the Armed Forces, which are a nation's military forces, exchange salutes in many situations when in uniform. The person who is saluted always returns the salute, unless he or she is unable to do so because of physical incapacity or when the right hand cannot be freed, as in carrying packages. A superior whose hands are full with packages, etc., need not return the salute. However, the junior member must salute and the senior member should nod in return or verbally acknowledge the salute. An exchange of verbal greetings is also appropriate if the junior member is carrying articles in both hands.

By tradition, if you are of junior rank, you salute first (the only exception to this occurs when a unit commander gives an official report to an adjutant who might be junior). If you are of junior rank, and see and recognize a military officer dressed in civilian clothes, you should salute the officer. Always return salutes by those of lower rank.

The basic rule is that, upon recognition, the military hand salute is rendered to all officers outdoors, with some exceptions. Below, you'll see some of these.

The military hand salute is not rendered indoors, except when performing a formal report to, or receiving a formal award from, an officer. This will be covered later in Lesson 6. Salutes are also exchanged at the conclusion of a conversation.

There often seems to be some misunderstanding about exactly when to salute. The following information should answer some common questions about when to salute.

Outdoors

Outdoor salutes are exchanged upon recognition of officers and warrant officers of the Armed Forces by JROTC cadets and enlisted personnel. The term *outdoors* means being outside a building, including areas such as open porches, covered sidewalks, bus stops, covered or open entryways, and reviewing stands. Salutes will be exchanged outdoors any time officers and warrant officers and JROTC cadets or enlisted members of the Armed Forces cross paths. The salute will be exchanged with a person on the sidewalk or with a person approaching or in the same structure. This applies both on and off military installations. Even when two out-of-uniform members of the military are outdoors and recognize one another, they usually exchange salutes (if the exchange of salutes is otherwise inappropriate). The salute is also rendered anytime you are outside and the National Anthem is playing. The salute is made from the position of attention, facing the Colors, or if not visible, facing the direction from which you hear the music.

Exceptions

Here are some special circumstances when salutes are not customarily exchanged:

Marked Government Vehicles/Staff Cars. Military pedestrians (including gate sentries) and officers in moving military vehicles do not have to exchange salutes. However, when the passengers in a vehicle are easily seen to be officers (for example, officers in appropriately marked vehicles), they must be saluted.

Standing in a Group. If you are part of a small group that is not in formation, the first person to see the officer calls the group to attention, and everyone should face the officer and salute. If an officer addresses the group or an individual in the group, everyone should remain at attention until the end of the conversation, unless otherwise ordered. At the end of the conversation, everyone should salute the officer.

In Formation. If you are in formation and an officer approaches, the person in charge of the group calls the members to attention and salutes for the group.

Work Details. If you are in charge of a work detail, salute for the entire group when you meet an officer.

Civilian Clothes. Saluting a person wearing civilian clothes is not required, but is recommended if you recognize the officer.

Proper Methods to Demonstrate Recognition and Respect

Even though you may not be able to distinguish the specific rank, you can recognize an officer by the:

- Service hat visor or band
- Hat or beret insignia
- Flight cap and insignia

In addition, marked government vehicles and staff cars may indicate that an officer is aboard.

Common acts of courtesy among all military personnel help maintain discipline and promote the smooth conduct of military affairs. When courtesy is not maintained within a unit, discipline also suffers and the success of the mission can be put in danger. Although many military courtesies involve the salute, other courtesies are also important.

Reporting to an Officer or Board

You are required to report to an officer anytime you have officially asked for and received permission to speak to the officer. You must also report if you have been notified that an officer wishes to speak to you. You must also use proper reporting procedures when reporting to any board, such as promotion or discipline. A **board** is *a group of persons having managerial, supervisory, and/or advisory powers*. The manner in which you report to an officer will create a good or bad impression. Remember that your advancement within JROTC depends partly on the impression you make on your instructors or board members. You will make a good impression if you report to an officer properly and demonstrate good military bearing. The reporting procedure is broken down into three separate steps: entrance, reporting, and departure.

Step 1—Enter and halt.

Courtesy of Michael Wetzel/ US Air Force JROTC

Entrance

Before entering the room or office, make sure your cell phone ringtone is set to silent or turned off. Knock once firmly and loudly enough to be heard in an average-sized room. If you don't get an answer in a reasonable amount of time, knock again. When told to enter, march in at the position of attention. Take the most direct route to the officer or board. Halt approximately two paces from the officer or from the desk if the officer is seated, or board members. Always halt in a way that places you squarely facing the officer or board.

Step 2—Reporting.
Courtesy of Michael Wetzel/US Air Force JROTC

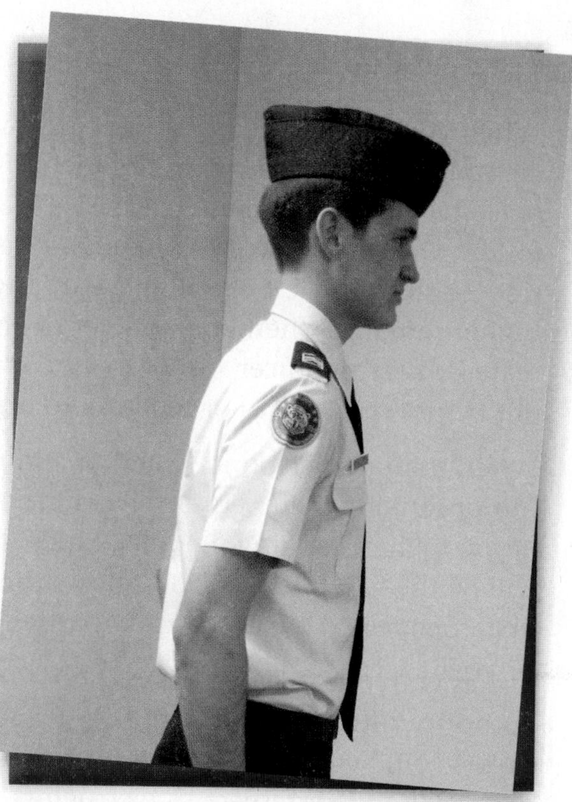

Step 3—Departure.
Courtesy of Michael Wetzel/US Air Force JROTC

Reporting Process

Reporting is the most critical step. Report in a military manner with snap and precision, but do not exaggerate the movements. The first thing to do is to salute properly. Begin your reporting statement at the time your hand reaches the saluting position. Speak in a clear, conversational tone of voice. If you were told to report, say "Sir/Ma'am, Cadet (your last name) reports as ordered." If you are reporting on your own, say "Sir/Ma'am, Cadet (your last name) reports." Hold the salute until you have completed the reporting statement and the officer, or highest-ranking board member has returned your salute. Stand at attention unless ordered otherwise. When the conversation is finished—or the officer or board has dismissed you—come to attention and properly salute. Hold the salute until the officer or highest-ranking board member returns it, and then drop the salute.

Departure

As soon as you drop the salute, complete the appropriate facing movement (about face, left face, right face, or a face in marching) and march or walk at the position of attention. Take the most direct route on the way out. Maintain proper military bearing at all times.

Personal Courtesies

When you are involved with officers—whether they are JROTC cadet officers or commissioned officers in any branch of the military—always take care to observe personal courtesies. These courtesies are usually simple acts of politeness anyone would follow. Only a few courtesies are unique to the military. As mentioned earlier, walk, ride, or sit to the left of a higher-ranking person. This means always give one who is higher-ranking, whether an officer or enlisted person, the place of honor. If you are seated when an officer speaks to you, stand. If you are in a parked vehicle, always get out before speaking to or replying to higher-ranking personnel not in the vehicle.

When military personnel enter an automobile, the highest-ranking member enters last. Junior-ranking members enter a vehicle first and take the seat that will be to the left of the highest-ranking member. Since the higher-ranking person gets in last, he or she will be the first one out. This allows the ranking officer or enlisted member to be the first one greeted by any waiting parties.

Just as with our military forces, JROTC cadets should not forget the proper lines of authority. Situations requiring close and frequent contact between instructors and cadets could create an air of informality. In such instances, cadets must remember to display proper respect to instructors, so the relationship stays the same between instructor and cadet. Instructor staff should practice common courtesy and good human relations with JROTC cadets. Instructors realize that cadets are valuable members of a JROTC unit, and must be treated as such. Instructors should also provide cadets with the proper amount of status, authority, and practical support to carry out their responsibilities.

The letters RHIP stand for "*rank has its privileges*." Why does higher rank come with additional privilege? This is because privilege and responsibility go hand-in-hand. The two are inseparable in the military, just as they are in civilian life. A person who assumes more responsibility should enjoy a few special privileges and courtesies. The President of the United States, as Commander-in-Chief, for example, enjoys privileges such as living in the White House. He also has government transportation and personal protection, paid for by our federal taxes.

Depending upon their rank and position, members of the Armed Forces also enjoy certain privileges. For example, most NCOs are exempt from manual labor while supervising work details. Senior ranking officials often receive reserved parking spaces. However, it's important to remember this precaution about RHIP. Positions must never be abused. NCOs who use junior-ranking service members to run personal errands are misusing their positions and their privileges.

Cadets need to remember that the mission of JROTC, along with the unit's morale, must come first. Whenever you are awarding or receiving privileges ask: How will this affect the mission and the unit? Problems may arise if members of the unit feel that

The Commander-in-Chief is given the place of honor.
Courtesy of Tech. Sgt. Eric Miller/Defense Video & Imagery Distribution System

a privilege has been undeservedly or unfairly given another. As a result, morale might decline, and disciplinary problems could arise that affect the mission. The privileges of rank and position are indeed worth working for and attaining. However, the best privileges are those you earn, not those you take and have not earned.

Use of Military Titles

Using correct titles is another important act of military courtesy. It shows respect for the individual's rank. You might wonder why the Armed Forces place so much emphasis on titles, but consider for a moment what a title is. It is *a formal name given to a person because of office, grade/rank, hereditary privilege, or as a mark of respect.* Individuals hold a title that matches a particular grade/rank. As members move from one grade/rank to the next, they also earn a title associated with each grade/rank. You will find that military personnel are proud of their titles because they signify hard work and success. When you address personnel by their titles, you are showing proper courtesy and respect to them as individuals as well as to their grade/rank. In addition, you are demonstrating your professionalism and discipline as a military member.

Even though the various services encourage the use of official military titles, higher-ranking members may address those under them by their first names. However, as you saw just above under Personal Courtesies, junior-ranking members must not communicate with higher-ranking individuals so informally. However, there are correct uses of military titles depending on whether communication is informal or formal.

If you are using written communication, you will use the individual's full title in the address line and salutation of formal, official correspondence: for example, The President, The Honorable (Governor, United States Senate, House of Representatives), Lieutenant Colonel, First Lieutenant, Chief Master Sergeant, or Technical Sergeant, etc.

When you speak to officers or NCOs, use their formal or abbreviated military titles, such as Lieutenant Colonel or Colonel; Second Lieutenant or Lieutenant; Chief Master Sergeant or Chief; Staff Sergeant or Sergeant. You may also use Sir or Ma'am, depending on the gender.

Address civilians as Mr., Mrs., Miss, or Ms. Address medical doctors and dentists, as well as veterinarians, as Doctor. A chaplain is officially designated Chaplain, regardless of rank or military service. A chaplain may also be called Father, Reverend, Rabbi, or by another title appropriate to the faith represented. Address other JROTC cadets as Mister/Miss, Cadet, or by their rank followed by the last name.

Retirees are a key part of the military. Treat them with the same respect and courtesies you show active duty members. By public law, they have earned and are entitled to enjoy certain benefits, rights, and privileges from the US government. One of these rights is that they are entitled to be addressed, both in written and verbal communication, by their retired rank.

keys to LEADERSHIP

Show respect to any person in authority. Recognize the person's presence by being courteous and respectful in bearing, behavior, and speech. An example of this is standing up and extending a verbal greeting when someone of higher rank enters the room or approaches, whether it is in an office area, classroom, or elsewhere. If you are on a cell phone or using another electronic device, hang up your cell phone and put it or the electronic device in a safe place out of sight. Your courtesy identifies your awareness of the value of respect in any organization and community.

Additional Courtesies

Calling a Room to Attention

When an officer or dignitary enters a room, stand at attention. If you are on a cell phone or other electronic device, hang up, put the device down, and wait until told to take a seat. If more than one person is present, the first person to see the officer or dignitary calls the group to attention. However, if an officer of equal or higher rank is already in the room, do not call the room to attention. Call the room to attention again as the officer or dignitary departs. If you are by yourself, do not call the room to attention; however, you must stand at attention until the officer or dignitary has departed.

Don't Keep People Waiting

One of the most valuable habits you can develop is to always be on time. Nothing is more irritating than being asked to be somewhere at a specific time and then having to wait because you or the other person is late. At times, you may not be able to avoid being late. If this happens, call ahead to inform those who are waiting for you that you are going to be late or to reschedule the appointment.

Dining-In and Dining-Out as Lessons in Courtesy

As a junior ROTC cadet, you will become familiar with the custom of dining-in and dining-out, which refer to formal military dinners. These are part of the traditional customs and courtesies you learn as a cadet. You will learn more about the etiquette of dining-in and dining-out as part of JROTC rules of etiquette later in Lesson 6.

Taboos

Avoiding taboos goes hand-in-hand with observing customs and courtesies. A taboo is *a prohibition excluding something from use, approach, or mention*. Taboos may be the result of long-held traditions or the requirements of good taste. You should not scoff at taboos, even when they strike you as being absurd. You may inadvertently offend someone or some group. Below are some taboos that are frowned upon in the military.

Showing Disrespect to the Uniform

Bad conduct in uniform is a longstanding taboo. Aside from the disrespect a person reaps as a result of bad conduct, it is a disgrace to the uniform and the branch of service represented. The good impression created by a large number of cadets who have dressed and behaved properly in public can be destroyed by just one cadet who presents a poor appearance or acts inappropriately.

Military members can be court-martialed for disgracing the uniform through bad conduct or by violating the regulations that govern wearing of the uniform. A court-martial is *a military or naval court of officers and, occasionally, enlisted personnel appointed by a commander to try offenders under military law*. Part of the Air Force mission is to keep citizens of the United States interested in airpower. As a result, anything that detracts from a favorable impression also detracts from the success of the Air Force mission.

Electronic Devices

Nothing shows greater disrespect to another person than to continue talking on your cell phone, or to use an electronic device while the other person is trying to have a conversation with you. This indicates to the other person that you are not interested in what they have to say. If you are using your electronic device while an officer or NCO is talking to you, this shows disrespect for authority and higher-ranking service members. This may detract from the favorable impression that higher-ranking members have previously held for you, and may affect your advancement in the unit.

Gossip

Gossip, because it often causes quarrels and disputes, is considered taboo. A unit's morale may be damaged by feuds that arise from gossip. With the growth of social media and blogs on the Internet, it is very easy to be tempted to believe everything you read. However, the Internet is not a center of integrity. More often than not, it serves as a huge rumor mill that can get you caught up in telling and passing half-truths or outright untruths about others, is considered a form of bullying and may be against the law. Indulging in this behavior can be very harmful to you and those you speak about.

Vulgar Conduct and Language

Vulgar conduct and language are taboo behaviors. Neither JROTC cadets nor instructors should lose their temper to the point of using profanity, particularly in addressing junior-ranking members of the unit. Instructors and cadets who use abusive and profane language to make a point show lack of self-control—not to mention a limited vocabulary. Cadets may risk receiving a reprimand if their conduct is poor, affecting their chance of advancement or the ability to hold their current position. Worse, any use of profane or abusive language by any members of the unit undermines their effectiveness as leaders.

Military Time

The most commonly used form of telling time in the world today is to use the 24-hour clock. In the United States, this is referred to as military time, which operates off the 24-hour clock, beginning at midnight. The first country to use the 24-hour clock was Italy in the 1800s, with the US Navy adopting the 24-hour clock in 1920 and the rest of the US Military by World War II.

Suppose you are told to be somewhere by 0600 ("oh-six-hundred"). It means that your arrival should be at 6:00 a.m., civilian time. All of the military services use military time, commonly known as *the 24-hour clock*. It is used in every facet of military life.

When you state time to a fellow cadet or instructor, you should pronounce time in one of four possible ways. If the time is 12:15 a.m., or 15 minutes past midnight, you would say "zero-zero-fifteen" or "zero-zero-fifteen hours." You may also say "oh-oh-fifteen," or "oh-oh-fifteen hours." Many military people use the term "zero" (such as "zero-three-fifteen") when the time is not exactly on the hour, or exactly on the half-hour. They will use "oh" for such times as "oh-eight-hundred" (8:00 a.m.) or "oh-nine-thirty" (9:30 a.m.).

Table 1.3 shows a basic conversion chart for civilian to military time.

Table 1.3 Military Time Conversion Chart

Standard	24-Hour	Standard	24-Hour
12 midnight	0000	12 noon	1200
12:01 a.m.	0001	12:01 p.m.	1201
12:15 a.m.	0015	2:15 p.m.	1415
12:30 a.m.	0030	7:30 p.m.	1930
12:45 a.m.	0045	11:45 p.m.	2345
1:00 a.m.	0100	1:00 p.m.	1300
2:00 a.m.	0200	2:00 p.m.	1400
3:00 a.m.	0300	3:00 p.m.	1500
4:00 a.m.	0400	4:00 p.m.	1600
5:00 a.m.	0500	5:00 p.m.	1700
6:00 a.m.	0600	6:00 p.m.	1800
7:00 a.m.	0700	7:00 p.m.	1900
8:00 a.m.	0800	8:00 p.m.	2000
9:00 a.m.	0900	9:00 p.m.	2100
10:00 a.m.	1000	10:00 p.m.	2200
11:00 a.m.	1100	11:00 p.m.	2300

Greenwich Mean Time (GMT)

When it comes to operational matters (such as communications, training exercises, deployments, ship movements, aircraft flights, etc.), the military often coordinates with bases and personnel located in other time zones. To avoid confusion, the military uses time called Greenwich Mean Time (GMT), *established to aid worldwide navigation and is based on the zero degree north/south line running through Greenwich, England.* At this time, there are currently 24 time zones around the world, with 12 time zones east of Greenwich and 12 west of Greenwich. The US Military refers to GMT as *Zulu Time*, and they attach the "Zulu" (Z) suffix, to ensure the time zone referred to is clear.

For example, two commanders may need to talk about an upcoming joint-base exercise. Although one commander is located in Germany and the other commander in California, they agree the commander in Germany will call at 1800 Z. By adjusting their respective local times to Zulu Time, the commander in California will know what time to expect the phone call. The commander in California would add 8 hours to his or her local time and the commander in Germany would subtract 2 hours from his or her local time. Therefore, the commander in California can expect a call at 1000 local and the commander in Germany will place the call at 2000 local.

More time zone locations and conversion charts can be found on the Internet on various sites including *http://wwp.greenwichmeantime.com*.

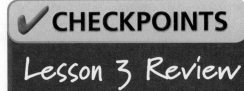

Lesson 3 Review

Using complete sentences, answer the following questions on a sheet of paper.

1. Why do people tend to obey customs?
2. In the military what does courtesy express?
3. Why do customs and courtesies help with mission success?
4. In early Europe, soldiers would raise their right hands to show what?
5. If you are wearing glasses, what should the right forefinger touch when saluting?
6. If you are outside, in uniform, what should do when you hear the National Anthem playing?
7. When reporting to a military officer or board what is the first thing you should before entering the room?
8. What should a cadet do when a military officer or dignitary enters a room?
9. What do cadets who use abusive and profane language show?
10. If you are told to report at 0730, what time is that using standard time?
11. Write the following times in military time: 12:15 a.m. and 12:15 p.m.; 3:00 a.m. and 3:00 p.m.

APPLYING YOUR LEARNING

12. Describe three ways you can demonstrate rank, recognition, and respect within your JROTC unit.

LESSON 4

Attitude, Discipline, and Respect

Quick Write

Based on the examples in the opening section on the importance of a positive attitude, list five words that you think best describe a positive attitude.

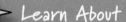

Learn About

- the importance of a positive attitude
- the importance of discipline

"There is very little difference in people, but that little difference makes a big difference. The little difference is attitude."

W. Clement Stone, businessman and motivational author

The Importance of a Positive Attitude

Attitude

Have you ever heard someone comment on another person's attitude? After a basketball game, for example, a coach might say, "Jim has a positive attitude. He's a real asset to the team." Or maybe you've heard someone say, "Bill won't succeed because he has a bad attitude." Did you ever wonder exactly what this means? Why is a positive attitude considered important for success in almost every activity? This lesson will explore the meaning and importance of a good attitude.

Attitude makes a difference in many facets of your personal life, and your life in the community. Good citizens reflect a positive attitude. It's more than just allegiance to their community and nation. They value and respect their responsibilities as citizens. In part, they do this by caring for others within their communities and beyond. In another way, they are ready and willing to defend the rights and privileges they have under the US Constitution. As good citizens, they are willing to give their time, effort, and money to help others and improve community life for everyone.

Examples of positive attitudes toward citizenship are everywhere. After Hurricane Katrina in 2005, hundreds of American citizens, many trained in emergency response, traveled long distances to New Orleans, Louisiana and surrounding areas. They helped people who lost power or their homes to flooding, or who were severely injured. Many just needed food, water, and basic shelter. Citizens who are Red Cross volunteers helped with these and other necessities. Police officers from other communities came voluntarily to help families and damaged businesses with security needs.

After Hurricane Sandy devastated the Maryland, Delaware, New Jersey, and Long Island shorelines in 2012, thousands of concerned citizens went to these areas to help. Many were construction workers trying to assist in rebuilding homes before government help could be obtained. Popular singers put on a huge live performance to raise funds to help the people start their massive cleanup and rebuilding efforts.

In future lessons, you will learn more about the need for citizens' involvement, and why it is so important. For now, let us explore just what is meant by attitude, and how you can develop a positive attitude to become a better citizen.

Attitude is *a state of mind*. It may be positive or it may be negative. Your attitude affects the success or failure of most of your activities. Your attitude reflects your personal philosophy of life and is shown through your actions. Your attitude is the frame of mind in which you view yourself, your work, and others.

Attitude is catching. One basketball player with a positive attitude, for example, can inspire a winning spirit for an entire basketball team. No matter how far the team is behind in a game, that person's hustle and drive—signs of positive attitude or energy—can energize a team's effort.

The late UCLA basketball coach, John Wooden, was known for his inspiring leadership. He coached his teams to rare undefeated seasons. "A leader's most powerful ally is his or her own example," he said. His teams were known for always having one or two players who inspired their teammates by their positive attitudes.

It is also true that a player who goes out onto the court and holds back because he or she feels it's not worth the effort can slow down the progress of the entire team. This negative attitude is just as contagious as a positive one.

It is especially important to have a positive attitude whenever you are in a leadership role. When you're in a position of leadership, those under you will reflect your attitude. In other words, if you convey an attitude of encouragement, those under and around you are more likely to be positive.

Vocabulary

- attitude
- integration
- foundation
- discipline
- en masse
- morale
- professional
- integrity

A Positive Attitude Can Achieve Great Things

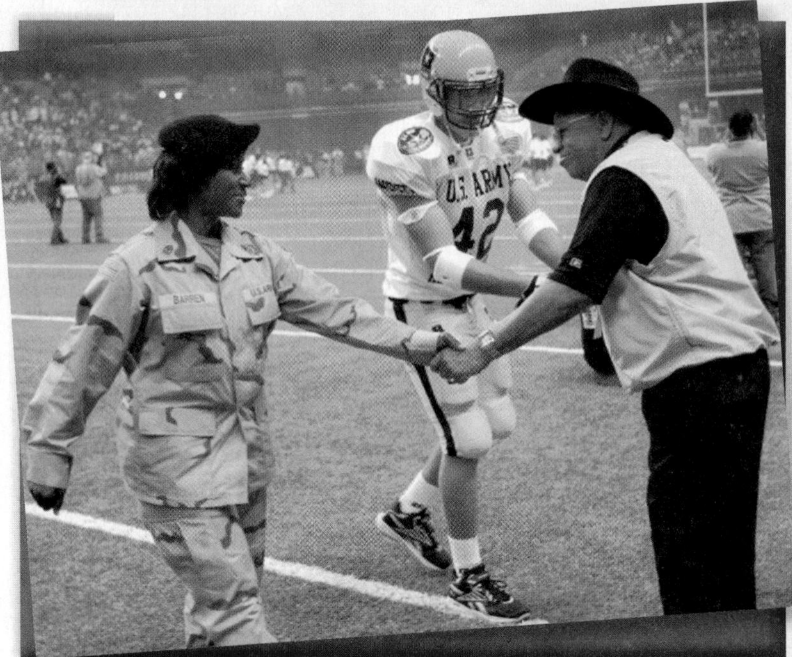

Herman Boone, far right, takes part in the US Army All-American Bowl in 2011. The trophy is named the Herman Boone Championship Trophy in his honor.

Courtesy of the US Army/www.army.mil

These two brief examples illustrate how a leader's positive attitude can achieve great things, despite the odds.

Herman Boone

It was 1971. With the United States still fighting a war overseas in Vietnam, there was another conflict at home over integration of schools through busing. Integration is *a federal law requiring the equal access to schools, buildings, or organizations regardless of the color of one's skin or ethnic background.*

Such was the case at T.C. Williams High School in Alexandria, Virginia. At T.C. Williams, the racial tensions were made more prominent by the fact that the school hired Herman Boone, a black man, known for his winning record at another school, to take over a high school football team—the Titans—that was newly integrated, and was playing against mostly all-white schools. It had been thought that another coach, Bill Yoast, who was white, and a long-time assistant coach at T.C. Williams, would be given the head coaching position. This added to the potential for strife among both players and coaches.

By demonstrating their ability to accept the situation and work together, Boone and Yoast set a positive example for the school and the team. However, as the fall playing season neared, tension among players from different backgrounds and cultures dampened the team's will to win. The coaches came to a point where they knew they needed to instill a spirit of cooperation among the players. One way to do that, Boone decided, was to start in training camp before his first season as head coach. On the first day of their annual training camp, all the black players started out sitting on one bus, while the white players occupied another. Coach Boone switched them around, placing the offense on one bus and the defense on the other, integrating the buses, and focusing the players on working together. It was one of the first of many techniques Boone incorporated to get his players to see each other as equal teammates and to become a winning unit.

Through his positive influence and attitude, Boone went on to lead his team to the state championship. In 2000, this episode became the subject of an award-winning film, *Remember the Titans*, starring the iconic actor Denzel Washington.

Oprah Winfrey

Television talk show host Oprah Winfrey built success out of a childhood of hardship. She came from a broken home, moved from place to place, and suffered abuse, ending up on the streets of Baltimore for a time. However, she rediscovered herself after moving back with her father, who insisted on reading, self-reliance, and education. Over thirty years she rose from obscurity to become a media icon worth almost $3 billion.

Oprah's success is based on a positive attitude that rubs off on all those she meets. This attitude allowed her to build a network—a trusted group of people around her who were talented, and who served as her mentors. After she accomplished this, she gave back—investing in her mentors, peers, employees, and audiences. Not only did she often spontaneously give to people in need who came on her show, she also established several charitable efforts that bettered the world. Her image and her world reputation as a leader continue to grow to this day. One of Oprah's favorite sayings reflects the power of a positive attitude: "My philosophy is that not only are you responsible for your life, but doing the best at this moment puts you in the best place for the next moment."

In some ways, Oprah was fortunate. For part of her young life, Oprah lived with her grandmother, who gave Oprah a love for reading. With the help of her father, Oprah was able to learn a sense of self-discipline and develop her natural talents at a local radio station. She could have gone a different direction entirely after being on the streets. However, she had a foundation of self-discipline and family on which to build. A foundation is *an underlying base or support*. Without a positive attitude that she could succeed, her story could have become tragic. Instead, she serves as a mentor and leader; her example is a model for young people all over the world.

These two examples illustrate how a positive attitude sets an example, whether you are a leader or a follower. Everyone has a role to play in life. Everyone can make a difference in his or her own way.

Oprah Winfrey.

Courtesy of Getty Open Content Images

If you find yourself in a leadership role, be especially careful to stay positive. Otherwise, the efficiency of your group will fall to the level of the attitude you display, or worse. This will limit the initiative and potential you could see achieved.

Attitude and Junior ROTC

Within a week of joining the JROTC program, your instructor can determine what your attitude is. How? By the expression on your face, your posture, your tone of voice, or the amount of effort you put into meeting grooming standards. Your attitude also influences the way you prepare for class, your quiz scores, and the manner in which you address the instructor or fellow cadets. Therefore, it's not hard to get a pretty good idea of how you feel about what you are doing just by observing you.

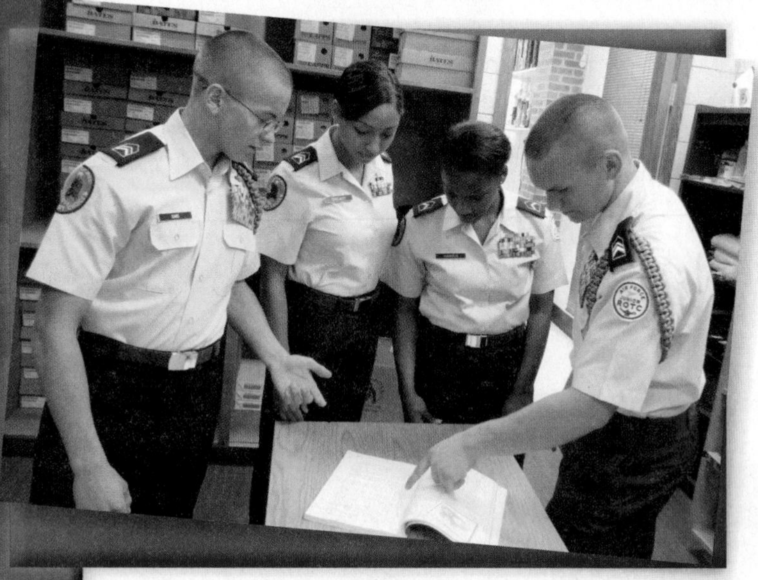

Your attitude is evident in your appearance and your actions.
Michael Wetzel/US Air Force JROTC

The JROTC program is built on the contributions of every individual. Every person in the program is a key to the success of his or her unit. If you have a positive attitude, demonstrated by working hard to reach your potential while actively participating in the program, you will be showing your willingness and ability to work with others and to share in the cooperative operation of JROTC.

However, if you have a negative attitude and fail to meet established JROTC standards, your actions could affect the success of your unit. You play an important role in your unit, so display a positive attitude in every aspect of JROTC.

How can you develop the proper attitude toward JROTC requirements and standards? The key to a positive attitude lies in understanding. You must try to understand the reasons behind JROTC activities and standards. For example, if you believe, as a cadet, that saluting, presenting a good appearance, or executing drill is a hassle, you are unlikely to develop a positive attitude toward the program. However, if you understand that there are standards that have been thought out completely and tested down through the years, you will be well on the way toward forming a positive attitude about JROTC. A positive attitude will greatly increase your chances of success in the JROTC program and all other areas of your life.

The Importance of Discipline

Discipline and the Military

The American Heritage Dictionary defines discipline this way—*training expected to produce a specific character or pattern of behavior.* According to George Washington, discipline is "the soul of an army," and indeed this applies to any military organization, from your JROTC program to our nation's armed forces at home and abroad.

People often misunderstand the real meaning of the term discipline. They tend to see it as restrictive, harsh, severe, or power for power's sake. Young people often look at discipline as classroom punishment or something found only in the military. It is seen as unpleasant and sometimes downright unreasonable.

Every soldier, sailor, marine, and airman serving in the US military trains to be a disciplined member of the armed forces. From the morning physical training session to afternoon specialized equipment training, all military members are taught to perform their duties as a well-disciplined unit. The following story illustrates how the training received by two US Army Delta Force members instilled the warfighting discipline needed on one fateful day, October 3, 1993. A Blackhawk helicopter piloted by Army Chief Warrant Officer 2 (CW2) Michael Durant was shot down by a rocket-propelled grenade while it was flying over Mogadishu, Somalia. Knowing that crewmembers were probably injured, Somali fighters began to surround and shoot at the downed helicopter and its crewmembers.

Flying over the crash site was another helicopter carrying two US Army Delta Force members, Sergeant First Class (SFC) Randall Shughart and Master Sergeant (MSG) Gary Gordon. Both agreed that if they did not assist the downed Blackhawk crewmembers, the crewmembers would not survive the attack. After receiving permission to help, Sergeants Shughart and Gordon took up fighting positions by the downed helicopter. Unfortunately, they found that only CW2 Durant had survived the crash. They removed him from the downed helicopter while still under attack from Somali fighters.

***Left*: Master Sergeant Gary Gordon.**
***Right*: Sergeant First Class Randall Shughart.**
Courtesy of US Army/www.army.mil

MSG Gordon gave CW2 Durant a weapon and ammunition, while he and SFC Shughart continued to receive heavy fire. These two highly disciplined, well-trained Delta Force members were committed to saving CW2 Durant. Although CW2 Durant survived, neither MSG Gordon nor SFC Shughart survived the battle with Somali fighters. Both men were recognized for their bravery, discipline, and selfless sacrifice by receiving the Congressional Medal of Honor, the highest combat medal any member of the armed forces can receive.

keys to LEADERSHIP

Discipline in military and civilian life brings rewards, such as promotions or pay raises. For civilians, the lack of discipline can mean failure or being fired. In the military, the lack of discipline can have a big impact on safety and morale. However, good discipline in the military also results in a reward greater than promotions or increased pay. It's the pride of protecting the safety of fellow Americans and the assurance for them to continue to enjoy the freedoms of American life.

The basic mission of the military is to protect the nation. This is a serious job. The armed forces, individually and as a whole, must be organized, trained, and equipped for combat that may last a long time. Our military forces have been engaged in combat operations in the Middle East for over 10 years. This broad responsibility means that members of all military branches must be trained to carry out that mission effectively and without hesitation. They must have discipline. Military discipline is an extension of what you have experienced in your civilian life, but adapted to what is required for the armed forces.

Discipline and Junior ROTC

What about discipline in JROTC? What is the purpose behind this discipline? What is the reason for shined shoes and drill, saluting and drill, inspections and drill? Why all the drill?

At one time, drill was absolutely necessary as training for war. When armies marched and maneuvered en masse, meaning *as a whole group*, and when the first muskets came into use, close order drill was an essential combat requirement.

Close order drill still has its place for teaching the basics of discipline, leadership, and teamwork. Drill, uniform dress, respect for higher-ranking individuals, and pride in appearance are among the important basics of your JROTC training. Here's why.

First, drill and specific performance standards teach you to act in unison with other cadets. By dressing alike and marching in formation, you begin to feel a part of something larger as each cadet begins to act as a member of a team. The effects of a mistake by a single member of the team are nowhere more apparent than on the drill field. It can be embarrassing when one cadet takes a wrong turn and marches off without the others. Learning that each individual is a vital member of a team is basic to training. The success of the group as a whole depends on every member of the formation working as one disciplined unit.

Discipline builds teamwork toward a common purpose.

Top: Courtesy of the Library of Congress Prints and Photographs Division Washington, DC 20540
Bottom: Michael Wetzel/US Air Force JROTC

Second, drill teaches individual cadets to respond instantly and subconsciously to a word or command. Close order drill teaches cadets to react like disciplined military members. If a cadet is marching and executes a right flanking movement when the command calls for a left flank, it will mean little more than embarrassment and perhaps a stubbed toe.

However, consider the tragic consequences to public safety at an Air Show highlighting the Army's Golden Knights, the Navy's Blue Angels, or the Air Force Thunderbirds if someone in the formation banked right when the commander quickly ordered to bank left. The discipline you acquire from drill can be used if you participate in sports such as football or basketball.

Discipline and teamwork are keys to success in today's high-tech military.

Clockwise, from top left: © Martijn Smeets/Fotolia.com; © Benjamin Kirk/Fotolia.com; Courtesy of US Army/www.army.mil

Third, the JROTC uniform, the drill, and the common requirements shared by all cadets give each cadet a feeling of belonging, a feeling of fellowship. You learned about this feeling of *esprit de corps* in Lesson 3. Once you realize that the ability of the group depends on the performance of each cadet, and that each cadet is judged by the group, you will feel more a part of a team. You will begin to work effectively toward common goals. Thus, esprit de corps raises individual morale, *a sense of common purpose*, and fosters teamwork within the unit.

Fourth, discipline from drill in JROTC should be viewed as self-discipline, not imposed discipline; the discipline should come from within, not from peers. If drill ever gets to be boring, if the uniform gets hot on a nice spring day, or if you are torn between shining your shoes or watching TV, remember why these things are necessary. See them as essential elements of personal discipline that can translate into success in many other areas of life.

Military history tells us from past events that discipline will determine how well a unit will perform and survive in combat. You are being taught discipline so that whether you are in the military or working in a retail store, you can be counted on to complete a task.

Attitude and discipline go hand in hand if a unit is to succeed. JROTC is the place where you and fellow cadets form initial attitudes toward the military. It is where you will develop basic concepts of military discipline. If you maintain a positive attitude, you will come out of the program well disciplined, and ready to take on challenges. When you finally choose a career, a positive attitude and self-discipline will give you a head start toward success.

Discipline and Respect

Respect for authority and discipline reinforce one another. However, discipline comes first. Self-discipline is the full and voluntary acceptance of authority. There will be rules, regulations, and standards in all areas of your adult life. JROTC will help you develop the self-discipline needed to respect fellow cadets and those in positions of authority. It will also help you become dependable in fulfilling responsibilities in other parts of your life.

Discipline and Integrity

The basic principles of integrity and conduct are guided by a sense of right and wrong. This sense is the internal compass that provides you the ability to do what is right even when no one is looking. A cadet's sense of right and wrong must be so strong that his or her behavior and motives are above suspicion. Integrity is the hallmark of a true professional, *one who conforms to a technical or ethical standard of a profession*, and there is nothing more important in the armed forces—or life, for that matter—than integrity.

Military organizations could not function without integrity, because others have to be trusted to do their jobs. Our nation has always depended on the integrity of people in the military who place the security of others ahead of their own self-interests. People have to be able to trust each other to make this sacrifice. Even in business, no employer could survive for long if they did not trust their employees. **Integrity** is *a moral compass, the inner voice, the voice of self-control, and the basis for trust.* In other words, integrity is honesty.

Integrity is not something you learn overnight. Most people have already incorporated integrity into their set of values. Your parents or guardians and schoolteachers, for example, have helped you understand the difference between right and wrong.

However, the military holds its members to a higher standard of honesty than much of society demands, so you must begin to build upon the foundation you have already established.

In the military, everyone relies on people to do their part. Often, the only way anyone knows what has been done is by another's word. Integrity is your word, your bond. Other people know when you say you did your job that they can bet their lives on it—and in the military, sometimes their lives *do* depend upon that trust. Integrity and self-discipline are cornerstones of JROTC. Integrity starts with the individual, and it starts with you right now.

Lesson 4 Review

Using complete sentences, answer the following questions on a sheet of paper.

1. What is attitude?
2. Why is a positive attitude important, especially in positions of leadership?
3. What are three ways your JROTC instructors can tell what your attitude is toward JROTC?
4. What is the definition of discipline?
5. What are three ways in which drill promotes discipline?
6. What is integrity?
7. What two terms are considered the cornerstones of JROTC?

APPLYING YOUR LEARNING

8. Attitude, responsibility, integrity, discipline: Choose one of these words and create a slogan for your JROTC unit that demonstrates the importance of that concept. Write a short paragraph explaining why you chose that word and what the slogan means to you.

LESSON 5

Ethics, Values, and Morals

Quick Write

Your best friend wants you to go with him/her to have some fun tonight. Jot down three personal guidelines you would use to decide whether it would be right or wrong to go with them.

Learn About

- ethics
- values
- core values of the US military services
- cultural and universal norms
- making ethical and moral decisions
- your personal code of conduct

"What lies behind us and what lies before us are small matters compared to what lies within us."

Ralph Waldo Emerson, American essayist, philosopher, and poet

Ethics

Adults make complex ethical decisions every day. We also know from psychology, which is *the study of the mind and of behavior,* that children at about the age of three begin to develop a conscience, a sense of right and wrong. So what is ethics and what effect does it have on us and others?

Ethics is a branch of philosophy, *the study of people's most fundamental and basic beliefs and how these beliefs are justified.* Not all philosophers agree on one definition of ethics. For our purposes, we define ethics as *the rules of conduct that people should follow.* The study of ethics helps us decide whether something we may do, say, choose, or think is right or wrong. While rules of conduct may change through the years to keep pace with changes in society, the fundamentals of ethics remain constant.

Conduct is a key word in the definition of ethics. Ethics assumes that we have the free will to make decisions and act on those decisions. You face ethical dilemmas every day you are at school. Over the course of a school year, you will take many exams to determine how much of the subject material you have learned. If your best friend sends you a text message with the answers to one of the exams, would you use the answers to cheat on the exam? When we decide whether to cheat or not to cheat, we are making a personal ethical decision about our conduct.

Four Basic Rules of Ethics

In general, philosophers agree that these four basic rules of ethics are enduring and universal:

1. Do good; avoid evil.
2. Be fair and unbiased, which means *free of favoritism.*
3. Respect the dignity of all people.
4. Be responsible for your thoughts and conduct.

The following list, derived from these four basic rules of ethics, contains a set of guidelines for human decency and well-being. Of course, this list does not contain every possible guideline. Also, a rule can be overridden if it is in conflict with another rule.

- Be honest.
- Keep promises.
- Obey and be loyal to proper authorities.
- Be courageous.
- Grow in knowledge.
- Be willing to work.
- Be moderate (don't do anything to excess).
- Maintain and enhance your health.
- Don't harm others.

Vocabulary

- psychology
- philosophy
- ethics
- unbiased
- integrity
- value system
- morals
- norms
- universal norms
- non-universal norms
- conscience

Ethics and Personal Standards

What comes to mind when you hear the word *ethics*? Are your first thoughts of laws, judges, and criminals? On the other hand, do you think of humane treatment of animals or equal treatment for all humankind? How about letting someone copy your homework or telling your best friend the latest gossip? All of these areas involve decisions based on ethics.

Willingness to work together is just one of the guidelines for human decency.
© Rido/Fotolia.com

Most of our moral beliefs are actually habits we learned as children. Doing the right thing brought praise, or at least no negative response. For example, when we walked on the rug with muddy shoes, our parents scolded us. With repetition, we learned to take off our shoes—or at least wipe them off before entering the house. We also learned that this type of behavior would keep us out of trouble.

For adults, the penalties and rewards of their habits are not so obvious—but they are just as real. Over the course of a lifetime, adults develop habits (good or bad) that can affect their reputation, social status, finances, or overall sense of well-being.

Even though habits are learned in social settings and reinforced by rewards and punishments, not all habits are right. Habits are right when they are ways of helping others and ourselves. That is, they help us to develop our best potential and to respect people's basic rights.

We use terms such as *right, good, should,* and *ought* in everyday conversations, but what do these terms mean? If we say an act is *right*, does that mean we approve of it? When we say we should not do something, is it because society disapproves of it? These are difficult questions. Both consequences and motives seem to be important in deciding what makes an act right or good. Philosophers continue to wrestle with these concepts. Meanwhile, each of us has an idea of what we believe to be right. Our beliefs may be based on what society or our parents believe or what our experiences have taught us. A combination of factors probably shapes many of our concepts. In any case, while we need to be tolerant of other people's concepts, beliefs, and feelings, we must also think and act according to our understanding of what is right and good.

As we said, not all decisions involve ethics. Nevertheless, many decisions that seem unrelated to ethics may actually have an ethical aspect. Consider the scientist who mixes together several harmless chemicals and then applies heat or pressure. The resulting products, such as plastic bags, are convenient for many types of shopping. The effect on the environment, however, can be very harmful. Plastic does not break down easily, and animals are harmed when they eat it. Thus, we must ask ourselves which we value more—the convenience of the disposable containers or the environment. These are not easy decisions to make. Technology continues to bring us new and better products; with these products come new and tougher decisions.

Concern for Others

Over time, we learn that our physical needs, such as food, air, and shelter, must be satisfied first. Once our basic needs are met, we are able to move on to higher-level needs, such as being able to recognize the needs of others, and being considerate of other people's opinions and feelings. Just like you, other people need recognition for a job or task well done; positive recognition is important to an individual's self-esteem. Receiving a pat on the back, earning a promotion, lettering in sports, or being applauded at a music recital are all examples of praise. Teachers encourage students to excel in academics. Coaches encourage their students to excel in drama, sports, music, or dance. Parents encourage their children to be the best they can be. Our friends cheer us on to make a touchdown or do well on college entrance exams. We all need a boost now and then. We need to know other people care about us, and they need to know we care about them.

Integrity

Along with showing concern for others, we should display a level of *integrity* in our daily activities that shows others that we are able to take a stand for something that we believe in. Integrity means *being honest and sincere with ourselves and with others, closely following a consistent code of ethics*. The key word here is *consistent*: not acting by one set of standards on Friday at school and another on Saturday night. It means not picking or choosing only those rules that benefit just you. It means doing what is right whether someone is watching or not. It also means having a disciplined, balanced approach to life. Being honest is sometimes painful. No one likes to admit to doing wrong or making a mistake. The following story portrays this point about personal integrity.

A high school volleyball player named Emmee Ashby admitted to the referee that a ball hit by her opponent actually touched her in bounds after the referee had called it out of bounds. This prompted a reversal of the referee's call and, in a very close game, changed the score to 23–22 in favor of Emmee's opponents.

We need to practice this kind of integrity every day. This involves our conscience, a topic that we will consider later in this lesson.

Closely related to the issue of integrity is the problem of putting success before honor. A fine line exists between a true concern for success in school or work and advancing at whatever the cost. We see examples of this kind of blind ambition in professional sports and in the financial world every day. Blind ambition can cloud our judgment. It can lead us to cover up mistakes in an effort to look good at all costs. It can also lead us to cover up for the person in charge. It takes a great deal of personal courage to say "I made a mistake" and take responsibility.

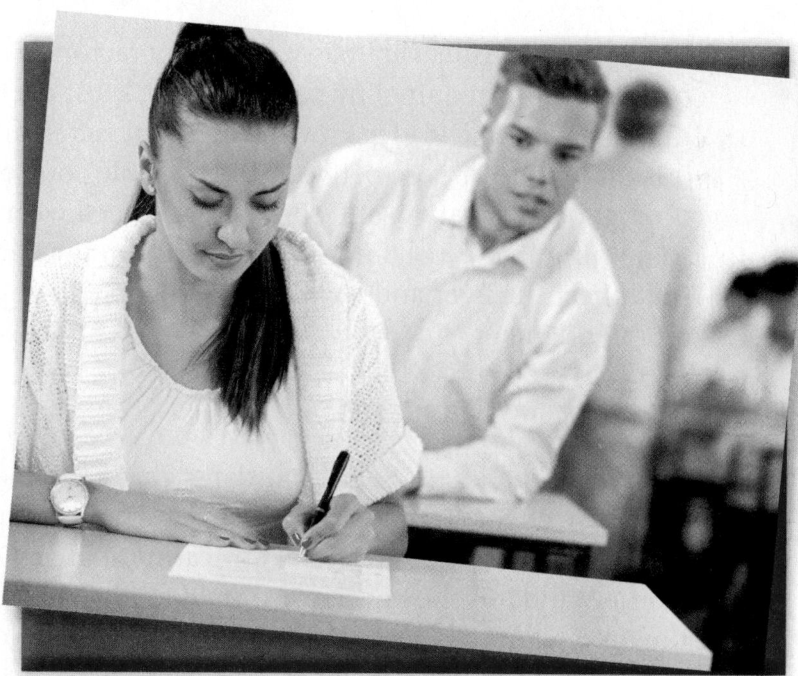

It's often tempting to cheat, but being honest with yourself defines your integrity.

© Igor Mojzes/Fotolia.com

Every JROTC program provides a *Cadet Honor Code* that each member is expected to learn and uphold. The *Cadet Honor Code* provides guidance for personal honesty and integrity that will remain with you throughout your life.

Ethical Qualities of Effective Leaders

We just finished a discussion of personal standards of ethics. Now, let's look at professional ethics—the ethics of leaders.

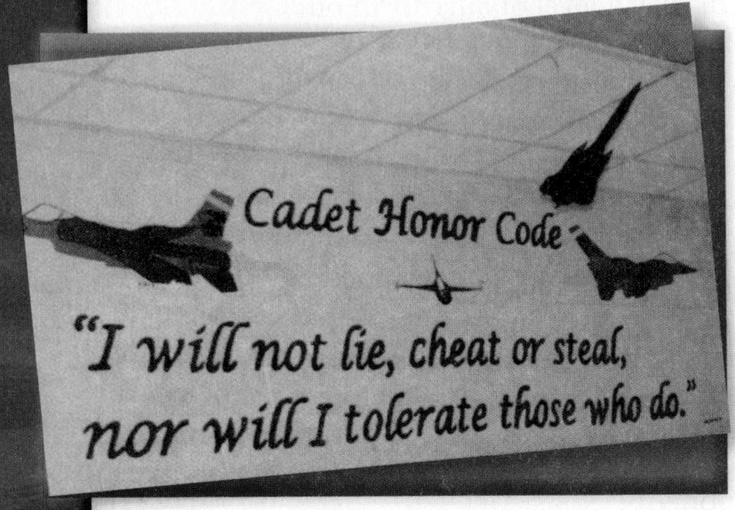

Cadet honor code.

Leaders are admired for their ability to influence others to achieve goals. Their ability to motivate people goes along with their knowledge in their field. Their technical and professional skills are finely tuned. They are able to evaluate complex situations and to determine the risks involved. They are willing to act on the judgments they make and to assume responsibility for the outcome. Continued success as a leader requires a great deal of self-discipline and personal stability. These qualities, to a large degree, are derived from the moral values and principles that influence their behavior.

Leadership decisions are based on many factors. These factors include all the considerations required by the situation. Most decisions require judgment that is influenced by the leader's own values, character, and background. In many cases, it is difficult to choose between the possible courses of action. Occasionally, there is no good alternative, and the leader is faced with having to choose between something that is bad and something that may be worse. All leadership decisions that affect the lives and well-being of people have ethical aspects and require moral judgment.

Professional Standards

Each profession has a set of standards that each member is expected to follow. When we choose to enter a profession (for example, teaching), we agree to abide by a prescribed set of professional ethical standards. Of course, we may not agree with all the standards; however, we should abide by all standards until we can work within the profession to change them. When we can no longer accept the standards, and find that we can't respect or choose to ignore them, we are ethically obligated to leave the profession—or we may be kicked out. Because professional ethical standards usually reflect the society the profession serves, disagreement with the standards is a serious action that requires serious thought. Every major action should be weighed against the effect it is likely to have on the profession, others around us, our self-respect, and the respect others have for us.

Right Choices

Right choices build confidence and self-respect; this is how integrity works. When we have taken proper action, we generally feel good about it. We regard ourselves as being worthwhile and capable. We have also earned the respect of those affected by our actions.

The ability to choose good behavior over bad behavior distinguishes effective leaders from average or poor leaders. Right choices are often difficult to make. The easy solution is frequently more attractive than the difficult, effective, and sound solution. Every day, we face situations that require action. Our choices in some situations may even call for inaction.

Here are twelve questions that may help you to make right choices.

1. If I do what I'm thinking of doing, would I be willing to have my action made into a law that requires everyone to act in the same way?
2. If I am considering using someone else for my own personal gain, would I allow myself to be used in the same way?
3. Would I be willing to explain to a jury why I chose this action?
4. Would I do this if I knew it would be on television news tonight or YouTube® tomorrow?
5. What would I think of this action if someone I disliked did it?
6. If my reason for acting this way is that everyone else does it, would I do it if no one else did it?
7. Would I do this if I knew I would have to explain my reasons to my family?
8. Would I be content with this action if it were taken by my boss or a member of my family?
9. Would I be content to have each of my followers behave exactly as I intend to in this situation?
10. My team could win the game by violating a rule. Before I call this play, would I be upset if the losing team took the same action?
11. If what I do hurts no one very much, would I be willing to let everyone do the same thing?
12. If there is very little harm in what I want to do, what kind of person will I become if it gets to be a habit?

Leaders who always try to make right choices show a great amount of ethical courage and maturity.

A key to building trust with your family, friends, and others you come into contact with is being able to *do the right thing*. If you follow the strategies in this lesson, you'll find that others will increasingly trust and value your judgment.

Cadets, more than most students, live with higher standards of order, obedience, and discipline.

Courtesy of Michael Wetzel/US Air Force JROTC

Rules and Principles of Ethical Decisions

Rules and principles have the greatest influence on our ethical decisions. When confronted with a decision that will affect others, we consciously or unconsciously ask ourselves, "What should I do?"

Society has standards for knowing what is right. The primary ethical standards in our culture are *telling the truth, keeping promises,* and *respecting people and property.* Cadets, more than most students, live with clear standards of order, obedience, and discipline.

Values

Our code of ethics is based upon our value systems, that is, our beliefs about what is and is not important to us as human beings. Freedom, happiness, equality, individualism, and volunteerism are some of the basic American values.

Every day, students add to their value systems. A value system consists of *our set of ideals, beliefs, interests, likes, and dislikes that we use every day to make decisions.* Activities like dating, skipping a school event, and even what we wear reflect our value systems. Deciding to date someone exclusively probably means we value that person's company. Skipping school band practice or a class indicates that we do not value the importance of getting an education.

Whatever the situation, ethics and value systems involve you in making individual choices, choices based on your own free will. Values do not involve involuntary behavior, such as blinking the eyes. Ethical conduct involves freely chosen behavior based on values that we individually, or as part of a group, believe to be very important.

Some people believe in doing whatever they want to do. Others believe in doing what helps other people, whether they really want to or not. Whatever the case, our beliefs are personal to each of us, and we are responsible for them. How do we know what values we have? One way is through voicing our likes and dislikes, and we do this fairly often. Another way is through positive or negative feedback on our behavior. Receiving an A on a test tells us we did well and may reflect the value we put on our studies.

One way we can begin to understand what we value as a society is through being aware of statistics on what we do and don't buy. For example, companies such as Nike® spend millions of dollars each year conducting research on what you buy and don't buy. This research will tell them which products are successful and which to eliminate.

Four Types of Values

The following four different types of values—personal, prudent, conventional, and moral—act as guidelines for our actions in all situations, whether at home, with friends, in school, while playing sports, or at work.

Personal Values

Our personal values guide our conduct. We get our personal values in many different ways. Parents, friends, family, church, and schools often affect our personal values. Freedom, happiness, equality, and peace, are some of the values that all Americans hold. Personal values may develop over time due to a number of different factors.

For the military professional, the greatest value is the public good. The aim of our defense forces is to ensure the security of the United States, and that may mean taking a new assignment every few years. On the personal side, individuals in the military want job satisfaction, a happy home, and an overall sense of fulfillment in life. Sometimes these personal and family values conflict with the values of the profession. So, our values are sometimes at odds with each other.

Prudent Values

Prudent values involve using good judgment when considering a likely course of action. These values may guide our behavior. For example, it is prudent to stay out of trouble with the law, to maintain your physical and mental health, and to establish a savings account. Sometimes people do not think ahead and therefore are not prudent. Sometimes they let values guide their conduct, such as spending money for the latest iPhone® instead of putting money in a savings account. Owning the latest and newest iPhone® may make you popular now, however, saving for the future may provide the money you need for college.

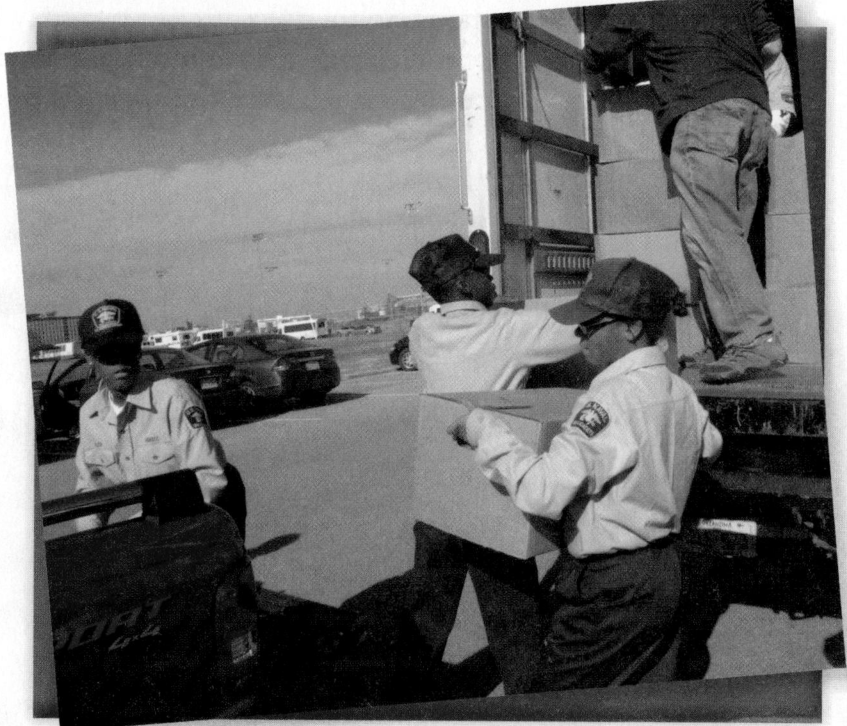

Our values are based on beliefs that are very important to us. Here US Naval Sea Cadets partner with Project Giveback, a DC-based food charity that helps feed needy families.

Courtesy of Joseph P. Cirone/Defense Video & Imagery Distribution System

Conventional Values

Conventional values are generally accepted and enforced within a given social order. They are binding upon the members of that social order. A social order might be as inclusive as a whole country or as specific as a sub-society within a larger group—such as members of a church, a high school or college community, or the United States Air Force. Respect for older people is an example of a conventional value.

Moral Values

While ethics are typically the basis for accepted rules of conduct in a society, as we stated earlier, ethics also have to do with the struggle between good and evil. The ethics of a society are written or stated to help us understand how we should act. On the other hand, the term morals refers to *our behavior, right or wrong*; often it is simply a substitute for the word *ethics*, but it may cover areas of conduct or thinking not related to ethics.

Moral values are rooted in a comprehensive view of human life, social living, and views of the ultimate purpose and meaning of life. People, even those who spend their lives devoted to the study of moral values, do not always agree completely about the nature of moral values. However, people with strong moral values believe they are the most important values to guide their lives. Moral values provide a point of view that people use to argue for social and personal change to an ideal set of values.

The moral code of Western society is based on Greek and Roman philosophy and the Judeo-Christian ethic. The Ten Commandments and the Golden Rule are Judeo-Christian contributions. So the rules we live by today have evolved through thousands of years. Some of our rules take the form of laws, such as laws against murder and arson. Others are customs, such as standing when the national anthem is played.

It is a custom to stand during the playing of the national anthem.

Courtesy of Petty Officer 1st Class Maurice Dayao/Defense Video & Imagery Distribution System

Still others are moral standards, such as rules against breaking promises (also covered by ethics) or gossiping about someone (which may or may not involve ethics).

Just as our living conditions change, our rules may change. For instance, we treat people with mental illness, people with disabilities, and people who struggle with alcoholism differently today from the way we did 50 years ago. Today, we better understand the causes of their disorders and what they need. In spite of changing conditions, however, we can agree on some common principles and rules of ethics. For example, in our society, we agree it is immoral for one of us to steal the worldly goods of another.

Some people say a moral code is meaningless because people always do what they believe is in their own best interest. They go on to say that we may claim we are interested in the welfare of others, but we always put ourselves first. For example, we tend not to conserve, preserve, or recycle unless laws force us to do so or we see a financial benefit in doing so. Some people won't conserve water unless the water rates are raised. Endangered species may have to be protected by law. Yet, we should be conserving, preserving, and recycling without these incentives, so future generations derive the same benefits we do from the environment. As a society, we need to find better solutions, ones that will meet everyone's needs. We need to internalize our moral and ethical values so completely that we *do unto others* automatically, without having to be urged or forced to do what is right.

At times we act selfishly on a personal level, despite what we may say or think we believe. When we drive our cars faster than the speed limit allows, we are breaking a rule set by society for the safety of all people on the highway. All of us are sometimes tempted to do what is in our own interest. If we are going to live together and develop into caring people, however, we must use good judgment in making moral decisions. This requires foresight, emotional control, and empathy, the ability to identify with another person's feelings and thoughts.

Rules and Values

We also use values, in addition to rules, to help us make ethical decisions. In discussing rules, we asked, "What should I do?" The questions here are "What is good? What value or ideal should I hold?" But values can sometimes be at odds with each other, too. The people who represent us in Congress must keep this philosophy in mind every time a bill comes up for a vote. Do we spend our tax dollars on landing a spacecraft on Mars and less on social programs? Do we need more aircraft carriers to keep our oceans safe and defend our coastlines, or do we need more research on diseases such as cancer and acquired immune deficiency syndrome (AIDS)? We have only a limited supply of tax money, so we should consider putting the money where it will do the most good for everyone affected by the decision.

Take football as an example. The main goal (value) is to score enough points to win the game. In doing so, the players and coaches choose among short-yardage plays, long-yardage plays, running, passing, kicking, and other plays to score a touchdown. All of these actions are governed by rules. If the ball is advanced but the rules are broken, the team can be penalized valuable yards. Thus, if we break the rules, we may not achieve our goals.

Sometimes the quarterback has to change the call made in the huddle. He must adjust to a changing situation. That type of call introduces us to a third element in ethical judgments—one based on the situation.

Our military has an additional set of values. The values of the individual men and women who serve in the military—and who come from every imaginable background—become values consistent with those of their organization, as they work with others toward the common goal of safeguarding our nation.

Core Values of the US Military Services

Consider how similar the core values of the nation's primary military services are, in spite of some differences in wording. Also consider how close these values are to your own beliefs, whether conscious or unconscious.

United States Air Force Core Values

Integrity first, *Service before self*, and *Excellence in all we do*. These are the Air Force Core Values. These values exist for all members of the Air Force family—officer, enlisted, and civilian; active reserve, Air National Guard, and retired; senior, junior, and middle management; civil servants; uniformed personnel; and contractors.

© Christopher Bradshaw/Fotolia.com

Integrity First

As you will recall from our earlier definition, integrity is the adherence to a moral code. A character trait, integrity is the willingness to do what is right even when no one is looking. It is the moral compass—the inner voice, the voice of self-control, the basis for the trust needed in today's society. People of integrity, for example, are capable of acting on convictions, or their strong beliefs. They can control their impulses.

Service Before Self

This statement tells us that professional duties that we choose to undertake have precedence over personal desires. This core value also states that it is better to give back, whether to our school or community. To do this will make our school and community a better place.

Excellence in All We Do

This core value states that for any undertaking we choose, we should give it our best effort; whether you are doing your homework, playing on the school baseball team, or wearing the uniform, anything less should be unacceptable. This expression also directs us to develop a passion for continuous improvement that will propel us into a long-term, upward spiral of accomplishment and performance.

United States Army Core Values

Many people know what the seven terms *Loyalty, Duty, Respect, Selfless Service, Honor, Integrity,* and *Personal Courage* mean. Soldiers in the Army learn these values in detail during their basic training. From then on, they live them every day in everything they do—whether they're on the job or off.

© Christopher Bradshaw/Fotolia.com

Loyalty

Bear true faith and allegiance to the US Constitution, the Army, your unit, and other Soldiers. Bearing true faith and allegiance is a matter of believing in and devoting yourself to something or someone.

Duty

Fulfill your obligations. Doing your duty means more than carrying out your assigned tasks. Duty means being able to accomplish tasks as part of a team.

Respect

Treat people as they should be treated. In the Soldier's Code, we pledge to "treat others with dignity and respect while expecting others to do the same." Respect is what allows us to appreciate the best in other people and ourselves.

Selfless Service

Selfless service is larger than just one person. In serving your community and country, you are doing your duty loyally without thought of recognition or gain.

Honor

Honor is a matter of carrying out, acting, and living the values of respect, duty, loyalty, selfless service, integrity, and personal courage in everything you do.

Integrity

Do what's right, legally and morally. Integrity is a quality you develop by adhering to moral principles. It requires that you do and say nothing that deceives others. As your integrity grows, so does the trust others place in you. The more choices you make based on integrity, the more this highly prized value will affect your relationships with family and friends, and, finally, the fundamental acceptance of yourself.

Personal Courage

Face fear, danger, or adversity (physical or moral). Personal courage has long been associated with our Army. Facing moral fear or adversity may be a long, slow process of continuing forward on the right path, especially if taking those actions is not popular with others. You can build your personal courage by daily standing up for and acting upon the things that you know are honorable.

© Christopher Bradshaw/Fotolia.com

© Sir_Eagle/Fotolia.com

United States Navy and Marine Corps Core Values

Throughout its history, the Navy has successfully met all its challenges. America's naval service began during the American Revolution, when on October 13, 1775, the Continental Congress authorized a few small ships. From those early days, the core values of the Navy and the Marine Corps have carried on to today. They consist of the three basic principles of *honor, courage*, and *commitment*.

Honor

"I will bear true faith and allegiance ...." Accordingly, we will: Conduct ourselves in the highest ethical manner in all relationships with peers, superiors, and subordinates; Be honest and truthful in our dealings with each other, and with those outside the Navy; Be willing to make honest recommendations and accept those of junior personnel; Encourage new ideas and deliver the bad news, even when it is unpopular; Abide by an uncompromising code of integrity, taking responsibility for our actions and keeping our word; Fulfill or exceed our legal and ethical responsibilities in our public and personal lives twenty-four hours a day. Illegal or improper behavior or even the appearance of such behavior will not be tolerated. We are accountable for our professional and personal behavior. We will be mindful of the privilege to serve our fellow Americans.

Courage

"I will support and defend ...." Accordingly, we will have: courage to meet the demands of our profession and the mission when it is hazardous, demanding, or otherwise difficult; Make decisions in the best interest of the Navy and the nation, without regard to personal consequences; Meet these challenges while adhering to a higher standard of personal conduct and decency; Be loyal to our nation, ensuring the resources entrusted to us are used in an honest, careful, and efficient way. Courage is the value that gives us the moral and mental strength to do what is right, even in the face of personal or professional adversity.

Commitment

"I will obey the orders ...." Accordingly, we will: Demand respect up and down the chain of command; Care for the safety, professional, personal, and spiritual well-being of our people; Show respect toward all people without regard to race, religion, or gender; Treat each individual with human dignity; Be committed to positive change and constant improvement; Exhibit the highest degree of moral character, technical excellence, quality and competence in what we have been trained to do. The day-to-day duty of every Navy man and woman is to work together as a team to improve the quality of our work, our people, and ourselves.

United States Coast Guard Core Values

The following core values are deeply rooted in the Coast Guard heritage. As the Coast Guard's website states, "They demonstrate who we are and guide our performance, conduct, and decisions every minute of every day. Because we each represent the Coast Guard to the public, we must all embrace these values in our professional undertakings as well as in our personal lives."

© Christopher Bradshaw/Fotolia.com

Honor

Integrity is our standard. We demonstrate uncompromising ethical conduct and moral behavior in all of our personal actions. We are loyal and accountable to the public trust.

Respect

We value our diverse work force. We treat each other with fairness, dignity, and compassion. We encourage individual opportunity and growth. We encourage creativity through empowerment. We work as a team.

Devotion to Duty

We are professionals, military and civilian, who seek responsibility, accept accountability, and are committed to the successful achievement of our organizational goals. We exist to serve. We serve with pride.

Cultural and Universal Norms

Cultural Norms

We all have certain habits of work, play, cleanliness, and eating. In each culture, people have definite ideas about personal conduct. All societies have morals, values, and concepts of human rights that have been accepted by the members of that group. They hold sacred certain institutions that meet their needs. While customs, habits, and institutions vary a great deal from one culture to another, they are alike in that they all have norms, *patterns of behavior considered acceptable or proper by a social group.*

Customs and values depend upon the culture in which we live. The norm—what is considered to be acceptable conduct—in one culture may be considered wrong in another culture. Women in many southwest Asian countries, for example, are required to cover their arms, legs, and faces in public. Most Americans have a different view of what women are allowed to wear in public. A culture's value systems are accepted as right for the people who live within that culture. We usually embrace our society's values as our own because we understand from early childhood that we are expected to act according to these values. The same is true of all people in different cultures the world over.

In addition to the broad set of cultural norms recognized by society, the groups to which we belong—such as family, school, or even JROTC—abide by a set of universal norms. It is important that we know and respect the guidance each of these groups offers.

Universal Norms

Universal norms are *the normal beliefs of people in most cultures.* Anthropologists have found that lying, stealing, violating a group's social codes, or committing murder are almost always condemned by people everywhere. One example of a universal norm is how communication is conducted between people. People of higher rank or positions of importance are spoken to in a more respectful manner than someone of lower authority or position. We tend to address our classmates or co-workers by their first names, however, citizens of a country commonly address their President or Prime Minister as Mr./Mrs. President or Mr./Mrs. Prime Minister. They would not address someone of a higher rank or authority by their first name. Another example is that students should not call teachers by their first name. A teacher or professor is considered the authority in the classroom and should only be addressed as Mr./Mrs./Ms. or Professor.

Another universal norm is how societies view theft. Many universal norms can be viewed differently when influenced by cultural norms—for example, theft is considered punishable in every society, some more harsh than others. However, cultural norms tend to override universal norms. For example, an American Indian who stole a horse from a fellow tribesman was severely punished. However, if he took a horse from an enemy tribesman, he was not punished. If he took a horse from a European settler, he was celebrated. The behavior was considered stealing only if he took the horse from his own people. The settlers, who thought of the Indians as thieves, would have been surprised to learn that the Indians did not think of themselves in the same way.

Without rules or norms, institutions would crumble. Keeping promises is a good example. We're all expected to do what we have said we will do. Most people keep their promises; if they didn't, society would fall into disorder. As citizens, we have an obligation to honor constitutional justice, civil law, and the moral norms of our communities.

Non-Universal Norms

Non-universal norms, by contrast, do not carry a universal moral obligation. These include *values such as duties specific to one's religion*—for example, worshipping, fasting, observing holy days and dress codes, and refraining from various activities—*toward which some people may feel a serious personal obligation.* This does not, however, mean that they should impose their personal obligations on others. Conflicts can be created when individuals try to impose their personal or non-universal norms on others.

Making Ethical and Moral Decisions

Ethics and morals present many tough questions. For instance, if acting according to a cultural norm harms someone, is this ethical? Is someone who does what is right simply out of fear of getting caught a moral person? Does the end result of a decision justify the means? Does the need to end a war quickly, for example, justify dropping an atomic bomb? We all must decide on the answers to such questions for ourselves. Nevertheless, how do we find answers to questions that may pose a moral dilemma? If you go through these four steps in this systematic process, it will to help you make the right ethical and moral decisions.

1. Consider all the facts, making sure to verify your information.
2. Determine the moral values or rules that apply to the situation.
3. Always make decisions and act in light of your knowledge of the values and facts in a way that is respectful of the life and well-being of all people.
4. Choose the lesser of two evils (or the least of many) when no better solution can be found. Ask, "Which of the possible choices I have will result in the greatest good for the greatest number of people?"

Students are faced with both simple and complex ethical decisions in their daily lives. Rules, principles, values, situations, and the possible results of our actions influence what we determine to be right. Exactly how do these affect our decisions?

Moral Courage and Maturity

One outstanding military leader, Vice Admiral William P. Lawrence, defined moral courage this way: To know right from wrong, to possess a firm set of values, and the strength to live by those values and do what is right regardless of the consequences.

Such courage is gained through knowledge and experience. The key to successful development of moral courage and maturity is the ability to set appropriate goals and achieve them. JROTC cadets should already possess:

- A conscience
- A sense of justice
- A personal code of conduct

The goals now are to refine our conscience, improve our sense of justice, and maintain a code of conduct sensitive to the right sort of values.

Conscience

Conscience is *the awareness of a desire to act properly and the awareness of guilt when improper acts are committed or intended*. Our conscience is not an automatic feeling or emotion. It is a product of knowledge and intelligence that allows us to judge right from wrong. The emotion of guilt is triggered by our conscience when we act in a manner contrary to what we know to be right. Our conscience is strengthened as our knowledge increases and we become more sensitive to important human values.

New facts, learned through experience and study, add to our ability to make right choices. Our moral courage is strengthened by our successes in attempting to act out our values. As our conscience continues to develop in the right ways and to mature, we become more realistic in judging the actions of others and more sensitive to their needs and motives. A properly informed conscience will allow us to be confident without being rigid and overbearing. It will give us the strength and purpose that build character.

Sense of Justice

A sense of justice is essential for effective leaders because it ensures fairness. As a leader, our sense of justice must prompt us to protect the rights of every individual. It must cause us to be aware of the need for fair distribution of benefits and burdens to all.

A sense of justice is developed from learning experiences over time. Just as our conscience goes through changes, our sense of justice must be allowed to mature. An effective beginning for developing an informed conscience and a true sense of justice is to be concerned with doing the right thing. It is also important to talk with other people about why our actions should be just and moral.

Personal Code of Conduct

Some guidelines on developing your personal code of conduct are offered in the following section.

Your Personal Code of Conduct

Our code of conduct need not be complicated or overly restrictive. It should not be a list of things we believe. Rather, it should be a list of reminders that cause us to practice acceptable behavior. We should state rules positively, as if they were goals that mean a great deal to us. The list should contain "I will" items. They can be as simple as, "I will do my best to be punctual and cause no one to wait for me," or "I will keep my room neat and orderly." Then we should put these rules or goals into daily practice.

Living right, that is, by a code of good conduct, has its own rewards. Among those rewards are developing good habits, having fewer occasions to apologize, possessing greater self-esteem, and earning the respect of others. Many opportunities that had been withheld will open to us. Our moral courage will increase and the frustration we experience when making choices will lessen in time. In short, we will be living a more fully human life.

Developing permanent good habits is very important. Dr. William James, an American physician and psychologist, stated that all of our behavior, our virtues and our vices, is really habit. As we repeat certain behaviors and thoughts, our nervous system "grows" in the ways we have used it, until we have a ready-made response to each sort of impression. We are bundles of habits.

Dr. James also said that if only young people could realize how soon they would become walking bundles of habits, they would pay more attention to how they were acting as their habits were being formed. Since children have no way of knowing these things, their teachers (and parents) must help them develop good habits. As we keep working to build our character in the right way, we get better and better at whatever we try. Dr. James offered these three practical steps to get rid of bad habits and to form good ones:

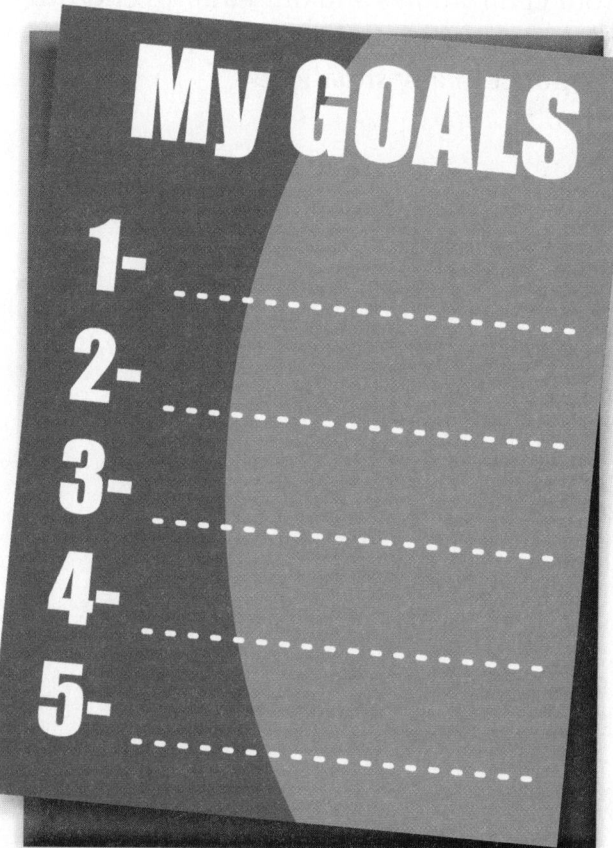

The ability to set appropriate goals and achieve them is the key to developing moral courage and maturity.

© photoestelar/Fotolia.com

1. To form a new habit or to get rid of an old one, begin the change in behavior as strongly as possible. Dr. James even recommended taking a public pledge, if possible. Consider the story of a man who advertised in his hometown newspaper a large reward to anyone who, after that date, should see him smoke a cigarette. The thought of having to pay the reward was a strong reason for him to stay away from cigarettes.
2. Never stop a new habit before it is firmly fixed in your life. Continuing to do the new behavior over and over helps make it a habit for life.
3. Take every chance you get to act on the change. Dr. James stated that the effects of practicing a new behavior communicate the new set of actions to the brain. Action, not simply the decision to change, builds the tendency to act in the new way you wish to behave.

Ethical behavior has been a key topic throughout history. Every culture has agreed that some actions are intolerable and some honorable. Consider the sources of guidance that are available to you. From the world's great thinkers and leaders, our civilization's and our nation's enduring values, and from your own use of the techniques in this lesson, you will develop your own system for responsible conduct in any situation.

✓ CHECKPOINTS

Lesson 5 Review

Using complete sentences, answer the following questions on a sheet of paper.

1. What is the definition of ethics?
2. What do we mean when we say someone is unbiased?
3. What is a value system?
4. What are the four types of values?
5. What are moral values?
6. Define the AF Core Value "Excellence in all we do."
7. What core value is commonly used by the Army, Navy, Marine Corps, and Coast Guard?
8. What is a cultural norm?
9. How do non-universal norms differ from universal norms?
10. How does the textbook define moral courage?
11. What does our conscience tell us?
12. How does an effective leader display a sense of justice?
13. Your personal code of conduct should be a list that will provide what for you?
14. To get rid of an old habit, what should you do with the new one?
15. Dr. James states that acting on a new behavior will communicate what to the brain?

APPLYING YOUR LEARNING

16. Think of one personal habit you would like to change. Using the three steps Dr. William James suggests to change this habit, write a plan to help you change the habit.

LESSON 6

Social Etiquette and Dining-In, Dining-Out

Quick Write

What do you think are good rules and practices for courtesy and etiquette in the 21st century? Make a list of five specific things that you do to show courtesy and etiquette in your everyday life.

Learn About

- etiquette and manners in formal and informal settings
- dining etiquette
- handling social invitations
- public courtesies
- Dining-In and Dining-Out

"Military courtesy is simply an application of common, everyday courtesy and common sense."

Richard S. Joslyn, 116th Pennsylvania Volunteer Infantry

Etiquette and Manners in Formal and Informal Settings

Through your Junior ROTC experience, you'll meet new people and interact in many different situations such as Dining-Ins and Dining-Outs, which will be discussed later in the lesson. Military social occasions are filled with tradition and ceremony. It is important that each cadet know how to properly prepare and conduct themselves at these occasions. When you know the rules of proper etiquette, you will feel more relaxed and confident in these situations. You will also have the chance to make a good impression on others.

Proper social conduct and behavior are important elements in your character development. Although this lesson concentrates on the etiquette and manners required at military social events, the information here is useful for other aspects of your life. **Etiquette** is *a code of behavior or courtesy based on rules of a polite society.* **Manners** are *socially correct ways of acting as shown in widespread customs*. Manners are based on kindness, respect, thoughtfulness, and consideration. The rules of etiquette may vary with the changing times, but good manners are timeless. As you read about the rules of proper etiquette and the practice of good manners, remember that social etiquette and good manners are nothing more than common courtesy, sincerity, and consideration for others. It is important to treat others in the same way we want others to treat us. This is the very foundation on which a polite society is built.

Social Introductions

How many times have you attended school activities or social events with friends and met up with their friends, only to awkwardly stand around because you were not introduced to the new people joining your group? In social occasions, introductions are important to make everyone feel welcome and part of the group. Introductions should be simple, direct, and dignified, and the act of making them should be a formal occasion. They should be made whenever people gather socially, even for a short period. Introductions should be made automatically and immediately when discovering that two people do not know each other; this helps establish a connection between two people who may be strangers. You may make these introductions or have someone else do it, if custom demands. If you neglect an introduction, however, you run the risk of being seen as rude. There is nothing mysterious about making introductions, unless you do not know what to do.

Vocabulary

- etiquette
- manners
- receiving line
- dignitary
- place card
- monopolize
- RSVP
- stilted
- netiquette
- Dining-In
- Dining-Out
- protocol
- comradeship
- President of the Mess

Introductions in a Formal Setting

Introductions at a formal reception, such as at a cadet Military Ball, may often include a receiving line. A **receiving line** is *a group of people, including the host and honored guests, who stand in line and individually welcome guests attending a function*. It is customary, and often mandatory, that all cadets and their guests go through the receiving line upon arrival. The people who would be in the receiving line include (in order):

1. The host (Senior JROTC Instructor or commander of the unit holding the reception)
2. The honored guest or, if there is no honored guest, the spouse of the host
3. The spouse of the host
4. The next ranking guest, with his or her spouse or guest
5. Other special guests with their spouses or guests

A receiving line is a customary way of ensuring that the hosts of an event meet everyone who attends.

Courtesy of Army Staff Sgt. Carlos M. Burger II/Defense Video & Imagery Distribution System

In a receiving line, such as that held for a Military Ball, which people are encouraged to attend as couples, the unit member precedes the guest through the receiving line. The member introduces the guest first to the Cadet Corps Adjutant or other corps representative, who often announces the names of all attendees to the host. If the couple attending the Military Ball are both JROTC cadets, the gentleman will precede the young lady and conduct the introductions. A cadet attending without a partner should introduce himself or herself to the adjutant. Even though the adjutant may be a friend of yours, do not shake his or her hand. The adjutant will announce your name to the host as you step in front of him or her.

A simple, pleasant greeting and a cordial handshake are all that is necessary when moving through a receiving line. Save lengthy conversation for later. Should your name get lost in the line, repeat it for the benefit of the person doing the greeting.

In the absence of an adjutant, the cadet still precedes the guest through the receiving line. The cadet introduces the guest first, and then introduces himself or herself directly to the host. After you have gone through the receiving line, you may proceed to the serving of refreshments or converse with other guests and await the signal for the next event. If the receiving and dining rooms are separate, do not enter the dining room until the signal to do so is given.

For the remainder of the event, you will be responsible for making introductions as you move around the room and during dinner and other activities. The following guidelines explain what you need to do.

Making Personal Introductions

When making a personal introduction, avoid using elaborate phrases. Remember that introductions should be simple and direct. The most generally accepted introductions are "Colonel Smith, may I introduce Ms. Breana Foster?" or "Colonel Smith, I would like you to meet Ms. Breana Foster."

The general rule is that you introduce juniors to seniors (this applies to age and military rank), gentlemen to ladies, and so on. However, the degree of formality used when making the introduction depends on the position of the persons involved or the occasion.

To introduce two people who are not near each other, you would typically take the lower-ranking individual to the senior-ranking person, the young lady to the older person, the gentleman to the lady, and so on.

Personal introductions should be simple and direct.
Courtesy of Petty Officer 3rd Class N.C. Kaylor/Defense Video & Imagery Distribution System

When introducing someone to a dignitary, *a person of importance or someone who holds a high office,* mention the dignitary first to show respect for the office he or she holds. Be sure that you use the correct formal title for the dignitary when making the introduction; if you don't know the person's title, ask someone, such as an instructor, who would most likely know. Here are a few guidelines for introductions of people with titles:

- Introduce military personnel by their rank. For example, when introducing your guest to one of your JROTC instructors, you might say, "Sergeant Allen, I would like you to meet Miss Jones."
- Introduce doctors, judges, or professors by their titles.
- Introduce members of Congress as "Senator" or "Representative."
- Introduce a Catholic priest as "Father." A Jewish rabbi is introduced as "Rabbi." Protestant clergy use titles such as "The Reverend," "Pastor," or "Doctor;" however, others prefer to be addressed as Mr., Mrs., Miss, or Ms.

Before making an introduction, it is a good idea to ask the individual how he or she prefers to be introduced. This action will not only save you from potential embarrassment, but will also cause you to be remembered as someone who is thoughtful and courteous.

If the situation arose where you had to introduce a teacher to a parent, you would use the teacher's name first. An example is "Major Cooper, I would like you to meet my mother, Mrs. Eastern." If both of your parents were there, you would introduce the woman first and then the man, such as "Major Cooper, I would like you to meet my parents, Mrs. Eastern and Mr. Eastern."

If seated, you should rise to acknowledge an introduction and remain standing while other members of the party are being introduced to one another. When being introduced to ladies or gentlemen who are seated, you need not rise if rising may inconvenience others at the table.

Introductions in Informal Situations

When introducing two people whom you know very well and who have heard you speak about the other, you may be more casual. For example, to introduce a cadet friend to your sister, you might simply say, "Susie, this is Pete." In this example, it is perfectly acceptable to make the introduction using the first names of both people. However, do not use the first name of an adult, a senior-ranking individual, or another important person when introducing that person.

Methods of Making Introductions

When making an introduction, speak each name slowly and clearly to be sure the names will be understood. When you are being introduced to someone, make a point of listening to the other person's name. Not remembering a name is common, and is easy to forgive. However, forgetting a name is not an excuse for not making an introduction. If you forget the name, or did not hear it, apologize and ask the person to restate his or her name. Then use the name several times in conversation to help you remember it. If necessary, ask for the person's name—with appropriate apologies—before starting an introduction to another person. For example, "I beg your pardon, sir (or ma'am), but I have forgotten your name.... Thank you, sir (ma'am). Colonel Smith, I would like you to meet Miss Jones."

When you are introduced to others, it is proper to return a courtesy such as "Nice to meet you," "Hello," "I am really glad to meet you," or "How do you do?" Additionally, when introduced to others, put your cell phone or electronic device away or down. Continuing to use your electronic device during introductions is rude and may give the other person the impression that you do not see them as important. When you introduce others, put your electronic device away before you make the introduction, and don't walk off and leave the two people staring at each other. As the person who made the introduction, you should either say something about each person to get a conversation started or excuse yourself so that you and your guest can continue to move about the room or participate in some other event.

To start a conversation, mention something of common interest to both parties. For example, "Major Davis, I would like you to meet Michael Knight. Major Davis is my Senior Aerospace Science Instructor, Michael. Sir, Michael hopes to enroll in JROTC next year." Before moving from the person whom you just introduced, your guest should respond with "Good-bye, I am very glad to have met you," or something to that effect.

When leaving a group, it makes no difference if you were introduced or just included in their conversation; you should politely and quietly say good-bye to anyone who happens to be looking at you, without attracting the attention of those who are unaware that you are leaving.

When in doubt whether two people have met, it is perfectly fine to ask whether they have met. Be sure to address the senior first, using a courtesy such as "Colonel Smith, have you met Miss Jones?" If they have not met, make the introduction. Usually, most people will consider your question as equal to an introduction, and will proceed with "how-do-you-do?" The biggest mistake people make is to assume that people know each other. There is no harm in introducing people who have already met, but it is inconsiderate to have strangers together without introducing them.

Remember to ask your friends if they have met, if you aren't sure if they have met before.

© diego cervo/Fotolia.com

Cadets sometimes assume, in error, that every cadet knows every other cadet. Do not hesitate to introduce cadets if you are not sure if they know each other.

In certain situations, you may find it necessary to introduce yourself to another person. If you are next to someone you do not know and no one is around to make an introduction, it is perfectly fine to introduce yourself. Use a greeting such as "Hello, I am Tom Frazier," while shaking that person's hand. Do not say, "What's your name?" A good reply to you would be "Ted Wentworth, nice to meet you." It is then up to both people to start their own conversation.

When and How to Shake Hands

When gentlemen are introduced to each other, they typically shake hands. Ladies who are JROTC cadets also shake hands during introductions. However, as a more general rule, whenever a lady or gentleman extends his or her hand as a form of greeting, the receiving party should extend his or her hand in return. Nothing could be ruder than to ignore a friendly gesture. At the end of the introduction or conversation, those who were drawn into it do not have to shake hands when parting; however, it is considered common courtesy to do so.

A proper handshake is brief, but the clasp should feel firm and warm. Maintain eye contact with the person whose hand you are shaking. Do not shake someone's hand violently, grasp the hand like a vise, keep the handshake going for a long time, or offer only your fingertips.

A JROTC cadet shakes hands at a Military Ball.

When being introduced to a lady outside, a gentleman in civilian clothes should remove his hat. If in uniform, do not remove your hat. In addition, a gentleman will ordinarily remove his glove to shake hands unless he is a member of a Color or Honor Guard. If a gentleman is confronted with a sudden introduction when he has gloves on and it is awkward to remove a glove while the other person has his or her hand outstretched, it is better to shake hands with the glove on with no apology. These are good rules to follow as part of general public behavior, even in casual situations.

Shake, Take, and Salute

During your time in JROTC you will have many opportunities to receive awards and recognition. This recognition may include certificates, ribbons, or medals for doing something good for your school or community. It is important that you know how to receive this recognition, especially in uniform.

If the award is being presented by the Aerospace Science Instructor (ASI), other enlisted personnel, or a civilian official such as the principal, follow these rules:

- Offer the left hand to receive the award.
- Offer the right hand to shake the presenting official's hand.

If the award is being presented by the Senior Aerospace Science Instructor (SASI) or other military officer, follow these rules:

- Offer the left hand to receive the award.
- Offer the right hand to shake the officer's hand.
- Finally, come to attention, face the officer, and render the proper hand salute. Be sure to hold your salute until the officer returns your salute.

Dining Etiquette

Table manners are an important part of social conduct. Proper manners around the table are not just reserved for special occasions; you should use them whenever you dine. Relaxed politeness is the key to any dining situation. When you know what to do, you can relax and enjoy yourself. This section will help you learn the rules of the table.

Manners and Courtesies Before Eating

A gentleman does not sit down until all the ladies at his table are seated. He can help with the seating by holding the chair for each lady—first for his guest, then for other ladies near him if the ladies outnumber the men. He does this by pulling out the lady's chair from the table far enough for her to move easily in front of it. Then, as the lady sits down, he gently pushes the chair under her until she is seated. When all ladies at the table are seated, he may then take his seat by going around the left side of his chair. Posture at the table should be straight, but not stiff.

If a lady leaves the table at any time, the gentleman who seated her rises and assists with the lady's chair. When the lady returns to the table, her escort or the gentleman who seated her rises and repeats the courtesies mentioned in the previous paragraph.

The polite dinner guest will not touch anything on the table, not even the napkin, until after the blessing (or invocation) has been said or until it is obvious that there will be no blessing. Then you may pick up your napkin and partially unfold it on your lap. Do this unnoticeably—do not unfold a dinner napkin completely or above the table.

POW-MIA Ceremony

The POW-MIA Ceremony is generally used in conjunction with the opening of a dinner function. Although no one is sure where this ceremony began, it is believed to have been started by naval crewmembers known as the Vietnam River Rats. The River Rats were US Navy service members who patrolled the deltas and rivers in small patrol boats during the Vietnam War. This solemn remembrance is for the men and women in all five services—Air Force, Army, Navy, Marines, and Coast Guard—who were prisoners of war and those who are missing in action. There are many different versions of the ceremony.

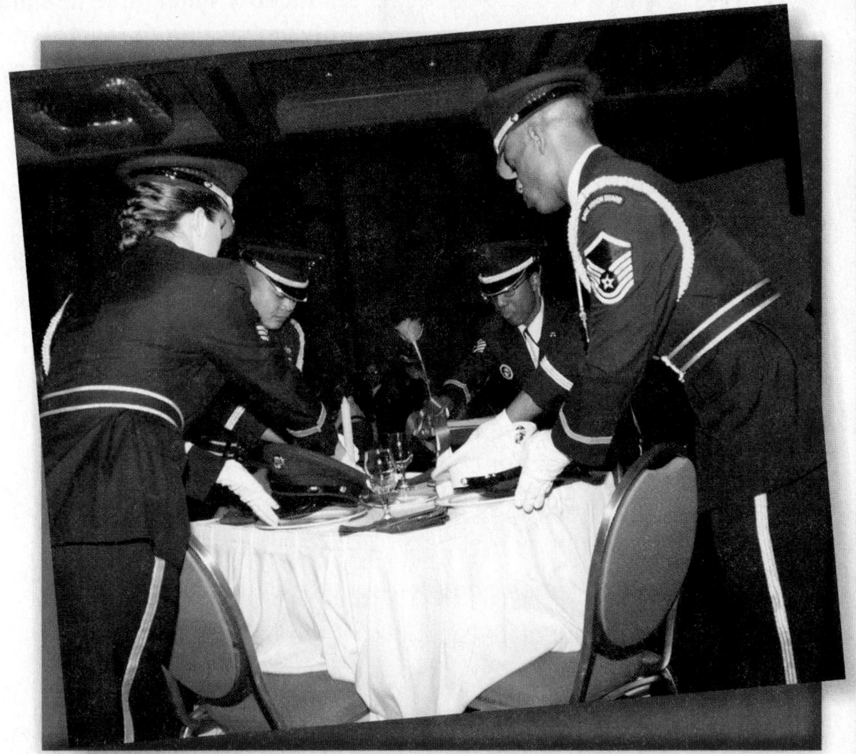

POW-MIA Honor Guard.
Courtesy of MSgt Dale C. Hanson II

The ceremony, in which wheel hats of all military services are placed at a table of honor, symbolizes those whose sacrifice prevents them from being at the function or with their loved ones. JROTC units often do not have access to wheel hats from other services and may choose not to use them.

The ceremony opens when a cadet narrator announces, "Ladies and gentlemen, please direct your attention to the center of our gathering. You may have noticed the table set before you. It is filled with symbolism. This table is set for our prisoners of war and those missing in action—from all wars. They are not with us today. Their chairs are empty, but saved for their hoped return. Let us remember their absence."

Once the Honor Guard members have placed the hats representing the missing members of the individual services at the unoccupied table, the cadet narrator explains the symbolism of the objects on the table. At the end of the evening, the POW-MIA table is retired by the Honor Guard as a symbol of both farewell and hope.

The intent of the ceremony is to recognize the presence, in spirit, of those POWs and MIAs whose sacrifice prevents them from being physically present. The ceremony also serves as a way of recognizing the powerful bond among all of those who serve our nation.

The POW-MIA Ceremony: A Cadet Narrator's Speech

© Christopher Nolan/Fotolia.com

As you entered the banquet hall this evening, you may have noticed a small table in a place of honor. This table is our way of symbolizing the fact that members of our armed forces are missing from our midst. They are commonly called POWs or MIAs. They are unable to be with us this evening and so we remember them.

The tablecloth is white, symbolizing the purity of their intentions to respond to their country's call to arms—so that their children could remain free.... Remember.

The lone candle symbolizes the frailty of a prisoner alone, trying to stand up against his oppressors.... Remember.

(A cadet lights the candle.)

The single rose in the vase symbolizes the blood that has been shed. It also reminds us of the loved ones and families of our comrades-in-arms who keep the faith and await their return.... Remember.

A slice of lemon is on the bread plate to remind us of their bitter fate—if we do not bring them home.... Remember.

(A cadet slices a lemon and places a slice on each bread plate.)

There is salt on the plate, symbolic of the family's fallen tears as they wait.... Remember.

(A cadet shakes salt onto each bread plate.)

The glasses are inverted. They cannot toast with us tonight—maybe tomorrow.... Remember.

The yellow ribbon tied around the vase is worn by family and friends; keeping the faith, while awaiting their return.... Remember.

The empty chairs at the table are a reminder that they are not here with us.... Remember.

As we look upon this empty table, do not remember ghosts from the past, remember our comrades.

Remember those whom we depended on in battle. They depend on us to bring them home.

Remember our friends. They are the ones we love—who love life and freedom as we do.

They will remember what we do. Please honor and remember them.

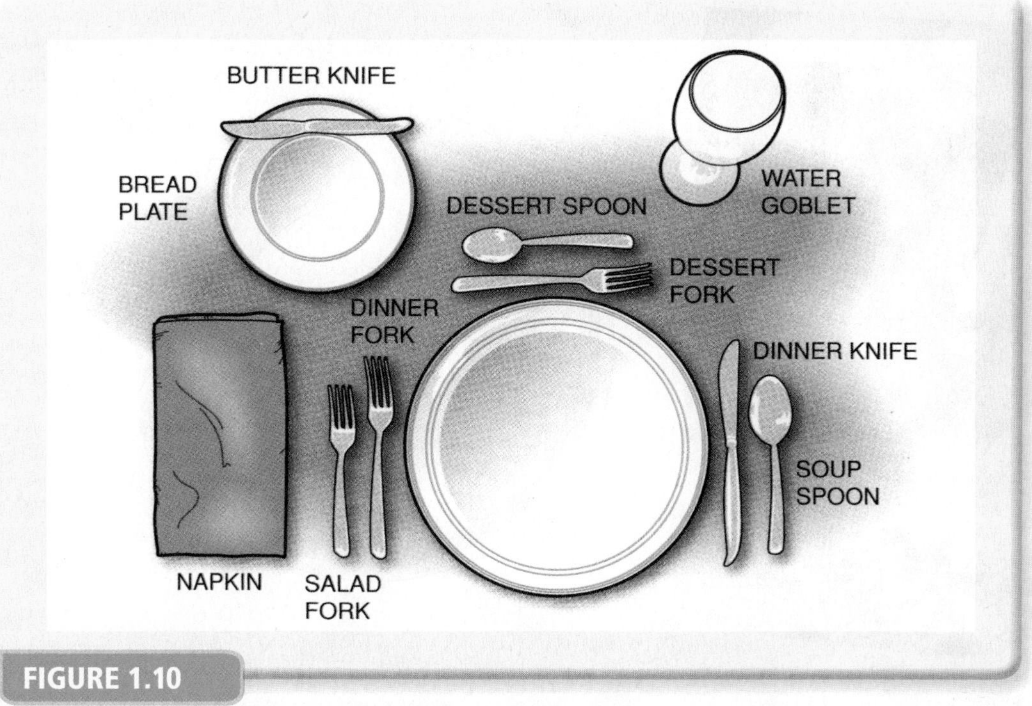

FIGURE 1.10

A formal place setting can be confusing if you are not familiar with it.

A Formal Dining Table Setting

At a large dinner, you may encounter a confusing array of silverware at your place setting, including one or two knives, two or three forks, and two or three spoons. A formal table setting is shown in Figure 1.10. If you have any doubt about the correct piece of silverware to use for a particular course, start with the outside piece of silverware and work inward. If you end up without a spoon or a fork, it is fine to ask for a replacement.

Specialized pieces of silverware include the butter knife, soup spoon, dessert fork and spoon, iced-tea spoon, oyster fork, and fish knife and fork. The number of pieces of silverware indicates the number of courses to expect. For example, a six-course meal might include soup, fish, sorbet (a fruit-flavored ice served to cleanse the palate, or clear your taste buds), salad, an entree, and dessert. The placement of the silverware indicates the order of these courses.

Proper Use of Silverware

In today's diverse social environment, you'll encounter different methods, manners, and courtesies of eating, depending on your host, the guests, and the occasion. To feel confident in any situation, you should be familiar with the proper use of silverware, how to eat with your fingers, how to handle a soup spoon, the differences between American and European styles of dining, and more.

FIGURE 1.11

The American style of eating and resting silverware.

Left: © Piotr Marcinski/Fotolia.com

In the American style of eating, food is cut as shown in Figure 1.11A. Hold the fork in your left hand, tines down, with your index finger on the back of the fork. Secure the food being cut with the knife, which is held in your right hand. Cut in front of the fork, not behind it. After cutting no more than two or three bites of food, place the knife on the plate and transfer the fork to your right hand. This is called the "zigzag" method.

When not using your knife and fork, place them separated across the top of your plate as shown in Figure 1.11B. This is the resting position. When you have finished the main course, place the knife and fork beside each other on the dinner plate diagonally from the upper left to lower right, or from the 10 o'clock to the 4 o'clock position. This is the "finished" position and indicates that your plate may be removed.

Various rules govern how to use silverware properly. These rules include:

- After you use a piece of silverware, do not place it back on the table.
- Do not leave a used spoon in a cup; place it on the saucer.
- Do not leave a soup spoon in a soup bowl. You may leave it on a soup plate if one is provided; otherwise, place it on the dinner plate when not in use.
- Do not lay a knife with the handle on the table and the tip of the blade on the edge of the plate. This also applies to the fork.
- Leave unused silverware on the table in its proper position.

How to Eat Soup and Finger Foods

When eating soup, the motion of the spoon should be away from you while filling it. Sip from the side of the spoon; do not slurp. If it is necessary to tip your soup bowl, tip it away from you. If your soup is too hot to eat, let it sit until it cools; do not blow on it.

Bread, rolls, biscuits, nuts, fresh fruit, olives, celery, radishes, raw carrots, cookies, and small cakes may be eaten with your fingers. Place finger foods on the bread plate if there is one. If there is no bread plate, use the salad or dinner plate.

As seen in Figure 1.12, break your individual servings of bread, rolls, and large biscuits into small pieces before buttering and eating them, one piece at a time. Do not cut these items. Buttering and eating a whole roll or whole slice of bread is also not appropriate.

Proper Use of Napkins

You should not tuck the napkin under your belt or wear it like a bib. Napkins are for dabbing lips, catching spills, and covering sneezes. Do not use a napkin to blow your nose. Never lick food from your fingers; always use your napkin. Before taking a drink of water or any other beverage, wipe your lips with your napkin to avoid leaving smears on the glassware. One quick, light pass with the napkin should be enough.

FIGURE 1.12

It is customary to break bread, rolls, and biscuits with your fingers before you butter them.

Left: © Lovrencg/Fotolia.com; Right: © gani_dteurope/Fotolia.com

If you must leave the table during dinner, say, "Excuse me, please," with no explanation, and rise, placing your napkin on your chair. When leaving the table after dinner, place the napkin on the table in loose folds to the right of your plate. Do not refold, crumple, or twist it. Always push your chair to the table when you leave it.

Basic Table Manners

The following list includes hints about table manners. Follow each one in any dining situation.

- If place cards are used, do not move or remove them. A place card is *a name card for a formal dinner.* In addition to showing the specific seating arrangement, place cards are used to make guests feel welcome and to help people get to know one another in large social settings.
- Take small bites. Large mouthfuls of food are unsightly. Do not chew with your mouth open or make loud noises when you eat. It is not polite to talk with food in your mouth.
- If you burp, say "Excuse me" (to no one in particular), and continue eating. Do not make a big deal out of it.
- Hats, gloves, cell phones, cameras, purses, sunglasses, and so on do not belong on the table. If it is not a part of the meal, do not put it on the table. Hats and gloves belong in the cloakroom. You may place cameras and purses under your chair. Unless you are expecting an emergency phone call, turn off your phone while in the dining room, and keep all electronic devices out of sight.
- Your hands should go no farther over the table than is necessary to eat and to pass things. Between courses, place your hands in your lap or at your side. Do not place your elbows on the table.
- If bread is placed in front of you, feel free to pick up the basket and offer it to the person to your right.
- Do not take the last piece of bread without first offering it to others.
- If you cannot easily reach something on the table, ask for it to be passed to you. Say "please" and "thank you." If you are the one passing something, place the items on the table for the person to pick up, if possible. When passing salt and pepper, pass them together.
- If food spills off your plate, you may pick it up with a piece of your silverware and place it on the edge of your plate.
- If you drop something, leave it on the floor until the meal is over; then pick it up. If a piece of your silverware falls onto the floor, pick it up if you can reach it and let the server know you need a clean one. If you cannot reach it, tell the server you dropped a piece of your silverware and ask for a clean one.

- Do not season your food before you taste it.
- Hold a long-stemmed glass with the thumb and first two fingers of your right hand at the base of the bowl or on the stem.
- It is not appropriate to ask for a "doggy bag" during a formal occasion.
- Do not scold or correct a server. Make any complaints to the person (cadet) in charge of the ballroom arrangements.
- If food gets caught between your teeth, and you cannot remove it with your tongue without being too noticeable, leave the table and go to the restroom where you can remove the food in private.
- At the end of dinner, after the host and honored guests have departed, make sure that you say good-bye to everyone at your table before departing.

Conversation During Meals

Conversation is an important part of social interaction around the table. It is perfect for the enjoyment of good companionship and a pleasant meal. A few important tips include:

- Try not to talk too quickly or too slowly.
- Keep the conversation light. Small talk includes casual, unofficial, interesting things in everyday life, such as the weather, music, upcoming events, movies, or sports. Keep topics of conversation safe and non-controversial. Avoid discussions about religion, race, politics, or any controversial issue. Avoid health issues, off-color jokes, and gossip.
- Answer respectfully when addressed.
- Be mindful of engaging in conversation with a person who has just taken a bite of food. Remember, do not talk with food in your mouth.
- Loud voices or laughter can be disturbing to others. Do not yell; use a pleasant tone of voice that can be heard only at your table. Do not use profane, abusive, or vulgar language.
- Be a good listener. Give others a chance to talk. Do not monopolize a conversation. To **monopolize** means *to take exclusive ownership or control*. Pay attention to the person speaking by making eye contact; do not look at other people when someone is talking to you.
- Do not interrupt. Allow the other person to finish what he or she is saying before speaking. If you and another person start talking at the same time, give way quickly in a friendly manner with a simple "Please go ahead."
- Do not ridicule or laugh at an unfortunate remark or someone's mistake. Although a person who makes good conversation does not contradict someone in a social setting, it is okay to state your opinion. When you do, always be tactful and respect the other person's point of view, especially when personal feelings are involved.

Handling Social Invitations

When you are invited to attend a social event, which could be a short afternoon visit, a dinner party, or a Military Ball, you have certain obligations that you must observe as a guest.

You must understand the invitation: what you are invited for, where it will be held, when you should be there, and what you should wear. A written invitation will usually spell out most of these things quite clearly. Certain things are implicit in an invitation, as you shall see.

RSVP

RSVP comes from the French expression "Répondez s'il vous plaît," which means "please reply." RSVP means that *you must reply to the hosts to let them know if you can or cannot attend the function to which you've been invited.* On many invitations, you will see RSVP followed by a telephone number or email address. In this case, the courtesy of a prompt reply by telephone or email is required to permit the host, hostess, or planning committee to plan the event properly. It is polite to call or send your message within two or three days to accept or decline the invitation. When telephoning, make your call between 9:00 a.m. and 6:00 p.m. Do not invite someone else unless the invitation clearly indicates the number and names of those invited.

Several variations on RSVP are coming into widespread use, especially on informal invitations. One variation is "RSVP Regrets Only." This notation means that the host or hostess is expecting you unless you notify him or her that you cannot come. If you can accept, you need not reply. Make sure to be there on time.

If your plans for that day are unsettled, do not pass this problem on to the host or hostess. It would be much better to decline the invitation than to give a complicated account of your social schedule. Even if the other arrangement or engagement is uncertain, it is best to decline the invitation. After you have declined, do not call back if your plans change.

When declining, it is enough to say to the host or hostess that a conflicting engagement prevents you from accepting. You can turn down an invitation because you do not want to go. However, use good judgment for the invitations you refuse.

Most written invitations will indicate exactly where the function is being held. Some invitations may include a small map for your convenience.

If the invitation is telephoned to you, repeat back all of the important information to be sure there is no misunderstanding when you accept the invitation. If you must first check your calendar before answering, get all the details and explain that you will call back as soon as you have looked at your schedule. Thank the caller for the invitation, make sure you have the phone number, and promise to call right back. Make sure you call back as you promised.

After you accept an invitation, if an illness or an absolute emergency prevents you from attending, call the host or hostess immediately with regrets and apologies. Invitations to dinners, receptions, and weddings will usually give a time. For dinners and receptions, this is the time at which you should arrive; do not arrive earlier or later. Plan your timing so you can be punctual. The time on a wedding invitation is the time the ceremony begins; allow enough time to be seated before the ceremony begins.

If you are invited to an open house from 3:00 p.m. to 6:00 p.m., you may arrive any time after 3:00 p.m. and depart before 6:00 p.m. You are not expected to stay the entire three hours. After a dinner party, you should stay at least an hour. If you do not, it hints of "eat-and-run" rudeness.

Regardless of the type of invitation, keep in mind that a delayed reply without reason, or no reply, or failure to attend the function after accepting are all serious breaches of etiquette.

Formal, Informal, or Casual Wear?

The invitation may specify what you should wear. For example, an Air Force JROTC cadet would most likely wear a semi-formal dress uniform to a Dining-In or Military Ball. In this situation, male guests should wear a suit, while female guests should wear either short or long evening attire.

Some invitations may simply indicate that the dress is formal, informal, or casual. Be sure that you understand what these terms mean. If you are in doubt, ask the host or hostess what to wear when you call to RSVP. As a general rule, use the following guidelines:

- **Formal**—For male cadets, the service dress or semi-formal service dress is expected. For a male guest, a suit may be acceptable, although a tuxedo equivalent is preferred. For female cadets, the service dress may be expected for Dining-Ins. For other formal occasions, a short or long evening gown may be appropriate for female cadets and female guests.
- **Informal**—For gentlemen, a sport coat and tie are appropriate; for ladies, a dress appropriate for daytime wear or a pants suit is acceptable.
- **Casual**—For gentlemen, nice slacks and a sport shirt are appropriate; for ladies, a sundress or pants and blouse are appropriate. In some situations, jeans or shorts and a shirt or blouse may be acceptable. Any form of sagging or revealing clothing is considered inappropriate for any gathering.

A cadet in semi-formal dress uniform receives an award at a Military Ball.

Courtesy of the US Air Force JROTC

Responsibilities to the Host

When attending a small gathering or dinner party, seek out and greet your host or hostess immediately upon arrival. Even at a large event, a crowded room should not keep you from properly greeting your host and hostess. You should also delay getting any refreshments until after you have properly greeted the host and hostess.

Because the host and hostess are in charge, let them run things. As a polite, unassuming guest, you can help by making conversation and joining wholeheartedly in whatever activities are planned. You should not sit when other guests are standing in your presence.

Before leaving, you must thank your host and hostess for a wonderful time. Even if there are still dozens of people present, you must seek out the host and hostess to say thank you and good-bye.

Writing Thank-You Notes

Be sure to write a thank-you note within two or three days, and no more than a week after you have been a guest at someone's home. A thank-you note should be handwritten in ink on nice writing paper. It is best to use stationery sets that provide matching paper and envelopes. Be conservative in the choice of color and design. Plain white is always acceptable. The requirements for a thank-you note include:

- Spell out the month—The 3/9/14 format is not used socially; this date would be written as March 9, 2014. Place the date in the upper-right corner, just below the fold line on the informal notepaper.
- Make sure the margins are large enough—Leave about $1\frac{1}{4}$ inches on the left side and about $\frac{3}{4}$ inch on the right, depending on the size of the paper.
- Place the salutation, such as "Dear Mrs. Elliott," at the left margin.
- Indent only the first line of each paragraph. Align the rest of the paragraph with the left margin.
- Place the closing about as far to the right as the date at the top of the page. "Sincerely," or "Sincerely yours," with your first and last names, are acceptable closings. Do not use "Yours truly," and use "Love" only for a family member or close friend, followed by your first name only.
- Do not use "Cadet" or your cadet rank in your signature.
- Place your return address on the envelope, not under your signature.

The thank-you note should be at least three paragraphs long. The first paragraph expresses your thanks specifically and in detail for the occasion. The last paragraph briefly summarizes your thanks. One or more paragraphs in the middle can be on any topic you choose about the occasion you attended. Be careful not to invite yourself back in your thank-you note.

How to Express Yourself

When expressing yourself, be yourself! If you do not normally speak a stilted or flowery language, do not sound that way in your note. Stilted means *stiffly or artificially dignified or formal, pompous, or lofty.* Sincerity is far more important than eloquence. For example, "I was overwhelmed by the sumptuousness of the repast in your exquisite domicile" will sound silly from most people. "I enjoyed the dinner in your attractive home" sounds much more natural. If you particularly enjoyed the soup or if the chocolate cream pie was out of this world, by all means say so in your note.

Sincerity is the first rule in social correspondence. Simplicity is the second rule. You can hardly go wrong with a few simple and direct statements about the things that pleased or amused you. Write just as you would say it to someone you know very well. Also, use correct grammar and spelling, and keep it neat.

The thank-you note is an individual responsibility. If more than one of you attended a dinner party at someone's home, it is not proper to send one thank-you note. Each of you should write your own note.

If you are on the planning committee for a Military Ball, you should also send thank-you notes to the special guests, any organizations that sponsored the event, and the organizations that provided services and entertainment.

Addressing Thank-You Notes

Make sure that you use a block style when addressing the envelope. Include the proper title with the name (such as Mr., Mrs., Miss, Dr., Colonel, MSgt, and so on). Place the city, two-letter state abbreviation, and zip code on the same line.

Place your return address on the front top left corner of the envelope. You may use an address label. You may also include "Cadet" in your title, but not your cadet rank. For example, Cadet John C. Scott is acceptable, but Cadet Captain John C. Scott is not correct.

Public Courtesies

Life is full of ways to show courteous behavior toward others. This section describes just a few ways you can act in a thoughtful and civilized manner.

Telephone Courtesy

In the 21st century, the telephone—especially the cell phone—has become the primary means of communication. We use it to keep in touch with friends and family, to shop, and to study, to name just a few. Because we now use our phone to communicate both in speech and in text, it's important to use proper netiquette, which means *the rules for communication using the Internet or electronic devices,* when talking and texting.

Here are some tips for proper voice telephone courtesy.

Avoid calling others during meal hours. If you are in doubt, ask the person you are calling if this is a convenient time, and offer to call back later if necessary. Let the phone ring at least six times to allow the person to reach the phone or to let the call go to voice mail.

Identify yourself when placing a call. Unlike talking to someone face-to-face, the person on the other end of the phone may not recognize your voice until you identify yourself. While talking on the phone:

In the 21st century, cell phone courtesy is as important as any other form of etiquette.

© javiindy/Fotolia.com

- Be polite. This applies to any conversation.
- Speak slowly and clearly. Do not eat, drink, or chew gum.
- Do not sneeze or cough into the receiver. Turn your head or excuse yourself.
- Do not carry on a conversation with someone in the room while talking on the phone.
- Call back immediately if you get disconnected from a call that you placed.
- When answering a call for someone else, say, "May I ask who is calling?" This sounds better than "Who is this?"
- If the phone number you are calling goes to voice mail, always leave a message identifying yourself, why you called, and what time you called. It is considered rude to call someone and hang up without leaving a message.

No matter how careful you are, you may still dial a wrong number. When that happens, apologize to the person who answers. That person is not interested in hearing a story about how you misdialed; just tell him or her, "I'm very sorry to have disturbed you," and hang up. Then make sure you have the correct number, and try again. It is rude to hang up without an apology.

When leaving a message, clearly state your name, the date and time of your call, and a brief message. Leave a phone number only if you need to be called back.

Cell Phone Common Sense

Because cell phones can be used virtually anywhere, cell phone users need to remember commonsense courtesy. Results from numerous nationwide surveys show that wireless users need to improve their phone etiquette and put people—and safety—before phone calls.

Here are a few tips to follow:

- Do not drive and use a cell phone. If you need to have a conversation while driving, be sure to pull off the road before talking or texting. This is an extremely dangerous activity and against the law in many communities and states.
- Use of cell phones may be prohibited in most schools and at school functions, check electronic device rules at your school prior to using your cell phone.
- Use of cell phones during social gatherings or appointments is not appropriate.
- Do not place a cell phone on the table during a meal. It is considered impolite to make or receive cell phone calls during a meal.
- Do not use a cell phone when it will inconvenience or disturb others.
- When in public places or at gatherings, limit your cell phone use. If you see a sign requesting you not use your cell phone, turn it off.

Texting while driving is dangerous and, in many states, it's also illegal.

Text Messaging Tips

Text messaging is convenient and quick, but also needs to be courteous. As the etiquette authority Emily Post's *Etipedia* states, "With it you can get a message to someone without causing their phone to ring at an inopportune time, ask a friend a question and let them respond at their leisure, or just shout out a quick greeting to someone without making a big deal about it." Here are a few of her text-messaging tips, along with some of our own.

- Do not read or send text messages while driving; it is extremely dangerous and against the law in most communities and states.
- Do not send a text message when a phone call would be more appropriate; this is considered rude.
- Make sure you are texting to the right phone number.
- Do not text anything confidential, private, or potentially embarrassing to you or anyone else.
- Just as you should not be answering your phone during a conversation, you should not send a text message when you are engaged with someone else. If you are with someone who will not stop text messaging during your conversation, feel free to excuse yourself until they have concluded their messaging.
- Avoid using text messaging when informing someone of sad news, urgent meetings, or other information that may be misunderstood in a brief text message.

- If you receive a text message that was sent to you by mistake, reply explaining that you aren't the intended recipient. You don't have to respond to anything else in the message.
- Do not let texting distract you from other activities, especially when safety is involved.

Email Netiquette

The same general principles of courtesy and etiquette that apply to text messaging also apply to email. However, since email has been with us much longer, and used as a more formal, way of communicating electronically, people who receive your messages will expect you to be a bit more formally courteous. Here are our current "top ten" tips for courteous email communication.

1. Check and answer your email on a regular basis; don't keep someone waiting for a response.
2. Check your addressee list before each mailing; the longer your addressee list, the easier it will be to send a message to the wrong person by mistake.
3. Assume that your email is permanent (it is) and could be read by anyone at any time.
4. Think twice before sending humorous remarks; avoid forwarding jokes.
5. Do not use email for confidential or personal information.
6. Use a clear subject line to identify your topic. When someone receives a message with an unclear or—worse—no subject line, they tend to delete or not read the message.
7. Refer clearly to the message to which you are responding. Consider setting your email program to include the original message in your response.
8. Spell words out completely, use spell check (and, if necessary grammar and style check) before you click "Send."
9. Avoid writing in FULL CAPS. Using FULL CAPS indicates directness or anger.
10. Never answer an email message in anger.

Assisting the Elderly and Disabled

One drawback of our current technology use is that it tends to draw in your attention so closely that you can easily ignore or miss what is happening around you. As our older population becomes more numerous, it is easier to find elderly individuals needing our assistance. If an older woman or gentleman wants some support, it is appropriate for you to offer your arm. The cadet does not offer his or her hand. Hand holding in public is not appropriate and is considered a public display of affection, which is improper when in uniform. A cadet may offer his or her hand only when it is not practical to offer the arm, for example, to help an elderly lady or gentleman out of a car. Offer your hand palm up, and do not force it upon the person to whom you are offering it. Withdraw your hand as soon as it is no longer needed.

When walking with a lady, a gentleman may walk on the curbside, or on her left if there is no curb.

Opening Doors for Others

If a gentleman arrives at a door first, he should open it and allow others to pass through. If a lady arrives at the door first and opens it, the gentleman may hold the door for her to continue.

If you are driving or riding to a social event in a privately owned vehicle, the gentleman should open the car door for your passenger to enter first on the right side of the car. Then go around the car and take your seat, either behind the wheel or in the back seat beside your guest. When you reach your destination, walk around the car and open the door for your guest if she has not already exited the vehicle. If the gentleman is a passenger in a car driven by a lady, he should always open the car door for the lady driver before taking his seat on the passenger side.

Being Responsible for Your Guest

Depending upon the nature of the social occasion, cadets should inform their guests about the traditions and courtesies of the occasion before arriving. For example, for the Military Ball, cadets should inform their guests about appropriate dress, conduct, the receiving line, traditions, and so on. Remember, if you invite a guest, you are responsible for your guest's behavior. If you have duties to perform after you arrive at the social, arrange for someone else to act as an escort for your guest until you are free. Introduce your friends and ensure that your guest is cared for.

Respect for Authorities and Senior Citizens

By this time in JROTC, you should not have any difficulty showing respect to military senior-ranking individuals; in fact, it should be automatic. You should also show respect for all adults, including parents, teachers, and others in a position of authority. In short, you should treat all persons with the utmost respect.

Just as it is unacceptable to use slang or poor grammar, such as "yeah," "nope," or "uh-huh" to a JROTC instructor, it is also socially rude to say these things to others.

You may encounter situations when adults address you by your first name. Although this may be flattering, you should never address an adult by his or her first name, unless that person specifically asks you to do so.

Chewing Gum

You may chew gum in public as long as you do it in a non-offensive way—quietly and inconspicuously. Do not chew gum in formal situations, in class, wearing your uniform, at work, if you are a host or hostess, or if you are around food.

Waiting in Line

When you are in public places with friends, do not make a lot of noise that might upset other people. Be respectful to others around you; do not engage in loud conversations with people around you or over a cell phone.

Do not push ahead of anyone. Wait your turn in line to go through a door, into an elevator, or onto an escalator.

Politeness

Use "Please," "Thank you," "You're welcome," "Excuse me," and "I'm sorry" naturally and sincerely in conversations. Say "Excuse me" if you accidentally brush against someone. You can also say, "I beg your pardon," but do not use the phrase, "Pardon me."

Hygiene and Grooming

Careful attention to all aspects of personal hygiene will help you be welcome in social situations. Be certain that you are well groomed every time you make a social appearance. One dirty or untrimmed fingernail may seem like a small thing to you, but it may be the basis for a negative impression. You never have a second chance to make a first impression. The following are just a few of the basics you should already be doing to make sure your appearance is up to standards.

- Make sure your hair is clean, neatly trimmed or styled, and combed at all times.
- Shower daily and use deodorant as part of your daily routine.
- Brush your teeth and floss daily. Try to brush after meals.
- For young men who already have to shave: if it is necessary for you to do so once or twice a day to be presentable, then do so.

Good grooming is an individual responsibility, it says a lot about your attention to detail. It should not be necessary for an instructor or an upper-class cadet to tell you to maintain proper personal hygiene. Additionally, cadets must make sure that their uniforms are clean, pressed, and presentable.

It's often said, you only get one opportunity to make a first impression. To make that first impression count, we have spent a lot of time in this lesson focusing on dining etiquette, how you should dress, and proper social behavior. While you are enrolled in JROTC, you will have many opportunities to make that first impression and put proper etiquette into practice. The last part of this lesson puts everything you have learned into practice. Attending a Dining-In or Dining-Out allows cadets to interact socially with other cadets and guests. It allows you to enjoy an evening filled with military traditions in a tasteful and dignified manner.

Dining-In and Dining-Out

You should be familiar with the terms *Dining-In* and *Dining-Out*, which refer to formal military dinners. **Dining-In** is *a formal dinner for members of the military only.* **Dining-Out** is *a formal dinner to which non-military guests are invited.* Many JROTC programs use Dining-Outs as their Military Ball since both are similar in tradition and activities. The protocol for these affairs often reflects long-standing traditions within a unit of the armed forces. **Protocol** is *a code of precedence in rank and status and of correct procedure in ceremonies; a form of etiquette observed in ceremonies; a combination of good manners and common sense that facilitates effective communication.* The intent is to promote cordiality, **comradeship**, which is *companionship*, and esprit de corps.

It is believed that Dining-In extends back to the Roman practice of holding great banquets to celebrate victory and parade the spoils of war. However, most historians believe that Dining-In began as a custom in English monasteries. It was then adopted by the early universities. Later, it spread to military units when the officers' mess began. The customs and traditions of our modern Dining-In come from those of the British Army Regimental Mess. The British mess was an occasion to observe the unit's longstanding customs and traditions. It also provided a time for solemn formality, horseplay, and an excuse for living beyond one's means. The first recorded American Dining-In occurred in September 1716 when Governor Spotswood of Virginia, along with a company of Rangers, celebrated after crossing the mountains and descending into the Shenandoah Valley. Air Force Dining-In began in the US Army Air Corps when the late General Henry H. (Hap) Arnold held his famous "wingdings." The custom also grew in popularity during World War II, when members of the US Army Air Corps participated in British Dining-Ins. The Dining-In is now recognized as an occasion where ceremony and tradition combine with good fellowship as an important element in Air Force life.

The primary elements are a formal setting, posting of the Colors, invocation, traditional toasts, a fine dinner, comradeship of cadets, benediction, and retirement of the Colors.

The Dining-In and Dining-Out provide an opportunity to recognize individual, flight, and unit achievements for the school year. They also give cadets an opportunity to honor teachers, principals, and other school personnel. The Dining-In may also be used to present individual and/or unit awards. As such, the Dining-In helps build esprit de corps within JROTC program; it also provides an enjoyable time for cadets. In addition, a Dining-Out may include entertainment after the formal portions, such as music and dancing.

Toasting at a Dining-In

Toasting is a universal custom. It is a simple courtesy to the person being honored. It is improper to drain the glass after each toast; it is also improper to raise an empty glass to make a toast. You need to know how many toasts are being given so you can gauge how much to drink with each toast. Toasts are made standing up. One person, usually the President of the Mess will present a toast by saying, "Ladies and gentlemen, the President of the United States" or "Ladies and gentlemen, I propose a toast to the President of the United States." All in attendance will then raise their glasses and say "The President" or "To the President." The President of the Mess is *usually the cadet group/wing commander hosting the Dining-In.* On the presentation and retirement of the Colors, face toward the Colors at attention until the ceremony is completed. Remain standing for the toasts and the invocation at the beginning of the program. You should rise again for the benediction at the end of the program.

The Military Ball

Another widespread custom in Air Force JROTC is the Military Ball. This formal event requires cadets to wear formal or semiformal service dress and guests to wear formal attire. The Military Ball presents certain rules, procedures, and protocol to be observed. For example, you must wear the uniform the JROTC instructors prescribe, and your date should also be dressed in appropriate attire. An important element of a Military Ball is the receiving line, which is made up of the official hosts and hostesses. You learned about the receiving line earlier in this lesson.

Cadets and guests at a Military Ball.

Courtesy of Michael Wetzel/US Air Force JROTC

Planning a Military Ball

Careful planning is needed to ensure that the Military Ball—or any social occasion—is successful. The first step is for the JROTC instructors to appoint a planning chairperson. This person should be given the authority to make many of the planning decisions, although some decisions may be subject to the instructor's approval. One of the chairperson's first duties should be to review the file reports on previous cadet organized Military Balls. These reports will provide the chairperson with details on what must be done to ensure a successful ball.

These activities include:

- Establishing committees, appointing committee leaders, and providing them with the necessary people and other resources. The chairperson also is responsible for supervising these committees. At a minimum, the chairperson will need to create the following committees:
  - Advertising
  - Decorating
  - Entertainment
  - Food
  - Fund-raising
  - Invitations, including the special guests
  - Program and seating arrangements
- Establishing short-term and long-term goals, identifying the tasks necessary for the achievement of these goals, and delegating the tasks to committees for execution.
- Identifying problem areas and lessons learned from previous cadet balls, and preventing them from reoccurring.

Invitations should be sent out as early as possible. If some guests do not accept, this allows time to invite others without offending them with a last-minute invitation. The invitation must clearly state the location, time, and dress requirements. Guests should know exactly what is being planned and what is expected of them. How to handle social invitations will be discussed later in this lesson.

Helpful Planning Tips

Helpful planning tips include:

- Be sure that all arrangements are carefully made for the special guests.
- Select a band that plays a variety of music, as well as music that does not offend anyone. Another option is a disc jockey (DJ). DJs can provide quality music at a reduced cost. If the ball is to be held during a holiday season, contact the band or booking agency at least six months in advance and provide them with a list of tentative dates.
- Arrange to have a photographer.

- Arrange to have several door prizes if you can find sponsors to donate them.
- Give credit in the program to all sponsors, as well as to individuals and organizations that helped put the ball together.
- Rehearse the Color Guard, POW/MIA ceremony, the sequence of events, and any special activities at the actual location at least one day prior to the actual event.
- Be sure that the staff at the site will prepare the correct number of meals and provide the correct number of chairs and tables, and check that the seating arrangements match the seating chart.

Other areas to consider include:

- Sign a contract that specifies the date, fees, and total hours the hall or ballroom will be available. The hours need to include time before the ball for decorating, as well as time after the ball for cleaning up. The band or DJ contract should specify the hours the band will play.
- Reserve the site and the band early, so you can be sure they are available on the desired date. A National Guard armory, officer or NCO club, American Legion hall or high school gym are some of the appropriate places for a cadet ball. The location you choose should include a kitchen.
- Set a working budget. Expenses include band or music fees, rent for the dance hall, security guard(s), decorations, tickets, food, flowers, invitations, and postage.
- Appoint a ticket chairperson if cadets are going to be charged in order to pay for the ball. Ticket sales should start early, and then be cut off at least one week before the ball. Ending sales a week before the ball gives you an accurate count of the number of people who will attend. Even if your unit has plenty of money, cadets should be charged a minimum amount for the ball, so they will value the event.
- Appoint a publicity chairperson to write up a series of news stories before and after the ball. Photos should be taken to go with the stories.
- The decorations chairperson should look over the site and start planning decorations. Supplies should be ordered or purchased at least one month in advance to ensure they are available. Major portions of the decorations should be completed no later than the day before the ball.
- Mail handwritten or engraved invitations to faculty members and special guests at least three weeks before the event. Keep a list of responses, and provide nametags for all expected guests.
- The food and refreshments chairperson must know how much money has been budgeted for food and refreshments. If catering is too expensive or inappropriate, cadets can contribute food items in lieu of paying for tickets.
- Formal dances often provide a commercial photographer to take pictures of cadets and their dates. If a photographer is hired for this purpose, be sure that everyone knows how much the pictures will cost before they are taken.
- If awards are to be presented, they should be ordered, engraved, picked up, and presentation scripts written.

Lesson 6 Review

Using complete sentences, answer the following questions on a sheet of paper.

1. What is the difference between etiquette and manners?
2. When introducing someone to a dignitary, who should be mentioned first?
3. When introductions are made, what is the biggest mistake people make?
4. Dinner guests will not touch anything on the table until when?
5. The POW-MIA table has a slice of lemon on it; what does the lemon represent?
6. Give three examples of proper dinner conversation topics.
7. What does "RSVP" mean in English?
8. If in doubt what to wear for an open house, who should you contact?
9. List two examples of courteous cell phone use.
10. List three tips for proper text messaging.
11. When a gentleman and lady approach a door, who should open the door?
12. Provide two examples for proper appearance.
13. When did the first recorded American Dining-In, hosted by Governor Spotswood of Virginia, take place?
14. If you are attending the JROTC Military Ball, what clothing should the cadet and a guest wear?
15. If you are planning to invite a speaker or other guests to the JROTC Military Ball, when should invitations be sent?

APPLYING YOUR LEARNING

16. You just attended a formal dinner party presented by your instructor and his or her spouse where you really enjoyed the dinner. Write a short thank-you note to the host or hostess indicating your appreciation.

CHAPTER 2

Courtesy of Michael Wetzel/US Air Force JROTC

Personal Behavior

Chapter Outline

“With self-discipline most anything is possible.”

Theodore Roosevelt, 26th President of the United States
and Lieutenant Colonel of the famed Rough Rider Regiment
during the Spanish-American War

LESSON 1

Note Taking and Study Skills

Quick Write

Write a short paragraph about one study habit that has helped you be successful on school exams.

Learn About

- note-taking strategies
- Thinking Maps®
- good study habits
- taking tests and exams
- how to do homework

"Education is the most powerful weapon which you can use to change the world."

Nelson Mandela, former President of South Africa and Nobel Peace Prize recipient

Note-Taking Strategies

There are many benefits for enrolling in the Junior ROTC program. One benefit of your experience is that you will be taught good study habits. This lesson will help you develop a study program that is orderly and efficient. The first step to any effective study program is learning how to take notes in class. If your notes are not well organized, the time you spend studying will not be used efficiently. In this section, we will cover basic concepts, or *the most basic understanding*, of good note taking.

Taking Notes

Taking notes helps you find and remember important ideas from your reading and from classroom presentations. It also gives you a way to look up these ideas quickly later if you didn't save an article or other published material you read. Notes are also important if you don't have time to read an entire article again or have trouble remembering points made by an instructor in class.

The temptation in taking notes is to try to write down every word said or read. Resist it! What is important is the idea or concept, not every piece of information.

Keep these rules in mind:

- Use your own words to make notes.
- Condense information.
- Always record the sources of your notes.

Hints for Good Notes

Start by assuming a position of mental and physical alertness. Prepare your mind and body. A good sitting posture and a mind that is alert and involved will help you avoid the temptation to wander into other thoughts or doodle in class.

There are other things to do to prepare for good note taking. For example:

- Develop a personal notehand. This is not the same as shorthand. Notehand is *something written down using an abbreviated form such as symbols*. You may wish you knew shorthand, but that could be a handicap because you would be tempted to take down everything. With notehand, you can take down only important things, faster and better. How do you use notehand? It is your own personal set of symbols for words: a plus sign for *and*, a check mark that means *for*, the letter C underlined for *with*. You can think of many others, especially if you use abbreviations and symbols when sending text messages. Englishman Samuel Pepys kept a now-famous diary from 1660 to 1669 about events in London, England, in a curious notehand of his own. President Woodrow Wilson developed a system of note taking when he was 14. Pope Pius XII left trunks full of notes taken in his own personal notehand.
- If given the opportunity, preview, which is *to review any notes or other material to help prepare for the day's assignment before you get to class*. Then you'll know what's in the text and be prepared for the day's lesson. You won't waste time during the class.
- Have plenty of notebook paper and a sharp pencil or working pen. If you have to stop to borrow supplies, you lose time and could miss something important.

Once class begins, instructors will often teach using key words or transition words like "because," "in addition," "later," "therefore," "also," "in spite of," "along with," and "on the other hand." They are keys to the relationships between the ideas the author or lecturer is presenting.

Vocabulary

- basic concepts
- notehand
- preview
- rule
- comprehension
- cause and effect
- context
- adjectives
- comparing and contrasting
- analogy
- metaphor
- test anxiety

Instructors often give a main point special emphasis by writing it on a blackboard, whiteboard, or Smartboard®, often repeating the same thought, so that may be a hint to put it in your notes. If an instructor uses words like "here are the main causes," "the point to remember is," "in conclusion," "in summary"—words that indicate the instructor is leading to or repeating the main point—you should take notes.

Always record the instructor's examples. Make a check by these and other key ideas the instructor emphasizes. Some students write "IMP" for "important" next to those key points. Do not hesitate to ask to have a point repeated during this time, or to raise questions in class when it is appropriate to do so.

Listen for clues—such as "the four causes were" or "to sum up." There may be something important to follow. In addition, note any major conclusion if the class gets into discussion.

Pay especially close attention to note taking in the last few minutes of class time. Often the instructor "saves the best for last."

Here are some other important hints for good note taking:

- Don't try to write down everything—only the main ideas. One page of good notes is worth ten pages of trivia.
- Write in outline form whenever possible. In outlining, you group ideas so that their relationships are clear. This means creating main categories under a general topic, then organizing the specific facts under them. Outlining can come in handy when reviewing for a test. Textbook chapter headings might serve as large categories for organizing what you've learned about each topic.

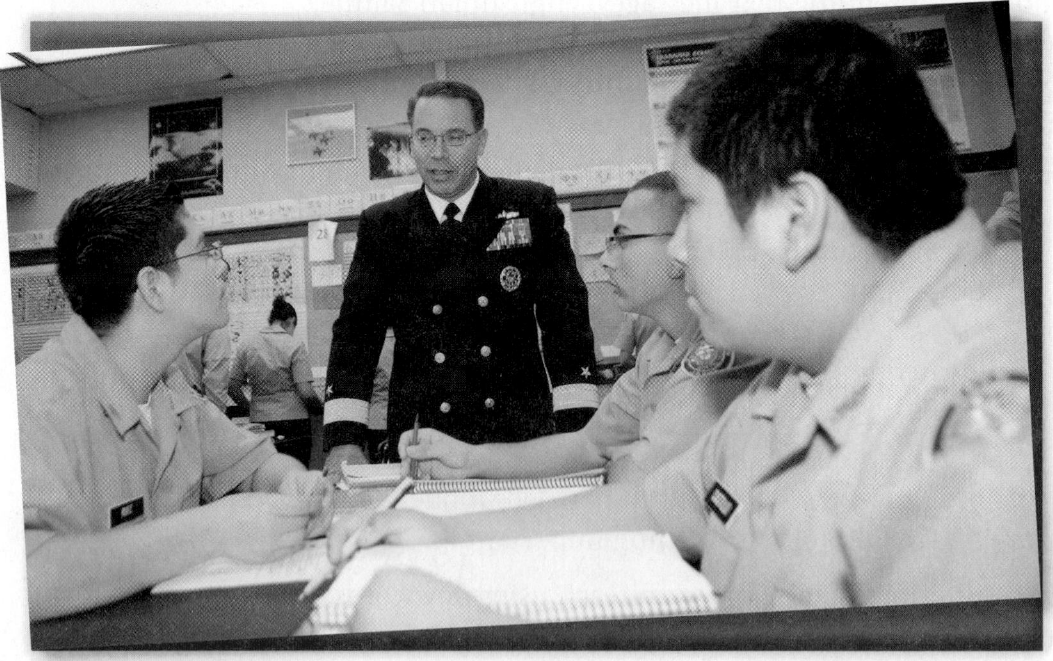

Taking notes helps you find and remember important ideas from your reading.
Courtesy of Scott A. Thornbloom/www.navy.mil

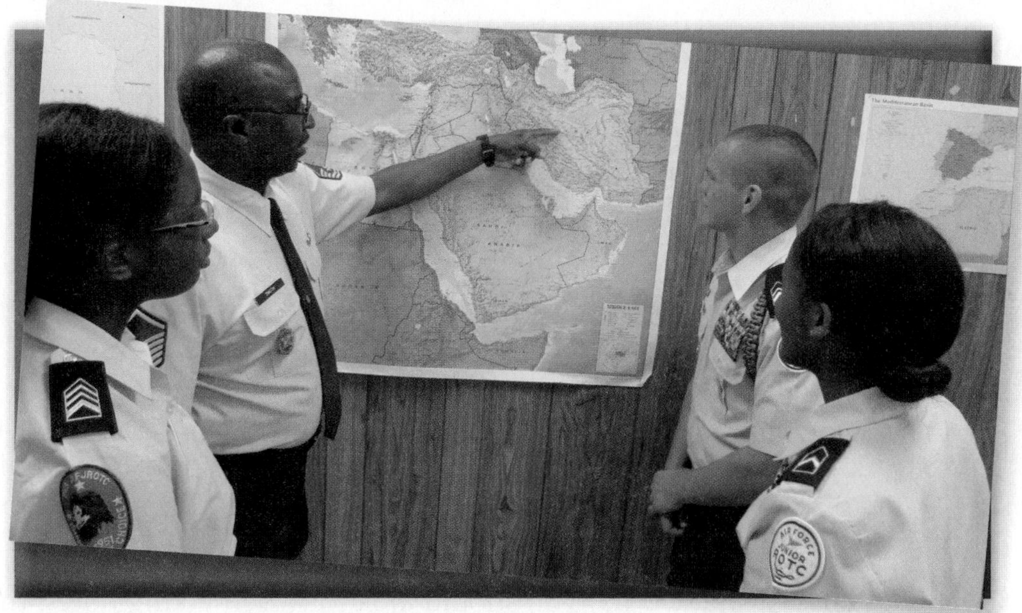

Cadets ask their instructor to explain an important topic after class.
Courtesy of Michael Wetzel/US Air Force JROTC

- Take notes in *your* words, not the instructor's. To do this, you must think, organize *your ideas*, and find your own words. If you don't understand the information well enough to express it in your own words, put a question mark in the margin and ask the instructor, after class, to explain it.
- Abbreviate words you know you will remember, try to use notehand, and remember to be consistent.
- Leave a blank line or two as you write. That gives you room to add a thought, key words, phrases, or ideas that are missed. Fill in these gaps later.
- Be sure your notes are readable. Don't scribble so fast that you can't read your notes the next day. Illegible handwriting costs businesses millions of dollars in delayed orders. Thousands of letters end up in the dead letter office because nobody can read the addresses. Students flunk exams because of unreadable notes.
- Copy *accurately* all formulas, rules, and assignments the instructor puts on the board. Do not be distracted by the speaker's mannerisms, method of delivery, or the quality of his or her voice. In other words, listen with the mind, not emotions.
- Include in your notes memos to yourself to dig deeper into subjects to find out more. For example, let's say you're studying exploring space. Should we have spent billions of dollars on problems here on earth, or have we gathered enough results from space trips to justify their cost? Get facts; seek different opinions. If you are studying African American history, find out what influence Gandhi had on Martin Luther King Jr. in the non-violent civil rights movement. What do the experts think?
- Many times, you will have to read material in the course of your studies. This material may be dull and boring; nonetheless, this is when taking the time to take good notes while reading becomes useful. It can heighten your attention by forcing you to actively engage with the material. It can also encourage you to put material into your own words and in a meaningful order.

Once you complete your notes, here are a few things to consider:

- If you have a clue column in your notes, this could be the key to higher marks. As soon as possible after taking notes, make time to read these over—not studying them, just reading them. Check now, while it is all still fresh, to see if anything important was left out or is incorrect, and then make changes. In the left-hand column, set down clue words near the topics in the notes. These clue words should not repeat information, but should designate or label the kind of information you find within the notes.
- Keep your notes well organized so you can quickly find what you need. These notes will make your papers clearer, your themes more interesting, and your exams better *illustrated*. Illustrated notes clarify or explain something by giving examples or making comparisons. Your class discussions will also become sharper and more relevant, all because you have become an expert taker of notes.

Now that we have covered how and what you should look for when taking notes, the next section will cover two methods of note-taking organization. The first method is the research-based 2-3-3-2 and 2-5-1 techniques, followed by a well-organized study system known as the Cornell method of note taking.

The 2-3-3-2 and 2-5-1 Techniques

If the course is one in which a presentation or lecture and text are closely related, use the 2-3-3-2 Technique. Start with a piece of 8 1/2 by 11-inch loose-leaf paper. Keep notes for each class on a single side of each page in a separate notebook, or section of a notebook. Put a topic heading on each page. Then take the time to **rule** the page, which is *drawing a line used to separate columns or create borders*:

- Make columns of 2 inches down the left-hand side for recall clues, 3 inches in the middle for lecture notes, and 3 inches on the right side for text notes. Leave a 2-inch space across the bottom of the page for observations and conclusions.

If it's a course where the presentation or lecture and the reading are not closely related, use separate pages for class notes and reading notes, following the 2-5-1 technique:

- Make columns of 2 inches at the left for clues, 5 in the middle for notes, and 1 inch at the right for observations. (After a while, drawing the actual lines will not be necessary.) In the center section or sections, take your regular notes in the form you've learned previously.

The Cornell Note-Taking System

Another widely used note-taking method is called the Cornell Note-Taking System. This system was developed Dr. Walter Pauk of Cornell University, New York, in the 1950s. The Cornell method is widely used in high schools, law schools, and universities, providing an excellent system for organizing and reviewing your notes, and increasing comprehension and critical thinking skills.

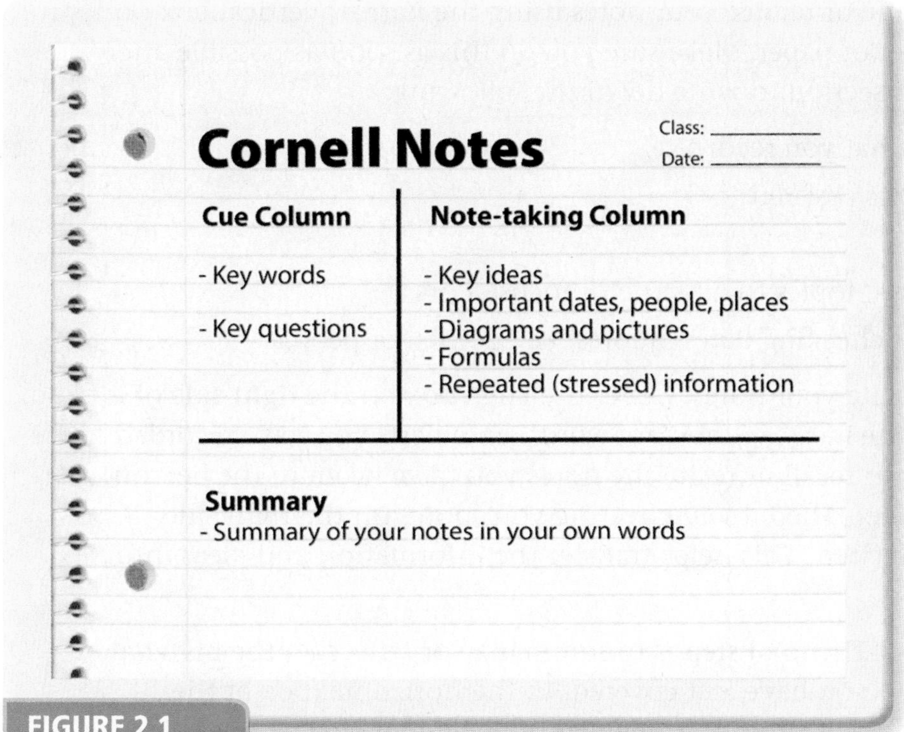

Cornell Notes

Class: ______
Date: ______

Cue Column	Note-taking Column
- Key words - Key questions	- Key ideas - Important dates, people, places - Diagrams and pictures - Formulas - Repeated (stressed) information

Summary
- Summary of your notes in your own words

FIGURE 2.1

Cornell Note-Taking System

The Cornell method is designed to save time, yet be highly efficient when done correctly. This method uses five main strategies for taking, condensing, and organizing notes.

The first step in using Cornell Notes (see Figure 2.1) is preparation. Using a sheet of notebook paper, you will first divide the sheet into three sections. First, draw a horizontal line about 2–3 inches from the bottom across the entire sheet of paper. Second, draw a vertical line $2\frac{1}{2}$ inches from the left side of the sheet. Across the top of the sheet, write down information such as class name, date, and period.

The second step is to capture your notes. Use the large box on the right side of the sheet to record your notes. Try to use notehand when taking your notes. Remember, do not try to write down every word spoken. Other useful techniques include:

- Make the notes brief.
- Put most notes in your own words.
- Skip lines to show the end of ideas or thoughts.
- Make sure you can read your own writing.
- Use graphic organizers or pictures when helpful.

The third step is to refine or reduce your notes using the narrow vertical box on the left side of the sheet of paper. Make sure you do this as soon as possible after the class ends. Use this section to write down the following:

- Questions about what you recorded
- Categories for topics covered
- Vocabulary words
- Review or test alerts; topics the instructor focused on
- Reminders such as checking dates, quotes, key points, or people

The fourth step is to recite your notes. Cover the large box on the right side of the paper. Now using the ideas, vocabulary words, and alerts you have recorded in the left column, try to recall or recite the notes you have taken in the box on the right side of the sheet. Then, by uncovering your notes on the right side, verify what you have recited. This helps transfer the information and ideas into your long-term memory.

To help reinforce the work you have put into your note taking, make sure you review your notes throughout the week. Brief review sessions will aid comprehension, or *understanding the meaning of something*, and retention of the material.

The final step is to summarize or reflect on the material you have just covered. In the horizontal box at the bottom of the page, write down experiences, ideas, important points of the lesson, or just summarize your notes. The summary is not a word-for-word rewriting of the notes, but is for reflection on the notes taken in your own words.

Sometimes it is difficult to describe an idea or concept. It can be even trickier when asked to describe main or supporting ideas for a story, or the cause and effect, meaning *the producer and the result*, of a specific action. This is where the use of Thinking Maps® can help you.

Thinking Maps®

Thinking Maps® were created to help organize and improve critical thinking, so that you can construct knowledge much like a doctor uses a certain set of tools to conduct surgery, with each tool being used for a specific task related to what the doctor is trying to accomplish. Thinking Maps® are visual learning tools. Each map is based on a fundamental thinking process such as classifying, describing quality, sequencing, and comparing and contrasting, and can be used to show relationships.

This section will cover eight types of Thinking Maps®, each serving a specific purpose for thinking processes.

Circle Map

Circle Maps (see Figure 2.2) are used for brainstorming ideas. They can be used to define in context, or *the setting for an event, statement, or idea, in terms of which it can be fully understood,* and answer a question, such as defining "What is a drill competition?" In the center circle, use a word, number, picture, or other sign or symbol to represent an object, person, or idea you are trying to understand or define. For example, in the center circle you could write "drill competition," and in the outer circle you could write words that are related to that concept, such as "awards," "participants," "uniform," "equipment," and so on. You can write or draw any information that puts this object, person, or idea into context. Circle Maps depict the most random type of thinking.

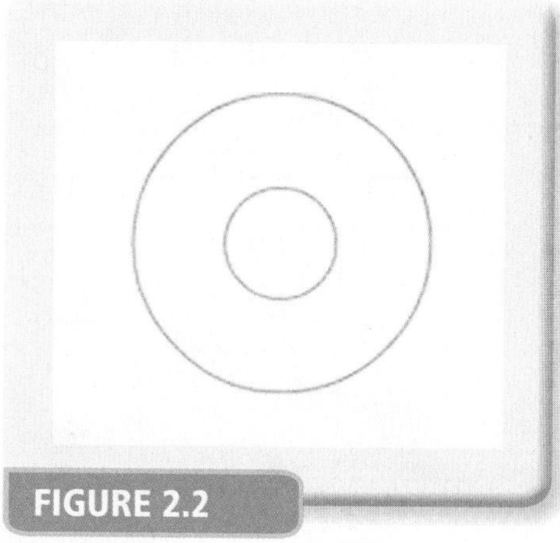

FIGURE 2.2

Circle Map

Bubble Map

Bubble Maps (see Figure 2.3) are used to describe qualities of a place, person, or thing. In the middle circle, you would write the name of the object you want to describe. For example, in the center circle you could write "JROTC," and in the surrounding circles you would write adjectives, *words that describe objects*, or an adjectival phrase. This answers the question, "Which adjective would best describe this object?" When you are done, your Bubble Map may look similar to a web or cluster. Bubble Maps are very useful for developing vocabulary, distinguishing between fact and fiction, or valuing/evaluating. Bubble Maps should not be used for brainstorming.

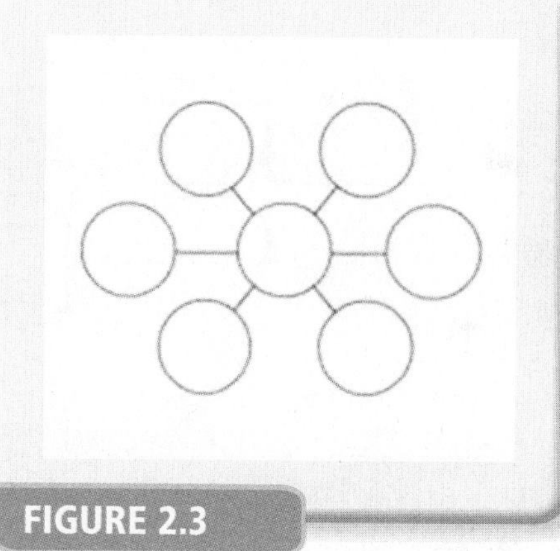

FIGURE 2.3

Bubble Map

Double Bubble Map

Double Bubble Maps (see Figure 2.4) are used for comparing and contrasting, which is *to examine two or more people, things, or ideas in order to discover similarities and differences between or among them.* In the center circles, write the words for two items or objects being investigated. In the middle bubbles, use *adjectives, adjectival phrases,* and other terms that show similarity between two objects and answer the question, "What are the similarities and differences?" In the outside bubbles connected respectively to the two objects, write the words that describe their different qualities.

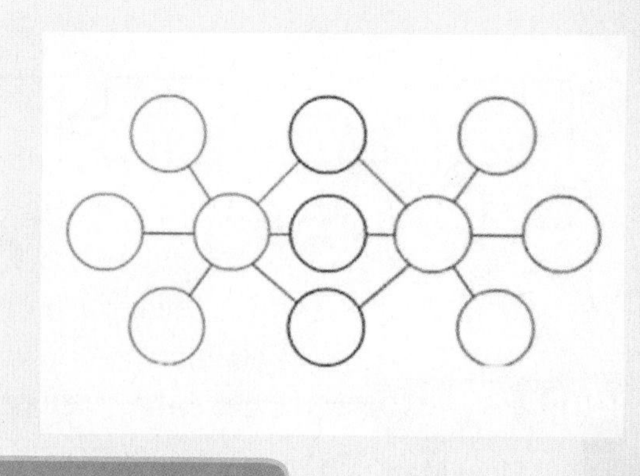

FIGURE 2.4

Double Bubble Map

Personal Behavior

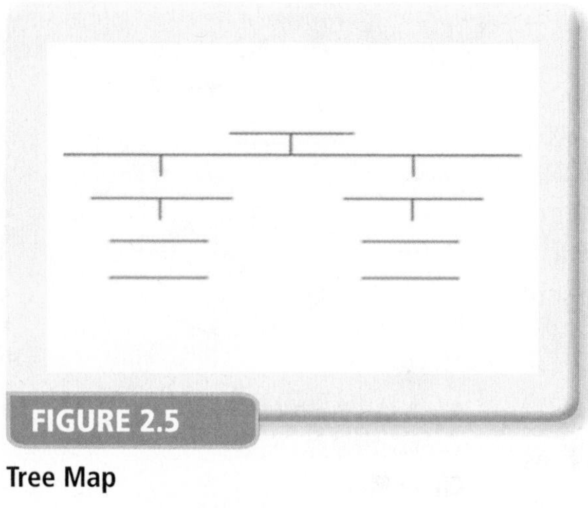

FIGURE 2.5

Tree Map

Tree Map

Tree Maps (see Figure 2.5) are used for classifying and categorizing objects and ideas according to common qualities and information about the category. A Tree Map answers the question, "What are the main ideas and supporting details of the topics?" On the top line, write a category name such as "animals." On the second level, list the subcategories such as "reptiles," "fish," "birds," and "mammals." On the next level, write the specific members of the subcategory; for example, for reptiles, write a subcategory list of frogs, lizards, etc. A Tree Map is an excellent tool for arranging objects in a formally ranked order as well as for informally grouping themes, concepts, and ideas.

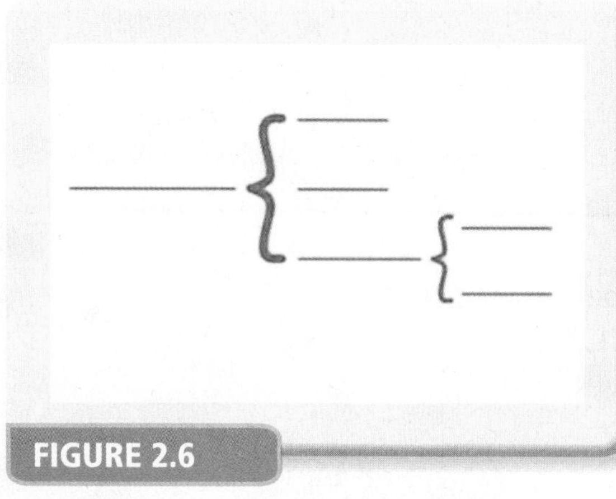

FIGURE 2.6

Brace Map

Brace Map

Brace Maps (see Figure 2.6) are used to analyze physical objects and part-whole relationships. A Brace Map answers the question, "What are the parts of the whole physical object?" On the line to the left, write the name of the whole object, such as "Air Force uniform." On the lines with the first brace to the right, write the major parts of the object, such as "shirt," "trousers," "shoes," "socks," "belt," and "hat." Then follow with the set of braces with the subparts of each major part. For example, the brace next to "shirt" would contain "name tag," "ribbons," "badges," and "rank insignia." Brace maps can also be used to identify the anatomy or physical structure of any object.

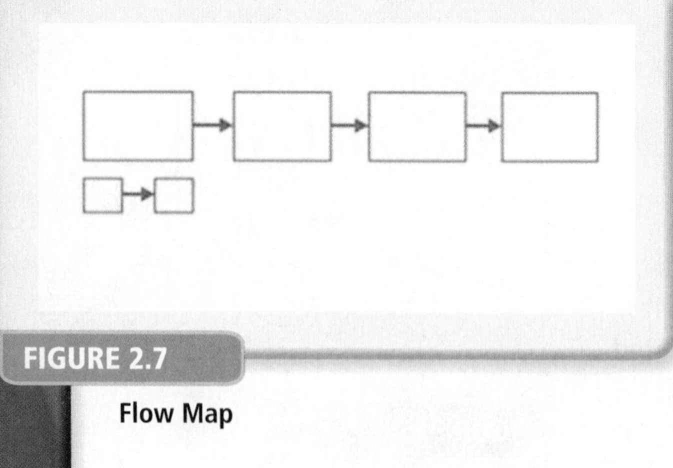

FIGURE 2.7

Flow Map

Flow Map

Flow Maps (see Figure 2.7) are used to sequence or order information. A Flow Map answers the question, "What happened?" In the outside rectangle, write the name for an event or sequence. In the larger rectangles, flowing from left to right, write in the major stages of the event. In the small rectangles below, write in the sub-stage of each major event. A Flow Map could be used to create a sequence of events needed to go on a school field trip.

Multi-Flow Map

Multi-Flow Maps (see Figure 2.8) are used for showing and analyzing cause-and-effect relationships. A Multi-Flow Map answers the question, "What are the causes and effects of an event?" In the center rectangle, write an important event that has occurred, such as "World War II." On the left side of the event, write the causes of the event such as "Japanese bombing Pearl Harbor" or "Germany attacking Great Britain." On the right side, write the effects of the event. For "World War II" this could be "millions of casualties," "war lasted 5 years," or "the atomic bomb was used." As you identify more causes and effects add them to the map. If you are studying a system, you will find that there are effects in the system that, in turn, influences initial causes. These circular cause-and-effect relationships are called *feedback loops*.

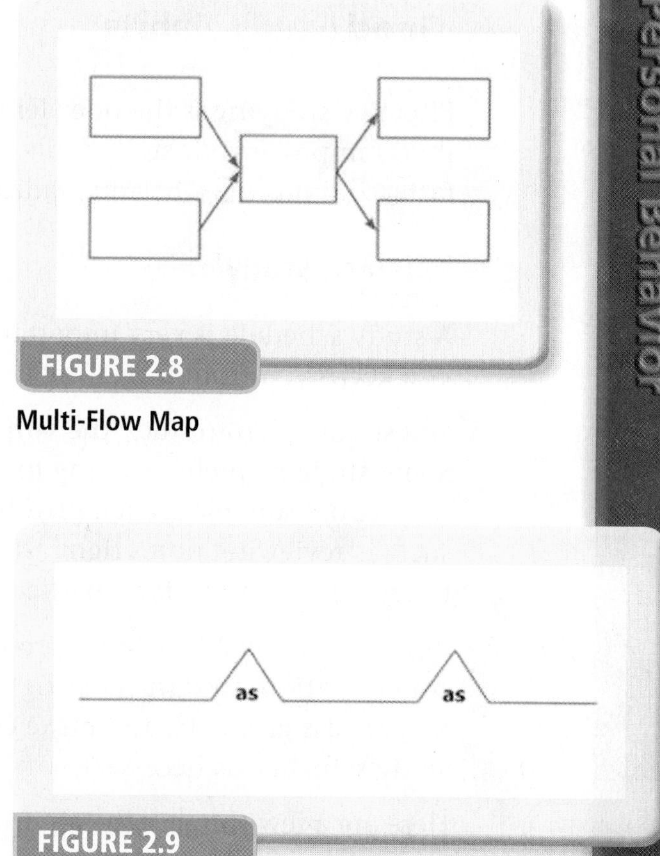

FIGURE 2.8
Multi-Flow Map

FIGURE 2.9
Bridge Map

Bridge Map

Bridge Maps (see Figure 2.9) gives you a tool for applying the process of seeing analogies. An **analogy** is *a comparison between two situations, processes, etc., that is intended to show that the two are similar.* It answers the question, "What is the guiding metaphor?" A **metaphor** is *a word or phrase that means one thing and is used for referring to another thing in order to emphasize their similar qualities*. On the line to the far left, write the relating factor. On the top and bottom of the left side of bridge, write the first pair of things that have this relationship. On the right side of the bridge, write the second pair of things that have the same relationship. This line of the bridge represents the relating factor that is "bridged over" from one side of the analogy to the other. An example of a Bridge Map is choosing two historical leaders and showing their relationship to important movements or conflicts.

Each Thinking Map® defined in this lesson was designed to help you develop a consistent way to process your thinking so you can learn effectively. Thinking Maps® are tools that can aid you in keeping your ideas organized and your research easy to read. Thinking Maps® are also excellent tools for stimulating critical thinking skills.

Thus far in this lesson, we have discussed two methods for effective note taking and how to use Thinking Maps® to improve critical thinking skills. However, for you to be successful on exams you will need an effective study routine. Studying doesn't have to be boring, dull, or difficult. It can be interesting, enjoyable, and useful.

Good Study Habits

Effective studying is the one element guaranteed to produce good grades in school. If you improve your study skills, studying will be more pleasant, learning will come faster and more easily, and grades will improve.

When to Study

A study schedule is very important to your academic success. It saves time and energy and keeps you from forgetting important things.

You should plan to study the same subject at the same time in the same place each day. Some students prefer evening for studying while others find studying right after class to be more suitable. When possible, you should study at the most productive time, such as reviewing notes right after class. If you know you will be called on to recite or to answer questions for a particular class, study your notes just before the class begins.

Big assignments like science projects and term papers require more time and concentration, so start those right away because you'll need time to gather materials, prepare assignments, and make corrections or revisions. Feel free to change your study schedule as necessary.

Here are a few things you can do to get the best use out of your study time:

- Avoid distractions during your scheduled study time such as computer games, text messaging, and Skyping® (unless used to form a study group), and other electronic distractions not being used directly for study.
- Make a chart for a full week. Block in all time that is committed, such as in-class hours, meetings, meals, regular chores at home, and work. Try to estimate how much time is needed each week to study for each subject and schedule those times.
- Use weekends for working on longer projects. Try to keep one afternoon open for work you can't finish on the weekend.
- Fit in health essentials—recreation, exercise, food, and sleep. They will help you get good results from studying.
- Take short breaks during long study sessions.
- Don't get stuck on one subject by spending too much time on it. Limit study time to approximately one hour per subject and only 20–30 minutes on memorizing.
- Begin with the most boring or hardest subject and work toward the easiest or the one that is most interesting.
- Study similar subjects at separate times to avoid confusion.
- Avoid studying when tired.

The OK4R Method

One way you can study effectively, as devised by Dr. Walter Pauk of Cornell University, is to employ the OK4R method. He is the same Dr. Pauk who developed the Cornell Note-Taking System.

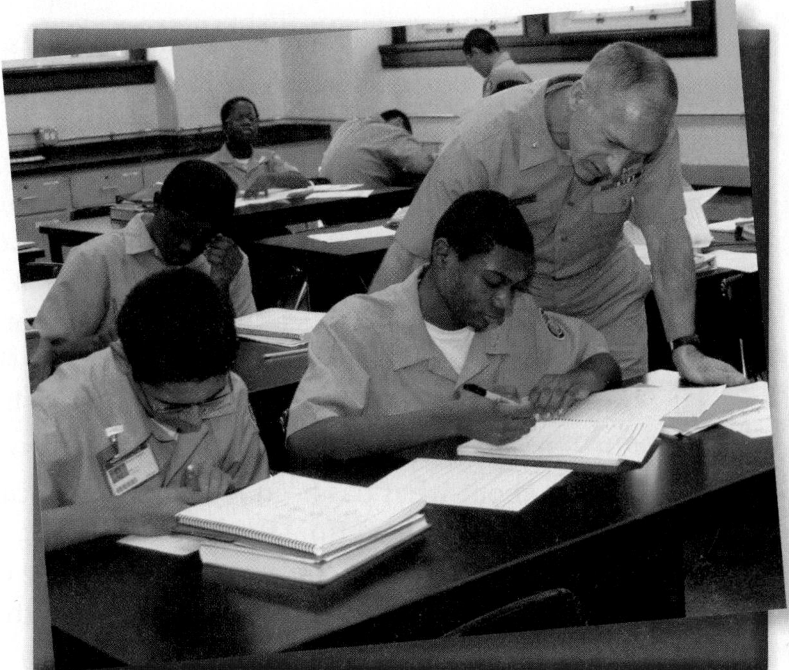

The OK4R method is an effective strategy for studying.
Courtesy of Mike Miller/www.navy.mil

- **O** = **Overview**—Read the title, the introductory and summarizing paragraphs, and all the headings included in the reading material.
- **K** = **Key Ideas**—Go back and skim the text for the key ideas (usually found in the first sentence of each paragraph). Also read the italics and bold type, bulleted sections, itemizations, pictures, and tables.
- **R1** = **Read**—Read assignments from beginning to end.
- **R2** = **Recall**—Put aside the text and say or write, in a few key words or sentences, the major points of what was read.
- **R3** = **Reflect**—The previous step helps to fix the material in the mind. To keep it there, relate it to other knowledge.
- **R4** = **Review**—This step is not done until just before the next quiz or test.

The PQRST Method

A similar method of study is a technique devised by Dr. Robin West, associate professor at the University of Florida called the PQRST method—a way to read a textbook so that what you read becomes part of your long-term memory. In this method, you follow five steps—Preview, Question, Read, State, and Test.

The first and last steps apply to each chapter or lesson itself. The middle three steps apply to every section within a chapter or lesson. You may find that many textbooks are compiled in a way that makes this method easy to apply.

- **P** = **Preview**—First of all, preview the entire chapter or lesson—skim through it to see what is coming later. One way to do this is read the chapter or lesson introduction, look at the headings, read the section introductions, then read the summary at the end of the chapter or lesson.

- **Q = Question**—As you read through each section, ask yourself what you need to learn in this section. Start by looking for a list of questions that may be found at the end of a chapter or lesson or reading assignment. Write down the questions while reading and study them when preparing for a test. The more you try to find the answers to good, intelligent questions while studying, the more you will improve your critical thinking skills. The questions help concentration by focusing attention on main points. As you become skillful in making up questions while studying, you will notice that more and more of the questions appear on tests and exams. As you become familiar with the testing habits of individual instructors, it becomes easy to spot more and more of their test questions.
- **R = Read**—The key to effective reading is *reaction*, that is, employing critical thinking skills about what has been read. Now, you can actually read that section in detail. This will be a good time to underline or highlight key words and thoughts. This is also a good time to take notes, and apply one of the two note-taking methods covered. Read the whole section first, and then summarize it later.
- **S = State**—Once you have finished reading, say aloud what has been read. It is important to do this recalling verbally. Speak the words aloud or quietly. The only way that you can tell whether you have a topic clearly enough in mind is to put it into words. The State step helps you comprehend and be able to put to use what you've studied.
- **T = Test**—So now you have finished studying the chapter or lesson or major section. It's time to test yourself and review all the material. If you took notes, review them. Think of review in terms of testing how much you remember. If you feel you are weak in some areas of the reading material, reread chapter or lesson summaries and portions of sections where your recall is not strong, rather than merely looking over notes or materials. Even though you have only just read the chapter or lesson, now is the best time to test yourself.

In the PQRST method, it is important to state out loud what you have read.

© AntonioDiaz/Fotolia.com

Every step in the PQRST method of study is a necessary link in a chain that leads to the most effective study process. It does not work miracles. Learning takes concentration, willingness to learn, and dedicated work.

In short, here's how you should think about the PQRST method:

- **Preview**—The lesson is about …
- **Question**—I'll need to learn …
- **Read**—Get the idea of …
- **State**—This paragraph says …
- **Test**—Monday's lesson and the reading said …

Memorizing

When an assignment calls for memorizing, try this method: memorize actively, not passively. Use as many senses as possible. Try to visualize in concrete terms and get a picture in the mind. Also use sound: say the words out loud and listen to the words being said. Use association: relate the fact to be learned to something personally significant, or find a logical tie-in. Ask questions in class until the lesson is understood. But don't detract from others who want to ask questions as well. If you don't understand the lesson, let the instructor know. If you dominate the entire class time with too many questions, the instructor may not have the opportunity to review the main points that will be on the test or exam.

Verbalizing some types of study may be helpful. Remember "S" for State. Repeat important dates and facts, and write them down. Each repetition makes it easier to recall the information. Write words, phrases, or formulas that must be memorized on individual 3-by-5-inch cards, and on the reverse side of each card, write the answer, meaning, etc. Study the cards until you know the material without hesitation.

Using Libraries

Learning to use the public or school library can make studying more interesting and effective. Most libraries have a reference section that has dictionaries, encyclopedias, atlases, and guides to magazines and newspaper articles. Short biographies of well-known people, medical and scientific dictionaries, bibliographies (list of books on various subjects), and yearbooks are also found in the reference section.

Libraries have become more technology-oriented so that when you are not studying, they are great places to browse. Computers help make searches for material much easier. You can also find such things as videotapes, records, microfilms, maps, filmstrips, and other visual materials that are helpful learning aids. Don't hesitate to ask the librarian for assistance. The librarian can help locate material and make suggestions on other things you might not know.

Many libraries and publicly accessible information search sites can now be found on the Internet. However, be very careful about who, where, and how this information was provided. More and more students are using the Internet to conduct research for assignments and studying. Usually, printed and online sources from public or university libraries have been thoroughly evaluated by subject matter experts to ensure material is accurate. However, when you are using an Internet search engine, recognize that there usually is no screening process or review of the material to ensure accuracy of information on websites; what seems to be fact may be just one person's point of view.

It is very important for you to know who is providing the information you are researching for an assignment or exam. Make sure to double-check the background of the author providing the information, and keep a record of trusted research websites in a "Bookmarks" or "Favorites" folder in your browser. It will not serve you well to learn inaccurate or wrong information.

Taking Tests and Exams

The best preparation for examinations is to keep up with assignments and study regularly. It's good to be concerned about taking a test, but it is not good to get test anxiety, *the excessive worry about doing well on a test,* which can mean disaster.

When reviewing, try to anticipate the questions the instructor might ask by checking in your notes for the main points the instructor seemed to emphasize in class discussions. Review the material under each heading and try to figure out what kinds of questions could be asked about it. Understand the information and relate it to what you already know.

If the test is objective (short answers), pay attention to details while you study. A more subjective essay test might emphasize relationships among different topics of the course material. You should pay attention to these relationships from your notes.

Above all, don't cram—that is, try to learn everything at one time the night before. It is very ineffective. Other things going on around you that cause you to lose sleep or place disorganization into your daily living habits may produce feelings of nervousness, tiredness, and confusion. These may tempt you to cram for your exams. However, cramming, at its worst, can cause you to lose the facts that you so frantically accumulated in a short time.

Once you sit down to take your exam, read directions carefully when the instructor hands out the test. If you don't understand the directions, ask the instructor to explain them.

You can take two important and effective steps to improve your grade, especially on a short-answer test.

1. **Survey the exam** for 30 seconds to see how many questions there are, how difficult each one is, and the grade value given to each question. If the number of right answers determines the score, guess at questions you do not know. Don't guess, however, if the wrong answers will be subtracted from the right answers. In this case, guessing will hurt your final score.
2. **Move along at a steady pace**—Skip difficult questions and come back to them later. Don't waste time worrying about them. If you have time at the end of the exam, return to any unanswered questions. Mark the questions you skipped so you can find them easily.

When your exam is returned, don't just look at the grade and the comments. Study in detail the questions missed and analyze the wrong answers. This will help you prepare more effectively for the next exam and improve your study habits.

Tips for Different Kinds of Tests

- **Completion**—Don't leave blanks. An answer thought to be wrong may be acceptable. Go back and check over the doubtful questions with a fresh viewpoint; this may eliminate a mental block.
- **True–False**—Guess if there is no heavy penalty on T–F questions.
- **Matching**—Answer the easy ones first to reduce the number of choices. Mark only one answer for each term.
- **Essay**—Keep these points in mind when preparing for an essay exam:
  - Read all the questions first and use the margin for noting phrases that relate to the answers. These phrases will help you write the essay answer.
  - Know the meaning of cue words such as these:

    Analyze—to examine critically to show essential features.

    Compare—to show differences or similarities between two or more things.

    Contrast—to show differences when compared.

    Define—to give a clear, not detailed, but precise meaning.

    Elaborate—to develop a theme or idea in greater detail.

    Evaluate—to appraise carefully, giving both the positive and negative aspects.

    Explain—to clarify and interpret the details of a problem, theory, etc.

    Illustrate—to explain or clarify by giving an example.

    List—to set down under each other a series of facts, dates, words, names, etc.

    Outline—to organize facts by arranging them in a series of headings and subheadings to show relationships.
  - Organize the answer; do not write haphazardly about the first idea that comes to mind.
  - Write legibly, writing what an instructor can't read may cause that instructor to mark the answer wrong.
  - Read and check what you wrote before you turn it in. Be sure to answer the questions that were asked.
- **Multiple Choice**—This is the most common method of administering assessments or exams; follow these tips:
  - If using a bubble sheet to record your answers, be sure your responses are numbered in the order of the questions, and be sure to fill in the bubbles completely.
  - Always cover up possible responses with a piece of paper or your hand while reading the question.
  - Have an answer in your head before looking at possible answers.
  - Read all the choices before choosing your answer.
  - Eliminate answers you know aren't correct.
  - Don't keep changing your answer; your first choice is usually the correct one.

- In a question with an "All of the above" choice, if you see at least two correct answers, then "All of the above" is probably the answer.
- Usually the correct answer is the one with the most information.
- Responses that use absolute words such as "always" or "never" are less likely to be correct.

Final Thoughts

To get the most out of any class you take, start by developing a positive attitude toward taking good notes and developing good study habits. Set some goals and work toward achieving them. We'll talk about setting goals later in the textbook.

Remember that good grades start with paying attention in class. Complete assigned reading on time. Do the same for homework assignments and proofread all material handed to the instructor. This will make classroom work, note taking, and study preparation for tests easier and more effective.

For your note taking, remember to have a system and order to the notes no matter what method is used. Give adequate attention to all notes. Divide them into several sections. Review them often—not just before a test. Set aside adequate time daily for review. This repetition may seem boring, but it is an effective learning method.

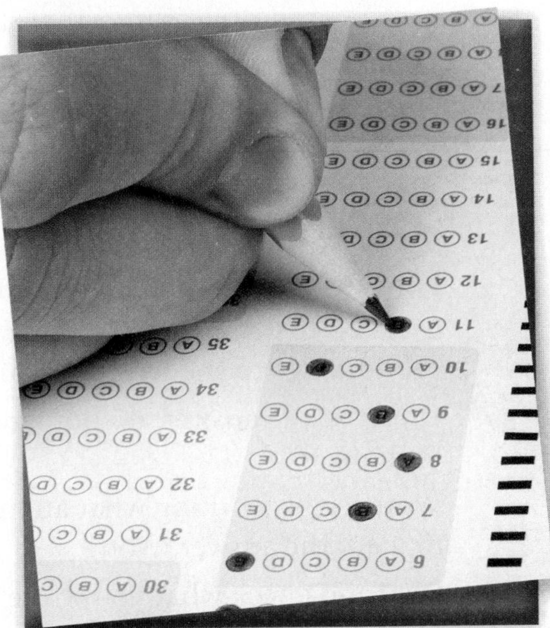

Your success as a student depends on studying that you do by yourself.

© VIPDesign/Fotolia.com

Also remember not to spend too much time studying all at once, a form of cramming. Take frequent breaks while studying (about every 15 minutes). Clear your head, or use the time to think about what you have learned or what you may have missed.

Before a test, review your notes one more time in order to organize your thoughts. This is not only a way to reinforce the notes; it is a good way to commit the material to your long-term memory.

How to Do Homework

Learning can be lonesome. Much of what you learn will come from the study you do in your own room. The homework assignments you complete, the required books you read, the TV documentaries you watch, the reports you work on, and the experiments you do—all of it is the heart and soul of your education.

You can cram with friends for an exam; however, as noted earlier, your success as a student depends on the steady, night after night, responsible effort you put in yourself. If the effort is not there, your work will show it.

Ignace Jan Paderewski, the great pianist, said, "If I miss one day's practice, I know; if I miss two days, other musicians know; if I miss three days, my audience knows."

There are always a few individuals around who brag that they didn't crack a book last night. However, when they want to get into a college, or get a good job, their ignorance will show.

Dr. James Conat, author, chemist, and former president of Harvard University, recommended each student do 15 hours of homework/study a week. That's three hours a night if you want your weekends free! Homework is your personal responsibility, not that of your parents or guardians. You don't learn the math if someone else works the problem. A science exhibit is not really yours if your brother did most of it.

A Homework Plan

If possible, have a regular time and place to study where you won't be interrupted. Study at the same place, same time, every night if possible. That conditions your mind to want to study as soon as you get there. It's best to have a room of your own. Your room should be physically comfortable. It should also be well lighted. Eyestrain brings on fatigue and nervous tension. Get glasses or contact lenses if you need them. Let fresh air circulate through the room to keep from getting drowsy. If needed, you can study at the kitchen table, as long as it's comfortable. The kitchen table may also be a good place to host your study group, as long as there are no distractions.

Get your tools: textbook, computer, notebook, sharpened pencil or pen, and everything else you need. A surgeon would not go into the operating room without his instruments "at the ready."

Using a computer could make your papers more readable and easier to do. Word processing programs will run spelling and grammar checks on your work for you, though they will not catch all errors. They also help you define words. However, if you do not have access to a computer, a good dictionary and encyclopedia are sound investments, too. Hearing the material over and over may be a good learning method for you. Reciting lessons on a recording device may help your memory of key lessons or homework material.

American novelist Sinclair Lewis, the first American writer to receive the Nobel Prize in Literature, believed that success in writing came largely from "applying the seat of the pants to the seat of the chair." The same applies for your homework. Have a comfortable chair, but don't slouch in it. Have a table to spread your work out on. Remove distracting objects from the area where you are doing homework or studying.

Maintain a personal bookshelf and a bulletin board to thumbtack clippings, pictures, memos, statistics, and anything that will add to your learning.

Turn off the radio and TV when it affects concentration. If your material is fascinating, it's possible to study even with radios, friends, or a marching band in the room. However, when the material is dull or difficult, a pin dropping could be distracting. Most learning takes everything you've got. So, concentrate!

If you are expected to discuss a topic or assignment in class the next day, do a trial run the night before. Watch yourself in the mirror while you speak. If you can, record it, then listen to see how you can improve it. During the next day's class, you will feel more comfortable when called on.

If you finish early, try to read something extra, just for pleasure, if for no other reason. Every bit of reading adds to your knowledge. When your homework is done, reward yourself with something you like!

Try to get your clothes and books laid out the night before. Be ready for a calm, unhurried start in the morning. Tomorrow is a brand new day and you're ready for it. You know more. You feel like a disciplined, organized person. You've done your homework!

Lesson 1 Review

Using complete sentences, answer the following questions on a sheet of paper.

1. What information should you be looking for when taking notes, resisting the temptation to write down every word said or read?
2. What are three rules to keep in mind for effective note taking?
3. List three things you can do to prepare for good note taking.
4. What is the advantage of taking notes during reading assignments?
5. What are the five main strategies in the Cornell Note-Taking System?
6. Name three thinking processes that Thinking Maps® are based on.
7. What type of thinking does a Circle Map depict?
8. What are Multi-Flow Maps used for?
9. Why is it so important to study effectively?
10. What are the five steps of the PQRST method of studying?
11. What are two important steps to improve your grade, especially on a short-answer test?
12. To get the most out of any class you take, what should you start with?
13. You should select a regular place and time for daily study. This will condition your mind to do what?
14. If you are expected to discuss a topic or assignment in class, what should you do the night before?

APPLYING YOUR LEARNING

15. Select one strategy from each of the five sections of this lesson to create a plan for improving your grades in a class in which you currently struggle.

LESSON 2

Managing Stress

Quick Write

Jot down at least two types of situations that are likely to cause you to feel stress.

Learn About

- positive and negative stress
- how your body responds to stress
- positive ways to manage stress
- methods to manage time

"Remember that stress doesn't come from what's going on in your life. It comes from your thoughts about what's going on in your life."

Andrew Bernstein, American author and philosopher

Positive and Negative Stress

The teen years are a time of many changes. Your body is changing, you are gaining new responsibilities, and you are forming new kinds of relationships. Stress is *your body's response to change* and a normal part of life. Stress happens when unusual situations, such as a threat or even a positive challenge, put pressure on your mind and body.

Stress is not necessarily bad. *Positive stress* can be healthy and provide a feeling of fulfillment. It can help motivate you to do your best and to reach certain goals. Positive stress creates excitement. It might help you to find the energy to score the winning goal in a soccer match, or to do exceptionally well on a school project.

Some stress can have unhealthy effects, however. This type of *negative stress* is called distress. Distress may cause you to have an upset stomach before giving a report, for example. It may also cause you to lose sleep after you argue with a friend. You can't always avoid negative stress, but you can learn to manage it.

Negative emotional stress distorts the way you view yourself, others around you, and the world in general. You may lose some of your self-esteem, which can make you feel less competent, unloved, or unworthy. Relating to people may become harder. Prolonged stress can make you feel listless, unable to enjoy life to the fullest, and may even cause illness.

What Causes Stress?

To handle stress, you need to know what causes it. *Anything that causes stress* is called a **stressor**. Stressors range from everyday annoyances to serious personal problems. They also affect different people in different ways. Whereas you might feel nervous about auditioning for a band, play, or choir, some of your friends might find the same situation exciting. Figure 2.10 shows you some of the things that may cause you stress as a teen.

Although positive changes are usually less stressful than negative ones, there are situations like competing for high grades or getting into a highly rated college that often cause great stress among teens.

Vocabulary

- stress
- distress
- stressor
- fight, flight, or freeze response
- relaxation response
- hypothalamus
- adrenaline
- resistance
- fatigue
- psychosomatic response
- stress-management skills
- assert
- physical activity
- endorphins
- time management
- procrastination

How Your Body Responds to Stress

When you perceive a situation or event to be a threat, your body begins a stress response. For example, if a car alarm suddenly goes off as you walk by, you may jump at the sound or feel your heart start to race. The sudden, loud noise is a stressor that makes you respond instantly, without even thinking about it. This response is largely involuntary, or automatic. It happens in three stages and can occur regardless of the type of stressor.

Alarm

Alarm is the first stage in the stress response. This is when your body and mind go on high alert. This **fight, flight, or freeze response** is *the body and mind's preparation to help us to respond to a tense situation or danger.* This includes a faster heart and breathing rate, increased blood flow to the muscles of our arms and legs, cold or clammy hands and feet, upset stomach, and/or a sense of dread. See Figure 2.11.

Although these events are common stressors, not everyone reacts to them in the same way.

somewhat STRESSFUL	*extremely* STRESSFUL
• Being popular • Moving to a new home • Going to a new school • Getting glasses or braces • Worrying over height, weight, or acne • Being named a captain of a team • Being tempted to use alcohol or other drugs • Losing a pet (disappearance or death) • Family member having a serious illness	• Parents/guardians separating or divorcing • Arguing with parents/guardians • Social media gossip or bullying • Negative thoughts and feelings about oneself • School demands and frustrations • Family financial problems • Family member's alcohol or drug problem • Getting arrested • Failing classes at school • Living in an unsafe environment or neighborhood • Problems with friends and/or peers at school that may involve bullying • Auditioning for the lead in a school play or a band • Taking on too many activities or having overly high expectations • Being sick or injured at a crucial time

FIGURE 2.10

Common Stressors for Teens

The same mechanism that turns on this stress response can also turn it off. As soon as we decide that a situation is no longer a cause for alarm, our minds and bodies change in ways that help us relax and calm down. This relaxation response is *the body's action to release tension, such as a decrease in our heart rate and breathing rate, and an increasing sense of wellbeing*. Teens who develop a "relaxation response" and other skills to manage stress feel less helpless and are more able to think clearly about the choices they have when responding to stress.

1. Alarm begins when a small area at the base of the brain called the hypothalamus receives danger signals from other parts of the brain. The **hypothalamus** is *sometimes referred to as the "master gland," as it controls important bodily functions such as our temperature and growth during childhood.*
2. The hypothalamus releases a hormone that acts on the *pituitary gland*.
3. The pituitary then secretes a hormone that stimulates the adrenal glands (triangular-shaped glands located on top of the kidneys that produce hormones such as testosterone and adrenaline). **Adrenaline** is *the "emergency hormone" that prepares the body to respond to a stressor.*

Physical Symptoms

- Dilated pupils
- Increased perspiration
- Faster heart rate and pulse
- Rise in blood pressure
- Faster respiration rate
- Narrowing of arteries to internal organs and skin
- Increased blood flow to muscles and brain
- Increased muscle tension

FIGURE 2.11

The Alarm Response

Resistance

If exposure to a stressor continues, the next stage of the stress response is resistance. **Resistance** is *your body adapting to the rush created by alarm and reacting to the stressor.* This is the stage in which you "fight," "take flight," or "freeze." In one sense, your body is briefly able to perform at a higher level of endurance. In the case of "fight," your ability to resist a physical challenge or attack may be enhanced. In the case of "flight," you may be able to run faster and farther than you normally could to escape from danger. This kind of resistance stage is why people in extremely high-stress situations have been known to accomplish incredible feats, such as lifting an automobile to save a child trapped underneath. However, in another kind of response, you may "freeze." This is when your mind goes blank when a teacher asks you a question or when your body freezes when it thinks the smallest move will be physically harmful. People afraid of heights sometimes react in this way.

Fatigue

Fatigue is *the body losing its ability to adapt to a situation when exposed to prolonged periods of stress*. During fatigue, the third stage of the stress response, an exhausted feeling takes over your mind and body. This lowers your level of activity. In this stage, your ability to manage other stressors effectively is very low.

Fatigue can affect your body in several ways:

- *Physical fatigue* results when your muscles work very hard for long periods, often leading to soreness and pain. Reaction time is impaired, and muscles tire very quickly.
- *Psychological fatigue* can result from many things. Among them are constant worry, overwork, depression, boredom, isolation, or feeling overwhelmed by too many responsibilities.
- *Pathological fatigue* is brought on when your body's defenses are overworked in fighting disease. Cold or flu, being overweight, and poor nutrition can bring on pathological fatigue. If you use drugs such as alcohol, this can intensify the feeling of fatigue.

Long-term stressful events can lead to illness. This is because changes take place in your body during any of the three stages of resistance. A recent study revealed that people who are always stressed release an excessive amount of a hormone called cortisol.

Symptoms of Stress in Teens

Physical Symptoms

- Lack of energy
- Fatigue
- Headaches
- Sweaty or cold hands and feet
- Ulcers
- Problems sleeping
- Nightmares
- Apathy
- Anxiety
- Depression
- Confusion
- Muscle tension
- Hives

Behavioral Symptoms

- Low self-esteem
- Inability to focus
- Irritability, anger, or tantrums
- Suicidal thoughts or attempts
- Withdrawal
- Crying
- Nail-biting or grinding teeth
- Overeating or under-eating
- Lying
- Moodiness
- Stealing
- Violence
- Chain smoking
- Drug or alcohol use

Cortisol normally helps a body's immune system response. However, people who are constantly stressed release too much cortisol. The body's immune cells then become insensitive to cortisol's normal regulatory effect. The research suggested that this reaction can promote disease, including the common cold.

Although a stress-related illness can be minor, such as sleep troubles or upset stomach, it can also be life-threatening. Over an extended period, high blood pressure can develop, or the risk of heart disease or stroke may increase. Even stressors that are often ignored, such as the hassles of a daily routine, can build up over time and cause physical and psychological problems.

Stress and Your Health

Stress is an unavoidable part of life. As mentioned before, stress can make life fun, exciting, enjoyable, and challenging. However, excessive or prolonged stress can have a negative impact on all aspects of your health.

Physical Effects

Sometimes stress can lead to a psychosomatic response. This is *a physical reaction that results from stress rather than from an injury or illness*. The prefix *psycho* means "of the mind," and *somatic* means "of the body." Psychosomatic responses may include sleep disorders, skin disorders, and stomach and digestive problems. Other health problems that may sometimes be stress-related include:

- **Headaches**—A headache caused by stress is the most common type of headache. When stressed, the muscles in the head and neck contract. Migraine headaches, which affect about one in ten people, may also be triggered by stress. During a migraine attack, inflamed blood vessels and nerves around the brain cause severe throbbing, which is often accompanied by nausea and vomiting.
- **Weakened immune system**—Extended exposure to stress can reduce your body's ability to fight disease by weakening the immune system. When your immune system is weakened, you may be more prone to colds, flu, or more severe infections. You may also experience a great deal of muscle tension and develop hives or other skin disorders.
- **Anxiety**—A feeling of severe anxiety can bring on other symptoms such as nightmares, confusion, and depression. It can even bring on stress-related ulcers.

Behavioral Effects

Stress can also have effects on mental, emotional, and social health. It can interfere with daily activities and relationships with others. For example, stress can make it hard to focus. This can cause some "self-put-downs" and the distorted belief that failure is inevitable.

The Impact of Tension-Related (Stress) Headaches

There are estimates that in any given year about 70 percent of some populations worldwide have at least one headache due to tension.

In the United States, about 30 to 80 percent of the adult population suffers from occasional tension headaches. Women are twice as likely to suffer from them as men are.

In a large 2001 British study, about 8 percent of 7-year-olds and 15 percent of 11-year-olds had headaches. Headaches occurred most often around age 13. The study further reported that many of these children tended to have headaches and other physical complaints when they grew up.

In the study, significant factors associated with childhood headaches included:

- Moderate or severe depression.
- Separation from the mother for more than a week.
- Chronic illness in the mother when the child was younger than 11.
- Mental illness in any family member.

Another study done in 2001 concluded that young people with headaches tended to be more emotionally rigid. They also tended to have more repressed anger than their peers.

Mood swings are also a common reaction to stress. Teens often experience mood swings as a result of hormonal changes and social and academic pressures. These emotional shifts from happy feelings to depression-like symptoms may put a strain on relationships with family and friends.

Stress can increase a person's vulnerability to alcohol, tobacco, or drug use. Many people give stress as the reason they started drinking or smoking. However, use of these substances actually increases stress and leads to even bigger problems.

In some cases, stress can lead to more serious behaviors like lying, stealing, and even physical violence.

Identifying Stress

The first step in stress management is to identify the source of the stress. To help identify your personal stressors, look at what is happening around you right now. Are any of the following causing you stress?

- **Life events**—These may include moving or relocating; adding family members by marriage, birth, or adoption; being ill; or parents' divorce or separation.
- **Physical stressors**—These may include being physically injured, lacking sleep or rest, using drugs or alcohol, eating or dieting excessively, or not getting exercise.
- **Daily hassles**—Feeling too many time or social pressures or having too many responsibilities are among these types of stressors, as well as conflicts with your surroundings, or with friends and fellow students, teachers, neighbors, or family.

Positive Ways to Manage Stress

There is no way to eliminate stress completely from your life; accept that throughout your life, you will encounter different levels of stress. To handle stress so that it has a positive result, you need a variety of stress management skills, or *ways to prevent and overcome problems related to stress*. One of the basic ways to manage stress is to follow a healthy lifestyle that includes a good diet, rest, and regular exercise. Problems are always easier to deal with if you feel well. You can also reduce your own stress by:

- Knowing how and when to relax
- Keeping a positive outlook
- Keeping a sense of humor
- Learning to be assertive
- Ignoring circumstances that can't be changed
- Being physically active
- Finding a hobby you enjoy
- Eating healthy
- Seeking supporters to help you cope
- Solving small problems to increase your confidence

Relax

When you relax, you reduce stress by slowing your heart rate. This makes you feel less tense. You can try a few of these techniques:

- **Relax your muscles**—Tighten and then relax one group of muscles at a time. Start at your toes and work your way up to your head.
- **Slow your breathing**—Take deep, even breaths for five minutes. Inhale through your nose, expanding your abdomen, and exhale slowly through your mouth.
- **Get enough sleep**—Feeling overly tired can make a stressful situation seem worse. It seems too simple, but things do seem better after a good night's sleep!
- **Try meditation**—Find a quiet place where you can be alone for 10 minutes. Sit on the floor or a chair, keeping your back straight, close your eyes, and try to empty your mind. Concentrate on slow breathing, focusing on a single word, image, or sound.

Keep a Positive Outlook

Think positively. When you are under stress, it is easy to feel hopeless. A minor problem can seem much bigger. In any stressful situation, take a moment to remind yourself to look at the big picture and keep things in perspective. Is it really the end of the world if you don't get to stay out as late as some of your friends do? Is your homework assignment really as difficult as you think?

Laughter is a great stress reliever.

© ryflip/Fotolia.com

Remember that some stress can be helpful. It can motivate you to take action. Say, for example, that you're nervous about doing well on an upcoming exam. The stress that you feel might motivate you to put in plenty of review and study time to build confidence.

Keep Your Sense of Humor

Don't let stress prevent you from seeing the funnier side of things. A good laugh is a great stress reliever. So have some fun. Take a little time out to do something enjoyable and relaxing. Listen to your favorite music, read a book, or watch a funny video.

Learn to Be Assertive

To assert, according to the *American Heritage Dictionary*, is to *state or express positively*. Asserting implies stating confidently without need for proof. This is a form of positive stress.

There is a distinct difference between being assertive and being aggressive. Aggression seeks to dominate. The idea is to win at the expense of another's feelings of self-esteem. Aggression produces mental and sometimes physical abuse. Being assertive, in contrast, is to be able to negotiate with regard to the feelings of all concerned. There is no eagerness to overpower, just a desire to be counted. Being assertive builds self-esteem and confidence. Assertive people do not force their issues or point of view, but calmly and positively state what has to be said.

Sometimes it seems easier to let people take advantage of you than to take a stand. It is easier to remain quiet than to state your position confidently. When subjected to unacceptable acts or words, the tendency is to suffer in silence. This action promotes negative stress, which contributes to emotional and physical ailments. For this reason, assertiveness is a very important behavior to learn. Learning to negotiate mutually satisfying solutions is a much better outcome than accepting the unacceptable.

Learn to speak up for your rights. Do not let others take advantage of you. Do not feel guilty when you have to say no. You have a responsibility to defend your rights as an individual. If your rights as a person are being violated, speak up positively and intelligently. You are important simply because you are a unique being, and there is no other like you.

Be persistent if you have a valid complaint. If you feel strongly and surely about something, do not back down. Don't be afraid to disagree with someone. When the need to disagree arises, do so in an appropriate manner. It is not necessary to be loud, crude, or belligerent.

If you don't understand what is expected of you, don't be afraid to be assertive and ask for clarification. No question is a dumb question if there is a need to know. It is better to understand than to live in confusion.

Ignore Circumstances That Can't Be Changed

Life offers certain circumstances that are beyond our control. When confronted with these situations, it is better to ignore them than to indulge in self-defeating behavior. Acknowledge that the situation exists, recognize that it is beyond your control, and proceed to things that are within your power.

> "I don't know the key to success, but the key to failure is trying to please everybody."
>
> Bill Cosby

Within your power is self-examination of your life. You can do this regardless of circumstances that are beyond your control. If you can take the time to reflect on your values and choices, and about whom you want to be or are called on to be, you can live with a more positive outlook. You can find purpose and live with integrity regardless of the seemingly large problems in the world that may cause you stress.

Be Physically Active

Physical activity, that is, *any movements that require your large muscle groups to work*, is a very good way to relieve stress. During exercise, you are benefitting your heart, lungs, and muscles. You also release **endorphins**, *tranquilizing chemicals*, in the brain. These trigger natural relaxation. They also produce feelings of pleasure and satisfaction that, during a good workout, can help reduce stress.

When you're feeling stressed, some good activities are running, lifting weights, bicycling, or skating. Organized sports like soccer, volleyball, or basketball give you many aerobic benefits. You may even try aerobic dance or the martial arts.

Physical activity helps calm you and increase your ability to handle stress. Physical activity improves your physical appearance and mood.

Medical experts say physical activity aids digestion and helps you sleep better. It also improves your immune system.

Physical activity can put you in control of your responses to life, setting a positive example for others.

Physical Activity and Stress

When you are under stress, physical activity can produce both physical and mental benefits.

Can you add other benefits to this list?

- **Improved Heart Function**
  Your heart rate and blood pressure stay steady
- **Better Mood**
  Your brain releases chemicals that make you feel happier
- **Increased Oxygen Supply**
  You can think more clearly
- **Improved Appearance**
  When you look better, you feel better
- **Improved Focus**
  Focus on a physical activity carries over to the classroom

© DragonImages/Fotolia.com

But there are more gains from fitness than what the mounds of research say about the health and social benefits. There is growing evidence that your cognitive (learning) skills improve from physical activity by teaching you how to focus. A University of Illinois study in 2009 showed students exhibited better attention in class and higher learning achievement after a morning workout.

Find a Hobby You Enjoy

Doing something that you really enjoy regularly can help reduce stress. These activities provide a creative outlet, lessen fatigue, and refresh the mind. Extracurricular activities at your school can be important stress-relievers. There should be numerous clubs and activities available in the community or the church, as well, which you can join.

Many activities can be done at home. Experiment with different hobbies. Computer games may be fine, but don't stay behind the computer screen for hours. Try something new and different that uses both your mind and body. You might find an interest you didn't know you had. You will be a healthier person for it.

Avoid Tobacco, Alcohol, and Other Drugs

Some people make the mistake of turning to tobacco, alcohol, or other drugs to relieve stress. However, these substances do not relieve stress. In fact, using them makes the body more prone to disease and has dangerous long-term effects. These negative effects of tobacco, alcohol, and drugs will be covered later in the textbook.

Eat Healthy

A balanced diet is important for overall health, but it's also important in dealing with stress. Poor eating habits can actually be a source of stress by causing fatigue, weakness, and a reduced ability to concentrate. Over- or under-eating can also put the body under additional stress. That kind of stress can cause poor absorption of vitamins and minerals, which can lead to deficiencies and health issues. Eating healthy will be discussed in more detail in another lesson.

Sweat Your Stress Away

When you're feeling stressed:

- Go running, bicycling, or skating, or lift weights.
- Play soccer, volleyball, or basketball.
- Participate in aerobic dance or martial arts.

Physical activity will:

- Calm you down
- Improve your mood
- Increase your ability to focus
- Improve your appearance
- Increase your ability to handle physical and emotional stress
- Aid digestion and help you sleep better
- Help you maintain a healthy weight
- Improve immune system function
- Remind you that you are in control of your responses to life

Seek Out Supporters to Help You Cope

Seek out support for your stress. Confide in someone you trust, such as a parent, guardian, sibling, teacher, or close friend. Just talking with someone about your problems may help you feel better.

Good Places to Turn to for Help

Friends, Parents, and Other Adults	Talking to friends lets you know you're not alone. Also, a parent, teacher, church leader, family doctor, or school nurse may be able to offer advice or give you the information you need.
School Counselors	School counselors are trained to help with all sorts of adolescent issues and provide positive alternate solutions or referrals to support groups.
Hotlines	If no other resources or assistance is available, pick up the phone and dial 411 for information or 911 for an emergency. Check the front of your phone book, if available, for hotline numbers. These can help you right away and guide you to other sources of help.

Your Stress Management Program

Regardless of the techniques used, the ultimate purpose of all stress management programs is to remove the stress response as soon as it is not needed. By returning the body and mind to a more harmonious and normal state, energy can be saved for more important tasks. Develop a stress management program to address your needs and make it a part of your daily routine. One of the major causes of stress in our lives is poor time management skills. By incorporating sound time management practices in our daily lives, we can be more productive and help reduce stress levels.

Methods to Manage Time

Learning skills in time management, or *using your time wisely*, can help you get more done and reduce stress. Time management combines planning with self-discipline. Managing your time involves figuring out which activities are most important to you. When you have a task to finish, stay focused. Avoid unnecessary interruptions, such as phone calls, visitors, and Internet distractions—unless they are needed for what you are working on—until you are ready to take a break. If you use your time wisely, you may be able to complete your tasks with time to spare for other activities.

Time Management Tips

Priority-Setting. You should always take on the most difficult or most important tasks first. Devise your own system of priorities that works for you. Sometimes, an "ABC" system is helpful. "A" is for the things you absolutely *need* to do; "B" is for the tasks you'd like to get done; and "C" is for tasks that can wait. Your priorities should reflect your goals. After you prioritize your tasks, think about the best, most effective way the tasks can be accomplished.

Don't do things that really don't matter. Busy work or doing low priority ("C") tasks might make a person look efficient. In reality, it makes a person ineffective and may put you far behind on a project that is important.

Don't tackle too many tasks at one time. Finish one task before starting another. This is important when you are prioritizing and planning. Also, learn how to say no. If you never say no, you will be overburdened with unnecessary work. Don't try to please everyone. Prioritize, plan, and schedule. Try keeping a time log for a week or two. Record all the activities you engage in during a period of time. Review the log for time wasters.

Avoiding Mistakes and "Do-Overs." One way to make sure you manage your time better is to do things right the first time. Learn from your mistakes—don't take it out on yourself if everything you do isn't perfect. On the other hand, mistakes made because you are careless or take shortcuts can waste a lot of time and may cause hardship for others.

Thinking, Planning, Communicating, and Listening. Part of the JROTC experience relates to self-discipline, especially when it comes to balancing your time available to accomplish projects.

You should always try to set aside time for *creative thinking*—a few minutes each day reviewing your goals and planning the next day's activities. This can be done before or after school, between classes, or for a short period at a scheduled time each day. It will improve your creative capacity and will help you to be innovative in planning and scheduling activities.

Planning comes from the ability to think through a problem. You may be presented with a project to plan during JROTC, like a Military Ball or some other event. Develop a plan for this or any project that requires time management. One of the benefits of planning is that it allows you to make allowances for the unexpected. No matter how well things are planned, unexpected problems or delays will arise. If you plan too tightly or delay implementing your plans, the unexpected will throw off your entire schedule.

You may have to put together a group or team to implement a plan. Don't try to involve everyone. Involve only those who really need to be involved and will be helpful.

Good *communication* is also important to manage time properly. For example, you may have to hold planning meetings with a group. If you want meetings to be effective, prepare for these meetings. If you are not properly prepared, the meeting may go too long and time will be wasted. Keep your communications as short and to the point as you can. This includes telephone calls or other meetings on the Internet. Be polite, tactful, and helpful, but be brief. Avoid wasteful and unnecessary conversation.

Listening is also a form of communication. The ability to listen carefully is a major contributor to using your time effectively and is important in formulating how you communicate responses to others. The average person's listening effectiveness is only 25 percent. If you improve your listening skills, you will avoid mistakes and misunderstandings. Listen for what is actually being said, and try not to form opinions until you hear the speaker out. This will help you be better understood by others and make the best use of your time, as well.

Good planning, listening, and communication skills help build effective teams.

How to Beat Procrastination

Procrastination is *to put off doing something, especially on a regular basis*. How many times have you waited until the last minute to study for an exam or work on a school project? One of the most significant obstacles to effective time management is procrastination. Many of the tools needed to complete your school assignments or study for exams have also created the greatest distraction from getting your work done. Watching TV, surfing the Internet, playing computer games, and talking or texting on a cell phone are major causes of procrastination. However, there are effective ways to overcome procrastination, such as these proven strategies:

- **Think positive thoughts**—When you study, push negative thoughts out of your mind.
- **Set a regular time and place to study**—Determine your best time and place to study. When and where do you get the most out of yourself?
- **Allow time for fun, down time, and sleep**—You don't have to be a bookworm; however, don't let your outside activities become a distraction from the work that needs to be done.
- **Break up big tasks into small ones**—When you have to complete a project or study for an exam, do a little each day. This will also reduce your stress level.
- **Jump in**—When it is time to work on a project or study, put away all distractions.
- **Be good to yourself**—Try to reward yourself when you have completed a big project or done well on an exam.

keys to **LEADERSHIP**

Track your progress. Keep your time-management schedule on hand as you go through the week. At the end of the week, evaluate your schedule and change it if necessary.

Finally, here are two more tips you should remember for managing your time:

- **Don't work with unclear instructions**—You will lose time if instructions are not understood or possibly cause mistakes that will force you to redo the work.
- **Deal with the causes of problems, not the symptoms**—Just addressing symptoms is a real time-waster. The problem will never be solved until the real cause is handled. Anything less is a waste of time.

Lesson 2 Review

Using complete sentences, answer the following questions on a sheet of paper.

1. What is stress?
2. What is distress?
3. Name the two common kinds of teen stressors, and provide two examples from each list.
4. What is the process known as the "fight, flight, or freeze" response?
5. What are four physical symptoms related to stress in teens?
6. Name four ways that you can reduce stress.
7. List four physical activities that can help reduce stress.
8. What does effective time management combine?
9. Define the "ABC" system for setting priorities.
10. List two tips that will help you overcome procrastination.

APPLYING YOUR LEARNING

11. Make a Bubble Map® that demonstrates positive ways of coping with the kinds of stress that teens experience.

LESSON 3

Making Positive Decisions

Quick Write

List three decisions you made since getting up this morning. Place a check next to those that had an influence on your health.

"Parents can only give good advice or put them on the right paths, but the final forming of a person's character lies in their own hands."

Anne Frank, Holocaust victim and famous diarist

Learn About

- a goal-setting process to arrive at healthful decisions
- impact of communication skills on leadership
- responsible use of electronic media

A Goal-Setting Process to Arrive at Healthful Decisions

Making Decisions and Setting Goals

Even a decision that may seem small can have great significance. Daniel, for example, agreed to take his younger brother to the nearby convenience store for some snacks. Because they were only driving around the corner, Daniel decided to call his girlfriend on his cell phone and became distracted as he made a left-hand turn into the store parking lot. An oncoming pickup truck slammed into Daniel's vehicle, leaving his brother with minor injuries. However, Daniel hit his head against the driver's side window, leaving him with a serious concussion. Because of this injury, Daniel is not allowed to play any type of contact sport such as football. This is particularly hard on Daniel since he was the defensive team captain. What Daniel thought was a minor decision has left him impaired for life. Impaired in this case means *having a condition that reduces physical or mental function.*

Decisions and Goals

Decision-making and goal-setting are two important health-related skills. Decision-making skills will help you make the best choices and find healthy solutions to problems. Goal-setting skills will help you take control over your life and give it purpose and direction.

People often think of goals as something academic or job-related. The fact is, health-related goals are also important. Goals that help you stay physically active and prevent injury will provide benefits throughout your life. Moreover, people who set and achieve goals for their health feel better about themselves and about their lives.

The Decision-Making Process

You can make better decisions by setting goals. You should understand that a decision is a process in itself. Decision-making is *the process of making a choice or finding a solution*. It involves a series of steps. Figure 2.12 illustrates these steps. If you follow these steps, you'll avoid a "snap" decision—one that does not take into account these steps, which may lead you to make bad choices.

Step 1 is to *state or identify the situation*. What choice do you need to make? How much time do you need to make your decision?

Steps 2 and 3 are about *listing your options and weighing the possible outcomes of each option*. When evaluating your choices, follow the HELP criteria below:

- **H (Healthful)**—Will it contribute to your health?
- **E (Ethical)**—Does it show respect for yourself and others?
- **L (Legal)**—Is someone your age allowed by law to do this?
- **P (Parent Approval)**—Would your parents or guardians approve? This leads to Step 4, your values.

In Step 4, *consider your values* and the values of society. Values are *the beliefs, ideals, and standards that guide the way a person lives*. For example, keeping a positive relationship with your family is probably one of your personal values. You know that if you decide to stay out past your curfew without permission, family members may lose trust in you. By considering your values, and getting home on time, you show respect and earn your family's trust. Respect and trust are also core ethical values generally shared by people around the world.

Vocabulary

- impaired
- decision-making
- values
- evaluate
- goal setting
- interpersonal communication
- body language
- mixed message
- eye contact
- active listening
- interpret
- feedback
- refusal skills
- assertive
- prejudice
- tolerance
- stereotyping
- consequences

Evaluating Your Decision

Step 5 is *making your decision and taking action*. If you have followed the first four steps, you can feel confident that the decision you have made and the action you have taken have been correct. On the other hand, how are you to be sure of this? This is where the final step of the decision-making process comes in.

Step 6 is about *evaluating the results*. How do you evaluate? From the concept of value, evaluate means *to determine the value of something*. To evaluate a decision, you should ask yourself the following questions:

- What was the outcome of my decision? Was it what I expected?
- How did my decision make me feel about myself?
- How did my decision affect others?
- How did my decision affect my health?
- What did I learn? Would I make the same decision again?

What should Kendra do?
Go through the six-step decision-making process to help her decide.

Kendra must make a decision. She and Michele have been best friends for a long time.

Recently, Michele has been spending time with other students who skip classes. Michele has even boasted of going with them once. Now she wants Kendra to join them too. Kendra doesn't want to lose Michele's friendship, but she knows that her parents trust her to obey school rules.

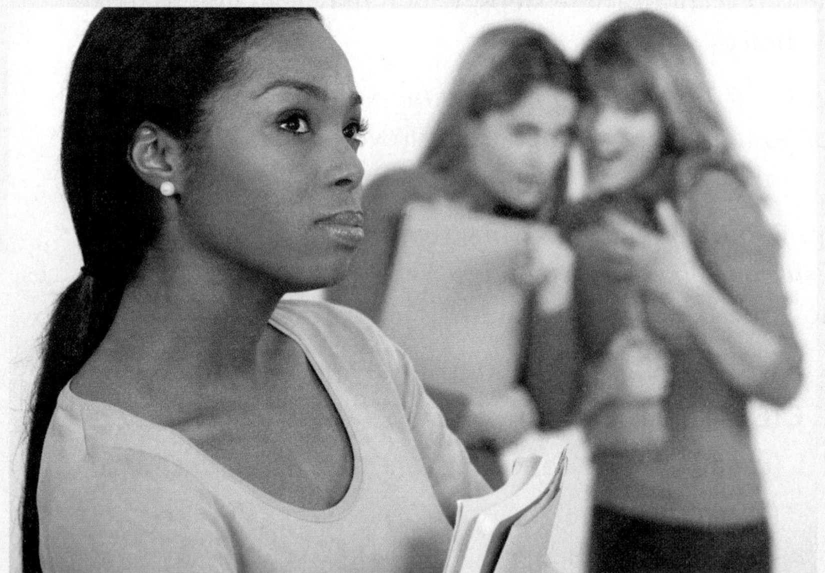

1. **State or identify the situation.**
2. **List the options.**
3. **Weigh the possible outcomes.**
4. **Consider your values.**
5. **Make your decision and act.**
6. **Evaluate the decision.**

FIGURE 2.12

The Decision-Making Process

As with any skill, decision-making gets easier with practice. For example, you might think about some problems that you or your family are facing. Think through all six steps of the decision-making process to find a healthy solution for each problem. This practice will help you with future decisions both during this school year and throughout your life.

Why Set Goals?

Goal setting is *the process of working toward something you want to accomplish.* Achieving a goal requires planning and effort, and it can give you a great sense of accomplishment and pride. Goals that you set for one area of your life often lead to the achievement of goals in other areas.

For example, if you work toward the goal of becoming a black belt in karate, you will achieve fitness goals, too. Along the way, you may also reach other goals such as making new friends, gaining more self-confidence, and learning more ways to manage stress.

However, there are other ways to think about goal setting. For example, do you feel that you do all you can do to protect your health? Is there room for improvement, like protecting yourself from injury or infection? Perhaps you need to work on family relationships. Setting goals will help you focus on the behaviors you want to change.

The Benefits of Setting Goals

Goals help you use your time, energy, and other resources wisely. They can help you identify what you want out of life.

There are three kinds of goals—short-term goals, intermediate goals, and those you want to reach over time, called long-term goals. Short-term and intermediate goals help you reach your long-term goals.

Short-Term Goals

Some short-term goals are just that: goals that you want to achieve within the next year. Your short-term goals may include earning an overall "A" in your math class this year. It may be to reach the rank of cadet Staff Sergeant in your JROTC class.

Other short-term goals are stepping stones to long-term goals. Suppose, for example, that your intermediate-term goal is to earn a track scholarship at one of the top schools in the United States. Your short-term goals might be to make the varsity team by the end of your freshman year. You may also want to eat healthier foods as part of your training to give you more energy.

Intermediate Goals

Intermediate-term goals are those things you want to achieve in one to five years. Suppose your long-term goal is to make the US Olympic team. So far, you have achieved your short-term goal by making the varsity track team. Now, your intermediate goal is to earn a track scholarship at a college with a successful track program.

Long-Term Goals

Reaching goals may take several weeks, months, or even years to achieve. You may want to become a professional track athlete or basketball player, or go into the same business that one of your relatives started. These are long-term goals. They will take time, planning, and dedication.

keys to LEADERSHIP

Following these steps as you set your own short-term goals will help you reach them.

1. Identify the goal and write it down;
2. List the steps you'll need to take to reach the goal;
3. Get help and support from others;
4. Set up some checkpoints to evaluate your progress;
5. Once the goal has been achieved, give yourself a reward.

Short-term and intermediate goals will help you achieve long-term goals. One example might be to get good grades in high school this year to start a pattern of preparation for acceptance to college later, where you can major in a degree that will allow you to start a career. For a basketball career, a short-term goal might be to become the best overall player on your high school team this season, so that later you may be able to earn a college scholarship, and eventually play professional basketball.

Figure 2.13 shows the steps one teen uses to set and pursue his goal of making the school basketball team.

Building Goal-Setting Skills

A national poll taken in 2011 found that a majority of American students lack faith in their ability to reach their goals. Only a little over a third said they believed they could find ways around obstacles to their goals. This may be due in part to students not having the proper guides or tools to set goals effectively.

Goal setting is important when it comes to reaching success, no matter if the objectives are in sports, school achievement, career planning, or personal life. Setting goals too high can make you frustrated and can tempt you to give up. Set them too low and you may never push yourself to reach your full potential.

As a teen, learning how to manage time, set goals, and make plans is especially important for making critical decisions that could affect the rest of your life.

Building skills in goal setting starts with adopting a plan or system. One proven method is the SMART goal-setting system, whose letters stand for **S**pecific, **M**easurable, and **A**ttainable goals, with clear **R**esults within a set **T**ime frame. Although the SMART system was introduced in the business world in the 1980s, it continues to work well for students.

Consider Katie, a real-life example. She set a goal to get straight As. She gave up time with her friends. She stayed after class to re-take tests. She also sought help from teachers. When she hit her goal, she was not only proud of the achievement, but she was able to strive for another goal—earning a perfect score playing her trumpet at a spring band competition. One week, she set a goal to get the rhythms right.

Here is one student's plan to achieve his goals using the SMART system.

Specific—**Identify a specific goal and write it down.**

Make the school's varsity track team.

Measureable—**List the steps you will take to reach your goal.**

Must be able to run 1 mile in 5 minutes or less to make varsity team.

Attainable—**Goals are realistic.**

Currently able to run 1 mile in 5 minutes and 30 seconds; reducing time by 30 seconds is a realistic goal.

Results—**Set up checkpoints to evaluate your progress.**

After 4 weeks of training, run a 1-mile time trial to check progress.

Time Frame—**12 weeks.**

Tryouts for the varsity track team are in 12 weeks, providing a clearly defined time frame to achieve goal.

Don't to forget to give yourself a reward once you have achieved your goal.

If I make the team, I will buy myself a new pair of running shoes.

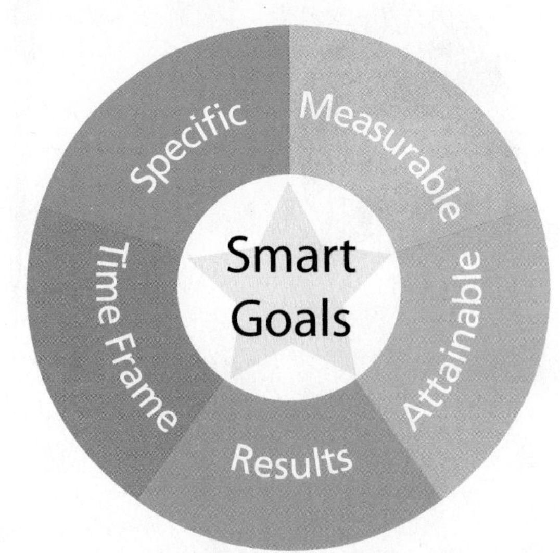

FIGURE 2.13

The SMART Goal-Setting Process

The next week she practiced hitting the higher notes. These goals were specific, measurable, and attainable, and she got results within the time she planned. Additionally, by achieving her short-term goals, Katie should be able to achieve her intermediate goal of earning a college scholarship.

Impact of Communication Skills on Leadership

You have probably discovered already that some people are better communicators than others. They have the ability to get their message across. However, they don't just say things well. They also listen to what others have to say and keep the lines of communication open. In short, they have good interpersonal communication skills.

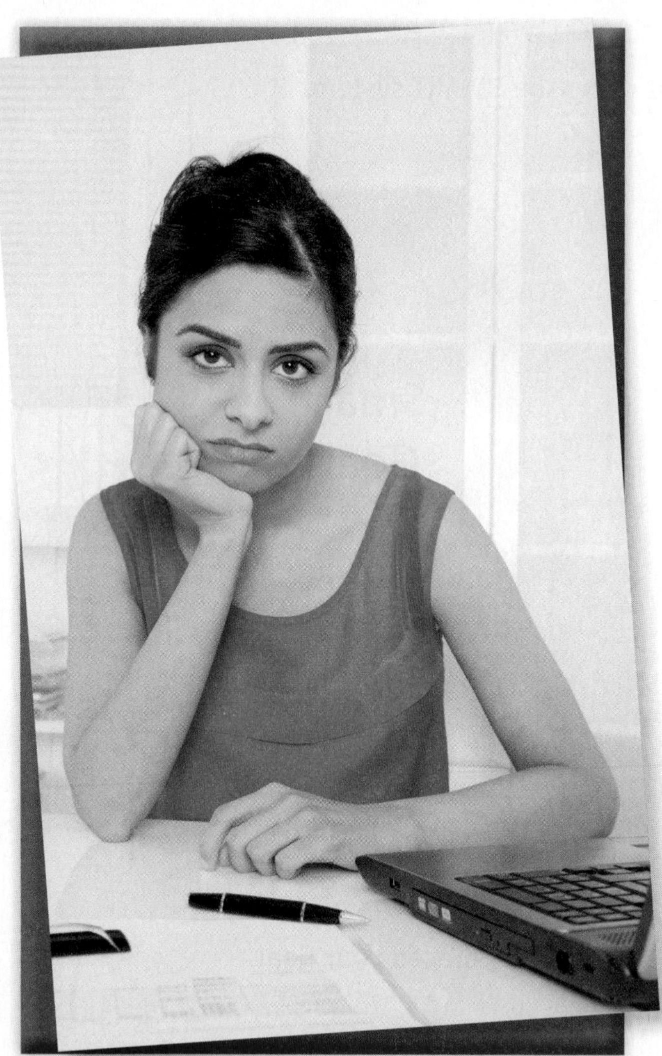

Body language can say more than words.
© Jeanette Dietl/Fotolia.com

Interpersonal communication involves *the exchange of thoughts, feelings, and beliefs between two or more people*. Like other skills, interpersonal communication must be learned and practiced. It is important because you use forms of communication in all of your relationships. Think about how often you talk with family members, friends, teachers, and classmates. Effective communication involves not just speaking and listening skills but use of body language, which sometimes says a lot without the use of words.

Body Language

As discussed in Chapter 1, your body language can communicate your thoughts and feelings. **Body language** is *a form of nonverbal communication*. For example, raised eyebrows might reflect curiosity, surprise, or interest. Drooping shoulders might indicate sadness, insecurity, or fear. It is important for speakers and listeners to be aware of body language. Some forms of body language, such as smiling and nodding, encourage communication. Other forms, such as frowning and crossing arms tightly across the chest, discourage communication. Sometimes your words and your body language don't communicate the same message.

A **mixed message** occurs *when your words say one thing but your body language says another.* For example, you might say "I'm not angry," but your frown and clenched jaw convey a different message. Your body language gives your true feelings away.

Using "I" Messages

Imagine your reaction if a friend said to you, "You're never on time!" or "You're so bossy!" These types of "you" messages place blame on the other person and often cause hurt feelings or an angry response. "You" messages can cause the listener to become defensive and stop any communication rather than solve a problem. Using "I" messages instead is a much more effective way to communicate. An "I" message is a statement in which a person uses the pronoun "I" to express an opinion or comment.

"I" messages usually contain four elements:

- How you feel about the behavior and its effects
- A description of the behavior; what actually happened
- The actual, concrete, tangible effects of that behavior on you
- The behavior you would prefer

A well-crafted "I" message is a powerful non-blaming communication tool. It states the situation and how you feel about it without putting blame on the other person. It also offers an explanation for your feelings. Finally, it states what we need or think. For example, you might say, "When we were late for the movie I felt disappointed. I'd heard that the opening sequence was funny and I didn't want to miss it. Next time we go to the movies, let's make sure we're early so I don't miss anything."

What does an "I" message do?

- Provides a high chance of changing the behavior of another person
- Protects the self-esteem or feelings of the other person
- Preserves the quality of the relationship
- Helps the other person to understand and improve

Of course, it would be much easier if we didn't have relationship problems with family, friends, or classmates. However, learning to manage the situation is your best hope. Using "I" messages to show annoyance, irritation, frustration, or anger is a more controlled way to indicate negative feelings. We are less likely to hurt feelings or cause negative reactions from the person whose behavior we are trying to change.

Speaking Skills

Interpersonal communication involves both giving and receiving messages. Speaking is the giving part. Good communication involves speaking clearly and carefully.

Here are some ways to improve your speaking skills:

1. **Use "I" messages**—Consider how your words will affect the other person, and express your concerns in terms of your own feelings. You'll be less likely to make others feel defensive.
2. **Make clear, simple statements**—Stick to the point and be specific. Make sure the other person understands what you're saying.
3. **Be honest with thoughts and feelings**—Say what you want to say. Be truthful and direct about your values while showing respect for your listener's values.
4. **Use appropriate body language**—Make sure your facial expressions, gestures, and posture match your message. Use eye contact, or *direct visual contact with another person's eyes*, to show that you are sincere.

Listening Skills

You might think that having good speaking skills means that you are a good communicator. In truth, though, being a good listener is equally important to interpersonal communication. A speaker's message has meaning only if the listener receives it. Good communication involves active listening. Active listening means *hearing, thinking about, and responding to the other person's message.*

The first part of active listening is important. Sometimes what you hear is based not so much on what the other person says, but on how it is said. It may be the tone of voice, use of eye contact, or body movements that affect what you hear.

Consider how you might respond if you heard the message below. State the sentence to yourself with the word in bold being emphasized.

"**I** didn't say that to Sally."

"I **didn't** say that to Sally."

"I didn't **say** that to Sally."

"I didn't say **that** to Sally."

In that one sentence, you can create or interpret four different meanings, depending on how you state it, and also how you hear it. To interpret is *to attribute a particular meaning or feeling*. Active listening means hearing the content and the tone of the message through verbal and nonverbal means.

How, then, can you improve your own listening skills?

First, listen carefully to what the other person has to say and *use appropriate body language* when you respond. You may disagree with what is said to you, but stay calm, maintain eye contact, and use facial expressions and gestures that show that you are interested.

Second, show that you are listening by nodding or asking questions. These things *encourage positive communication* in return. Say things like "Really?" or "What happened next?" to show that you are paying attention.

Third, repeat what the person said as a way of confirming what you heard. This is how you *mirror the other's thoughts and feelings*, another way you show interest. However, do not repeat everything that is said; this can be become annoying to the speaker and may inadvertently end communication. Then, offer feedback when appropriate. Feedback is *a response by the listener to what the speaker has said.*

Finally, *ask questions*. After the person has finished speaking, ask questions or add your own comments or opinions.

Say No and Mean It!

Your body language can speak as loudly as your words do. These teens are emphasizing their points of view with strong body language.

This teen is showing refusal with a firm, resistant body posture response. Others will clearly understand that she means "No!"

© 9nong/Fotolia.com

© Elenathewise/Fotolia.com

This teen's crossed arms send a clear visual signal that his refusal is to be taken seriously.

Refusal Skills, or How to Say "No"

During your high school years, there will be times when friends or acquaintances may want you to do something that you do not want to do. Maybe you're just not interested. Maybe you don't have the time or money. Maybe it's something that is unhealthy or that goes against your values. In these situations, saying no can be difficult. That's why refusal skills can be important.

Refusal skills are *strategies that help you say no, effectively.* When you feel pressured to do something, good refusal skills let others know that you mean what you say. Like other skills, they take practice. Nevertheless, using them will help you be true to yourself. You can resist temptation to "go along" without feeling guilty or uncomfortable. Other people will respect you for being honest and holding to your values.

keys to LEADERSHIP

A key for remembering refusal skills is to keep in mind the letters in the word STOP.

- **S**ay no in a firm voice.
- **T**ell why not.
- **O**ffer other ideas.
- **P**romptly leave.

One of these skills is to be assertive. Assertive means *behaving with confidence and clearly stating your intentions*. Words and actions show someone that you mean what you say. Speak clearly, calmly, and in a firm tone of voice to show the other person that you mean what you say. Your body language, including eye contact, helps you to do this. Be sure that your body language and gestures match your words. If you stare at the floor or shift your weight from one leg to another, you won't seem very assertive or confident. If you have a smile on your face and a teasing look in your eyes, the person pressuring you won't believe that you're serious. Instead, use eye contact, put a serious or neutral look on your face, and stand or sit up straight.

Eliminating Communication Barriers

Have you ever heard the saying, "A chain is only as strong as its weakest link"? The same is true of communication. If one person in a relationship has good communication skills but the other person does not, the entire communication process suffers. Sometimes a person's beliefs or attitudes can make communication difficult.

Obstacles to clear communication take several forms:

- **Image and identity issues**—Many teens spend at least part of their teen years searching for an identity—a sense of who they are and their place in the world. If someone is unsure of his or her values, the uncertainty can complicate the communication process.
- **Unrealistic expectations**—Imposing unrealistic expectations on your listener can cause the individual to become frustrated or defensive.
- **Lack of trust**—Good communication is built on trust between two people. If you don't trust a person—if you believe that you can't count on him or her to tell you the truth or to keep in confidence—communication is very difficult.
- **Prejudice**—Some individuals have a prejudice or *an unfair opinion or judgment of a particular group of people*. Prejudice prevents a person from having an open mind and listening to new information. To avoid developing prejudices, you can demonstrate tolerance, or *the ability to accept others' differences and allow them to be who they are without your expressing disapproval*. Being tolerant helps you understand the differences among people and recognize the value of diversity.
- **Gender stereotyping**—Gender stereotyping is a type of prejudice. Stereotyping involves *having an exaggerated or oversimplified belief about a group of people*. Assuming that all males like sports and that all females enjoy cooking are examples of this. In the military, a recent policy decision has allowed women into combat roles. This came about only after a long history of gender stereotyping. For a long time women were thought not to be able, physically or mentally, to handle the stress of combat. Eliminating such stereotyping allows people to communicate more honestly and openly.

Good communication skills help you form healthy relationships.

© Igor Mojzes/Fotolia.com

Responsible Use of Electronic Media

How we communicate with others has continued to dramatically change since the invention of the telephone and computer. Prior to this, if you wanted to communicate with someone else, you either had to talk with them face-to-face or write a note or letter.

With the invention of computer communications came a change in how we communicated with other people. People could email others without having to talk directly to them. In the late 1980s the mobile or cell phone appeared, allowing us to keep in constant contact with other people. Today's technological improvements allow you to communicate with anyone, from anywhere, at any time. You can Tweet®, text, post messages, email, and send many other forms of communication without actually having to talk directly to the other person. Some experts believe that not only has this changed the way we communicate, it has actually created barriers to effective communication. In this section, we will explore responsible use of the most popular form of communication for young people today: social networking.

Using a cell phone, laptop or desktop computer, tablet, or other mobile device, it is easier than ever to stay in touch with your friends, family, school, or even your place of work. Young people have been the first to adopt new technologies and in doing so, have become the largest population of social media users today. Social networking sites such as Facebook®, Twitter®, and Instagram® provide easy-to-use tools that allow users to explore the Internet and connect with others with the same interests. This also allows individuals to connect with others 24 hours a day, seven days a week.

Studies have shown that only 7 percent of communication is based on the verbal or written word. That means 93 percent is based on non-verbal body language. When we can hear the tone of someone's voice and see the expression on his or her face, we really know how that person feels about a topic or situation. The use of social media has allowed anyone to hide behind a text, email, tweet, or Facebook® post.

Safe Social Networking

The last thing young people want to hear is another set of rules; it seems everywhere you turn there are rules. The school you attend has rules, the home where you live has rules, and the society we live in has rules. So, instead of calling these suggestions rules, think of them as guidelines for responsible social networking. After all, irresponsible social networking comes with consequences, or *the direct results of your actions*. It could cost you that college scholarship you were hoping to receive or that job you really wanted. Irresponsible social networking could cause you to be arrested or expelled from school. Worst of all, it could cause harm to someone you really care about.

For responsible and safe social networking, do not become involved in:

1. **Posting information on illegal activities**—Never post information on any activity that is illegal, such as underage drinking, drug use, or any other abuse of the law. To do so could result in expulsion from school or criminal arrest.
2. **Bullying**—This is a serious problem in schools and society today. Hateful words or actions using social networking could result in violence, and you could face expulsion or criminal arrest. Bullying will be covered in more detail in a later lesson.
3. **Trashing your teachers or school**—After all, teachers and the school you attend will ultimately provide the support you may need to earn the grade and receive recommendations that may result in the scholarship or job you badly wanted.
4. **Posting objectionable content from school computers or network**—Follow school policies when using computers, whether at home or school. By accessing school networks, you are held to the school's policies for computer use.
5. **Posting confidential or personal information**—Do not share any personal information about yourself over social networks. Be especially careful about sharing your address, social security number, phone number, student ID, full name, or birthday over social networks. These networks are accessible by anyone. Too much information could lead to someone stealing your identity or showing up where you live. Doing this over a cell phone is okay as long as you know the person you are providing the information to; however, it still has risks, so know who you are texting or talking to. Always check with your parents or guardians before releasing any confidential or personal information to anyone.
6. **Providing overly specific locations when communicating**—Just as you would with your personal information, if you are using a social network site to check in with friends and family, do not be too specific about your location, especially if you are alone.

7. **Lying, cheating, or plagiarizing**—Lying and cheating—in any environment, whether online or face-to-face—reflect on your character and may result in people no longer trusting you. Plagiarizing is claiming or using someone else's work as your own. Doing this in high school will result in a failing grade, and doing this in college may result in expulsion from school.
8. **Threatening violence**—Threatening another person or group is an extremely serious offense. Doing so over the phone or the Internet can, and most often does, result in an investigation and many times an arrest of the person who posted the threat. Avoiding and preventing violence will be covered in a later lesson.
9. **Ignoring school-specific policies**—School policies vary from state to state and public or private institutions. Know your school's electronic use and networking rules. Ignoring these rules could result in loss of privileges, suspension, or even expulsion.
10. **Portraying unprofessional public profiles**—Whether you are a high school student applying for a job at McDonald's or you are hoping to earn a scholarship at a top-rated university, posting or sending questionable photos of yourself or your activities could raise red flags about your values or character to potential employers or universities looking to offer scholarships. It may also be illegal.
11. **Relying on privacy settings to keep you 100 percent safe**—Although social networks provide security settings, these may be complicated to use or not fully effective when used. The bottom line is to protect your personal information. If you don't want it seen, don't post it.
12. **Posting emotionally**—Everyone has said and done things they regret. Sometimes we overreact and say and do the wrong thing. Our friends and family have made us all angry from time to time. Remember, how you respond using social media tools has consequences. Posting or sending an angry message cannot be taken back once it's out there for all to see. So, before you hit the post or send button, take a moment to breathe and think about what you are about to do. Would you want someone doing this to you?

Using a cell phone or computer requires responsible behavior.

© warnerbroers/Fotolia.com

The best way to communicate with another person is still to talk directly to them. Whether you call them on a phone or meet with them face-to-face, this is still the best way to express yourself or understand how someone else feels. However, it seems more and more people prefer social media networks to communicate their views, feelings, and messages. Make sure you follow responsible guidelines when using this method of communication; your personal information and reputation may be at stake.

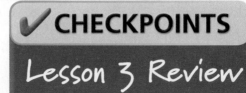

Lesson 3 Review

Using complete sentences, answer the following questions on a sheet of paper.

1. Define the term decision-making.
2. What are the six steps of the decision-making process?
3. What are three questions you can ask yourself when you evaluate a decision?
4. Define interpersonal communication.
5. List four elements of an "I" message.
6. What are four tips for improving speaking skills?
7. List two social networking sites.
8. Define the word consequences.
9. Write down four guidelines for responsible social networking.

APPLYING YOUR LEARNING

10. You have just created your first Facebook® account, which comes with a lot of responsibility. Describe what information you would provide for others to read and what information you would leave off.

Emotional and Mental Health Care

Quick Write

Briefly describe in writing two situations in which you experienced one of the following: fear, anger, happiness, guilt, or mixed emotions.

Learn About

- identifying and understanding emotions
- mental and emotional problems
- getting help

"If you don't have self-awareness, if you are not able to manage your distressing emotions, if you can't have empathy and have effective relationships, then no matter how smart you are, you are not going to get very far."

Daniel Goleman, author of *Emotional Intelligence*

Identifying and Understanding Emotions

What Are Emotions?

Your emotions are *your feelings created in response to thoughts, remarks, and events*. For example, how do you react to something you really like? How do you react to being ignored? How do you react when someone you like is hurt?

Your responses to these questions bring into play your basic emotions. These are often called primary emotions, those *common emotions felt and expressed by everyone in all cultures*. Happiness, sadness, and anger are the primary emotions you feel every day. For example, if you really like something, you will probably feel happiness. If you are ignored, you might feel anger. If someone you care for is hurt, say, in a car accident, you might feel sadness.

Fear, guilt, happiness, jealousy, anger, and sympathy are the kinds of emotions that are learned. They can influence most aspects of your life, and how you behave. Learned emotions are *emotions not common to all peoples and are expressed according to the culture and environment in which a person grows up*.

Understanding Emotions

To correctly understand your emotions, you first need to learn about emotional intelligence. Emotional intelligence is *the ability to accurately sense, assess, and manage your emotions.*

Emotional intelligence allows you to process information of an emotional nature and use it to guide your thoughts, actions, and reactions. Emotions are neither good nor bad, nor right nor wrong. However, the ways in which you express your emotions are another matter. You can't always choose when an emotion will build up inside you, but you can choose how to handle it. Learning to understand emotions and to express them in healthy ways is an important part of a healthy mental and emotional outlook. People who are mentally and emotionally healthy control their responses and express their emotions in ways that promote positive outcomes for any situation.

You have probably already seen how people express emotions in different ways. Most likely, you have observed this through others who are close to you, such as family members. However, you may not always understand why people around you express emotions the way they do. You may feel confused about your own ways of expressing emotions. This is a common and normal part of growing up. Understanding the emotions that you experience will help you deal with them. Consider the primary emotions mentioned above and think about the ways you experience them daily.

- **Happiness** is a sense of well-being. When you are happy, you feel good about life in general.
- **Sadness** is a normal, healthy reaction to an unhappy event, such as a good friend moving away or a family member dying. When you are sad, you may feel easily discouraged and have less energy. The more serious the event, the deeper your sadness may become, and the longer it may last.
- **Anger** is a common reaction to being emotionally hurt or physically harmed. Anger can come from an event that affects you in a harmful way. On the other hand, it can be internal, like when you expect to hit a game-winning home run but strike out. In this case, you may feel both anger and sadness—anger for missing the pitch you should have hit out of the park, and sadness for letting your team down when you could have won the game.

Vocabulary

- emotions
- primary emotions
- learned emotions
- emotional intelligence
- shyness
- panic
- resilience
- emotional needs
- symptom
- anxiety disorder
- personality disorder
- schizophrenia
- mood disorder
- bipolar disorder
- desolate
- clinical depression
- psychotherapist
- antidepressants
- suicide
- therapy
- family therapy
- psychologist
- psychiatrist

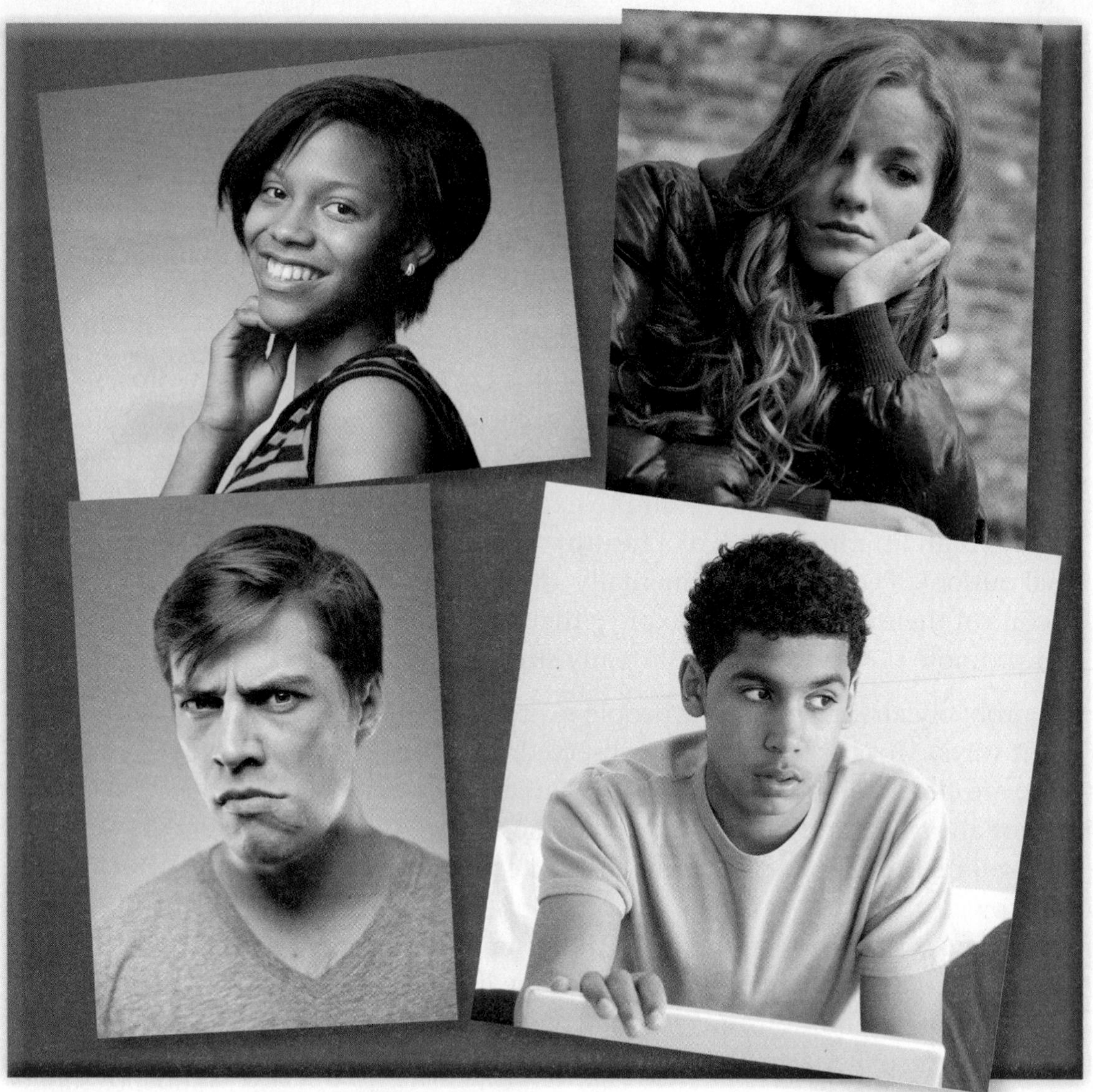

Emotions are expressed in many different ways.

Clockwise, from top left: © Konstantin Sutyagin/Fotolia.com; © Martinan/Fotolia.com; © Monkey Business/Fotolia.com; © camrocker/Fotolia.com

Your learned emotions depend, in part, on the kind of society in which you are raised. More than likely, your geographic area and family history will influence these emotions.

- **Fear** is a very unpleasant or disturbing feeling caused by the presence of danger. Fear is an emotion that can help keep you safe from danger. However, some fears, such as the fear of failure, may keep you from doing things you want or need to do. The source of your fear may be real or imagined.
- **Guilt** is the feeling of blame or being held responsible for the act of doing something wrong or illegal or not doing something you were supposed to do. Guilt is often associated with an inner fear.
- **Love** is a combination of caring and affection that binds one person to another.

- **Empathy** is the ability to understand and share another person's feelings.
- **Jealousy** is a feeling of resentment or unhappiness at another's good fortune.
- **Sympathy** means understanding and sharing another's problems or sorrow.
- **Anxiety** is a state of uneasiness and apprehension, much like fear, especially about future uncertainties. Anxiety can keep you from doing or being your best.

Expressing Emotions

We all have felt these emotions from time to time, which is quite normal. We'll now discuss how expressing some of these more common emotions can be healthy and beneficial when done correctly.

Expressing Anxiety and Fear

Have you ever felt fear or anxiety before giving a report or taking a test? When you feel these things, you often express them by taking shorter breaths. Your heart beats faster, and your muscles tense. Anxiety can help you accomplish more by releasing energy. However, too much anxiety and fear can cause you to accomplish less. You could lose sleep or even panic. To handle these emotions, stay optimistic about the situation. Practice self-talk, make a habit of complimenting yourself, and create a plan for success from what you have learned in previous lessons. Shyness and fear are how some individuals show their anxiety and fear of situations they can't control. We'll look at how shyness and panic are expressions of anxiety and fear.

Shyness is an emotion characterized by *a feeling of apprehension and anxiety in social situations, especially with unfamiliar people and situations*. Many people experience some degree of shyness. Shyness can be confined to one situation, such as being in a large group or meeting someone important like the school superintendent or state governor. Shyness can limit your potential if you hesitate to speak up for yourself or avoid situations where you would need to be a leader or speak publicly. To overcome shyness, especially in social situations, start by having a short conversation with someone you don't know. If you slowly push yourself out of your comfort zone, you will overcome your shyness.

Panic, *a feeling of sudden, intense fear*, can have some very negative physical effects on you. You may feel symptoms such as dizziness and a pounding heart. When you feel panic, it is best to seek out someone trustworthy to help you ease this feeling. Sometimes, just admitting to a family member or friend that you feel anxious will help you feel better. Other people may give you the reassurance and encouragement that you need.

Overcoming your anxiety will help build your resilience. Resilience is *the ability to adapt to and recover from disappointment, difficulty, or crisis*. Resilience is also known as the "bounce-back" factor. We all experience disappointment from time to time; people who develop resilience can bounce back from setbacks and disappointments.

Expressing Anger

Anger is also a normal emotion, but some people express their anger in unhealthy ways. Yelling, hitting, and threatening are not healthy ways to express anger. If it gets out of control, anger can be destructive and damage relationships. It is also not healthy to hold anger inside or to deny how you feel. Bottled up anger can raise your tension level and leave you feeling defensive. Here are some steps you can take when you feel angry that will ease your tension.

- Take a deep breath and stay calm. If needed, excuse yourself from the situation that made you angry until you are ready to address what made you angry.
- Focus on exactly what made you angry. Sometimes it is just one thing.
- Think of words to express your true feelings.
- Tell the other person in a calm way how you feel, and explain what it was that caused you to feel this way. Avoid criticism, threats, or placing blame.
- Tell the person what you expect from him or her in the future.

Expressing Your Emotions

Expressing your emotions in healthy ways helps improve your overall mental health.

1 Identify the Emotion
Amy and Hannah used to be best friends. Now Amy feels angry with Hannah and avoids her. She realizes that it is because she is jealous of Hannah.

2 Understand the Cause
Amy had expected to get the lead role in the school play. Instead, Hannah got the lead, and Amy just has a small part.

3 Respond in a Healthy Way
Amy recognizes that her jealousy is ruining a good friendship. She congratulates Hannah and offers to help her learn her lines.

© Gelpi/Fotolia.com

© Gelpi/Fotolia.com

Disagreements can be settled without arguments.
© *diego cervo/Fotolia.com*

In the heat of an argument, it is often hard not to respond harshly when anger is directed toward you. Even so, if you focus on these steps as best you can, you will help ease the tension for yourself and for whomever or whatever circumstance may have caused you to become angry.

Understanding Your Emotional Needs

Everyone has physical needs, such as water, food, and sleep. You also have emotional needs. These are *needs that affect your feelings and sense of well-being.* Your basic emotional needs include the following:

- **The need to feel worthwhile**—You need to feel that you make a difference in the world, and that you are making a contribution. Working toward short-term, intermediate, and long-term goals will give you a sense of accomplishment.
- **The need to love and be loved**—You need to feel that you are cared for and that you are special to people—family, friends, classmates, and teammates.
- **The need to belong**—You need to know that others accept and respect you as you are. Find friends who are accepting, reliable, and trustworthy.

Meeting Emotional Needs in Healthy Ways

Recognizing your emotional needs will help you meet them in healthy ways. Meeting your emotional needs in healthy ways means making the choice to engage in healthful behavior. Emotionally healthy people think in ways that help them adjust and reach their goals. They have four helpful thinking styles—realistic optimism, meaningful values, coping, and healthy explanations.

Realistic Optimism

When emotionally healthy people apply realistic optimism, they:

- Set and work toward goals that are challenging but obtainable
- Recognize what can and cannot be controlled in their life
- Have faith in themselves and hope that events will work out for the best

Meaningful Values

Emotionally healthy people make sure their actions are based on their personal values. They view disadvantages as challenges to be overcome. Emotionally healthy people:

- Develop values that guide their thinking and behavior
- Reflect on their own feelings and thoughts instead of worrying about how others might judge them
- Face and overcome disadvantages
- Find meaning in their work or actions

Coping

People respond, or react, to stress in two ways—avoidance or coping. Sometimes avoidance is the best response, especially if someone is trying to harm you. However, avoidance will not remove the stress. If you continue to avoid a problem, you may develop symptoms of an illness. A symptom is *a bodily reaction that signals an illness or a physical problem*. For example, you may be anxious about an upcoming science exam. You avoid the feeling by playing video games to try to forget about the exam. This may cause you to develop physical symptoms such as a headache or an upset stomach. Coping with the actual stress will help deal with and remove stress and anxiety. Emotionally healthy people cope by:

- Learning from experiences, mistakes, and successes
- Knowing when to change behaviors that are not working
- Asking for help from family members, teachers, school counselors, or other trusted adults
- Trying again after a failure

Healthy Explanations

Sometimes a loss or other disappointment can result in stress. Resilient people tend to bounce back or recover quickly from misfortune or hardship. They have a positive way of looking at disappointments. They cope by talking to friends and family. They often volunteer in their communities and give back to others less fortunate. Emotionally healthy people use a positive thinking style to explain events. For example, you may receive a failing grade on a recent math test. One reaction may be to say the test was not fair.

A positive reaction would be would be to say, "That was a hard test and I will spend more time studying for the next one so that I can do better." Emotionally healthy people with positive attitudes cope by:

- Looking on the positive side
- Talking with friends, family, or trusted adults
- Helping someone else or volunteering in the community
- Letting go of worries about things they cannot control

Resilient people believe they have some control over their lives, but they accept that they cannot control everything. Lead by example by offering to help someone without being asked. Ask a friend how his or her day went and really listen to the answer. Show affection for family members or volunteer for a good cause. Get to know other people better by sharing everyday experiences with them. All of these actions contribute to others' emotional well-being, as well as your own.

Mental and Emotional Problems

Have you ever witnessed someone being called "crazy"? What did you think that meant at the time? Have you ever wondered about the difference between mentally healthy and unhealthy behavior? Mental health covers a wide range of behaviors. Everyone has problems from time to time. Most people overcome their problems and are able to function well at home, school, and work. However, about one person in five is unable to cope with stress or disappointment, or may have a mental disorder. Calling someone "crazy" is never acceptable. Mentally unhealthy people need understanding and help or treatment in order to regain their mental health.

Three common types of mental health problems affect people by triggering their worries, fears, or other emotions that interfere with their daily lives. These are anxiety disorders, personality disorders, and mood disorders.

Anxiety Disorders

Most people experience anxiety from time to time. It's a normal reaction to challenging or worrying situations. Some people, however, have unreasonable or excessive anxiety. These people have an anxiety disorder, *a condition in which intense anxiety or fear keeps a person from functioning normally.* Table 2.1 describes the five categories of common anxiety disorders and their symptoms.

Anxiety disorders involve many different kinds of problems. Some are physical and some psychological. Physical problems can be treated with medicine prescribed by a doctor. Psychological problems can be treated with counseling that includes behavior modification. In counseling, a person will talk over his or her problems with a qualified therapist or counselor. Behavior modification teaches a person to replace less effective behavior patterns with more effective ones. For example, a person can learn to relax by being taught deep breathing to help avoid panic.

Table 2.1 Types of Anxiety Disorders

Disorder	Symptoms
General Anxiety Disorder	Restlessness, tiredness, difficulty concentrating, irritability, muscle tension, sleep disturbance
Panic Attacks	Pounding heart, sweating, trembling, shortness of breath, nausea, fear of losing control
Phobia	Intense and exaggerated fear of a specific situation or object. Examples: fear of animals, flying, heights, or insects
Obsessive-Compulsive Disorder	Obsessions such as a need to perform behaviors over and over; compulsions such as hand-washing, counting, hoarding, and arranging possessions
Post-Traumatic Stress Disorder (PTSD)	Withdrawal or depression after a distressing experience such as sexual abuse, natural disaster, accident, or witnessing violence

Personality Disorders

Personality disorders include *a variety of psychological conditions that affect a person's ability to get along with others*. People with personality disorders behave in unexpected ways. These disorders affect their thinking, moods, personal relationships, and control of sudden urges.

One of the most serious personality disorders is schizophrenia. Schizophrenia (skit·zoh·FREE·nee·uh) is *a severe mental disorder in which people lose contact with reality*. They may experience hallucinations in which they see or hear things that are not actually there. They may have delusions involving false personal beliefs that are unreasonable. People who have schizophrenia may not be able to sort out what is important from what is not. They may also be unable to separate what is really happening from what they imagine. For example, they may believe that they are other people, such as celebrities or historical figures.

Mood Disorders

People who feel sad when life is good, or happy for no apparent reason, may suffer from a mood disorder. A mood disorder is *a disorder in which a person undergoes changes in mood that seem inappropriate or extreme*. Mood disorders include bipolar disorder (also called manic-depressive disorder) and clinical depression. Bipolar disorder is defined as *going from one extreme of feeling upbeat and energetic to feeling desolate and tired for no apparent reason*. Desolate means *the feeling of sadness, depression, and hopelessness*.

Teen Depression

Everyone feels "down" or "blue" from time to time. Many teens, for example, become depressed about their looks, about their relationships, or about getting bad grades. This kind of depression is usually short-lived and not very serious. At such times it's a good idea to identify the cause of your depression and to talk about it with someone you trust.

Clinical depression is much more serious. **Clinical depression** is *a major mood disorder in which people lose interest in life and can no longer find enjoyment in anything.* The National Institute of Mental Health estimates that every year, about 5 percent of teens experience clinical depression. Some depressed teens abuse alcohol or drugs. Some try to harm themselves.

Self-injury has become common among young people. A study reported in the journal *Pediatrics* in 2012 stated that even children in third grade might engage in self-injury. About 7 percent of third-grade boys and girls were doing so. By sixth grade, boys (6 percent) are far more likely than girls (2 percent) are to harm themselves. By ninth grade, the trends are reversed, with 19 percent of girls and just 5 percent of boys reportedly injuring themselves.

Most people who are injuring themselves are usually trying to feel better. They are causing themselves physical pain in search of temporary relief from emotional stresses and pain in their lives. However, this is a symptom of a mood or anxiety disorder and they should seek professional help.

Symptoms of clinical depression are described in Table 2.2. A teen who has three or more of the symptoms described for more than two weeks should be checked for clinical depression.

Table 2.2 Warning Signs of Clinical Depression

Symptoms	Warning Signs
1. Depressed Mood	"I never feel happy anymore."
2. Lack of Energy	"I'm always tired."
3. Inability to Concentrate	"I can't think anymore."
4. Withdrawal	"I don't want to see anyone."
5. Change in Sleep Pattern	"I wake up a lot every night."
6. Feelings of Worthlessness	"I can't do anything right."
7. Indifference	"I don't care what happens."
8. Pessimism	"Things will never get any better."
9. Irritability or Anger	"You just don't understand."
10. Thoughts of Death or Suicide	"Sometimes I wish I just wouldn't wake up, ever."

If you think that you are seriously depressed, don't just wait and hope the feeling will go away. Instead, talk to a parent, teacher, counselor, or other adult you trust about how you feel. These adults can get you the help you need. If you have clinical depression, the treatment may be counseling, medication, or a combination of the two. The National Institute of Mental Health has reported that treatment that involves a combination of psychotherapy and antidepressant medication appears to be the most effective treatment for adolescents with major depression. A **psychotherapist** is *someone who treats individuals with mental disorders by using intense counseling methods.* **Antidepressants** are *drugs used to prevent or reduce depression.*

Teens who receive this kind of treatment are usually able to go on to enjoy life again and feel better about themselves.

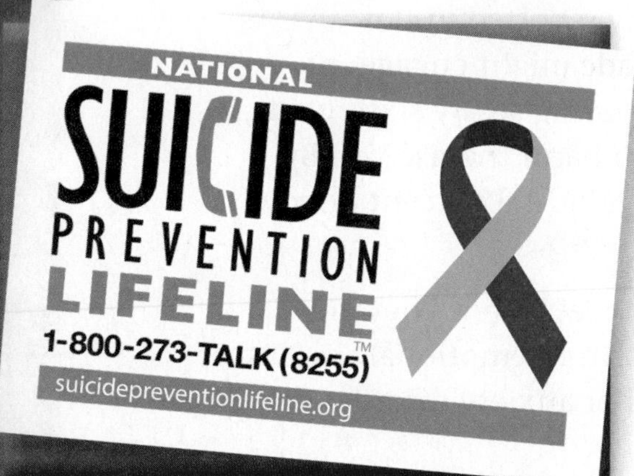

The National Suicide Hotline is a resource that is always available if you or someone you know has suicidal thoughts.

Suicide Prevention

Suicide, or *the act of intentionally killing oneself,* is a serious problem in the United States, especially among teens. Suicide is the third leading cause of death among young people ages 15 to 24, and accounts for 20 percent of all deaths annually. Every day, 12 young people between the ages of 15 and 24 years take their own lives.

Warning Signs of Suicide

You may know someone who has said things like "The world would be better off without me," or "I'd be better off dead." Most people who commit suicide talk about it beforehand. Anyone who talks about suicide should be taken seriously. Tell a trusted adult immediately if you hear someone speak like this.

People who are thinking about suicide may show signs, at first, of depression or a noticeable downturn in mood. Once they decide to end their lives, they may feel better because they think that they have solved their problems. They may start giving away valued possessions. People who reach this point are in great danger. Other warning signs of suicide include:

- Lack of energy
- Inability to let go of the feeling of grief or sadness
- Withdrawal from friends and family
- No longer taking interest in favorite activities
- No longer taking interest in personal appearance
- Talking about or taking unnecessary risks
- Expressing suicidal thoughts, self-hatred, or talking a lot about death

If anyone you know talks of suicide...

Do...

- Trust your feelings
- Take the threat seriously
- Say how concerned you are
- Listen carefully
- Talk calmly
- Involve a trusted adult
- If needed, stay until help arrives

Do not...

- Judge the person
- Analyze openly the person's motives
- Dare the person to go ahead with the suicide attempt
- Argue or offer reasons not to attempt suicide
- Leave the person alone, if at all possible

What You Can Do

With most people, a suicide attempt is a cry for help. They don't really want to die, but they feel so much emotional pain that they can't see any other course of action. They need to be convinced that even though the pain seems unbearable, it will not last forever.

Things to Remember When You're Down

Everyone has tough times and feels depressed now and then. If it happens to you, don't wait. Talk to someone about how you feel. Just remember you are not alone. There are people who understand how you feel and will try to be helpful.

Also, take care of your physical needs—get enough sleep, eat regular and healthy meals, and participate in regular physical activity.

Most of all, avoid alcohol and other drugs, even caffeine. They will only add to your depressed feelings.

Don't wait—talk to someone about how you feel.

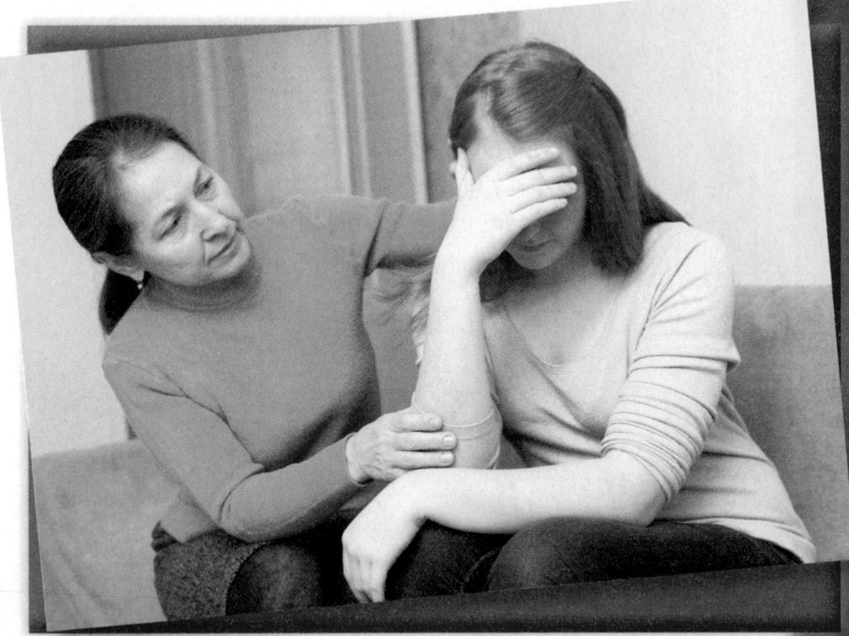

Family and friends can be a source of help and support for teens who are having difficulty handling their problems.

© JackF/Fotolia.com

Getting Help

Talking about your thoughts and feelings may be difficult at first. You may feel frightened or embarrassed. You may feel that any adult you approach will be shocked or annoyed at what you have to say. However, most adults understand and want to help. Sometimes all you need to do is let someone know that you need help. It is nothing to be ashamed of; the mistake is not asking for help.

Seeking Professional Help

How can you tell if a problem is serious enough to discuss with a professional? Learning the warning signs that indicate you need help with mental health problems is an important first step. The following box shows some signs that may indicate when a mental health issue may require a professional's help.

Signs That You May Need Professional Help

If you experience several of these signs, and if they last a long time, you may need to talk to a professional.

- Feeling sad or angry for no reason
- Being tired all the time
- Waking up too early or sleeping too much
- Finding it impossible to concentrate
- Losing interest in activities you usually enjoy
- Getting lower grades than usual
- Having aches or pains for no reason
- Losing or gaining a lot of weight
- Disregard for personal appearance
- Avoiding friends or family and wanting to be alone
- Thinking that you just can't fit in anywhere
- Feeling that you can't deal with life
- Feeling hopeless, guilty, or ashamed
- Using alcohol or other drugs

© Lisa F. Young/Fotolia.com

Therapy Methods

There are various methods of therapy, or *treatment*, for mental health problems. These fall into two broad types: talk therapy and biological therapy. Talk therapy includes a variety of counseling methods. Biological therapy involves using medications to treat mental health problems.

The goal of any mental health treatment is to help patients find positive change in their lives so that they can handle their problems better. Some professionals use only counseling. Others rely mostly on medication. Still others use both types of therapy. A teen who is clinically depressed after the death of a close friend, for example, may receive counseling to deal with the loss or may be given medication to help improve his or her mood if counseling is unsuccessful.

Mental Health Counseling Goals

In counseling, an individual talks with a mental health professional to learn positive ways of thinking or behaving. Changing someone's thoughts or behavior is not easy. However, once these changes have been made, they lead to changes in feelings. By learning, or re-learning, to think or behave in healthy ways, the person improves his or her mental and emotional health. Some people feel much better after just a few sessions with a mental health professional. Others may need months of counseling.

Some people choose to talk alone with a counselor. Others prefer to take part in group therapy. In group therapy, the counselor meets with several people at once who have the same or similar problems. Some people find that they benefit from the empathy and support that comes from other members of the group.

A variation on group therapy is family therapy. Family therapy is *counseling that seeks to improve troubled family relationships*. Family therapists are trained to help relieve family problems, strengthen family relationships, and solve small problems before they get bigger. The therapy sessions may involve all or some family members.

Mental Health Counseling Methods

Counseling that focuses on helping people think more positively about themselves can be especially helpful for people who experience depression. The professional helps the depressed person identify negative thoughts that are contributing to the depression. From that point, the person can be guided to more positive ways of thinking. Teens who are depressed because they focus on their weaknesses or mistakes, for example, can learn to focus on their strengths and achievements instead.

Counseling may also focus on changing behavior. This type of therapy is especially helpful to people with anxiety disorders such as phobias. The individual learns to stay calm while facing the situation he or she fears. Imagine, for example, a girl who has a severe fear of giving speeches. She might begin by learning to stay calm while giving a brief talk to a few friends. Her therapist might then encourage her to speak for a little longer and to more people. Eventually, she might be able to speak in front of a large group without feeling any fear. Adults face similar difficulties, such as stage fright, or being camera shy on television. Some famous people have had to do extensive therapy to overcome these fears.

Prescription Drug Treatments

Some mental health disorders can be treated with prescription drugs. Different types of prescription drugs are used to treat different kinds of illnesses. People with anxiety disorders may take anti-anxiety drugs, which affect the central nervous system. Those who have clinical depression may take antidepressant drugs, which affect brain activity. Prescription drug treatment is highly individualized. A drug or dose that may help one person could seriously harm another. The medications used to treat mental disorders can be prescribed only by a medical doctor or a psychiatrist.

Sources of Help

People in a variety of roles and professions can help with mental health problems. If you need help or want to help someone else, seek out the following people:

- **Parent or other adult family member**—You might be able to get all the help you need by talking with a parent or guardian, older brother or sister, or other adult family member with whom you have a special bond.
- **Clergy member**—A leader of a church, synagogue, or mosque may have formal training in counseling. Even those who do not have such training usually have a lot of experience in counseling people of all ages.
- **Teacher or school counselor**—Teachers and school counselors are trained to help students with mental and emotional problems. Some counselors are specially trained to deal with problems that concern students.
- **Family counselor**—Instead of counseling individuals, family counselors see family members together. Most family counseling sessions focus on improving communication between family members in order to improve their relationships with each other.
- **School nurse**—If you are not sure what kind of help you need, a talk with the school nurse is a good place to start. School nurses are trained to deal with all health problems. A nurse can guide you to the help you need.

- **Social worker**—Many schools have social workers who help students and their families with social and personal problems that interfere with learning. They help students develop coping, social, and decision-making skills.
- **Psychologist**—A psychologist (sy·KAH·luh·jist) is *a mental health professional who is trained and licensed by the state to provide counseling*. Psychologists treat mental health problems by using one or several types of counseling.
- **Psychiatrist**—A psychiatrist (sy·KY·uh·trist) is *a medical doctor who treats mental health problems*. A psychiatrist is the only mental health professional who can prescribe drugs.

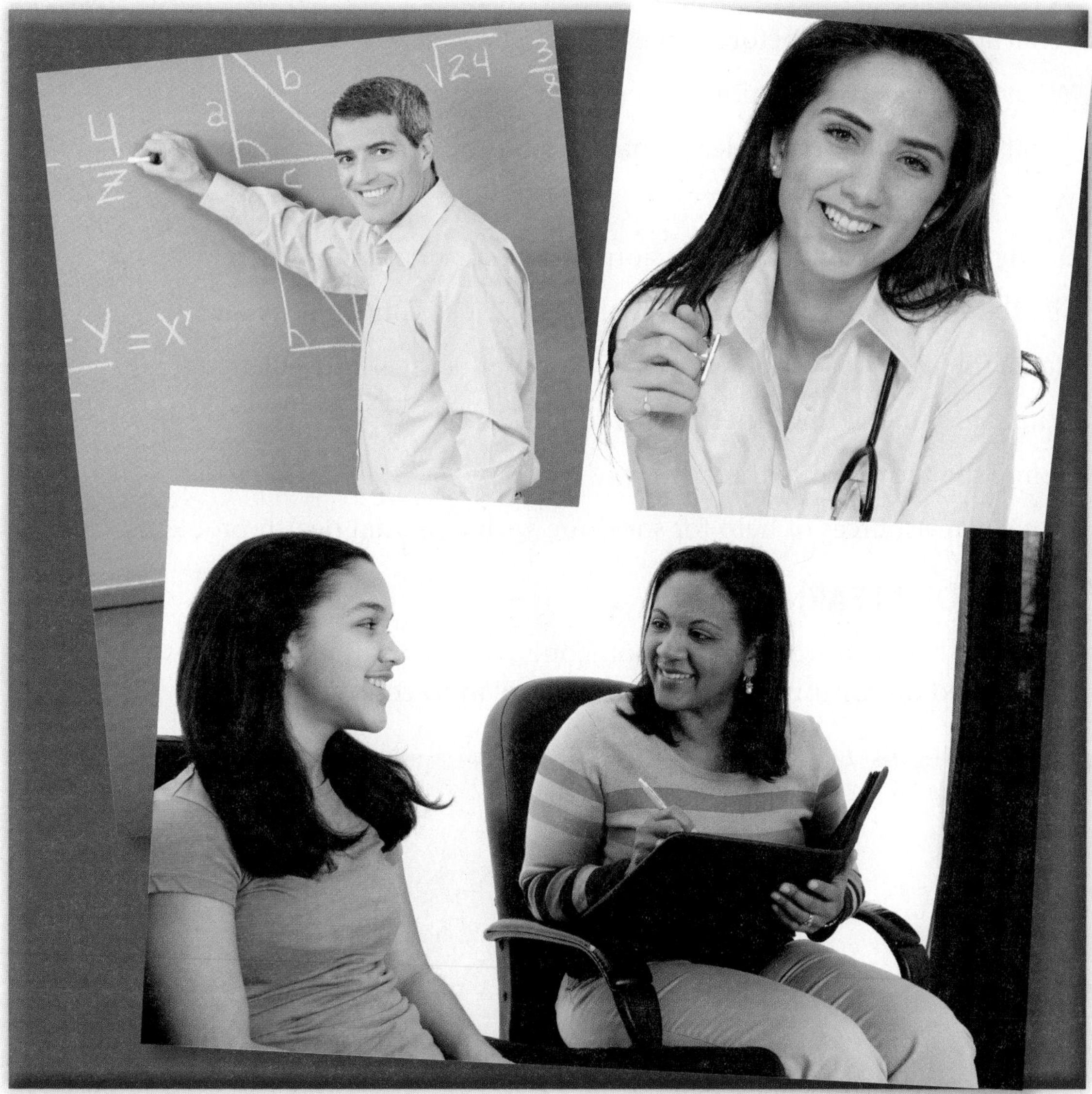

There are many sources of help for teens with emotional and mental problems.

Clockwise, from top left: © Tyler Olson/Fotolia.com; © Studio-FI/Fotolia.com; © Rob/Fotolia.com

Lesson 4 Review

Using complete sentences, answer the following questions on a sheet of paper.

1. List the three primary emotions.
2. What is the difference between empathy and sympathy?
3. Why is resilience sometimes called the "bounce-back" factor?
4. What should you do before you express your anger?
5. What are two basic emotional needs that everyone has?
6. What kind of mood disorder is characterized by extreme mood swings?
7. What is clinical depression?
8. Briefly state why clinical depression is a serious mental disorder.
9. List the warning signs of someone thinking of committing suicide.
10. Name the two broad types of therapy for mental health problems.
11. What are some of the benefits of group therapy?
12. Define the term family therapy.
13. Name three sources of help for someone with a mental health problem.

APPLYING YOUR LEARNING

14. Describe steps you would take if someone you know appeared depressed and started discussing with you how they plan to commit suicide.

LESSON 5

Avoiding and Preventing Violence

Quick Write

Write a short paragraph explaining why you think some young people resort to violence to settle differences.

Learn About

- violence in our society
- school and campus violence
- protecting yourself from rape or sexual violence

"Non-violence is not a garment to be put on and off at will. Its seat is in the heart, and it must be an inseparable part of our being."

Mahatma Gandhi, Nonviolent civil rights activist who led India's independence from British rule

Violence in Our Society

Hitting someone is clearly an example of violence, but what about threatening to hit or hurt someone? Is that violence? What about destroying property or yelling mean and hurtful words at someone? Is that violence? The answer is yes. **Violence** is *any act that causes physical or psychological harm to a person or damage to property.* **Homicide**, *the killing of one human being by another,* is violence at its worst. While in recent years the numbers of homicides and other violent acts have statistically declined, the increase in acts of violence in schools is unacceptably high. According to the Centers for Disease Control and Prevention (CDC), homicide remains a leading cause of death among young people.

Violent crime has many costs. One cost is money; other costs are the physical and mental harm to people. Victims of violence may be hurt permanently. For example, injuries may cause permanent brain damage or leave an individual paralyzed. Victims of violence may also suffer from mental health problems. Witnesses of violent crime may be left with a feeling of fear and may never feel safe again.

Everyone ends up paying for violent crimes. The added costs for police officers, courts, and prisons go up each year. Federal and local governments are often forced to raise taxes to help pay for these additional costs. Everyone becomes the victim.

Various factors have been suggested as causes for the high rates of violence. Some people point to the violent acts shown on television, music, video games, movies, and on the Internet as contributing factors. Others cite changes in family structure that tend to leave children unsupervised for hours at a time. Many also believe the availability of guns to be a major cause of violence. Poverty also plays a role in higher rates of violent crime. Communities with poor housing, high unemployment, and limited community services tend to have higher rates of violence.

Vocabulary

- violence
- homicide
- bullying
- extort
- cyberbullying
- gang
- zero tolerance policy
- mediation
- peer mediation
- rape
- victim

Factors that Contribute to Teen Violence

Too much violence in America involves teenagers. In 2002, more than 877,700 young people ages to 10 to 24 were injured from violent acts, according to the Centers for Disease Control and Prevention (CDC). Of these, one out of every thirteen incidents required hospitalization. Teens are not just victims, however. Each year, more than 120,000 youths are arrested for committing violent crimes. Teen violence often involves bullying, gangs, guns, alcohol and drugs, or rape.

Bullying and Cyberbullying

Bullying can happen to anyone. Bullying behavior can be directed at the shy, quiet student, or the class tough guy. There is no one characteristic that determines who will be bullied. Someone who was bullied one day might be the person who makes fun of the shy girl the next day. Students who bully can be any size, age, grade, race, or gender.

In a 2009 study of students in grades 9 through 12, nearly 20 percent reported having been bullied on school property within the past year. Bullying is *the use of threats or physical force to intimidate and control another person*. A bully will choose as his or her victim someone who is less powerful in terms of physical strength or status among peers. Through name-calling, physical force, and pressure on others to isolate the victim, a bully's goal may be to extort, or *obtain something by force, threats, or other unfair means*, or simply take pleasure from someone else's embarrassment or humiliation. Three types of bullying occur in our society:

1. Verbal bullying is saying or writing mean things. Verbal bullying includes:
    - Teasing
    - Name-calling
    - Inappropriate sexual comments
    - Taunting
    - Threatening to cause harm
2. Social bullying, sometimes referred to as relational bullying, involves hurting someone's reputation or relationships. Social bullying includes:
    - Leaving someone out on purpose
    - Telling other students not to be friends with someone
    - Spreading rumors about someone
    - Embarrassing someone in public
3. Physical bullying involves hurting a person's body or possessions. Physical bullying includes:
    - Hitting/kicking/pinching
    - Spitting
    - Tripping/pushing
    - Taking or breaking someone's personal belongings
    - Making mean or rude hand gestures

Are you a victim of bullying? What should you do? If you feel that you are being bullied or you witness someone else being bullied, here are some things you should do:

There is no place for bullying.
© Rob/Fotolia.com

- Talk to someone you trust, such as a teacher, school counselor, school administrator, parent, older relative, or friend.
- Be persistent. If the first person you talk to doesn't help, don't give up. Speak to someone else.
- If possible, write down everything that has been said or done to hurt you or someone else. Be careful to write down only things that have really happened.
- Ask the person you talk to not to do anything without telling you about it first. You have the right to know what is being done on your behalf.

- If you find it difficult talking to an adult, ask one of your friends to come with you, or ask someone to talk to an adult on your behalf.
- If you feel that the act of bullying may cause you or someone else immediate physical harm and you are not at school, call 911.
- Most importantly, do something! Sometimes it only takes action on your or someone else's behalf to stop the bullying. However, doing nothing will cause the bullying to continue until someone gets hurt.

Cyberbullying is *bullying via email, text or instant messaging, Facebook®, or other social media outlets*. It may not be immediately physical, but is especially damaging because the bullies can harass their victims at home or anywhere else at any time of day or night. Cyberbullies frequently will make threats or spread rumors about the victim.

Cyberbullying is different than other types of bullying because:

- Cyberbullying can happen 24 hours a day, 7 days a week, and can reach the victim even when he or she is alone. It can happen any time of the day or night.
- Cyberbullying messages and images can be posted and distributed quickly to a very wide audience. It can be difficult and sometimes impossible to trace the source.
- Deleting inappropriate or harassing messages, texts, and pictures is extremely difficult after they have been posted or sent.

Just as with any type of bullying, when cyberbullying happens, it is important to document and report the behavior so it can be addressed. There are also additional actions you need to take to stop cyberbullies.

1. Steps to take immediately:
   - Don't respond to and don't forward cyberbullying messages.
   - Keep evidence of cyberbullying. Record the dates, times, and descriptions of instances when cyberbullying has occurred.
   - Save and print screenshots, emails, and text messages. Use the evidence to report cyberbullying to web and cell phone service providers.
   - Block the person doing the cyberbullying from your email or social media account.
2. Report the cyberbullying to online service providers:
   - Review the terms and conditions or rights and responsibilities sections of Internet accounts. Cyberbullying often violates the terms of service established by social media sites and Internet service providers.
   - Visit social media safety centers to learn how to block users and change settings to control who can contact you.
   - Report cyberbullying to the social media site so they can take action against users abusing the terms of the service agreement.

3. Report cyberbullying to law enforcement—when cyberbullying involves any of the following activities, it is considered a crime:
   - Threats of violence.
   - Child pornography or sending sexually explicit messages or photos.
   - Taking a photo or video of someone in a place where he or she would expect privacy.
   - Stalking or hate crimes.
4. Report cyberbullying to your school:
   - Cyberbullying can create a disruptive environment at school and is often related to in-person bullying. The school can use the information to help with prevention and response strategies.
   - In many states, schools are required to address cyberbullying in their anti-bullying policy. Some state laws also cover off-campus behavior that creates a hostile school environment.

Cyberbullying is harmful.
© micromonkey/Fotolia.com

Any type of bullying produces a climate of fear and disrespect at schools. It can cause increased levels of anxiety and depression in not only the victims, but also in other students, teachers, and administrators. While most victims suffer in silence, a few strike back, usually causing further harm to themselves and others.

Bullying can have devastating consequences; teen suicide is one. There are too many stories of young people bullied to the point that they see no way out but to take their own lives. The following story is just one of the many examples of someone who felt this way.

Sarah Lynn Butler, a seventh grader from Hardy, Arkansas, committed suicide on September 26, 2009. Sarah, who had just been voted Queen for her upcoming Fall Festival, was teased at school, and later on received bullying messages on her social networking page.

Sarah's mother said she often checked her daughter's social network page to make sure there wasn't anything inappropriate being sent or received. When she noticed that Sarah was getting some messages about rumors at school, she talked with her about it. But Sarah then removed her mother from her list of friends and she was no longer able to read her page.

On the morning of her suicide, Sarah stayed home while her family was out and logged on to her social networking page. The last message Sarah read said that she was easily forgotten, and that she was just a stupid little naive girl and nobody would miss her.

When her parents returned home, they found that Sarah had hanged herself. She left a suicide note that said she couldn't handle what others were saying about her.

No one should have to pay the price of another person's careless hatred. The best way to deal with bullying is to stop it before it starts and get others involved. A bully who senses that others perceive his or her actions as unacceptable will quickly lose motivation.

For further resources on preventing bullying and cyberbullying, go to the US Department of Health and Human Services website at *http://www.stopbullying.gov/*.

Gossip harms relationships, and that's why it's bad. What seems innocent can eventually cross the line and become bullying if it damages friendships and causes people to dislike or harm someone.

Gangs

Although gang activity was once associated with large cities, it is now a national problem. A **gang** is *a group of criminals who associate with one another to take part in criminal or antisocial activity*. Gangs will display their membership and unity by wearing similar types of jewelry and clothing and using certain types of language and hand signals. Typical gang activities include vandalism, graffiti, robbery, and drug dealing. Because gangs don't readily associate with people they perceive as different, their members are often isolated from the rest of the community.

In recent years, gangs have started recruiting younger members because young offenders receive less severe penalties. Many young people join gangs due to the influence of their classmates, neighbors, or family members. Some young people join gangs for excitement; they feel bored at home or they don't receive positive feedback from parents or guardians.

Because gang members often carry weapons, they make areas unsafe for everyone. In addition, some of their actions, such as random shootings, are unpredictable. As a result, innocent people are injured or killed. The presence of gangs in a school or community causes people to live in fear instead of confidence about their safety.

Gangs hurt communities.
© aijohn784/Fotolia.com

Gang members, especially recruits, often know of no way other than gang membership to gain a sense of belonging. However, once in a gang, members often find themselves caught in an environment of intimidation and crime they may not be able to escape. One way to reduce gang violence is to offer other choices, such as Community Boys and Girls Clubs, sports, school-supported clubs and activities, and JROTC, which do not lead to violence.

Guns

While many people disagree about the relationship between weapons and violence, most agree that when weapons are used in fights, fights are more deadly. This is especially the case with firearms.

According to NBC News Research, in the United States, handguns are used in the majority of homicides and suicides. Every 17 minutes someone in the United States dies from a gunshot wound. Firearm injuries are the second leading cause of death for young people ages 10 to 24. For every one person killed by a firearm, four are wounded. A survey of young people who had been shot revealed that 35 percent of them were carrying guns when they were wounded.

Strategies to prevent firearm accidents include controlling gun ownership and installing safety devices on guns. Gun owners are also advised to keep their firearms unloaded and to store ammunition in a separate, locked place. When people buy guns for hunting or protection, they are highly encouraged or may be required to take a safety course to learn how to handle the guns.

Alcohol and Drugs

Alcohol, drugs, and violence tend to go hand in hand. Drug users who are desperate for money to support their drug habit often turn to illegal and violent behavior. Drugs also affect a user's ability to think clearly and have good judgment. While under the influence of drugs, a person might shoplift, steal a car, or commit a violent crime.

Although alcohol is not legal for purchase or consumption for individuals under the age of 21, this has not stopped the problem of underage drinking. According to the Centers for Disease Control and Prevention, alcohol use by persons under the age of 21 is a major public health problem. Alcohol is the most commonly used and abused drug among youth in the United States, more than tobacco and illegal drugs. One study conducted by the US Department of Justice found that alcohol was a factor in 40 percent of all violent crimes. Another study published in the *Annual Review of Public Health* examined drinking on college campuses over a two-year time frame. This study reported that 600,000 students reported being hit or assaulted by another student who'd been drinking.

According to a study conducted by the Surgeon General of the United States, each year approximately 5,000 young people die as a result of underage drinking. Sixteen hundred of these deaths are a result of homicides.

Underage drinking affects everyone, including those who don't drink. Everyone can make a difference to help eliminate alcohol and illegal drugs from schools and communities. Schools and communities should deliver a message that alcohol and illegal drugs are not okay. When young people are actively involved in sports programs, school academic programs, or community projects, they are less likely to become involved in alcohol or illegal drugs.

School and Campus Violence

School violence is not easy to understand. There is no single reason why students become violent. Some follow behavior they have seen at home, in their neighborhoods, or on TV, movies, and video games. Sometimes, young people who have been the victim of bullying can't take it anymore and will do anything to make it stop. The Centers for Disease Control and Prevention (CDC) provides a list of risk factors for those who commit violent crimes on school campuses:

- History of violent abuse
- Attention disorders, such as hyperactivity or learning disorders
- History of early aggressive behavior
- Involvement with illegal drugs, alcohol, or tobacco
- Poor behavior control
- High emotional distress
- Emotional problems
- Antisocial beliefs and attitude
- History of violence and conflict in the family
- Gang involvement
- Social rejection by classmates

School violence gets a lot of publicity, but the vast majority of schools experience little or no violence.
© mertcan/Fotolia.com

Incidents of violence in schools have led to increased security measures. Many schools now keep all or most doors to the school locked. In some schools, students must pass through metal detectors to enter the school. School officials may search lockers and students' belongings if they have reasonable suspicion that someone is planning a violent act.

Many schools have adopted a zero tolerance policy for weapons or weapon look-alikes, illegal drugs, and violent behavior. A zero tolerance policy is *a policy that makes no exceptions for anybody for any reason.* Any student found guilty of bringing any prohibited items to school, or of behaving violently, is automatically expelled.

Become an Advocate for Preventing Violence

Schools work very hard to create a safe, supportive environment for students to be academically and socially successful. Students must also help with keeping schools and campuses safe from violent acts. You can help prevent school violence by acting responsibly and encouraging others to do their part. Here are some actions that you can take and advocate.

- Refuse to bring a weapon or weapon look-alike to school, to carry a weapon for another person, or to keep silent about those who carry weapons.
- Immediately report any violent incidents or threats of violence to school authorities or the police.
- Learn how to manage your own anger.
- Help others settle arguments through proper conflict mediation. Mediation is *both sides in a dispute working to reach a peaceful agreement.*
- Welcome new students and get to know students who are often left out.
- Sign (or start) a pledge of non-violence in which students promise to settle disagreements using mediation and to work toward a safe campus.

Peer Mediation Programs

Many schools use peer mediation to help reduce the risk of violence that occurs from unresolved conflicts. Peer mediation is *a process in which trained students help other students find fair ways to resolve conflicts and settle their differences*. Such programs are effective because they are kept confidential and help prevent or reduce punishment for those students involved. By putting pressure on those who are involved in a conflict to settle their differences peacefully, you have taken a step in the right direction to prevent violence and become a mediator. To become a mediator, check with your school about their peer mediation program and the possibility of joining or starting one. All mediators and involved students should follow a checklist and set guidelines during the mediation process. Below are some guidelines to follow to successfully mediate a conflict:

- Let both sides know that you are not taking either side of the conflict.
- Set some rules, such as using calm, reasonable talk.
- Let each person state his or her feelings without being interrupted.
- Allow each person to ask reasonable questions of the other.

- Encourage both people to figure out different ways to solve the problem.
- Ask both people to discuss each way and to agree on one idea.
- Work at finding a compromise; do not let them give up without really trying.

Even with the best intentions, violent conflicts still happen. If other people get into a fight, do not cheer them on. Having people around and cheering on the situation raises the chances that things will quickly get out of control. Do not try to end any violent conflict yourself because you may get hurt. You should be the one who seeks assistance from a school administrator or other school staff member.

Ways to Protect Yourself from Violence

No one ever wants to be the victim of violence or crime, and there are some things you should do to reduce your chances of becoming a victim. You can protect yourself from violence and unsafe situations. First, develop self-protection habits by being alert to what is going on around you and trusting your instincts. If a situation feels dangerous, it probably is. Be ready for threatening situations before they arise by anticipating possible problems and planning appropriate responses. With the adults in your family, identify some dangerous situations that could happen. Figure out what you could do to get out of those situations safely. If you suspect or hear a student talking about violence, report it to school authorities. Many cases of school violence could have been prevented because the attackers provided information to others about their intentions.

Choosing your friends wisely is another way to protect yourself. Avoid people who have a low commitment to school, participate in illegal activities, or use alcohol or drugs. Figure 2.14 suggests other ways to protect yourself from violence.

Protecting Yourself from Rape or Sexual Violence

Rape is *any kind of unlawful sexual intercourse against a person's will.* Over half of all rape victims know their attackers. Whenever a person is forced to have sex, whether with someone he or she knows or with a stranger, a rape has occurred. Rape is always an act of violence, and never legal. To protect yourself from rape, avoid situations in which an attack is possible. Here are some suggestions:

- If you go out alone with someone, make it clear that you're not interested in any sexual activity.
- Always let your parents or guardians know where you will be.
- Avoid secluded places.
- Don't drink alcohol or use other drugs, and don't date people who do.
- Always carry money so you can take a cab or bus home if you feel unsafe.

Follow these precautions to protect yourself from violence.

OUTDOORS	AT HOME
• Do not walk alone at night. • Avoid poorly lit streets. • If you think someone is following you, go into a store or other public place. • Never hitchhike or accept a ride from strangers. • Avoid entering an elevator alone with a stranger. • Don't look like an easy target. Stand tall and walk with confidence. • If someone wants your money or possessions, give them up. • If you are attacked, scream and get away any way you can. • Do not carry a firearm or other weapon. • Do not loiter or give the appearance that you are lost. • If you are on public transportation, avoid displaying expensive items such as smartphones, watches, and jewelry.	• Lock doors and windows when you are home alone. • Open the door only to people you know well. • Do not give personal information over the telephone or computer. • Never agree to meet alone with a person you met online. • If someone comes to the door or window and you are frightened, call 911 or the police. • Never shoot firearms or pick them up, even if they are unloaded. • When you come home, have your key ready before you reach the door. Do not enter if the door is ajar or appears to have been tampered with. • Never tell a stranger that you are home alone. Instead, say that your parents are busy and can't come to the door or phone.

FIGURE 2.14

Reduce your chances of becoming a victim—know your surroundings.

Images © Arcady/Fotolia.com

What You Should do if You are a Victim of Sexual Violence

Young people ages 16 to 19 are more than three times as likely to be a victim of sexual violence than people aged 20 or older. Reporting a rape or other sexual violence is often very hard for the victim. A victim is *someone who is hurt by somebody or something, especially in a crime, accident, or disaster.* Experts think that only half of these violent acts are reported. Sometimes, the victim may know the attacker and doesn't want to get them into trouble. Unfortunately, many times the victim is afraid that the attacker will come after them again. Fear or the thought of getting someone into trouble does not stop the need to report any acts of sexual violence.

Schools and many communities have police officers who are trained to help and talk with victims. The individual who has suffered an attack needs to know they are the victim. While most states and schools provide different reporting procedures for victims of sexual violence, the following information is provided for those individuals who do not know what to do:

- Get to a safe place: home, school, police station, fire station, or hospital.
- Report the crime; notify the police or a trusted adult.
- Call a friend, family member, or someone you can trust.
- Get medical care as soon as possible.
- If you suspect you have been given any type of drug, ask the hospital or medical care provider to check for drugs.
- Write down everything you can remember, including a description of the attacker.
- Talk to a counselor who is trained to assist victims of sexual violence or contact the closest rape crisis center in your area.

✓ CHECKPOINTS

Lesson 5 Review

Using complete sentences, answer the following questions on a sheet of paper.

1. Define violence.
2. List two things you should do if you are victim of bullying.
3. Name two examples of cyberbullying.
4. List three risk factors that contribute to violent crimes on school campuses.
5. What happens to a student who violates a school's zero tolerance policy?
6. Name two things you can do to help keep your school campus safe.
7. What are three basic ways you can protect yourself from violence?
8. List two actions that you can take to help protect yourself from rape.
9. List three actions you should take if you are a victim of sexual violence.

APPLYING YOUR LEARNING

10. In one paragraph, describe what can be done in your community to discourage teens from joining gangs.

CHAPTER 3

Courtesy of Michael Wetzel/US Air Force JROTC

Be Health Smart

Chapter Outline

LESSON 1

Your Body Systems

LESSON 2

Nutrition

LESSON 3

The Benefits of Physical Activity

LESSON 4

Understanding Your Body Image

LESSON 5

First Aid

"To keep the body in good health is a duty... otherwise we shall not be able to keep our mind strong and clear."

Buddha, Indian religious leader and founder of Buddhism

LESSON 1

Your Body Systems

Quick Write

"Health is a state of complete physical, mental, and social well-being, and not merely the absence of disease...."

World Health Organization

The human body is made up of several different systems that work together as one unit. What do you think is the most amazing thing about how your body works?

Learn About

- functions of the human skeletal system
- how your muscular system works
- the human circulatory system
- the human respiratory system
- how the nervous system and sense organs work
- the human digestive system
- the body's waste disposal system

The Human Body

Your body system is an amazing organization of systems that work together to keep you in good health. This lesson will tell you about your body's systems—the skeletal and muscular systems, the circulatory and respiratory systems, the nervous system and sense organs, and the digestive and waste disposal systems—and how they work together.

Two major body systems that work together closely to keep you moving throughout the day are the skeletal and muscular systems. The skeletal system is *your body's system of connected bones, or your skeleton.* It is the frame that supports your body and protects your organs. Attached to this skeletal frame is the muscular system, which *includes the tissue that connects the bones and other parts of your body, allowing your body to move and to maintain posture.*

Functions of the Human Skeletal System

Have you ever seen a house under construction, before the roof and outside walls go on? Like a building, your body needs a framework to give it shape and support. Your body's framework is your skeletal system. Your skeletal system has these three main functions.

Support and Protection. Your skeleton provides support and protection for your muscles and other body parts. As you can see in Figure 3.1, your skeleton is made up of all of the bones in your body, both large and small. Your skeleton gives your body its basic shape and provides the support that you need as you move through the activities of the day.

Your spine, or vertebral column, is *the center of your skeleton.* The spine consists of 33 bones called vertebrae (VUR tuh bray). The vertebrae support your head and give flexibility to your neck and back.

Many bones of the skeletal system protect internal organs. Your ribs and breastbone, for example, form a protective cage around your heart and lungs. Your spine protects the *spinal cord,* which runs through the vertebrae. The hard, thick skull protects your brain.

Movement. In coordination with your muscular and *nervous system,* your skeletal system is jointed to allow you to move. A joint is *a place in your body where two or more of your bones come together.* Joints allow an amazing range of movements from the simple striking of a key on a keyboard to the complex coordination of actions in sports such as pole vaulting or ice skating.

Storage and Production of Materials. Within the skeleton, your bones store substances essential for your health, such as phosphorous (found in corn, poultry, and nuts, among other foods) and calcium (found in milk, cheese, and yogurt, to name a few sources). Your bones release these substances when other parts of your body need them.

What Is the Purpose of Bones?

Your body has more than 200 bones. Your bones provide your body's structure. They also protect your organs, store important minerals, and produce certain blood cells.

Bones are living material. They are made of cells, *the smallest independently functioning unit of the human body.* Each cell has its own job to do. Cells that do the same job form tissues. Bone cells make up bone tissue. Because bones are living tissue, they need nutrients, which are *parts of food that help the body function and grow properly,* just as other parts of your body do. You get nutrients from the food you eat. Your blood carries the nutrients to your bones.

Vocabulary

- skeletal system
- muscular system
- spine, or vertebral column
- joint
- cells
- nutrients
- ligaments
- cartilage
- marrow
- smooth muscles
- skeletal muscles
- tendon
- cardiac muscles
- tendonitis
- circulatory system
- platelets
- clotting
- pulse
- blood pressure
- systolic pressure
- diastolic pressure
- respiration
- trachea, or windpipe
- bronchi
- lungs
- alveoli
- diaphragm
- chest cavity
- inhale
- exhale
- cerebrum
- instinctive thinking

continued on next page

Vocabulary

continued

- cerebellum
- brain stem
- medulla
- spinal cord
- peripheral nervous system
- reflexes
- sense organs
- cornea
- optic nerve
- iris
- eardrum
- auditory nerve
- tinnitus
- receptor cells
- taste buds
- skin
- digestion
- saliva
- enzyme
- esophagus
- villi
- diabetes
- excretory system

The size of the bones in your body ranges from large to very small. There are four basic kinds of bones:

- Long bones, which are in your arms and legs
- Short bones, in such places as wrists and ankles
- Flat bones, in such places as the ribs
- Irregular bones, in such places as fingers and toes

How Are Bones Joined?

Long bones have larger ends that form a joint with another bone. Joints allow for several kinds of movement. For example, the joint that has the greatest range of motion is the ball-and-socket joint. You have a ball-and-socket joint in each of your hips and shoulders. This joint allows you to move your arms and legs forward and backward. It also allows your legs and arms to move from side to side and in a circle.

Your knee joint is a hinge joint. It is similar to a hinge on a door. You can bend your leg back at the knee, but you can't bend it forward after you straighten it again. Pivot joints are in your elbows and between your head and spinal column. They move in the same way hinge joints do but also can rotate.

Ligaments are *tough bands of stretchy tissue that hold joints together and keep organs in place*. **Cartilage** is *a strong but flexible material found in some parts of the body such as the joints, nose, and ears*. Ligaments move easily, but can tear if stretched too far.

Long bones are somewhat hard on the outside. Inside, however, is a soft substance called **marrow**, which is *a type of tissue that fills in the spaces in bones*. Bone marrow forms red blood cells and white blood cells. As these cells become worn out or damaged, the marrow replaces them.

Maintaining Healthy Bones

Caring for your skeletal system is something you should do every day. You can start by eating foods that contain nutrients and vitamins such as calcium, vitamin D, and phosphorus. These help maintain the strength of your bones and lower the risk of certain skeletal issues. You can find phosphorus in dairy products, dark green leafy vegetables, beans, and whole grains. Milk is fortified with vitamin D and contains calcium. Another way to strengthen your bones is to do regular physical activity. Never forget to wear protective gear such as a helmet and padding to reduce the risk of injury. Proper nutrition for a healthy body will be covered in more detail in the next lesson.

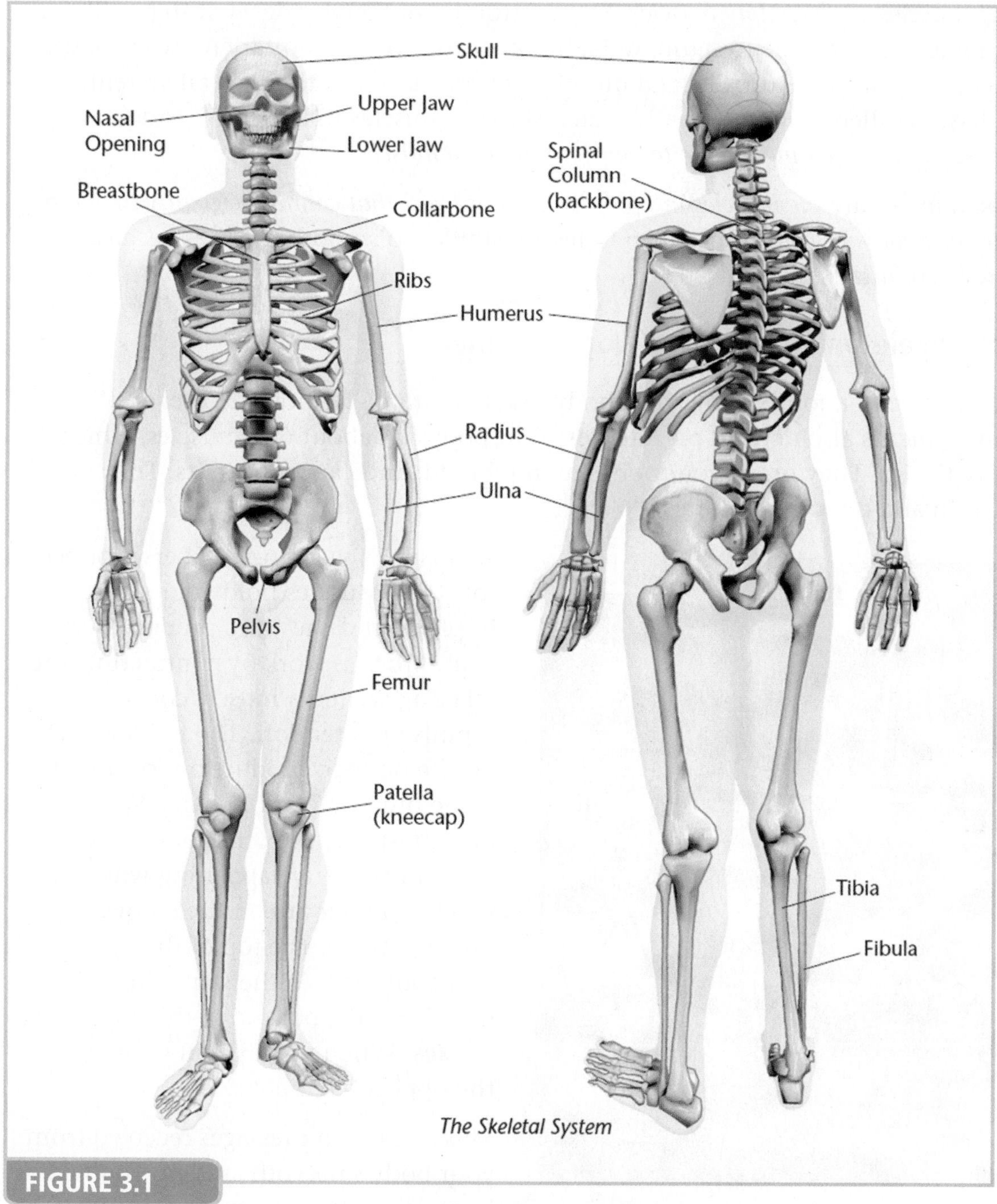

FIGURE 3.1

Your skeleton provides a framework that supports and protects many other body parts.

How Your Muscular System Works

The muscular system is made up of three basic types of muscles—smooth, skeletal, and cardiac. Smooth muscles are *involuntary muscles*. They work even though you don't think about making them work. Some smooth muscles are in the walls of your stomach, blood vessels, passageways to the lungs, and bladder. They move food, waste, and blood through your body.

Skeletal muscles are *voluntary muscles*. You control them. You decide what they will do. For example, if you decide to stand, walk, jump, or run, your voluntary muscles move. They react to your decision. Skeletal muscles are connected to the skeletal system. Tough tissues called tendons usually attach skeletal muscles to bones. A **tendon** is *a strong set of fibers joining muscle to bone or muscle to muscle*.

Cardiac muscles are *the muscles in the walls of your heart that contract regularly to pump blood throughout your body*. Cardiac muscles are similar to smooth muscles because they are involuntary.

How the Skeleton and Muscles Work Together

As described earlier, joints allow your body's skeletal frame to move. However, all body movements also depend on muscles. Your body has about 600 muscles, which do many things. They move your bones, pump blood, and carry nutrients. They also move air in and out of your lungs.

Muscles make it possible for you to play basketball.
© Nikokvfrmoto/Fotolia.com

A muscle is made up of fibers grouped together. Muscles hold your skeleton in place, and they also produce body heat. Muscles work by contracting and relaxing. When a muscle contracts, it pulls on a tendon. The tendon acts on the bone to produce a movement. Some muscles work in pairs. When one contracts, the other one relaxes. You can feel this happening when you bend your arm at the elbow. The muscle on the top of the upper arm contracts. At the same time, the muscle on the bottom of the upper arm relaxes. When you extend your arm, the opposite happens.

Muscles act on messages received from your body's nervous system. You will learn about the nervous system later in this lesson.

What Is Muscle Tone?

Some muscles never relax completely. They are somewhat contracted all the time. This is because of muscle tone. When you are in good health, a constant flow of messages runs from your nerves to your muscles. This helps you keep good muscle tone. Exercise and healthy eating are important for good muscle tone.

Care of the Muscular System

Daily regular physical activity is the best way to keep your muscles strong and healthy. Muscles that are not used for long periods will decrease in size and strength. Muscle tone is also lost. Physical activity and fitness planning will be covered in Lesson 3.

Common Muscle Injuries

When you engage in physical activity, your muscles work very hard. If your muscles become overworked or are not warmed up properly, you are increasing the chances of injury. Recovery time varies with the type and severity of the injury. Common injuries to muscles are strains or sprains. A strained muscle results when a muscle is stretched or partially torn from overexertion. A sprain is an injury to the ligament in a joint and usually requires medical attention. Another common injury is tendonitis, which is *an inflammation of a tendon*. Signs of tendonitis include joint pain or swelling that gets worse with more activity. The best treatment is rest and proper medication. Treating muscle injuries will be covered in more detail in Lesson 5.

Muscles move more freely when you warm up before vigorous exercise. A proper warm up prepares the muscle for exercise, and keeps you from hurting yourself.

The Human Circulatory System

All systems in your body work together. Think of the circulatory system as your body's transportation system. The circulatory system includes the heart and three kinds of blood vessels that will be covered later.

Why Does the Body Need Blood?

The circulatory system is *the system that moves blood through the body*. Blood carries food and oxygen to every cell. Cells use the food and oxygen to do their work. The blood also carries waste products away from the cells.

Blood is made up of red blood cells, white blood cells, and platelets, *small particles in the blood that help clotting*. Red blood cells carry oxygen to all parts of your body. They also remove carbon dioxide gas, a waste product made when the body breaks down food for energy. White blood cells work to keep your body healthy by fighting disease and germs. Most of the time your body has fewer white blood cells than red blood cells, but the number of white blood cells increases when your body is fighting germs. Platelets are the smallest parts in blood. They prevent the body from losing blood through a wound by clotting, or *sticking together to form a plug to stop bleeding*.

How Does Blood Move Through the Body?

Your heart pumps blood to all parts of your body. Your heart has been beating every minute since you were born, and even before that. In fact, the average heart beats about 72 times a minute. This *regular beat of your heart* is your **pulse**.

Your heart is in the left side of your chest. It has four chambers—two on the left side and two on the right. Blood from all parts of your body flows into the right side of your heart. This blood contains carbon dioxide. The blood must get rid of the carbon dioxide through the lungs. The right side of your heart pumps the blood to the lungs, where you breathe out the carbon dioxide.

In your lungs, blood gets rid of carbon dioxide and picks up oxygen. Then the blood travels to the left side of your heart. From there, your heart pumps blood to all parts of your body to get oxygen to the cells.

Blood vessels distribute blood, or send it, throughout your body. You have three kinds of blood vessels—arteries, capillaries, and veins. Arteries are the largest blood vessels and carry blood away from your heart. They have thick, three-layered walls. Arteries branch into smaller vessels. These small branches regulate, or control, the flow of blood into the capillaries.

Capillaries are the smallest blood vessels. Capillaries connect the arteries and veins. They have thin walls. These walls allow nutrients and oxygen to pass from the blood to the body cells. Capillaries also pick up waste products from the cells.

When blood leaves the capillaries, it travels to veins. Veins carry the blood back to your heart. Veins that receive blood from capillaries are small. They become larger, though, as they come closer to your heart. This passage of the blood throughout your body happens quickly. It takes about one minute for blood to travel through your whole body. Figure 3.2 shows the network of blood vessels in your body.

Blood Pressure and Anger

Understanding your body can help you live a longer, healthier life. When you get really angry and feel like you are about to explode, this feeling is from an increase in blood pressure. When you feel yourself getting angry, calm your anger by taking a few deep breaths. Then evaluate and calmly express what's upsetting you. Once you feel calmer, you'll see solutions not apparent when you were angry.

What Is Blood Pressure?

Blood pressure is *the force of blood on the walls of blood vessels and arteries*. Pressure is created as your heart pumps blood to all parts of your body. As blood is forced out of the heart into your arteries, the artery walls are stretched under the pressure. Between heartbeats, the pressure decreases in preparation to pump more blood into the arteries. Blood pressure can be measured with an instrument called a sphygmomanometer (sfig mo muh NAH muh ter). As the heart contracts to push blood through arteries, the systolic pressure is measured. **Systolic pressure** is *the maximum pressure placed on your arteries*. This is recorded as the upper number representing blood pressure. *As the heart relaxes to refill, blood pressure is at the lowest point*, called

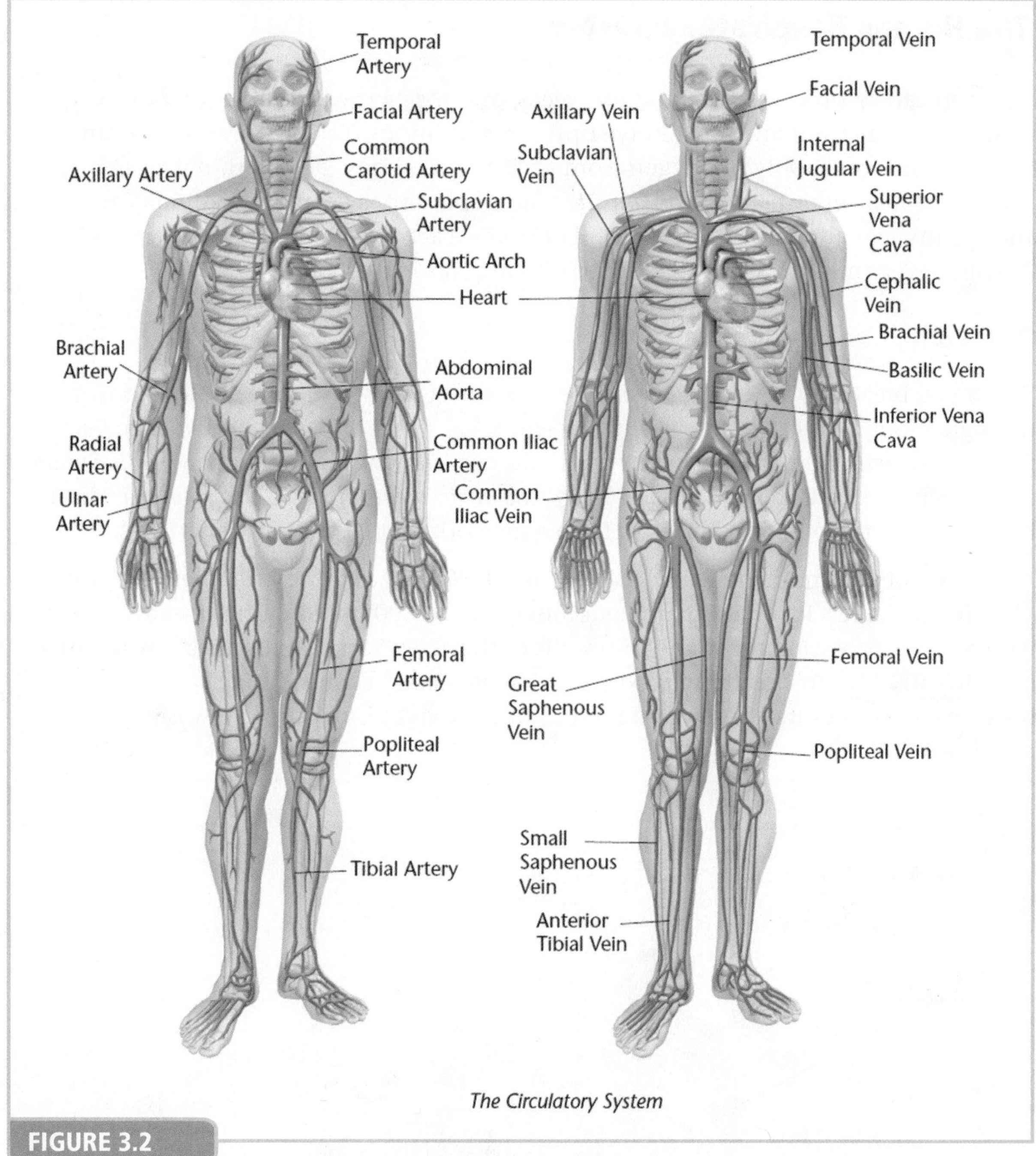

FIGURE 3.2

The circulatory system is your body's transportation system.

the diastolic pressure. This is recorded as the lower number in a blood pressure reading. Blood pressure consistently recorded above 140 over 90 is considered high because it places a strain on the heart as it pumps blood. Your body needs to keep a certain level of blood pressure for proper blood circulation. Preventing high blood pressure includes maintaining a healthy weight through a healthy diet, exercising regularly, and avoiding tobacco, alcohol, and drugs.

The Human Respiratory System

A person can survive without food for weeks, and for days without water. However, without oxygen, humans can survive only a few minutes. Your respiratory system brings a constant supply of oxygen from air into your body. Respiration is *breathing in oxygen and breathing out carbon dioxide*. The respiratory system is a system of tubes and organs that allows you to breathe. For routine activity, your body breathes about 20 times every minute. Figure 3.3 shows the respiratory system.

Oxygen In, Carbon Dioxide Out

When you breathe, you take in air through your nose or mouth. The air flows down through a long tube called the trachea, or windpipe, which is *a long tube running from your nose to your chest*. The trachea divides into two branches called bronchi, or *breathing tubes*. Each one leads into one of the lungs, *the major breathing organs in your body*. In the lungs, each of the bronchi divides to form a network of tubes called bronchioles.

At the end of each bronchiole is *a cluster of tiny balloon-like air sacs with thin walls*, called alveoli. You have a lot of alveoli in your lungs—about 300 million. The alveoli are covered with a network of capillaries. The thin walls of the alveoli and capillaries allow the two gases involved in the breathing process to change places. That is, the oxygen goes in to break up nutrients into energy, and then carbon dioxide comes out as a waste product.

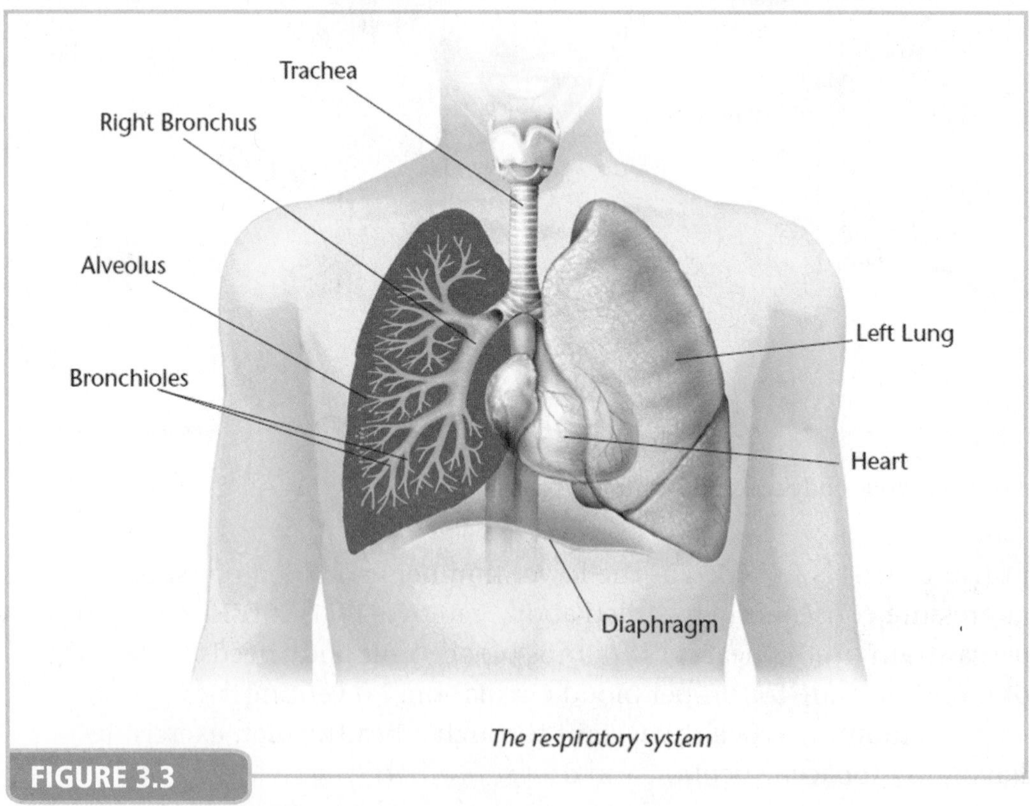

The respiratory system

FIGURE 3.3

The respiratory system brings outside air into the body. It also removes carbon dioxide from the body.

Your lungs get help from your diaphragm and chest cavity. The diaphragm is *a band of muscle tissue beneath your lungs*. Your chest cavity *includes ribs and muscles that surround your heart and lungs*. When you inhale, or *breathe in*, your rib muscles and diaphragm contract. This enlarges your chest cavity and allows air to rush in. When you exhale, or *breathe out*, your rib muscles and diaphragm expand. This forces the air out.

How the Circulatory and Respiratory Systems Work Together

The blood that the circulatory system carries to all areas of your body delivers oxygen to the cells. Cells need oxygen to break up nutrients, which provide energy to the cells. The respiratory system gets the oxygen into your body. It also gets rid of carbon dioxide, a waste product. Together, the respiratory and circulatory systems give all your cells the oxygen they need to survive.

The respiratory, circulatory, muscular, and skeletal systems all work together to keep us healthy and functioning day and night. To do that, they depend on the nervous system, the body's communication network.

How the Nervous System and Sense Organs Work

The nervous system sends messages throughout your body. The nervous system has two parts—the central nervous system and the peripheral nervous system. Figure 3.4 shows the nervous system. The central nervous system is made up of the brain and the spinal cord.

How Does the Brain Control the Body?

Your brain receives messages from your nerves and sends messages through the nerves to all parts of your body. Your brain is like a computer and a chemical factory combined. It can process and store information. It produces and uses chemicals to send signals. The brain has three main parts that work together to control your body: the *cerebrum*, *cerebellum*, and *brain stem*. Figure 3.5 shows the parts of the brain.

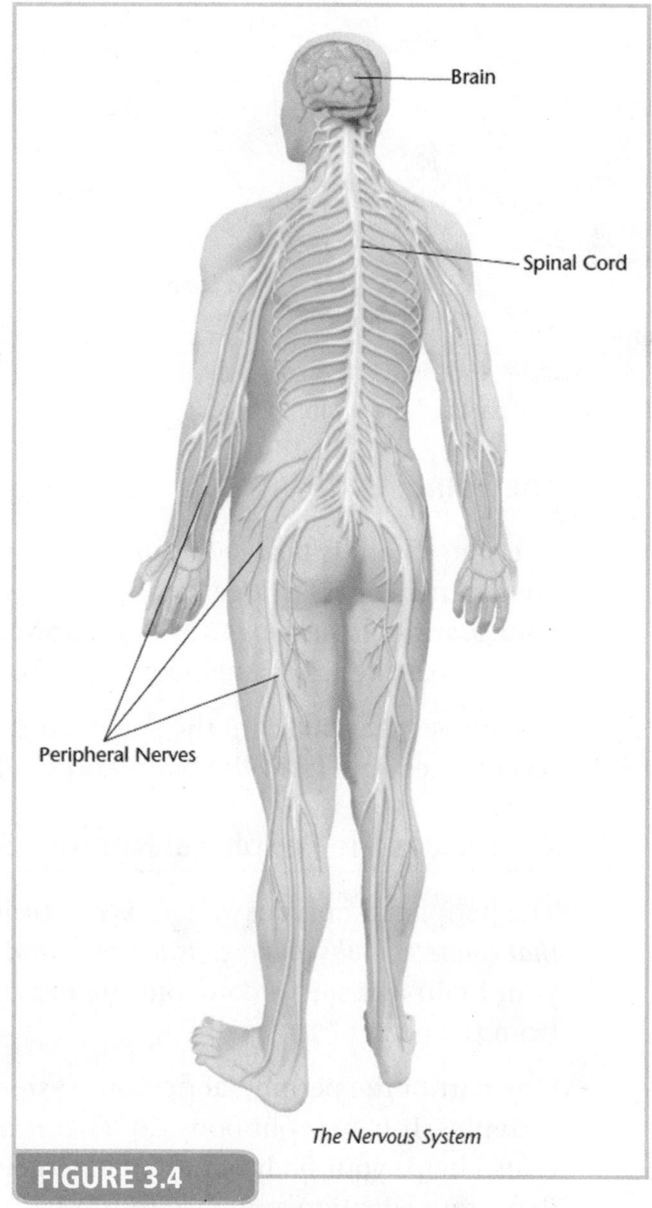

FIGURE 3.4

The human nervous system is the body's communication network.

The cerebrum is *the part of the brain that lets a person read, think, and remember*. It is the largest part of the brain. The cerebrum is divided into two halves. The right half controls the movement on the left side of your body. It also is the site for artistic skills and instinctive thinking. Instinctive thinking *relates to actions that happen instantly without your thinking consciously about them*. An example of instinctive thinking is the first answer that pops into your head when someone asks you a question, or it could be that gut feeling you get. The left half controls the movement on the right side of your body. It is the site for math and language skills and logical, or sensible, thinking.

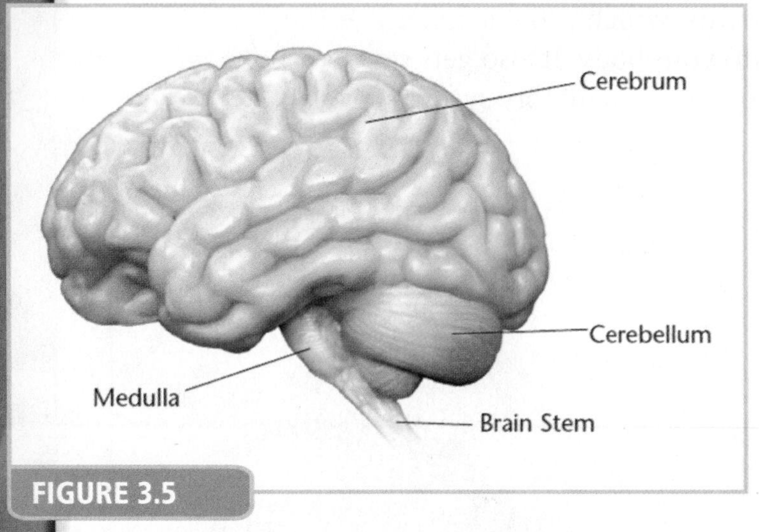

FIGURE 3.5

The primary parts of the brain.

The other two parts of your brain are much smaller than your cerebrum. They are the cerebellum and brain stem. The cerebellum lies between the cerebrum and brain stem. Your cerebellum is *the part of the brain that controls balance and helps coordinate muscular activities such as walking*. The brain stem *connects the cerebrum to the spinal cord*.

One part of the brain stem is the medulla, which *controls the body's automatic activities*. These include breathing, digesting food, circulating blood, swallowing, coughing, and sneezing.

The Spinal Cord

The spinal cord is *the major pathway your brain uses to send messages to your body*. Your spinal cord is a large batch of long nerve cells wound together. It connects to your brain stem and extends to the lower part of your back. The spinal column is made up of a series of small bones. These bones surround and protect your spinal cord.

The nerves that make up the spinal cord send and receive messages. These nerves receive messages from the brain and send them to other sets of nerves.

What Does the Peripheral Nervous System Do?

The peripheral nervous system is *a network of nerves outside the central nervous system that connects limbs and organs to the central nervous system*. They carry messages between your brain and spinal cord and the rest of your body. Peripheral means "located away from the center."

One part of the peripheral nervous system helps control your body's automatic activities. It helps your body do what it must to remain stable, or under control. It also helps your body act in an emergency. For example, suppose you are in a dangerous situation and need to run fast. The peripheral nervous system signals your body to speed up your breathing and heartbeat so you can act on the signal to run.

This happens during the body's stress response. Afterward, the peripheral nervous system slows the workings of your body and returns your body to normal.

A special part of your peripheral nervous system controls your reflexes. Reflexes are *automatic responses to something such as heat or pain*. For example, when you touch something hot, you jerk your hand away without thinking. Your nerves have sent a message to the muscles in your hand. A person cannot stop reflex actions from happening.

How Do the Sense Organs Work?

Nerves throughout your body carry messages to your brain. Your brain receives messages and then sends signals to other parts of your body. When messages come from outside your body, your sense organs receive them. Sense organs are *specialized parts of your body that function as receivers of outside information*. Human sense organs are your eyes, ears, tongue, nose, and skin.

The Sense of Sight

Your eye is your organ of sight. Figure 3.6 depicts the parts of the eye. How does the eye work? First, light enters the eye through the cornea. The cornea is *the transparent membrane that covers the pupil of the eye*. The cornea sends the light to the pupil, the dark center of the eye. The pupil can adjust its size. It gets smaller in bright light and larger in dim light. This allows the pupil to let the right amount of light into the eye.

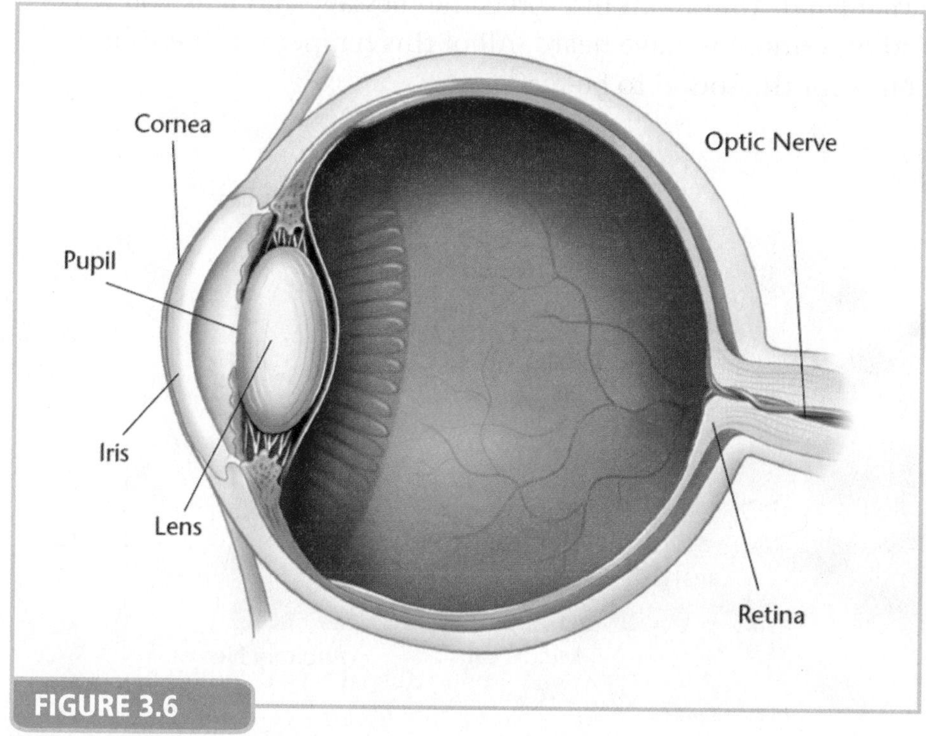

FIGURE 3.6

Cross-section of the human eye.

Behind your pupil is the soft, clear tissue called the lens. The lens helps direct the light energy onto the retina. The retina contains special cells that send the light information to the optic nerve, which is *the nerve that sends the information received by the eye to the brain*. Then the brain changes the light information into understandable pictures. This entire process happens faster than you can blink.

Another part of your eye is the iris. The iris is *the part of the eye surrounding the pupil that gives your eye its color*.

It is important to protect your eyes when involved in activities where the eye can be damaged. Keep dirty hands or objects away from your eyes to reduce the possibility of damage or infection. Maintain a balanced diet that includes vitamin A to help prevent night blindness, reducing your ability to see in dim light.

The Sense of Hearing

You may not notice that the air vibrates, or shakes, when a sound is made. Your ears, however, do notice. Figure 3.7 shows the parts of the ear. Your outer ear picks up air vibrations and sends them through the ear canal to your eardrum. Your eardrum is *a thin piece of tissue stretched across the ear canal*. When your eardrum receives the vibrations, it also vibrates. Eardrum vibrations cause three small bones in the middle ear to vibrate. These bones—the *hammer*, *anvil*, and *stirrup*—pass the vibrations to a snail-like organ in the inner ear. There, tiny cells transfer the vibrations to your auditory nerve, which is *the part of the ear that sends information to your brain*. Your brain interprets the message and tells you what kind of sound you have heard. All of this happens in the time it takes for the sound to be made.

keys to LEADERSHIP

Protecting your hearing while you are young will help prevent hearing damage and medical problems as you get older.

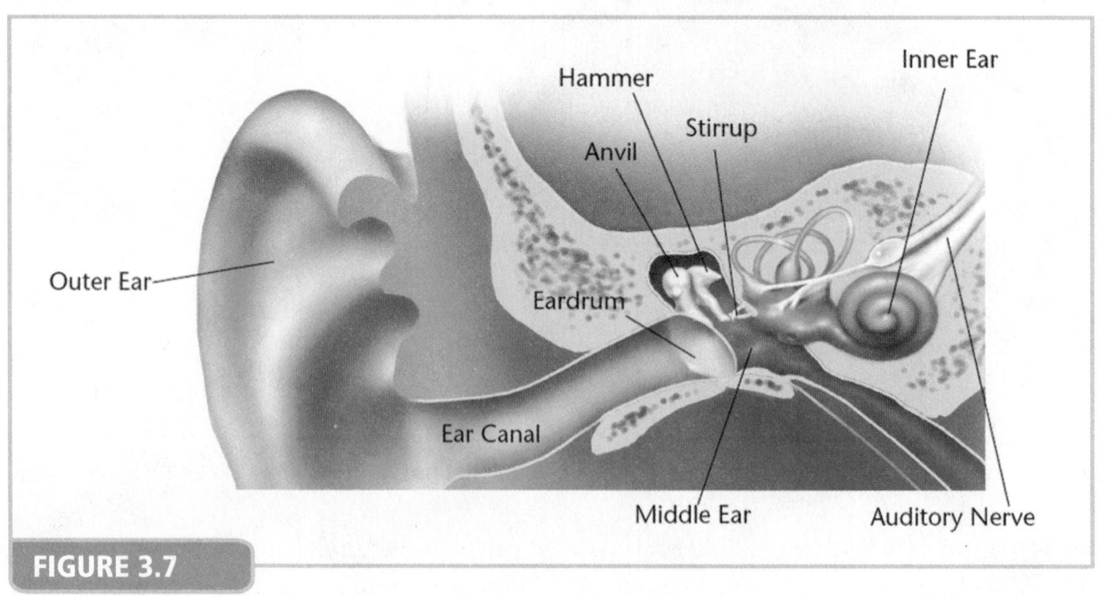

FIGURE 3.7

The ear.

It is important to protect your hearing from things such as loud noises and impact injuries. Always wear a helmet that protects the face and ears when playing sports. The most serious injury to your hearing is damage caused by overexposure to loud noises or music. This can lead to tinnitus, which is *a condition in which a ringing, buzzing, whistling, roaring, hissing, or other sound is heard in the ear*. To protect your hearing, lower the volume of music and wear hearing protection when around loud machinery.

The Senses of Smell and Taste

Both your tongue and your nose contain receptor cells, or *cells that receive information*. The receptor cells in your nose send messages through nerves. These nerves include the olfactory nerve. Your olfactory nerve is connected to your brain. Your nose can pick up thousands of different odors.

Your tongue, however, can recognize only four kinds of taste. The four tastes are sweet, salty, sour, and bitter. Different taste buds are *receptors for each kind of taste*. The taste buds send messages to your brain through your nerves. The taste buds are located on different parts of your tongue. They tell you how something tastes. Different parts of your tongue can recognize each of the four tastes.

The Sense of Touch

Your skin, your *sense organ for touch*, is your body's largest organ. Sense receptors all over your skin receive different sensations. You have receptors for touch, pressure, pain, heat, and cold. Your sense receptors send messages through the nerves to your spinal cord and brain. This is how you determine whether something is hot, cold, rough, or smooth. Your fingertips and lips are the most sensitive parts of your body because they have the greatest number of sense receptors.

The Human Digestive System

Your body needs food for energy, growth, and repair. Your body must break down food into substances that cells can use. *Breaking down food into smaller parts and changing it to a form that cells can use* is called digestion. The digestive system is the system that breaks down food for your body's use. Figure 3.8 shows the digestive organs.

How Does the Digestive System Break Down Food?

When your mouth waters at the sight, smell, or thought of food, it produces saliva, *a liquid in your mouth*. Saliva contains an enzyme, *a special chemical that breaks down food*. Enzymes are in all your digestive organs. When you take a bite of an apple, your tongue pushes the food around. Your teeth help you chew the food into small pieces. The chewing is part of mechanical digestion, when food is physically broken into smaller pieces. When the food in your mouth mixes with saliva, the enzyme in saliva begins to break down the food chemically.

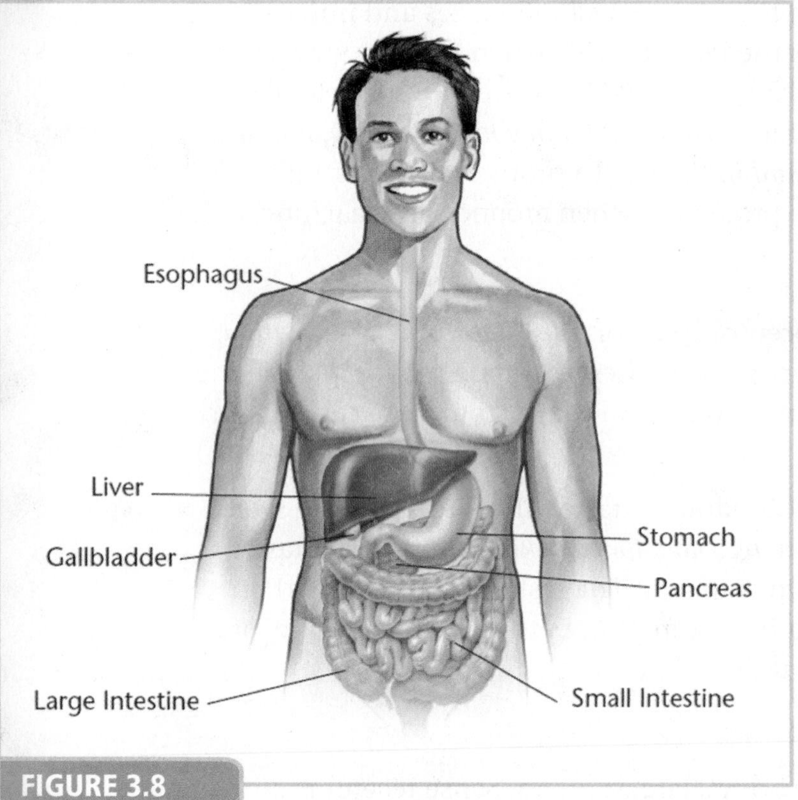

FIGURE 3.8

The digestive system breaks down food for your body's use.

Food next enters your esophagus, *a long tube that connects your mouth and your stomach*. Muscles in the walls of your esophagus push the food along to your stomach. Your stomach walls give off juices containing enzymes that break down food more. Your stomach also breaks down food through twisting and churning it. Food stays in your stomach for three to four hours. During that time, the enzymes change solid food into a partly liquid form.

From your stomach, food enters the small intestine. The small intestine is a curled-up tube just below your stomach. Most of the breakdown of food into chemicals takes place in your small intestine. The small intestine is lined with millions of villi (singular, *villus*), which are *tiny, fingerlike projections that absorb the food that has been broken down into chemicals*. Villi contain tiny blood vessels that are connected to the rest of your bloodstream. The chemicals from the broken-down food enter your blood vessels in the villi. Your bloodstream then sends the chemicals to all parts of your body.

Your liver and gallbladder are also digestive organs. Your liver is a large organ that produces bile, a liquid stored in the gallbladder that breaks down fats, such as butter. Your gallbladder is a small pouch attached to the liver. When bile is needed for digestion, it is pushed into the small intestine.

Your pancreas also helps in digestion. This gland produces a hormone called insulin, which helps cells regulate the level of sugar in the blood. Your pancreas also gives off enzymes that break down foods. Most food moves through your small intestine in one to four hours. Some foods are digested very quickly.

In the next two lessons, we will learn how beneficial eating a proper diet and having an active lifestyle are for our bodies. One of the most serious medical issues Americans face today is diabetes. Diabetes is *a serious disease in which the body cannot properly control the amount of sugar in your blood because it does not have enough insulin*. If the pancreas is not producing the correct amount of insulin, your cells will not be able to use the sugar they need. If diabetes is allowed to get worse, it causes changes to blood vessels. These changes may cause strokes and loss of eyesight, as well as damage to the kidneys and the circulatory system.

There are two common types of diabetes today, type I and type II. Type I diabetes is also known as insulin-dependent diabetes. This type of diabetes usually starts at childhood, when a young person's white blood cells attack the pancreas. When this happens, cells in the pancreas are not able to produce insulin. Sugar levels are not controlled and can cause you to pass out.

Type II diabetes is called noninsulin-dependent diabetes. The most common form of diabetes, type II usually happens as you get older. With type II diabetes, your pancreas makes insulin but your body cells cannot use the insulin properly. For years, type II diabetes has been linked to heredity. Lately, however, type II diabetes is becoming more common in younger people due to lack of activity and being overweight. Type II diabetes can cause blurry vision, slow-healing sores, and being tired all the time.

If you have diabetes, sometimes it can be controlled simply by changing your diet, but in some cases, it may require treatment with insulin. Only your doctor will know if you have diabetes through a medical checkup with tests that check for diabetes.

You can help prevent type II diabetes by eating a healthy diet and staying active every day.

The Body's Waste Disposal System

Once the digestive system has retrieved all the nutrients it can from food and liquids, waste products must be removed from the body. The body disposes of waste solids and liquids through the excretory system. The excretory system is *a system of organs that work to remove waste from the body.* Anything that the villi do not absorb in the small intestine moves on to the large intestine. The large intestine is a tube connected to the small intestine. It helps your body by gathering and removing waste materials that are left over after digestion. Through its walls, the large intestine absorbs water and nutrients from the waste material.

The solid material left in the large intestine is called feces. Feces are stored in the rectum, or lower part of the large intestine. Feces leave the body through an opening called the anus.

How Does the Body Get Rid of Liquid Waste?

Your body is good at using nutrients it needs. It can also eliminate, or get rid of, the rest. The excretory system allows the body to eliminate liquid and solid waste. Figure 3.9 shows the excretory system. This system removes water and salts through your sweat glands.

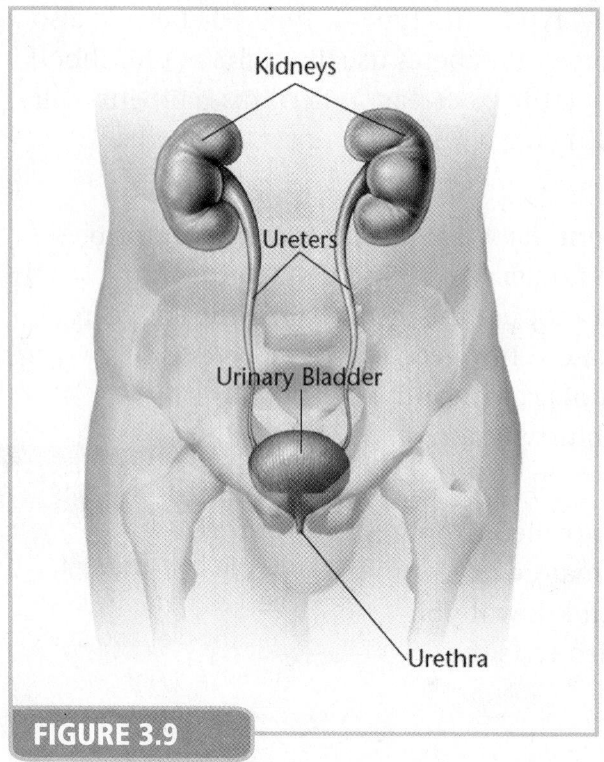

FIGURE 3.9

The excretory system allows the body to eliminate liquid and solid waste.

The excretory system also takes waste products out of your blood. The main excretory organs that do this are your two kidneys. The kidneys are on either side of your spine in your lower back. The kidneys take waste products out of your blood. Then they return water and minerals to your blood.

As your blood supplies nutrients to your cells, the cells form waste products. These wastes flow through cell walls into your bloodstream. When blood circulates through your kidneys, wastes are strained out. The blood then travels back to your heart through your veins.

Waste products move out of your kidneys through tubes called ureters to your urinary bladder. This bag can stretch to hold this liquid waste, which is called urine. Urine passes out of your body through the urethra.

As you can see, your body is a remarkable "system of systems." Being aware of how your body's separate systems work together can help you function more confidently throughout the day. Your body's "home team" is made up of your skeletal and muscular systems, nervous system and sense organs, circulatory and respiratory systems, and digestive and excretory systems. In the next lesson, you'll learn how to make healthy eating choices to keep your body systems in top shape.

Lesson 1 Review

Using complete sentences, answer the following questions on a sheet of paper.

1. What two body systems are joined to the skeletal system and allow coordinated movement?
2. What is the name of the tough bands of tissue that hold joints together?
3. State the three basic types of muscles in your body.
4. How do muscles work to allow movement?
5. What do white blood cells do?
6. How is pressure created in your blood vessels and arteries?
7. What are the major breathing organs in your body?
8. What is needed by cells to break up nutrients?
9. What makes up the central nervous system?
10. What part of the brain controls balance and helps to coordinate muscular activities?
11. What happens when your mouth waters?
12. Where does the breakdown of most food into partial chemical form take place?
13. What type of diabetes is a result of insulin not being used properly by the body?
14. What allows the body to eliminate liquid and solid waste?
15. What is the main excretory system organ?

APPLYING YOUR LEARNING

16. Your body has approximately 600 muscles. Explain how muscles are used to allow movement of your body, such as your leg or arm.

LESSON 2

Nutrition

Quick Write

What is your idea of healthy eating? Create a list of foods you eat during a normal day of school and at home. Don't forget to include anything you drink and snacks. After completing this lesson, consider what changes you may need to make in your food and drink choices.

Learn About

- what influences food choices
- nutrients and how the body uses them
- making wise food choices

"Let thy food be thy medicine and thy medicine be thy food."

Hippocrates, ancient Greek physician

What Influences Food Choices

Why is making healthy food choices so difficult for young people? One reason may be that healthier food usually takes longer to prepare and costs a little more than fast food. It is also due to the exposure and advertisement of fast foods that make them seem more appealing. One of the most difficult things for young people to do is to eat healthy. That's because they are constantly exposed to many unhealthy food choices and not enough healthier choices. The Kaiser Family Foundation studied 13 television networks and found that 34 percent of food and drink commercials were for candy and snacks. Another 29 percent were for cereal, and 10 percent for beverages. Only 8 percent were for dairy and prepared foods. Combine this advertising with the easy access to fast food stores and drive-thru restaurants that offer tasty but unhealthy foods with high amounts of sugar and fat, and it's easy to see why so many people eat poorly.

Appetite and Hunger

When you smell popcorn, does the pleasant odor make you want to try some? Does the sight of fresh strawberries make your mouth water? Do you like something crunchy to chew—maybe a good apple, or a fresh carrot? These are signs of your appetite at work. Your **appetite** is *the psychological desire for food.* It may be stimulated by the smell, sight, or texture of food.

Appetite is different from hunger. **Hunger** is *the physical need for food.* When you are hungry, your brain sends a signal to look for something to eat. You may hear your stomach growl or feel a little discomfort. Sometimes that's called a hunger pain. You may also feel tired or light-headed. These signs indicate that your body's supply of food energy and nutrients is running low.

When you eat, the hunger gradually goes away. Your stomach needs about 20 minutes to send a message back to the brain to turn off the hunger switch. This may cause some people to overeat if they eat too fast while their hunger switch is on. Therefore, it's best to eat slowly to allow time for your brain to receive the message that your hunger has been satisfied.

Vocabulary

- appetite
- hunger
- calories
- nutrients
- nutrition
- nutrient deficiency
- carbohydrates
- nutritionist
- proteins
- amino acids
- complete proteins
- incomplete proteins
- fats
- saturated fats
- unsaturated fats
- triglycerides
- vitamins
- minerals
- hydration
- electrolytes
- fiber
- *trans* fats
- cholesterol
- Dietary Guidelines for Americans
- foodborne illness
- Percent Daily Value

Food and Emotions

Food can meet emotional needs, too. Do certain foods make you happy? Maybe it's something you eat at a special event like a birthday party or at a Thanksgiving dinner. Perhaps you have favorite foods that make you feel more comfortable when stressed or depressed. Using food to deal with negative emotions is not a healthy way to respond to these feelings. People who eat to relieve stress or boredom may fall into a pattern of overeating; to stay healthy, they need to develop better ways to cope with such feelings.

When you are able to make healthy choices about foods, you are more likely to look, feel, and perform your best.

Obesity in Young People

Have you ever heard the saying, "you are what you eat"? According the US Department of Health and Human Services, the current high rates of overweight and obesity among young people in the US is primarily the result of individual behaviors that lead to excessive calorie intake. **Calories** are *units of heat that allow us to measure the energy used by the body and the energy that foods supply to the body*. Many factors contribute to excessive calorie intake. Here are just a few:

- Increased consumption of sugar-sweetened beverages
- Increased snacking
- Larger portion sizes
- More meals purchased or eaten away from home
- More exposure to advertising that encourages food consumption
- Less nutritious foods at fast food locations

From this list, it is easy to see why fast foods are much more popular than eating healthy at school or home. By the end of this lesson, you should have a better understanding of why foods that are better for you should be your first choice in meeting your hunger and appetite needs.

Why the Body Needs Nutritious Foods

Foods that provide adequate **nutrients**, *substances in food that your body needs*, are essential. Nutrients have many important roles. They give you energy. They build new body tissues and repair cells. They also help your body's processes and systems run smoothly.

You need a wide variety of healthy foods to get all the nutrients your body needs. Good nutrition is one of the main factors in building and maintaining good health. **Nutrition** is *the process of using food and its substances to help your body have energy, grow, develop, and work properly.*

One important reason you eat is to take in calories. You need this energy for everything you do—from running laps to doing your homework.

This lesson will discuss how nutrients benefit the body and how making correct food choices will lead to a healthier lifestyle. You'll be asked to consider the foods you already eat and what you can do to make changes. Now, think about the foods that you like the most. Do you know why you make these food choices? Just as with calorie intake, there are many factors influencing your food choices. Table 3.1 describes some of these factors.

Nutrients and How the Body Uses Them

Everyone needs the same nutrients to maintain good health, but the amount of nutrients needed depends on a person's age, gender, state of health, and level of activity. When you do not get enough of a particular nutrient, you could have a **nutrient deficiency**, *a shortage of a necessary nutrient.* As a young person, you need more calcium than older people do. Calcium helps build strong bones. If you don't eat enough foods that supply calcium, over time, the calcium deficiency could affect the strength of your teeth and bones. In some cases, an eating pattern that lacks calcium-rich foods can lead to osteoporosis, a disease in which bones become brittle and easier to break.

Iron is also important for you because your body makes more red blood cells as you grow. A shortage of iron can lead to a blood disease called anemia.

Table 3.1 Factors That Influence Food Choices

Factors	Description
Family and friends	You may prefer certain foods because you have grown up eating them at home. Other choices may be influenced by your friends. Still other choices you make may be due to a favorite place to eat in your neighborhood.
Cultural background	Different cultures have different traditions about what they eat, and perhaps where, how, and with whom they eat. For example, Mexican-American families eat a lot of beans, corn, and tortillas, while Italian-American families often favor pasta dishes. Consider some of your own family traditions in eating. In addition, many Americans enjoy trying a variety of foods from different cultures.
Food availability	Some foods are regional, growing only in certain areas. Some are seasonal and available only in certain months. Fresh blueberries, for example, are plentiful in summer but hard to find in the winter months. Still, modern transportation and growing methods have expanded the food supply and your choices. Many foods that were once regional or seasonal are now available in many areas year-round.
Time and money	Schedules and budgets can greatly affect a family's food choices.
Resources	Eating fast foods is often less expensive, and the convenience often means it takes less time than preparing a meal at home. Some families buy bulk foods that provide more meals for the dollar.
Advertising	Have you ever tried a food because you heard about it from radio or television, or saw an Internet ad? Ads can influence our choices to buy certain brands and products over and over. They may also persuade us to try new kinds of foods.
Knowledge of nutrition	The more you know about the nutrients in different foods, the better you are at choosing foods that supply the nutritional benefits that you need.
Personal physical or medical factors	Some people have allergies or medical conditions that restrict what they can choose to eat. Among the foods that most often cause allergic reactions are milk, peanuts, wheat, and shellfish.
Personal preferences	Your personal likes and dislikes, and overall health goals, contribute to your food choices. You will have a healthier and more enjoyable eating experience if your preferences include foods that provide nutrients.

keys to LEADERSHIP

Nutritional knowledge and a healthy eating plan are key defenses against long-term health problems. A healthy eating plan gives your body the nutrients it needs every day. It will lower your risk in later years for heart disease as well as other health conditions, especially those related to obesity.

As a young person, you generally need more of most nutrients to support your continued growth and to satisfy your needs for energy. Most people in the United States get plenty of food, yet many still do not get the nutrients they need. This is partly the result of their lifestyles. They often center their eating habits on fast foods and foods high in fat and sugar. Unfortunately, choosing to eat low-nutrient, high-fat foods, along with overeating, can lead to heart conditions, stroke, cancer, diabetes, and other diseases, not to mention the lack of physical fitness that comes with being overweight.

The Six Categories of Nutrients

Foods provide you with nourishment from more than 40 different nutrients. These nutrients are grouped into six categories: carbohydrates, proteins, fats, vitamins, minerals, and water. Eating a variety of foods that supply a good balance of these nutrients is essential to good health.

Carbohydrates

Carbohydrates are *the sugars and starches that provide your body with most of its energy.* Carbohydrates can be either simple or complex.

Simple carbohydrates, or sugars, are found in fruit, milk, and honey. Sugar is also added to candy, cookies, and other foods.

Complex carbohydrates, or starches, are found in breads, cereals, pasta, rice, potatoes, dry beans, corn, and other starchy vegetables. As your body digests complex carbohydrates, it breaks them down into simple sugars, which are absorbed into the bloodstream to provide energy. Complex carbohydrates break down slower than simple carbohydrates, therefore providing a steady level of energy.

Nutritionists recommend that 45 to 65 percent of your daily calories come from carbohydrates derived from fruits, vegetables, and whole grains. A nutritionist is *someone who studies or is an expert in nutrition.*

Proteins

Proteins are *nutrients your body uses to build, repair, and maintain cells and tissues.* They also help your body fight disease, and they provide energy when your body doesn't get enough from other sources.

Amino acids are *small units that make up protein.* Your body can produce most amino acids on its own. The remaining ones, called essential amino acids, must come from the food you eat.

Foods from animal sources, such as meat, fish, poultry, eggs, milk, cheese, and yogurt, contain complete proteins. These are *proteins that provide all the essential amino acids.* Foods from plant sources, such as soybeans, nuts, peas, and dry beans, contain incomplete proteins, which are *proteins that lack one or more of the essential amino acids.* By consuming a variety of plant foods, such as beans, rice, nuts, and peas, you combine incomplete proteins from different sources, making complete proteins that provide essential amino acids. You don't need to eat these foods at the same meal to get the benefit. Just have a good variety throughout the whole day.

Fats

Fats are *nutrients that provide energy and perform many functions for your body.* They carry certain vitamins and promote healthy skin and normal growth. Foods that are high in fats also tend to be high in calories. For this reason, health experts generally recommend that any eating plan include only moderate amounts of fat.

Saturated fats are *fats that are solid at room temperature.* They are found mostly in animal and dairy products such as red meat, butter, cheese, and whole milk. An eating pattern that includes too many saturated fats can increase a person's risk of heart disease.

Unsaturated fats are *fats that remain liquid at room temperature.* They come mainly from plant sources. Foods containing mostly unsaturated fats include vegetable oils, nuts, avocados, and olives. Unsaturated fats lower cholesterol levels and are considered healthier than saturated fats.

Triglycerides are *the chemical form in which most fat exists in food and the chief form of fat storage in the body.* Triglycerides are derived from fats eaten in foods or made in the body from other energy sources such as carbohydrates. Triglycerides are long chains of fatty acids that provide much of the energy your body's cells need to function. High levels of triglycerides circulating in the bloodstream have been linked to heart disease in some people.

A meal that includes beans, rice, and a leafy vegetable can provide essential vitamins and minerals, along with protein.

© chas53/Fotolia.com.

Vitamins

Vitamins are *substances needed in small quantities to help regulate body functions.* Because our bodies cannot produce enough of the vitamins we need, we should get our vitamins from food sources. There two types of vitamins, water-soluble and fat-soluble.

Water-soluble vitamins, such as vitamin C and B, dissolve in water, and will not be stored in your body. They need to be replaced often as part of your daily eating plan.

Fat-soluble vitamins, including vitamins A, D, E, and K, dissolve in fat and can be stored in body fat until needed. Use caution when taking fat-soluble vitamins, because they are stored; too much of these vitamins can cause health problems.

Vitamins keep your immune system in top shape. They help produce white blood cells to fight infections, and they maintain the health of your brain, bones, and heart.

Minerals

Minerals are *elements needed in small quantities for forming healthy bones and teeth, and for regulating certain body processes.* Calcium, phosphorus, and magnesium help build strong bones and teeth. Iron plays a vital role in making red blood cells. Adequate potassium levels help cells function efficiently. Potassium also helps to regulate heartbeat, encourage normal muscle contraction, regulate kidney function, and promote normal body growth. See Table 3.2 for more information about functions and sources of important vitamins and minerals.

Water

Water is a nutrient that is vital to your life and health. It makes up over half of your body and serves many important functions. Water transports nutrients through your body. It helps you digest food, lubricates your joints, removes wastes, and helps regulate body temperature. You lose water every day in urine and sweat, requiring you to replace it continually. A combination of thirst and normal drinking behavior—especially consuming fluids with meals—is usually enough to maintain normal hydration. Hydration is *providing enough water for somebody or something in order to reestablish or maintain a correct fluid balance.* However, if it is particularly hot or you're involved in prolonged physical activity, it is important to drink fluids regularly during and after the activity. Drink plenty of water or other replenishment fluids such as fruit juices, milk, soup, or electrolyte drinks. Electrolytes *help to control fluid levels and maintain normal potassium levels in the body.*

Beverages with high levels of caffeine or added sugar should be avoided.

Table 3.2 Vitamins and Minerals: Functions and Sources

Functions	Sources
Vitamin A Promotes healthy skin and normal vision	Dark green leafy vegetables (such as spinach); dairy products (such as milk); deep yellow-orange fruits and vegetables (such as carrots, winter squash, apricots); eggs; liver
B Vitamins A group of eight vitamins needed for a healthy nervous system; helps with energy production	Meat; poultry; eggs; fish; whole grain breads; fruits, cereals, and oats
Vitamin C Needed for healthy teeth, gums, and bones; helps heal wounds and fight infection	Citrus fruits (such as oranges and grapefruit); cantaloupe and strawberries; mangoes; tomatoes; cabbage and broccoli; potatoes
Vitamin D Promotes strong bones and teeth and the absorption of calcium	Fortified milk; fatty fish (such as salmon and mackerel); egg yolks; liver; vegetables
Vitamin K Helps blood clot	Dark green leafy vegetables (such as spinach); egg yolks; liver; some cereals
Calcium Needed to build and maintain strong bones and teeth	Dairy products (such as milk, yogurt, and cheese); dark green leafy vegetables (such as spinach); canned fish with edible bones (such as sardines)
Fluoride Promotes strong bones and teeth; prevents tooth decay	Fluoridated water; fish with edible bones
Iron Needed for hemoglobin in red blood cells	Red meat; poultry; dry beans (legumes); fortified breakfast cereal; nuts; eggs; dried fruits; dark green leafy vegetables
Potassium Helps regulate fluid balance in tissues; promotes proper nerve function	Fruits (such as bananas and oranges); dry beans and peas; dried fruits; dark green leafy vegetables; yogurt; fish
Zinc Helps heal wounds; needed for cell reproduction	Meat; poultry; eggs; dry beans and peas; whole grain breads and cereals

Other Substances in Food

Other than the major nutrients, foods have other substances. One is fiber, which is important to your health and should be part of your everyday food choices. However, there are also substances that are not good for you in large quantities, including hidden fats, bad cholesterol, added sugars, salt, and caffeine.

Fiber

Fiber is *the part of fruits, vegetables, grains, and beans that your body cannot digest.* It helps move food particles through your digestive system. Including high-fiber foods in your eating plan may help lower your risk of certain types of cancer and reduce your risk of heart disease. Foods high in fiber include whole grain breads and cereals, fruits and vegetables, and dry beans and peas.

Hidden Fats

The Centers for Disease Control and Prevention recommend that no more than 25 to 35 percent of teens' daily calories come from fat. It's easy to cut down on the fats you can see. For example, put a smaller amount of butter on your baked potato, or trim the fat from meats. However, fats are often hidden in processed and prepared foods. It's harder to cut down on hidden fats, but it can be done. Reduce the amount of fried food you eat and switch from whole to low-fat milk. Carefully read the labels on packaged foods to check for fats and oils.

***Trans* fatty acids**, or *trans* fats, are *artificial fats made when hydrogen gas reacts with oil.* They can be found in cookies, crackers, icing, potato chips, margarine, and microwave popcorn. *Trans* fats are created when liquid vegetable oil and hydrogen are combined to make oils solid. *Trans* fats pose a higher risk of heart disease than saturated fats, which were once believed to be the worst kind. *Trans* fats not only raise total cholesterol levels, they also deplete high-density, or good cholesterol (HDL), which helps protect against heart disease.

Cholesterol

Cholesterol is *a waxy substance used by the body to build cells and hormones, and to protect nerve fibers*. Most cholesterol is produced in your liver and circulates in the blood. Cholesterol is also found in foods of animal origin, including meats, chicken, egg yolks, and dairy products. Eating foods high in cholesterol can affect the levels of cholesterol in your blood. The low-density, or bad cholesterol, LDL, can leave deposits on the walls of your blood vessels. This buildup raises the risk of heart attack or stroke. To help reduce LDL levels in your blood, medical experts recommend you limit intake of foods that are high in saturated fat. Many studies have found that regular aerobic physical activity also helps prevent LDL buildup.

HDL can help lower LDL levels. Most of the fat that you eat should come from unsaturated sources: nuts, vegetable oils, and fish are sources of unsaturated fats. Just the opposite of LDL, many studies have shown that regular aerobic physical activity raises HDL levels.

Added Sugar

Here's an amazing fact. The average American eats about 100 pounds of sugar a year! Try lifting a bag containing 100 pounds of sand or other material. Or just try moving it a few inches along the floor.

Sugar occurs naturally in fruit and milk, and it does provide some good food energy. Sugar is not harmful in moderate amounts. Unfortunately, it is added to many prepared foods such as soft drinks, cookies, candy, breakfast cereal, and even spaghetti sauce. The reality is that you are eating more sugar in an average day than you realize. If you don't pay attention to the amount of added sugar you take in, it may cause you to gain weight from the additional calories, or develop health problems over time.

Refined sugar is found in many prepared foods.
© bit24/Fotolia.com

Sodium

Sodium is another necessary nutrient that helps control the balance of fluids in the body. It occurs naturally in salt, in various foods, and in many prepared sauces. It is also used extensively in processed foods to flavor or preserve the food. Most Americans eat much more sodium than they need. For some people, too much sodium may contribute to high blood pressure and fluid retention. You can lower your sodium intake by substituting spices for salt. There are many tasty spices that can make your meals healthier. Also, use food labels as a guide for how much salt you consume. Food labels will be covered later in the lesson.

The American Heart Association recommends you not consume more than 1,500 milligrams (mgs) of sodium per day. Animal and human studies have shown that excess sodium intake leads to problems with the heart and kidneys.

Caffeine

Caffeine is a substance that stimulates the nervous system and can become habit-forming. It is an ingredient in "energy drinks," cola, and some other soft drinks. Coffee, tea, and chocolate also have it. Caffeine stimulates the heart rate and the appetite. It can perk you up, but then it makes you feel drowsy so that you want more. For this reason, it's best to limit your intake of products containing caffeine.

Making Wise Food Choices

How do you know you're getting the nutrients you need? The US government has developed nutrition tools to help Americans make wise food choices. Two such tools are the Dietary Guidelines for Americans and the Nutrition Facts panel. Also, check out ChooseMyPlate.gov.

Dietary Guidelines for Americans

The Dietary Guidelines for Americans are *recommendations about food choices for all healthy Americans age 2 and over.* The guidelines were revised in 2010. They focus on balancing calories with physical activity, consuming more healthy foods like vegetables, seafood, fruits, whole grains, fat-free and low-fat dairy products, and taking in less sodium, saturated and *trans* fats, added sugars, and refined grains.

Make Smart Choices from Every Food Group

The best way to give your body the balanced nutrition it needs is by eating a variety of nutrient-packed foods every day. Just be sure to stay within your daily recommended calorie needs. Setting the proper goal for the calories you take in will help you maintain a proper body weight.

Your plan should emphasize:

- Fruits, vegetables, whole grains, and fat-free or low-fat milk and milk products
- Lean meats, poultry, fish, beans, eggs, and nuts
- Low quantities of saturated fats, trans fat, cholesterol, salt (sodium), and added sugars
- Controlled portion sizes

Don't Give In When You Go Out. It's important to make smart food choices and watch portion sizes wherever you are—at the grocery store, in your favorite restaurant, or running errands. Try these tips:

- At the store, plan ahead by buying a variety of nutrient-rich foods for meals and snacks throughout the week.
- When grabbing lunch, have a sandwich on whole grain bread and choose low-fat or fat-free milk, water, or other drinks without added sugars.
- In a restaurant, choose grilled, steamed, or broiled dishes instead of those that are fried or sautéed in crème sauce.
- On a long trip, pack some fresh fruit, cut-up vegetables, string cheese strips, or a handful of unsalted nuts—to help you avoid impulsive, less healthful snacks.

Also see the box, "Tips for Eating Healthy When Eating Out," for some additional advice on making smart eating choices when you're eating out.

Tips for Eating Healthy When Eating Out

- As a beverage choice, ask for water or order fat-free or low-fat milk, unsweetened tea, or other drinks without added sugars.
- Ask for whole-wheat bread for sandwiches.
- In a restaurant, start your meal with a salad packed with veggies to help control hunger and feel satisfied sooner.
- Ask for salad dressing to be served on the side. Then use only as much as you want.
- Choose main dishes that include vegetables, such as stir fries, kebabs, or pasta with a tomato sauce.
- Order steamed, grilled, or broiled dishes instead of those that are fried or sautéed.
- Choose a small or medium portion. This includes main dishes, side dishes, and beverages.
- Order an item from the menu instead of heading for the all-you-can-eat buffet.
- If main portions at a restaurant are larger than you want, try one of these strategies to keep from overeating:
  - Order an appetizer-sized portion or a side dish instead of an entrée.
  - Share a main dish with a friend.
  - If you can chill the extra food right away, take leftovers home in a doggy bag.
  - When your food is delivered, set aside or pack half of it to go immediately.
  - Resign from the "clean your plate club"—when you've eaten enough, leave the rest.
- To keep your meal moderate in calories, fat, and sugars:
  - Ask for salad dressing to be served on the side so you can add only as much as you want.
  - Order foods that do not have creamy sauces or gravies.
  - Add little or no butter to your food.
  - Choose fruits for dessert most often.

Source: United States Department of Agriculture, 2014. http://www.choosemyplate.gov/healthy-eating-tips/tips-for-eating-out.html.

Mix Up Your Food Choices within Each Food Group

Focus on Fruits. Eat a variety of fruits—whether fresh, frozen, canned, or dried—rather than a fruit juice. For a proper diet, you should have two cups of fruit each day. When buying canned fruit, choose fruits with no added sugar.

Vary Your Veggies. Eat more dark green and dark, leafy green vegetables. Vary your choices between broccoli, kale, and others. Eat orange vegetables such as carrots, sweet potatoes, pumpkins, and winter squash. Don't forget beans and peas. Eat a variety of pinto beans, kidney beans, black beans, garbanzo beans, split peas, and lentils.

Count on Your Calcium. Get three cups of low-fat or fat-free milk—or an equivalent amount of low-fat yogurt and/or low-fat cheese—every day. One-and-a-half ounces of cheese equals one cup of milk. If you don't or can't drink milk, you can try lactose-free milk products as an alternative. Also choose calcium fortified foods and beverages.

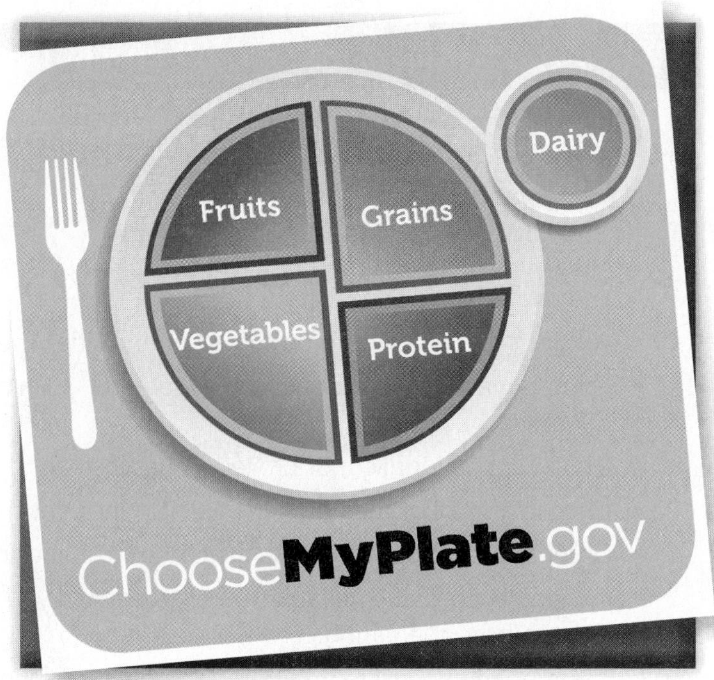

Guidelines for a balanced diet.

Courtesy of www.ChooseMyPlate.gov

Make Your Grains Whole. Eat at least three ounces of whole grain cereals, breads, crackers, rice, or pasta every day. One ounce is about equal to one slice of bread, one cup of breakfast cereal, or one-half cup of cooked brown rice or pasta. Look to see that grains such as wheat, rice, oats, or corn are referred to as "whole" in the list of ingredients.

Go Lean with Protein. Choose lean meats and poultry. Bake it, broil it, or grill it. And vary your protein choices—with more fish, beans, peas, nuts, and seeds.

keys to LEADERSHIP

Your food and physical activity choices affect your health—how you feel today, tomorrow, and in the future.

- Make at least half your grains whole grains
- Vary your veggies
- Focus on fruit
- Get your calcium-rich foods
- Go lean with protein

Start with these ideas for a healthy diet. Changes that you can make today can pave the way to better health, more energy, and a new, fitter you.

Find Your Balance Between Food and Physical Activity

Becoming healthier isn't just about eating well—it's also about physical activity. Regular exercise is important for your overall health and fitness. It helps you control body weight by balancing calories you take in as food with the calories you use up every day. The President's Council on Fitness, Sports, and Nutrition recommends being physically active for 60 minutes every day. Increasing the intensity level of your physical activity brings even greater health benefits and body weight control. We will discuss more about the benefits of physical activity in the next lesson.

You should set a goal to maintain a healthy weight that helps you look and feel good. It lowers your risk for heart disease, some cancers, and diabetes. Your doctor or health care provider can determine if you are at a healthy weight for your height and age.

Get the Most Nutrition Out of Your Calories

Active young people need to take in a fairly large number of calories. The US Department of Agriculture's Dietary Guidelines define *active* as a lifestyle that includes moderate physical activity equivalent to walking more than three miles per day at a pace of three to four miles per hour. This is in addition to the normally light physical activity one does each day.

Using this guideline, active female teens should consume approximately 2,400 calories a day. Active male teens should consume 2,800 to 3,200 calories a day. However, the entire calorie intake could be used up on a few unhealthy, empty-calorie items. Empty calories are foods that have high amounts of sugar and fats, and don't contain the full range of vitamins and nutrients the body needs to be healthy. For the best benefits, you should try to eliminate foods that are high in fats, sugars, and salt.

To get the most nutrition out of your calories, do the following:

- Choose foods packed with vitamins, minerals, fiber, and other nutrients, but lower in calories. Pick foods like fruits, vegetables, whole grains, and fat-free or low-fat milk and milk products more often.
- Choose foods that are low in saturated fat, *trans* fat, and cholesterol, and moderate in total fat. Foods high in saturated fat (such as butter and whole milk) and *trans* fat (such as cookies, chips, and margarine) raise blood cholesterol levels.
- Choose beverages and foods that reduce your intake of sugars. Soft drinks provide many calories but few nutrients. They can also contribute to tooth decay. Try to limit your intake of drinks and foods containing added sugar. Check the ingredient list on packaged foods. If sucrose, corn syrup, honey, fructose, or other sweeteners are listed first or second, these foods are high in sugars.
- Choose and prepare foods with less salt. High salt or sodium intake can contribute to high blood pressure and cause calcium loss. If you normally add salt to food, try using herbs such as basil or oregano or spices such as paprika instead.

Play It Safe with Food

You should know how to prepare, handle, and store food safely. Part of good nutrition habits involves making sure that foods are safe from harmful bacteria and other contaminants. Doing so reduces the risk of foodborne illness, *a sickness that results from eating food that is not safe to eat*. Here are some important things to remember:

- Thoroughly clean your hands, food-contact surfaces, fruits, and vegetables. Avoid washing or rinsing raw meats and poultry near other foods, or you could spread bacteria.
- Separate raw, cooked, and ready-to-eat foods when shopping, preparing, or storing them.
- Cook meat, poultry, and fish to safe internal temperatures to kill harmful microorganisms.
- Chill perishable foods promptly and thaw foods properly, according to their directions.

Nutrition Labeling

All packaged foods carry a label titled "Nutrition Facts." These labels provide valuable and important information for making healthy food choices. Food labels compare products to the Percent Daily Value, *the percent of the recommended daily amount of a nutrient provided in a serving of food.* The Percent Daily Value is based on an intake of 2,000 calories per day. Understanding how to read a food label, like the one shown in Figure 3.10, can help you select more nutritious foods to maintain a properly balanced eating pattern.

A Vegetarian Diet

A vegetarian is a person who eats mostly or only plant foods. Some people are vegetarians for religious or cultural reasons. Others may make this choice because of concern for the environment or for how animals used as food are raised or slaughtered. However, there are many people who become vegetarians for health reasons. By cutting out the saturated fats and cholesterol found in many animal products, vegetarians may reduce their risk of cardiovascular disease and some cancers and control their weight. Also, vegetarians tend to consume more fruits, vegetables, and whole grains—foods that are linked to a smaller risk of many health problems. No matter which plan a person follows, a vegetarian eating style still involves choosing nutritious foods. Table 3.3 describes four separate vegetarian eating styles.

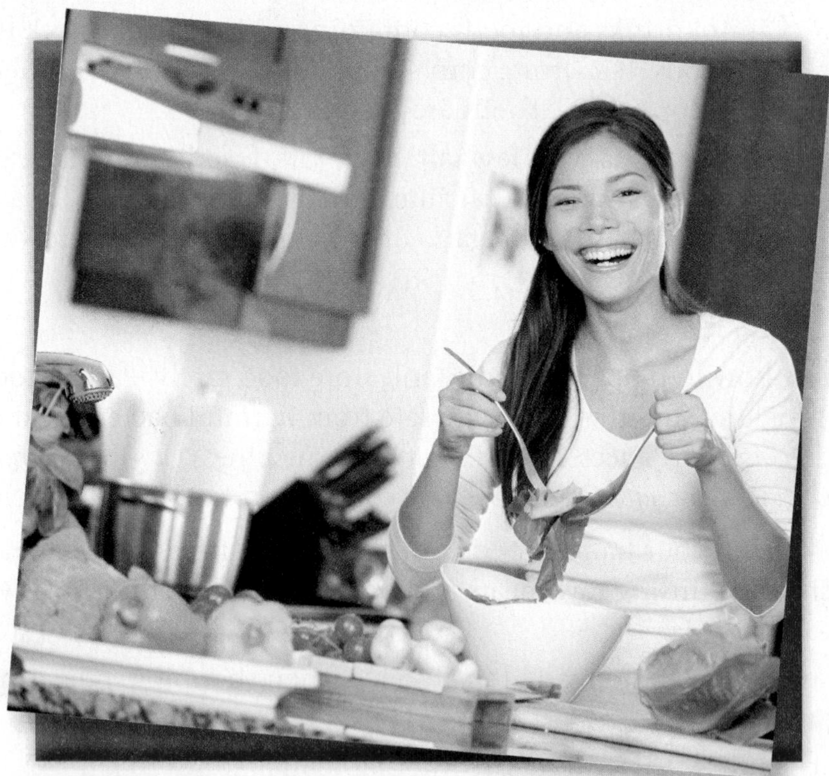

Many people become vegetarians for health reasons.
© Ariwasabi/Fotolia.com

Food labels provide important nutritional information that can help you make sensible food choices.

Nutrition Facts

Serving Size 2/3 cup (55g)
Servings Per Container About 8

Amount Per Serving	
Calories 230	Calories from Fat 72
	% Daily Value*
Total Fat 8g	**12%**
Saturated Fat 1g	**5%**
Trans Fat 0g	
Cholesterol 0mg	**0%**
Sodium 160mg	**7%**
Total Carbohydrate 37g	**12%**
Dietary Fiber 4g	**16%**
Sugars 1g	
Protein 3g	
Vitamin A	10%
Vitamin C	8%
Calcium	20%
Iron	45%

* Percent Daily Values are based on a 2,000 calorie diet. Your daily value may be higher or lower depending on your calorie needs.

	Calories:	2,000	2,500
Total Fat	Less than	65g	80g
Sat Fat	Less than	20g	25g
Cholesterol	Less than	300mg	300mg
Sodium	Less than	2,400mg	2,400mg
Total Carbohydrate		300g	375g
Dietary Fiber		25g	30g

1. **Serving size**—The nutrient content of the food is calculated according to its serving size. If you double the servings you eat, you double the calories and nutrients, including Percentage of Daily Value.
2. **Calories (and calories from fat)**—Calories provide a measure of how much energy you get from a serving of this food. Remember, the number of servings you consume determines the number of calories you actually eat.
3. **Nutrients (fats and sodium)**—The amount of total fat in one serving is listed, followed by the amount of *trans* and saturated fat. The calories from fat are shown to the right of the total calories per serving. Sodium and cholesterol amounts are also provided. Eating too much fat, saturated fat, *trans* fat, cholesterol, and sodium may increase your risk of certain chronic diseases such as heart disease, cancer, or high blood pressure.
4. **Nutrients (vitamins, fiber, and minerals)**—Most Americans don't get enough dietary fiber, vitamins, calcium, and iron in their diets. Eating enough of these nutrients can improve your health and help reduce the risk of some diseases and conditions.
5. **Percentage of Daily Value (%DV)**—The %DV can help you determine if a serving of food is high or low in a nutrient. You can use the %DV as a frame of reference whether you consume more or less than 2,000 calories a day. The %DV helps you interpret grams and milligrams by using a uniform scale for the day (0–100%DV). Each nutrient is based on 100 percent of the daily requirements for that nutrient. By referring to these numbers, you can tell whether foods are high or low in certain nutrients.
6. **Understanding footnote on bottom of nutrition facts label**—The footnote in the lower part of the nutrition label tells you percentage (%) of Daily Values is based on a 2,000 calorie diet. This statement must be on all labels. The entire footnote may not be there if the package is too small. However, all labels must contain the first line after the asterisk (*).

You can find more information about Nutrition Facts Labels by going to: **http://www.fda.gov/Food/IngredientsPackagingLabeling/LabelingNutrition/default.htm**.

FIGURE 3.10

What the Food Label Tells You

Table 3.3 Vegetarian Eating Plans

Plan Name	Foods Included
Lacto-ovo vegetarianism	Dairy (*lacto*) foods and eggs (*ovo*) in addition to foods from plant sources.
Lacto vegetarianism	Dairy foods in addition to foods from plant sources.
Ovo vegetarianism	Eggs in addition to foods from plant sources. Fortified soy milk and soy cheese are often substituted for dairy products.
Vegan	Foods from plant sources only. Fortified soy milk and soy cheese are often substituted for dairy products.

The main concern for vegans is getting enough protein without consuming any red meat, poultry, or seafood. Vegans are able to get their protein requirements through plants: grains, vegetables, nuts, and seeds. When meals and snacks contain a variety of plant-based foods and calorie intake is sufficient to meet energy needs, protein needs are also met.

✓ CHECKPOINTS

Lesson 2 Review

Using complete sentences, answer the following questions on a sheet of paper.

1. What is the difference between appetite and hunger?
2. What are calories? What do they measure?
3. What is nutrition?
4. Name four factors that contribute to food choices.
5. Why is protein important to your body?
6. Why is calcium needed in your diet?
7. What are *trans* fats?
8. What kinds of foods contain added sugars?
9. Name two foods from each of the five food groups identified in the Dietary Guidelines for Americans.
10. How much physical activity should you do each day?
11. Define foodborne illnesses. How can foodborne illness be prevented?
12. How is nutrient content on the nutrition fact label calculated?
13. What foods are included in a lacto vegetarian plan?

APPLYING YOUR LEARNING

14. Read the Nutrition Facts panel on the label of three foods you eat during a typical day. Compare the nutritional content on these labels with the recommended Dietary Guidelines for Americans. How does your daily intake compare? Write a short paragraph comparing your daily intake with the recommended Dietary Guidelines.

LESSON 3

The Benefits of Physical Activity

Quick Write

Write a short paragraph describing how you would measure a person's fitness level. According to these criteria, would you consider yourself physically fit?

"Lack of activity destroys the good condition of every human being, while movement and methodical physical exercise save it and preserve it."

Plato, ancient Greek philosopher

Learn About

- the benefits of an active lifestyle
- increasing your level of fitness
- aerobic capacity, muscular strength and endurance, and flexibility: three elements of fitness
- setting fitness goals
- the three stages of exercise
- monitoring your progress
- sports safety
- avoiding performance-enhancing drugs (PEDs)

The Benefits of an Active Lifestyle

Physical fitness is an official and integral part of every Junior ROTC program. Physically fit cadets are more capable of serving their communities and nation. Air Force Junior ROTC provides a wellness program as a tool to help you achieve personal fitness goals and national standards calculated for student age and gender. The objective of every AFJROTC fitness program is to motivate cadets to lead active, healthy lifestyles in school and at home.

In 2008, the US government set a standard for young people to do 60 minutes or more of physical activity each day. In a 2013 survey, it appeared that the guidelines were not being met. The survey found that only 29 percent of high school students participated in such activity for 60 or more minutes a day.

A recent review of 14 studies conducted by the medical staff of Peak Fitness® found that physical activity and academic performance are closely linked. Physical activity benefits both your body and mind. Besides promoting your overall health, it helps you look and feel better. When these activities involve other people, you also get social benefits of interacting with other people your age.

Physical activity provides academic and emotional benefits. Being active lets you clear your mind and "burn off" stress. It also helps you feel good about yourself. The "Benefits of Physical Activity" box lists many of the physical, academic/emotional, and social benefits of physical activity.

✓ CHECKPOINTS

Lesson 2 Review

Using complete sentences, answer the following questions on a sheet of paper.

1. What is the difference between appetite and hunger?
2. What are calories? What do they measure?
3. What is nutrition?
4. Name four factors that contribute to food choices.
5. Why is protein important to your body?
6. Why is calcium needed in your diet?
7. What are *trans* fats?
8. What kinds of foods contain added sugars?
9. Name two foods from each of the five food groups identified in the Dietary Guidelines for Americans.
10. How much physical activity should you do each day?
11. Define foodborne illnesses. How can foodborne illness be prevented?
12. How is nutrient content on the nutrition fact label calculated?
13. What foods are included in a lacto vegetarian plan?

APPLYING YOUR LEARNING

14. Read the Nutrition Facts panel on the label of three foods you eat during a typical day. Compare the nutritional content on these labels with the recommended Dietary Guidelines for Americans. How does your daily intake compare? Write a short paragraph comparing your daily intake with the recommended Dietary Guidelines.

LESSON 3

The Benefits of Physical Activity

Quick Write

Write a short paragraph describing how you would measure a person's fitness level. According to these criteria, would you consider yourself physically fit?

Learn About

- the benefits of an active lifestyle
- increasing your level of fitness
- aerobic capacity, muscular strength and endurance, and flexibility: three elements of fitness
- setting fitness goals
- the three stages of exercise
- monitoring your progress
- sports safety
- avoiding performance-enhancing drugs (PEDs)

"Lack of activity destroys the good condition of every human being, while movement and methodical physical exercise save it and preserve it."

Plato, ancient Greek philosopher

The Benefits of an Active Lifestyle

Physical fitness is an official and integral part of every Junior ROTC program. Physically fit cadets are more capable of serving their communities and nation. Air Force Junior ROTC provides a wellness program as a tool to help you achieve personal fitness goals and national standards calculated for student age and gender. The objective of every AFJROTC fitness program is to motivate cadets to lead active, healthy lifestyles in school and at home.

In 2008, the US government set a standard for young people to do 60 minutes or more of physical activity each day. In a 2013 survey, it appeared that the guidelines were not being met. The survey found that only 29 percent of high school students participated in such activity for 60 or more minutes a day.

A recent review of 14 studies conducted by the medical staff of Peak Fitness® found that physical activity and academic performance are closely linked. Physical activity benefits both your body and mind. Besides promoting your overall health, it helps you look and feel better. When these activities involve other people, you also get social benefits of interacting with other people your age.

Physical activity provides academic and emotional benefits. Being active lets you clear your mind and "burn off" stress. It also helps you feel good about yourself. The "Benefits of Physical Activity" box lists many of the physical, academic/emotional, and social benefits of physical activity.

Physical Fitness and the Benefits of Physical Activity and Exercise

The terms *physical fitness*, *activity*, and *exercise* are closely related, but each has its own meaning. Physical fitness is *the ability to perform moderate to vigorous levels of activity, and to respond to physical demands without excessive fatigue.* Physical activity is *any kind of movement that uses up energy.* You use energy by exercising and playing sports. You also use energy by any movements that are part of an active lifestyle. This can include biking to the store, raking leaves, or walking up and down the stairs. Exercise is *a planned and organized session of physical activity that you do to improve or maintain your physical fitness.* How do you become fit? Every expert agrees it is done with regular exercise, sound nutrition, and an active lifestyle.

Vocabulary

- physical fitness
- physical activity
- exercise
- obese
- metabolism
- aerobic exercise
- anaerobic exercise
- sedentary
- aerobic capacity
- cross-training
- strength
- muscle strength
- muscle endurance
- flexibility
- pulse
- warm-up
- exertion
- cool-down
- sports conditioning
- dehydration
- anabolic steroids

Physical Activity and Weight Control

You can become healthier and have a more productive life by raising your level of fitness and maintaining your weight at the recommended range.

Currently, the number of overweight people in the US continues to grow. In 2012, the Center for Disease Control and Prevention (CDC) reported that about two-thirds of all Americans are considered overweight. More than 36 percent are obese. Obese is *having a body weight more than 20 percent greater than recommended for a person of a certain height.* Among teenagers (ages 12 to 19), more than a third are overweight or obese. This growth can be traced to people having inactive lifestyles and overeating.

It is important for all of us to be physically active and develop good eating habits in order to stay within a healthy weight range. Understanding your metabolism, the way the food you eat is converted into energy, can help you maintain a healthy weight.

Metabolism is *the process by which your body gets energy from food.* As we learned from the previous lesson on nutrition, food's energy value is measured in units of heat called calories. Your body needs to take in enough calories each day to function properly. If we consume too many calories, the additional calories must be burned through physical activity or they will be stored in the body as fat. By being physically active, your metabolic rate rises, and your body burns more calories than when it is at rest. The number of calories burned depends in part on the nature of the activity. When you stop being active, your metabolic rate slowly returns to normal. The good news is however, for several hours after being physically active, you will continue to burn more calories than you did before you began the activity. Table 3.4 shows how many calories are burned during common physical activities at both moderate and vigorous levels.

Benefits of Physical Activity

Physical Benefits

- Strengthen heart and lungs
- Strengthen bones
- Manage weight
- Control blood sugar
- Control blood pressure
- Increase strength and stamina
- Improve flexibility and muscle tone
- Improve balance, the feeling of stability and control over your body
- Develop coordination, the smooth and balanced movement of body parts at the same time
- Improve reaction time
- Increase body's defense to diseases
- Improve sleep

Academic/Emotional Benefits

- Feel more alert and energetic
- Reduce stress
- Learn to focus on completing tasks, such as homework
- Learn new things
- Get a sense of accomplishment
- Lessen mental fatigue
- Build a positive self-image
- Increase self-confidence and self-esteem

Social Benefits

- Engage in enjoyable activities
- Meet and interact with new people
- Use abilities to work with others as a team
- Get support from friends
- Share goals and achievements with others

Table 3.4 Calories Used per Hour in Common Physical Activities

	Approximate Calories per 30 Minutes for a 154-lb Person[1]	Approximate Calories per Hour for a 154-lb Person[1]
Moderate Physical Activity		
Hiking	185	370
Light gardening/yard work	165	330
Dancing	165	330
Golf (walking and carrying clubs)	165	330
Bicycling (<10 mph)	145	290
Walking (3.5 mph)	140	280
Weightlifting (general light workout)	110	220
Stretching	90	180
Vigorous Physical Activity		
Running/jogging (5 mph)	295	590
Bicycling (>10 mph)	295	590
Swimming (slow freestyle laps)	255	510
Aerobics	240	480
Walking (4.5 mph)	230	460
Heavy yard work (chopping wood)	220	440
Weightlifting (vigorous effort)	220	440
Basketball (vigorous)	220	440

1. Calories burned per hour will be higher for persons who weigh more than 154 lbs (70 kg) and lower for persons who weigh less.

Source: Adapted from Centers for Disease Control and Prevention: Dietary Guidelines for Americans.

Increasing Your Level of Fitness

The first step to increasing your level of fitness is acknowledging that physical activity is important to your lifelong health and well-being. The next step is to move more! Make physical activity part of your daily life. Becoming more active is easy. Just look around. Instead of using elevators and escalators, take the stairs. Walk or ride a bike when possible, rather than asking your friends, parents, or guardians for a ride.

In addition to looking for everyday opportunities to put your body to work, plan regular exercise. Start in sessions of 10 to 15 minutes at a time. Gradually work up to about 60 minutes 5 to 7 days of the week. If you feel that you do not have time to spare, break down your activity into multiple shorter sessions during the day. Three 10-minute exercise sessions will provide the same benefit as one covering 30 minutes.

Choosing the Right Activities

The second step is to choose activities that you enjoy and will give you the benefits you want. There are two main types of exercise: aerobic and anaerobic. **Aerobic exercise** is *rhythmic, nonstop, and moderate to vigorous activity that requires large amounts of oxygen and improves the cardiorespiratory system.* Running, walking, biking, and swimming are forms of aerobic exercise. **Anaerobic exercise** is *intense physical activity that requires little oxygen but uses short bursts of energy.* Sprinting, weightlifting, and gymnastics are examples of anaerobic exercise. Each type of exercise benefits the body in a particular way. You can combine both types of exercise to achieve optimum fitness. By choosing a variety of activities, you can receive the benefits of both types of exercise.

Technology has certainly made our lives simpler, easier, and more fun. Yet, technology has a downside. It has replaced many of the physical activities that were once part of daily life. People ride instead of walk. They use machines to do the work that used to be done by hand. They sit at home, watching TV, playing games on a computer, or engaging in hours of social media conversation, instead of being outside playing. They send email or text messages instead of walking over to a friend's house.

Think about your own lifestyle. Estimate how many hours a week you watch television or sit at a computer screen. Compare that to the number of hours you spend doing something physically active. Compare the totals. Are you active most of the time or sedentary? **Sedentary** involves *a lot of sitting and very little exercise.* Because you know that physical activity and exercise are essential to fitness, this comparison may make you stop and think about how you spend your time.

Aerobic Capacity, Muscular Strength and Endurance, and Flexibility: Three Elements of Fitness

Exercise is used to develop fitness in four ways. One is aerobic capacity. Another is muscle strength and endurance. The other two ways are flexibility and body composition. We will cover the first three in this lesson, and the fourth, body composition, in Lesson 4. AFJROTC utilizes a tracking program based on the Presidential Fitness Challenge to help cadets track fitness level. Each cadet will establish a fitness baseline and then work toward improvement over the school year. Once cadets establish their fitness baseline, instructors and cadets will be able to assess their improvement at the end of the school year. The physical fitness baseline for cadets is measured from five fitness activities:

- Curl-ups (or partial curl-ups)
- Shuttle Run
- Endurance run/walk
- Pull-ups
- V-sit reach (sit and reach)

Aerobic Capacity

Aerobic capacity refers to *the ability of your heart and lungs to supply the muscles of your body with oxygen.* Heart and lung capacity is important in all kinds of exercise—running, biking, jumping rope, swimming, and walking. Measuring aerobic capacity, including how far you can run without stopping, or how long you can play basketball without tiring, are indicators of your heart and lung endurance. Learn to pace yourself so that you can walk or jog without stopping. The best way to build up heart and lung endurance is by doing moderate to vigorous exercise for at least 60 minutes on most days. This is called cardiovascular exercise because it raises your breathing and heart rates. This increase benefits your heart and the blood vessels that make up the cardiovascular system. Some cardiovascular improving exercises are:

- **Walking/jogging/running**—Start off slowly, and then gradually increase your pace. Work up to a 30-minute walk, or alternate walking and jogging until you can jog or run for 20 minutes without stopping.
- **Swimming**—Swimming provides a total body workout. Gradually work up to 20 minutes of continuous swimming. Swim at a steady pace and vary your routine by using different strokes.
- **Jumping rope**—As you jump, guard your joints against unnecessary strain by raising your feet just high enough to allow the rope to pass. Gradually build up your ability until you can jump rope for 60 seconds without stopping.

It's also a good idea to vary your exercise routines. Cross-training, or *switching between different exercises* has benefits over doing one exercise all the time. Whatever exercises you choose, try to vary them equally, and don't overdo it. Cross-training can also help reduce boredom of doing one type of exercise over and over again. It can also help reduce the chance of injury by working different muscle groups instead of overusing one group, as may happen if your only exercise is running. Overuse of one muscle group can cause weakness in another area of the body, possibly resulting in injury. A good form of cross-training for someone who runs is to include weightlifting. Weightlifting provides muscular strength while running improves heart and lung endurance.

Muscle Strength and Endurance

The ability of your muscles to exert a force is called strength. Muscle strength is *the most force you can exert or weight you can lift at one time.* Muscle endurance is *the ability of a muscle to repeatedly exert a force over a prolonged period.* The greater your muscle strength, the more force your muscles can exert. The greater your muscle endurance, the longer your muscles can exert force.

Three basic strengthening exercises help improve strength and endurance of your abdominal area and upper body. These include push-ups, curl-ups, and step-ups:

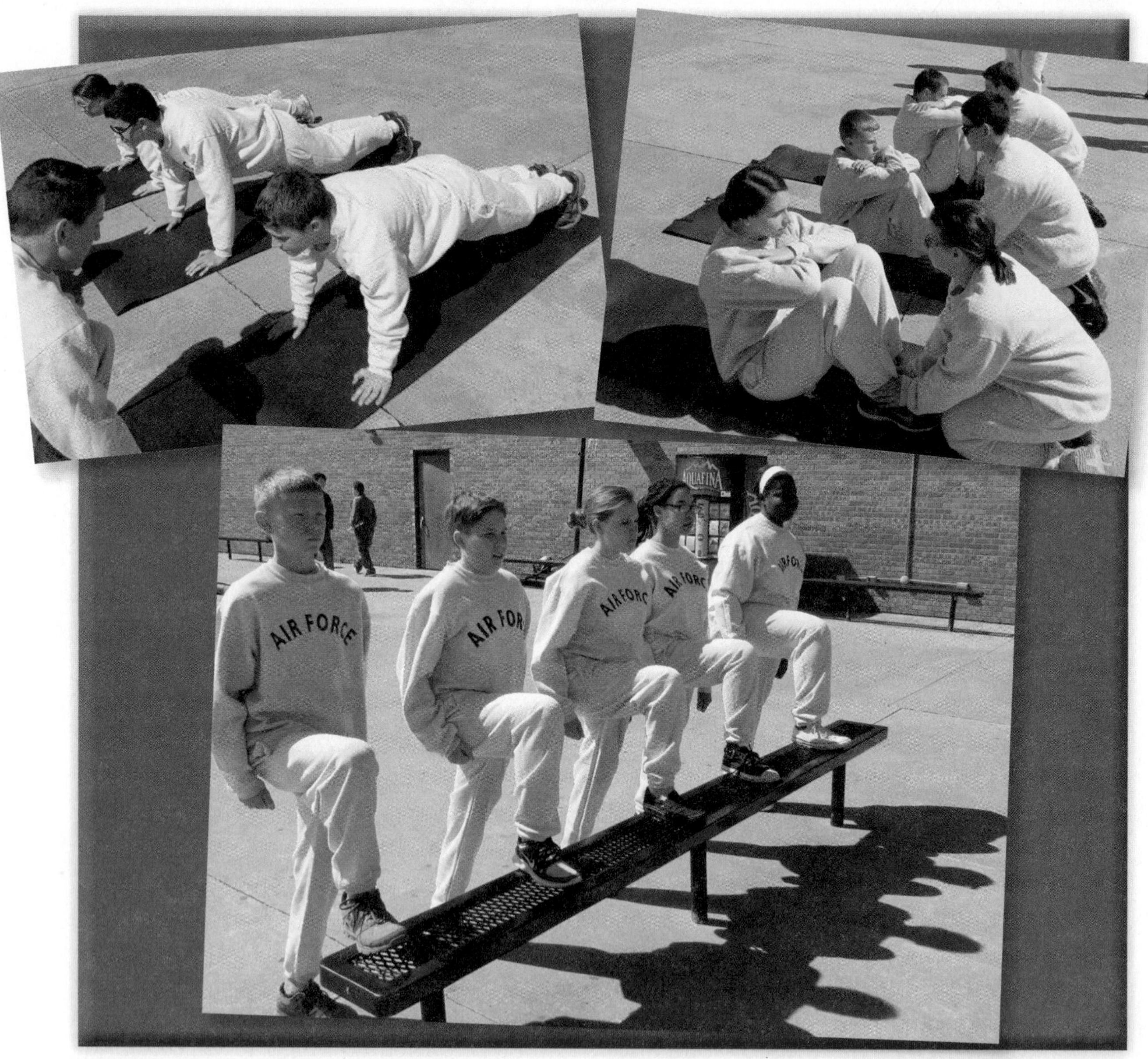

Push-ups, curl-ups, and step-ups are three basic strengthening exercises.
All photos courtesy of Michael Wetzel/US Air Force JROTC

- **Push-ups strengthen muscles in your arms and chest**—Lie face down on the floor. Bend your arms and place your palms flat on the floor beneath your shoulders. Straighten your arms, pushing your entire body upward, and then lower your body to the floor. Repeat.
- **Curl-ups strengthen your abdominal muscles**—Lie on your back with your knees bent and your heels on the floor. Cross your arms over your chest. Curl your upper body forward so that both shoulder blades come off the floor. Uncurl and repeat.
- **Step-ups strengthen your leg muscles**—Step up onto a step with your left foot and then bring your right foot up. Step down with your left foot and bring the right foot down. Repeat, alternating between feet.

Many high school-age students become interested in weight training because it's a good way to build muscle strength. You should start with lifting light weights multiple times. Make sure, however, that you learn from an expert, such as a fitness trainer or physical education teacher. Lifting weights properly prevents injury and provides the best chance for improvement.

keys to LEADERSHIP

Weight training is an important aspect of fitness that you should start during high school and continue throughout your life.

Flexibility

The third step of fitness, **flexibility**, is *the ability of your body's joints to move easily through a full range of motion*. When you have good flexibility, you can easily bend, turn, and stretch your body. People with limited flexibility may move stiffly or strain parts of their body.

Figure 3.11 shows how to measure the flexibility of muscles in your lower back and the back of your legs. You can improve your flexibility through regular stretching, bending, and twisting exercises. Move slowly and gently, and improve the flexibility of different muscle groups gradually. One tool used to measure flexibility is the V-sit reach testing as explained in Figure 3.11.

Your Target Heart Rate

Finally, the Centers for Disease Control and Prevention (CDC) recommends that you monitor your heart rate during exercise to ensure you reach target heart rates. When you are exercising, you should increase your heart rate to at least 50 percent of your maximum rate to provide a benefit for your heart and lungs. The **pulse** (or heart rate) is *the regular expansion and contraction of an artery, caused by the heart pumping blood through the body*. The heart rate that will safely provide the greatest benefit when exercising is between 60 and 80 percent of your maximum rate. This is your target pulse rate (also known as target heart rate).

Here's how you perform V-sit reach testing:

- A straight line two feet long is marked on the floor as the baseline.
- A measuring line four feet long is drawn perpendicular to the midpoint of the baseline extending two feet on each side and marked off in half-inches. The point where the baseline and measuring line intersect is the "0" point.
- Student removes shoes and sits on floor with measuring line between legs and soles of feet placed immediately behind baseline, heels 8 to 12 inches apart.
- With hands on top of each other, palms down, the student places them on measuring line.
- With the legs held flat by a partner, the student slowly reaches forward as far as possible, keeping fingers on the measuring line and feet flexed.
- After three practice tries, the student holds the fourth reach for three seconds while that distance is recorded.

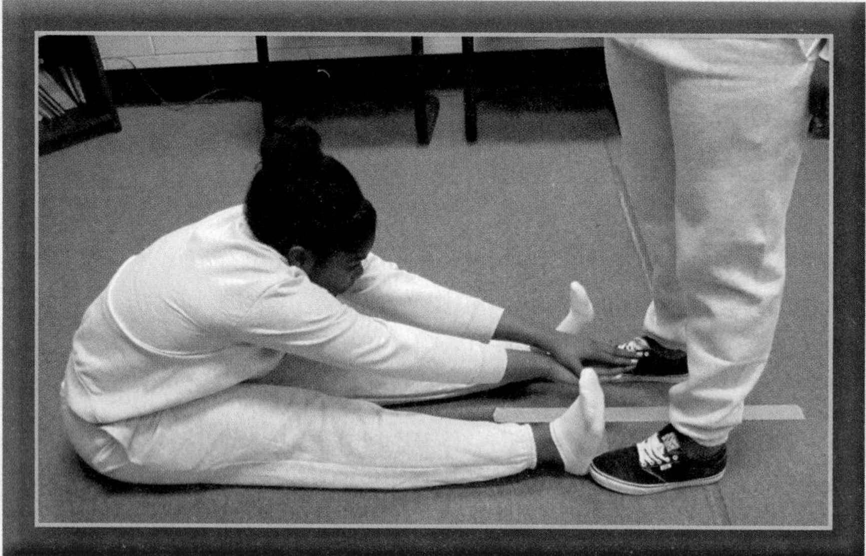

Courtesy of Michael Wetzel/US Air Force JROTC

V-sit reach tip:

Participants are most flexible after a warm-up run. Best results may occur after performing a good warm-up.

FIGURE 3.11

V-sit Reach Testing

For moderate-intensity physical activity, a person's target heart rate should be 50 to 70 percent of his or her maximum heart rate. This maximum rate is based on the person's age. An estimate of a person's maximum age-related heart rate can be obtained by subtracting the person's age from 220. For example, for a 16-year-old person, the estimated maximum age-related heart rate would be calculated as 220 − 16 years = 204 beats per minute (bpm). The 50 percent and 70 percent levels would be:

- **50 percent level**—204 × 0.50 = 102 bpm
- **70 percent level**—204 × 0.70 = 143 bpm

For vigorous-intensity physical activity, a person's target heart rate should be 70 to 85 percent of his or her maximum heart rate. To calculate this range, follow the same formula as used above, except change "50 and 70 percent" to "70 and 85 percent." For example, for a 17-year-old person, the estimated maximum age-related heart rate would be calculated as 220 − 17 years = 203 beats per minute (bpm). The 70 percent and 85 percent levels would be:

- **70 percent level**—203 × 0.70 = 142 bpm
- **85 percent level**—203 × 0.85 = 173 bpm

Thus, vigorous-intensity physical activity for a 17-year-old person will require that the heart rate remain between 142 and 173 bpm during physical activity.

Measuring Your Heart Rate

The CDC recommends the following method to determine whether you are exercising within the heart rate target zone. You must stop exercising briefly to take your pulse. You can take the pulse at the neck, the wrist, or the chest. We recommend the wrist. You can feel the pulse on the artery of the wrist in line with the thumb. Place the tips of the index and middle fingers over the artery and press lightly. **Do not use the thumb**. Take a full 60-second count of the heartbeats, or take for 30 seconds and multiply by 2. Start the count on a beat, which is counted as "zero." If this number falls between 102 and 143 beats per minute in the case of the 17-year-old person, he or she is active within the target range for moderate-intensity exercise.

Measuring pulse at the wrist.

© ia_64/Fotolia.com

After two weeks, ask yourself, "Was my heart rate generally within the range of my target heart rate? Which forms of exercise produced the highest rate? The lowest?"

After reading this section and completing the physical activities described, you should have a clearer idea of your aerobic capacity, muscle strength and endurance, and flexibility. Are you as physically fit as you should be? Are you as fit as you would like to be? If you want to raise your level of physical fitness, you'll need to set goals for yourself and then decide how to achieve these goals. Remember to consider your limits, though. Some people improve faster than others, and some people have a higher fitness potential than others.

The role of heredity and overall health are also important in your physical abilities. For example, if you have asthma, you may become short of breath when exercising. If you have a physical impairment, you may not be able to participate in all activities. To develop a realistic plan that is right for you, check with your doctor before pursuing specific fitness goals.

Setting Fitness Goals

A personal fitness plan can help you achieve the level of fitness that will improve your general health and improve your endurance. However, a plan can become confusing. You may wonder which exercises or other physical activities will best help you reach your fitness goals. Maybe you're not sure how to do an exercise. You can, however, turn to your instructor, a physical education teacher, or coach for help. Any of these experts can show you how to get started, what equipment to use, and how to exercise safely. An expert can also help you stay motivated. You can get an idea of how to proceed by looking at Table 3.5, which compares different types of activities for their benefits.

Whatever your fitness goals may be, try to do one or more forms of physical activity or exercise each day. Being fit and healthy means performing exercises that will improve endurance, flexibility, and strength. Setting goals is an important step in starting a fitness program. Keep in mind that the goals you set should be reasonable and realistic. Using the SMART system will help you set reachable goals.

Example of Setting a SMART Goal

Specific:
Be able to run three miles

Measurable:
Log activity each week

Attainable:
Run/walk for 30 minutes three times a week

Results:
Run a 10-minute mile by the end of the month

Time Frame:
I want to be able to do this by the end of the month

Table 3.5 Rating Different Activities*

Exercise	Muscle Strength and Endurance	Lung Strength and Endurance	Heart Strength and Endurance
Handball	High	High	High
Swimming	High	Medium	High
Jogging	Medium	High	High
Bicycling	Medium	High	High
Tennis	High	Medium	Medium
Brisk walking	Medium	High	High
Slow walking	Low	Medium	Medium
Softball	Medium	Low	Low
Weight training	High	High	Low

*The ratings in this chart show the benefits of activities done for 30 minutes or more.

Be Active Every Day

Even if you don't set specific fitness goals, you should look for opportunities to be active every day. Take time away from the computer or other mind-stimulating but sedentary activities in favor of activities requiring body movement. Take stairs instead of an elevator or escalator. Bike to a friend's house. Walk to the store (if it's safe). Do outdoor work like raking leaves or shoveling snow.

Preparing an Activity Plan

If you feel confident enough to do your own fitness planning, a weekly activity outline like the one in Figure 3.12 can be helpful. A written plan will keep you on track and help you exercise consistently. There are two things to do when developing your plan. First, write down all of your scheduled physical activities or exercise sessions. These would include gym periods, team practices, and drill practice. Second, pencil in a variety of physical activities and exercises. Try to balance your schedule so that every day you have some activities listed, but no single day is overloaded. Also, be flexible, and include some choices. For example, you might write, "Jog or bike ride," and then decide which activity you prefer when that day comes.

Keep in mind that your activity plan should meet your personal fitness goals. You may also find that it is not that hard to stay active.

A written plan will help you include a balance of activities in your weekly schedule.

Sunday	Monday	Tuesday	Wednesday	Thursday	Friday	Saturday
Bike ride **1 hr.**	Gym class **50 min.**	Basketball or jog after class **40 min.**	Gym class **50 min.**	Basketball or jog after class **40 min.**	Gym class **50 min.**	Soccer game **1 hr.**
	Soccer practice **2 hrs.**	Karate class **1 hr.**	Soccer practice **2 hrs.**	Karate class **1 hr.**	Walk home from school **20 min.**	Karate class **1 hr.**
	Walk home from practice **20 min.**	Drill practice **1 hr.**		Drill practice **1 hr.**		
TOTAL **1 hr.**	TOTAL **3 hr. 10 min.**	TOTAL **2 hr. 40 min.**	TOTAL **2 hr. 50 min.**	TOTAL **2 hr. 40 min.**	TOTAL **1 hr. 10 min.**	TOTAL **2 hr.**

FIGURE 3.12

A Sample Weekly Activity Plan

The Three Stages of Exercise

Every exercise program should have three stages: the beginning warm-up, the workout itself, and then the cool-down. Because all three stages are important, it's important not to skip any of them.

Warming Up

A **warm-up** is *a period of low to moderate exercise to prepare your body for more vigorous activity*. You should start every exercise session with a warm-up lasting about 10 minutes. During this warm-up, your heart rate should gradually increase, and your body temperature should start to rise.

As the flow of blood to your muscles increases, they become more flexible, which makes them less prone to injury during exercise. You should begin a warm-up with gentle aerobic activities, such as a fast walk or light jogging, followed by stretching exercises. When you stretch, move slowly, and stretch the muscles little by little. Be careful not to overstretch or bounce as you stretch, which can damage body joints or tissues. Figure 3.13 shows two typical stretching exercises. Some stretches are not good for your joints, so ask your instructor or teacher for a good stretching routine.

Another way to warm up is to do the actual movements of your planned activity but at a slow and easy pace. For example, if you plan to play softball or baseball, you might want to warm up by gently throwing the ball back and forth with a teammate. Then, do some light jogging and finally a variety of stretching exercises.

Working Out

Once you have warmed up, you're ready to work out. Your workouts should start at a comfortable level of exertion, and then build up gradually. **Exertion** is *the act of strenuous exercise or effort*. Some guidelines for starting and increasing your workout program include:

- **Frequency**—Gradually increase the number of times you exercise per week. Start by exercising two or three times the first week and work your way up to exercising daily.
- **Intensity**—This refers to the difficulty of your physical activity or exercise session. The most common way of gauging intensity is in terms of heart rate. You can usually increase intensity by speeding up—running faster, for example, or doing more sit-ups in less time. You can also increase intensity by making yourself work harder. For example, it's a lot harder to bike up a hill than along a flat road.
- **Duration**—Limit your workout sessions to about 10 to 15 minutes at first. Gradually increase the time until you're exercising for about 45 to 60 minutes each session. Remember to aim for 60 minutes of physical activity on most days.

Different stretching exercises benefit different parts of the body. These exercises stretch calves and shoulders.
How do you warm up before you exercise?

Calf Stretch

Lean against a wall for support, as shown, and place your palms flat against the surface. Bend one leg, and keep the other leg extended. While keeping the heel of the extended leg on the ground, move your hips forward until you feel a stretch in the calf muscle.

Shoulder Stretch

Stand with your feet shoulder width apart. Reach back with your left or right hand, trying to touch your spine. Use the opposite hand to gently put pressure by placing it on the elbow, as shown in photo. Gently apply pressure to stretch shoulder muscles. Alternate with other arm.

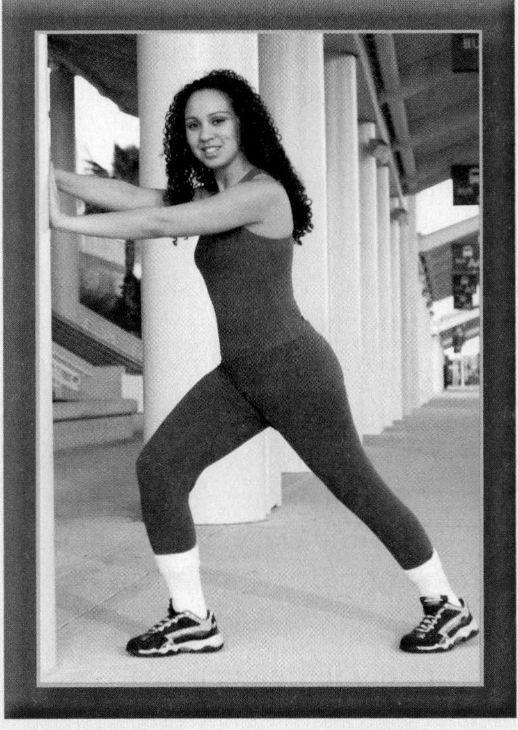

Calf stretch.
© Frank Herzog/Fotolia.com

Shoulder stretch.
© Nicholas Piccillo/Fotolia.com

FIGURE 3.13
Stretching Exercises

- **Order**—If you're doing both aerobic and strength-building exercises during a workout session, perform the aerobic exercise first. Your muscles will work more smoothly after aerobic activity. If you want to build on your workout, do it gradually. Change only one element at a time. For example, if you increase the duration of your workout, keep frequency and intensity the same.

Cooling Down

Just as a warm-up should precede your workout, a cool-down should follow it. A cool-down is *a period of low to moderate exercise to prepare your body to end a workout session.* Cooling down helps return blood circulation and body temperature to normal.

If you end a workout abruptly, your muscles may tighten up and you may feel faint or dizzy. To avoid such effects, slow your body down gradually. Continue the movements of your workout activity, but at a slower, easier pace. A cool-down should last about ten minutes, and it should include gentle stretching exercises.

Monitoring Your Progress

As you work toward your fitness goals, monitoring your progress becomes important. Remember that change comes gradually. You can't expect to cut 30 seconds off your mile time after only a week of working out. Here are some suggestions for evaluating your progress.

- Keep an exercise log or journal, making performance notes after each workout.
- After four to six weeks of workouts, you should notice some improvement in your overall fitness. Depending on the exercises you have been doing, you should feel stronger. You should have more endurance and greater flexibility. You will probably also feel better overall, look more fit, and have more energy.
- If you see no significant change after six weeks, you need to evaluate the situation. Have you been exercising regularly? Do you need to modify your fitness goals? Another measure of fitness is your resting heart rate, the number of times per minute your heart beats when your body is at rest. The average heartbeat rate ranges from 72 to 84 beats per minute. A resting heartbeat rate less than 72 is generally associated with good physical fitness.
- Once you reach your fitness goals, you might consider setting new goals for yourself.

Choosing the Right Activity

Think about the kinds of activities you enjoy most. There may be a number of individual or team sports that can provide personal satisfaction and a way to stay active, or one sport may suit your needs better than others. No matter what choice or choices you make, playing sports has many benefits.

Individual Sports

Individual sports that you do on your own or with a friend, like biking, running, walking, swimming, golf, and skating have more time flexibility than team sports. You can do them whenever you feel like it, and you can do them for as long as you wish. However, there are two major disadvantages of individual sports. You have to set your own time to do the activity and stick to it. You also have to motivate yourself to keep that schedule once set. Some people find it hard to stick to a plan if they have to do it on their own.

Team Sports

You may prefer, as many young people do, organized team sports. In high school, there are many opportunities for team sports such as softball, baseball, soccer, basketball, volleyball, and football. Other team sports such as track, tennis, golf, swimming, and wrestling are also common. These require individual performances, but they contribute to a team's overall scores or match wins.

Although schools offer a variety of team sports, most of these sports are also offered through local recreation departments and community centers. Other youth programs through churches and synagogues offer sports, as do some sports and fitness centers.

Advantages of team sports are several. Many young people like the excitement of competition. You have the companionship and support of teammates and coaches as you work together toward a common goal. Playing on a team also gives you an opportunity to develop communication and social skills. You learn about cooperation, compromise, and good sportsmanship.

Of course, having a schedule that requires several team practices and games after school every week and on weekends may interfere with family and school commitments. If these commitments prevent you from participating in team sports, individual sports may offer a better fitness alternative.

Playing sports provides an academic and emotional impact as well as a physical one. Playing sports raises your body temperature, which also has calming emotional effects. In addition, playing sports teaches the mind to focus on a game or competition rather than other worries and anxieties. This ability to focus may carry over to your academics if you use the same strategies learned from sports.

Sports Conditioning

Whether you choose an individual sport or a team sport, you need to be physically fit to do your best. It takes time and effort to be in good physical condition for sports.

Sports conditioning is *regular physical activity or exercise to strengthen and condition muscles for a particular sport.* In addition, proper conditioning requires you to eat healthy, learn safety rules, and use the right kind of equipment. Whether you choose to participate in team or individual sports, it is important to work with a coach or sports trainer to develop a conditioning program for the sport in which you participate. The correct conditioning program will properly prepare you to get the most out of your sport or exercise.

Living an active lifestyle helps you feel good about yourself.
Courtesy of Michael Wetzel/US Air Force JROTC

Sports and Nutrition

An important part of sports conditioning is having a balanced, nutritious diet. Just as you learned from the previous lesson, your choice of foods should include a wide variety that gives you energy but has a limited amount of fat. Here are some things to remember about your diet when conditioning:

- **Carbohydrates**—Your body needs extra energy to play sports. Fruits, vegetables, pasta, and whole-grain breads provide the needed carbohydrates as an energy source.
- **Vitamins and minerals**—If you play any sport actively, you'll need to get plenty of calcium, potassium fiber, magnesium, and vitamin E. These nutrients are essential to a balanced diet and to sports conditioning. Calcium, for example, strengthens bones, while iron helps provide muscles with oxygen during physical activity.
- **Protein**—Athletes need protein, but no more than anyone else, as long as their diets include enough nutritious foods. Even though protein helps to build muscle tissue, it is only through exercise and training that you can fully develop your muscles.
- **Water**—If you play sports, your body will lose water through sweating. To maintain fluid balance, take in plenty of fluids during the activity, and drink several glasses of water or other fluid after practice or a game. Your goal is to avoid dehydration, *an excessive water loss from the body*, which can lead to dizziness, muscle cramps, and possible serious medical problems.

Sports Safety

Whenever you exercise or participate in sports, you increase the risk of injury. To reduce that risk, you need to employ safe behavior; use safe, proper equipment; and know your physical limits.

Safe Behavior

Many sports-related injuries can be prevented by always promoting safety:

- **Exercise where and when it's safe**—A soft, even surface is easier on your legs, knees, and feet. You should exercise with another person and avoid deserted places. Protect yourself during hot weather by drinking plenty of fluids, using sunscreen outdoors, and exercising in the cooler mornings or evenings.
- **Always warm up and cool down**—Gradually get your body ready to begin an exercise routine with a proper warm-up. Then, end your workout by cooling down.
- **Practice your sport regularly**—Practices, whether with a team, or with just a playing partner, help you maintain physical fitness levels and help you and your teammates learn to work together effectively and safely.
- **Learn the proper techniques and rules of the game**—Following the rules and regulations of a sport promotes both safety and good sportsmanship.
- **Keep your emotions under control**—Anger or frustration can lead to unsafe or risky actions. Try to stay calm and relaxed.

Safe Equipment

Your clothing and equipment choices will affect your safety. Here are some examples of what you should do:

- **Wear loose-fitting or stretchable clothes**—For some sports, clothing that fits loosely gives you freedom of movement and helps you stay cooler. For other sports, tight, stretchable clothes are more appropriate.
- **If you exercise outdoors, make yourself visible**—Wear light-colored and reflective clothing so you'll be visible to drivers, especially during the hours of darkness.
- **When exercising in cold weather, dress in layers**—You can easily add or remove layers as needed during your workout.
- **Wear protective equipment**—Different sports require protection for different parts of the body. Always wear the right protective gear for the sport you are playing.
- **Choose shoes carefully**—Shoes should fit properly, feel comfortable, provide adequate support, and be suitable for the activity you have chosen.
- **Select your equipment wisely**—Whether you're picking skates, a helmet, or a baseball glove, take the time to make a wise choice.

Know Your Limits

When exercising or playing sports, it's important to recognize your limits. Exceeding your personal limits could lead to injury:

- **Listen to your body**—Exercise can cause discomfort, like mild loss of breath or tired muscles, but pain is not normal. If you're feeling pain, your body is telling you to slow down, rest, or stop completely. If pain persists, see a doctor.
- **Stop if you get injured or feel ill**—If you get hurt while exercising or while playing in a game, don't continue until someone checks you out. Consult a coach, fitness trainer, school nurse, or doctor. Also, don't play sports if you're not feeling well.
- **Rest, Ice, Compress, and Elevate (RICE) injured areas**—Follow the RICE formula if you have a minor sports injury like a sprained ankle. First Aid will be covered in more detail in a later lesson.

Avoiding Performance-Enhancing Drugs (PEDs)

According to the National Center for Drug Free Sport®, performance-enhancing drugs are any substance taken to perform better athletically. Some athletes from high school all the way through the professional ranks in sports have either experimented with or started regular use of PEDs. Although there are many forms of PEDs, one common drug used is anabolic steroids; these are *drugs that cause muscle tissue to develop at an abnormally fast rate*. PEDs provide the ability for athletes to perform at a higher level by increasing their strength, endurance, and recovery from injury. However, the use of these drugs is both dangerous and, in almost every sport, illegal. In addition, athletes who test positive and admit to having used these drugs eventually find their reputations and their ability to participate in sports are negatively affected.

Among the physical and medical side effects users of PEDs may experience are:

- Weakening of tendons, leading to joint or tendon injuries
- Cardiovascular damage and high blood pressure, raising the risk of heart attack
- Mental and emotional effects, such as anxiety, severe mood swings, uncontrolled rage, and delusions
- Severe acne
- Trembling
- Bone damage
- Liver and brain cancers
- Facial hair growth in females and breast development in males

A complete list of PED side effects and health concerns can be found on the United States Anti-Doping Agency website: *http://www.usada.org/effects-peds/*.

Performance-enhancing drugs have no place in a healthy fitness plan. Besides damaging your body, they can destroy a potential career in athletics.

✓ CHECKPOINTS

Lesson 3 Review

Using complete sentences, answer the following questions on a sheet of paper.

1. What are three examples of the academic/emotional benefits of physical activity?
2. Define physical activity.
3. Why does the body need calories?
4. What is the difference between aerobic exercise and anaerobic exercise?
5. Name two activities technology has replaced that once were part of our daily lives.
6. What is the downside of technology in terms of our general physical fitness?
7. Define aerobic capacity.
8. What is the best way to build up heart and lung endurance?
9. What is the difference between muscle strength and muscle endurance?
10. What should be a person's target heart rate for moderate-intensity physical activity?
11. List three activities that can help you achieve fitness goals.
12. What activity is rated highest in all three categories for achieving fitness if done for 30 minutes or more?
13. Why should you have a written physical activity plan?
14. What are the three stages of an exercise workout?
15. Why should you always have a cool-down stage when exercising?
16. What should you notice about your fitness progress after four to six weeks of workouts?
17. If you don't see a noticeable change of fitness after six weeks of workouts, what should you do?
18. What should you keep in mind when preparing an activity plan?
19. What is sports conditioning?
20. Define dehydration.
21. When you participate in sports, why is it important to practice regularly?
22. What three areas should you consider when exercising so that you stay within your physical limits?
23. What are performance-enhancing drugs (PEDs)?
24. What are three negative side effects of taking PEDs?

APPLYING YOUR LEARNING

25. Create a weekly physical activity plan using Figure 3.12 as a guide. As part of your plan, write down what safety measures you would use for each activity to reduce your chance of injury.

LESSON 4

Understanding Your Body Image

Quick Write

Many magazines and electronic media sources alter body images of young people and adults so they appear in the photo as thinner, heavier, or taller than they really are. Are these photos realistic? Should this really be done? Write down your opinions on this topic.

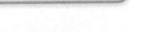

"The next time you look into the mirror, try to let go of the story line that says you're too fat or too shallow, your eyes are too small or your nose too big; just look into the mirror and see your face. When the criticism drops away, what you will see then is just you, without judgment, and that is the first step toward transforming your experience of the world."

Oprah Winfrey

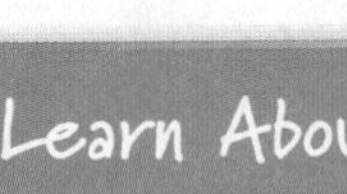

Learn About

- what is body image?
- weight problems and diet
- managing your appropriate weight
- the dangers of eating disorders

What Is Body Image?

How do you react when you look at yourself in the mirror? How do you feel about your appearance? *The way you see your physical self* is called your **body image**. Someone who feels good about his or her looks is more likely to have a positive self-image. Trying to look the same as a model, athlete, or anyone else can be unhealthy and unrealistic.

You should recognize that no individual weight or body type is ideal for a specific age. Your body will grow and change throughout your teen years. A few extra pounds now, for example, could disappear in a few months after you grow an inch. Someone who feels too skinny may gain weight after he or she stops growing. Physical activity will also have an effect on your body weight and shape.

Your Appropriate Weight

Many factors influence your **appropriate weight**, or *the weight that is best for your body*. Gender, height, age, body frame (small, medium, or large), and, during your teen years, your growth pattern are among these factors.

Body Composition

In Lesson 3, you learned about the first three elements of fitness. They are aerobic capacity, muscular strength and endurance, and flexibility. The fourth element is body composition, *the ratio of body fat to lean body tissue, such as bone, muscle, and fluid.* One way to measure body composition is to use Body Mass Index (BMI), *a measurement that allows you to assess your body size, taking your height and weight into account.* BMI is a reliable indicator of body fatness and can be used to identify possible weight problems in young people and adults. BMI is used to compare your weight relative to your height and to estimate your total body fat. Here is how to calculate your BMI: $w(lbs)/h(in)^2$:

STEP 1 Write down your weight in pounds (lbs)

STEP 2 Write down your height in inches (in)

STEP 3 Square your height (height × height)

STEP 4 Divide your weight by your height squared: $w(lbs)/h(in)^2$

STEP 5 Multiply by 703 to find BMI

Example:

Body Mass Index can be calculated using pounds and inches with this equation:

$$\text{BMI} = \frac{\text{(Weight in pounds)}}{\text{(Height in inches)} \times \text{(Height in inches)}} \times 703$$

For example, a person who weighs 220 pounds and is 6 feet 3 inches tall has a BMI of 27.5.

$$\frac{\text{(220 lbs)}}{\text{(75 in)} \times \text{(75 in)}} \times 703 = 27.5$$

BMI Considerations

BMI is used as a screening tool to identify possible weight problems for young people. Centers for Disease Control and Prevention (CDC) and the American Academy of Pediatrics (AAP) recommend the use of BMI to screen for overweight and obesity in young people beginning at two years old.

Vocabulary

- body image
- appropriate weight
- body composition
- Body Mass Index (BMI)
- overweight
- underweight
- malnutrition
- osteoporosis
- anabolism
- catabolism
- endocrine system
- Basal Metabolic Rate (BMR)
- fasting
- obsession
- eating disorders
- anorexia nervosa
- bulimia nervosa
- binge eating disorder

keys to LEADERSHIP

The best ways to improve and maintain a healthy body composition are by eating nutritious, low-fat, low-sugar foods, and participating in regular physical activity.

For young people, BMI is used to screen for obesity, overweight, healthy weight, or underweight. However, BMI is not a diagnostic tool. For example, a young person may have a high BMI for their age and sex.

You are more likely to feel good about yourself and have the energy you need for peak performance if your weight is at an appropriate level.

Weight Problems and Diet

Being overweight or underweight is unhealthy. People who are **overweight** *weigh more than the appropriate weight range for gender, height, age, body frame, and growth pattern*. People who are **underweight** *weigh less than the appropriate weight range for gender, height, age, body frame, and growth pattern*. Because of pressure placed on young people from family, friends, and social images, they can become overly concerned that they have a weight problem. In reality, most young people don't need to lose or gain weight. In fact, unnecessary dieting can interfere with normal growth and development.

Overweight

Eating foods with high amounts of sugar and fat or eating more food than needed can lead to weight gain. This is especially true for people who are *sedentary,* a term we learned from the previous lesson involves a lot of sitting and very little exercise. Many times, people tend to eat foods with empty calories or low nutritional value; this may result in overeating because you may not feel full. As we learned from Lesson 2, *empty calorie* foods have high amounts of sugar and fats, and do not contain the full range of vitamins and nutrients the body needs to be healthy.

Many young people tend to grab food from fast-food places and convenience stores. Much of this food is high in fat, sugar, and empty calories. Some fast-food restaurants even allow supersize portions, which attract people to them through bargain prices and other selling techniques. These supersize portions may come at a bargain price, but they also come with much more fat, sugar, and calories.

If you have a sedentary lifestyle, this may make you more prone to weight gain. Many jobs require people to spend their day sitting at a desk. At home, many people watch too much television, play video games, or stay on a computer for long periods. These activities burn fewer calories than those involving physical movement.

As we have discussed in previous lessons, excess weight puts strain on the heart and lungs. Overweight people have an increased risk of developing high blood pressure, diabetes, heart disease, cancer, and stroke. If you think that you are overweight, check your BMI, review the results, and if necessary check with a health care professional. You may just be gaining weight before getting taller. This is the body's way of storing up extra energy for growing.

Underweight

Young people who appear skinny are not necessarily underweight. Some are simply growing taller first. After reaching a certain height, the body may take time to catch up and add shape and muscle.

Some people are underweight because they do not consume enough nutrients, eating mostly empty calorie foods. Others are underweight because of extreme dieting or excessive exercise. As we have learned in previous lessons, foods with the right amount of nutrients and calories provide the best foundation for staying healthy. Being underweight increases health risks just as much as being overweight.

Being underweight may indicate **malnutrition**, *a condition in which the body doesn't get the nutrients it needs to grow and function properly*. Being underweight may lower your body's ability to recover from illness, fight infections, and heal wounds.

According to a study published in 2010 in *The Baltic Journal of Health and Physical Activity*, underweight people have lower bone mass densities. This may lead to **osteoporosis**, *a condition marked by bone loss, brittle and fragile bones, bone pain, and increased risk of fractures to bones*. Although seen more in older people, being underweight can lead to osteoporosis in young people.

People who often feel tired due to lack of nutrients that supply energy may be more likely to develop medical issues such as anemia, which is related to this low nutrient intake. Anemia is a deficiency of red blood cells. As we learned from a previous lesson, red blood cells help transport oxygen to our organs and muscles. Being underweight can also lower your immune system, making you more likely to catch colds or the flu.

The Role of Calories

The calories you take in and use every day affect your weight. As you remember, calories measure both the energy available in food and the energy your body uses. The more calories a food contains, the more energy it provides.

You consume calories whenever you eat and drink. When you take in the same number of calories that your body burns, your weight should remain the same. When your body burns more calories than you take in, you should lose weight. When you take in more calories than your body burns, you will gain weight. Your body converts and stores the extra calories as fat.

When you're thirsty, choose water instead of a soft drink. A 12-ounce can of cola may have 150 empty calories.

A healthy eating plan is based on foods rich in nutrients rather than the number of calories they contain. Instead of eating two slices of pizza for lunch at 375 calories per slice, try a different approach. Eat one pizza slice (375 calories), a garden salad (180 calories), an apple (110 calories), and an orange (85 calories). Each choice totals 750 calories, but the nutrients in the second choice are far greater.

The body is good at storing fat cells for future energy use. Storing fat above or below your BMI is unhealthy, and can lead to medical problems. On average, teen females require 2,200–2,400 calories per day, and teen males require 2,800–3,200. If you are counting calories, eating too much or too little in a given day is less important than focusing on your average intake over the long term.

Managing a healthy weight also requires more than counting calories. Make sure you consider the nutrient value of the foods you eat and stay away from empty calorie foods.

Managing Your Appropriate Weight

An earlier recommendation suggested that if you think you might be over or under your appropriate weight, you should check with a health care professional. This person can analyze your situation and suggest the best approach for you to manage weight. Most successful weight-change programs combine increased physical activity with a healthy eating plan that includes nutrient-dense foods.

Increasing Physical Activity

There is one key ingredient whether you are trying to lose or gain weight. Physical activity is the key to keeping a healthy weight. As you learned earlier, physical activity helps tone muscles and reduce body fat. You can also burn more calories by increasing your level of activity. The following box lists some of the other benefits of regular physical activity.

Adjusting Your Calorie Intake

Whether the goal is to lose or gain weight, eating foods with nutritional value will provide the best chance for reaching your goal. Instead of fried foods, you should eat foods that are broiled, baked, or steamed. If you do a little of your own cooking, you can add flavor by using herbs and spices instead of oils or cream sauces. Drinking fewer drinks with high amounts of sugar or caffeine will also help. Drinking more water or drinks that replenish nutrients will also help manage your intake of calories.

When you are increasing or reducing calorie intake, it's always best to eat more servings of lean and low-fat foods, including those with complex carbohydrates, such as whole grain breads, pastas, and fresh vegetables. Whether you want to reduce or increase calorie intake, use information from the Dietary Guidelines for Americans or ChooseMyPlate.gov.

Physical Activity and Your Weight

Physical activity helps you manage your weight and stay healthy.

How do you stay physically active?

Physical Activity...

- **A** Helps you manage stress.
- **B** Can help strengthen and firm muscles.
- **C** Helps your heart and lungs work better.
- **D** Burns calories and helps you maintain a healthy weight.
- **E** Helps you feel good, have more energy, and develop higher self-esteem.

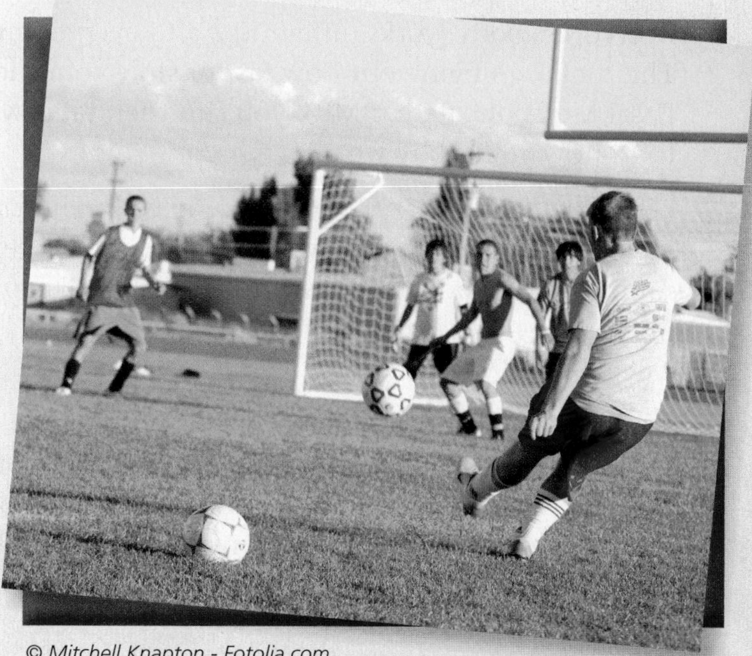

© Mitchell Knapton - Fotolia.com

Managing Weight Change

There are no shortcuts to managing your weight. Exercise and a good diet provide the best chance for success and long-lasting results. Experimenting with fad diets, pills, and other "procedures" that promote quick weight loss can be dangerous to your health. Most of these are short-term solutions at best, and they cannot replace informed, healthy choices about weight change. In fact, these "quick fix" techniques may lead to an unhealthy loss of water and lean muscle instead of fat. The majority of fad diets promote eating very few calories, eliminating certain healthy foods, or skipping meals altogether. Most of these "diets" are ineffective and not medically proven. Among other problems, they can lead to serious nutritional deficiencies.

When you're trying to manage your weight, it's good to understand how your body uses the food you eat. As we have learned, metabolism is the way your body processes everything you eat and drink, changing sugar, protein, and fat into energy. It's a never-ending, two-part process of anabolism and catabolism. Anabolism is *when energy is created and stored from food*. Catabolism is *when energy is released for use*. All of this is controlled by the endocrine system, *the system in charge of many of our body's processes, from cell and tissue growth and repair to reproductive functions and mood regulation.*

While you can't directly control how your metabolism works, you can control what you eat, how much you eat, and how much physical activity you get every day. These three factors influence your metabolism. It always comes back to diet and exercise, doesn't it?

Everyone's body works differently, and everyone will have a different *metabolic rate*. The trick is to figure out how fast or slow your metabolism is. If you measure your Basal Metabolic Rate (BMR), you can then tailor your caloric and exercise needs to fit how your body works.

Basal Metabolic Rate (BMR) *measures how many calories you burn when you're doing nothing*. (Remember, even when you're not active, your body is still using energy for breathing and other basic functions that keep you alive.) It's calculated based on your age, gender, height, and weight factors. Figure 3.14 shows the formula for calculating BMR.

Your metabolism is individual to you, based on a combination of your genetics, age, gender, muscle mass, and certain environmental factors. While your best friend who is able to eat anything and still stay slim seems to have a faster metabolism, it's not likely her metabolic rate that's creating such a difference. She's working with a balance of how many calories she eats, how much she exercises, how much muscle mass she has, and how much she sleeps.

Basically, weight management comes down to this: the more active you are, the more calories you burn. That means how much physical activity you get in a day has more impact on your weight loss and gain than a fast or slow metabolism. When you're trying to lose or maintain weight, physical activity is one of the most important factors because it's under your control—you choose how sedentary or active you want to be. Figure 3.15 shows how to use the Harris Benedict Equation to determine your daily calories needs.

The **BMR formula** uses the variables of height, weight, age, and gender to calculate the Basal Metabolic Rate (BMR). This is more accurate than calculating calorie needs based on body weight alone. The only factor it omits is lean body mass and the ratio of muscle to fat a body has. Remember, leaner bodies need more calories than less lean ones. Therefore, this equation will be very accurate in all but the very muscular (will underestimate calorie needs) and the very overweight (will overestimate calorie needs).

BMR Formula:

Women: BMR = 655 + (4.35 × weight in pounds) + (4.7 × height in inches) – (4.7 × age in years)

Men: BMR = 66 + (6.23 × weight in pounds) + (12.7 × height in inches) – (6.8 × age in years)

FIGURE 3.14

Basal Metabolic Rate (BMR)

The **Harris Benedict Equation** is a formula that uses your BMR and then applies an activity factor to determine your total daily energy expenditure (calories). The only factor omitted by the Harris Benedict Equation is lean body mass. Remember, leaner bodies need more calories than less lean ones. Therefore, this equation will be very accurate in all but the very muscular (will underestimate calorie needs) and the very overweight (will overestimate calorie needs).

Harris Benedict Formula:

To determine your total daily calorie needs, multiply your BMR by the appropriate activity factor, as follows:

Little or no exercise: Calorie calculation = BMR × 1.2

Light exercise/sports 1–3 days/week: Calorie calculation = BMR × 1.375

Moderate exercise/sports 3–5 days/week: Calorie calculation = BMR × 1.55

Hard exercise/sports 6–7 days a week: Calorie calculation = BMR × 1.725

Very hard exercise/sports and physical job: Calorie calculation = BMR × 1.9

Total Calorie Needs Example:

If you are sedentary, multiply your BMR (1745) by 1.2 = 2094. This is the total number of calories you need in order to maintain your current weight.

FIGURE 3.15

BMR Calculator » Harris Benedict Equation

Muscle mass makes us strong, and it also helps us burn calories—during and after workouts. Strength training applies resistance to help build muscle mass. It usually includes exercises such as weightlifting or using a resistance band. Adding strength training to your workout routine will help build muscle mass and keep your bones strong. One pound of muscle burns about 15 calories a day, and while that's still not much, it's more about your total weight from muscle mass.

A University of Chicago study found that when we don't get enough sleep, our endocrine system's functions change. That includes our metabolism. And it's not good. Getting half of the recommended sleep—four instead of eight hours of sleep each night—for just six nights alters how our bodies regulate blood sugar levels and store energy so much that otherwise healthy participants suddenly began to show early symptoms of diabetes.

If you average seven or eight hours of sleep per night, an hour more or less won't make much of a difference. However, if you're getting only four or five hours, another two or more hours will promote weight loss.

Developing healthful eating habits will help you maintain a healthy weight.
© Igor Mojzes/Fotolia.com

Another factor that can affect our metabolic rate is how well hydrated we are. A study at the University of Utah found that people who are better hydrated have higher metabolic rates. Eight to twelve 8-oz. glasses of water every day will help your metabolic rate.

If you skip meals or severely reduce the number of calories you eat, your body compensates by slowing down your metabolism. This allows your body to save calories to handle basic functions. When you eat too many calories without also increasing your physical activity, those unused calories can mean weight gain.

Fasting, or *not eating for long periods,* is also a potentially dangerous way to lose weight. Fasting slows your metabolism, causing side effects including muscle tissue loss, heart damage, digestive problems, and stunted growth. Diet pills can be addictive and can have serious side effects. Body wraps cause water loss rather than loss of fat. With all these methods, weight may drop temporarily but usually returns quickly.

Recognize the Risks

Keeping in mind what you have just read about successful ways to manage your weight, here are some bad decisions that may put your health at risk:

- Following weight-loss programs that promise quick results
- Relying on special products or formulas
- Trying to lose more than $^1/_2$ to 1 pound per week
- Eating fewer calories a day than recommended from BMR calculation
- Skipping meals

Weight Management Tips

Maintaining a healthy weight means learning to eat smart and staying active for a lifetime. Working with a health care professional can help you develop a safe weight management program. A professional can assist you in setting realistic goals that are both safe and effective. Managing your portions will allow you to balance the calories you take in with those you burn. A good program of enjoyable physical activities like bike riding, dancing, volleyball, or swimming will help you burn enough calories to help you manage your weight.

A healthy weight management plan is not difficult to establish. You can maintain a healthy weight by first calculating your BMR, choosing nutritionally balanced meals, and getting regular exercise.

The Dangers of Eating Disorders

Many young people spend a great deal of time worrying about their weight or other problems. Sometimes these worries get out of control. An obsession can develop. An obsession is *an emotional state in which something seems so important that you are always thinking about it.* If food intake is coupled with mental and emotional problems, eating disorders can be the result. Eating disorders are *extreme and damaging eating behaviors that can lead to sickness and even death.*

Eating disorders can be triggered by many psychological factors. These include low self-esteem, poor body image, and depression. Young people are at risk because of the normal stresses during the teen years and the natural growth patterns of their bodies. Eating disorders are serious; they can be fatal. People with eating disorders need professional help.

Three dangerous eating disorders are anorexia nervosa, bulimia nervosa, and binge-eating disorder.

Anorexia Nervosa

Anorexia nervosa is *an eating disorder characterized by self-starvation leading to extreme weight loss. Anorexia* means "without appetite," and *nervosa* means "of nervous origin." Teenage girls and young women seem to be especially susceptible to this disorder, though men and teenage boys can also experience it.

Signs of anorexia nervosa include:

- An intense fear of gaining weight or being overweight.
- A highly distorted body image that continues to see fat where none exists.
- A refusal to maintain a normal body weight.
- A refusal to eat, or eating patterns that tightly restrict food intake.

Even when they are very thin, people with anorexia nervosa see themselves as fat.
© Alina Isakovich/Fotolia.com

Many also have trouble coping with everyday stresses, such as high expectations, the need to achieve, or the need to be popular.

Because people with anorexia nervosa eat very little, they suffer malnutrition and develop shrunken organs, bone loss, low body temperature, low blood pressure, and a slowed metabolism.

Some people with anorexia can develop an irregular heartbeat that may lead to cardiac arrest. Treatment for anorexia nervosa may require a stay at a hospital or clinic. There, the affected person will receive treatment and the nutrients needed to restore physical health. Counseling is also provided to address underlying problems causing the disorder.

Bulimia Nervosa

Another type of eating disorder is bulimia, or bulimia nervosa. **Bulimia nervosa** is *a condition in which a person eats large amounts of food and then tries to purge*. Many people with bulimia force themselves to vomit. Others take laxatives to force the food quickly through their body. Although bulimia is more common among young women and teenage girls, young men and teenage boys can also develop the disorder. People with bulimia are extremely concerned about being thin and attractive. They have an overwhelming need to maintain control over their bodies. They might gorge on large amounts of food. Then, fearing that they are losing control of their bodies, they may take drastic steps to regain control. Some go on crash diets, including fasting, to try to make up for overeating.

Bulimia damages the body in many ways. Stomach acids from frequent vomiting can damage teeth and injure the mouth and throat. Vomiting can also cause the stomach to rupture. Repeated use of laxatives can damage the kidneys and liver, causing long-term health problems. Many people with bulimia suffer from malnutrition as a result of emptying the body of nutrients.

Signs of bulimia nervosa include:

- Regular binge eating episodes, at a rate of at least two per week for several months.
- Binges followed by purging, strict dieting, or excessive exercise to prevent weight gain.
- Using self-induced vomiting or laxatives as part of purging.
- An obsession with weight and body shape.

Binge Eating Disorder

Another eating disorder is binge eating disorder, or *the rapid consumption of an excessive amount of food*. This disorder may be the most common eating disorder, affecting one to two million Americans. People with binge eating disorder eat unusually large amounts of food at a time. Unlike people with bulimia, though, they do not rid their bodies of the food. Afterward, they often feel a sense of guilt and shame.

People with binge eating disorder may use food as a way of coping with depression and other mental or emotional problems. However, the guilt and shame they feel after bingeing adds to the depression. This creates a cycle that can be difficult to break without professional help. Because binge eating disorder often leads to excess weight, it contributes to many health problems, such as obesity, diabetes, and heart disease.

Signs of binge eating disorder include:

- Eating large amounts of food in a relatively short period, whether you are hungry or not, at least twice a week.
- Eating until you feel overly full.
- Eating large amounts of food when you are alone.
- Eating personal "comfort foods," such as a certain type of cookies, ice cream, or other foods you find especially pleasurable, during sessions of excessive eating.

Other Unhealthy Eating Behaviors

There are other unhealthy eating behaviors that do not qualify as full-blown eating disorders. However, they still have serious effects on weight, mental health, and well-being. These behaviors are classified as disordered eating, a range of habits in which food is used primarily to deal with emotional issues.

- **Compulsive overeating**—Feeling the need to eat constantly and quickly, even when full. Often snacking around the clock instead of eating meals at a set time.
- **Extreme dieting**—Dieting and weight loss that become obsessions focused on each bite of food eaten and every pound of weight shed. While extreme dieters do not lose enough weight to have anorexia nervosa, they are at greater risk for developing anorexia nervosa.

Help for People with Eating Disorders

Eating disorders are potentially life-threatening. They affect people's emotional and physical health. People who have eating disorders usually need professional help. Sometimes this help can come from a counselor or psychologist. Help is also available at community clinics and through support groups such as Overeaters Anonymous. A useful online resource is The National Eating Disorders Association (NEDA) website.

If a friend develops an eating disorder, you might want to speak to a school nurse or counselor. It is natural to want to solve your friend's problem by yourself. However, you can help most by showing support. Guide this individual to a health professional, if possible. Family and friends can also provide much-needed support for a person with an eating disorder. Often their role is to encourage the person to seek help. The box below takes a closer look at the role that family and friends can play.

Helping Someone with an Eating Disorder

Someone you know may have an eating disorder. Following these steps may enable you to help him or her.

Ⓐ Encourage the person to seek help.

A person with an eating disorder may not be aware of the seriousness of the condition. The person may also deny that the problem exists and may not want to be helped.

Ⓑ Tell an adult.

You can talk to your parent or guardian, the school nurse, a counselor, or another trusted adult to see if they can help the person get the needed help.

Ⓒ Get professional help.

Psychological problems are usually the cause of eating disorders. The person with the disorder requires professional help. Sometimes family members are also encouraged to meet with the counselor.

Ⓓ Encourage the person to join a support group.

Support groups provide encouragement to people with eating disorders and help them on the road to recovery.

Ⓔ Recommend a follow-up.

Eating disorders can recur and could become lifelong problems. Follow-up visits to counselors and support groups are an important part of the recovery process.

© Lisa F. Young/Fotolia.com

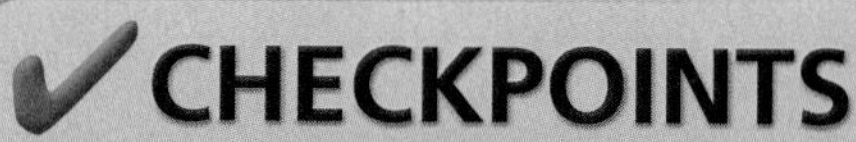

Lesson 4 Review

Using complete sentences, answer the following questions on a sheet of paper.

1. Define body image.
2. What factors determine "appropriate weight"?
3. What can lead to weight gain?
4. Define malnutrition.
5. When managing weight, what else should you consider besides counting calories?
6. What do most successful weight management programs combine?
7. What is anabolism?
8. What does BMR measure?
9. What is an eating disorder?
10. Name four signs of anorexia nervosa.
11. Name four ways in which bulimia nervosa can damage your body.

APPLYING YOUR LEARNING

12. Based on what you have covered in this lesson, describe on paper a plan you would use to make healthy food choices and increase physical activity over the next seven days. Include whether this plan would be used to lose, gain, or maintain weight.

LESSON 5

First Aid

Quick Write

Suppose you witnessed a car accident. List the actions you would take to provide help, and the order in which you would take them.

Learn About

- what is first aid?
- how to recognize and treat common emergencies
- when minutes count: severe emergencies

"I may be compelled to face danger, but never fear it, and while our soldiers can stand and fight, I can stand and feed and nurse them."

Clara Barton, nurse and founder of the Red Cross

What Is First Aid?

Even with precautions, accidents and injuries will still happen, whether it's falling and scraping your knee or a serious car accident. Millions of people are injured every day, and how you handle the situation often determines how well you or someone else will recover. In an emergency, knowing and applying first aid skills can possibly save a life, or at least ease a person's pain and personal suffering. First aid is *the immediate emergency care given to a sick or injured person before professional medical care can be provided*. If you ever find yourself in a position where someone needs first aid assistance, knowing what to do during certain common emergencies can prevent further injury and may even speed the person's recovery. Equally important, though, is knowing what *not* to do. In serious cases, providing the correct first aid can make the difference between life and death.

Ways to Prepare for an Emergency Situation

First aid might be needed anywhere, at any time, and without warning. The first key to preparation is learning basic first aid skills. These skills will help you handle most common emergencies.

Another way to be prepared is to keep a list of emergency numbers near all landline phones or entered into the contacts lists for cell phones—on speed dial, if possible. A study conducted by New York's Albany Medical Center found that many emergency medical facilities often have difficulty contacting family members in cases where the victim is unconscious. A very simple remedy is to put the word "ICE" beside the name of any individual or family member you want called in an emergency. ICE stands for "in case of emergency."

All family members should know where family health records are kept. If a family member has certain allergies, for example, that information may be needed during an emergency. You can enter them into a cell phone's text message inbox as a note, or in some other easily reachable database.

It is also highly recommended that you keep first aid supplies at home and in the car, and that you know how to use them. You can assemble your own first aid kit or buy a packaged kit. The box titled "First Aid Supplies" provides suggestions for basic first aid supplies. If a family member has a medical condition, specific medicines may need to be added to the kit.

Universal Precautions for First-Aid Providers

Universal precautions are *actions taken to prevent the spread of disease by treating all blood as if it were contaminated.* These actions include wearing protective gloves when treating a victim. People infected with HIV or hepatitis carry the virus in their blood. Because these diseases are easily transferred, touching contaminated blood carries a risk. For this reason, it is important to protect yourself when giving first aid. **Human Immunodeficiency Virus (HIV)** is *a virus that infects and destroys cells of the immune system.* **Hepatitis** is *a disease that can cause inflammation of the liver and sometimes be fatal.* It is especially important to wear disposable gloves, if you have them available. Many first aid kits contain gloves.

Other universal precautions include using a facemask or shield when giving first aid for breathing emergencies. Also, cover any open wounds on your body with sterile dressings. Avoid touching any object that had contact with the victim's blood. In addition, always wash your hands thoroughly after giving first aid.

Vocabulary

- first aid
- universal precautions
- Human Immunodeficiency Virus (HIV)
- hepatitis
- sprain
- fracture
- open fracture
- closed fracture
- heat cramps
- heat exhaustion
- heatstroke
- Heimlich Maneuver
- shock
- tourniquet
- cardiopulmonary resuscitation (CPR)
- sudden cardiac arrest (SCA)
- arrhythmias
- ventricular fibrillation (v-fib)

keys to LEADERSHIP

The most important quality you can display any time first aid is needed is remaining calm. Doing so will allow you to better help the victim.

First Aid Supplies

Keeping a first aid kit in your home will help your family be prepared for emergencies.
What other supplies might you add to this kit?

- **Instruments**
  Tweezers, scissors
- **Equipment**
  Thermometer, cotton swabs, blanket, cold pack
- **Medications**
  Antiseptic ointment, sterile eyewash, activated charcoal, hydrogen peroxide, aspirin
- **Dressings**
  Gauze pads, adhesive tape, adhesive bandages, triangular bandage
- **Miscellaneous**
  Small flashlight, tissues, hand sanitizers, disposable gloves, face mask, biohazard waste bags

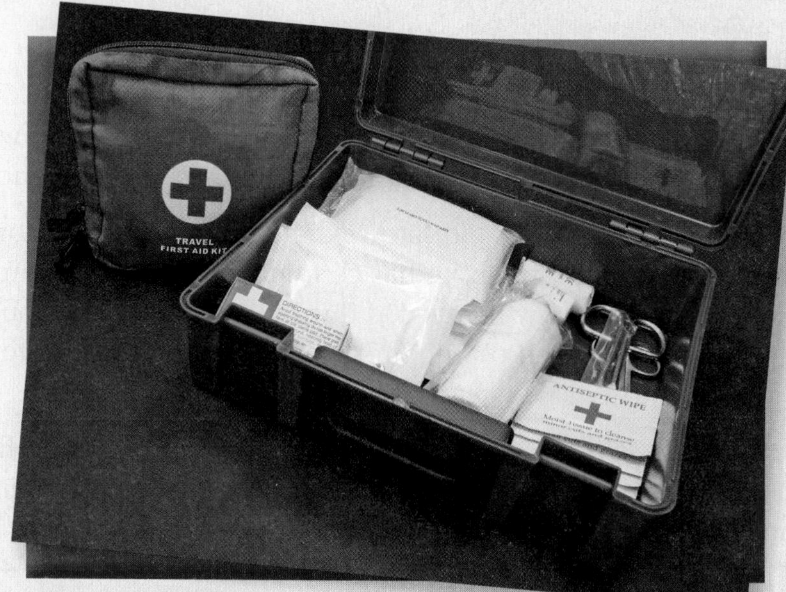

© stocksolutions/Fotolia.com

The Basic Guidelines for First Aid

Every emergency situation is unique. However, there are four steps to take for most emergency situations, as recommended by the American Red Cross. The following guidelines should be followed when administering first aid.

Recognize the Signs of an Emergency

Your senses of hearing, sight, and smell will alert you to most emergencies. Be alert and aware. Look around your immediate surroundings to see if there are any dangers to either you or the injured person. Listen closely if you hear people calling out. Are they in trouble? Be aware of sudden loud or unusual noises, such as shattering glass or explosions.

Sometimes the first sign of an emergency is an odor, such as the smell of smoke. Be especially aware of any strong smell that makes your eyes sting, causes you to cough, or makes breathing difficult. These sensations can signal a chemical spill or toxic gas release.

In any event, before you decide to take action, make sure the emergency scene is safe for you, the victim, and anyone nearby who may be watching out of curiosity.

Your first responsibility is to protect your own safety. Move the injured person only in case of immediate danger, such as a fire or oncoming traffic. Never put your own life in danger to help someone else. Be sure to consider your own strengths and limitations. For example, unless you are trained as a rescue swimmer or lifeguard, don't dive into a lake to rescue someone who is drowning. Instead, throw the person a life preserver or some other object that floats.

Decide to Act

Once you have considered the situation, it's time to act. Find out if the person is conscious, or awake. Tap them on the shoulder. You can also loudly ask if the person is all right. Ask permission to give help. Check the person's whole body for injuries. If the person is not conscious, do not leave, unless you are also in danger. Ask someone to go for help. Check for any medical identification, such as a bracelet, or card. The identification will tell you if the person has any medical problems or allergies to medicines.

Check the person for bleeding. If you have latex gloves, put them on. Latex gloves are very thin gloves made of a special type of rubber. The latex gloves protect from any viruses or diseases in the blood. After putting on the gloves, press down on any bleeding wound. This will help stop the bleeding. If no gloves are available, use several layers of cloth or a sheet of plastic to protect yourself from the blood.

You should not hesitate to help others because you are afraid of doing something wrong. Almost all states have Good Samaritan laws, which protect rescuers from legal action when they act responsibly.

Call for Help

In an emergency, you can always call for help, which is often the best and only action for you to take. This alone can possibly save a life. So when in doubt, make the call. If you are alone, quickly make the call. If you have to leave the area to make a call, return to the injured person as soon as possible.

In the United States, the number to call for all emergencies is **911**. Dialing **0** for the operator is also an option and may be necessary in some small towns. When you call, stay calm. Be ready to tell the emergency operator the following information:

- Nature of the emergency
- The street address or the closest intersection or landmark if the address is not known (you may be able to get your location from the map function on a cell phone)
- Whether the emergency is ongoing
- Who is involved (including descriptions, if possible)
- The number of victims (so that the correct number of ambulances can be sent)
- Status of the victims (are they breathing, bleeding, or conscious)
- Whether any weapons were involved

The operator will notify the police, fire department, or emergency medical services. Stay on the phone until the operator has the necessary information and tells you that you can hang up.

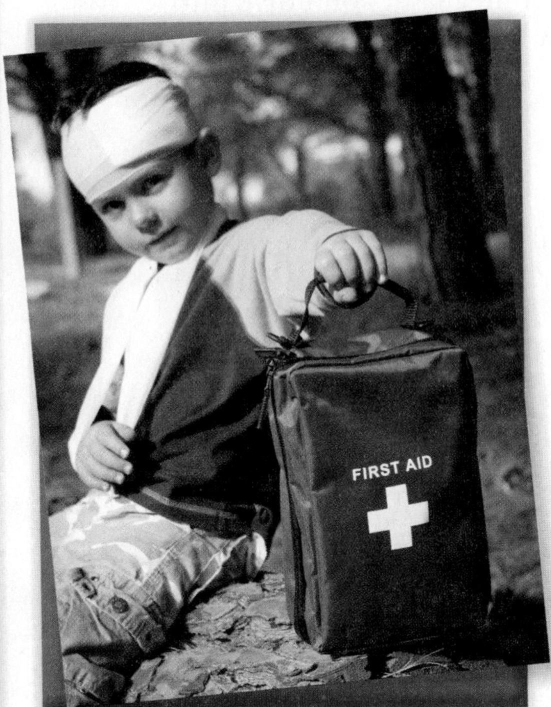

It's a good idea to take along a first-aid kit; you never know when you will need it.

© *MrSegui/Fotolia.com*

Provide Care Until Help Arrives

Once you have called for help, stay with the injured person. Keeping the victim quiet may protect the person from further injury. Helping the person maintain normal body temperature is also important. If you can provide a coat or blanket, that will help. You should also carefully loosen any tight clothing, and provide shade from the sun if necessary. Reassure the victim that help is on the way.

In general, you should not try to move a victim because it could cause pain or further injury. Wait for professional help to arrive. Remember, the only situation in which a victim should be moved is if he or she is in danger, such as in the path of fire or oncoming traffic.

If the victim is unconscious and unresponsive, cardiopulmonary resuscitation (CPR) may be needed. This technique for dealing with life-threatening emergencies is described later in this lesson.

How to Recognize and Treat Common Emergencies

Sprains, bruises, and broken bones are a few of the common emergencies you may encounter. Others include insect bites, burns, poisoning, foreign objects in the eye, nosebleeds, fainting, heat cramps, and heatstroke. Learn how to treat these conditions properly. Also recognize the difference between a minor condition that you can treat, and a more serious condition that needs professional medical assistance.

Sprains

A sprain is *a condition in which the ligaments that hold the joints in position are stretched or torn*. Sprains usually result from a sudden force, often a twisting movement. Ankles and knees are the most commonly sprained joints. You can often recognize sprains by swelling and bruising around the injured area. A medical professional should treat serious sprains. However, you can treat minor sprains by using the R.I.C.E. method:

- **Rest**—Rest the affected joint for 24 to 48 hours.
- **Ice**—Apply ice to reduce swelling and pain. Place a cloth between the skin and the bag of ice in order to reduce discomfort.
- **Compression**—Compress the injured part by wrapping it in an elastic bandage.
- **Elevation**—Elevate, or raise, the injured part above the level of the heart to reduce swelling.

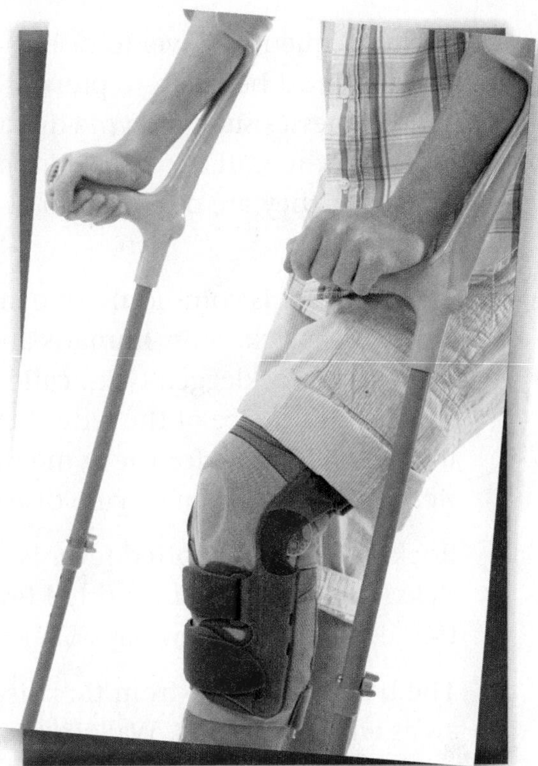

Ankles and knees are the most commonly sprained joints.

© Alexander Raths/Fotolia.com

Broken Bones

A fracture is *a break in a bone*. Fractures are common; the average person has two in a lifetime. Fractures occur when the physical force exerted on the bone is stronger than the bone itself. Although fractures are common in young people, they usually are not serious and can heal properly when the correct treatment is applied. As you get older, however, your bones become more brittle and you are more likely to suffer fractures from falls.

An open fracture is *a complete break, with one or both sides of the bone piercing the skin*. A closed fracture is *a break that does not pierce the skin and may be difficult to identify*. Some of these hard-to-identify fractures are called *hairline fractures*.

With a closed fracture, there are telltale signs. These include pain, swelling, and a deformed appearance. Sometimes, however, a broken bone causes no immediate pain. The only way to be sure a bone is broken is to have it X-rayed.

Insect Bites and Stings

Insect bites or stings often cause pain and swelling at the site of the bite or sting. However, for a person who is allergic to them, the situation is much more serious—possibly life-threatening. If a rash develops, or if there is difficulty breathing, signs of shock, or a history of being allergic to stings, the victim needs professional medical help immediately.

First aid for insect bites involves washing the affected area and applying a special lotion for bites. For insect stings, you first need to remove the stinger by scraping against it with your fingernail. If you have ever had a splinter under the skin, it is a similar process. Once the stinger is out, apply ice or a cold pack to relieve pain and prevent swelling.

If you frequently travel to or live in a wooded area where ticks are common, caution must be taken to prevent tick bites. Some ticks transmit bacteria that cause illnesses such as Lyme disease or Rocky Mountain spotted fever. Ticks attach to the skin and draw blood. Although ticks can attach to any part of the body, they are often found in hard-to-see areas such as the groin, armpits, or scalp.

Lyme disease is commonly transmitted through the bite of the blacklegged tick or deer tick. Most humans are infected through the bites from the immature blacklegged ticks, called nymphs. Nymphs are very small (less than 2 mm), or the size of the letter "D" on a dime. The nymphs must be attached for 36 to 48 hours for the Lyme disease to be transferred. Although adult deer ticks can also transmit Lyme disease, they are much larger and easier to detect.

Rocky Mountain spotted fever is another disease that can be transmitted by ticks. Rocky Mountain spotted fever can be a severe or even fatal illness if not treated in the first few days of symptoms.

The best prevention from tick diseases is awareness. Avoid wooded or bushy areas with high grass. Walk in the center of trails. Use insect repellents on exposed skin and clothing for protection that lasts up to several hours. Use products that contain permethrin to treat clothing and gear such as boots, pants, socks, and tents. Be sure to use insect repellents that are safe for human use and registered with the Environmental Protection Agency.

Bathe or shower within two hours after coming inside to wash off or easily find ticks that may be crawling on you. Conduct a full-body check of yourself after returning from tick-infested areas. Also check clothing, pets, and equipment. Tumble dry your clothing, if possible, on high heat for one hour to kill ticks hiding in your clothing.

If a tick is attached to your skin, there's no need to panic. Remove the tick very carefully following the procedures provided in Figure 3.16.

Animal Bites

Animals, including even small pets, carry bacteria that can cause illness after a bite or deep scratch. People who are bitten sometimes react with a fever and other symptoms after such an incident.

To provide first aid for an animal bite, first control any bleeding. Then, wash the wound with soap and water as soon as possible, and apply an antiseptic such as hydrogen peroxide. Then cover the wound with a sterile dressing or bandages.

If you find a tick on your body, have an adult follow the method shown to remove it.

1. Using a pair of pointed, smooth-tipped tweezers, grasp the tick by the head or mouthparts right where they enter the skin. Do not grasp the tick by the body.
2. Without jerking or twisting, pull firmly and steadily directly upward.
3. Place the tick in alcohol to kill it. Clean the bite wound with disinfectant.
4. If possible, seal the tick in a container and place in freezer. Your doctor may want to see the tick if you develop symptoms.

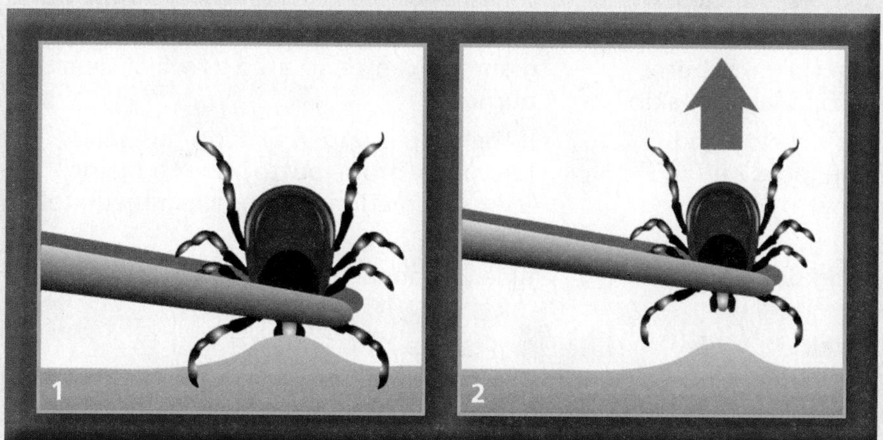

FIGURE 3.16

How to Remove a Tick

Courtesy of the National Institute of Environmental Health Sciences/http://ehp.niehs.nih.gov

A person who is bitten by an animal with rabies is at risk of suffering severe nervous system reactions if not treated soon after the bite. Call the local animal control facility and pinpoint the location of the incident. Don't try to catch the animal yourself. You or the victim should follow up with animal control soon after the incident to see if the animal was caught and had rabies. Further treatment may be needed if the animal is not located. If bitten by any animal and it is not known whether the animal has rabies, you should be seen by a medical professional as soon as possible.

Burns

First aid for burns depends on the amount of skin burned, the location, and the depth of the burn. Burns to the eye or airway and burns caused by chemicals or electricity require special first aid procedures, which are not covered here. Table 3.6 explains how to recognize and treat three classifications of burns. Treatment for burns depends on the severity of the burn.

Table 3.6 Three Degrees of Burns

Type of Burn	Description	Treatment
First-Degree	• Affects only the outer layer of the skin. • The skin is usually red, but the outer layer has not been burned through. • There may be swelling and pain.	• Cool the burn with running water. • Immerse the burn in cold water, or apply cold compresses for at least 15 minutes. • Cover the burn with a sterile bandage.
Second-Degree	• Burns through the first layer of skin and burns the second layer of skin. • Blisters develop and the skin looks red and splotchy. • Usually there is severe pain and swelling.	• A burn no larger than 2 to 3 inches in diameter can be treated as a first-degree burn. • If the burn is larger, or is on the hands, feet, face, groin, buttocks, or a major joint, get medical assistance immediately. • Do not use ice or put any type of bandage on the burn.
Third-Degree	• Involves all layers of skin and muscle; affects fat and bone. • The burned area may be charred, burned black, or appear dry and white. • There may be little or no pain felt at this stage.	• Call 911 for medical assistance immediately. • While you are waiting, treat the victim for shock. • Do not remove clothing. • Cover the area of the burn with a cool, moist, sterile bandage or clean cloth. • Do not apply cold water to the burns. • Elevate the burned area, above heart level if possible. • Keep the victim still and help him or her to sip fluids.

Poisoning

Poisons can cause severe bodily harm. They can be swallowed, inhaled, absorbed through the skin, or injected. About half of all poisonings involve medicines or household products. Anyone who has been poisoned needs immediate treatment. If a victim indicates having been poisoned, you should call the nearest poison control center. This is a 24-hour hot line that provides emergency medical advice on treating these victims. Be prepared to give information about the individual and about the suspected poison. The person at the poison control center will tell you what action to take. You may be instructed to give the victim large amounts of water or milk to dilute the poison. Or you may need to give the victim activated charcoal; this helps prevent the poison from being absorbed into the stomach lining.

If the victim's skin comes into direct contact with a poisonous chemical such as a pesticide or household cleaning agent, remove any clothing that has come into contact with it. Remove as much of the chemical from the surface of the skin as you can by flooding the area with water for 15 minutes. While the skin is being flooded, call the nearest poison control center.

Foreign Object in the Eye

Something that gets into your eye can be as common as an eyelash or something more severe. If you get a foreign object in your eye, do not rub the eye. Rubbing can possibly cause injury. Your first action should be to try to flush the object out of your eye with clean water. Hold the rim of a small, clean glass filled with water against the base of your eye socket. Keeping your eye open, gently pour the water into the eye. If the object isn't washed out, repeat the process. If you cannot clear your eye after several attempts, it is best to get assistance.

To help somebody else who has a foreign object in the eye, you should first locate the object. Gently pull the lower lid downward while the person looks up. If you do not see the object, hold the upper lid open and examine the eye while the person looks down. If the object is floating on the surface of the eye, lightly touch the object with a moistened cotton swab or the corner of a clean cloth. If you cannot remove the object or the victim is too sensitive to direct contact with his or her eye, seek medical assistance immediately.

Nosebleed

Nosebleeds are fairly common. They can be caused by an injury, by being in a very dry place, or even by a cold. If you experience a nosebleed, sit upright and lean forward; this will reduce pressure on the veins in your nose. Pinch your nose shut with your thumb and index finger and breathe through your mouth. Keep the nose pinched for 5 to 10 minutes. If bleeding lasts more than 20 minutes, there is a lot of blood, or the nosebleed was caused by an injury such as a fall, get medical assistance immediately.

Fainting

Have you ever stood up too fast and felt lightheaded? Fainting occurs when the brain's blood supply is cut off for a short amount of time. Someone who faints loses consciousness briefly. If you feel faint, lie down or place your head between your knees if sitting down.

To help someone else who faints:

- Leave the victim lying down. Check the airway. If the person is breathing, raise the legs above the level of the head.
- Loosen any tight clothing. Sponging the face with cool water may also help.
- If the person does not regain consciousness in one to two minutes, call for help.
- If the person is not breathing, call for help and start CPR if you are trained (see the end of this lesson).

Losing consciousness after a head injury is not fainting—call for help or 911 if this occurs. Immediate CPR is needed if there are no signs of breathing.

Heat-Related Illnesses

Heat-related illnesses include heat cramps, heat exhaustion, and heatstroke. **Heat cramps** are *painful, involuntary muscle spasms that usually occur during heavy exercise in hot weather.* People who experience heat cramps should rest, cool down, and as you learned from Lesson 2, drink water or a replenishment drink that contains electrolytes. Gentle stretching exercise and gentle massage may help relieve the cramps.

It is important to cool down, rest, and drink water when suffering heat cramps.

© expressiovisual/Fotolia.com

Heat exhaustion is *a condition characterized by faintness, nausea, rapid heartbeat, and hot, red, dry, cold, pale, and clammy skin or heavy sweating.* If you are with someone who shows signs of heat exhaustion, take the person to a shady or air-conditioned place. Have the person lie down and slightly elevate the feet. Loosen clothing. Have the person drink cold, but not iced, water. Cool the person by spraying him or her with cool water and by fanning. Keep careful watch. Heat exhaustion can quickly become heatstroke, which is the most serious form of heat illness because it is potentially life threatening. **Heatstroke** is *a serious condition that results from heat exhaustion that remains untreated and the victim continues to overheat.* Heatstroke can cause the body's normal processes for regulating heat to be impaired or to shut down. The most serious symptom of heatstroke is a body temperature that rises to 104 degrees or higher. Signs of heatstroke may also include dizziness or vertigo, fatigue, or convulsions. Move the victim to a cooler location or shady area immediately. The victim may have hot, red, dry, or moist skin, and a rapid and strong pulse. The victim may be unconscious, or have a severe headache or rapid and shallow breathing. Heat stroke is a medical emergency and you should call 911 immediately. Try to reduce the person's body temperature with cool cloths or even a cold bath until medical help arrives. Do not give the victim any liquids if they are vomiting or unconscious.

If you think someone may have heatstroke, immediately call for emergency medical help (911), while treating the victim.

When Minutes Count: Severe Emergencies

In a life-threatening emergency, a person may have only minutes to live unless the right treatment is provided. If you can provide appropriate first aid in such a situation, you may save a life. For all life-threatening emergencies, your first actions are to stay calm, and call for help.

Remember, when you encounter an emergency, make sure the area around you is safe for you and the victim. Life-threatening conditions you should look for are: severe bleeding, unconsciousness, or difficulty breathing.

Choking

More than 4,600 people die from choking every year. Choking occurs when a person's airway becomes blocked by a piece of food or some other object. Choking prevents oxygen from getting to the lungs and the brain. If this situation lasts for more than four minutes, and the object is not removed, it may result in brain damage or death. It is important for you to recognize and know how to handle choking both at home and in public places. A choking person usually has an expression of fear and may clutch his or her throat—the universal sign for choking. He or she may wheeze or gasp, turn reddish purple, have bulging eyes, and become unable to speak. If the person can speak or cough, it is not a choking emergency.

A choking person needs immediate help. You may be able to clear the object from an adult's or child's throat by using the technique shown in Figure 3.17. The technique shown is the Heimlich maneuver. Dr. Henry Heimlich is credited with inventing the maneuver in 1974. Dr. Heimlich was a Navy surgeon who developed the Heimlich maneuver as a way to save choking victims. This is an emergency procedure used to treat choking victims that is responsible for saving thousands of lives each year. The Heimlich maneuver is *a series of abdominal thrusts to force out an obstruction blocking the airway*. It is done by applying pressure under the diaphragm in a thrusting motion, inward and upward to dislodge the object. The first aid procedure for a choking infant is different from the adult technique. If you have infants in your household, check with a first aid manual to learn how to help infants.

Before you perform the Heimlich maneuver, or abdominal thrusts, on someone you think is choking, you should first determine if the person is actually choking by asking the individual if he or she can speak.

A Stand behind the person who is choking. Wrap your arms around the person's waist and tip the person slightly forward. Make a fist with one hand. Place the fist just above the person's navel but below the breastbone and diaphragm. Position the fist so the thumb side is against the victim's abdomen. Grasp your fist with your other hand.

B Quickly, thrust inward and upward. The motion is similar to one you would use if you were trying to lift the person off the ground. Repeat thrusts until the food or object is dislodged. If the person becomes unresponsive, call for medical help and begin CPR.

FIGURE 3.17

First Aid for a Choking Adult or Older Child Abdominal Thrusts—The Heimlich Maneuver

Courtesy of www.nlm.nih.gov

If you are alone and find yourself choking, you can use the Heimlich maneuver on yourself. There are two ways to do this. First, make a fist and position it slightly above your navel. Grasp your fist with your other hand and thrust inward and upward into your abdomen until the object pops out. The second technique is to lean over a firm object, such as the back of a chair, and press your abdomen into it.

Shock

Shock is *a life-threatening condition in which the circulatory system fails to deliver enough blood to vital tissues and organs*. A person can go into shock when they suffer an injury, burn, severe infection, heat illness, poisoning, blood loss, broken bones, and heart attack. Because shock can result from a medical emergency, you should look for signs of it when providing first aid. Watch for cool, clammy, pale, or gray skin; weak and rapid pulse; and slow, shallow breathing. The person's pupils may be dilated or enlarged, and the eyes may have a dull look or seem to stare. If conscious, the shock victim may feel faint, weak, confused, and anxious. If you think the victim is in shock or in danger of going into shock, call 911 for medical help and take these precautions.

- Have the person lie down on his or her back. Raise the victim's feet higher than the head. Try to keep the person from moving.
- Loosen tight clothing.
- Keep the person warm. Use a blanket, coat, or whatever is available as a cover.
- Do not give the person anything to drink.
- If the person vomits or bleeds from the mouth, roll the person to his or her side to help prevent choking.

If you think a person is in shock or in danger of shock, check symptoms, and then call for medical help immediately.

Severe Bleeding

To stop severe bleeding, have the victim lie down. If possible, raise the location of the bleeding above the level of the heart. When treating anyone who is bleeding, use protective gloves whenever possible. Bleeding can usually be stopped by applying direct pressure to the wound, using a clean cloth. If that is unsuccessful, apply pressure to the artery that supplies blood to the area of the wound. See Figure 3.18. A last resort method to stop severe bleeding is to apply a tourniquet. A **tourniquet** is *a constricting band placed around an arm or leg to control bleeding*. The tourniquet should not be used unless applying pressure to the wound does not stop the bleeding. Using a tourniquet is very dangerous and should only be considered as a last resort.

This illustration shows the areas on arms and legs that can be pressed against a bone to stop circulation to the arm or leg.

Arm

Use four fingers to press on the inside of the upper arm at the area circled in the diagram. You will press the artery at this point against the arm bone. To find the artery, feel for a pulse below the round muscle of the biceps.

Leg

Keeping your arm straight, use the heel of your hand to press the groin at the area shown in the diagram. You will press the artery at this point against the pelvic bone. You may need to use both hands to apply enough pressure.

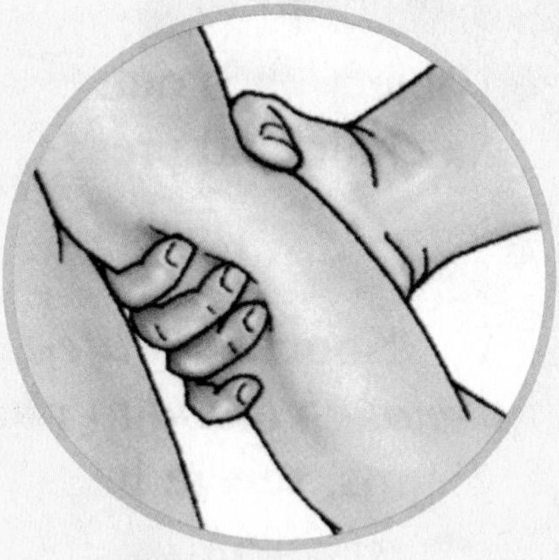

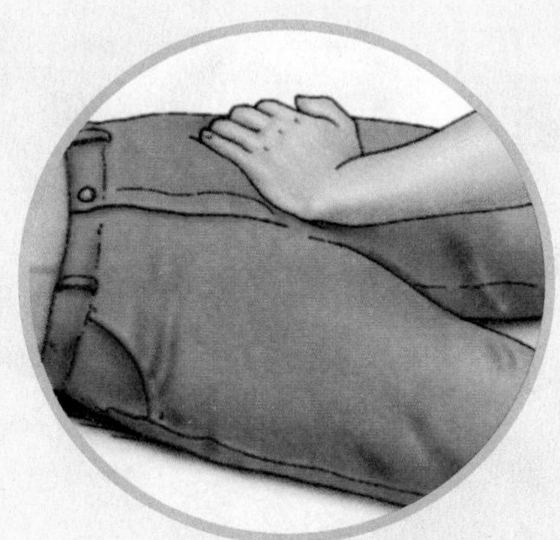

FIGURE 3.18

Pressure Point Bleeding Control

The ABCs of Cardiopulmonary Resuscitation (CPR)

The first steps of CPR involve assessment and rescue breathing. If you have an available breathing mask, follow the directions that came with the mask.

1. **Airway**—Look inside the victim's mouth. If you see anything blocking the airway, remove it. Lay the person flat on a firm surface. Gently tilt the head back with one hand and lift the chin with the other. If you suspect head or neck injuries, do not move the victim's head. Open the airway by lifting the jaw instead.
2. **Breathing**—Look, listen, and feel to find out if the victim is breathing. *Look* for chest movement. *Listen* at the victim's mouth for breathing sounds. *Feel* for exhaled air on your cheek. If the victim is not breathing, begin rescue breathing. Pinch the person's nostrils shut, take a normal breath, and place your mouth over the victim's, forming a seal. Give two breaths, each about one second long. The victim's chest should rise with each breath. If chest does not rise, reposition the head again and make sure air passageway is clear.
3. **Circulation**—Check for circulation by watching for some response to your rescue breaths, such as breathing, coughing, or movement. If there are no signs of circulation, a person trained in CPR should begin chest compressions immediately (see Figure 3.19). If the victim responds but is not breathing normally, give two rescue breaths after every 30 chest compressions.

What Is Cardiopulmonary Resuscitation (CPR)?

Based on the injuries and illnesses we have covered in this lesson, having to provide CPR for someone is a real possibility. Everyone should be trained to perform CPR and many states have required training prior to getting your driver's license. You can also receive training for CPR through your local Red Cross, American Heart Association (AHA), or online from OnlineAHA.org or www.firstaidweb.com.

Imagine that you are in an emergency situation in which somebody loses consciousness. You gently shake the victim and shout, "Are you OK?" but the victim does not respond. If a victim is unresponsive and not breathing, he or she needs immediate CPR. Cardiopulmonary resuscitation (CPR) is *a first aid procedure that combines rescue breaths with chest compressions to restore breathing and circulation.* Only people who have received the proper training should perform CPR.

The first step in any emergency is to call 911 immediately. If there is someone else with you that can provide assistance, have them call or send them for help. The next step is to administer CPR. First check the ABCs—airway, breathing, and circulation, as recommended by the American Heart Association. If you have not received formal training for infant CPR check a first aid manual to learn how to help younger children and infants. Figure 3.19 illustrates the process for combining rescue breaths with chest compressions.

CPR involves both chest compressions and rescue breaths. It should be administered only by people who are properly trained.

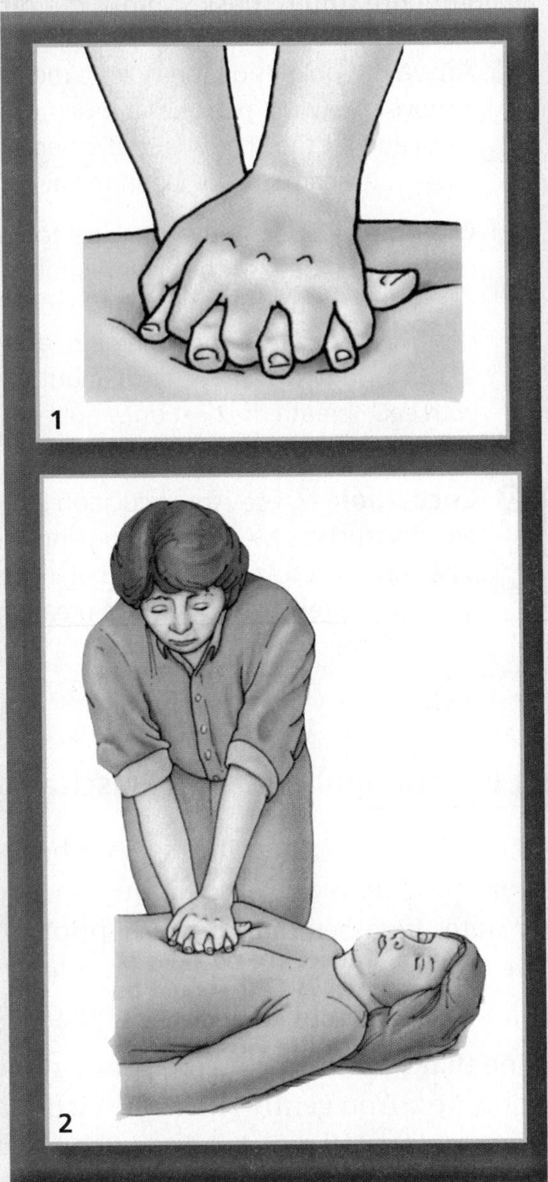

1. **Position your hands**—Prepare to start chest compressions by finding a spot on the lower half of the victim's breastbone. Place the heel of one hand on that point, and interlock the fingers with the fingers of the other hand. Do not allow your fingers to rest on the victim's ribs.

2. **Begin chest compressions and rescue breathing**—Lean over the victim until your shoulders are over your hands. Lock your elbows, then press down firmly and release, allowing the chest to spring back. Without pausing, give 30 chest compressions at a rate of about 100 per minute. Pause to give two rescue breaths (see the box titled "The ABCs of Cardiopulmonary Resuscitation"). Check for signs of circulation after four cycles, then every few minutes as you continue. Give CPR until the victim revives or medical assistance arrives.

3. In 2010 the American Heart Association recommended the following actions if you are a bystander without CPR training. You can still provide compression-only CPR for an adult victim. The bystander positions both hands on the center of the chest, applying compressions at a rate of about 100 per minute without stopping until medical assistance arrives. Although not as effective as compressions and breaths, this method keeps blood circulating to the brain.

FIGURE 3.19

CPR for Adults

Courtesy of www.nlm.nih.gov

Automated External Defibrillator (AED)

A new life saving device used to revive victims of sudden cardiac arrest is the automated external defibrillator or AED. Sudden cardiac arrest (SCA) is *a condition in which the heart suddenly and unexpectedly stops beating*. Usually death will occur if not treated within minutes. Using the AED on someone who is having SCA may save the person's life.

The heart has an internal electrical system that controls the rate and rhythm of the heartbeat. With each heartbeat, an electrical signal spreads from the top of the heart to the bottom. As the signal travels through the heart, it causes the heart to contract and pump blood.

Problems with the internal electrical system can cause abnormal heart rhythms called arrhythmias (ah-RITH-me-ahs). During an arrhythmia, the heart can beat too fast, too slow, or with an irregular rhythm. Some arrhythmias can cause the heart to stop pumping blood to the body. These arrhythmias cause SCA.

The most common cause of SCA is an arrhythmia called ventricular fibrillation (v-fib). *In v-fib, the ventricles (the heart's lower chambers) don't beat normally*. Instead, they quiver very rapidly and irregularly.

In people who have arrhythmias, an electric shock from an AED can restore the heart's normal rhythm. Doing CPR on someone having SCA can also improve his or her chance of survival.

AEDs are lightweight, battery-operated, portable devices that are easy to use. Each unit comes with instructions, and the device will even give you voice prompts to let you know if and when you should send a shock to the heart.

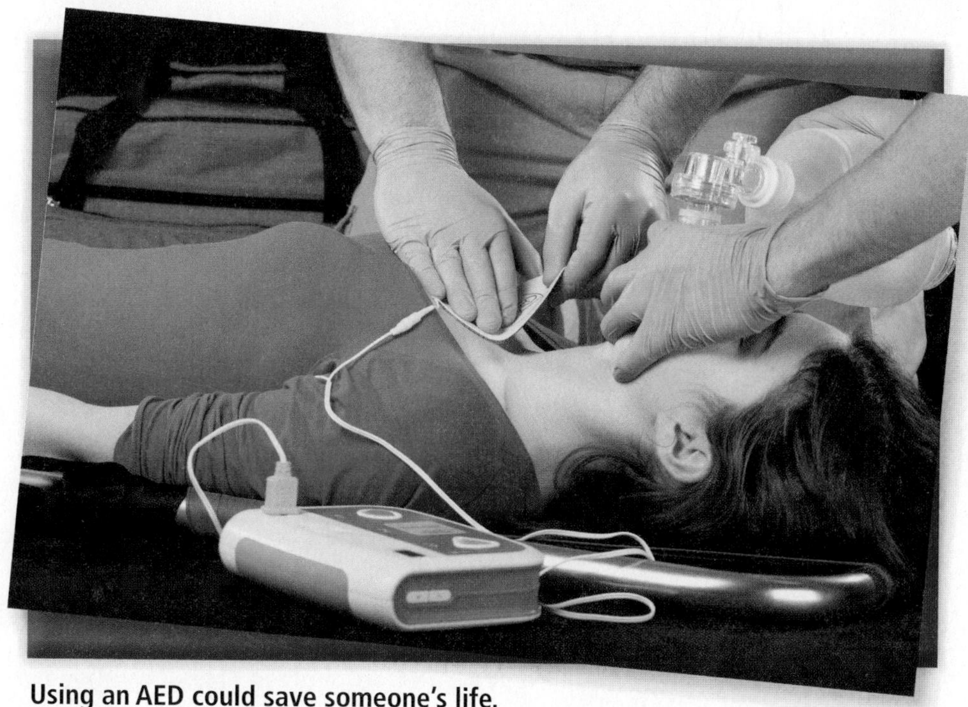

Using an AED could save someone's life.

© Photographee.eu/Fotolia.com

An AED can check the person's heart rhythm and determine whether an electric shock is needed to try to restore a normal rhythm.

You often find AEDs in places with many people, such as shopping malls, golf courses, businesses, airports, airplanes, casinos, convention centers, hotels, sports venues, and schools.

Learning how to use an AED and taking a CPR course are helpful. However, if trained personnel aren't available, untrained people also can use an AED to help save someone's life. Ninety-five percent of people who have SCA die from it within minutes. Rapid treatment of SCA with an AED provides the best chance for survival.

✓ CHECKPOINTS

Lesson 5 Review

Using complete sentences, answer the following questions on a sheet of paper.

1. What is first aid?
2. Name four universal precautions to take when giving first aid.
3. Give three examples of ways you can provide help to an injured person until professional help arrives.
4. How do you treat minor sprains?
5. Explain the process for removing a tick from a person's body.
6. What action should you take if you or someone else has a second-degree burn?
7. What action should you take for a victim of heat exhaustion?
8. What is the Heimlich maneuver?
9. List the ABCs of CPR.
10. What does the AED check prior to providing an electrical shock?

APPLYING YOUR LEARNING

11. A driver walks out after a car crash and says that he is all right. However, his skin is gray, his pupils are dilated, and his breathing is shallow. From what condition might the driver be suffering? What should you do?

CHAPTER 4

Making Safe, Drug-Free Decisions

Chapter Outline

"Drugs are a waste of time. They destroy your memory and your self-respect and everything that goes along with your self-esteem."

Kurt Cobain, singer and songwriter

LESSON 1

Medicines and Drugs

Quick Write

Write what you would say in a short email to a younger brother, sister, or cousin explaining the most important reason young people should avoid drug use.

Learn About

- how medicines differ from drugs
- drug misuse and abuse
- help for drug users
- living drug free

"Good medicine always tastes bad."

Ron Hall, author

How Medicines Differ From Drugs

What do you think of when you hear the words *medicine* and *drugs*? Many people use the terms interchangeably. The difference is extremely important, however. **Medicine** is *a type of drug we use to treat or prevent disease and other conditions.* All medicines are drugs, but not all drugs are medicines. **Drugs** are *substances other than food that change the structure or function of the body or mind.* You will learn more about drugs later in this lesson.

Medicine Safety

In the United States, the Food and Drug Administration (FDA) is responsible for ensuring that all medicines are safe and effective. When someone discovers or creates a new medicine, it must go through a very long process (sometimes several years) of testing before it can be sold legally. Here are the steps:

1. A potential new medicine is discovered or created.
2. Researchers conduct experiments to help decide how the new medicine might be used to treat an illness. They test the drug on animals to determine whether the medicine has any harmful effects.
3. The FDA reviews the preliminary research on animals and the test results. If approved, the new medicine is studied in humans.
4. If the testing on humans shows the medicine is safe and effective and the FDA agrees that the medicine is safe and effective for its intended use, the FDA approves it.
5. Once approved, the medicine can be made available for physicians to prescribe or for consumers to purchase.

In addition to reviewing and testing new medicines for safety, the FDA decides how the people who need the medicine can obtain it and classifies it into two major categories:

Prescription Medicines

Some medicines are very strong and potentially harmful if taken improperly or by people who do not need them. Only doctors can write prescriptions for them. These prescription medicines are *medicines that can be sold only with a written order from a physician.* Figure 4.1 shows the information that must appear on all prescription medicine labels. Only a pharmacist can fill a prescription written by a doctor. A pharmacist is *someone trained and licensed to prepare and sell medicines that a doctor prescribes.* A pharmacist will also read the prescription to make sure it is given correctly. *Always* read the instructions before you start taking any kind of medication. Many people do not take prescription medicine properly. There are five common mistakes made by individuals:

- Taking the incorrect dosage
- Taking the medicine at the wrong time
- Forgetting to take a dose (missing prescribed times for taking medicine)
- Failing to take all the medicine
- Failing to ask questions about how to use their medicine

Over-the-Counter (OTC) Medicines

Have you ever been given cough syrup or nasal spray when you were sick? These over-the counter (OTC) medicines are *medicines that are safe enough to be taken without a written order from a physician.* However, just like prescription medicines, OTC medicines can cause harm if not used as directed.

OTC medicines are available at pharmacies, supermarkets, and other stores that sell medicine. However, just because a medicine is available without a prescription does not mean

Vocabulary

- medicine
- drugs
- prescription medicines
- pharmacist
- over-the-counter (OTC) medicines
- vaccines
- antibodies
- antibiotics
- analgesics
- side effect
- tolerance
- overdose
- narcotics
- addiction
- stimulants
- attention deficit hyperactivity disorder (ADHD)
- amphetamine
- methamphetamine
- narcolepsy

continued on next page

Never take medicines that are not specifically prescribed for you; this can cause unhealthy side effects and if mixed with other medicines, can be deadly.

Vocabulary

continued

- Parkinson's disease
- schizophrenia
- club drugs
- depressants
- street drug
- coma
- hemp
- THC (tetrahydrocannabinol)
- misdemeanor
- felony
- synthetic
- spice
- hallucinogens
- psychological dependence
- inhalants
- physical dependence
- withdrawal
- detoxification

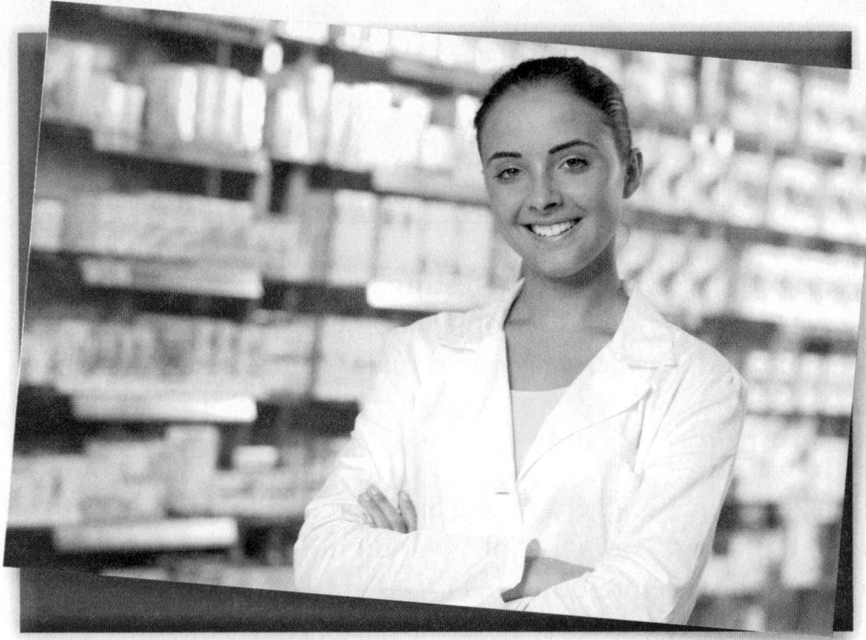

Talk to a pharmacist before taking over-the-counter (OTC) medicines.

© stokkete/Fotolia.com

it can't hurt you. OTC drugs present many of the same problems as prescription drugs. The Food and Drug Administration (FDA) warns against the misuse of these drugs. Always check with an adult before using any OTC or other medicine. Be sure to read and understand the information provided on an OTC medicine label.

Medicine labels provide important information:

- Prescription number
- Date prescription was written
- Date prescription was filled
- Name of patient
- Name of medicine
- Pharmacy's name, address, and phone number
- Name of prescribing doctor
- Warning labels/special instructions
- Number of refills remaining
- Directions from doctor
- Expiration date of the prescription

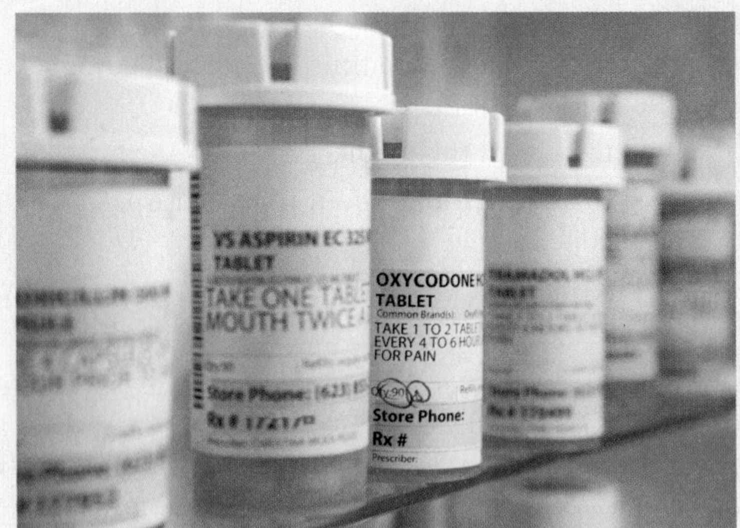

© JJAVA/Fotolia.com

FIGURE 4.1

Prescription Medicine Label

Types of Medicines

There are different types of medicines, and each type affects the body in specific ways. The most common uses for medicines include preventing disease, fighting infection, and relieving pain.

Medicines to Prevent Diseases

Some medicines, known as vaccines, *prevent a disease from developing*. Traditional vaccines contain dead or weakened germs of the disease you want to prevent. Having these germs in the body causes the immune system to produce antibodies, which are *proteins that attack and kill or disable specific germs that cause disease.*

Some vaccines last many years or even a whole lifetime and protect you from diseases such as whooping cough, measles, mumps, rubella, chicken pox, pneumonia, and hepatitis A and B. These vaccines provide long-lasting protection. Other vaccines, such as the flu shot, protect you for only a year or so because new variants of the flu virus appear each year, requiring new vaccines.

Medicines to Fight Infection

Many germs and diseases cannot be prevented with vaccines because they are caused by bacteria rather than viruses. Instead, certain medicines called antibiotics (an·ti·by·AH·tiks) fight these illnesses. Antibiotics are *medicines that reduce or kill harmful bacteria in the body.* Each type of antibiotic fights only certain types of bacteria. For example, penicillin (pen·uh·SI·luhn) is highly effective in killing the bacteria that cause strep throat and pneumonia.

Medicines to Relieve Pain

Many people take *medicines that help relieve pain*; these are called analgesics. When the body feels pain, such as that from a headache or toothache, pain messages travel along the nerves and spinal cord to the brain. The role of pain medicines is to block these pain messages or lessen their effect.

Acetaminophen (found in Tylenol) and ibuprofen (found in Motrin) are two of the most commonly used mild analgesics for treating minor pain or reducing fevers. Occasionally, a serious illness or a chronic disease will cause serious pain. In this case, a doctor may prescribe stronger analgesics such as codeine or morphine. We'll discuss codeine and morphine in greater detail later in the lesson.

Remember, however, that pain relievers and fever reducers do not actually fight the problem; they only ease the symptoms. You may feel better after taking Tylenol, for example, but you still need rest, fluids, and possibly other medicine.

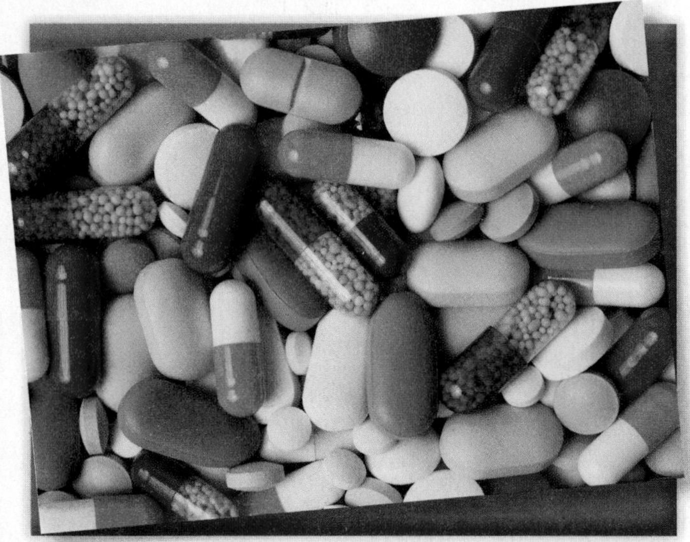

Never mix medicines without asking.

The FDA has published warnings against overuse of the analgesic Tylenol. Taking more than the recommended dose can lead to serious liver damage. This is one reason why following dosage recommendations is important.

Other Medicines

A variety of medicines are available to treat people with certain health problems or conditions. Specific medicines are used by people with chronic (ongoing) conditions, including heart and blood pressure problems, diabetes, and allergies.

How Medicines Affect the Body

The effects of a medicine in the body depend on the type and amount of medicine taken. The way a medicine is taken will also affect how quickly it begins to work in the body. In addition, medicines will affect each person differently. That is why it is important for medicine to be used only as prescribed or directed, and only by the person who needs the medicine. Figure 4.2 illustrates the four main ways in which medicines can enter the body.

Side Effects

In addition to their intended effects, some medicines also cause one or more side effects. A side effect is *any effect of a medicine other than the one intended*. Some side effects, such as kidney failure, can be harmful, but others are minor and may be temporary until the body adjusts to the medicine. Common side effects include headaches, rashes, an upset stomach, and drowsiness. Some people may be allergic to certain medicines and may need to see a doctor about a replacement.

Tolerance

When used over a long period, certain medicines can cause a person to develop a tolerance. For medicine, tolerance is *a condition in which a person's body becomes used to the effect of a medicine and needs greater and greater amounts of it in order for it to be effective*. In some cases, the medicine ceases to be effective and the doctor must prescribe a different type of medicine.

The way medicines enter the body depends on their form.

Ingestion

Medicine in the form of pills, tablets, capsules, and liquids is ingested, or swallowed. The medicine moves through the stomach and small intestine and is absorbed into the bloodstream and circulated throughout the body. You can also take cold medicines this way.

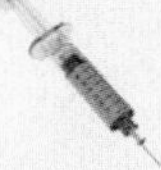

Injection

Medicine given through injection goes directly into the blood. Some injections are given in a vein, others under the skin or into a muscle. If you have diabetes, you may need to give yourself daily injections. Vaccines are examples of medicines given through injections.

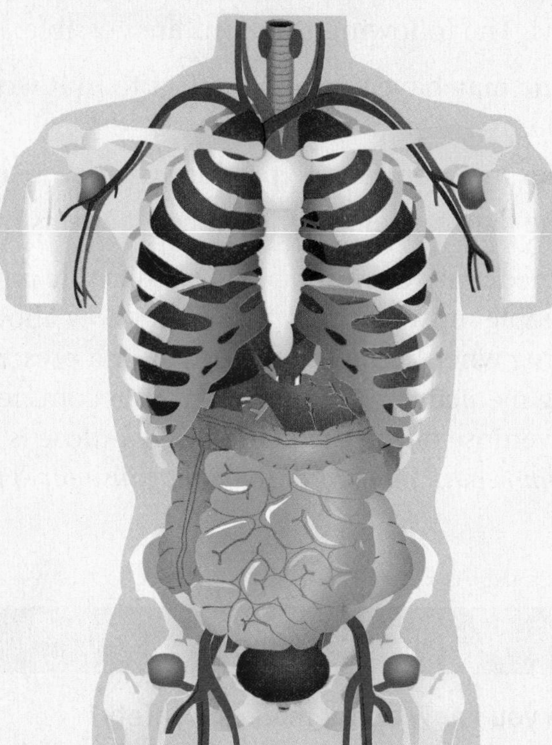

© rudall30/Fotolia.com

Inhalation

When a liquid medicine is changed into a fine mist, it can be inhaled, or breathed in. If you have asthma, you may need an inhaler.

Absorption

Creams and ointments are applied to the skin or scalp and absorbed by the body. Skin patches are applied to the skin and release medicine over time. If you have a rash, for example, you may rub ointment or lotion on the rash to reduce itching.

FIGURE 4.2

How Medicines Enter the Body

(Ingestion) © Vadym Tynenko/Fotolia.com; (Injection) © mipan/Fotolia.com; (Inhalation) © Andrzej Tokarski/Fotolia.com; (Absorption) © blueringmedia/Fotolia.com

Overuse of Medicines

If medicines are overused, they can lose their ability to fight diseases. For example, the use of penicillin became widespread in the 1940s. Penicillin is an antibiotic used to fight infections. Within just a few years, new strains of bacteria had developed. The new bacteria were resistant to penicillin. The more often antibiotics are used, the more likely it is that bacteria will develop a resistance to them. This risk is another reason you should always use medicines wisely and in moderation.

Mixing Medicines

When two or more medicines are taken at the same time, the combined effects may be dangerous. The following reactions are possible:

- Each medicine may have a stronger effect than it would have if taken alone.
- The medicines may combine to produce unexpected effects.
- One medicine may cancel out the expected effects of the other.

Because mixing medicines can produce unpredictable and sometimes even deadly results, people must let their physician know about any medicines they are presently taking when receiving treatment or a prescription for additional medicine. Mixing medicines without a doctor's recommendation or consent can easily cause an overdose of the medicine. An overdose is *when you take more than the normal or recommended amount of something, usually a prescribed medicine or illegal drug.*

Medicine Safety in the Home

How much do you know about medicine safety?
Follow these tips to store, use, and dispose of medicines safely:

- Store medicines in a cool, dry place.
- Keep medicines safely sealed in childproof containers, and keep them out of the reach of children.
- Keep certain medicines in the refrigerator. Check the label to see if refrigeration is required.
- Do not share prescription medicines. They could cause serious harm to someone else.
- Do not use nonprescription medicines for more than ten days at a time unless you check with your doctor.
- Before taking two or more medicines at the same time, get your doctor's approval.
- Know what medicines are in your home and what they are used to treat. Keep only those that are currently needed.
- Do not use medicines that have passed their expiration date.
- To safely dispose of outdated or unused liquids or pills, contact your city or county government's household trash and recycling service to see if there is a medicine take-back program in your community and learn about any special rules regarding which medicines can be taken back.

Drug Misuse and Abuse

Remember, medicines are a type of drug intended to help people with certain illnesses and conditions. However, medicines can be harmful if misused. Other types of drugs are not medicines and can be even more dangerous. Drug *misusers* take legal drugs in an improper way, either for a reason not intended or by a person without a prescription. Drug *abusers* take legal or illegal drugs in a way that is harmful to your health.

Drug Misuse

The following are forms of drug misuse:

- Using a drug without following the directions
- Combining medicines without a physician's advice
- Taking more of a drug than the doctor ordered
- Using a drug prescribed for someone else
- Giving your prescription to someone else
- Using a drug for longer than a physician advises
- Using a medicine when you do not need it

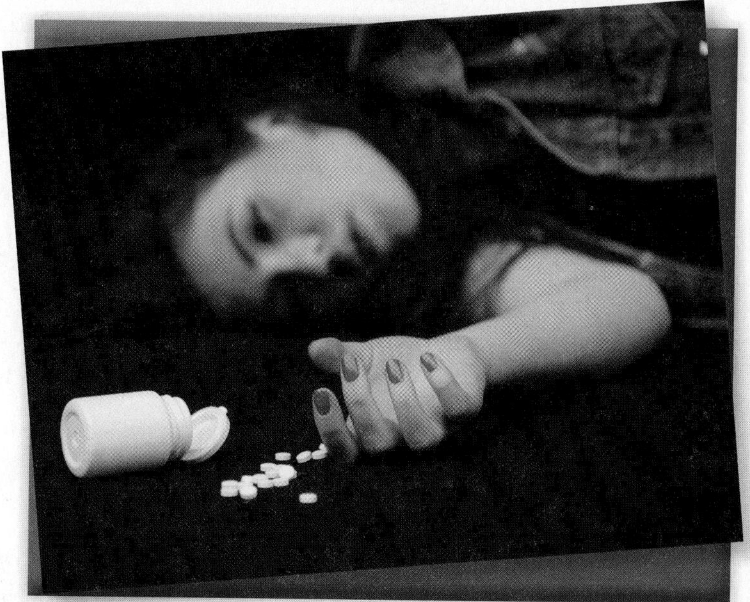

Misuse of medicines can lead to serious medical problems.
© Photobank/Fotolia.com

Drug Abuse

The following are forms of drug abuse:

- Using any illegal drug
- Taking a substance that was not meant to enter the body
- Using a drug for purposes other than medical treatment
- Faking health problems to obtain or renew a prescription

How Drugs Affect the Brain

The brain is the command center of your body. It controls just about everything you do, even when you are sleeping. When drugs enter the brain, they can interrupt the work and actually change how the brain performs its jobs. These changes are what lead to compulsive drug use and addiction.

Drug abuse affects three primary areas of the brain:

- **The brain stem** is in charge of all of the functions our body needs to stay alive—breathing, circulating blood, and digesting food.
- **The limbic system** links together a bunch of brain structures that control our emotional responses, such as feeling pleasure when we eat chocolate. The good feelings motivate us to repeat the behavior.
- **The cerebral cortex** is the mushroom-like outer part of the brain (the gray matter). In humans, it is so big that it makes up about three-fourths of the entire brain. The front part of the cortex, known as the frontal cortex or forebrain, is the thinking center. It powers our ability to think, plan, solve problems, and make decisions.

Drugs are chemicals. They work in the brain by tapping into its communication system and interfering with the way nerve cells normally send, receive, and process information. Different drugs—because of their chemical structures—work differently. In fact, some drugs can change the brain in ways that last long after the person has stopped taking drugs, maybe even permanently. This is more likely when a drug is taken repeatedly.

There are three categories of illegal drugs that are being used today: narcotics, stimulants, and depressants. All three affect the brain differently and can ultimately lead to addiction and death.

Narcotics

Narcotics are *specific drugs that are obtainable only by prescription and are used to relieve pain.* Doctors may prescribe the narcotics morphine or codeine, for example, to treat extreme pain. Narcotics can be safe when taken under a physician's supervision, but they are so addictive that their sale and use are controlled by law. People with an **addiction** have *a physical or psychological need for a drug.* Pharmacists must keep records of all sales of narcotics.

Morphine

Morphine is a medication used to relieve pain. It reduces the intensity of pain signals reaching the brain and affects those brain areas controlling emotion, which reduces the effects of a painful stimulus such as a burn or broken bone.

Morphine also suppresses the immune system, the body's defense against infections. Because of this effect, doctors weigh the pain-relief benefits against the added risk of infection, particularly for those being treated for severe burns or certain cancers. Morphine abusers, many of whom are already infection-prone due to unclean needles, repeated injections, and poor nutrition and living conditions, are rendered even more vulnerable by these drugs.

Codeine

Codeine is used to relieve mild to moderate pain. It is also used, usually in combination with other medications, to reduce coughing. Combination products that contain codeine should not be used in teens younger than 16 years of age. Codeine will help relieve symptoms but will not treat the cause of symptoms or speed recovery. Codeine belongs to a class of medications called narcotic analgesics. When codeine is used to treat pain, it works by changing the way the brain and nervous system respond to pain. When codeine is used to reduce coughing, it works by decreasing the activity in the part of the brain that causes coughing.

Codeine can slow or stop your breathing. Never use this medicine in larger amounts, or for longer than prescribed. Codeine may also be habit-forming, and should only be used as prescribed.

Stimulants

Stimulants (STIM·you·lunts) are *substances that speed up the body's functions*. Stimulants come in a variety of forms, all of which are very dangerous if abused. Stimulants make the heart beat faster, increase breathing rate, and raise blood pressure. The effects of some stimulants are so mild that people may not even realize they are using a drug. Caffeine, for instance, is a stimulant found in cocoa, coffee, tea, energy drinks, and many soft drinks. It is a legal drug that is not harmful in very small doses; however, it can be harmful and addictive if you take too much of it.

Some stimulants may be prescribed to help people with certain physical or emotional problems. However, stimulant abuse can be very dangerous. High doses of strong stimulants may cause blurred vision, dizziness, anxiety, loss of coordination, or collapse. Stimulants such as amphetamine, *cocaine*, and *crack* (defined below) can also become habit-forming, and you can become addicted quickly. Table 4.1 describes some common stimulants and their harmful effects.

Do Prescription Stimulants Make You Smarter?

A growing number of teenagers and young adults are abusing prescription stimulants to boost their study performance in an effort to improve their grades in school, and there is a widespread belief that these drugs can improve a person's ability to learn.

Prescription stimulants do promote staying awake; however, studies published by the National Institute on Drug Abuse (NIDA) have found that stimulants do not enhance learning or thinking ability when taken by people who do not actually have **Attention Deficit Hyperactivity Disorder (ADHD)**. ADHD is *a common childhood disorder that includes symptoms such as not staying focused or paying attention, difficulty controlling behavior, and hyperactivity*. Also, research has shown that students who abuse prescription stimulants actually have lower GPAs in high school and college than those who don't.

Amphetamine

Amphetamine (am·FE·tuh·meen) is *a drug that stimulates the central nervous system.* Doctors may prescribe amphetamines to treat hyperactivity and ADHD. Amphetamines are highly addictive, however. People who use or abuse amphetamines can develop a dependence on the drugs, needing larger and larger doses to get the desired effect. If you have a prescription for these, do not take more than your assigned dosage.

Methamphetamine (Meth)

Methamphetamine (meth·am·FE·tuh·meen) is a stimulant similar to amphetamine. Doctors prescribe methamphetamines to treat diseases such as narcolepsy, Parkinson's disease, and obesity. Narcolepsy is *a condition that causes individuals to suffer frequent, brief, and uncontrollable deep sleep.* Parkinson's disease is *a progressive nervous disorder where the individual shows symptoms of trembling hands, lifeless face, and a slow shuffling walk.* Using this drug heavily or over a long time can lead to serious side effects such as aggression, paranoia, kidney problems, brain damage, depression, weakening of the immune system, convulsions, and schizophrenia. Schizophrenia is *a very serious mental illness in which someone cannot think or behave normally and often experiences delusions.*

Table 4.1 Effects of Stimulants

Substance	Other Names	Forms	Methods of Use	Harmful Effects
Amphetamine	Blue or black mollies, speed, footballs, whiz, uppers, louee, goey	Pills, powder, chunky crystals	Swallowed, snorted up the nose	Uneven heartbeat, rise in blood pressure, physical collapse
Methamphetamine	Meth, crank, ice, shabu, crystal	Pills, powder, crystals	Swallowed, snorted up the nose, smoked, injected	Memory loss, damage to heart and nervous system, seizures, death
Cocaine	Coke, C, dust, snow, flake, blow, girl, nose candy	White powder	Snorted up the nose, injected	Damage to nose lining, liver, and heart; heart attack; seizures; stroke; and death
Crack	Crack, freebase rocks, rock, 24-7	Off-white rocks or chunks	Smoked, injected	Damage to lungs if smoked, seizures, heart attack, and death

In recent years, methamphetamine (meth) has appeared in "club drugs." Club drugs are *dangerous, illegal substances available at dance clubs and all-night parties*. You'll learn more about club drugs later in the lesson. Meth is a white, bitter powder and easily dissolves in water or alcohol. Sometimes it's made into a white pill or a shiny, white or clear rock called crystal meth that is smoked in a pipe.

Meth can quickly lead to addiction. It causes medical problems that include:

- Making your body temperature so high that you pass out
- Severe itching
- "Meth mouth"—broken teeth and dry mouth
- Thinking and emotional problems

Cocaine

Cocaine is a powerful, illegal stimulant. Its abuse has become a major health problem in the United States. Some people use cocaine because it makes them feel happy and energetic. This feeling is short-lived, however, and is followed by depression as the drug wears off. Users often take more cocaine to relieve the depression, thus forming an addiction to it. Powdered cocaine is a white powder (which scientists call a hydrochloride salt) made from the leaf of the coca plant. Street dealers generally mix cocaine with other substances like cornstarch, talcum powder, or sugar. Cocaine is a dangerous drug, and an overdose can lead to a heart attack or stroke.

Crack

Crack cocaine is a concentrated form of cocaine that can be smoked. Smoking crack has the same effects on the body as using cocaine, only stronger. Crack reaches the brain within seconds and produces an intense high. The high lasts only for a few minutes, though, and is followed by an equally intense low. Using crack makes you crave even more of the drug to relieve these intense bad feelings. For these reasons, the National Institutes of Health (NIH) lists crack as one of the most addictive and dangerous drugs used in the United States today.

Depressants

Depressants are *substances that slow down the body's functions and reactions*. These substances, which are often called sedatives, lower blood pressure and slow down heart rate and breathing. Doctors sometimes prescribe depressants for relief of anxiety, tension, nervousness, and sleeplessness. There are three main kinds of depressants:

- **Tranquilizers** (TRAN·kwuh·lie·zerz), when used as prescribed by a physician, can help reduce anxiety and relax muscles.
- **Barbiturates** (bar·BI·chu·ruhts) are powerful sedatives that produce a feeling of relaxation.
- **Hypnotics** (hip·NAH·tiks) are very strong drugs that bring on sleep.

Table 4.2 Effects of Depressants

Substance	Other Names	Forms	Methods of Use	Harmful Effects
Tranquilizer	Valium, Librium, Xanax	Pills or capsules	Swallowed	Anxiety; reduced coordination and attention span. Withdrawal can cause tremors and lead to coma or death.
Barbiturate	Downers, barbs, yellow jackets, reds, goof balls, pink ladies	Pills or capsules	Swallowed	Causes mood changes and excessive sleep. Can lead to coma and death.
Hypnotic	Sonata, Ambien, Ambien CR, ProSom	Pills or capsules	Swallowed	Impaired coordination and judgment. High doses may cause internal bleeding, coma, or death.

Any depressants should be taken only under a doctor's supervision. Even drugs authorized or prescribed by a doctor can, if taken over an extended period, cause dependence and a need for more and more of the drug. Do not deviate from the prescription instructions when taking such drugs. If abused, depressants can have many harmful effects on the body, up to and including death.

Depressants produce effects similar to those produced by alcohol, which itself is a form of depressant. When depressants are combined with alcohol, the effects increase, and the risks multiply. The results can be deadly. Table 4.2 provides more information about depressants and their effects on the body. Lesson 3 of this chapter discusses alcohol use in greater detail.

Street Drugs

Companies that manufacture drugs sold as medicines must follow strict government regulations. These laws ensure that the medicines are pure and consistent in strength, known risks, and side effects. *Any drug that is made or sold illegally* is considered a **street drug**.

Street drugs include illegally made, packaged, or sold legal drugs, such as amphetamines and meth. Street drugs also include illegal drugs, such as heroin, hashish, and marijuana. There are no guarantees that street drugs contain what they claim to contain. People who use them don't know how much of the drug they are actually taking. As a result, they risk being poisoned and dying of accidental overdose.

Heroin Is Addictive and Not Selective in Whom It Kills

Many famous people have died as a result of their heroin addiction. Their age at the time of death is listed beside their name:

Cory Monteith (31)—TV actor from "Glee"
Kurt Cobain (27)—Nirvana lead singer
Jim Morrison (27)—Lead singer of the band The Doors
Janis Joplin (27)—One of the greatest female folk-rock singers of all-time
John Belushi (33)—Saturday Night Live comedian and movie star
Lucy Grealy (39)—Poet
Philip Seymour Hoffman (46)—Award-winning actor
Chris Kelley (34)—Member of rap duo Kris Kross
Bradley Nowell (28)—Lead singer for the band Sublime
Dee Dee Ramone (50)—Founder of band The Ramones
Sid Vicious (21)—Bassist for the punk band The Sex Pistols
Rachel Whitear (21)—College student
Paula Yates (41)—British television personality and writer

Heroin

Heroin (HAIR·uh·win) is an illegal narcotic that is made from the pain killer morphine, a natural substance in the seedpod of the Asian poppy plant. This section discusses overdose due to heroin. An overdose may result in serious, harmful symptoms or death.

Heroin is a white or brown powder or black, sticky goo. It can be mixed with water and injected with a needle. Heroin can also be smoked or snorted up the nose. All of these ways of taking heroin send it to the brain very quickly. This makes it very addictive.

It is the most commonly abused narcotic. When users do not get the heroin they need, they feel severe pain. Heroin depresses the central nervous system and can lead to coma or death. Other effects include:

- Feeling sick or itchy
- Having trouble breathing
- Going into a coma, *a deep state of unconsciousness*
- Increased risk of contracting hepatitis or HIV because drug users often share dirty needles

Marijuana and Hashish

Marijuana is the most commonly used street drug. Marijuana is a dry, shredded green and brown mix of leaves, flowers, stems, and seeds from the hemp plant *Cannabis sativa.* Hemp is *a strong stemmed plant used for making rope; marijuana is made from types of hemp. The main mind-altering chemical in marijuana* is THC (tetrahydrocannabinol). THC harms the brain in many ways, as described below.

Although some users mix marijuana with food and eat it, most choose to smoke it. As a result, marijuana smokers experience many of the same lung problems as tobacco smokers. These include persistent coughing, bronchitis symptoms, and frequent colds. Marijuana smoke contains three to five times the amount of tar and other cancer-causing substances found in tobacco smoke.

Research clearly demonstrates that marijuana has the potential to cause problems in daily life or make a person's existing problems worse. In fact, heavy marijuana users generally report lower life satisfaction, poorer mental and physical health, relationship problems, and less academic and career success compared to their peers who came from similar backgrounds. For example, marijuana use is associated with a higher likelihood of dropping out from school. Several studies published by the National Institute on Drug Abuse (NIDA) also associate workers' marijuana smoking with increased absences, tardiness, accidents, workers' compensation claims, and job turnover.

Hashish, which is made from the same plant, is much stronger than marijuana because it contains more THC. The box on the following page lists the effects of marijuana. Hashish consists of the THC-rich material of the cannabis plant, which is collected, dried, and then compressed into a variety of forms, such as balls, cakes, or cookie-like sheets. Pieces are then broken off, placed in pipes, and smoked.

Implications of Possession of Marijuana in States That Have Legalized It

You may have heard that in some places marijuana use is legal. As of 2013, 18 states and the District of Columbia had passed laws allowing the sale and use of marijuana as "medicine" for certain conditions. Among these, Colorado and Washington have made recreational (general, non-medical) use legal for people over 21. These new laws may make it *seem* as if it's safe or "okay" to use marijuana. However, it's not okay! The associated physical and mental health issues have not gone away.

Even though some states are allowing some people to use marijuana, it is not legal for minors (under 21). In addition, *marijuana use is still illegal under federal law.* You could be charged with a misdemeanor for simply having marijuana in your possession—even if you haven't used it! A **misdemeanor** is *a crime less serious than a felony that results in a less severe punishment*. If you have sold or helped sell it, the crime and the punishment are now considered a felony. A **felony** is *a more serious crime than a misdemeanor that violates federal laws and can lead to severe punishments, such as being sentenced to prison.*

It is true that the cannabis plant contains some chemicals that can temporarily ease pain, as some medicines do; however, there are more efficient, less harmful ways to get those same effects. And whether or not it is legal in your state, *marijuana is extremely dangerous, especially for young people.*

Remember, the voting adults who live in a state, not the medical or drug researchers, make and vote on the laws. They do not necessarily understand how harmful a substance like marijuana is. The Food and Drug Administration (FDA) has a scientific review process for determining whether a drug is safe, and even after enormous and ongoing research, the FDA has not found marijuana to be safe or effective as medicine.

NIDA research shows that as a young person, you are almost twice as likely as an adult to become addicted to marijuana if you use it.

Marijuana and other illicit drugs are addictive and unsafe especially for use by young people. As stated by officials with the NIDA, drug addiction is a progressive disease and the earlier one starts, the more likely the chances of developing a substance use disorder.

Synthetic Marijuana (Spice)

A recent way illegal drug makers have tried to get around the laws against selling naturally occurring drugs like marijuana is to develop synthetic versions that have similar effects. Synthetic means *to be made from artificial materials or substances, not natural ones*. Spice is *a term for a variety of mixtures of plant material and chemicals that create mind-altering effects like marijuana*. Some versions of spice even claim to be "natural" on the label, but this refers to the plant material inside, not the harmful chemical mixed with it. Like marijuana, spice is mainly taken through smoke inhalation. Sometimes it is drunk like a tea. Be careful: some spice products are sold as incense. A friend or acquaintance might light some "incense," claiming it is harmless and legal, when in fact it could be a synthetic drug or even have marijuana mixed into it.

What Does Marijuana Do to You?

- Weakens your memory, reaction time, and coordination; clouds your judgment
- Lowers your initiative and ambition
- Increases your heart rate and appetite
- Lowers your body temperature
- Damages your heart and lungs
- Interferes with your normal body development by changing hormone levels
- May cause addiction

Common street names for marijuana include pot, grass, weed, joint, and herb.

Easy access and the belief that spice products are "natural" and therefore harmless have contributed to its popularity. The Department of Defense has determined that spice is illegal and punishable.

Research into the effects of spice is very limited right now, but people who use it have reported anxiety, paranoia, and hallucinations as well as rapid heart rate, vomiting, agitation, and confusion.

Spice goes by a number of nicknames, including blaze, fake weed, genie, Yucatan fire, and K2, among others. According to the National Institute on Drug Abuse, spice is also often labeled "not for human consumption" and contains dried, shredded plant material and chemical additives that cause psychoactive (mind-altering) effects.

The Dangers of Hallucinogens

Hallucinogens (huh·LOO·sin·uh·jenz) are *drugs that distort moods, thoughts, and senses.* Hallucinogens can have many harmful effects on the body, up to and including death. Like other types of drugs, they can have both physical and psychological effects on users. Physical effects of hallucinogens include increased heart rate and blood pressure and lack of muscle coordination. Hallucinogens can also cause decreased sensitivity to pain, which can result in serious self-injury.

A psychological effect of taking a hallucinogen is to hallucinate, which is to see things that are not really there. In addition, sometimes these drugs can trigger uncontrolled, violent behavior. Hallucinogens also cause people to lose their sense of direction, distance, and time. These effects often lead to misjudgments that result in serious injuries and death.

PCP

Phencyclidine (fen·SI·kluh·deen), commonly called PCP, is a powerful and dangerous hallucinogen whose effects last a long time. PCP produces strange, destructive behavior, which causes many users to end up in hospital emergency rooms. PCP use often leads to **psychological dependence**, *an addiction in which the mind sends the body a message that it needs more of a drug.* Table 4.3 provides more information about PCP. Among the adverse psychological effects reported are:

- Symptoms that mimic delusions, hallucinations, unorganized thinking, and a sensation of an out-of-body experience, as if floating above your surroundings.
- Mood disturbances: Approximately 50 percent of individuals brought to emergency rooms because of PCP-induced problems reported significant elevations in anxiety.
- People who have abused PCP for long periods have reported memory loss, difficulties with speech and thinking, depression, and weight loss. These symptoms can persist up to one year after stopping PCP abuse.

PCP is addictive—its repeated abuse can lead to craving and compulsive PCP-seeking behavior, despite severe adverse effects.

LSD

LSD is an abbreviation for lysergic (luh·SER·jik) acid diethylamide (dy·e·thuh·LA·myd), another powerful hallucinogen. Use of LSD often produces rapid mood swings and hallucinations. Some users have terrifying thoughts and feelings, such as a fear that they are dying or going crazy. Many LSD users experience flashbacks. During a flashback, the effects of LSD may recur days, months, or years after the drug was taken. The user's sense of time and self is altered. Experiences may seem to "cross over" different senses, giving the user the feeling of hearing colors and seeing sounds. These changes can be frightening and can cause panic. Table 4.3 gives additional information about LSD.

The effects of LSD depend largely on the amount taken. LSD causes dilated or enlarged pupils; can raise body temperature and increase heart rate and blood pressure; and can cause profuse sweating, loss of appetite, sleeplessness, dry mouth, and tremors.

Table 4.3 Effects of Hallucinogens

Substance	Other Names	Forms	Methods of Use	Harmful Effects
PCP	Angel dust, supergrass, killer weed, rocket fuel	White powder; tablet, capsule, liquid	Applied to liquid or leafy materials and smoked	Loss of coordination; increase in heart rate, blood pressure, and body temperature; convulsions, heart and lung failure, or broken blood vessels; bizarre or violent behavior; temporary psychosis; false feeling of having super powers
LSD	Acid, blotter, microdot, white lightning	Tablets; squares soaked on paper	Eaten or licked	Increase in blood pressure, heart rate, and body temperature; chills, nausea, tremors, and sleeplessness; unpredictable behavior; flashbacks; false feeling of having super powers
Psilocybin	Magic mushrooms, shrooms	Dried form or mixed with tea	Dried, eaten, or brewed in a tea	Hallucinations, an altered perception of time, an inability to discern fantasy from reality, panic; long-term effects such as flashbacks, risk of psychiatric illness, impaired memory

Psilocybin (Mushrooms)

Mushrooms containing psilocybin (sil·a·sy·bin) are available fresh or dried and are typically taken orally. It can produce muscle relaxation or weakness, uncoordinated muscles, excessive pupil dilation, nausea, vomiting, and drowsiness.

Individuals who abuse psilocybin mushrooms also risk poisoning if one of many existing varieties of poisonous mushrooms is incorrectly identified as a psilocybin mushroom.

How Inhalants Affect the Body

Not all dangerous drugs are illegal street drugs. Inhalants are *substances whose fumes are sniffed and inhaled to produce mind-altering sensations*. Household products that come in aerosol spray cans are commonly used as inhalants.

Abusers of inhalants breathe them in through the nose or mouth in a variety of ways (known as "huffing"). They may sniff or snort fumes from a container or dispenser (such as a glue bottle or a marking pen), spray aerosols (such as paint or computer cleaning dusters) directly into their nose or mouth, or place a chemical-soaked rag in their mouth. Abusers may also inhale fumes from a balloon or a plastic or paper bag. Although the high produced by inhalants usually lasts just a few minutes, abusers often try to prolong it by continuing to inhale repeatedly over several hours. These substances are not meant to be taken into the body and can be very dangerous.

When inhalants are breathed in, their harmful fumes go directly to the brain. These fumes commonly cause headache, nausea, vomiting, and loss of coordination. Just one use can result in sudden death. Inhalant use can also lead to physical dependence, *a type of addiction in which the body itself (rather than just the mind, as with psychological dependence, defined above) feels a direct need for a drug*. Long-term inhalant use can damage the liver, kidneys, and brain. There is a common link between inhalant use and problems in school, including failing grades, chronic absences, and general lack of interest. Other signs include the following:

- Paint or stains on body or clothing
- Spots or sores around the mouth
- Red or runny eyes or nose
- Chemical breath odor
- Drunk, dazed, or dizzy appearance
- Nausea, loss of appetite
- Anxiety, excitability, irritability

Dangers of Skittle Parties

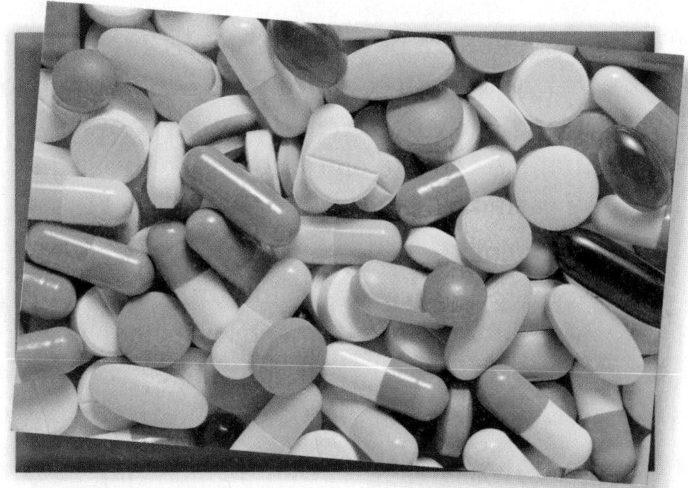
Mixing any type of drug is not safe.

A Skittle party is a slang term for a party (or just a drug-taking gathering) at which people, typically teens, take a variety of drugs without knowing what they are taking, such as you might grab a handful of Skittle candies without caring what flavors you get. Perhaps someone will even mix Skittle candies in with the drugs to make the drug taking appear more fun. *Don't be deceived; you could die at that party.*

A Skittle party is just one type of situation where you could find people your age using drugs you never thought you would even come across. You must be on guard against situations that can tempt or lead you to take drugs, even if you were not intending to at first. Pressure from friends can make you feel as though the dangers discussed in this lesson mean little compared to how good you imagine you will feel to be "part of the group." On the other hand, you may not even realize that others are giving out or taking drugs until you have taken some yourself.

Club Drugs

Club drugs get their name from being associated with nightclubs, concerts, and all-night dance parties occasionally called "raves." Other terms for drugs associated with these activities are "designer drugs" and "look-alike drugs." The term "designer drug" often refers to a synthetic version of a natural drug. Look-alike drugs are drugs that resemble and are passed off as another drug.

Some club drugs are colorless, tasteless, and odorless. These properties have led to the dangerous practice of drug "slipping," which means placing a drug in someone's food or beverage without that person's knowledge. Some people have used drug slipping to help them sexually assault or rape someone; therefore, some club drugs are sometimes called "date rape drugs." Commonly used club drugs include the following:

- **Ecstasy**, also called E, X, and XTC, is a stimulant and a hallucinogen in pill form. It can cause confusion, depression, anxiety, nausea, faintness, chills, or sweating. Ecstasy can cause permanent brain damage.
- **GHB** is a depressant, and its street names include Liquid Ecstasy, Liquid X, Georgia Home Boy, and Grievous Bodily Harm. Available in powder and liquid form, GHB is especially dangerous when taken with alcohol or other drugs. The combination may result in sleep, coma, and death.

- **Rohypnol** is a powerful sedative. It's also called the date rape drug, Roofies, and R-2. Rohypnol is typically a small white tablet, which when dissolved in liquid, has no taste or odor. The drug's short-term effect is a sleepy, relaxed feeling that lasts two to eight hours. The user might also black out and have loss of memory.
- **Ketamine** is an anesthetic used for medical purposes, mostly in treating animals. Misused as a club drug, Ketamine is often sold as a white powder to be snorted, like cocaine, or injected. The drug is also smoked with marijuana or tobacco products. Ketamine causes hallucinations and dreamlike states. It can also cause high blood pressure or death through respiratory failure.

Synthetic drugs and **bath salts** refer to another, newer type of man-made drug aimed at avoiding detection. These bath salts have nothing to do with taking a bath; they are usually in a white or brown powder form and are sometimes disguised as "plant food," "jewelry cleaner," or "phone screen cleaner." They are given several different nicknames, including Ivory Wave, Bloom, Cloud Nine, Lunar Wave, Vanilla Sky, White Lightning, and Scarface.

Bath salts are typically taken orally, inhaled, or injected, with the worst outcomes associated with snorting or needle injection. Bath salts have been linked to an alarming surge in visits to emergency departments and poison control centers across the country. Common reactions reported for people who have needed medical attention after using bath salts include cardiac symptoms (such as racing heart, high blood pressure, and chest pains) and psychiatric symptoms including paranoia, hallucinations, and panic attacks.

Bath salts affect the brain much in the same way that methamphetamines do. Don't let anyone deceive you with talk about "legal drugs"; whether legal or not, these are harmful drugs and can be highly addictive.

Help for Drug Users

Drug addiction is a complex illness characterized by intense and, at times, uncontrollable drug craving, along with compulsive drug-seeking and use that persists even in the face of devastating consequences. While the path to drug addiction begins with the voluntary act of taking drugs, over time a person's ability to choose not to do so becomes compromised, and seeking and consuming the drug becomes compulsive. This behavior results largely from the effects of prolonged drug exposure on brain functioning. Addiction is a brain disease that affects multiple brain circuits, including those involved in reward and motivation, learning and memory, and control over behavior.

Kicking the Habit

Kicking the drug habit once addicted is *much harder* than resisting the pressure to start. The first step is for the drug user to recognize that a problem exists. The next step is to start the recovery process. A person who has become physically or psychologically addicted to a drug will suffer withdrawal during the recovery process. Withdrawal includes *the physical and psychological symptoms that occur when someone stops using an addictive substance.*

Withdrawal symptoms vary depending on the drug used but may include vomiting, headaches, chills, and hallucinations. Withdrawal is often a painful process, and medications are usually given to ease the withdrawal symptoms. In addition to ridding one's body of the addictive substance, the recovering drug user must change his or her thinking and the habits that led to the drug use. Although withdrawing from drugs is difficult, the benefits of becoming drug free are well worth the effort.

Getting Help

Drug users can rarely recover alone; they need help. Most communities offer support groups and treatment programs for drug addiction. A support group is a group of people who share a common problem and work together to help one another cope and recover. Common support groups for drug addiction include Narcotics Anonymous and Cocaine Anonymous. Nar-Anon (not the same as Narcotics Anonymous) provides help for those who have been affected by *someone else's* drug use, most commonly family members or close friends. If you are uncertain whether it may be necessary for a friend or family member to get help, consider the following warning signs of addiction that may indicate the need for help:

- Significant changes in weight
- Poor personal hygiene
- Fights with friends and family members
- Promises to get help that are not kept
- Withdrawal from family functions
- Lying about where they have been
- Accusations of petty crimes
- Denial of drug and/or alcohol use

A good drug treatment program uses trained experts who provide education and support and who can help the user through the withdrawal period. Withdrawal often requires detoxification (dee·tocks·i·fi·KAY·shuhn), *the physical process of freeing the body of an addictive substance.* "Detox" also involves helping the user overcome psychological dependence on the substance and regain health. A variety of treatment programs are available to help people recover from drug abuse:

- **Detox units** are usually part of a hospital or other treatment center. Addicts remain under a doctor's care while going through detoxification.
- **Inpatient treatment centers** are places where people stay for a month or more to fully concentrate on recovery.
- **Outpatient treatment centers** are places where people get treatment for a few hours each day. Then they return to their homes and regular surroundings.
- **Individual and group counseling** focuses on reducing or stopping illicit drug or alcohol use; it also addresses related areas of impaired functioning—such as employment status, illegal activity, and family/social relations—as well as the content and structure of the patient's recovery program.

Remember: It is much harder to stop once you start than it is to never start.

Reasons to be Drug Free

- You will *not be breaking the law.*
- You will have *better concentration and memory.*
- You will make *wiser decisions.*
- You will be able to *focus on improving* your talents and enjoying your interests.
- You will have more *natural energy.*
- You can reach your *full growth potential.*
- You can be as *healthy as possible.*
- You will *look better* because drugs will ruin your appearance.
- You will have *better control* of your feelings and actions.
- You will *not regret foolish actions* caused by drug-impaired judgment.
- You will *not waste money* on drugs.
- You will have *better relationships* with friends and family members.
- You will *respect yourself* for taking care of your body and mind.
- You will be able to *succeed in education.*
- Your *mental and emotional development* will not be cognitively delayed.

Being drug free allows you to have more success in your life.

Courtesy of Michael Wetzel/US Air Force JROTC

Living Drug Free

You have the responsibility—to yourself, to your loved ones, and to the community you live in—to be the healthiest person you can be. The best way to meet that responsibility is to make wise choices that have a positive effect on your health. One of the most important decisions you can make is to be drug free. One of the best ways to avoid becoming addicted to drugs is through education. The National Family Partnership (NFP) is a national leader in drug prevention and education. NPF has organized the Nationwide Red Ribbon Campaign. The Red Ribbon Campaign mobilizes communities to educate youth and encourage participation in drug prevention activities. The box on the preceding page shows some of the many advantages of avoiding drugs.

Ways to Live Drug Free

Choosing to live drug free will provide lifelong benefits. You will find that there are many exciting ways to spend your time.

If you feel lonely, depressed, or bored:

- Learn a new sport or hobby or join a club.
- Start a regular physical activity routine like running, bicycling, or swimming. You should challenge yourself by setting goals using the SMART system.
- Volunteer to help people in your community.

If you need help solving personal problems:

- Talk to a school counselor or an adult you trust.
- Contact a hot line or support group.
- Seek counsel through your church, temple, or mosque.

If you are tense and anxious:

- Learn relaxation techniques like yoga or tai chi.
- Meditate.
- Get enough rest and physical activity and eat properly.
- Use time management skills to avoid overscheduling your time.

Learning a new hobby is just one drug-free way to feel better about yourself.

© Sabphoto/Fotolia.com

Lesson 1 Review

Using complete sentences, answer the following questions on a sheet of paper.

1. What are five mistakes people make when taking medicines?
2. What is an antibiotic?
3. Name the four ways medicines enter the body.
4. What is a side effect?
5. List the three possible reactions that can result from taking more than one medicine at the same time.
6. Name five forms of drug *misuse*.
7. What is addiction?
8. What is morphine used for?
9. List four medical problems caused by using meth.
10. What is spice?
11. Define the term hallucinogen.
12. Name two hallucinogens known by their initials.
13. Name four ways you may be able to identify someone who uses inhalants.
14. What are club drugs?
15. Why are some club drugs called date rape drugs?
16. Define the term withdrawal.
17. Name three types of drug treatment programs.
18. What is one of the best ways to prevent drug addiction?
19. List eight reasons why you should stay drug free.

APPLYING YOUR LEARNING

20. You suspect that your best friend has starting huffing aerosol paint. List the signs for someone who may be huffing and what you should do to help your friend become drug free.

LESSON 2

Tobacco

Quick Write

Why do some teenagers begin using tobacco? List all of the reasons you can think of, including those from friends you know who are now smoking.

Learn About

- history of tobacco use
- harmful substances in tobacco
- the costs of tobacco to society
- how to avoid tobacco use

"Of every three young smokers, only one will quit, and one of those remaining smokers will die from tobacco-related causes. Most of these young people never considered the long-term consequences associated with tobacco use when they started smoking."

Report of the Surgeon General of the United States, 2012

History of Tobacco Use

Tobacco was grown by Native American Indians before the Europeans came from England, Spain, France, and Italy to North America. Native Americans smoked tobacco through a pipe for special religious and medical purposes. They did not smoke every day.

Tobacco was the first crop grown for money in North America. In 1612, the settlers of the first American colony in Jamestown, Virginia grew tobacco to make money. It was their main source of income. Other cash crops were corn, cotton, wheat, sugar, and soya beans. Tobacco helped pay for the American Revolution against England. Also, the first President, George Washington, grew tobacco.

A Native American Indian with a ceremonial tobacco pipe.

John K. Hillers/J. Paul Getty Museum/Getty Search Gateway Open Content Images

It was not until a cigarette-making machine was invented in 1881 that cigarette smoking became widespread. Up until that point, those who smoked hand-rolled their cigarettes and cigars, or smoked tobacco in a pipe. The new machine was able to make up to 120,000 cigarettes a day. Sales of cigarettes were in the beginning directed mainly at men.

During World War I and World War II, soldiers fighting overseas were given free cigarettes. By 1944, members of the military purchased or received free almost 75 percent of all cigarettes produced. In 1964, the US Surgeon General, who is appointed by the President of the United States, published the first report on the dangers of smoking.

In 1984, Congress passed a law called the Comprehensive Smoking Education Act. It stated that cigarette companies had to change the warning labels on cigarette packs every three months. Since the 1980s, federal, state, and local governments as well as private companies have been taking actions to restrict cigarette smoking in public places.

Tobacco is a plant that grows best in warm, humid climates. The leaves of a tobacco plant are dried, aged for two or three years, mixed with chemicals, and then made into a product for smoking or chewing. Tobacco use—once thought to be healthful—is now known to be a major cause of early and preventable death. Although banned in many public places throughout the world as a nuisance and a danger, many people still use tobacco on a regular basis.

How Tobacco is Used

Tobacco products now come in many different forms, including cigarettes, cigars, and smokeless tobacco (chewing or dipping). Regardless of the form, all tobacco products are harmful. That's why there are laws to control the advertising and sale of tobacco products. Some of the new products on the market, such as e-cigarettes, are being added to the list that the government considers important to regulate because of their harm on the nation's health.

Vocabulary

- therapeutic
- hydrogen cyanide
- ammonia
- nicotine
- addictive drug
- tar
- cilia
- carbon monoxide
- cancer
- deoxyribonucleic acid (DNA)
- emphysema
- physical dependence
- psychological dependence
- secondhand smoke
- mainstream smoke
- sidestream smoke
- cold turkey
- nicotine patch

Cigarettes

According to statistics published by the Centers for Disease Control and Prevention (CDC), cigarettes are the most common form of tobacco used in the United States. More than 42 million people smoke cigarettes. That's 18 percent of the population. Cigarettes put smokers at risk for a host of life-threatening conditions. These include cancer, infertility, stroke, and lung and heart diseases that will be covered in more detail later in this lesson. Each year more than 480,000 people in the US die from diseases caused by cigarette smoking. Another 16 million suffer from some disease associated with cigarette smoking.

Cigars and Pipes

Cigars contain the same dangerous substances as cigarettes, but in much larger quantities. One large cigar can contain as much tobacco as a pack of cigarettes. Cigar smokers are 4 to 10 times more likely to contract cancer of the mouth, larynx, and esophagus than nonsmokers, and they have a greater risk of dying from heart disease. Cigar smokers can also develop emphysema and episodes of chronic bronchitis, diseases that affect the lungs. About one in six high school boys are reported to be cigar smokers.

Some people smoke pipes, using loose tobacco. Pipe smokers usually inhale less than cigarette and cigar smokers do, but pipe smoking still increases the risk of cancer. Cancers of the lip, mouth, and throat are common among pipe smokers.

Smokeless Tobacco

Smokeless tobacco is tobacco that is chewed, dipped, or sniffed. Chewing tobacco comes in a couple of forms. There are long strands of loose leaves or twists of tobacco. There are also pieces that are called *plugs*, *wads*, or *chew*. These pieces are chewed or placed between the cheek and gum or teeth. Common names for smokeless tobacco also include *snus* (sounds like "snoose") and snuff. Many people believe that smokeless tobacco is safer than other tobacco products because the user doesn't inhale tobacco smoke. This is not true. Users of smokeless tobacco still absorb poisonous substances through the mouth or nose. Smokeless tobacco has been linked to cancers of the mouth, esophagus, larynx, stomach, and pancreas. Chewing tobacco also stains the teeth and causes tooth loss and gum disease. Moreover, tobacco chewers need to spit out tobacco juice from time to time—a habit that many people find offensive.

Youth Risk Behavior Survey found that use of smokeless tobacco among high school kids is even higher than for young adults. They found that about 13 percent of male high school students and more than 2 percent of female high school students had used chewing tobacco.

For a long time, pro baseball players found it convenient, and a bit of a status symbol, to chew tobacco. Young athletes followed their example and youth coaches did little to discourage their players from the practice. Chewing also gave players a sense of a "manly" appearance. However, the documented negative health impacts of chewing tobacco have been alarming. Professional baseball players have since turned to chewing gum, nuts, sunflower seeds, and other less dangerous forms of chewing "pleasures" on the field. In a sense, they had to do so because Major League Baseball took the step in 2011 to prohibit teams from providing tobacco products to players. League policy strongly discourages clubhouse attendants from purchasing tobacco for players. Players also may not do televised interviews while using the products or they can be fined.

Specialty Cigarettes

The use of *bidis* and *clove* cigarettes has increased in the United States. Bidis, sometimes called "beedies," are flavored, unfiltered cigarettes from India. They are popular for their fruit-like or licorice flavorings. Despite the attractive flavors that are added, some bidis contain pure tobacco with seven times as much nicotine and twice as much tar as regular cigarettes. As of October 2009, federal laws were enacted banning such cigarettes from sale in the United States.

Clove cigarettes, also called *kreteks*, are made in Indonesia. They contain tobacco and ground cloves. Clove cigarettes contain 60 to 70 percent tobacco, along with ground cloves, clove oil, and other additives. Users often have the mistaken belief that smoking clove cigarettes is safer than smoking regular cigarettes. However, they have the same health risks as regular cigarettes. In fact, clove cigarettes deliver more nicotine, carbon monoxide, and tar than regular cigarettes. The chemicals in cloves have also been linked to asthma and other lung diseases.

Hookah is another form of tobacco smoking that started in the Middle East. Users burn flavored tobacco (called *shisha*) in a water pipe and inhale the smoke through a long hose. It has become popular among young people who pass the pipe around—a kind of social event. But it is no safer, even though the percentage of tobacco is low. People often think the water filters out the toxins. This is false. In fact, hookah smoke contains more nicotine, carbon monoxide, tar, and heavy metals than regular cigarette smoke.

Several types of cancer have been linked to hookah smoking, including lung, mouth, and bladder cancer. Hookah use is also linked to the spread of infectious diseases by sharing the pipe or through the way the tobacco is prepared.

Electronic Cigarettes

Electronic cigarettes have become especially popular among teens. E-cigarettes look much like traditional cigarettes but they usually use a heat source that is battery powered to turn "e-liquid," a liquid that usually contains nicotine from tobacco and flavorings, into an aerosol. The aerosol is inhaled. The amount of nicotine in the aerosol may vary by brand.

Unlike other smokeless products, little scientific information about the safety of electronic cigarettes exists because regulations are still pending.

So far, not enough evidence has been collected to suggest that e-cigarettes may be safer than regular cigarettes. On the other hand, with regular cigarettes, the biggest danger is the smoke.

Tests of e-cigarettes to this point show that the levels of dangerous chemicals they give off are less than what you'd get from a real cigarette. But it's the nicotine inside the cartridges that is addictive. When you stop using nicotine, you can get withdrawal symptoms. You can feel irritable, depressed, and restless. Your stress level can be raised. These products can also be harmful to people with heart problems.

Nevertheless, it's a big business—a booming, billion-dollar industry that is on track to outsell tobacco products within a decade. The number of young people using these products doubled between 2011 and 2012.

Currently the US Food and Drug Administration (FDA) regulates therapeutic e-cigarettes, cigarettes, cigarette tobacco, roll-your-own tobacco, and smokeless tobacco. Therapeutic means *anything used in the treatment of disease or disorders*. The FDA has recently proposed a new rule that would extend its authority to regulate products like electronic cigarettes, cigars, pipe- and waterpipe tobacco, gels, and certain dissolvables that are not "smokeless tobacco." Once the proposed rule becomes final, the FDA will be able to set possible age restrictions on their use, and use an array of scientific studies and reviews on new tobacco products.

Harmful Substances in Tobacco

Tobacco and tobacco smoke contain approximately 4,000 chemicals, of which 250 are known to be harmful, including hydrogen cyanide, carbon monoxide, and ammonia. Hydrogen cyanide is *an extremely poisonous, colorless liquid or gas with a characteristic smell of almonds*. Ammonia is *a poisonous gas with a strong unpleasant smell mainly used in cleaning products*. Nicotine and tar are especially damaging to the human body.

Nicotine is *an addictive drug found in tobacco leaves and in all tobacco products*. An addictive drug is *one that is capable of causing a user to develop intense cravings for it*. When smoked or chewed, nicotine takes less than 7 seconds to reach the brain, where it creates a feeling of stimulation. About 30 minutes later, when the chemicals have left the brain, the user begins to feel discomfort. The desire to recapture the feeling and avoid the feeling of discomfort causes the user to crave more tobacco.

The nicotine in tobacco changes the brain's chemistry. This change makes the user want more and more tobacco.

Despite the high personal costs and health risks of tobacco use, a number of people continue to smoke or chew tobacco. They may want to stop but find it difficult or frustrating. This is because they have formed an addiction to the nicotine in tobacco.

As defined in the previous lesson, an addiction is the physical or psychological need for a drug. Addiction develops from regular use of a drug. Nicotine addiction can occur in a short amount of time.

Tar is *a dark, thick, sticky liquid that forms when tobacco burns*. When smokers inhale, tar gets into their lungs. It leaves a residue that destroys **cilia**, *the tiny hairs in the nose and air passages that help protect the lungs*. Over time, it also destroys the air sacs in the lungs. The presence of tar can make breathing difficult. It is known to cause emphysema, other lung diseases, and cancer.

Carbon monoxide is *a colorless, odorless, poisonous gas that is produced when tobacco burns*. The carbon monoxide in smoke passes through the lungs into the bloodstream. There, it reduces the amount of oxygen the blood cells can carry. A reduced oxygen supply weakens muscles and blood vessels, which, in turn, may lead to heart attacks and stroke.

Diseases Attributed to the Use of Tobacco Products

Many diseases have been attributed to the use of tobacco products since the Surgeon General of the United States in 1964 first published a report on the dangers of smoking. In this lesson, we will discuss diseases linked to tobacco use and how they affect the human body. Figure 4.3 lists the short- and long-term effects of tobacco use on the body.

Cancer-causing Chemicals in Tobacco

Nearly 80 chemicals in tobacco are potentially cancer-causing, including the following:

- Arsenic (ar·sen·ik) (a poisonous chemical used to kill weeds and pests)
- Benzene (ben·zeen) (also found in vehicle emissions and gasoline fumes)
- Beryllium (buh·ril·ee·um) (a toxic metal)
- Cadmium (kad·mee·um) (a toxic metal)
- Chromium (kroh·mee·um) and nickel (metallic elements)
- Ethylene oxide (eth·uh·leen ok·sahyd) (a chemical used to make antifreeze and pesticide)
- Polonium-210 (puh·loh·nee·um) (a radioactive chemical element)
- Vinyl chloride (vahyn·l klohr·ahyd) (a substance used to make plastics)

Other toxic chemicals in tobacco smoke are suspected to cause cancer, including formaldehyde (fawr·mal·duh·hahyd) and toluene (tol·you·een), (a strong-smelling, colorless liquid used to make gasoline and other types of fuel, paint, paint thinner, fingernail polish, glue, and rubber.

Tobacco use is particularly damaging to young people because their bodies are still growing and developing. Some of the effects of tobacco use are evident almost immediately. Others become apparent over time.

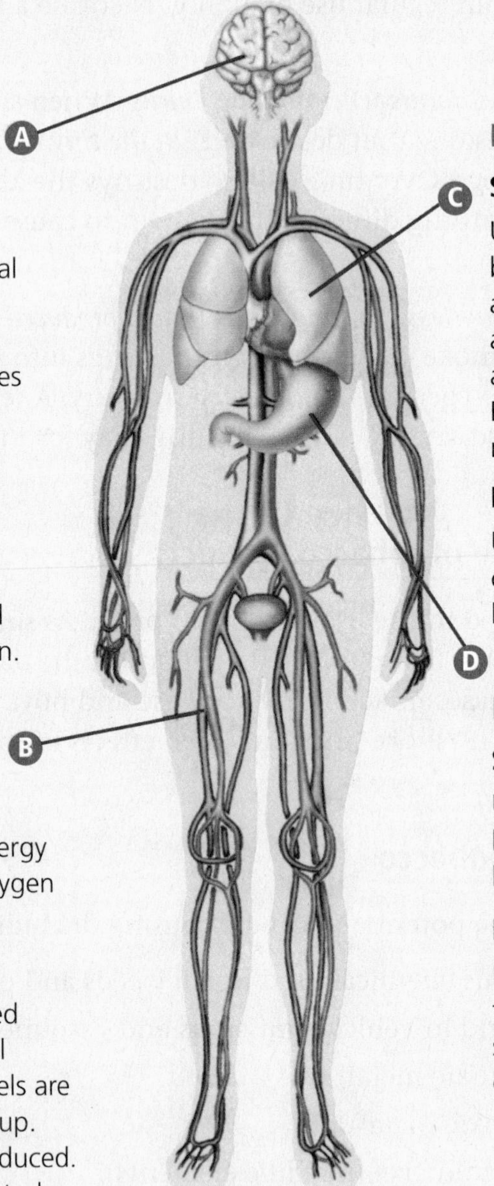

Nervous System (A)

Short-term Effects:

Changes take place in brain chemistry. Withdrawal symptoms (nervousness, shakes, headaches) may occur as soon as 30 minutes after the last cigarette. The heart rate and blood pressure increase.

Long-term Effects:

There is an increased risk of stroke due to decreased flow of oxygen to the brain.

Circulatory System (B)

Short-term Effects:

Heart rate is increased. Energy is reduced because less oxygen gets to body tissues.

Long-term Effects:

Blood vessels are weakened and narrowed. Cholesterol levels increase. Blood vessels are clogged due to fatty buildup. Oxygen flow to heart is reduced. Risk of heart disease and stroke is greater.

Respiratory System (C)

Short-term Effects:

User has bad breath, shortness of breath, reduced energy, coughing, and more phlegm (mucus). Colds and flu are more frequent. Allergies and asthma problems increase. Bronchitis and other serious respiratory illnesses increase.

Long-term Effects:

User faces high risk of lung cancer, emphysema, and other lung diseases.

Digestive System (D)

Short-term Effects:

User has upset stomach, bad breath, stained teeth, dulled taste buds, and tooth decay.

Long-term Effects:

Risk of cancer of the mouth and throat, gum and tooth disease, stomach ulcers, and bladder cancer increases.

FIGURE 4.3

Short-term and Long-term Effects of Tobacco Use

Cancer refers to *diseases in which abnormal cells divide out of control and are able to invade other tissues*. Smoking can cause cancer and then block your body from fighting it:

- Poisons in cigarette smoke can weaken the body's immune system, making it harder to kill cancer cells. When this happens, cancer cells keep growing without being stopped.
- Poisons in tobacco smoke can damage or change a cell's deoxyribonucleic (dee·ok·si·rahy·boh·noo·klee·ik) acid (DNA). **Deoxyribonucleic acid (DNA)** is *the cell's "instruction manual" that controls a cell's normal growth and function*. When DNA is damaged, a cell can begin growing out of control and create a cancer tumor.

Doctors have known for years that smoking causes most lung cancer. It's still true today; nearly 9 out of 10 lung cancers are caused by smoking cigarettes. In fact, smokers have a greater risk for lung cancer today than they did in 1964, even though they smoke fewer cigarettes. One reason may be changes in how cigarettes are made and what they contain.

According to the CDC, using tobacco products and smoking can cause cancer almost anywhere in your body, including the:

- **Mouth, nose, and throat**
- **Larynx**—part of the throat that contains the vocal chords
- **Trachea**—tubes by which air passes to and from the lungs
- **Esophagus**—tube that leads from the mouth through the throat to the stomach
- **Lungs**—the basic respiratory organs
- **Stomach**—the organ where food goes and begins digestion
- **Pancreas**—the large gland near the stomach that produces insulin
- **Liver**—the organ that secretes bile and provides changes to substances contained in the blood
- **Kidneys and ureters**—organs that remove waste products from blood and create urine
- **Bladder**—the organ that holds urine after it passes through the kidneys
- **Colon and rectum**—organs that remove nutrients and transfer waste products
- **Cervix**—tissue that connects the female sex organ to the uterus
- **Bone marrow**—spongy tissue inside your bones
- **Blood**—circulating fluid that provides the body's cells with nutrition and oxygen, and carries waste materials away from the cells

Buerger's Disease

Buerger's disease affects blood vessels in the arms and legs. Blood vessels swell, which can prevent blood flow, causing clots to form. This can lead to pain, tissue damage, and even gangrene (the death or decay of body tissues). In some cases, amputation may be required.

Almost everyone with Buerger's disease smokes cigarettes. However, Buerger's disease can occur in people who use other forms of tobacco, like chewing tobacco. People who smoke one-and-a-half packs a day or more are most likely to develop Buerger's disease.

Researchers are working to understand how tobacco increases the risk for Buerger's disease. One theory is that chemicals in tobacco irritate the lining of the blood vessels and cause them to swell.

The most common symptoms of Buerger's disease are:

- Pale, red, or bluish hands or feet
- Cold hands or feet
- Pain in the hands and feet; may be severe
- Pain in the legs, ankles, or feet when walking—often located in the arch of the foot
- Skin changes, painful sores, or ulcers on the hands or feet

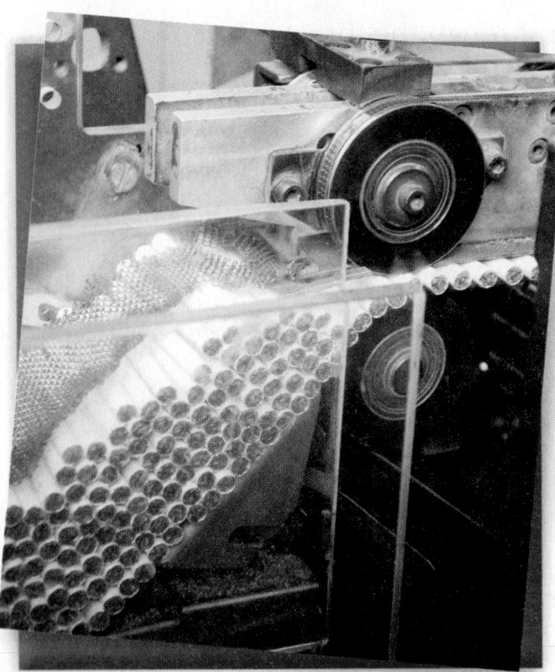

Despite tobacco's harmful effects, tobacco companies continue to produce billions of tobacco products every year, with a lot of advertising directed at young adults to influence their decisions about smoking.

Chronic Obstructive Pulmonary Disease (COPD)

COPD is a serious lung disease that gradually makes it harder and harder to breathe. COPD includes emphysema and chronic bronchitis. Emphysema (em·fuh·see·muh) is *a chronic medical disorder of the lungs in which the air sacs are dilated or enlarged and lack flexibility.*

COPD most often occurs in people age 40 and older with a history of smoking (either current or former smokers). However, as many as one out of six people with COPD have never smoked. Smoking during childhood and teenage years can slow how lungs grow and develop. This can increase the risk of developing COPD in adulthood.

With COPD, less air flows through the airways—the tubes that carry air in and out of your lungs—because of one or more of the following:

- The airways and tiny air sacs in the lungs lose their ability to stretch and shrink back.
- The walls between many of the air sacs are destroyed.
- The walls of the airways become thick and inflamed (irritated and swollen).
- The airways make more mucus than usual, which can clog them and block air flow.

The chemicals in tobacco and tobacco smoke can cause damage to many of your body's systems. Even nonsmokers who are forced to inhale the chemicals released by smoke can suffer the effects.

How Tobacco Affects Appearance

Most of the damage caused by tobacco use occurs inside the body. However, tobacco use also harms a person's outer appearance. Every time a person uses a tobacco product, the smell of tobacco lingers on his or her hands, breath, hair, and clothing.

Over time, sometimes in as little as 10 years, tobacco use leads to stained teeth. Also, the nicotine in cigarettes causes blood vessels to narrow in your skin's outer layers, causing premature wrinkling of the skin. Additionally, your skin doesn't get as much oxygen and important nutrients, such as vitamin A.

Shortness of breath and frequent coughing are also symptoms that indicate smokers are generally less physically fit than nonsmokers. Smokeless tobacco users often develop cracked lips, inflamed gums, and sores in their mouths.

Appearance can also tend to affect social relationships. There are many people who are offended by a tobacco user's smelly breath, hair, and clothing, and they don't want to get close to that person.

Physical and Psychological Addiction to Tobacco

Nicotine causes two types of addiction. One is a **physical dependence**, *a type of addiction in which the body feels a direct need for a drug*. Nicotine affects body temperature, heart rate, digestion, and muscle tone. Once the nicotine level drops or the nicotine leaves the body's systems, the body craves more. Tobacco users don't feel normal unless their bodies are under the influence of nicotine.

The other kind of addiction is a **psychological dependence**, *an addiction in which the mind sends the body a message that it needs more of a drug*. Certain events, situations, and habits trigger a desire to use tobacco. Young people might think they need to smoke a cigarette to help them relax at a party or to help them be more alert before a test. Many smokers feel the need for a cigarette every time they talk on the telephone or finish a meal.

According to the CDC, nicotine addiction is the most common form of drug addiction in the United States. Nicotine is more addictive than heroin or cocaine. Younger people are more likely to develop a higher level of addiction than people who begin to use tobacco at a later age.

The Costs of Tobacco to Society

It is easy to see that people who use tobacco are harmed by its effects. But there are also physical and sometimes psychological impacts on those who must endure tobacco use near them. Often these effects of tobacco are very costly to a family, and more generally, to society as a whole.

Harmful Effects of Secondhand Smoke

Secondhand smoke is *air that has been contaminated by tobacco smoke*. There are two kinds of secondhand smoke. Mainstream smoke is *smoke that a smoker inhales and then exhales*. Sidestream smoke is *smoke given off by the burning end of a cigarette, cigar, or pipe*. Sidestream smoke contains twice as much tar and nicotine as mainstream smoke.

Secondhand smoke can kill!
© *goce risteski/Fotolia.com*

Nonsmokers can develop respiratory illnesses such as pneumonia and bronchitis as a result of secondhand smoke. Infants and young children who are constantly exposed to secondhand smoke have more colds, ear infections, allergies, and asthma than children who grow up in smoke-free homes. Secondhand smoke can also lead to lung disease, heart disease, and cancer in nonsmokers. The CDC reports that since 1964, 2.5 million nonsmokers have died from exposure to secondhand smoke.

Who Buys Tobacco?

Tobacco is a big business in the United States. In 2008, tobacco companies spent over $10 billion on marketing and advertising campaigns worldwide. That's almost $27 million every day! And although tobacco use among adults has declined significantly in recent decades, tobacco companies want to attract new users to replace those who have either quit or died, and are placing emphasis on reaching the youngest audiences.

In the eyes of the tobacco industry, children and teens represent the most profitable market. People who become addicted to nicotine at a younger age are more likely to spend thousands of dollars on tobacco products in their lifetime. Because of lawsuits settled in 1968, tobacco companies have agreed not to use cartoon characters and other advertising methods that might attract children and teens. Nevertheless, the industry continues to find ways to lure young smokers.

An Expensive Habit

Tobacco use is not only an unhealthy habit but also an expensive one. People who use tobacco frequently pay higher health insurance rates. They generally have more doctor and dental bills because of tobacco-related illnesses. There is also the cost of the tobacco product itself. On average, and partly depending on where you live, a cigarette will cost 33 cents, a pack of cigarettes costs approximately $6.50, and a carton will cost you $50 to $60. At that rate, smokers who smoke a pack a day will spend almost $2,400 each year just on cigarettes.

Public Health Costs

According to the US Surgeon General, cigarette smoking alone costs the nation $96 billion in direct medical costs and an estimated $97 billion in lost productivity by the nation's workers each year. Each day, the cost of tobacco smoking is $260 million in direct medical spending and $270 million in lost productivity due to premature death from tobacco-related diseases.

Tobacco users must pay higher rates for health insurance to cover these costs. Taxpayers also must pay a large portion or all of the medical bills for those who lack health insurance.

Costs to the Nation's Economy

People who miss work because of tobacco use produce fewer goods and services. As a result, companies earn less money. Productive time is also lost when tobacco users leave their workstations to have a cigarette. Even more time is lost when workers have to leave for extended periods to be treated for a tobacco-related illness.

Pregnancy and Tobacco

Women who smoke when pregnant increase their risk of having a low-birth-weight baby or a premature delivery. Nicotine and carbon monoxide keep needed nutrients and oxygen from the unborn baby. Sudden Infant Death Syndrome (SIDS) is also reported higher in homes where parents smoke.

Why Teenagers Start to Use Tobacco

The CDC reported in 2012 that 6.7 percent of middle school and 23.3 percent of high school students used tobacco products, including cigarettes, cigars, smokeless tobacco, pipes, dissolvable tobacco, and electronic cigarettes.

keys to LEADERSHIP

Tobacco use does not fit in with a healthy lifestyle; it reduces your stamina and your ability to exercise properly and play sports.

The good news is that the majority of young teens—over two-thirds—don't smoke. In addition, smoking among high school students began to decline in 2000. The bad news is that each day, more than 3,200 teens smoke their first cigarette. Of this group, 2,100 will become regular smokers. Depending on which study you use, about one-third to nearly one-half of these regular smokers will eventually die of smoking-related illnesses.

There are many influences that cause teenagers to make the choices they do. Most are positive and some are negative. The following information provides some background on the role internal and external influences play on a young person's choice to use tobacco products.

Internal Influences

- **Stress**—Teens don't realize that the symptoms of withdrawal from nicotine, which occur as often as every 30 minutes, will add to, not reduce their daily stresses.
- **Weight**—Some teens wrongly believe that using tobacco will help them maintain a healthy weight. Instead, its use reduces the capacity for aerobic exercise and sports.
- **Image**—Using cigarette lighters and blowing smoke makes some teens feel grown up. However, mature teenagers know that lifelong health is more important than looking "cool."
- **Peer acceptance**—Teens may think they need to smoke in order to fit in with their friends. However, most teenagers today don't want anything to do with tobacco users.
- **Independence**—Tobacco use may appear to be a sign of independence. However, it's just the opposite. Tobacco users become dependent, and it's unhealthy and costly.

External Influences

- **Imitating a role model**—Some teenagers want to be like a friend, a celebrity, or some other role model who uses tobacco. They don't realize that most of those role models want to "kick" their tobacco habit.
- **Peers**—Peers, siblings, and friends are powerful influences. Many teenagers try their first cigarette with a friend or relative who already smokes.

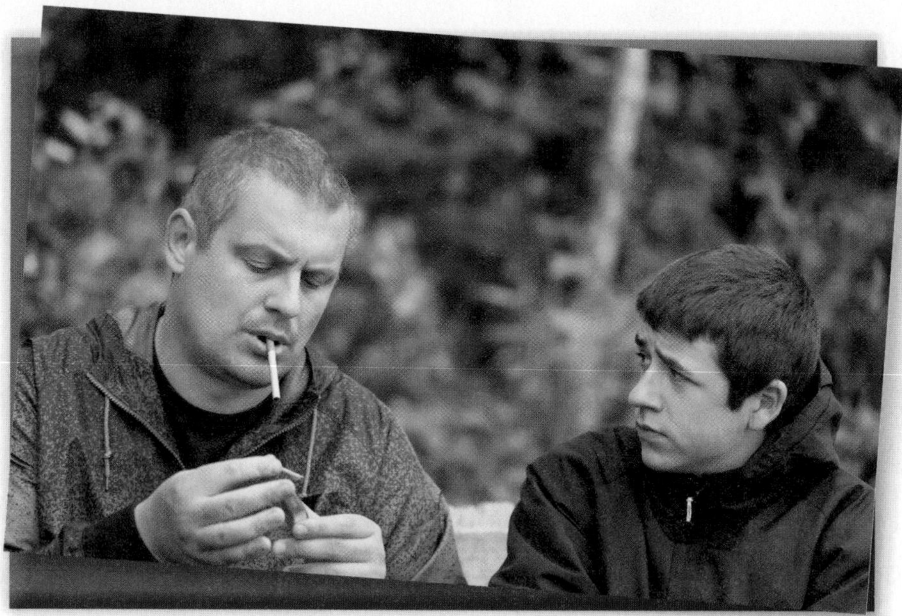

Smoking is not healthy, even if someone you look up to does it.
© lukasvideo/Fotolia.com

- **Entertainment**—Movies and television shows often portray tobacco use in ways that appeal to teenagers. Tobacco companies pay millions of dollars to have their products featured in movies.
- **Advertising**—Strong evidence has shown that tobacco advertising influences teens. One survey published by the National Cancer Institute found that 81 percent of young people who smoke prefer the three most heavily advertised brands.
- **Family members and other adults**—Some teens see their parents and other adults using tobacco and think that it's all right for them to use it, too.

How to Avoid Tobacco Use

The best way to lead a tobacco-free life is to never start using tobacco products. About 90 percent of adult smokers began smoking before the age of 21, and over half of them had become regular smokers by age 18. If you avoid using tobacco during middle or high school, there's a good chance you'll never start. Resisting peer pressure to use tobacco can be difficult. However, you can use several strategies to help you.

- **Choose friends who don't use tobacco**—If you don't spend time with people who use tobacco, you won't be pressured to use it yourself.
- **Avoid situations where tobacco products may be used**—You may be invited to a party where you know your peers will be smoking or chewing tobacco. Give your reasons for not going and then do something fun with tobacco-free friends instead. Even when you don't smoke at these parties, you are still inhaling secondhand smoke.

- **Use refusal skills**—If tobacco users urge you to try tobacco, you can simply say no. If the pressure continues, however, you can explain your reasons for avoiding tobacco products. Just as you learned from an earlier lesson, be assertive! If your friends or peers continue to pressure you, leave.

Ways to Quit

A variety of strategies are available to help someone break the tobacco habit. One way is to quit gradually by reducing the number of cigarettes smoked, or the frequency of using smokeless tobacco, over a period of time. Another way to quit is cold turkey, or *stopping all at once*. Cold turkey is thought to be more effective than trying to quit gradually. However, just like any other addictive drug, those who have suddenly quit smoking can experience *withdrawal* symptoms.

Tobacco users, no matter what age, may need products such as a nicotine patch or nicotine gum to help them through withdrawal. The nicotine patch is *a medication that allows tobacco users to give up tobacco right away while gradually cutting down on nicotine.* The patch is available both by prescription and over the counter. Nicotine gum is available over the counter, and it works in a similar way as the patch.

Choosing friends who don't use tobacco helps you avoid peer pressure to smoke.
© william87/Fotolia.com

Tobacco users who want to quit may seek help from local support groups and organized programs or from professional counselors. The American Lung Association, the American Heart Association, and the American Cancer Society, as well as hospitals and health groups, offer programs to help tobacco users quit. There are also websites dedicated to helping young people stop smoking, such as http://teen.smokefree.gov.

Withdrawal

Quitting is not easy. In order to quit, tobacco users have to go through withdrawal. However, it is important to remember that these withdrawal symptoms are short-term. As you learned from the previous lesson, withdrawal is the physical and psychological symptoms that occur when someone stops using an addictive substance. Physical symptoms of nicotine withdrawal include the craving to use nicotine, headaches, shakiness, fatigue, increased appetite, and nausea. Psychological symptoms include feeling irritable, nervous, anxious, and sad.

People going through withdrawal may have trouble thinking during the day and sleeping during the night. The intensity of withdrawal symptoms and the length of time they last vary from person to person. An inability or reluctance to cope with withdrawal is often the main obstacle to quitting tobacco use.

However, people who have quit most often say they feel both physically and psychologically stronger because of having overcome the withdrawal symptoms.

You Can Quit!

Two-thirds of adults who smoke say that they would like to quit, and 50 percent of teen smokers also want to quit. In the year 2000, a survey showed 70 percent of teen smokers said they regretted having started. It is also important to remember that many people are unable to quit smoking the first time they try, but don't give up. The benefits of not smoking far outweigh the health risks of smoking.

It's never too late to quit smoking.
© ryanking999/Fotolia.com

Lesson 2 Review

Using complete sentences, answer the following questions on a sheet of paper.

1. What law did congress pass in 1984 that affected how cigarettes are labeled?
2. Name the most common forms of tobacco use.
3. Why is using smokeless tobacco just as harmful as smoking cigarettes?
4. Define nicotine.
5. Define the term cancer.
6. Who is more likely to suffer from COPD?
7. How does nicotine cause a physical dependence to tobacco?
8. Name two types of smoke that nonsmokers might inhale.
9. On average, how much do smokers spend on cigarettes yearly?
10. List external influences that affect tobacco use.
11. What are three strategies for resisting peer pressure to use tobacco?
12. What is meant by "cold turkey" when trying to quit smoking?
13. What are the physical symptoms of nicotine withdrawal?

APPLYING YOUR LEARNING

14. Your best friend wants to experiment with cigarettes because he or she thinks it's cool when an actor is smoking in a movie. Using what you have learned in this lesson, write a short paragraph on what you would say to stop them from smoking.

LESSON 3

Alcohol

Quick Write

You have just been invited to a party this weekend. You find out that the parents are not going to be home, so there is a good chance alcohol will be available at the party. As a member of the school baseball/softball team you were required to sign a character contract stating you would not drink alcohol any time during the scheduled season. Write a brief paragraph stating refusal skills you would use to avoid the pressure to drink alcohol.

Learn About

- alcohol: a threat to everyone
- alcoholism
- why some teens drink alcohol

"Avoid using drugs, cigarettes, and alcohol as alternatives to being an interesting person."

Marilyn vos Savant, American writer

Alcohol: A Threat to Everyone

Alcohol is *a drug that is produced by a chemical reaction in fruits, vegetables, and grains*. Alcohol is a chemical substance that is toxic to the body. The key ingredient for every alcoholic drink is ethanol. **Ethanol** is *a colorless liquid used in alcoholic beverages, gasoline, and cleaning solutions*.

Alcohol use is widespread in American society. According to the Centers for Disease Control and Prevention (CDC), approximately 88,000 deaths are caused by excessive alcohol use each year. Close to 14 million adult Americans have physical, social, and psychological problems related to alcohol use. It causes premature death from a variety of diseases.

Alcohol is also used in gasoline for your car.

© M.studio/Fotolia.com

It also contributes to unnecessary deaths and injuries on the roads and in the home. The economic cost of excessive alcohol consumption in 2006 was estimated at $223.5 billion.

Vocabulary

- alcohol
- ethanol
- binge drinking
- underage drinking
- blood alcohol concentration (BAC)
- intoxicated
- fetal alcohol spectrum disorders (FASD)
- alcoholism
- recovery
- detoxification
- sobriety
- alternatives

How the Media Influences Our View of Alcohol

Alcohol's wide availability makes it relatively easy to obtain. Alcohol use is also seen as generally acceptable in people who are over 21—even though it can be dangerous at any age. Alcoholic beverage producers use a wide range of media outlets to influence choices made about alcohol consumption. In this section, we will examine the three main media outlets used to target users.

Television

Companies that sell alcohol bombard the public with advertisements for beer, wine, liquor, and other beverages. Television commercials and magazine ads often show drinkers in beautiful outdoor settings, at fun-filled parties, or enjoying sports. Although the ads never show underage drinking, the scenarios tend to appeal to teens as much as to adults.

Usually the message accompanying an alcohol ad says nothing about the product. Unlike ads for some drugs, alcohol ads are not required to list negative side effects. Instead, the ads promote a one-sided image of drinkers as athletic, healthy, and successful. The ads give the false impression that drinking will make you more popular and attractive. If you were to believe these hidden messages, you might think that it is normal, smart, and sophisticated to drink.

Movies

Alcohol use is common in movies, even those intended for young children and teenagers. Movies tend to portray alcohol use positively most of the time, which may influence teenage use. Alcohol use in movies does not focus on just one audience as alcohol commercials do on television. Many believe this is because teenagers spend much less time watching movies than

Responsible leaders make mature choices about alcohol. Alcohol related incidents may prevent you from obtaining established goals.

they do watching television. Surveys published by the US National Library of Medicine found that the average teenager watches 20.2 hours of television each week. Teenagers in the same group spend an average of only 4.7 hours each week watching movies. It is stated in this report that more studies need to be done in this area before experts can say movies have an influence on whether young people choose to drink.

Music and Music Videos

In a survey conducted in 2010 on adolescent binge drinking published in the journal *Alcoholism: Clinical & Experimental Research*, researchers from Dartmouth College and the University of Pittsburgh studied how alcohol brands mentioned in music could affect young people's drinking behaviors. Binge drinking is *the consumption of several alcoholic drinks in a very short period of time*. Binge drinking is especially dangerous. Alcohol is a depressant; it slows body systems down. Binge drinking can also lead to alcohol poisoning and possibly death.

Researchers found that music is the fastest growing form of media for young people today. Young people are listening to about 2.5 hours of music each day. They are hearing approximately 14 references to drinking per song and about eight brand names of alcohol mentioned.

The researchers also surveyed 2,541 young people, ages 15 to 23, to assess what role the association of alcohol and music played in their lives. Researchers wanted to know whether participants had ever drunk a whole drink, if they had ever engaged in binge drinking, and whether they had suffered any injuries or memory loss after drinking. A surprising result from the researchers' analysis of the survey was a strong association between recalling the alcohol brands in popular music and alcohol drinking in young people. Young people who could name at least one alcohol brand in the music were at a higher risk of having a drink or even binge drinking.

Seeing Through Media Messages

Keep in mind that alcohol companies spend billions of dollars each year promoting their products. Their advertisements focus on people's activities while using these products, rather than on the products themselves. Alcohol products mentioned in music provides free advertisements for these companies.

Young people using the latest technologies are being exposed to alcohol advertising 24 hours a day, seven days a week; these technologies include cell phones and social networking sites. Advertisers of alcohol develop advertising experiences. For example, Anheuser-Busch Company, an American brewery, spends millions of dollars each year to develop and broadcast their annual Bud Bowl. Held each year at the same time as the National Football League's Super Bowl, all characters in this Super Bowl type of production are beer bottle figures. Young people are led to believe through these experiences that things such as alcohol and sports go together, and that to be popular or have fun you should consume alcohol products.

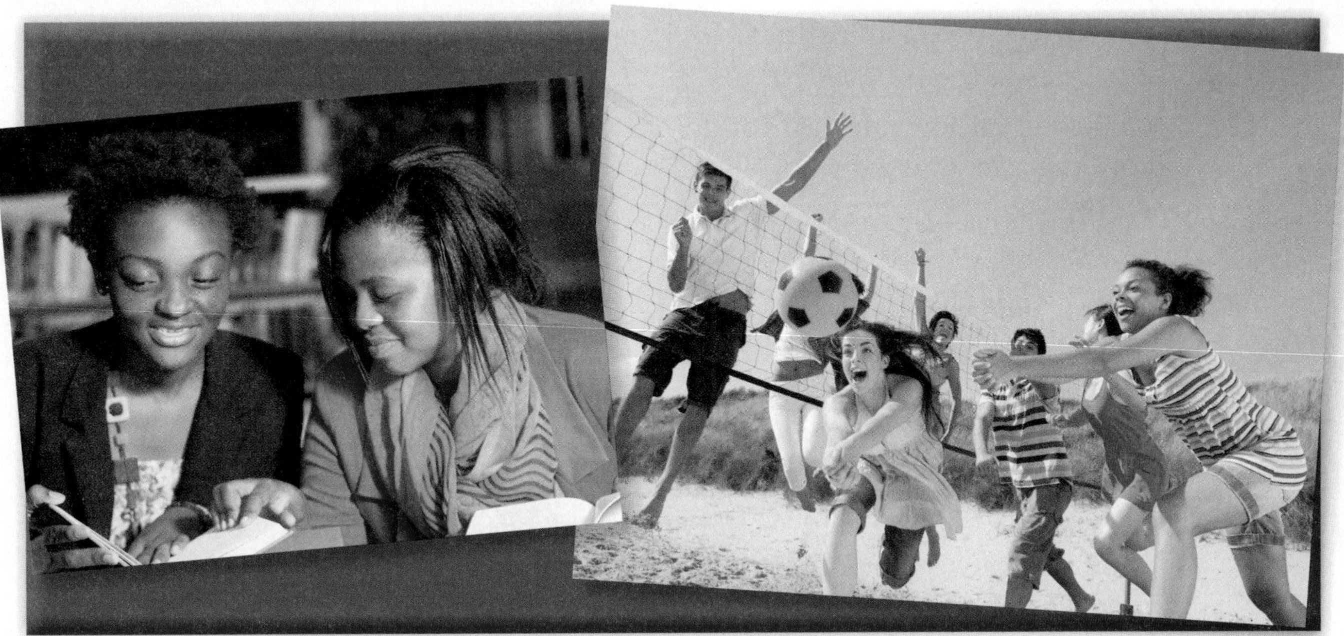

Refusing alcohol and choosing alternative activities go hand-in-hand for success in school and with friends.

Left: © vlam1/Fotolia.com; right: © micromonkey/Fotolia.com

When you see ads for alcohol, use your own judgment to evaluate them. Will an alcoholic drink really make you more attractive or more popular? Will your relationships be successful and problem-free as a result of drinking? The harsh realities of alcohol use that you will learn in this lesson are not shown by alcohol manufacturers.

Drinking and Injuries

Drinking and driving is a dangerous, and potentially deadly, combination. Drinking alcohol impairs a person's vision, reaction time, and physical coordination. Consequently, a person who has been drinking should never get behind the wheel of a car. According to the US Department of Transportation, in 2011, there were 43,668 fatal car crashes. Of these, 4,347 involved young people between the ages of 15 to 20. Thirty-two percent or approximately 1,360 of these people were found to have alcohol in their system.

Alcohol causes other kinds of unintentional injuries as well. It impairs a person's ability to ride a bicycle or skateboard. About one-third of all bicyclists and pedestrians who die in motor vehicle collisions have been drinking. Alcohol is also linked to about one-third of all drowning deaths and about half of all deaths by fire.

Alcohol use by young people has many serious consequences, the first of which is that it is illegal. Underage drinking is *when anyone under the minimum legal drinking age of 21 drinks alcohol.*

According to the National Institutes for Health, underage drinking risks include:

- **Death**—5,000 people under age 21 die each year from alcohol-related car crashes, homicides, suicides, alcohol poisoning, and other injuries such as falls, burns, and drowning. Almost one-half of all traffic deaths of people under age 25 involve alcohol.
- **Serious injuries**—More than 190,000 people under age 21 visited an emergency room for alcohol-related injuries in 2008 alone.
- **Impaired judgment**—Drinking can cause young people to make poor decisions, which can then result in risky behavior like drinking and driving, sexual activity, violence, or other criminal activity. Nearly a quarter of all violent crimes committed by teens involve alcohol.
- **Increased risk for physical and sexual assault**—Young people who drink are more likely to carry out or be the victim of physical or sexual violence. Research has found that between one-third and two-thirds of date rape cases among teens and college students involve alcohol.

How Alcohol Affects the Body

Alcohol is a depressant that has powerful effects on the body. In the United States, the law prohibits alcohol use by anyone under the age of 21. Adults, however, can choose whether to drink alcohol. To make responsible decisions about alcohol use, people should understand how alcohol affects the body.

Alcohol, like other depressant drugs, slows down the functions of the brain and other parts of the nervous system. It also affects the digestive and urinary systems. Excessive use of alcohol over a long period can damage almost every organ in the body. Figure 4.4 shows some of the short-term and long-term effects of alcohol consumption.

Alcohol and the Individual

The effect that alcohol has on a person is influenced by a number of factors, including:

- **Body size**—The same amount of alcohol has a greater effect on a small person than it does on a larger person.
- **Gender**
  - Men have a greater ratio of muscle to fat than women. Muscle has a large amount of blood that flows through the muscle tissue. Fat has a much smaller amount of blood. The difference this makes is that alcohol is more diluted in a man's body, due to the larger volume of blood.
  - Women have a naturally higher percentage of body fat than men do. Due to this, each drink is more concentrated in a woman's blood. This results in a higher blood alcohol level for women compared to men.
  - If a 140 lb male drinks two drinks in one hour, his blood alcohol level is .038. If a 140 lb female drinks two drinks in one hour, her blood alcohol level is .048.

Short-term effects occur within minutes of drinking alcohol. Long-term effects develop over time.

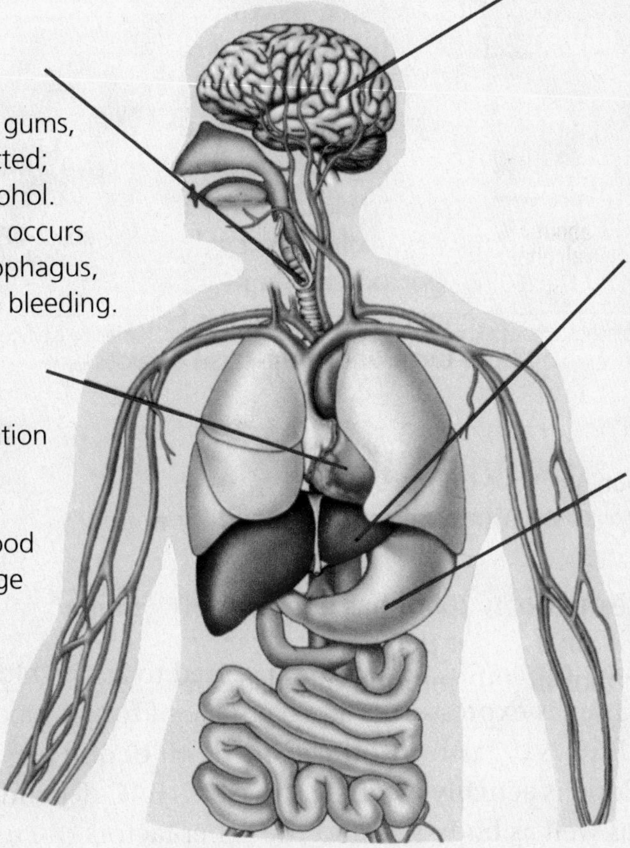

Mouth and Esophagus

Short-term: Tongue, gums, and throat are affected; breath smells of alcohol.
Long-term: Damage occurs to tissues of the esophagus, resulting in possible bleeding.

Heart and Blood Vessels

Short-term: Perspiration increases and skin becomes flushed.
Long-term: High blood pressure and damage to the heart muscle is common. Blood vessels harden and become less flexible.

Brain and Nervous System

Short-term: Speech is slurred and vision is blurred. Drinker has difficulty walking.
Long-term: Brain cells, many of which cannot be replaced, are destroyed. Damage occurs to the nerves throughout the body, resulting in numbness in the hands and feet.

Liver

Short-term: Liver changes alcohol into water and carbon dioxide.
Long-term: Liver is damaged, possibly resulting in cirrhosis (suh·ROH·sis), which is the scarring and destruction of the liver.

Stomach and Pancreas

Short-term: Stomach acids increase, which often results in nausea and vomiting.
Long-term: Irritation occurs in the stomach lining, causing open sores called ulcers. Pancreas becomes inflamed.

FIGURE 4.4

Effects of Alcohol on the Body

- **Time frame**—A person who drinks a lot in a short period is more likely to become intoxicated. Rapid drinking overwhelms the liver's ability to break down the alcohol.
- **Amount**—Drinking a large quantity of alcohol causes alcohol levels in the bloodstream to rise. If the levels become too high, alcohol poisoning can occur. Figure 4.5 shows the alcohol content of some common alcoholic beverages.
- **Food**—Food in the stomach slows down the passage of alcohol into the bloodstream.
- **Medicine**—Alcohol can interfere with the effects of medicines, and medicines can intensify the effects of alcohol.

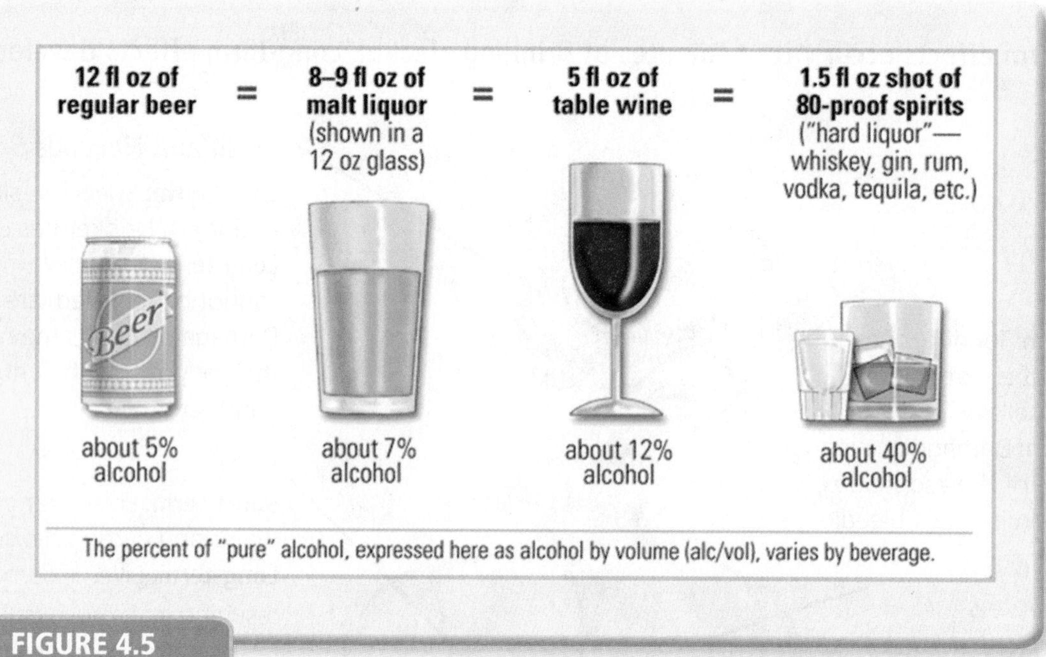

FIGURE 4.5

Alcohol Content of Common Alcoholic Drinks

Courtesy of the National Institute on Alcohol Abuse and Alcoholism/http://www.niaaa.nih.gov

Blood Alcohol Concentration

The amount of alcohol in a person's bloodstream is referred to as the blood alcohol concentration (BAC). BAC is expressed as a percentage of total blood volume. For example, if a person's BAC is 0.1 percent, then one tenth of one percent of the fluid volume of his or her blood is actually alcohol. A person's BAC depends on the amount of alcohol consumed as well as body size and the other factors discussed earlier.

A person with a BAC of 0.1 percent—or in most states, 0.08 percent—is considered legally intoxicated, or *physically and mentally impaired by the use of alcohol*. Driving while intoxicated can result in a jail term and, in some states, loss of driver's license. For anyone under 21, a BAC above 0 percent is illegal. If a young person is found guilty in a court of law for underage drinking, most states will now suspend all driving privileges until the age of 21. This does not include all the court costs and fines you will also have to pay.

Alcohol's Effects on Teens

Alcohol can interfere with a young person's mental and physical growth processes. Research shows that brain development, which continues well into a person's 20s, can be affected by alcohol use. For example, a long-term study reported by the National Institutes of Health indicates that teens who abuse alcohol have poorer language skills than other teens. Research also suggests that exposure to alcohol during the teen years reduces levels of certain hormones essential to normal physical development.

According to a recent *New York Times* article, young people who are at the highest risk for early drinking include those with a history of abuse, family violence, depression, and stressful life events. A family history of alcoholism also raises the risk of beginning to drink before the age of 20 and becoming an alcoholic. Such drinkers are also reported to be more apt to underestimate the effects of drinking and to make judgment errors, such as going on binges or driving after drinking, than young drinkers without a family history of alcoholism.

The Effects of Alcohol on a Fetus

When a pregnant woman drinks alcohol, it passes from her body into her developing baby's bloodstream. A fetus exposed to alcohol in this way may be born with fetal alcohol spectrum disorders. Fetal alcohol spectrum disorders (FASD) is *a range (spectrum) of alcohol-related birth defects that include both physical and mental problems*.

FASD is the leading known cause of intellectual disabilities and birth defects in the United States. The good news is that FASD is entirely preventable. Since even small amounts of alcohol can harm a fetus, the only safe decision for a pregnant woman is not to drink any alcohol at all.

People with FASD often have difficulty in the following areas:

- Coordination
- Emotional control
- School work
- Socialization
- Holding a job

Alcoholism

Alcohol can become addictive. Alcoholism is *a progressive, chronic disease involving a mental and physical need for alcohol*. People with this disease are called alcoholics. Alcoholics cannot control their drinking. They drink even when they know they are harming their health and hurting others. An addiction to alcohol is both psychological and physical. As we found out in a previous lesson, with a psychological addiction, the mind sends the body a message that it needs more and more alcohol. With physical addiction, the body develops a direct need for the drug. Either way, an alcoholic feels very uncomfortable when alcohol is withheld for even a brief period.

More than half of the drivers killed in nighttime automobile collisions are legally drunk.
© Duncan Noakes/Fotolia.com

Stages of Alcoholism

The seven stages of alcoholism are as follows:

STAGE 0: Non-drinker—No alcoholic behavior or symptoms.

STAGE 1: Social drinking—Up to one or two drinks per day routinely, depending on body mass, with no alcoholic behavior.

STAGE 2: Non-social drinking to reduce stress or tension—The first signs of alcoholic behavior begin to appear, including an urgent need for the first drink of the day, and more than one or two drinks per day on a routine basis.

STAGE 3: Frequent "relief drinking" to escape stress—More alcoholic behavior manifests: relief drinking most days to escape something, feelings of guilt about drinking, needing more drinks to get the desired result.

STAGE 4: Routine daily drinking to excess—Significant alcoholic behavior and symptoms manifest: memory blackouts, hidden drinking.

STAGE 5: Alcohol dependence—A wide range of additional alcoholic behaviors and symptoms manifest: more frequent memory blackouts, true dependence on alcohol, finding excuses to drink, unwillingness to discuss the problem, dramatic mood and behavior changes. Someone at this stage also continues to drink when others have stopped, repeatedly fails to follow through on commitments, tells lies, avoids family and friends, finds non-drinkers boring, and has difficulty keeping a job or managing money.

Stage 6: End stage alcoholism—Obsessed with drinking, seldom eats, stays drunk for long periods of time, increasingly amoral behavior, health deteriorates, highly resentful of anything or anybody that interferes with their drinking, excessively emotional.

Stage 7: Death

How Alcoholics Can Recover

A person who is addicted to alcohol is dependent on it. However, the addiction can be treated. *The process of learning to live an alcohol-free life* is called **recovery**. The steps of recovery are shown in Figure 4.6.

Step 1—Admission

The alcoholic admits to having a problem and asks for help.

Step 2—Detoxification

The alcoholic goes through detoxification, a process in which the alcoholic's body adjusts to functioning without alcohol.

Step 3—Counseling

The alcoholic receives counseling on how to live without alcohol.

Step 4—Recovery

The alcoholic takes responsibility for his or her own life.

FIGURE 4.6

Steps to Recovery

© DOC RABE Media/Fotolia.com

Recovering from alcoholism is difficult, but it can be successful. Just like drug addiction, the recovery process may involve withdrawal. Withdrawal symptoms include nausea, sweating, shakiness, and anxiety. Treatment for alcoholism depends on the severity of the alcoholism and the resources available in your community. Treatment may include detoxification, *the physical process of freeing the body of an addictive substance*. "Detox" also involves helping the user overcome psychological dependence on the substance and regain health. Varieties of treatment centers are available to help people recover from alcoholism.

- **Detox units** are usually part of a hospital or other treatment center. Alcoholics remain under a doctor's care while going through detoxification.
- **Inpatient treatment centers** are places where people stay for a month or more to fully concentrate on recovery.
- **Outpatient treatment centers** are places where people get treatment for a few hours each day. Then they return to their homes and regular surroundings. Treatment may also include taking prescribed medications to help prevent a return to drinking (or relapse) once drinking has stopped and individual and/or group counseling. Such counseling often involves teaching alcoholics to identify situations and feelings that trigger the urge to drink and to find new ways to cope that do not include alcohol use.

Many alcoholics join support groups to help them be successful. These support groups help someone live a life of sobriety. Sobriety, which is *living without alcohol*, is a lifelong challenge. One of the best known of these support groups is Alcoholics Anonymous (AA). AA is an organization of recovering alcoholics who know firsthand the difficulty of beating alcohol addiction. Most communities have chapters of AA. Listings for AA and other support groups for alcoholism can be found on the Internet or in the Yellow Pages of the phone book, usually under the heading "Alcoholism."

Help for the Family

The harmful effects of alcohol do not affect only the drinker. The drinker's family members and friends suffer as well. One in four families in the United States is affected by alcoholism. Alcohol abuse is a factor in the breakup of many families. Many cases of spousal abuse and child abuse involve someone who has been drinking.

A growing number of young people are living with a person who is addicted to alcohol. These teens may not realize that they need help for themselves as well as for the problem drinkers in their lives. The first step to take is to admit that the problem exists. The second is to reach out for help.

Many alcohol treatment centers offer help to family members of the alcoholic. These programs teach family members about alcoholism and provide individual and family therapy. Some family members join support groups where they can talk with other people who have faced the same problems. Two of these support groups are described here:

- **Al-Anon** helps family members and friends of alcoholics. Al-Anon members learn how to help themselves as well as the person dependent on alcohol.
- **Alateen** helps young people cope with having a family member or friend who is an alcoholic. Its members share their experiences and work together to improve their lives.

Listings for Al-Anon, Alateen, and other support groups for family members and friends of alcoholics can be found on the Internet at www.al-anon.alateen.org or by putting these terms into a search engine, as well as by looking in the Yellow Pages of the phone book, usually under the heading "Alcoholism."

How You Can Help

If a friend or family member has a problem with alcohol, he or she needs help. Always remember, however, that your most important responsibility is to yourself. If you are close to an alcoholic, try not to let that person's drinking problem change your own behaviors and attitudes. Below are some suggested ways provided by the National Council on Alcoholism and Drug Dependence, Inc. (NCADD) you may want to use to help an alcoholic:

- **Learn all you can about alcoholism and drug dependence**—Utilize the resources we have provided including Learn About Alcohol, and Learn About Drugs and Family Education.
- **Speak up and offer your support**—Talk to the person about your concerns and offer your help and support, including your willingness to go with them and get help. Like other chronic diseases, the earlier addiction is treated, the better.
- **Express love and concern**—Don't wait for your loved one to "hit bottom." You may be met with excuses, denial, or anger, but be prepared to respond with specific examples of the behavior that has you worried.
- **Don't expect the person to stop without help**—You have heard it before—the person promises to cut down or stop, but it doesn't work. Treatment, support, and new coping skills are needed to overcome addiction to alcohol and drugs.
- **Support recovery as an ongoing process**—Once your friend or family member is receiving treatment, or going to meetings, remain involved. While maintaining your own commitment to getting help, continue to support their participation in continuing care, meetings, and recovery support groups. Continue to show that you are concerned about their successful long-term recovery.

Here are some things you *don't* want to do:

- **Don't preach**—Don't lecture, threaten, bribe, preach, or moralize.
- **Don't be a martyr**—Avoid emotional appeals that may only increase feelings of guilt and the compulsion to drink or use other drugs.
- **Don't cover up**—Don't lie or make excuses for them and their behavior.
- **Don't assume their responsibilities**—Taking over their responsibilities protects them from the consequences of their behavior.
- **Don't argue when they are using**—Don't argue with someone who is drinking or using drugs; at that point they can't have a rational conversation.
- **Don't feel guilty or responsible for their behavior**—It's not your fault.
- **Don't join them**—Don't try to keep up with them by drinking or using drugs.

Why Some Teens Drink Alcohol

You have learned that alcohol will harm your physical and mental/emotional health, and that drinking alcohol is against the law for teens. Why, then, do some young people experiment with alcohol? The following box lists some statements teens may give, followed by what they should know about alcohol.

Reasons to Refuse Alcohol

At least one-third of Americans do not drink alcohol at all, and many who used to drink have stopped. As people become aware of the physical and emotional damage that drinking can cause, fewer choose to start drinking. More and more young people are choosing not to drink also. Here are some of their reasons:

What Teens May Say and What Teens Should Know

What Teens May Say	What Teens Should Know
"I'll look more grown-up with a drink in my hand."	You won't look mature getting in trouble for illegal underage drinking.
"If I drink, I'll be able to forget my problems."	The problems will still be there when the effects of the alcohol wear off.
"I'm stressed out about this test. A drink will help me relax."	Alcohol does not relieve stress; it disrupts sleep, creating more stress.
"My friends keep pressuring me to try alcohol."	Real friends won't pressure you to do something harmful.
"The ads make drinking look like fun."	Alcohol companies want people to spend money on their products.

- **It is illegal**—Drinking is against the law for anyone under age 21. Obeying the law requires maturity and taking responsibility, and makes life easier and safer for everyone.
- **It interferes with your activities**—As a teen, your life is full of activities. You go to school, and you have family responsibilities and friendships. Teens who choose not to drink will be better able to meet these challenges.
- **It promotes foolish behaviors**—Drinking can make people sick. It can also cause them to embarrass or endanger themselves.
- **It is not smart**—Smart teens know that drinking does not enhance popularity. Drinking does not make a person more mature. Acting responsibly is a sign of maturity.
- **It disappoints those who care about you**—Teens who drink alcohol have to hide their behavior. Many young people would rather not have to be dishonest with people they care about.
- **It harms your health**—Drinking alcohol harms body organs, particularly the liver, and increases the chance for injuries.

As stated earlier in this lesson, for teens and others under the age of 21, using alcohol is illegal. In addition, schools have adopted a zero-tolerance policy. Under such a policy, students face stiff consequences, including suspension, starting with the first time they are caught with alcohol.

"We" is a key to success in refusal.

If you see a friend being pressured to take a drink, use reverse peer pressure by saying:

- *We* don't need to drink to have fun.
- *We* don't want to drink.
- *We*'ve got something else to do.

Resisting peer pressure can make a young person feel very alone. But when the solitary "me" becomes a "we," peer pressure loses its strength.

Alternatives to Drinking Alcohol for Fun and Relaxation

Why do some teens give in to the pressure to drink alcohol? One reason is that they have not thought about alternatives. Alternatives are *other ways of thinking or acting.*

There are plenty of alternatives to drinking. A few of them are suggested here:

- **Become good at something that requires a steady hand**—Assemble a model airplane, play a video game, or paint a picture. Then congratulate yourself—a person whose senses are dulled by alcohol could not accomplish what you have.
- **Join other teens for alcohol-free fun**—Plan an alcohol-free party or outing, or have a basketball or volleyball game. Make sure all invited know that alcohol use will not be tolerated.

- **Volunteer to help others**—Volunteer at a hospital or nursing home, or lend a hand to a community improvement organization such as Habitat for Humanity.
- **Learn something new**—You might learn a musical instrument, computer program, or foreign language. Learn a sport you have never tried before, such as karate or kickboxing.
- **Advocate**—Volunteer to speak to an elementary school class about the dangers of alcohol and the benefits of remaining alcohol-free. Younger children look up to teens like you as role models.

Lesson 3 Review

Using complete sentences, answer the following questions on a sheet of paper.

1. Define the term alcohol.
2. What are the three media outlets used to influence choices made about alcohol?
3. What is binge drinking?
4. Define the term alcoholism.
5. What is Stage 1 alcoholism?
6. Define the term sobriety.
7. Name two support groups for families and friends of alcoholics.
8. What is the main reason someone under the age of 21 should not drink?
9. List five fun and relaxing things you could do that do not involve alcohol.

APPLYING YOUR LEARNING

10. One of your friends has a drinking problem. From the information you have read in this lesson, list three things you would do to encourage your friend to get help and why they would be helpful. Also list four things you should not do and why those things would not help your friend.

LESSON 4

Environmental Health

Quick Write

Write a short statement about how you feel after being in a smoky room, or in an outdoor place where the air is heavily polluted from an industrial plant.

"When the earth is sick and polluted, human health is impossible....To heal ourselves we must heal our planet, and to heal our planet we must heal ourselves."

Bobby McLeod, Australian Koori Aborigine activist

Learn About

- the effects pollution has on health
- methods for reducing and preventing pollution

The Effects Pollution Has on Health

You may not realize that your entire life is a constant interaction with the physical environment around you. The environment is *the place in which people live and work.* As you learned from earlier lessons, there are things you can control to have better health. Drugs, alcohol, and tobacco products are among those things you can choose to avoid.

However, other kinds of daily contacts with the environment aren't so easy to control. There are involuntary things you experience every day, like breathing the air. No, you can't stop breathing, but you can find ways to avoid breathing pollutants, *substances that are harmful to your environment.*

You may also encounter toxic waste material that could be harmful to people, animals, or the environment. You may live in a community where manufacturing or other industries exist. The US Environmental Protection Agency (EPA) tightly controls most industries. Nonetheless, members of your community may still suffer from diseases, injuries, or other disabilities due to exposure to manufacturing byproducts. Manufacturing byproducts are materials that are left over or not useable, and must be disposed of.

Basically, our environment is made up of natural resources. Natural resources include *the air, water, land, and living things.* When something happens to one resource, it can directly affect others. As we will see in this lesson, the earth's environment thrives best when its natural resources are protected.

In this lesson, you will learn about people's impact on the environment and on your health. You will also learn what the government does to protect the environment and things you can do within your own community.

The two most important natural resources we need for our survival as humans are the air we breathe and the water we drink. If our air or water is unhealthy or polluted, we can suffer severe consequences.

What is pollution? Pollution is *the presence of harmful materials in our soil, water, and air.* Most pollution is caused by a combination of natural events and human activities. Human activities such as manufacturing, drilling for oil, and construction have upset the balance of nature by overusing Earth's resources and producing pollution. On the other hand, when all parts of the environment work together, a healthy balance of nature is maintained. This is why a clean, healthy environment is needed for human and animal life.

Pollution is harmful to all life.

Vocabulary

- environment
- pollutants
- natural resources
- pollution
- extinct
- ecology
- clinical ecology
- air pollution
- sulfur dioxide
- ground-level ozone
- smog
- ozone layer
- chlorofluorocarbons (CFCs)
- particulates
- radon
- carbon monoxide (CO)
- mold
- ecosystem
- runoffs
- shellfish
- algae
- pharmaceutical waste
- sewage
- pesticides
- lead
- land pollution
- groundwater
- e-waste
- toxins
- deforestation

continued on next page

Vocabulary

continued

- greenhouse gas (GHG)
- noise pollution
- light pollution
- radiation
- tsunami
- solar energy
- ethanol
- hydrogen
- natural gas
- recycling
- biodegradable
- conservation

It may seem unlikely that pollution will make a great difference in your life. However, scientists predict that large numbers of animal and plant species will be extinct by the end of the current century. *An animal or plant that does not exist anymore* is **extinct**. As the earth's population growth accelerates, the rate of human-created pollution could grow very quickly and cause much greater harm to the environment.

However, damage to our environment can be reversed. The first step is understanding the problem. Earth's natural resources such as oil and gas will eventually run out. We need to understand that the conditions needed to keep humans alive—air, water, animals, and soil—are all linked. However, this link is fragile. There have been new branches of science created to deal with problems within the environment, and its health. **Ecology**, *the study of how living things and the environment work together and depend on each other,* has expanded into new areas in recent years. One important new area is **clinical ecology**, *the science dealing with the harmful effects of human-made and natural materials on humans.*

Air Pollution

Air pollution is *a mixture of natural and human-made substances in the air we breathe.* Much of it is made up of fine particles produced by manmade activities.

Outdoor Air Pollution

A main source of outdoor air pollution is burning fossil fuels. Fossil fuels come from the earth; coal, oil, and natural gas are refined for our everyday uses. Fossil fuels are formed from prehistoric animals and plants that died and were gradually buried in layers of rock. These refined substances pollute our environment. Factories that burn oil and coal produce smoke that can harm your lungs over time, or cause other reactions. A gas byproduct from many factories and power plants, **sulfur dioxide**, is *a poisonous gas that gets into the air from the burning of fossil fuels.* There are also gases released into the air from the evaporation of gasoline and paint thinners that affect our senses and our health.

When it's time to purchase your first car, look for a vehicle that is fuel efficient and low in maintenance requirements.

Our cars and trucks burn fuels that emit exhaust fumes. If we don't keep our cars and trucks in proper running condition, the dirty exhaust will contribute to air pollution. Furnaces can create a smoky environment when waste or coal is burned. Even burning leaves generates a lot of smoke, creating air pollution.

Natural and human-made changes, such as the eruption of Mount St. Helens, affect the balance of nature.

Fires are another environmental hazard that can destroy property and life. Natural disasters like volcanic eruptions and wildfires produce unhealthy air. However, the destruction caused by fires and other natural disasters does not necessarily destroy the balance of nature. Prairie fires, for example, are good for the environment. Because the roots of prairie plants grow deep into the ground, fire does not completely destroy them. In fact, prairie fires prevent brush and trees from taking over the prairie. After a fire, prairies are alive with prairie plants that serve nature.

Volcanic eruptions, while devastating initially, have proven to be shorter-term problems. When Mount St. Helens in the state of Washington erupted in 1980, scientists thought that the destruction would be long-term—but in just a few years, the mountain started showing growth of trees and other plant life. As plant life returned, so did the fish population in Spirit Lake on the mountain. Elk, rainbow trout, and birds have come back in surprisingly large numbers.

Air pollution also comes from ground-level ozone, which is *a reactive form of oxygen that emits harmful gases*. These gases include sulfur dioxide, nitrogen oxides, carbon monoxide, and chemical vapors. Ground-level ozone is also the primary source of the smog that you see around cities or near certain industries. Smog is *a brownish haze that forms when the pollutants in the air react to sunlight*. It can be very difficult to breathe normally in a condition of intense smog. Some people experience soreness in the eyes, sinus conditions, and even severe breathing difficulties.

In Table 4.4, you can see the major sources of air pollution and their health effects.

Table 4.4 Pollutant Sources and Effects

Pollutant	Sources	Effects
Ozone—A gas that can be found in two places. Near the ground (the troposphere), it is a major part of smog. The harmful ozone in the lower atmosphere should not be confused with the protective layer of ozone in the upper atmosphere (stratosphere), which screens out harmful ultraviolet rays.	Ozone is not created directly, but is formed when nitrogen oxides and volatile organic compounds mix in sunlight. That is why ozone is mostly found in the summer. Nitrogen oxides come from burning gasoline, coal, or other fossil fuels. There are many types of volatile organic compounds, and they come from sources ranging from factories to trees.	Ozone near the ground can cause a number of health problems. Ozone can lead to more frequent asthma attacks in people who have asthma and can cause sore throats, coughing, and breathing difficulty. It may even lead to premature death. Ozone can also hurt plants and crops.
Carbon monoxide—A gas that comes from the burning of fossil fuels, mostly in cars. It cannot be seen or smelled.	Carbon monoxide is released when engines burn fossil fuels. Emissions are higher when engines are not tuned properly, and when fuel is not completely burned. Cars emit a lot of the carbon monoxide found outdoors. Furnaces and heaters in the home can emit high concentrations of carbon monoxide, too, if they are not properly maintained.	Carbon monoxide makes it hard for body parts to get the oxygen they need to run correctly. Exposure to carbon monoxide makes people feel dizzy and tired and gives them headaches. In high concentrations it is fatal. Elderly people with heart disease are hospitalized more often when they are exposed to higher amounts of carbon monoxide.
Nitrogen dioxide—A reddish-brown gas that comes from the burning of fossil fuels. It has a strong smell at high levels.	Nitrogen dioxide mostly comes from power plants and cars. Nitrogen dioxide is formed in two ways—when nitrogen in the fuel is burned, or when nitrogen in the air reacts with oxygen at very high temperatures. Nitrogen dioxide can also react in the atmosphere to form ozone, acid rain, and particles.	High levels of nitrogen dioxide exposure can give people coughs and can make them feel short of breath. People who are exposed to nitrogen dioxide for a long time have a higher chance of getting respiratory infections. Nitrogen dioxide reacts in the atmosphere to form acid rain, which can harm plants and animals.
Particulate matter—Solid or liquid matter that is suspended in the air. To remain in the air, particles usually must be less than 0.1 mm wide and can be as small as 0.00005 mm.	Particulate matter can be divided into two types—coarse particles and fine particles. Coarse particles are formed from sources like road dust, sea spray, and construction. Fine particles are formed when fuel is burned in automobiles and power plants.	Particulate matter that is small enough can enter the lungs and cause health problems. Some of these problems include more frequent asthma attacks, respiratory problems, and premature death.

Table 4.4 Pollutant Sources and Effects, continued

Pollutant	Sources	Effects
Sulfur dioxide—A corrosive gas that cannot be seen or smelled at low levels but can have a "rotten egg" smell at high levels.	Sulfur dioxide mostly comes from the burning of coal or oil in power plants. It also comes from factories that make chemicals, paper, or fuel. Like nitrogen dioxide, sulfur dioxide reacts in the atmosphere to form acid rain and particles.	Sulfur dioxide exposure can affect people who have asthma or emphysema by making it more difficult for them to breathe. It can also irritate people's eyes, noses, and throats. Sulfur dioxide can harm trees and crops, damage buildings, and make it harder for people to see long distances.
Lead—A blue-gray metal that is very toxic and is found in a number of forms and locations.	Outside, lead comes from cars in areas where unleaded gasoline is not used. Lead can also come from power plants and other industrial sources. Inside, lead paint is a significant source of lead, especially in houses where paint is peeling. Lead in old pipes can also be a source of lead in drinking water.	High amounts of lead can be dangerous for small children and can lead to lower IQs and kidney problems. For adults, exposure to lead can increase the chance of having heart attacks or strokes.

Air pollution is a big problem in modern cities.

There is another area of ozone that is located very high up in the earth's atmosphere. This is the ozone layer, *a protective layer in the atmosphere that absorbs harmful ultraviolet light from the sun.* A damaged ozone layer allows too many ultraviolet rays from the sun to reach the earth's surface. Many scientists believe it is the source of increased cases of skin cancers worldwide. If you live in a city, you've probably seen weather reports that give regular air quality updates. Breathing poor air every day can damage the lungs and lead to conditions like bronchitis and emphysema, which cause difficulty in breathing. Many large cities post air quality index categories on the Internet, announce the status of air quality to the news media, or use message boards at key locations to caution pedestrians and drivers. Figure 4.7 shows the air quality index levels.

Air Quality Index Levels of Health Concern	Numerical Value	Meaning
Good	0 to 50	Air quality is considered satisfactory, and air pollution poses little or no risk.
Moderate	51 to 100	Air quality is acceptable; however, for some pollutants there may be a moderate health concern for a very small number of people who are unusually sensitive to air pollution.
Unhealthy for Sensitive Groups	101 to 150	Members of sensitive groups may experience health effects. The general public is not likely to be affected.
Unhealthy	151 to 200	Everyone may begin to experience health effects; members of sensitive groups may experience more serious health effects.
Very Unhealthy	201 to 300	Health warnings of emergency conditions. The entire population is more likely to be affected.
Hazardous	301 to 500	Health alert: everyone may experience more serious health effects.

FIGURE 4.7

Air Quality Index Colors

Courtesy of www.airnow.gov

There are certain pollutants we put into the air ourselves that are damaging to the ozone layer. *Aerosol sprays and cooling fluids for refrigeration, among other products, give off damaging chemicals* called CFCs, or chlorofluorocarbons (klor·oh·FLOOR·oh·car·buns). The federal government has taken steps to regulate the use of these materials, and CFCs are now banned in new commercial products.

Many other pollutants we breathe are called particulates, *tiny pieces of solid materials such as dust, ash, dirt, and soot that float in the air.* Some particulates can carry gases and pesticides that can cause allergic reactions, or worse. They often bother your eyes, nose, throat, and lungs. Particulates are also found in pollutants we see indoors, such as lead paint and other household cleaners and insect sprays.

The National Institutes of Health has reported on university and medical studies about the negative effects of air pollution over the past 30 years. The research has found repeatedly that respiratory diseases (such as asthma), cardiovascular diseases, changes in lung function, and death result from the effects of air pollution.

Indoor Air Pollution

We are conditioned by so much reporting about pollution outdoors that we forget about pollution that occurs indoors. Our homes, the schools we attend, and places we go to meet friends can be more polluted than the outdoor environment around us. Buildings, for example, are constructed to shut off air leaks and drafts from the outside. In doing so, some materials were often used that have been found to harm humans and the environment.

Before laws were passed to deal with many of these conditions, people suffered from the effects of indoor smoking, aerosol sprays, and fireproofing materials such as asbestos (as·BES·tus). Asbestos was later found to cause serious diseases of the lungs when people breathed its dust. Asbestos is no longer used in construction of homes or buildings. Radon, *a natural, radioactive gas in the ground* that leaks into building foundations and structures is also shown to be destructive to personal health. Thousands have died from lung cancer caused by radon.

Speaking of lung cancer, you learned in a previous lesson that tobacco and tobacco smoke contain about 250 chemicals known to be harmful to the human body. Smoking tobacco not only causes lung cancer in many regular smokers, but also leaves a trail of pollutants in the air that often cause "secondary" smoke-related diseases.

In homes, and even businesses where heavy smoking is allowed, the impacts can be devastating to human health. This is why laws are now being passed in almost all states that ban smoking in most stores, restaurants, and other buildings where many people eat or share work spaces.

Carbon monoxide (CO) is *a gas that has no odor or color.* But it, too, is very dangerous. It can cause sudden illness and death. CO is found in the fumes created by cars and trucks. However, lanterns, stoves, gas ranges, and heating systems also emit CO fumes. These fumes can build up and you can be poisoned by breathing them in, especially in places that have little or no air ventilation.

You may have also heard of mold. A **mold** is *a type of fungus*. Some fungi reproduce through tiny spores in the air. You can inhale the spores or they can land on you. Molds like to grow in warm, damp, humid conditions. In your house, the basement or bathroom is the most likely place for mold to grow.

Molds can cause health problems. Inhaling or touching mold or mold spores may cause allergic reactions or asthma attacks. Fungal infections often start in the lungs or on the skin. You are more likely to get a fungal infection if you have a weakened immune system or take antibiotics. More generally, mold exposure can irritate your eyes, skin, nose, throat, and lungs.

Causes of Indoor Air Pollution

We usually think of air pollution as being outdoors, but the air in your home, school, or activity area could also be polluted with:

- Mold and pollen
- Tobacco smoke
- Household products and pesticides
- Gases such as radon and carbon monoxide
- Materials used in the building, such as asbestos and lead
- Fuel-burning indoor heaters and gas stoves
- Dust mites

Usually indoor air quality problems only cause discomfort. Most people feel better as soon as they remove the source of the pollution. However, some pollutants can cause diseases that show up much later, such as respiratory diseases or cancer.

Making sure that a building is well-ventilated and free of pollutants can improve the quality of the air indoors.

—Environmental Protection Agency

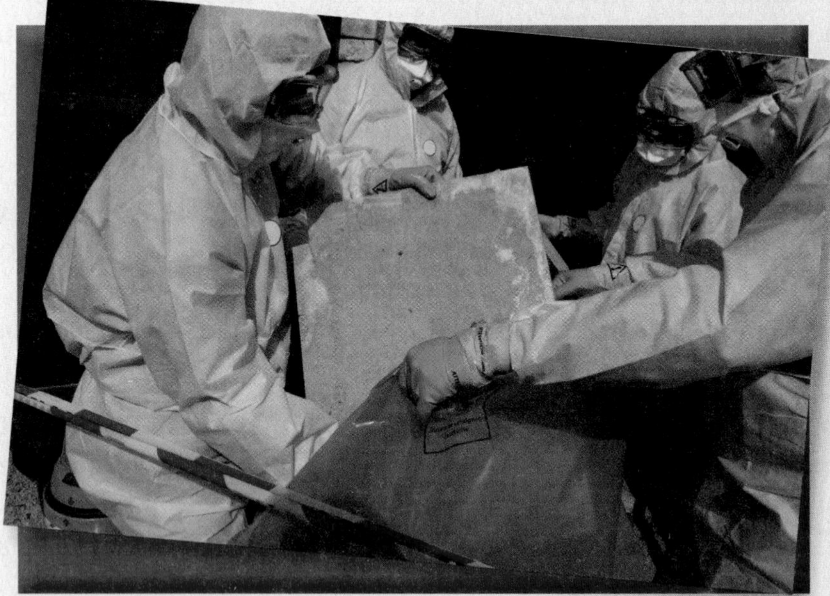

Indoor air pollutants such as asbestos are dangerous and need careful removal.

© Bernard MAURIN/Fotolia.com

Text adapted from the US National Library of Medicine and the National Institutes of Health. National Institutes of Health/http://www.nlm.nih.gov/medlineplus/indoorairpollution.html

Water Pollution

You may have already seen the results of many natural disasters. Hurricanes, earthquakes, major floods, and oil or chemical spills often are the cause of dirty, and in some cases, highly toxic water that people can't drink or use because of the threat of disease or death. Dirty water is considered one of the world's biggest health risks, and affects us all, in and around our own communities.

In our daily lives, we may rarely see natural disasters. Nevertheless, the sources for polluting the water we use and drink are still all around us. Water from normal rain and melting snow that runs off rooftops and roadways and through farm fields will pick up enough toxic chemicals, dirt, trash, and organisms to cause health issues or disease.

For example, rain and snowfall can contain large amounts of sulfuric (sul·fu·ric) or nitric (ni·tric) acids. These acids, when they mix with the wet air, create what is popularly known as "acid rain." Acid rain is created by factories and can travel through the air as far as the United States from China, or the Southeast, New England, and eastern Canada from the Midwest United States. The harm it causes is extensive when you consider how many waterways, including plant and animal life, are affected by it. In Germany, major forests have been destroyed by acid rain.

When streams and lakes become very acidic from polluted rain, fish can't lay eggs, and they may even die. In other cases, the water may accumulate mercury and lead that contaminate fish, making them unfit to be eaten.

In spite of ongoing efforts by government, corporations, environmental organizations, and concerned individuals, much of our water remains unprotected. Air pollution from the processes of farms, industrial plants, and fuel mining activities also pollute the water.

Much of our water remains unprotected from pollution.

Sources of Water Pollution

Water pollution comes from sources that are both direct and indirect. Factories, refineries, and waste treatment plants are some of the sources that send or redistribute fluids directly into streams or rivers that often serve as water supplies for cities and even small towns. Despite regulations, there is no "perfectly clean" water where there is any industry.

The effects of oil spills are disastrous, as we have seen from recent oil spills in Alaska and the Gulf of Mexico. Birds, fish, and other marine life have been devastated by such spills. Often, the ecosystems take decades to recover. Ecosystem is *the interrelationship between living organisms and their environment*. The spilled oil is ingested by birds, fish, and some animals, allowing the pollutants to enter the food chain. Commercial fishing can be halted or severely reduced in the area of a spill.

Indirect water pollution can come from underneath the surface of the earth and in our soils. Use of pesticides and fertilizers causes pollution of runoffs, *water that drains from land into streams and other water sources*. Rain and snow will also pick up pollutants from factories, industrial operations, and vehicle exhausts, among other sources.

An especially severe problem is water pollution from livestock. Large livestock farms, which can house hundreds of thousands of pigs, chickens, or cows, produce vast amounts of manure. The Natural Resources Defense Council (NRDC) estimates that the manure from a large livestock farm can generate the same amount of waste as a small city. However, unlike human waste, this waste is not processed through a sewage treatment plant. Pollution from livestock farms is a serious threat to the health of humans, fish, and ecosystems.

Facts about Pollution from Livestock Farms

Here are some livestock-generated water pollution events that have occurred within the United States:

- In 1995, an eight-acre hog-waste lagoon in North Carolina burst, spilling 25 million gallons of manure into the New River. The spill killed about 10 million fish and closed 364,000 acres of coastal wetlands to shellfishing. Shellfish are *ocean creatures that have a hard shell around them; examples are crabs, mussels, and oysters*.
- In 2010, nutrients in animal waste caused blooms of oxygen-absorbing algae, *a plantlike organism* that uses up oxygen, in the water of the Gulf of Mexico. This led to a "dead zone" that destroyed aquatic life in an area of over 7,700 square miles.
- In 2011, an Illinois hog farm spilled 200,000 gallons of manure into a creek, killing over 110,000 fish.
- In 2012, a California dairy left over 50 manure-covered cow carcasses rotting around its property that polluted nearby water supplies.

Another fast-growing and worldwide pollution problem is pharmaceutical (phar·ma·ceu·ti·cal) waste. **Pharmaceutical waste** is *the byproduct of drugs and medicines used by humans and animals*. Millions of doses of drugs are prescribed to people each year. Even more antibiotics are given to livestock. Those chemicals eventually make their way into the water supply. In addition to the risk to human health, these wastes may allow for the eventual growth of superbugs. Superbugs are bacteria that are immune to antibiotics.

You should be aware that even your own home generates wastes that get into the water. **Sewage** is *the waste material carried from toilets and drains*. Sewage wastes come from your sinks, your clothes washer, and spray bottles carrying pesticides and other treatments for garden pests and plant growth.

Things you can do on your own to become aware of the effects of water pollution are:

- Learn about the water resources in your area and surrounding industries
- Do things that will prevent possible unhealthy runoffs from your home
- Find out more about how your drinking water is tested, treated, and protected

Other Pollutants Indoors and Outdoors

Products for cleaning, carpentry, auto repair, and other indoor and outdoor household uses may have toxic ingredients. Oven and drain cleaners, laundry powders, paint thinners, and arts and crafts supplies may have ingredients that can affect your health if they are inhaled, swallowed, or absorbed through the skin. To avoid problems with these products, it's best to keep them in the containers they come in and use them exactly as the label says. If you are exposed directly, follow the label's directions immediately for treating the exposed part of your body, and get medical help, if necessary.

Pesticides are another pollution source. They are used both outdoors and indoors. **Pesticides** are *products that contain chemicals that kill insects, and are also used to control weeds, rodents, mildew, and germs*. Many household products contain pesticides. While the chemicals in pesticides can protect your health by killing germs, animals, or plants that could hurt you, they can also be harmful if you are exposed to them in any significant amounts.

Another pollutant found mostly indoors, but that may also be in outdoor plumbing and other fixtures, is **lead**, *a metal that occurs naturally within the earth*. Older homes still have lead-based paint. Water pipes in older homes still may have lead that can get into drinking water. Lead can affect almost every organ and system in your body. It is especially dangerous for children. A child who swallows large amounts of lead may develop anemia, severe stomachaches, muscle weakness, and even brain damage. Even at low levels, lead can affect a child's mental and physical growth.

Land Pollution and Deforestation

Land pollution is *the depositing of solid or liquid waste materials on land or underground in a manner that can contaminate the soil and groundwater.* At worst, land pollution threatens the health of the public. At best, pollution on land is visually unpleasant and can be a nuisance, as when people dump trash near public locations.

Solid waste, such as trash you see along roadways, is land pollution, as is debris from construction or demolition sites. Most solid waste is nonhazardous, like garbage, rubbish, and trash from homes, schools, industrial facilities, or commercial businesses. Garbage is often moist and decomposes, like food waste. Rubbish is mostly dry like paper, plastic, and glass. Around cities, you often see large trash items that are illegally dumped. These may include discarded mattresses, appliances, or pieces of furniture. These don't break down, and become very unsightly. Discarded construction materials can also be very unpleasant to see over time. These include wood and metal objects, and concrete or asphalt, among others.

Hazardous wastes are more dangerous. They can include toxic substances that come from liquids, solids, or sludge-like materials. They come from various manufacturing operations that produce chemicals, fuels, and paper products. Moreover, as mentioned above, the emission of particulates from some of these processes can cause mild to severe health problems over time.

Hazardous wastes are also generated by a host of local, small businesses you see around you, like machine shops, dry cleaners, and automobile repair shops. Improperly disposed, these hazardous wastes can contaminate groundwater, *the water located within the earth that supplies wells and springs*. Hazardous materials collected or used around your home that are not properly disposed of may also leak into local groundwater.

A new category of hazardous waste is e-waste, which is *hazardous waste generated by the production or disposal of electronic or digital devices*. In the electronic age we now live in, the amount of e-waste is growing because the useful lifespan for electronic products is getting shorter. Consumers are always looking for the next best thing in technology. This requires companies to update and improve devices quicker than ever before. The National Safety Council predicts that 250 million computers will become obsolete in the next five years. Cell phones are also replaced at a rate of 130 million per year.

Why is e-waste hazardous? Old computers, for example, can contain toxins and heavy metals. Toxins are *poisonous substances that cause disease*. Heavy metals are considered toxic and include lead, mercury, or copper. These are just some of the toxins found in discarded electronic products. When e-waste is not properly disposed of, it adds to land pollution and possible contamination of groundwater. The EPA website provides information for recycling and disposing of e-waste materials. Before throwing your old laptop into the trash, review the EPA recommendations for e-waste recycling at their website: http://www.epa.gov/epawaste/conserve/materials/ecycling/faq.htm.

Logging and land clearing are quickly depleting our rain forests.

Deforestation, *the cutting down and clearing away of trees from forests* for commercial use, is another human activity that scientists say is destroying the environment. The statistics are staggering. More than 80 percent of the earth's natural forests already have been destroyed, according to the World Resources Institute. The two largest surviving regions of rain forest in Brazil and Indonesia are disappearing rapidly. The forests are being cut down for the logging industry and for agriculture and cattle. The burning of these forests is adding to air pollution and destruction of the ozone layer, in addition to the harm done to the local wildlife.

If you consider just land animals and plants, more than two-thirds live in forests. Rain forests help generate rainfall in otherwise drought-prone areas of the world. Studies have shown that the destruction of rain forests led to two decades of droughts in the interior of Africa. Droughts lead to great hardship and lack of food among the human population.

Greenhouse Effect

Greenhouse gas (GHG) is *any gas that absorbs infrared radiation in the atmosphere.* Destruction of trees pumps a combination of carbon dioxide and methane into the atmosphere, two of the most familiar of the greenhouse gases. Scientists call it "the greenhouse effect." Carbon dioxide, researchers say, is causing Earth to act like a greenhouse. You have probably seen a greenhouse where plants are grown in a warm, damp enclosure. It has a glass ceiling that traps the sun's heat. Earth is surrounded by a carbon dioxide cloud from pollution, which in turn also traps the sun's heat. Methane, a colorless, odorless gas that is a product of decomposing organic matter such as garbage and manure, also contributes to this effect.

Recycling is important for preserving our natural resources and limiting pollution.
© Photographee.eu/Fotolia.com

These and other substances act like the glass ceiling in a greenhouse, trapping heat and dampness inside Earth's atmosphere. It's an unnatural event, causing Earth's atmosphere to get warmer, and its impact is in several areas. For one, even small rises in the temperatures around the world affect rainfall everywhere. Less rainfall in some areas can cause crops to fail and make more deserts. More rainfall in other areas can cause serious floods and soil erosion. Sea levels could rise, flooding areas along the coast and mixing saltwater with freshwater that could harm aquatic life.

Earlier, you learned about the ozone layer and air quality. However, there is more to this issue than simply the quality of the air.

The ozone layer, an area 6 to 30 miles above the earth's surface, has become thinner. A thinner ozone layer allows more of the sun's harmful rays to reach Earth, and causes an increase in the average temperature. These rays may damage crops, forest growth, animal life, and human health.

In 1985, scientists discovered a hole the size of the United States in the ozone layer over Antarctica. Later studies found an ozone loss over the Arctic polar region that is threatening the polar bear population, among other problems, such as the threat of rising sea levels around the world.

Some scientists believe global warming will upset the balance of nature and cause serious changes in the weather.

Other Forms of Pollution

Most traditional forms of pollution discussed in this lesson are those that can harm the environment and cause disease or death. In addition to these, our increasingly crowded planet has generated newer forms of pollution that create further cause for concern.

Noise Pollution

Our ears are constantly exposed to noisier, more crowded streets; numerous loud engines; or music turned up too loud, causing hearing loss. Many of these increasing noises in our environment have caused a rising level of noise pollution.

Noise pollution is *the constant presence of loud, disruptive noises in an area*. Noise pollution is unpleasant and can be dangerous for humans and even wildlife. Some songbirds, such as robins that live around cities, are unable to communicate or find food in the presence of heavy noise pollution. In the oceans, sound waves produced by some vessels can disrupt the sonar or sound waves used by marine animals to communicate or locate food.

There are other impacts from too much noise. Stress is increased. People experience problems such as high blood pressure, tension, anger, or fatigue.

Light Pollution

Look around you at night. Even if you live fairly far out into the country, there are spots in the sky where town or city lights are reflected. If you are closer to a city, the glow can be quite bright from the effects of lights on streets, in parks, around factories and office buildings, and where security has been increased. Neon lights have been overtaken by large, digital signs that have moving pictures and bright graphics, and halogen lamps. These sources of light are brighter and more efficient, but also increase **light pollution**, *the excess amount of light in the night sky*.

While increased lighting provides many conveniences, the pollution it causes can disrupt ecosystems by confusing the distinction between night and day for animals who roam at night. Too much light may disrupt sleeping and hunting patterns for these animals. On the other hand, animals that are active during daylight hours may remain active well into the night. Feeding and sleep patterns may be confused. Migrating birds have been known to fly into lighted towers.

For humans, too much light also has its effects. The American Medical Association (AMA) concluded recently that light could disrupt sleep patterns, affecting our normal biological clocks much as it does for animals. The AMA also said that the glare from roadways, property, and other artificial lighting sources could create unsafe driving conditions, especially for older drivers. Light pollution is a relatively new issue; more studies are being done to understand the impact of light pollution, including psychological effects and the effects on people with chronic diseases.

In 2007, Congress passed the Energy Independence and Security Act. A requirement of this new law stated that light bulbs had to use 25 percent less energy by 2012. Newer bulbs provide a wider range of colors and brightness, while using less energy. Prior to the passing and implementation of this new law, studies found that older incandescent light bulbs lost about 90 percent of the electricity they used to heat. Incandescent light bulbs produce light by making the wire within the glass enclosure very hot.

According to the EPA, if every American home replaced its five most frequently used light bulbs with "Energy Star" qualified lighting, this would save America $8 billion each year in energy costs, and would reduce greenhouse gases. Energy Star is a voluntary EPA program that helps businesses and individuals save money and protect our environment.

Radiation

Radiation is *energy that comes from a source and travels through space in the form of waves.* All living creatures are exposed to a natural level of radiation in the environment. We are also exposed to low levels of radiation when we get X-rays for an injury or to look for possible diseases. However, factories and power plants use high levels of radiation to generate power for our homes and businesses. People working in nuclear power plants are exposed to these higher levels of radiation. Those who are exposed to too much radiation get radiation sickness. This includes symptoms like upset stomach, vomiting, headache, diarrhea, hair loss, or fatigue. Some can get cancer from too much exposure.

Many people have died from radiation. Atomic bombs dropped during World War II caused tens of thousands of deaths from exposure to radiation. More recently, the nuclear accident in 1986 at Chernobyl in the former Soviet Union caused many people to die immediately. Many more had to deal with sickness and disease afterward. The prevailing winds from the accident carried radiation through the air to other parts of Europe, which may eventually cause some people many hundreds of miles from the scene to die from cancer, according to scientists.

The losses from a natural disaster such as the tsunami that hit Japan in 2011 are greatly multiplied when it causes the release of radioactive and other human-made pollutants.

© KABUGUI/Fotolia.com

More recently, the Great East Japan Earthquake of 2011 caused a tsunami that resulted in the destruction of three of the six nuclear reactors at the Fukushima Daiichi (fuu·kuu·SHEE·ma daa·ii·chi) Nuclear Power Plant. A **tsunami** is *a series of ocean waves caused by sudden displacement of the ocean floor, usually from an earthquake*. This tsunami also killed 19,300 Japanese citizens and residents. The resulting failure of the Fukushima Daiichi Nuclear Power Plant required the evacuation of approximately 185,000 people. As of 2014, radioactive water is still leaking from the power plant.

Plastics

Many plastics are toxic. Some with polyvinyl chloride (PVC) can cause cancer. Others can cause insulin resistance or have been linked to heart disease. The problem with plastic materials is they do not break down (biodegrade). In some cases, plastic products may last for hundreds of thousands of years as waste. Excessive use of plastics has become a worldwide problem.

Plastics and other human-made pollution destroy our oceans.
© vladimirfloyd/Fotolia.com

Huge islands of plastic trash have been known to accumulate in the world's oceans. The Great Pacific Ocean Garbage Patch, made up of plastic bags, bottles, and debris, stretches out for hundreds of miles. Another such patch has been found in the Atlantic Ocean. Among the kinds of debris being found is a growing number of abandoned plastic fishing nets. These may entangle seals, sea turtles, and other animals, drowning them. More fishermen from developing countries are now using plastic. It's inexpensive, but once abandoned, these nets can continue to trap fish for months or years. Plastic bags are often eaten by sea turtles that mistake the bags for jellyfish, which are the turtles' main food source.

Floating plastic waste is another problem. As sunlight breaks it down, the surface water thickens with plastic "bits" that contains toxic chemicals linked to various environmental and health problems, and can be very poisonous to marine life when ingested.

Methods for Reducing and Preventing Pollution

Protecting the environment is everyone's job—the world community, governments, businesses and factories, local communities, and individuals. There are many current actions being taken by world and local governments and by groups and individual citizens to help reduce pollution. You can play a major role in this effort by getting involved.

Laws That Protect the Environment

The United States and other governments around the world have become sensitive to the need to protect the environment.

The US government has passed several laws, starting in 1970 with the Clean Air Act, which regulates the allowable amount of air pollution. The law also requires each state to have a plan to meet the standards of the US Environmental Protection Agency (EPA). Some states have laws about how much exhaust cars can make as one way to meet these standards. In these states, cars must pass an emissions test every year.

Another law, the National Environmental Policy Act, requires federal agencies to take into consideration how their plans and activities will affect the environment. Before any agency can begin a new project, it must file an environmental impact statement and hold public hearings about the environmental effects of the project.

There are other US environmental laws that set standards for water safety and ways to get rid of solid and hazardous wastes. They require polluters to manage the cleanup of chemical spills and toxic waste. The US Department of Energy and the Nuclear Regulatory Commission oversee the proper use and safety of nuclear energy and work with the EPA on proper disposal of nuclear energy wastes.

Because so many environmental problems affect the entire world, nations have joined together to try to agree on solutions. For example, an international meeting in Senegal in 2005 studied ways to keep the ozone layer from thinning. Many nations have agreed to stop using CFCs and other materials that may further damage the ozone layer.

In 1992, the United Nations (UN) General Assembly started the Conference on Environment and Development. It brought together leaders from 178 countries. They talked about ways to live well and protect the environment at the same time. Today, the UN keeps looking for ways to protect the environment.

Reducing Existing Pollution

Scientists are working on ways to protect the environment from further harm. For example, they are searching for ways to use solar energy, *a source of energy that comes directly from the sun*. Solar energy is clean and environmentally safe. Wind energy is another energy source that is becoming more popular.

As you've learned, most of our oil, gas, and electricity now come from fossil fuels. Although fossil fuels help provide energy we need for production, transportation, and in your home, they come with a heavy price to the environment. If we use solar and wind energy, we can reduce the use of fossil fuels in our homes by as much as 70 percent, according to scientists.

Scientists have also found other fuels to lessen exhaust from cars and trucks. One of these fuels is ethanol, or *alcohol made from corn*—a renewable resource. Many states now use ethanol mixed with regular gasoline.

Hydrogen and natural gas are also examples of clean-burning fuels that are being used in new ways. Hydrogen fuel is *produced from water and fossil fuels, providing a cleaner alternative*. Although hydrogen can be produced from fossil fuels, its manufacturing byproduct has a much smaller impact on the ozone layer. Natural gas is also *a fossil fuel formed in the same way as coal and oil, but provides a cleaner burning fuel*. Hybrid cars also run on a mix of gasoline and electricity that reduces gasoline use and lessens harmful exhausts. Solar energy may one day be a common way to power cars, and would totally eliminate the need for gasoline fuels.

California law requires new cars sold in that state to use less fuel. If automobiles can't meet the required mileage expectations, the buyer will have to pay an additional fee. California and many other states have high-occupancy vehicle (HOV) lanes that require users to carry multiple riders to their workplaces or other places where traffic is normally congested. Having fewer cars on the road is one way to lessen car exhaust.

Effective Methods of Preventing Pollution

Recycling has become common in most communities. Recycling means *reusing materials instead of buying new ones*. Recycling means less solid waste in our landfills. Because of recycling, our natural resources aren't used up so quickly. We can "renew" many products, from newspapers and cardboard to aluminum cans and glass, through recycling.

Scientists are working on new plastic materials made from corn that biodegrade in less than 60 days, instead of plastics in use now that can take hundreds or thousands of years to break down.

Corn-based plastic cups can be crushed with decaying plants and vegetables to make compost. Compost added to dirt improves the soil for growing. The idea here is if you combine recycling with the use of biodegradable plastics, the environment is protected and the life span of landfills can be increased. Biodegradable products are *capable of being slowly destroyed and broken down into very small parts by natural processes*.

Another way to prevent pollution is by using less of what creates waste in the first place. People are beginning to pass up using plastic bags at grocery, clothing, and other shops to slow down the dumping of those non-biodegradable bags into the environment.

In addition, instead of using things like cardboard boxes and paper one time, then throwing them away, there are ways to recycle these products. Empty jars can be cleaned and reused for storage.

Community Actions to Reduce and Prevent Pollution

As the usable land on Earth shrinks due to population growth and development of natural resources increases to meet population demands, pollution is becoming worse. In cities, for example, the rapid increase of pavement causes more rain to run off instead of soaking into the soil. Runoff picks up pollutants and distributes them into nearby lakes and streams.

Farming communities have a different problem, as farmlands disappear and more food has to be grown more efficiently in smaller spaces.

Communities are addressing concerns like these through **conservation**, *an effort to preserve and protect the environment by managing natural resources*. Some communities are developing zoning regulations that try to make the best possible use of land within their borders. Community planners are also being more environmentally conscious about developing land for new construction.

Community standards about recycling have often changed attitudes toward the environment. Many communities pick up recyclable products at the curb. Other communities have recycling centers. In many communities, people can get cash for glass, plastic bottles, aluminum, and other metals.

What hasn't changed within many communities is the lack of control over many individuals' wasteful and pollution-generating habit of throwing out trash on the sides of roadways. Much of this trash is not biodegradable, and this littering has reached epidemic proportions in many communities.

keys to LEADERSHIP

As a young person, you can help set an example for a clean environment by getting involved in your community. There are three ways to do this—become informed, volunteer your time, or be an advocate, which means speaking out or writing about an issue or problem.

Maybe you'd want to join a group to adopt a roadway to clean up trash and then write about it for a school project. For a speech class or civics, give a talk about your experiences on such a cleanup crew and what you see as a need to educate the community about the harmful effects of littering.

Other Things You Can Do

Everything you do makes a difference. Every individual can work to protect the environment. Here are some additional actions you and others can take to protect the environment:

- Turn off the lights when you leave a room.
- Take shorter showers.
- Do not run hot water if you do not need to.
- Use fewer things that need to be thrown away. For example, use a glass cup instead of a paper or plastic cup, or use cloth towels instead of paper towels.
- Find out what recycling services are in your community and use them.

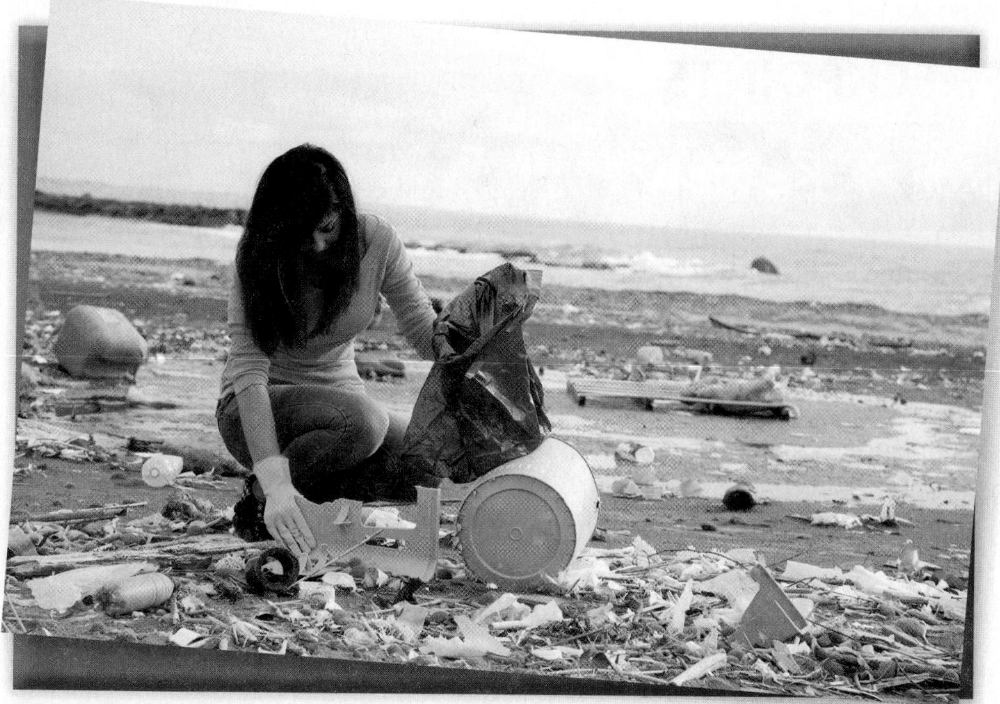

There are many things you can do to help protect the environment.
© fmarsicano/Fotolia.com

- Reuse items such as paper.
- Buy products that have refillable containers, such as beverages in glass or plastic bottles.
- Look for products with the recycled symbol. This symbol shows that recycled materials were used in making them.

For now and in the future, protecting the environment is everyone's job. Get involved with environmental issues in your community, and take care of the little things in your home, school, and the places you go. All these things will go far to protect the earth.

Lesson 4 Review

Using complete sentences, answer the following questions on a sheet of paper.

1. What is pollution?
2. What is clinical ecology?
3. What kinds of fires are actually good for the environment?
4. Why is it harmful for the earth to have a damaged ozone layer?
5. What is e-waste?
6. Why is exposure to lead especially harmful to children?
7. What does the US Department of Energy oversee?
8. How does recycling help the environment?
9. What is conservation?
10. What are three things you can do right now to protect the environment?

APPLYING YOUR LEARNING

11. Write a short paragraph on acid rain and its effects on the environment. Explain why acid rain is so dangerous to communities far from the original point where pollutants entered into the atmosphere and were picked up by the moisture in the air.

CHAPTER 5

The Foundations of United States Citizenship

Chapter Outline

LESSON 1

The American Flag and Other National Symbols

LESSON 2

Civics

LESSON 3

The Constitution of the United States

LESSON 4

Interpreting the Bill of Rights and Other Amendments

LESSON 5

US National Government

"Our citizenship in the United States is our national character. Our citizenship in any particular state is only our local distinction. By the latter we are known at home, by the former to the world. Our great title is AMERICANS..."

Thomas Paine, Founding Father and influential writer during the Revolutionary War

LESSON 1

The American Flag and Other National Symbols

Make a list of everything you know about the design of the American flag. Then write a summary of what the American flag and other patriotic symbols mean to you.

"Our great modern Republic. May those who seek the blessings of its institutions and the protection of its flag remember the obligations they impose."

Ulysses S. Grant, 18th President of the United States

Learn About

- history of the American flag
- courtesies rendered to the flag of the United States
- courtesies rendered to the National Anthem, Pledge of Allegiance, and American's Creed
- the Great Seal of the United States and the military services' seals

History of the American Flag

After fighting broke out between the American colonists—*those who settled in America from Europe*—and the British army in Massachusetts, representatives from the 13 original colonies met in 1775 for the Second Continental Congress. This meeting in Philadelphia led to several things. One was the drafting of the Declaration of Independence, which we cover in Lesson 3. Another was the formation of a Continental Army. Yet another was the approval of an official American flag. Called the "Stars and Stripes" and "Old Glory," this new national symbol was adopted on June 14, 1777. We now celebrate June 14 as Flag Day.

The resolution for this new flag offered by the Congressional Marine Committee read:

> *Resolved: that the flag of the United States be thirteen stripes, alternate red and white; that the union be thirteen stars, white in a blue field representing a new constellation.*

The number 13 represented the original Thirteen Colonies. This resolution gave no indication as to how many points the stars should have or how to arrange the stars on the blue field, called the union. The union is *the upper left corner of the flag, representing a group of states that join together.* Some original flags had stars scattered on the blue field without any specific design, some had the stars arranged in rows, and some in a circle. The first Navy Stars and Stripes had the stars arranged in staggered formation, in alternate rows of threes and twos on a blue field. Other Stars and Stripes flags had stars arranged in alternate rows of four, five, and four. Some stars had six points while others had eight.

There is strong evidence that Francis Hopkinson of New Jersey, a signer of the Declaration of Independence, was responsible for the stars in the American flag. At the time that the flag resolution was adopted, Hopkinson was Chairman of the Continental Navy Board. Hopkinson also helped design other devices for the government, including the Great Seal of the United States.

Vocabulary

- colonists
- union
- patriot
- ensign
- halyard
- half-staff
- executive or military department
- member of Congress
- bunting
- retreat
- reveille
- page
- heraldry
- obverse
- authenticate
- ratification
- die
- symbolism
- amphibious

The Betsy Ross Flag

During the Revolutionary War, several patriots made flags for our new nation. A patriot is *someone who has strong feelings of love, respect, and duty toward their country.* Cornelia Bridges, Elizabeth (Betsy) Ross, and Rebecca Young, all from Pennsylvania, and John Shaw of Annapolis, Maryland were among the flag makers. Betsy Ross was the best known of these persons. She made flags for 50 years. The claim that she designed the first flag of the United States is based on family traditions. What is known is that she made flags for the Pennsylvania State Navy in 1777. The flag known as the "Betsy Ross flag," in which the stars were arranged in a circle, did not appear until the early 1790s.

William J. Canby, a grandson of Betsy Ross, brought her to public attention in 1870. In a paper he read before a meeting of the Historical Society of Pennsylvania, Canby stated:

> *Colonel Ross with Robert Morris and General Washington, called on Mrs. Ross and told her they were a committee of Congress, and wanted her to make a flag from the drawing, a rough one, which, upon her suggestions, was redrawn by General Washington in pencil in her back parlor. This was prior to the Declaration of Independence. I fix the date to be during Washington's visit to Congress from New York in June, 1776 when he came to confer upon the affairs of the Army, the flag being no doubt, one of these affairs.*

The Betsy Ross Flag.

The Grand Union Flag

The first flag of the colonists that looked similar to the present Stars and Stripes was the Grand Union Flag. This is sometimes referred to as the Congress Colors, the First Navy Ensign, and the Cambridge Flag. An ensign is *a national flag displayed on ships and aircraft, often with the special insignia of a branch or unit of the armed forces.*

Grand Union Flag.

The Grand Union flag had 13 stripes, alternately red and white, representing the original Thirteen Colonies. It had a blue field in the upper left corner, bearing the red cross of St. George of England with the white cross of St. Andrew of Scotland. As the flag of the revolution, it was used on many occasions. The ships of the Colonial Fleet were the first to display this flag on the Delaware River. On December 3, 1775, John Paul Jones, a Navy lieutenant, raised this flag aboard Captain Esek Hopkins' flagship *Alfred*. Later, the flag was raised on the liberty pole at Prospect Hill, which was near General George Washington's headquarters in Cambridge, Massachusetts. It was the unofficial national flag and ensign of the Navy until June 14, 1777, when the Continental Congress authorized the Stars and Stripes.

The Final Flag Design

There were several changes to the American flag before the final design was accepted. The first change was in 1794, when Congress passed an act requiring that the flag consist of 15 white stars on the blue field and 15 stripes, alternating red and white. This change took into account the newly admitted states of Vermont in 1791, and Kentucky in 1792. This became the official flag from 1795 to 1818. It played a role in many historic events. When Fort McHenry was attacked in 1814, Francis Scott Key was inspired to write "The Star Spangled Banner," a poem that later became the national anthem. It was the first flag to be flown over a fortress of the Old World when American Marine and Naval forces raised it above the pirate stronghold in Tripoli in 1805. It was the ensign of American forces in the Battle of Lake Erie in September 1813. In January 1815, General Andrew Jackson flew it in the final battle of the War of 1812. Capt. Samuel C. Reid, USN, realized that the flag would become difficult to carry if it had a stripe for each new state, and suggested to Congress that the stripes remain 13 in number to represent the Thirteen Colonies. He also suggested that a star be added to the blue field for each new state coming into the union.

On April 4, 1818, President James Monroe signed a bill requiring that the American flag have a union of 20 stars for the number of states at the time, white on a blue field. The new law also said that each time a new state came into the union, one star would be added to the union of the flag. This would happen on the Fourth of July following the date each state was admitted. The 13 alternating red and white stripes would remain unchanged. This act set the standard for the basic design of the flag while making sure that the growth of the nation would be properly symbolized.

Stars and Stripes.
© Joanne Stemberger/Fotolia.com

Eventually, the country grew to the point where it had 48 stars. This happened when Arizona and New Mexico were admitted to the union in 1912. Alaska became a state in 1959, which added a 49th star to the flag. Hawaii, in 1960, became the 50th state. With the newest 50-star flag, President Dwight Eisenhower, by executive order, directed a new design and arrangement of the stars. A national banner with 50 stars became the official American flag.

A symbol of liberty, the American flag has carried the message of freedom to many parts of the world. Sometimes the flag was flying at a crucial moment in our history, and at other times it was flown elsewhere to symbolize our continued struggles for the same cause of liberty. By paying proper respect to this symbol, your actions mark you as a leader.

The colors used in the American flag are symbolic. White is for purity and innocence. Red is for hardiness and valor. Blue is for vigilance, perseverance, and justice.

The flag that flew over the Capitol in Washington on December 7, 1941, when Pearl Harbor was attacked was the same flag raised on December 8, when war was declared on Japan. It was raised again three days later when war was declared against Germany and Italy. President Roosevelt called it the "flag of liberation." He carried it with him to the Casablanca Conference and on other historic occasions. It flew from the mast of the *USS Missouri* during the formal Japanese surrender on September 2, 1945. It also was used in 1945 at the United Nations Charter meeting in San Francisco, California, and at the Big Three Conference at Potsdam, Germany.

The Flag Today

Today's American flag has 13 horizontal stripes—seven red and six white, alternating—and a union of white stars of five points on a blue field. The blue field is in the upper quarter of the flag next to the staff, and extends to the lower edge of the fourth red stripe from the top. The number of stars equals the number of states in the Union. The flag in its current design was raised for the first time at 12:01 a.m. on July 4, 1960, at the Fort McHenry National Monument in Baltimore, Maryland.

Courtesies Rendered to the Flag of the United States

Flag Presentation

When it is appropriate to present the flag at a ceremony or other occasion, a brief explanation of the importance of the event should be given, followed by the presentation of the flag. Afterward, all attendees in uniform should salute the flag, and those in civilian clothes should place their right hand over their heart, recite the Pledge of Allegiance, and sing the National Anthem.

Flag Laws and Regulations

Prior to June 14, 1923 there were no federal or state regulations governing display of the American flag. It was on this date that the National Flag Code was adopted by the National Flag Conference, which was attended by representatives of the Army and Navy who had evolved their own procedures, and some 66 other national groups. This purpose of providing guidance based on the Army and Navy procedures relating to display and associated questions about the American flag was adopted by all organizations in attendance.

The US Code contains the laws relating to the American flag. Title 4, Chapter 1 is about the flag and seal, seat of government, and the states. Title 18, Chapter 33 is about crimes and criminal procedures. Title 36, Chapter 10 is about patriotic customs and observances. There are also executive orders and presidential proclamations that add to these laws.

Displaying and Using the Flag

The flag is usually displayed only from sunrise to sunset on buildings and on stationary flagstaffs in the open. However, you can display the flag 24 hours a day for a patriotic effect. A law signed on July 7, 1976, permits the display of an all-weather American flag all day and night, if proper lighting is provided during hours of darkness.

The flag should be hoisted briskly and lowered ceremoniously. It should not be displayed in bad weather, except when using an all-weather flag. The flag can be displayed on all days, especially on the following holidays:

- New Year's Day, January 1
- Dr. Martin Luther King's Birthday, January 15
- Inauguration Day, January 20
- Abraham Lincoln's Birthday, February 12
- Presidents' Day (George Washington's Birthday), the third Monday in February
- Easter Sunday (the exact date varies each year)
- Mother's Day, the second Sunday in May
- Armed Forces' Day, the third Saturday in May
- Memorial Day (half-staff until noon), the last Monday in May
- Flag Day, June 14
- Independence Day, July 4
- Labor Day, the first Monday in September
- Constitution Day, September 17
- Columbus Day, the second Monday in October
- Navy Day, October 27
- Veteran's Day, November 11
- Thanksgiving Day, the fourth Thursday in November
- Christmas Day, December 25
- Other days as proclaimed by the President of the United States
- State birthdays (date of admission and state holidays)

The flag should be displayed daily on or near the main administration building of every public institution. It should be displayed in or near every polling place on election days, and it should be displayed during school days in or near every schoolhouse.

Flag Day

The Second Continental Congress authorized a new flag on June 14, 1777 to symbolize our new nation, the United States of America. The Stars and Stripes is celebrated each year on June 14, the same day as its birthday.

The Stars and Stripes first flew in a Flag Day celebration in Hartford, Connecticut. This was in 1861, during the first summer of the Civil War. The first national observance of Flag Day was on June 14, 1877, the centennial of the original flag resolution.

By the mid-1890s, the observance of Flag Day was a popular event. Mayors and governors began to issue proclamations in their jurisdictions to celebrate the date. In the years to follow, public sentiment for a national Flag Day observance grew further. In 1916, President Woodrow Wilson issued a proclamation calling for a nationwide observance of Flag Day on June 14.

Many patriotic societies and veterans' groups got involved with Flag Day. Their main objective was to inspire patriotism among the young, so schools were the first to become involved in activities honoring the flag. In 1949, Congress made the day a permanent observance. Its resolution said: "The 14th day of June of each year is hereby designated as Flag Day." President Truman signed the measure into law. Although Flag Day is not celebrated as a federal holiday, Americans everywhere continue to honor in various ways the history and heritage the day represents.

Ways to Position and Display the Flag

When carrying the flag in a procession with another flag or flags, make sure it is either on the marching right—that is, the flag's own right—or, if there is another line of flags, in the front and center of that line.

Other guidelines for proper display of the flag include:

- Do not display the flag on a float in a parade, except from a staff or suspended with folds falling free.
- Do not drape the flag over the hood, top, sides, or back of a vehicle, railroad train, or boat. When displaying the flag on a motorcar, fix the staff firmly to the chassis or clamp it to the right fender.

A color guard displaying the flag.

Courtesy of Chief Warrant Officer Donnie Brzuska/Defense Video & Imagery Distribution System

- Do not place any other flag or pennant above or, if on the same level, to the right of the American flag. The only exception is during church services conducted by naval chaplains at sea, when the church pennant may be flown above the flag.
- Do not fly any flag or pennant above the American flag, except the United Nations flag at the United Nations Headquarters.
- When using the American flag for ceremonies by motorized and mechanized organizations, make sure they are carried on vehicles specifically designed for color and color guards. The position in line from right to left will be as follows: the American flag, the organizational flag, and the individual's flag (displayed only when a general officer is commanding).
- When displaying the American flag with another flag against a wall from crossed staffs, make sure the American flag is on the right—the flag's own right—and that its staff is in front of the staff of the other flag.
- In general, display the American flag flat or hanging free. Do not drape it over doorways or arches, tie it in a bow, or fashion it into any other shape.
- When the American flag is among a group of flags—of states or localities, or pennants of societies—that are displayed from staffs, make sure the American flag is at the center, highest point of the group.
- The American flag should always be at the peak when flown on the same halyard with flags of states, cities, and localities (or pennants of societies). A halyard is *a rope for hoisting and lowering things*. When the flags are on adjacent staffs, hoist the American flag first and lower it last. Do not place any other flag or pennant above the American flag or to its right.
- When displaying flags of two or more nations, fly them from separate staffs of the same height. Make sure the flags are approximately equal in size. International usage forbids the display of the flag of one nation above that of another nation in time of peace.
- When displaying the American flag from a staff that projects horizontally or at an angle from a windowsill, balcony, or front of a building, place the union of the flag at the peak of the staff unless the flag is at half-staff.
- When the flag is suspended over a sidewalk from a rope extending from a house to a pole at the edge of the sidewalk, hoist the flag out from the building, union first.
- When displaying the flag horizontally or vertically against a wall, make sure the union is uppermost and to the flag's own right—that is, to the observer's left. The same applies when displaying the flag in a window.

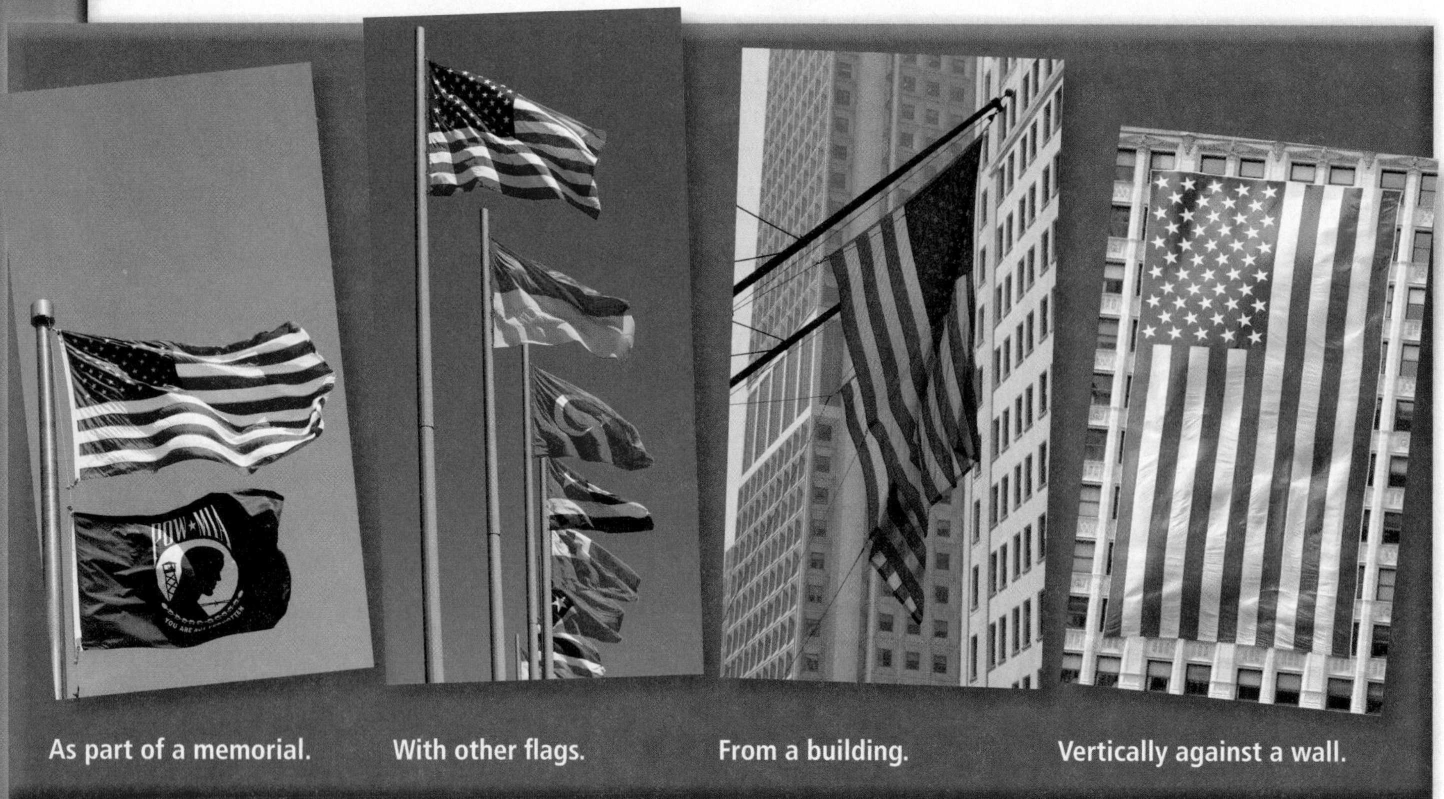

As part of a memorial. With other flags. From a building. Vertically against a wall.

The American flag displayed in various positions.

Left to right: © Leonard Zhukovsky/Fotolia.com; © Nobilior/Fotolia.com; © apeschi/Fotolia.com; © KNSTUDIOS/Fotolia.com

- When displaying the flag over the middle of the street, suspend it vertically with the union to the north in an east-west street, or to the east in a north-south street.
- When using the flag displayed flat on a speaker's platform, display it above and behind the speaker. When displaying the flag from a staff in a church or public auditorium, make sure it holds the position of superior prominence. The position should be in front of the audience and in the position of honor at the right of the clergyman or speaker as he or she faces the audience. Place any other flag to the left of the clergyman or speaker, or to the right of the audience.
- The flag should be a distinctive feature of a ceremony for unveiling a statue or monument. Never use it as the covering for the statue or monument.
- When flying the flag at half-staff, first hoist it to the peak for an instant, and then lower it to the half-staff position. Raise the flag to the peak again before it is lowered for the day. Half-staff means *the position of the flag when it is one-half the distance between the top and bottom of the staff*. On Memorial Day, display the flag at half-staff until noon only, and then raise it to the top of the staff.
- By order of the president, fly the flag at half-staff upon the death of principal figures of the United States Government, as a mark of respect to their memory. Do the same for the governor of a state, territory, or possession.

The American flag is lowered to half-staff.

Photo by Tech. Sgt. Brian Christiansen/Defense Video and Image Distribution System

In the event of the death of other officials or foreign dignitaries, the flag should fly at half-staff. Follow the instructions or orders set by the president, or those customs or practices that are consistent with law. If a present or former official of the government of any state, territory, or possession of the United States dies, the governor of that entity may decide to fly the national flag at half-staff. The flag should fly at half-staff in the following situations:

- For 30 days after the death of the president or a former president.
- For ten days after the day of death of the vice president, the chief justice, a retired chief justice of the United States, or the speaker of the house of representatives.
- From the day of death until internment of an associate justice of the Supreme Court, a secretary of an executive or military department, a former vice president, or the governor of a state, territory, or possession. Executive or military department means *any agency listed under sections 101 and 102 of title 5, United States Code.*
- On the day of death and the following day for a member of Congress. Member of Congress means *a senator, a representative, a delegate, or the resident commissioner from Puerto Rico.*
- When using the flag to cover a casket, place it with the union at the head and over the left shoulder. Do not lower the flag into the grave or let it touch the ground.

The American flag is known around the world as a symbol of liberty and freedom.

© luchschen_shutter/Fotolia.com

Displaying the United Nations Flag

When the American flag and the United Nations flag are on display together, the American flag is on the right—best identified as "the marching right." The American flag will be equal in size or larger, in the position of honor on the right (observer's left), and above the United Nations flag. The United Nations flag will be carried only for occasions honoring the United Nations or its high dignitaries. When carried in this way, the United Nations flag will be on "the marching left" and below the American flag.

Showing Respect for the American Flag

Always show respect to the American flag. Never dip the flag to any person or thing. Only regimental colors, state flags, and organization or institutional flags are dipped as a mark of honor. The only circumstance in which the American flag would be dipped is when a US Naval vessel receives this type of salute from a vessel registered by a nation formally recognized by the United States.

- Never display the flag with the union down, except as a signal of dire distress when extreme danger to life or property exists.
- Never let the flag touch anything beneath it, such as the ground, the floor, water, or merchandise.
- Never carry the flag flat or horizontally; always carry it aloft and free.
- Never use the flag as wearing apparel, bedding, or drapery. Always allow it to fall free. Never put things on it, pull it back or up, or drape it in folds.
- When using the bunting of blue, white, and red, always arrange it with the blue above, the white in the middle, and the red below. A **bunting** is *a lightweight, loosely woven fabric used mainly for flags and festive decorations*. Some common uses for bunting are for covering a speaker's desk, draping the front of a platform, and decoration in general.
- Never fasten, display, use, or store the flag a way in which it can be easily torn, soiled, or damaged in any way.
- Never use the flag as a ceiling covering.
- Do not place or attach any mark, insignia, letter, word, figure, design, picture, or drawing on the flag.
- Never use the flag as a receptacle for receiving, holding, carrying, or delivering anything.
- Never use the flag for advertising purposes. Do not embroider it on cushions, handkerchiefs, and other personal items. Do not put it on paper napkins, boxes, or anything that is used temporarily and discarded. Do not fasten advertising signs to a staff or halyard from which the flag is flying.

- Do not use any part of the flag as a costume or athletic uniform. However, a flag patch may be affixed to the uniform of military personnel, firemen, policemen, and members of patriotic organizations. The flag represents a living country and is itself considered a living thing. Since the lapel flag pin is a replica, wear it on the left lapel near the heart.

Retiring the National Flag

The flag, when it is in such condition that it is no longer a fitting emblem of display, should be destroyed in a dignified way, preferably by burning. First cut the blue field from the flag, then completely burn the two pieces. After the flag has completely burned, you may bury the ashes. Always perform this ceremony with respect and feeling.

During the ceremony, there can be appropriate music, singing, and comments about freedom and liberty or other topics dealing with the flag as an American symbol.

Always treat the flag with respect.
Photo by Petty Officer 3rd Class Loumania Stewart/Defense Video & Imagery Distribution System

Flag Folding Ceremony

In the US Armed Forces, a flag folding is done at a retreat ceremony where the flag is lowered, folded in a triangle fold, and kept under watch throughout the night as a tribute to our nation's honored dead. Retreat *signals the end of the official duty day and also serves as a ceremony for paying respect to the flag.* The next morning the flag is brought out and, at the ceremony of reveille, raised again. Reveille is *the signal for the start of the official duty day.*

A funeral honors detail performs a flag folding at a funeral ceremony. It includes the folding of a American flag and its presentation to the veteran's family. The playing of "Taps" follows the flag folding ceremony by a bugler who is a member of the detail. If a bugler is not available, a recorded version of "Taps" is played.

The source and the date of origin of this flag folding procedure is unknown. Some sources attribute it to the Gold Star Mothers of America, while others to an Air Force chaplain stationed at the United States Air Force Academy. It is provided as a patriotic service to all. See Figure 5.1 for the traditional method of folding the flag.

When the flag is completely folded, the stars are uppermost, reminding us of our national motto: "In God We Trust."

The traditional method of folding the flag is a carefully performed procedure:

STEP 1—Straighten out the flag to full length and fold lengthwise once.

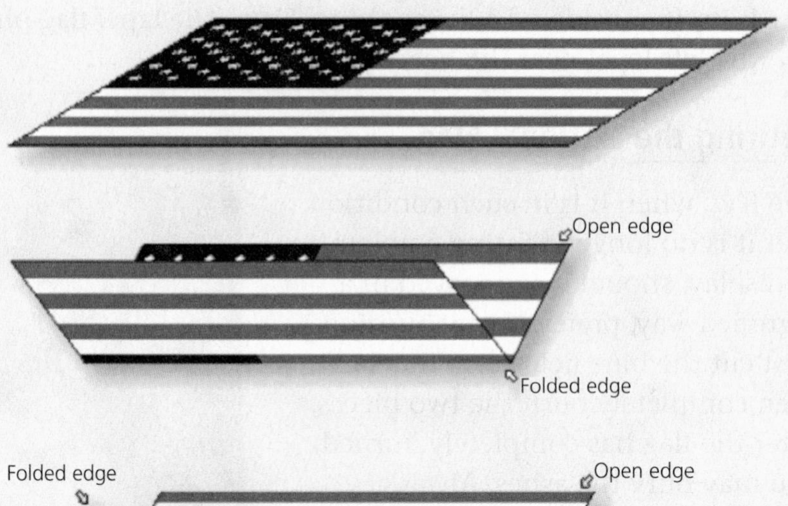

STEP 2—Fold it lengthwise a second time to meet the open edge, making sure that the union of stars on the blue field remains outward in full view. (A large flag may have to be folded lengthwise a third time.)

STEP 3—Make a triangular fold by bringing the striped corner of the folded edge to the open edge.

STEP 4—The outer point is then turned inward, parallel with the open edge, to form a second triangle.

STEP 5—Triangular folding is continued until the entire length of the flag is folded in this manner.

STEP 6—When the flag is completely folded, only a triangular blue field of stars should be visible.

FIGURE 5.1

Flag Folding Procedure

After the flag is completely folded and tucked in, it has the appearance of a cocked hat, ever reminding us of the soldiers who served under Gen. George Washington and the sailors and Marines who served under Capt. John Paul Jones and were followed by their comrades and shipmates in the US Armed Forces, preserving for us the rights, privileges, and freedoms we enjoy today.

The portion of the flag denoting honor is the field of blue containing the stars representing states our veterans served in uniform. The field of blue dresses from left to right and is inverted only when draped on the casket of a veteran who has served our country honorably in uniform or highly regarded State and National figures.

Military and Civilian Courtesies to the Flag

Below are the special courtesies that all who wear the military uniform are expected to render to the American flag.

When in Uniform and in Formation. When you are in uniform and in formation, but not part of a ceremony, the unit commander commands "present arms" during the National Anthem or "To the Colors." The unit should be facing the flag before being given "present arms." Hold the salute until unit commander gives the command "order arms."

When in Uniform, Outdoors, but Not in Formation. At any outdoor ceremony that uses the American flag, come to attention, face the flag in the ceremony, and salute. At sporting events, if the flag is visible, face the flag and salute. If the flag is not visible, face the band and salute in its direction. If the music is recorded, face the front and salute. At all other outdoor occasions follow the same general principle: come to attention, face the flag (if it is visible), and salute. If the flag is not visible, face the music and do the same. Salute on the first note of music and hold the salute until the last note.

When in Uniform, Indoors, and the National Anthem or "To the Colors" is Played. When you are indoors and the National Anthem or "To the Colors" is played, face the flag (if it is present) and assume the position of attention. If no flag is present, assume the position of attention while facing the music.

When Indoors or Outdoors in Civilian Clothes. When in civilian clothes and the National Anthem or "To the Colors" is played, stand at attention, face the flag, and place your right hand over your heart. If the flag is not visible, face the music and do the same. A male will remove his hat with the right hand and hold it at his left shoulder with his right hand over his heart. A female does not remove her hat, however, and salutes by standing at attention and placing her right hand over her heart. Male cadets without hats salute in the same way as female cadets. Salute on the first note of music and hold the salute until the last note. Veterans may render the military salute or place right hand over heart. When you are indoors and the ceremony is outdoors, you do not need to face the flag or salute. The same rule applies during ceremonies that are broadcast over radio or on television.

To an Escorted Flag Outdoors. If you are at any outdoor event and an uncased flag is escorted past you, stand at attention, face the front, and render the appropriate salute. Render the salute approximately six paces before the flag is even with you, and hold the salute until the flag is approximately six paces past you.

On a Stationary Flagstaff. Salute flags on stationary flagstaffs only at reveille, retreat, and special occasions. Do not salute small flags, flags at half-staff, or cased and folded flags.

By Vehicle Passengers. At the first sound of the music, all vehicles come to a complete stop. Occupants of a civilian or military vehicle, including the driver, should sit quietly until the music ends.

At Half-Staff. When the flag is at half-staff, it is to honor and pay respect to deceased personnel of national importance. The Chiefs of Staff of the military services set the number of days or periods to keep the flag at half-staff. The flag is flown at half-staff on all bases that make up the command of the deceased commander. Deceased cadets may also be honored in the same way.

Miniature Flags. Do not salute miniature flags, such as those displayed at downtown parades and sporting events.

Conduct During Hoisting, Lowering, or Passing of the American Flag. During the ceremony of hoisting or lowering the flag, or when the flag is passing in a parade or in review, everyone except those in uniform should face the flag and stand at attention with the right hand over the heart. Those in uniform should render the military salute. Veteran's may render the military salute or place right hand over heart. Male cadets who are not in uniform should remove their hat with their right hand and hold it at the left shoulder with the hand over the heart. A female does not remove her hat, however, and salutes by standing at attention and placing her right hand over her heart. When the flag is in a moving column, salute at the moment the flag passes.

Courtesies Rendered to the National Anthem, Pledge of Allegiance, and American's Creed

National Anthem

The American flag and National Anthem are symbols of all the people, their land, and their institutions. When we salute these symbols, we are saluting the nation. We show the same respect to flags and national anthems of friendly foreign nations.

The National Anthem is played at most flag ceremonies. Sometimes "To the Colors," a bugle call, is used instead, and it must be given the same respect as the National Anthem. "To the Colors" can be used when a band is not available or during bad weather. During these ceremonies, all military and civilian personnel render the proper courtesies.

As mentioned earlier in this lesson, Francis Scott Key, a 35-year-old lawyer and poet, wrote our National Anthem. As the British fleet attacked Fort McHenry in Baltimore Harbor on September 13, 1814, Key watched from the deck of a British prisoner-exchange ship. He had gone to seek the release of a friend, but they were refused permission to go ashore until after the attack. As the battle stopped on the following morning, Key turned his telescope to the fort and saw that the American flag was still waving. The sight so inspired him that he pulled a letter from his pocket and began to write a poem, originally titled, "Defense of Fort McHenry." Later that year the title was changed to "The Star-Spangled Banner." Key returned to Baltimore later that day, where he rented a room at a tavern to complete the poem. Later, the poem was put to the music of an old English song. It would later be named as the National Anthem of the United States by Congress in 1931. Although the original work has four verses, only the first is sung for the National Anthem. In the box are the words to the National Anthem, as originally written by Francis Scott Key.

Original Lyrics of the National Anthem

The Star-Spangled Banner

O! say can you see, by the dawn's early light,
What so proudly we hail'd at the twilight's last gleaming?
Whose broad stripes and bright stars, thro' the perilous fight,
O'er the ramparts we watched were so gallantly streaming?
And the rockets' red glare, the bombs bursting in air,
Gave proof thro' the night that our flag was still there.
O! say does that Star-Spangled Banner yet wave
O'er the land of the free and the home of the brave?

On the shore, dimly seen thro' the mist of the deep,
Where the foe's haughty host in dread silence reposes,
What is that which the breeze, o'er the towering steep,
As it fitfully blows, half conceals, half discloses?
Now it catches the gleam of the morning's first beam,
In full glory reflected now shines on the stream.
'Tis the Star-Spangled Banner. O long may it wave
O'er the land of the free and the home of the brave.

And where is that band who so vauntingly swore,
That the havoc of war and the battle's confusion
A home and a country should leave us no more?
Their blood has wash'd out their foul footstep's pollution.
No refuge could save the hireling and slave
From the terror of flight or the gloom of the grave,
And the Star-Spangled Banner in triumph doth wave
O'er the land of the free and the home of the brave.

O thus be it e'er when freemen shall stand
Between their lov'd home and war's desolation,
Blest with vict'ry and peace, may the Heav'n-rescued land
Praise the pow'r that hath made and preserv'd us a nation.
Then conquer we must, when our cause it is just,
And this be our motto, "In God is our Trust."
And the Star-Spangled Banner in triumph shall wave
O'er the land of the free and the home of the brave.

The Pledge of Allegiance to the Flag

The Pledge of Allegiance recited today was developed from the original version drawn up in August 1892. It was created in the offices of *Youth's Companion* magazine in Boston, Massachusetts. It was written to celebrate the 400th anniversary of the discovery of America. It was first published in the September 8, 1892 issue of the magazine. Public schools first used it to celebrate Columbus Day on October 12, 1892.

The Pledge of Allegiance to the Flag

I pledge allegiance to the flag of the United States of America *(pause)*, and to the republic for which it stands *(pause)*, one nation under God *(pause)*, indivisible *(pause)*, with liberty and justice for all.

I:	You and me; an individual; a person.
PLEDGE:	Take a vow; an oath; a promise.
ALLEGIANCE:	Duty owed to your country; observance of obligation.
TO THE FLAG:	A symbol of liberty; freedom; that which we as free men and women do so cherish.
OF THE UNITED STATES:	Joined together; combined; produced by two or more persons; a union our forefathers put together in 1776 to make us a united people free of a tyrant or an oppressor.
OF AMERICA:	A land blessed with brotherhood from sea to shining sea; a land full of natural resources; a land where anyone can do what he or she wants as long as it does not violate the rights of another.
AND TO THE REPUBLIC:	A state in which the supreme power rests in the body of citizens entitled to vote and is exercised by elected representatives.
FOR WHICH IT STANDS:	A flag known throughout the world as a symbol of freedom; a nation in which people can worship as they please, speak and not be afraid of being censored for what they say, express an opinion in writing and not be afraid of being arrested for writing what they feel.
ONE NATION:	A body of people associated with a particular territory, who are conscious of their unity; one body of people speaking the same language and yet opening doors to those foreign to us and saying, "Welcome."
UNDER GOD:	Meaning we have been so blessed.
INDIVISIBLE:	Incapable of being divided; even with our own internal problems, our people, when sensing someone trying to take away our freedom, will answer the call to put down an adversary; we will unite.
WITH LIBERTY:	Freedom from outside control; freedom from captivity; freedom from dictatorship; the right to choose our own government.
AND JUSTICE:	The quality of being just; equitable, fair treatment for all, regardless of social background or economic standing; the right to be heard, to see our accusers, and to question why.
FOR ALL:	Not for just a chosen few, but for everyone in the land.

Two people claimed to be the author of the first draft. One was James B. Upham, a partner in the firm that published the magazine. The other was Francis M. Bellamy, a former minister and a member of the magazine staff at the time. Although this is still debated, the 79th Congress recognized Mr. Bellamy as the author in December 1945. At that time, his work was officially designated as the Pledge of Allegiance to the Flag by Public Law 287. In 1942, when the 77th Congress set rules pertaining to the use and display of the flag, it also gave official recognition to the Pledge of Allegiance.

In its original version, the pledge read "my flag" instead of "the flag of the United States." The 1923 National Flag Conference adopted the change in the wording. This change was made to help foreign-born children and adults to think of the American flag when reciting the Pledge.

The most recent change, authorized by Congress on June 14, 1954, added the words "under God." In signing the act, President Eisenhower remarked:

> *In this way we are reaffirming the transcendence of religious faith in America's heritage and future; in this way we shall constantly strengthen those spiritual weapons which forever will be our country's most powerful resource in peace and war.*

The Pledge is a vital expression of every American's patriotism and loyalty to the flag. It is also an expression of the freedoms it represents for every citizen. Finally, it represents a nation that recognizes God as its superior and the source of its strength. The Pledge is a reminder of the solemn duty as a nation to preserve, at any cost, our precious heritage of liberty and justice for all citizens. The Pledge should be recited daily in classrooms and at all meetings and ceremonies at which the flag is displayed.

The stance for reciting the Pledge of Allegiance is to come to attention and face the flag. When not in uniform, cadets will remove their hats with their right hand and hold it at the left shoulder. Cadets in uniform may remain silent, stand at attention, face the flag, and salute if outdoors; if indoors, stand at attention. Uniformed members may also recite the Pledge, if civilians are present.

The American's Creed

William Tyler Page of Friendship Heights, Maryland, wrote the American's Creed in 1917, as part of a nationwide contest as World War I was taking place in Europe. Reaction to the war was significant at the time, and this contest came about to reinforce the feeling of patriotism and respect for the flag, especially at this critical point in history.

Mr. Page was a descendant of President John Tyler and Representative John Page, who served in Congress from 1789 to 1797.

Mr. Page began his own government career as a congressional page in December of 1881. A page is *a student whose job is to help a member of the Congress*. In 1919, he was elected Clerk of the House of Representatives and held that position until December of 1931.

It was just prior to his election as the House Clerk that he created what is now called the American's Creed. Being a student of history, Mr. Page had become familiar with the great documents of the United States. He worked on the creed almost daily until it was finally completed to his satisfaction.

The creed was sent to the Committee on Manuscripts for the contest in August 1917. Seven months later, in March 1918, Mr. Page received notice from the committee that he had successfully won the competition from among more than three thousand contestants. The creed was accepted on the part of the United States by the Commissioner of Education and by the Speaker of the House of Representatives.

In a historical accounting, Mr. Page said, "The American's Creed is ... not an expression of individual opinion upon the obligations and duties of American citizenship or with respect to its rights and privileges. It is a summary of the fundamental principles of American political faith as set forth in its greatest documents, its worthiest traditions and by its greatest leaders."

After Mr. Page's departure as House Clerk in 1931, and out of respect for him, a new post, Emeritus Minority Clerk, was created for Mr. Page in the House, which he occupied until his death on October 20, 1942.

keys to LEADERSHIP

Today, the American's Creed is recited by many patriotic groups to open meetings, ceremonies, and other events. It is sometimes recited for flag retirement ceremonies. It also appears as one of the official United States national symbols detailed in Title 36, Chapter 10 of the US Code.

The American's Creed

I believe in the United States of America as a Government of the people, by the people, for the people; whose just powers are derived from the consent of the governed; a democracy in a republic, a sovereign nation of many sovereign states; a perfect union, one and inseparable; established upon those principles of freedom, equality, justice, and humanity for which American patriots sacrificed their lives and fortunes.

I therefore believe it is my duty to my country to love it; to support its constitution; to obey its laws; to respect its flag; and to defend it against all enemies.

The Great Seal of the United States and the Military Services' Seals

The Great Seal of the United States

It was on July 4, 1776, just after members of the Continental Congress signed the Declaration of Independence, that a committee was formed to create a seal for the new United States of America. The mission was to reflect the Founding Fathers' beliefs and values, and the sovereignty of the new nation. It would take several years of work before the seal was adopted by the Continental Congress in 1782.

In devices of heraldry like seals and insignias, each element and color has a specific meaning. Heraldry is *a system of designing and recording of any coats of arms*. The colors red, white, and blue did not have meanings for the Stars and Stripes when it was adopted in 1777. However, the colors in the Great Seal did have specific meanings. Charles Thompson, then Secretary of the Continental Congress, reported to its members the intended meanings of the colors for the first time, saying: "The colors of the pales (the vertical stripes) are those used in the flag of the United States of America; white signifies purity and innocence; red, hardiness and valor; and blue, the color of the chief (the broad band above the stripes) signifies vigilance, perseverance and justice."

The obverse of the Great Seal—which is used 2,000 to 3,000 times a year—authenticates the president's signature on many official documents. Obverse means *the front of*; in this case, the front of an official seal or insignia. Authenticate means *to establish or prove as real or true*. The obverse of the Great Seal appears on documents like treaty ratifications, international agreements, appointments of ambassadors, and communications from the president to heads of foreign governments. Ratification is *an approval or sanction*.

The American bald eagle is prominently featured on the front of the Great Seal. The eagle supports a shield of 13 red and white stripes representing the Thirteen Original States, with a blue bar uniting the shield and representing Congress. The motto of the United States is the Latin phrase *E Pluribus Unum* (meaning "out of many, one"), which refers to this union. The olive branch and 13 arrows grasped by the eagle symbolize peace and war and the powers solely vested in the Congress. The constellation of stars symbolizes the new nation taking its place among the sovereign powers.

The design of the obverse of the Great Seal is the US coat of arms. It can be shown on coins, postage stamps, passports, monuments and flags, and in many other ways. You are probably most familiar with the obverse design and the less familiar reverse on the one-dollar bill.

(Left) The obverse (front side) of the Great Seal; (right) the reverse (back side) of the Great Seal.

(Left) © Speedfighter/Fotolia.com; (right) © blackboard1965/Fotolia.com

The pyramid on the reverse of the Great Seal signifies strength and duration. The eye over it and the motto, the Latin phrase *Annuit Coeptis* (meaning "He [God] has favored our undertakings"), allude to the many interventions of providence, or a powerful force that some people believe causes everything that happens to us in favor of the American cause. The Roman numerals below are the date of the Declaration of Independence. The Latin words under it, *Novus Ordo Seclorum* (meaning "a new order of the ages"), signify the beginning of the new American era in 1776.

The Great Seal die, counter die, press, and the cabinet in which they are housed are kept at the US Department of State's Exhibit Hall in Washington, DC. In manufacturing or in the printing industry, a die is *a block of metal used for pressing or cutting something into a shape or pattern*. An officer of the department's presidential appointments staff performs the actual sealing of documents after the secretary of state has countersigned the president's signature.

The Seals of Each Military Branch

Every branch of the United States military has its own seal. As with the American flag, each seal is filled with historical symbolism and significance. Symbolism is *the use of symbols to represent a thing, idea, or quality*.

The Air Force Seal

Although the US Air Force was formally established on September 18, 1947, the Department of the Air Force Seal was first created in July of 1947. President Truman approved the final design on November 1, 1947. The seal has been in use ever since. The official Air Force Seal was developed for the new air service that was formed after World War II.

The Air Force Seal has colors of ultramarine blue and Air Force yellow that appear prominently. The circular background of the seal is ultramarine blue. The outer trim is Air Force yellow. These colors were carried down from the Army Air Corps. The coat of arms in the center of the seal has two parts. The crest consists of the eagle, wreath, and cloud formation. The American bald eagle, in its natural colors, symbolizes the United States and its air power. The wreath under the eagle is made up of six alternate folds of metal (white, representing silver), and light blue. These colors are incorporated into the basic design of the shield. The white clouds behind the eagle show the start of a new sky—the Department of the Air Force.

The Air Force Seal.
Courtesy of the US Air Force/www.wpafb .af.mil

The shield below the eagle represents the clouds, in which there is a yellow thunderbolt that portrays striking power through the use of aerospace.

The 13 white encircling stars represent the original Thirteen Colonies. The yellow Roman numerals under the shield read 1947, the year the Department of the Air Force was established. The band encircling the whole design is white, edged in Air Force yellow, with black lettering. The inscriptions read "Department of the Air Force" on the top part and "United States of America" on the lower part.

The Air Force Emblem (which contains the Coat of Arms) and the Department of the Air Force Seal are very similar in appearance and are often confused. The emblem is an acceptable substitute for internal Air Force use when the use of the Seal is not authorized. But only the emblem may be used for public or commercial use, and this requires an official licensing agreement.

The Air Force Emblem.
Courtesy of the US Air Force/www.af.mil

Air Force Symbol

The Air Force Symbol is the official symbol of the United States Air Force. It honors the heritage of our past and represents the promise of our future. Furthermore, it retains the core elements of our Air Corps heritage, the "Arnold" wings and star with circle, and modernizes them to reflect our air and space force of today and tomorrow.

The Air Force Symbol.
Courtesy of the US Air Force

The symbol has two main parts. In the upper half, the stylized wings represent the stripes of our strength—the enlisted men and women of our force. In the lower half are a sphere, a star, and three diamonds. The sphere within the star represents the globe. It reminds us of our obligation to secure our nation's freedom with Global Vigilance, Reach, and Power. The star has many meanings. Its five points represent the components of our Total Force and family—our active duty, civilians, Guard, Reserve, and retirees. The star symbolizes space as the high ground of our nation's air and space force. The rallying symbol in all our wars, the star also represents our officer corps, central to our combat leadership. The star is framed with three diamonds, which represent our core values—integrity first, service before self, and excellence in all we do.

The Army Seal.
© Speedfighter/Fotolia.com

The Army Seal

The Army Seal was used originally only to authenticate documents. It was used from the Revolutionary War until it was renamed the Seal of the Department of the Army by the National Security Act of 1947.

The central element, the Roman cuirass, is a symbol of strength and defense. The sword, esponton (a type of half-pike formerly used by subordinate officers), musket, bayonet, cannon, cannon balls, mortar, and mortar bombs are representative of Army implements. The drum and drumsticks are symbols of public notification of the Army's purpose and intent to serve the nation and its people. The Phrygian cap (often called the Cap of Liberty) supported on the point of an unsheathed sword and the motto, "This We'll Defend," on a scroll held by the rattlesnake is a symbol depicted on some American colonial flags and signifies the Army's constant readiness to defend and preserve the United States.

The Army Emblem.
Courtesy of the US Army/www.army.mil

The Army Emblem was established in January 1974. It became the first Army display item to identify the service. Derived from the Army Seal, the emblem differs from the seal in several respects, including its use for display in color.

On the emblem, the American flag is on its own right (observers' left) to reflect the current custom for the display of flags. The Army flag pattern has been added to the other flag. The Roman numerals MDCCLXXVIII, which indicate the date the Army seal was adopted, were replaced with the date "1775" to reflect the date the Army was established.

The Navy Seal

The first American naval seal was adopted by the Continental Congress on May 4, 1780 for the Board of Admiralty, the name given to the Continental Navy before the Navy Department came into existence.

The Continental Navy of the American Revolution went out of existence in 1785 with the sale of the last ship, USS Alliance. When a separate Navy Department was founded in 1798, the Board of Admiralty seal was no longer used. Naval officer commissions from 1798 to 1849 carried a distinctly different seal, which contained the basic elements of the current official seal—the sea, ship under sail, eagle, and anchor.

The seal again underwent changes around 1850, as the design came closer to that which is in use today. However, after the 1850 design, there were many variations that shifted the position and shape of the eagle, ship, and anchor. After seeing this range of seal variations, Navy officials expressed the need for a uniform design. The final seal design was approved by President Eisenhower by Executive Order in October 1957.

The seal is placed on a circular background of fair sky and moderate sea with land. A three-masted square-rigged ship appears. "Department of the Navy" is at the top, and "United States of America" is at the bottom, separated on each side by a mullet (five-point star) and within a rim in the form of a rope; the inscription, rope, mullet/star, and edges of the seal are all gold. An American bald eagle rises to the front of the ship with one foot on the ground, the other resting on the anchor near the shank.

The Navy Seal (left) and Emblem (right).

(Left) courtesy of the US Navy/www.navy.mil; (right) courtesy of the US Department of Defense/ www.defense.gov.

Land in the design symbolizes the Navy's supporting shore facilities as well as the fleet's amphibious strike capabilities. The wording "Navy Department" used on earlier seals had generally come to signify only the headquarters activities in Washington. So the inscription was changed to "Department of the Navy" in order to embrace the Navy's total worldwide operations on the sea, in the air, and ashore.

The seal was to serve as the main feature of the official US Navy Flag adopted in 1959.

The Marine Corps Seal

The US Marine Corps Seal traces its roots to the designs and ornaments of early Continental Marines as well as British Royal Marines. The general design of the emblem was probably derived from the British Royal Marines' "Globe and Laurel."

The traditional Marine Corps emblem—eagle, globe, and foul anchor—forms the basic device of the Seal. Of these three, the eagle and the foul anchor date from 1800 when they first appeared on the Marine uniform button—a button which has remained to this day virtually unchanged from its original form. Influenced strongly by the design of the emblem of the British Royal Marines, the US Marines adopted in 1868 as their emblem a globe showing the Western hemisphere. To this was added the spread eagle and foul anchor from the button. Twelve years later the motto, "Semper Fidelis," ("Always Faithful") completed the design.

The globe on the US Marine emblem signifies service in any part of the world. The eagle also indirectly signifies service worldwide, although this may not have been the intention of the designers in 1868. The eagle, which was selected for the Marine emblem, is a crested eagle, a type found all over the world. On the other hand, the eagle pictured on the Great Seal and the currency of the United States is the bald eagle, strictly a North American variety.

The Marine Corps Seal.
Courtesy of the US Department of Defense/ www.defense.gov

The image of the anchor, whose origin dates back to the founding of the Marine Corps in 1775, indicates the amphibious nature of Marines' duties. Amphibious means *capable of being used both on water and on land.*

On June 22, 1954, President Dwight D. Eisenhower signed an Executive Order that approved the design of an official seal for the United States Marine Corps. The new seal consisted of the traditional Marine Corps emblem in bronze; however, an American bald eagle replaced the crested eagle depicted on the 1868 emblem. It is depicted with wings displayed, standing upon the western hemisphere of the terrestrial globe, and holding in his beak a scroll inscribed with the Marine Corps motto "Semper Fidelis" ("Always Faithful"), with the hemisphere superimposed on a foul anchor.

The seal is displayed on a scarlet background encircled with a Navy blue band edged in a gold rope rim and inscribed "Department of the Navy, United States Marine Corps" in gold letters. The scarlet and gold surrounding the emblem are the official Marine Corps colors. These in turn are enclosed by Navy blue and gold, signifying the Marine Corps as an integral part of the naval team.

Coincident with the approval of this seal by the President, the emblem centered on the seal was adopted in 1955 as the official Marine Corps Emblem.

The Marine Corps Emblem.
Courtesy of the US Marine Corp/www.marines.mil

The Coast Guard Seal

The creation of an official Coast Guard seal confirmed the existence of a symbol that had evolved over the decades. The Revenue Cutter Service, the Life-Saving Service, and the Lighthouse Service all had their own unique devices. The Bureau of Marine Inspection and Navigation used drawings of ships and marine equipment on licenses and stationery. But it wasn't until 1927, after Treasury Secretary Andrew Mellon approved a design, that the Coast Guard had its first official seal/emblem.

At that time, the seal and emblem were one and the same. It was designed by civilian Coast Guard draftsman Oscar H. Kee.

Executive orders defined the Coast Guard Seal as:

a. Two identical crossed golden anchors, mirrored to each other at 45-degree angles.
b. A shield bearing seven white stripes and six red stripes, with a blue cap field.
c. A white circular plate obscuring the anchors, reading "United States Coast Guard" above and "1790" beneath.
d. An inscription in red surrounding the shield, reading "Semper" above and "Paratus" below the shield, which means "Always Prepared."
e. A field of blue surrounded by a gold rope border.

The Coast Guard Seal.
Courtesy of the US Department of Defense/www.defense.gov

The central device of the seal is the emblem of the United States Coast Guard. Over the years, the seal and emblem became two different devices.

The Coast Guard Emblem.

Courtesy of the US Coast Guard/www.uscg.mil

The design of the Coast Guard Emblem is defined as follows:

a. On a disc, the shield of the Coat of Arms of the United States circumscribed by an annulet edged and inscribed "United States Coast Guard 1790," in front of two crossed anchors.

b. The emblem in full color is described as follows: White anchors and white ring all outlined in medium blue (Coast Guard blue), letters and numerals medium blue (Coast Guard blue), white area within ring, shield with medium blue (Coast Guard blue) chief and 13 alternating white and red (Coast Guard red) stripes (7 white and 6 red), with narrow medium blue (Coast Guard blue) outline.

In 1967, a Coast Guard instruction set the definitions for use of both the seal and emblem that still exist. The seal is used for official documents and records. It is also found on invitations, programs, certificates, diplomas, and greetings. It may also be used for things like jewelry and stationery at the discretion of the Commandant.

Lesson 1 Review

Using complete sentences, answer the following questions on a sheet of paper.

1. What two names were given to the American flag at the time of adoption?
2. What was the date when the official American flag was adopted?
3. What is an ensign?
4. Which section of the US code covers patriotic customs and observances of the American flag?
5. At what times of the day is the American flag usually displayed?
6. How should the flag be positioned when displayed on a wall?
7. What is half-staff?
8. What do the American flag and National Anthem symbolize?
9. What does the Pledge of Allegiance express?
10. When was the American's Creed written?
11. What does the white portion of the Great Seal of the United States represent?
12. How is the front (obverse) of the Great Seal used by the president?
13. Why was the Air Force Seal originally developed?
14. What do the stylized wings of the Air Force Symbol represent?
15. What was the US Army seal originally used for?
16. What does the anchor on the US Marine Corps Seal symbolize?

APPLYING YOUR LEARNING

17. William Tyler Page wrote the American's Creed in 1917. After reading it, write a short paragraph about what the creed means to you.

LESSON 2

Civics

Quick Write

What sets America today apart from other countries? What do you think are the most important responsibilities Americans have toward one another and toward the nation as a whole? Write down what you know about our democratic government. Consider how living in a democracy affects your life.

Learn About

- civics
- the need for government
- citizenship and the naturalization process
- duties and responsibilities of citizenship, including volunteerism

"The legitimate object of government is to do for a community of people whatever they need to have done, but cannot do...for themselves—in their separate and individual capacities. In all that the people can individually do as well for themselves, government ought not to interfere."

Abraham Lincoln, 16th president of the United States

Civics

Civics is *the study of the rights and duties of citizens*. This lesson discusses different aspects of what it means to be a United States citizen. As you move through your high school years and into adulthood, you will find yourself more and more connected to the society around you. A society is *a group of people living together in organized communities with shared laws, traditions, and values*. You will begin to fulfill more and more civic responsibilities, *legal or social obligations to your community*. In just a few years, at age 18, you will gain some responsibilities, like registering for the draft (required for males) and voting (optional for all but important). Still, even at your present age, you can contribute in many valuable ways to your community and nation through volunteer work.

Think about the United States. It shares a border with Canada. Can you walk across the border anytime you'd like? If you do, do you become a Canadian? What makes the United States separate from Canada to the north, Mexico to the south, or from a country across the ocean? Why is crossing a national border a bigger deal than crossing the border of a state, county, or city?

While these questions relate to the differences between governments, it is the people who make a society—a nation, state, county, city, or town—what it is. You are part of a community, *a group of people united by common government, location, interest, or activity*. In fact, you are part of many communities. Communities are most often defined by their governments. Nations, states, and cities come into being because a certain group of people agree to live near one another, depend on one another, buy and sell things together, and abide by a common set of rules—laws. Other communities, such as schools or participants in a sport or profession, arise as people unite behind a common activity or cause. The members of a community do not have to agree on everything. But they do share things in common with one another that they do not share with other communities.

Citizens are *community members who owe loyalty to the government and are entitled to protection from it*. Citizens are a part of a country. However, being a citizen means much more than just living in a country. American citizens who live in other countries are still citizens of the United States; just crossing the border does not change your status as a citizen of your own country. The idea of citizenship dates back more than 2,500 years to ancient Greece and Rome. In those days, only a few people—men with property—could be citizens. This elite group helped govern the city and enjoyed other privileges that the common people did not share. Today, gender and wealth are no longer requirements for citizenship. Indeed, most people are citizens of the country in which they live. But all citizens have certain rights and duties.

The Need for Government

To set rules and use authority over something or someone else is to govern. Thus, government refers to *the people and system for exercising authority over a community*. Any organization that has the power to make and enforce laws and decisions for its members acts as a government. For thousands of years, people have formed governments. Thomas Hobbes, an English political thinker during the 1600s, believed that without government life would be "solitary, poor, nasty, brutish, and short." Hobbes claimed that human beings naturally compete for territory, resources, and power. If each of us could do whatever we wanted, fighting would be common, and survival would depend on strength and cunning.

Vocabulary

- civics
- society
- civic responsibilities
- community
- citizens
- government
- terrorist
- public policy
- budget
- bylaw
- dictatorship
- democracy
- direct democracy
- representative democracy
- political party
- majority rule
- naturalization
- aliens
- immigrants
- deport
- duties
- responsibilities
- draft
- Selective Service System
- jury
- tolerance
- bureaucracies
- welfare
- volunteerism

Serving on a Jury

When Americans vote or serve on a jury, their actions as citizens are based on ideas that people had in the fourth century B.C. In examining how people act, Aristotle wrote these words: "If liberty and equality, as is thought by some, are chiefly to be found in democracy, they will be best attained when all persons alike share in the government to the utmost."

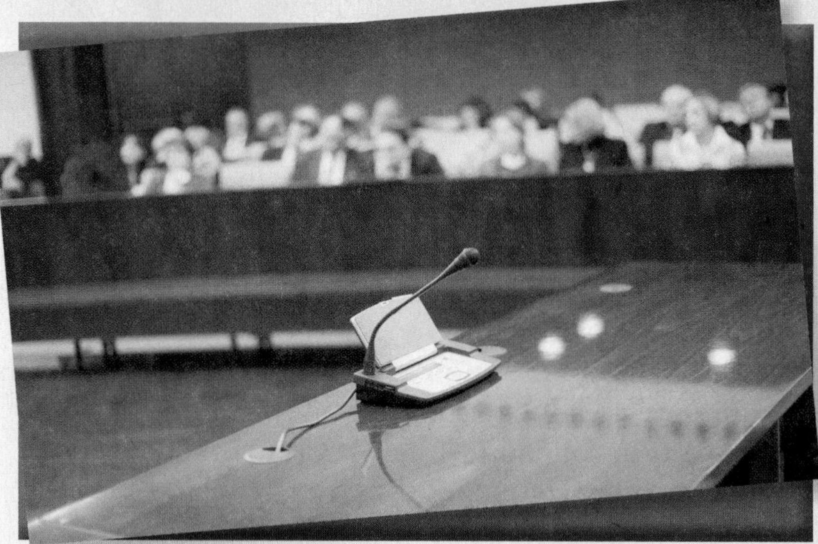

Americans serving on a jury practice an important function of citizenship.

© aerogondo/Fotolia.com

Think about trying to play basketball with no rules or referees. How would players know what to do and what not to do? How would you decide who wins? The game would probably be a chaotic free-for-all. Similarly, if there were no government to make and enforce laws, we would live in a state of confusion, violence, and fear. We would also struggle to meet our needs entirely on our own. Government can help people live together peacefully and productively.

The Functions of Government, Including Security and Public Safety

Governments serve many purposes and offer citizens many benefits. In any community, there will be criminals who steal, cheat, and hurt others. And there will be unavoidable disasters like floods and fires. These and other problems are best solved when people work together. Governments help keep order, settle conflicts, and protect the community. They provide services that individuals could not supply independently. They also guide the community and plan for its future by setting policies, making budgets, and interacting with other communities.

Keeping Order and Providing Security

Conflicts are unavoidable when people live together in a community. Citizens may disagree on all sorts of matters—their choice of leaders, the best way to raise or spend money, the rightful owner of certain property, and so on. Governments make laws to help prevent conflicts and to settle the conflicts that do arise. Governments have the power to enforce the laws. For example, to make sure that drivers obey traffic regulations, police officers are empowered to ticket or arrest violators. When someone is accused of a serious crime, like stealing, who is to say the person is actually guilty? We have courts with systems for trials and with judges and juries who decide whether those accused of crimes are guilty and what their punishment should be. In addition to law and order come concerns about community security—defending citizens and their land from enemies. The armed forces exist to protect our nation and other nations we are partners with around the world.

Terrorism Awareness in the Community

In addition to general law and order, one security problem has become more important in recent years: terrorism. While experts disagree about what makes someone a terrorist, in general, a terrorist is *someone who seeks to use violence or the fear or threat of violence to send a message or to get what he or she wants.*

Even though terrorism has existed for centuries, ever since the attacks on the World Trade Center in New York City and the Pentagon in Washington, DC on September 11, 2001, the United States has been especially concerned with protecting its citizens from terrorists. Within our borders, the Office of Homeland Security helps protect us from terrorists and other major threats to the safety of our country. The Transportation Security Administration (TSA), whose airport officials will make you take your shoes off and walk through the metal detector, provides for your security in this way. So are thousands of people you never see who study reports and images on computer screens trying to catch terrorists who may be planning an attack.

Although the government employs many people to fight terrorism, everyone in the country, including you, can help fight it as well. You don't need weapons or a uniform to do so, either; you just need alertness and common sense. For example, if you see a box, briefcase, or a small bag sitting by itself on a bench at the mall, go tell someone from mall security or even a store worker. Sure, the bag was probably left behind by a shopper by accident, but it could be a bomb planted by a terrorist. You might not think much of a stranger walking down your street or standing outside of a local post office one morning, but if you start seeing that person in the same place every day, bring it to an adult's attention.

The nationwide "If You See Something, Say Something™" public awareness campaign encourages citizens to report suspicious activity. Citizens should report, for example, a package or backpack left unattended in a public place or someone trying to break into a building to local law enforcement. As a JROTC cadet and future leader, your awareness can help keep your community and nation secure.

Providing Public Services

Governments provide many services that would not be available without cooperation and coordination. Governments create and manage libraries, schools, hospitals, parks, and recreation centers. They develop mass transit systems like subways and city busses and supply water to our homes and businesses. Government workers build and repair streets and bridges, collect garbage, and deliver the mail.

Our government in action.
© Andrea Izzotti/Fotolia.com

The goal of many government services is to keep the public healthy and safe. Local communities set up fire departments and ambulance services, for example. State governments test drivers before issuing licenses, and doctors must show their state they are properly trained before receiving a license to practice medicine. Other government agencies protect us from dangerous drugs or spoiled food. Government inspectors check for safety problems ranging from factories to day care centers to amusement park rides. Governments also give help to needy people; in each of the 50 states, poor families and people who are out of work can receive affordable nutrition assistance. Government agencies also supply affordable housing, health care, job training, and special programs for people with disabilities.

Guiding the Community

Another function of government is to develop public policy. **Public policy** is *a course of government action to achieve community goals*. For example, when government leaders decide they want to protect consumers from unsafe medicine or strengthen national security, they are setting public policy goals. When they pass laws or develop guidelines to reach these goals, they are making public policy. Most public policy decisions involve some financial planning as well.

Governments have limited amounts of money, and they must use it wisely. Creating a budget is key to the success of the community. A **budget** is *a plan for collecting and spending money.*

Another part of guiding the community is developing relations. Governments often communicate and cooperate with other governments for the benefit of their citizens. International trade, travel, and military pacts or agreements are all part of public policy. These would all be impossible if national governments were not concerned about foreign relations.

The Levels of Government

When you hear the phrase "the government," what do you think of? People usually mean the national government. However, there are three different government levels in the United States and each level exercises authority over a different group of people. The highest, broadest level in the United States is the national government, also called the *federal government*, centered in the nation's capital, Washington, DC. The federal government makes and enforces laws for the entire country.

Secondly, each of our 50 states has its own *state government* as well, which makes laws for the people in that state. Sometimes state laws and federal laws on the same issue are different. For instance, as discussed earlier in the textbook, several states have made marijuana use legal for adults for medical purposes, but using it is still against laws of the federal (national) government. A person might not get in trouble for using the drug in his or her own state, but a federal law enforcement agent from the Department of Drug and Alcohol (DEA) or the Federal Bureau of Investigation (FBI) could still arrest the person.

A third level of government is called local government. Local governments include counties, cities, and towns. The people who lead and serve your various local governments probably live and work fairly close to you, unlike the president of the United States, who is the leader of all citizens but is a neighbor only to the citizens who also live in downtown Washington, DC.

As a citizen of the United States, you are under the authority of the federal government. As a resident of your state—Ohio for example—you are also under the authority of the laws of Ohio. While you are in a particular town or city, you must also follow the laws of that city, even if you do not actually live there.

On a much lower level, organizations can also have bylaws through which they govern. A bylaw is *a rule made by an organization for its members*. For example, your school may have a student government or student body council, and if you choose to belong to a club, you respect that organization's bylaws. These bylaws or rules, however, are not as binding as state and federal laws. State and local governments, as well as governments of organizations, cannot take actions that go against the laws and authority of the national government.

Democratic Government

In some parts of the world, governmental power lies in the hands of just a small group or even a single person. For example, the government of Cuba is a dictatorship. A dictatorship is *a government controlled by one person or a small group of people*. In the United States, all citizens share in governing and being governed. This kind of *government, in which the people rule*, is called a democracy. The foundations of democracy are more than 2,500 years old. Democracy began in ancient Greece, most famously in the city of Athens. Every citizen of Athens had the right and responsibility to participate in the city's government, and all citizens had an equal voice. This was a direct democracy, *a governmental system in which all the citizens met to debate government matters and vote firsthand*. This method worked for Athens partly because not everyone in the country was a citizen and because it was a small country. Direct democracy is not practical for most countries today because of their large sizes and large populations. Many countries have representative democracies instead. In representative democracies, *the citizens choose a smaller group to represent them, make laws, and govern on their behalf*, but the people remain the source of the government's authority.

The United States is the world's oldest representative democracy. For more than 225 years, Americans have elected presidents, members of Congress, state lawmakers, and other leaders to speak and make decisions for their communities. Citizens express their views to these leaders in person, by voting, over the phone, through blogs and other social media, by email or regular mail, and through public opinion polls and political groups.

E-Government

Using the Internet, individuals now have access to federal, state, and local government websites. Hundreds of websites exist at the federal level for access to branches of government, or resources such as the Smithsonian Institution museums. These sites provide access to documents, pictures, and videos for our federal government in action.

E-government is making it much easier for citizens to learn about public policy, check on elected officials, request services, and participate in government directly. State and local government websites are helping people do everything from obtain marriage licenses to comment on performances of elected officials.

Many states allow residents to register to vote, request ballots, view the state constitution, see the state budget, or obtain fishing and hunting licenses online. Having federal, state, and local governments provide easy access websites for citizens and residents holds officials and offices more accountable for their actions.

"Government of the people, by the people, for the people."

Abraham Lincoln, 16th president of the United States

Principles of American Democracy

Abraham Lincoln, America's sixteenth president, described our democracy as a "government of the people, by the people, for the people." Let's look at what President Lincoln meant by this statement.

His words make three important points. "Of the people" means that the people who lead and work in the government come from among the citizens themselves. The president, state governors, mayors of small towns, and heads of school boards are all regular citizens. In America, a person doesn't have to be born into a certain family or a family of a certain race or social status to qualify for a role in the government if you desire.

"By the people" means that Americans citizens, acting through their representatives, give the government its authority. We agree to abide by the laws those leaders make, and if we disagree, we have a specific process for trying to get enough others to agree with us to make the change. Americans often disagree with and even criticize some of their leaders, but those leaders are only in their positions because the people have agreed to let them lead. Because democratic governments exist by the people, all genuine democracies have free, fair, and competitive elections.

Finally, "for the people" means that the purpose of the government is to serve the citizens—to make the United States a better place for those who live here. This purpose might seem obvious, but for some people, it is not. Too many leaders around the world and throughout history have used their authority to serve or enhance their own goals—to get rich, to hold power over others, or to change laws in ways that personally benefited themselves. The government does not exist for its own sake or for the sake of the leaders themselves; it exists to help take care of its people.

These phrases in Lincoln's famous speech at the Gettysburg battleground help express our ideal vision of who can participate in the government. Another way you can participate, once you are of age, is through voting. Through free elections, citizens have the chance to choose their leaders and voice their opinions about various issues. What makes an election fair and free? First, everyone's vote must carry the same weight. This principle is often expressed in the phrase "one person, one vote." Second, all candidates have the right to express their views freely to the public. It would not be right if the President, for example, ordered the police to arrest someone who wanted to run against him in the next election and gave a speech criticizing his policies.

Voting rights must be equally available to all, with only very basic restrictions: you must be 18, you must be a US citizen, and for state and local elections, you must be a resident of the state or community you vote in. Other factors, like race, gender, and ethnic and religious background, cannot be used to keep a person from voting. A final voting right we have is the right to vote by secret ballot, without fear that the government will punish us for the way we voted. In some countries today, many of these basic rights of participating in government are denied to citizens.

Each vote matters! You may feel that your one vote among millions of others' votes cannot possibly make a difference. However, if everyone felt that way and decided not to vote, we couldn't have an election. Yours may be just one among many, but you owe it to your country, yourself, and those whose views you share (those whom your vote supports) to make your preference heard. Many elections, especially for state and local leaders, are won and lost by closer margins than you might think. As former President Franklin D. Roosevelt said, "The ultimate rulers of our democracy are not a president and senators and congressmen and government officials, but the voters of this country."

Principles of American Democracy

Our American democracy is built on these fundamental principles:

- **Rule of Law**
  All people, including those who govern, are bound by the law.
- **Limited Government**
  Government is not all-powerful—it may do only those things that people have given it the power to do.
- **Consent of the Governed**
  American citizens are the source of all governmental power.
- **Individual Rights**
  In the American democracy, individual rights are protected by government.
- **Representative Government**
  People elect government leaders to make the laws and govern on their behalf.

A **political party** is *a group of individuals with broad, common interests who organize to support candidates for office and determine public policy.* Competitive elections and competing political parties are important parts of democracies. Competing political parties give voters a choice among candidates. Also, the parties out of power help make those in power pay more attention to the needs of the people who don't agree with them. Citizens in America are free to support any candidate or issue they believe in.

Another principle of our democracy is majority rule. **Majority rule** means that *when differences of opinion arise, all members of a group, community, or nation will abide by what most people want.* At the same time, however, we insist on respect for the rights of those in the minority.

Respect for minority rights is sometimes difficult to maintain, especially if society is under a great deal of stress. For example, the United States government imprisoned more than 100,000 Japanese Americans in relocation camps during World War II. Government leaders feared that these Americans would be disloyal. This relocation program caused severe hardships for many Japanese Americans and deprived them of basic liberties. In 1988, Congress admitted the "grave injustice" of the relocation camps and offered payments of $20,000 to those Japanese Americans still living who had been relocated. After the terrorist attacks of 2001, President George W. Bush realized that many people might turn their anger against Muslims in the United States. Therefore, soon after the attacks, he visited the Islamic Center in Washington, DC. He explained that Islam is a peaceful religion and urged Americans to treat Muslim Americans fairly.

Citizenship and the Naturalization Process

Who Are America's Citizens?

Citizens are people with certain rights and duties under a government, who owe allegiance to that government. Every country has rules about how people gain citizenship. In the United States, the 14th Amendment defines a US citizen as anyone "born or naturalized in the United States." Therefore, the US Constitution establishes two ways to become a citizen: by birth and by naturalization. Naturalization is *the legal process by which citizens from another country can choose to become American citizens.*

Citizenship by Birth

If you were born in any of the 50 states or the District of Columbia, you automatically became an American citizen at birth. The same is true if you were born outside the country but in American territory, such as Puerto Rico, Guam, or on a US military base overseas. Even if you were born elsewhere, you could still claim American citizenship if your parents are both citizens or if one parent is a citizen who has actually lived in the United States. Children born on American soil to non-US citizens also become US citizens at birth. An exception to this rule is made for children born to foreign diplomats—official government representatives—living in the United States. Such children keep the citizenship of their parents. Under some circumstances, Americans may hold dual citizenship. This means that they enjoy rights in the United States and in another country at the same time. For example, a child born abroad to American parents may be both a US citizen and a citizen of the country of his or her birth.

The Naturalization Process

Several million legal aliens, *people who are not citizens*, have gained authorized entrance to live or work in the United States. Some come to study, work, or visit relatives for a while. Just as you would remain a US citizen during an exchange summer in the country of South Korea, these aliens remain citizens of their own countries and eventually return home. Other legal aliens, however, plan to settle here and become naturalized citizens. More than half a million immigrants gain American citizenship each year.

Aliens who have entered the United States legally lead lives much like those of American citizens. Legal aliens may hold jobs, own property, attend public schools, and receive other government services.

Rita M. Rodriguez

Dr. Rodriguez, a former director of the Export-Import Bank of the United States, was born in Oriente, Cuba in 1942, and came to the United States at the age of 15. She graduated from the University of Puerto Rico, and received her master's degree in business administration and her PhD from the New York University Graduate School of Business. In 1969, she became the first woman hired to teach at the Harvard Business School, and she remained there until 1978. Then Dr. Rodriguez became a professor of international finance at the University of Illinois. In 1982, she was confirmed by the US Senate as one of the five directors of the Ex-Im Bank, an independent agency whose chief purpose is to improve US trade with other countries. She retired in 1999.

They pay taxes and are entitled to legal protection. Legal aliens do not have full political rights, however. They may not vote in elections or run for office. They may not serve on juries or work in most government jobs. In addition, unlike US citizens, legal aliens must carry identification cards at all times.

Oscar Handlin, a well-known American historian, described what immigration has meant to America: "Once I thought to write a history of the immigrants in America. Then I realized that the immigrants were American history." Immigrants are *people who leave one country to settle permanently in another country.* Immigrants who want to become United States citizens must first submit an Application for Naturalization to the United States Citizenship and Immigration Service (USCIS), an agency of the Department of Homeland Security. For most immigrants, the next step comes after living in the United States for at least five years. (Aliens who are married to citizens wait only three years.) During this time, many immigrants take special classes to prepare for citizenship. If the immigrant is at least 18 years old and has lived for at least three months in the state where he or she seeks naturalization, he or she may apply for citizenship, which requires an interview with USCIS officials. Agency officials want to be sure the alien meets all requirements and has a good moral character. The applicant must also take a citizenship exam that includes questions about reading, writing, and speaking English. The exam also asks basic facts about United States history and government. Afterward, USCIS makes its decision. If the application is granted, the final step in naturalization is attending a ceremony and pledging an oath of allegiance. The individual swears to be loyal to this country above all others, to obey the Constitution and other laws, and to perform military or other duties if needed. Then the person signs a document and is declared a citizen of the United States. If he or she has children under 18, they automatically become naturalized citizens, too.

Tom Castillo

He thought he was an American citizen. He was drafted in 1969 and served two years in the US Army during the Vietnam War; but when Tom Castillo was about five, he, his mother, and his two siblings moved from Mexico to Texas. His mother kept his birthplace a secret, wanting him to grow up American. Later, at age 52, Castillo became a naturalized citizen of the United States. It was a natural step for Castillo, who says, "I've always considered myself an American first."

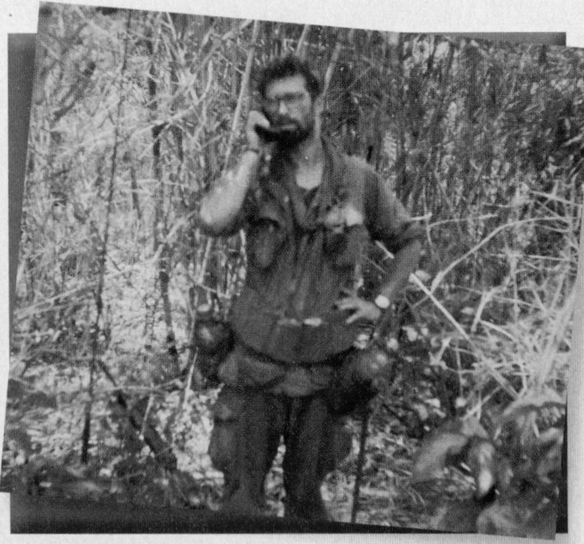

American soldier during the Vietnam War.

Photo by Staff Sgt. Caleb Barrieau/Defense Video & Image Distribution System

Another pathway to citizenship is through military service. Current members and recently discharged members of the military may also have their naturalization process expedited if they meet the requirements and qualifications provided by USCIS. These include good moral character, knowledge of the English language, knowledge of US government and history, and taking an Oath of Allegiance to the US Constitution. President George W. Bush also signed an executive order on July 3, 2002 that expedited naturalization, authorizing all noncitizens who had served honorably with the US armed forces on or after September 11, 2001 to immediately file for citizenship. Since 2002, over 89,000 noncitizens have become naturalized United States citizens.

A Lifelong Privilege

Whether they are naturalized or native-born, most Americans keep their citizenship forever. Only the federal government can both grant citizenship and take it away. Although state governments can deny a convicted criminal some of the privileges of citizenship, such as voting, they do not have the power to deny citizenship itself. The federal government may strip naturalized citizens of their citizenship if it was not obtained properly. However, in most cases, the only way to lose US citizenship is to voluntarily give it up. This must be done in a foreign country, with a formal oath signed before an appropriate American official. There is no going back for those who take this step. They cannot later change their minds and regain citizenship. They also remain liable for old debts and any crimes they may have committed in the United States.

Consider what goals or priorities would be satisfying to pursue as you mature as a US citizen. Then start to put those goals into action by discussing them with your family and classmates. Doing so is an important step toward becoming a leader in your community.

The Impact of Immigrants in America

The United States restricts the number of immigrants who can enter the country. Millions apply, but only about 680,000 per year have been naturalized. Traditionally, the relatives of US citizens and people with needed job skills have received the highest priority. Family members still get special consideration. However, because of the Immigration Act of 1990, emphasis has shifted toward welcoming "those who want to work and produce and contribute," as one member of Congress put it. The new policy benefits people with particular skills, talents, or the money to invest in our economy.

The Impact of Illegal Aliens

Despite immigration limits, as of 2011 approximately 11.5 million illegal aliens were living in the United States. Some are refused permission to immigrate; others never applied for permission because they feared a long, slow process or being turned down. Illegal aliens come to the United States in a variety of ways. A few enter the country as temporary visitors and never leave. Others risk capture and arrest by illegally crossing our borders with Mexico and Canada. Other illegal aliens are foreigners who have stayed in the United States after their legal permits have expired.

Oath of Allegiance to the United States

All citizenship applicants must take the citizenship oath to become a naturalized citizen.

I hereby declare, on oath, that I absolutely and entirely renounce and abjure [reject] all allegiance and fidelity to any foreign prince, potentate, state, or sovereignty, to whom or which I have heretofore been a subject or citizen; that I will support and defend the Constitution and laws of the United States of America against all enemies, foreign and domestic; that I will bear true faith and allegiance to the same; that I will bear arms on behalf of the United States when required by law; that I will perform noncombatant service in the armed forces of the United States when required by law; that I will perform work of national importance under civilian direction when required by law; and that I take this obligation freely without any mental reservation or purpose of evasion; so help me God.

Whatever the method, the reason is usually the same. "I came for work and for a better life," explained one South American immigrant. Despite this kind of high expectation, illegal aliens often have a difficult time in the United States. Many have no friends or family here, no place to live, and no sure way to earn money. It is against the law to hire illegal aliens, and those who do find work usually receive little pay and no benefits. Every day they live with the fear that government officials will discover and deport them. To deport people is *to send them back to their own country.* The United States Customs and Border Patrol (CBP) is the border enforcement arm of the Department of Homeland Security. You will learn more about the Department of Homeland Security in LE 300. Its main responsibility is to detect and prevent the illegal entry of aliens into the United States. CBP patrols the 6,000 miles of Mexican and Canadian international land borders and 2,000 miles of coastal waters surrounding the Florida Peninsula and the island of Puerto Rico.

Duties and Responsibilities of Citizenship, Including Volunteerism

When you think of your community, do you think of your neighborhood or perhaps your town? Actually, each of us belongs to many communities—our school or workplace; our church, synagogue, or mosque; our state; and our country. On the broadest level, we are also members of the global community, more connected than ever before to people around the world.

We all have a stake in making our communities safe and successful. Thus, we all have certain duties and responsibilities to fulfill. Duties are *things that we must do.* Responsibilities are *things we should do; they are obligations that we fulfill voluntarily.*

A Citizen's Legal Duties

As American citizens, we have legal duties that we are required to perform. National, state, and local governments require Americans to perform certain duties established by laws. If we fail to perform them, we are subject to legal penalties, such as fines or imprisonment. By accepting all of these responsibilities and duties, we strengthen our communities and help secure our rights. Some countries require their citizens to perform many duties, such as serving a certain number of years in the military. Although the US government asks less of its citizens, it does require that they fulfill the following duties.

Obey Laws

Following the law is a citizen's most important duty. Our laws are designed for specific purposes—to help people get along, to prevent accidents, to see that resources are used fairly, and so on. If we do not obey the law, then governments cannot maintain order or protect our health, safety, and property.

Pay Taxes

Taxes pay for the government's activities. Without them, the federal government could not pay its employees, maintain armed forces to defend the country, and help those in need. Your local government could not hire police officers or firefighters, and your state could not pave roads or maintain parks.

Citizens pay taxes in several ways. The federal government and some states and cities collect income taxes—a percentage of what people earn. Most states and some cities collect taxes on the sale of goods and services—the sales tax you pay at the store, or when you buy or register your automobile. Most local governments collect taxes on the residential and commercial property within school districts.

"A Nation That Serves Goals Larger Than Self"

On September 11, 2001, terrorist acts killed thousands of Americans. President George W. Bush led the nation during this troubled time, and in 2002 proclaimed: "After America was attacked, it was as if our entire country looked in the mirror and saw our better selves. We were reminded that we are citizens, with obligations to each other, to our country, and to history. We began to think less of the goods we can accumulate and more about the good we can do… In the sacrifice of soldiers, the fierce brotherhood of firefighters, and the bravery and generosity of ordinary citizens, we have glimpsed what a new culture of responsibility could look like. We want to be a nation that serves goals larger than self. We have been offered a unique opportunity, and we must not let this moment pass."

Defend the Nation

You may have heard of the draft, *the action by the government of selecting those required to serve in the military.* Although the US has not drafted service members since the Vietnam War ended in 1975, the government keeps a record of eligible young men in the event of a national crisis requiring more people than the regular active and reserve armed forces can supply. *The agency that keeps these records and executes the draft if it is ever needed* is called the Selective Service System. US Law requires all men who are citizens or residents to register no later than 30 days after they turn 18. Men are eligible to be drafted until they turn 26.

In a few years, you will probably receive a notice in the mail informing you of this requirement. Even if you do not receive that notice, however, *you must still register.* Registering does NOT mean you will automatically be drafted. Some countries, like South Korea, Israel, and Mexico require all young men to serve in the military for a year or two. The US government prefers to make the military an all-volunteer force. The government sees drafting people as a last resort for providing additional troops needed in a crisis. More detailed information about the Selective Service System will be covered in LE 300.

Serve in Court

Another civic duty of all US citizens is jury duty. Even if you have never sat in on a trial, perhaps in a book or film you have seen the group of 12 people near the front, the jury, listening to the arguments presented by lawyers. A jury is *a group of adult citizens who listen to the evidence in a court case and decides which side is in the right.* The use of a jury comes from one of America's most fundamental values: that everyone has a right to a fair trial if accused of a crime. To make trials fairer, a jury is made up of ordinary people chosen from their local area to serve on that particular trial. These people have regular jobs, but they are required to serve on the jury to provide the fairest perspective possible on the evidence from the common person's point of view. Another duty of citizens is to serve as witnesses at a trial if called to do so.

Once you become an adult (18 or older), you will be eligible to be called for jury duty. Unlike voting and the draft, however, you do not actually have to register for jury duty. By being registered as a resident of your state and county (through getting a driver's license, paying state and local taxes, or registering to vote), you place your name in a long list of residents who are eligible to serve on a jury in your area. Jurors are selected randomly to be available for a short period of time, typically a week, for trials in their area that come up while they are on duty. More detailed information about jury duty will be covered in LE 300.

Attend School

Most states require young people to attend school—or be home schooled—until age 16. This requirement benefits both you and the government. Knowledge and skills can help you make wise decisions, and our democratic system of government needs informed citizens with a basic education to operate well. In school, you should gain an understanding of history, government, science, and other important subjects. You should also learn to think through problems, form opinions, and express your views clearly.

"Education is the key to unlock the golden door of freedom."

George Washington Carver, scientist and educator

A Citizen's Civic Responsibilities

Several responsibilities of citizenship are voluntary obligations rather than legal duties. If you ignore these, you won't be arrested or punished. Yet if you fulfill them, you can help our democracy flourish and reap personal benefits as well.

Be Informed

Every day government leaders make decisions that affect your life. The state legislature, for example, might pass a law changing the rate of sales tax you pay. Your school board might vote to start the school day earlier. Your town council might set aside funds for a new recreation center. As a citizen, you have a responsibility to know what the government is doing so that you can voice your opinions on matters you feel strongly about. In addition, you have a duty to obey the laws whether or not you know what they are, so you should stay informed.

As mentioned earlier in this lesson, you can learn more about local and national issues and leaders. You can read books, websites, newspapers, and magazines. You can also listen to the news on television or radio and talk with your teachers, family, and friends. However, not all websites, articles, or friends (or other types of sources) are accurate, so you must be sure you are receiving correct information. Don't trust all statistics you read and don't assume people you know well have all of the facts. Crosscheck information with other sources.

Being informed also includes knowing your rights. For example, people accused of crimes have the right to be represented by a lawyer. If people were unaware of that right, they might not receive fair trials.

Citizens' Rights, Duties, and Responsibilities

Rights

- Security—protection by government
- Equality—equal treatment under the law
- Liberty—rights guaranteed under the Constitution

Duties

- Obey the law
- Pay taxes
- Defend the nation
- Serve in court
- Attend school

Responsibilities

- Be informed and vote
- Participate in your community and government
- Respect the rights and property of others
- Respect different opinions and ways of life

Respect Others' Rights

To enjoy your rights to the fullest, you must be prepared to respect other people's rights. For example, if you own a dog, you have an obligation to keep it from becoming a nuisance to your neighbors. If you're in the library, you should not interfere with anyone's right to work quietly. However, if the library caught on fire, you do have a responsibility to interrupt everyone you could and warn them the building is on fire.

Citizens also have a responsibility to show respect for public property and for the property of others. Some people might claim that no one gets hurt when they litter in a park or paint graffiti on a school wall. However, that public property belongs to us all, and we all pay through our taxes if it is damaged. Vandalism and littering are actually more than disrespectful acts; they are crimes. Many of our laws have been enacted to encourage people to respect others' rights. If you have a party that gets out of hand, for example, you could be arrested for disturbing the peace.

Respect Diversity

In a democratic society like ours, with such a diverse population, it is especially important to respect the civil liberties of others. Although you may disagree with people or disapprove of their lifestyles, they have an equal right to their beliefs and practices. *Respecting and accepting others, regardless of their beliefs, practices, or differences,* is called **tolerance**. Treating others politely and respectfully is thus part of being a good citizen. One of America's strengths has always been the diversity of its people.

Immigrants have brought a variety of religions, traditions, and lifestyles to this country, and they continue to do so. As citizens, we have a responsibility to respect the practices and traditions of others when they are different from our own, just as we expect them to respect our differences. There are no levels of citizenship in the United States. All citizens are considered equal and entitled to be treated the same.

Contribute to the Common Good

Responsible citizens care about others. They are willing to contribute time, effort, and money to help other people and to improve community life for everyone. Think about what your community would be like if no one donated to charities, volunteered in after-school programs, or lent a hand at the local health clinic. What if no one ever spoke out about community problems? Communities and governments need people to participate. If we want our communities to thrive, all American citizens must be active participants and not just idle bystanders. In the next section, you will read about ways to contribute, like volunteering, in more detail.

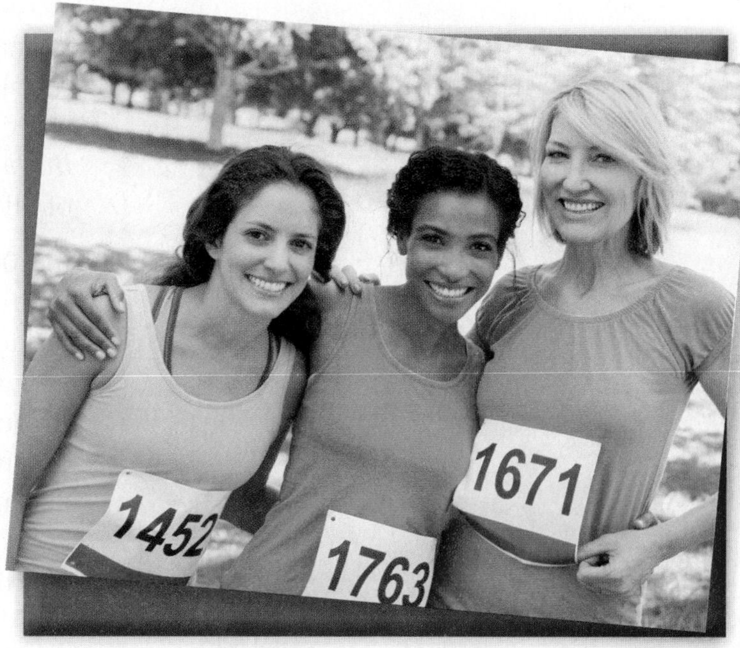

There are no limitations on contributing to the common good. Charity walks/runs are a great example of this.
© WavebreakmediaMicro/Fotolia.com

The Need for Citizens' Involvement

As stated in Chapter 1, Lesson 1, all JROTC programs encourage and provide opportunities for community involvement. Just doing your schoolwork, playing sports or band practice, going to work, and catching a movie once in a while with friends may seem like all you have time for. However, you may be surprised at the variety of ways and the ease with which you could contribute to the good of your community, grow as an individual, and have fun doing so.

So what should you do if you want to get involved in your community? Where should you start? Starting with something already organized will help you learn what volunteering is like and what kinds of things you enjoy doing. Through JROTC or other community service group, you might find, for example, that you really enjoy reading to elderly people or at the local elementary school—something you may never have thought of doing—but that you don't enjoy volunteering at a health clinic as much as you expected.

As you have seen, government provides a wealth of services. We rely on government for everything from local police protection to national defense, and from collecting household trash to ensuring clean water and air nationwide. Citizens, however, also share responsibility for meeting community needs. The government, after all, has limited resources. In addition, governments are bureaucracies—*complex systems with many departments, rules, and people in the chain of command*. Therefore, the government cannot always respond quickly or efficiently to social problems.

Courtesy of the Library of Congress/www.log.gov

"Ask not what your country can do for you; ask what you can do for your country."

President John F. Kennedy, 1961

In many cases, private citizens can solve problems or meet needs better. Good citizens are concerned about the welfare—*the health, prosperity, and happiness*—of all members of the community.

In 2001, President George W. Bush called for a renewed commitment to community service. He noted that we can show "the world the true values of America through the gathering momentum of a million acts of responsibility and decency and service." More recently, President Barack Obama has asserted that community service is one way Americans can "make this country stronger." Every year more than half of all Americans do volunteer work to help make their communities better places to live. These volunteers include more than 14 million students in grades 6 through 12. Without the efforts of so many private citizens, many important social needs simply would not be met.

Donating Time and Money

People contribute to their communities in countless ways, working independently or as part of volunteer groups, both large and small. You probably know a mom or dad who is active in the PTA (Parent Teacher Association), coaches soccer, or leads a Scout troop. Neighbors might spend a Saturday afternoon cleaning up a vacant lot or preparing holiday baskets for needy families. Retirees mentor schoolchildren, record books for the blind, and lead museum tours. You or your fellow students might visit nursing home patients, volunteer in an animal shelter, or collect canned goods for a local food pantry. Contributing your time to work on community projects is the heart of volunteerism—*the practice of offering your time and services to others without payment.*

In addition, Americans may also support worthy causes by contributing money. In 2011, America was ranked as the most charitable country in the world. According to the National Philanthropic Trust (NPT), a charity advising organization, Americans gave $316 billion to charity in 2012. Much of this money came from small donations by average citizens. The typical American donates about two percent of his or her income to charity.

Korczak Ziolkowski

Without Korczak Ziolkowski, there would be no Crazy Horse Memorial. Ziolkowski, born of Polish decent in Boston, became famous as a mountain carver, but it is his life and dedication that have inspired the people who learn about him. Ziolkowski assisted Gutzon Borglum at Mount Rushmore, and then dedicated his life to sculpting the Crazy Horse Memorial. Crazy Horse was a Native American leader who bravely defended his people and their way of life. Ziolkowski carved Crazy Horse as a memorial to the leader's spirit. Ziolkowski worked on the memorial—the world's largest sculpture—for 36 years until his death in 1982. He refused to be paid for his work. Ziolkowski's wife and family continue his work on the Crazy Horse Memorial.

Honoring Crazy Horse.

© Jim Parkin/Fotolia.com

Many companies, too, believe in giving something back to the community. Small businesses may sponsor a recreational sports team or donate prizes for a charity's fund-raiser. Large companies often contribute millions of dollars to community projects, like building a new public swimming pool or putting on a free concert. They frequently match the charitable donations of their employees, chipping in a dollar of corporate funds for every dollar that a worker gives to charity. Many companies make a special commitment to investing in young people. They may offer college scholarships to students or give their employees time off to volunteer in the schools.

Volunteers in Action

Community involvement tends to be rooted in individual action and informal groups. People are more likely to participate when they feel a personal connection to a cause or know others involved. Thus, they join their Neighborhood Watch or become active at their child's school. They reach out to the community through their religious congregations or service clubs like the Lions and Kiwanis.

Some people, however, volunteer through more formal channels such as charitable organizations, school-based programs, and national service programs (Figure 5.2).

"Volunteer work brings real change, change you can be a part of, change you can see with your own eyes. You don't need politicians or police to tell you things are better. You can see it and feel it for yourself and know you were a part of it.... There's a real pride involved. We're part of a community."

John Gatus, a retired steamfitter who volunteered for an anti-gang neighborhood patrol

OVERVIEW

- **26.5 percent of US residents volunteer**
- **32.4 volunteer hours per resident**
- **64.5 million volunteers**
- **7.9 billion hours of service**
- **51 percent of US residents donate to charity**
- **9 percent of residents participate in public meetings**
- **$175 billion of service contributed**

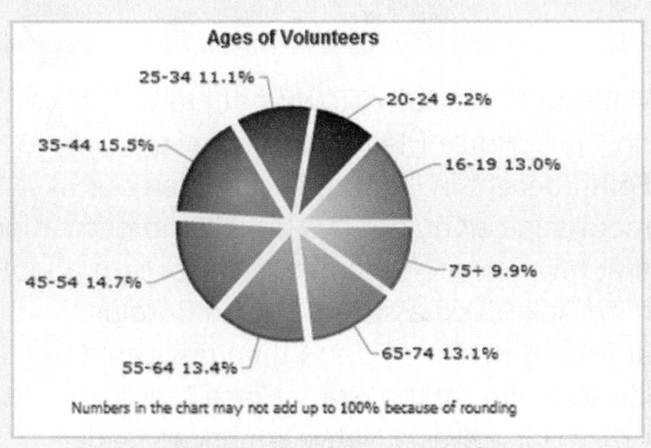

www.volunteeringinamerica.gov/national

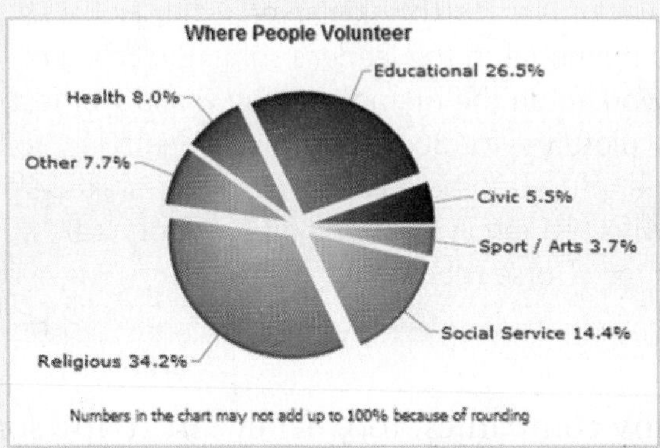

www.volunteeringinamerica.gov/national

HOW YOU CAN VOLUNTEER

Places to Volunteer

- Homeless shelters
- Food banks
- Hospices and hospitals
- Special Olympics
- Habitat for Humanity
- State and local parks
- City parks
- Schools or after-school programs
- Libraries
- Senior citizen centers
- Animal shelters
- Environmental organizations
- Political campaigns
- Red Cross and Salvation Army
- Local charities and organizations
- Your school or community government

Sample Volunteer Activities

- Prepare and distribute meals
- Help organize a food drive
- Talk with families and kids
- Help raise funds or lead activities
- Help build a house
- Clean up trails or pick up trash
- Assist with recreational activities
- Tutor a child or new immigrant
- Read to children or reshelve books
- Deliver meals to homebound seniors
- Take care of animals
- Lead hikes or lobby for a cause
- Lend a hand at the campaign office or join a letter-writing campaign
- Help out in an emergency
- Create a website
- Hold an elective office, attend a city council or school board meeting or public hearing and voice your opinion

WHY SHOULD YOU VOLUNTEER?

- To help others
- To learn something new about an activity or organization
- To meet people and make friends
- To beat boredom
- To better deal with a loss you have experienced (such as the death of a loved one)
- To learn something new about life
- To explore careers

There are many volunteering opportunities in your local community. All volunteers are valuable resources to their communities.

FIGURE 5.2

American Volunteers in Action

Justin Dart, Jr.

Justin Dart, Jr. had a message to deliver: "People with disabilities are fully equal." To spread that message, he traveled to all 50 states at least four times and to nations around the world. Stricken with polio at age 18, Dart used a wheelchair and knew personally the hurdles that people with disabilities must overcome. He worked to tear down these hurdles by launching, along with his wife Yoshiko Saji Dart, the disability rights movement.

Dart advised governors, presidents, and the US Congress on the subject of disabilities. However, he relied on grassroots support—the support of ordinary people—to bring about change. "Get into politics as if your life depended on it," he told one audience.

In 1990, Dart's grassroots army won the passage of the Americans with Disabilities Act. The act prohibits discrimination against people with disabilities. In 1998 Dart received the Presidential Medal of Freedom, the nation's highest civilian award. At the beginning of the 21st century, Dart announced a new goal—to carry the disability rights movement worldwide.

Justin Dart, Jr. (1930–2002)
US Department of Labor/www.dol.gov

Charitable Organizations

More than one million charities are officially registered with the federal government. Many are small and locally based. They often work on one or two projects, such as helping the victims of domestic abuse or preserving historic landmarks. Other organizations, such as the United Way, the Boys and Girls Clubs of America, and Big Brothers Big Sisters, are large, national bodies with varied activities serving millions of people. All of these groups depend on ordinary people who give their time freely. Most, however, also have some staff—who are paid through financial donations to the organization—who help set organizational goals, manage the budget, and oversee operations.

School-Based Programs

Across the country, more than half of all schools now arrange community service for students in grades 6 through 12. Several hundred school districts even require it. In Atlanta, Chicago, and the entire state of Maryland, for example, high school students must volunteer a set number of hours to earn a diploma. Some people believe that community service is less meaningful when it is required. According to one school official in Atlanta, however, the "students think it's a neat idea, and for many of them it is nothing new." Many have already been active volunteers in the community.

Also, in more than 3,400 high schools across America and overseas, more than 550,000 JROTC cadets are actively involved with community service projects. JROTC cadets contribute more than 10 million hours of community service, from reading to elementary students to maintaining hiking trails. Without this volunteerism, most of these services would not get done. Being part of a JROTC program should be a source of pride for cadets who give back to their community.

National Service Programs

Over the years, the federal government has created various national programs to encourage volunteerism. In 1961, for example, the Peace Corps was launched by President John F. Kennedy to help people in the poorest corners of the world. The Peace Corps has sent tens of thousands of Americans to over 100 countries, where they advise farmers, teach children, dig wells, help start small businesses, and fight the spread of AIDS and other serious diseases.

For those who want to volunteer but not leave the country, the government provides community service opportunities through AmeriCorps and the Senior Corps. More than 80,000 Americans participate each year in AmeriCorps. Most work through local and national organizations to meet community needs. Under the guidance of the American Red Cross, for example, volunteers help victims of floods, fires, earthquakes, and other disasters. Working with other groups, they might clean up polluted rivers, immunize children, or assist people with disabilities. In return for a year of full-time service, AmeriCorps volunteers receive an allowance to live on and money to help pay for college.

Lions Clubs International and Rotary International (RI) are two additional groups you can volunteer with: large, worldwide organizations with tens of thousands of local clubs. Both organizations aim to improve the quality of life for people in need in the US and all over the world. These well-known groups and others like them organize activities like collecting food and clothes for street children, repairing playgrounds, setting up after school programs, and raising money to help pay for immunizations. They seek to help the poor and promote health, education, and goodwill among the countries of the world. The Lions Club has youth and young adult programs such as Alpha Leo Clubs for ages 12 to 18 and Omega Leo Clubs for ages 18 to 30.

RI has Interact clubs for ages 12 to 18 and Rotaract for ages 18 to 30. Both of these organizations offer rewarding service opportunities, individual and leadership development, conferences, and valuable interaction with other like-minded young people. See http://www.lionsclubs.org or http://www.rotary.org for more information about Lions and RI and the many ways you can help serve.

The Benefits of Volunteering

The United States has always been a nation of volunteers. When Alexis de Tocqueville, a French political writer, visited America in the 1830s, he was amazed to see citizens pitching in to solve community problems rather than relying on the government. He explained it as "self-interest rightly understood." In other words, by banding together to serve the community, we also serve ourselves.

When you volunteer, you benefit both yourself and others. Volunteer work helps you build skills that one day may help you get into college or launch a career. You may also benefit from working with people you might not otherwise meet who could turn out to be future colleagues, bosses, and friends.

As you become an adult, you become more responsible for contributing to the well-being of the communities you live in. Whether the responsibilities are required by law or voluntary, think of them as privileges instead of obligations. Because others in the past have dedicated so much, today we can exercise the privileges of voting, joining the military, serving on a jury, or making a difference as a volunteer. By volunteering, we make our communities better places to live while gaining new opportunities to learn, make friends, and improve our teamwork, leadership, and problem-solving skills. It is satisfying to know that you can make a difference in someone else's life, as well as your own.

Lesson 2 Review

Using complete sentences, answer the following questions on a sheet of paper.

1. What is civics?
2. What is meant by the phrase "to govern"?
3. What security problem has become more important in recent years?
4. What are the three levels of government?
5. How does the 14th Amendment define a US citizen?
6. Define naturalization.
7. What requirements and qualifications must immigrants serving in the US military complete to become a naturalized citizen?
8. Which level of government has the power to grant or take away someone's US citizenship?
9. What are some specific purposes for laws?
10. Use of a jury comes from one of America's fundamental values. What is that value?
11. Why is it important for citizens of the United States to be informed about what the government is doing?
12. Define tolerance.
13. What is volunteerism?
14. Community involvement is rooted in what?
15. What program was launched by President Kennedy in 1961 to assist people in the poorest parts of the world?

APPLYING YOUR LEARNING

16. In a short paragraph, describe the process of how an immigrant can become a US citizen.

LESSON 3

The Constitution of the United States

Quick Write

"The people made the Constitution, and the people can unmake it. It is the creature of their own will, and lives only by their will."

John Marshall, Chief Justice, US Supreme Court

How do you think the Constitution of the United States protects your rights and freedoms as an American citizen? Write down everything you know about the Constitution of the United States.

Learn About

- the Constitution of the United States—a remarkable document
- the process of amending the Constitution
- how the Constitution is interpreted

The Constitution of the United States—A Remarkable Document

The Constitution of the United States was one of the first written constitutions in modern history. A constitution is *the system of fundamental laws and principles that prescribes the nature, functions, and limits of a government or other institution.* The framers wanted to produce a written plan for a strong central government that would unify the country, while preserving the ideals of the Declaration of Independence written a few years earlier. The document they wrote formed the basis for our democracy. It created:

- A representative legislature
- The office of president
- A system of courts
- A process for adding amendments when and if the people saw the need for change in how the government carried out its responsibilities

For over 225 years, the strength and flexibility of the Constitution has guided the nation's political leaders. The document has become a symbol of pride and a force for national unity. In the following sections, you will see the entire text of the Constitution and its amendments. Passages that have been set aside or changed by the adoption of amendments are printed in blue. Read closely the notes on meanings of the passages. A passage is *a short section of a book, article, poem, or music*. These help clarify the meaning of each article and section.

The "Father of the Constitution"

Even in his day, James Madison, the nation's fourth president, was known as the "Father of the Constitution." Madison protested: "You give me credit to which I have no claim… It ought to be regarded as the work of many heads and many hands." However, when it came to creating a constitution, Madison had few equals. He not only played a leading role in shaping the Constitution, he wrote many of the Federalist papers defending it. Federalists were *supporters of ratification for the US Constitution*.

James Madison (1751–1836)

© Georgios Kollidas/Fotolia.com

Vocabulary

- constitution
- passage
- Federalists
- preamble
- legislature
- framers
- majority
- enumeration
- impeachment
- president pro tempore
- impeach
- indictment
- quorum
- adjourn
- immunity privilege
- emoluments
- bills
- revenue
- veto
- resolution
- duties, imposts, and excises
- naturalization
- tribunals
- letter of marque
- reprisal
- insurrections
- militia
- appropriations
- devolve
- jurisdiction
- appellate jurisdiction

continued on next page

The Constitution and Its Parts

Men with strong but often opposing ideas about the role of government shaped the US Constitution. Even modern-day presidents understand that our Constitution is a remarkable document.

Vocabulary

continued

- treason
- extradition
- amendments
- ratification
- engagements
- The Bill of Rights
- income tax
- abridging
- quartered
- warrants
- probable cause
- common law
- bail
- emancipation
- apportionment
- vacancies
- suffrage
- interpretation

For example, Harry S. Truman, our 33rd president, stated, "It's a plan, but not a straitjacket, flexible and short." In just a few pages, the Constitution manages to provide an adaptable framework for government that has held up for more than 225 years.

Although the main purpose of the Constitution is to provide a framework for the US government, it does much more than that. It is the nation's highest authority. It is the basic law of the United States. The powers of all the branches of government come from the Constitution. Like the American flag, the Constitution is also a symbol of our nation. It represents our system of government and our basic beliefs and ideals, such as liberty and freedom.

The Constitution has three main parts. First is the Preamble, *an introduction that states the goals and purposes of the government.* Next are seven articles that describe the structure of the government. Third are 27 amendments, or additions and changes, to the Constitution.

Every American president takes an oath to "preserve, protect, and defend the Constitution of the United States." George Washington and Barack Obama were sworn in as the first and forty-fourth presidents.

Photo by Master Sgt. Cecilio Ricardo/Defense Video & Imagery Distribution System

Misspelled Words in the Constitution?

The Constitution was handwritten in 1787. At that time, the American spelling and capitalization of words was inconsistent at best, and several words are spelled using British spelling. In colonial days, writers did not have the benefit of spell checkers or easy editing. Since there was no standard spelling of words in that period, most misspellings were accepted and stayed in the document, even today.

The Constitution was hastily written after the Constitutional Convention of 1787 was concluded. Words such as "chuse," "controul," "defence," and "labour" are examples of misspelled words or words using British spelling. Using current standardized American spelling, we would spell these words "choose," "control," "defense," and "labor."

The Preamble

The Preamble is the opening section of the Constitution, which tells why the Constitution was written. It sets forth the general purposes for which the government was established and declares that the power of the government comes from the people. In the single, concise sentence that begins and ends as follows, you can see how carefully the words were chosen to make clear this principle:

> *We the People of the United States...do ordain and establish this Constitution for the United States of America.*

This statement that the government depends on the people for its power and exists to serve them is unique among nations and has endured as the primary guiding principle for the nation.

The middle part of the Preamble states six purposes of the government:

- **"To form a more perfect Union"**—To unite the states more effectively so they can operate as a single nation, for the good of all
- **"To establish Justice"**—To create a system of fair laws and courts and make certain that all citizens are treated equally
- **"To insure domestic Tranquility"**—To maintain peace and order, keeping citizens and their property safe from harm
- **"To provide for the common Defense"**—To be ready militarily to protect the country and its citizens from outside attacks
- **"To promote the general Welfare"**—To help people live healthy, happy, and prosperous lives
- **"To secure the Blessings of Liberty to ourselves and our Posterity"**—To guarantee the freedom and basic rights of all Americans, including future generations (posterity)

Preamble

"We the People of the United States, in Order to form a more perfect Union, establish Justice, insure domestic Tranquility, provide for the common defence, promote the general Welfare, and secure the Blessings of Liberty to ourselves and our Posterity, do ordain and establish this Constitution for the United States of America."

The actual printed text of the Constitution shows the punctuation of the original document on parchment.

The Preamble introduces the Constitution and sets forth the general purposes for which the government was established.

© SOMATUSCANI/Fotolia.com

The Articles

The seven articles that follow the Preamble explain how the government is to work.

Articles I–III

The first three articles describe the powers and responsibilities of each branch of government—legislative, executive, and judicial—in turn.

Articles IV–VII

The remaining articles address more general matters. In Article IV of the Constitution, the framers shifted their focus to the states. The article says that all states must respect each other's laws, court decisions, and records. Article IV also explains the process for creating new states, and it promises that the federal government will protect and defend the states.

Article V reveals the foresight of the framers. They realized that in a changing world, the Constitution might need modification over time. Thus, they specified how amendments are to be made.

Article VI contains a key statement declaring the Constitution the "supreme Law of the Land." It adds that if state laws or court decisions conflict with federal law, the federal law shall prevail.

In Article VII, the framers dealt with practical matters. They wrote that the Constitution would take effect when nine states had ratified it.

Articles

Creation and Powers of the Legislative Branch

It is no accident that the first article deals with the legislative branch. The framers of the Constitution intended the legislature, or *elected lawmaking body,* to take the leading role in government. Framers were *the group of delegates who drafted the United States Constitution at the Constitutional Convention in 1787.* In the United States, the legislature is the Congress. Article I says that a Congress shall be made of two houses—the Senate and the House of Representatives—which will have all lawmaking authority. The article then describes how members of each house will be chosen and what rules they must follow in making laws. For example, a majority, or *more than half,* of both senators and representatives must vote for a bill before it can become a law.

Article I also lists specific powers that Congress does and does not have. For example, Congress may collect taxes, regulate foreign and interstate trade, coin money, and declare war. It may not tax exports, however, or favor one state over another.

Article I: The Legislative Branch

Section 1. Legislative Powers; The Congress

All legislative Powers herein granted shall be vested in a Congress of the United States, which shall consist of a Senate and House of Representatives.

Section 2. House of Representatives

[1.] The House of Representatives shall be composed of Members chosen every second Year by the People of the several States, and the Electors in each State shall have the Qualifications requisite for Electors of the most numerous Branch of the State Legislature.

[2.] No person shall be a Representative who shall not have attained to the Age of twenty five Years, and been seven Years a Citizen of the United States, and who shall not, when elected, be an Inhabitant of that State in which he shall be chosen.

What it means

Article I. The Legislative Branch. The Constitution contains seven divisions called articles. Each article covers a general topic. For example, Articles I, II, and III create the three branches of the national government—the legislative, executive, and judicial branches. Most of the articles are divided into sections.

What it means

Clause 1. The term "electors" refers to voters. Members of the House of Representatives are elected every two years. Any citizen allowed to vote for members of the larger house of state legislation can also vote for members of the house.

What it means

Clause 3. The number of representatives from each state is based on the size of the state's population from the latest census or enumeration. Enumeration is *a census or population count*. Each state is entitled to at least one representative. "All other persons" meant slaves, and each slave counted as three-fifths of a person. This issue became meaningless when slaves were freed by the Thirteenth Amendment and were counted as a free person.

[3.] Representatives and direct Taxes shall be apportioned among the several States which may be included within this Union, according to their respective Numbers, which shall be determined by adding to the whole Number of free Persons, including those bound to Service for a Term of Years, and excluding Indians not taxed, three fifths of all other Persons.

The actual Enumeration shall be made within three Years after the first Meeting of the Congress of the United States, and within every subsequent Term of ten Years, in such Manner as they shall by Law direct. The Number of Representatives shall not exceed one for every thirty Thousand, but each State shall have at Least one Representative; and until such enumeration shall be made, the State of New Hampshire shall be entitled to chuse three, Massachusetts eight, Rhode-Island and Providence Plantations one, Connecticut five, New-York six, New Jersey four, Pennsylvania eight, Delaware one, Maryland six, Virginia ten, North Carolina five, South Carolina five, and Georgia three.

What it means

Clause 4. Executive authority means the governor of a state. If a member of the House leaves office before his or her term is up, the governor must call for a special election.

[4.] When vacancies happen in the Representation from any State, the Executive Authority thereof shall issue Writs of Election to fill such Vacancies.

What it means

Clause 5. The House elects a Speaker. Only the House has the power of impeachment, or *the process of removing from office a government official accused of wrongdoing*.

[5.] The House of Representatives shall chuse their Speaker and other Officers, and shall have the sole Power of Impeachment.

What it means

Electing Senators. Originally, senators were chosen by the state legislators of their own states. The Seventeenth Amendment changed this, so that senators are now elected by the people. There are 100 senators, 2 from each state. The vice president serves as president of the Senate.

Section 3. Senate

[1.] The Senate of the United States shall be composed of two Senators from each State, chosen by the Legislature thereof, for six Years; and each Senator shall have one Vote.

[2.] Immediately after they shall be assembled in Consequence of the first Election, they shall be divided as equally as may be into three Classes. The Seats of the Senators of the first Class shall be vacated at the Expiration of the second Year, of the second Class at the Expiration of the fourth Year, and of the third Class at the Expiration of the sixth Year, so that one third may be chosen every second Year; and if Vacancies happen by Resignation, or otherwise, during the Recess of the Legislature of any State, the Executive thereof may make temporary Appointments until the next Meeting of the Legislature, which shall then fill such Vacancies.

What it means

Clause 2. Every two years, one third of the senators run for reelection. Today, thanks to the Seventh Amendment, the governor of a state may choose a senator to fill a vacancy that occurs between elections.

[3.] No Person shall be a Senator who shall not have attained to the Age of thirty Years, and been nine Years a Citizen of the United States, and who shall not, when elected, be an Inhabitant of that State for which he shall be chosen.

[4.] The Vice President of the United States shall be President of the Senate, but shall have no Vote, unless they be equally divided.

John Adams, the first vice president.

Courtesy of the National Park Service/ www.nps.gov

[5.] The Senate shall chuse their other Officers, and also a President pro tempore in the Absence of the Vice President, or when he shall exercise the Office of the President of the United States.

What it means

Clause 5. The president pro tempore is *the presiding officer of the Senate who serves when the vice president is absent.*

[6.] The Senate shall have the sole Power to try all Impeachments. When sitting for that Purpose, they shall be on Oath or Affirmation. When the President of the United States is tried, the Chief Justice shall preside: And no Person shall be convicted without the Concurrence of two thirds of the Members present.

What it means

Clause 6. One of Congress's powers is the power to impeach— *to put federal officials accused of wrongdoing on trial, and if necessary remove them from office.*

[7.] Judgment in Cases of Impeachment shall not extend further than to removal from Office, and disqualification to hold and enjoy any Office of honor, Trust or Profit under the United States: but the Party convicted shall nevertheless be liable and subject to Indictment [*charging a person with an offense*], Trial, Judgment and Punishment, according to Law.

Section 4. Elections and Meetings

What it means

Clause 1. State legislatures can decide when and how congressional elections are held. However, in 1872, Congress decided that congressional elections must be held in every state on the same date in even-numbered years.

[1.] The Times, Places and Manner of holding Elections for Senators and Representatives, shall be prescribed in each State by the Legislature thereof; but the Congress may at Any time by Law make or alter such Regulations, except as to the Places of chusing Senators.

[2.] The Congress shall assemble at least once in every Year, and such Meeting shall be on the first Monday in December, unless they shall by Law appoint a different Day.

Section 5. Legislative Proceedings

The unique gavel of the United States Senate has an hourglass shape with no handle. The current gavel was presented by the Republic of India in 1954.

Courtesy of the United States Senate/ www.senate.gov

[1.] Each House shall be the Judge of the Elections, Returns and Qualifications of its own Members, and a Majority of each shall constitute a Quorum [*minimum number of members that must be present to conduct sessions*] to do business; but a smaller Number may adjourn [*suspend a session*] from day to day, and may be authorized to compel the Attendance of absent Members, in such Manner, and under such Penalties as each House may provide.

[2.] Each House may determine the Rules of its Proceedings, punish its Members for disorderly Behaviour, and, with the Concurrence of two thirds, expel a Member.

[3.] Each House shall keep a Journal of its Proceedings, and from time to time publish the same, excepting such Parts as may in their Judgment require Secrecy; and the Yeas and Nays of the Members of either House on any question shall, at the Desire of one fifth of those Present, be entered on the Journal.

[4.] Neither House, during the Session of Congress, shall, without the Consent of the other, adjourn, nor to any other Place than that in which the two Houses shall be sitting.

Section 6. Compensation, Immunities, and Disabilities of Members

What it means

Compensation. To strengthen the federal government, the Founders set congressional salaries to be paid by the United States Treasury rather than by members' respective states. Originally, members were paid $6 per day. In 2013, members of Congress received a base salary of $174,000 per year.

Immunities. While Congress is in session, a member is free from arrest in civil cases and cannot be sued for anything they say on the floor of the Congress. This allows for freedom of debate. However, a member can still be arrested for a criminal offense.

[1.] The Senators and Representatives shall receive a Compensation for their Services, to be ascertained by Law, and paid out of the Treasury of the United States. They shall in all Cases, except Treason, Felony and Breach of the Peace, be privileged from Arrest during their Attendance at the Session of their respective Houses, and in going to and returning from the same; and for any Speech or Debate in either House, they shall not be questioned in any other Place [members have immunity privilege, *whereby they cannot be sued or prosecuted for anything they say in Congress*].

[2.] No Senator or Representative shall, during the Time for which he was elected, be appointed to any civil Office under the Authority of the United States, which shall have been created, or the Emoluments [*payments for holding office*] whereof shall have been encreased during such time; and no Person holding any Office under the United States, shall be a Member of either House during his Continuance in Office.

> **What it means**
>
> **Clause 2.** A member of Congress cannot hold another federal office during his or her term in Congress.

Section 7. Revenue Bills, President's Veto

[1.] All Bills [*drafts of proposed laws*] for raising Revenue [*income raised by government*] shall originate in the House of Representatives; but the Senate may propose or concur with Amendments as on other Bills.

> **What it means**
>
> **Clause 1.** All tax laws must originate in the House of Representatives.
> This ensures that the branch of Congress that is elected by the people every two years has the major role in determining taxes.

[2.] Every Bill which shall have passed the House of Representatives and the Senate, shall, before it become a Law, be presented to the President of the United States; If he approve he shall sign it, but if not he shall return it, with his Objections to that House in which it shall have originated, who shall enter the Objections at large on their Journal, and proceed to reconsider it. If after such Reconsideration two thirds of that House shall agree to pass the Bill, it shall be sent, together with the Objections, to the other House, by which it shall likewise be reconsidered, and if approved by two thirds of that House, it shall become a Law. But in all such Cases the Votes of both Houses shall be determined by Yeas and Nays, and the Names of the Persons voting for and against the Bill shall be entered on the Journal of each House respectively. If any Bill shall not be returned by the President within ten Days (Sundays excepted) after it shall have been presented to him, the Same shall be a Law, in like Manner as if he had signed it, unless the Congress by their Adjournment prevent its Return, in which Case it shall not be a Law.

> **What it means**
>
> **Clause 2.** A bill may become a law only by passing both houses of Congress and by being signed by the president. The president can check Congress by rejecting—vetoing—its legislation.
> A bill can also become law without the president's signature or veto if each house of Congress passes the bill again by a two-thirds vote. To veto is *to exercise the right to reject a bill or measure.*
> If the president refuses to sign the bill and Congress adjourns within 10 days, then the bill dies through the President's inaction. This is called a "pocket veto."

[3.] Every Order, Resolution [*a formal expression of the majority at a meeting and usually as the result of a vote*], or Vote to which the Concurrence of the Senate and House of Representatives may be necessary (except on a question of Adjournment) shall be presented to the President of the United States; and before the Same shall take Effect, shall be approved by him, or being disapproved by him, shall be repassed by two thirds of the Senate and House of Representatives, according to the Rules and Limitations prescribed in the Case of a Bill.

Section 8. Powers of Congress

What it means

Clause 1. Expressed powers are those powers directly stated in the Constitution. Most of the expressed powers of Congress are listed in Article I, Section 8. These powers are also called enumerated powers because they are numbered 1–18. Duties, imposts, and excises are *forms of collected taxes on products brought in or sold in the United States.*

[1.] The Congress shall have the Power to lay and collect Taxes, Duties, Imposts and Excises, to pay the Debts and provide for the common Defence and general Welfare of the United States; but all Duties, Imposts and Excises shall be uniform throughout the United States;

[2.] To borrow Money on the credit of the United States;

[3.] To regulate Commerce with foreign Nations, and among the several States, and with the Indian Tribes;

[4.] To establish an uniform Rule of Naturalization [*procedure by which a citizen of a foreign nation becomes a citizen of the United States*], and uniform Laws on the subject of Bankruptcies throughout the United States;

Congress determines the value of printed money.

© ekostsov/Fotolia.com

[5.] To coin Money, regulate the Value thereof, and of foreign Coin, and fix the Standard of Weights and Measures;

[6.] To provide for the Punishment of counterfeiting the Securities and current Coin of the United States;

[7.] To establish Post Offices and post Roads;

[8.] To promote the Progress of Science and useful Arts, by securing for limited Times to Authors and Inventors the exclusive Right to their respective Writings and Discoveries;

[9.] To constitute Tribunals [*courts of law*] inferior to the supreme Court;

[10.] To define and punish Piracies and Felonies committed on the high Seas, and Offences against the Law of Nations;

What it means

Clause 11. Only Congress can declare war. Declarations of war are granted at the request of the president. Letters of Marque and Reprisal are no longer used.

[11.] To declare War, grant Letters of Marque [*letters giving authority to a citizen to outfit an armed ship and use it to attack enemy ships in time of war*] and Reprisal [*taking by force property or territory belonging to another country or its citizens*], and make Rules concerning Captures on Land and Water;

[12.] To raise and support Armies, but no Appropriation of Money to that Use shall be for a longer Term than two Years;

[13.] To provide and maintain a Navy;

[14.] To make Rules for the Government and Regulation of the land and naval Forces;

[15.] To provide for calling forth the Militia to execute the Laws of the Union, suppress Insurrections [*rebellions*] and repel Invasions;

[16.] To provide for organizing, arming, and disciplining the Militia, and for governing such Part of them as may be employed in the Service of the United States, reserving to the States respectively, the Appointment of the Officers, and the Authority of training the Militia according to the discipline prescribed by Congress;

[17.] To exercise exclusive Legislation in all Cases whatsoever, over such District (not exceeding ten Miles square) as may, by Cession of particular States, and the Acceptance of Congress, become the Seat of Government of the United States, and to exercise like Authority over all Places purchased by the Consent of the Legislature of the State in which the Same shall be, for the Erection of Forts, Magazines, Arsenals, dock-Yards, and other needful Buildings;

And

[18.] To make all Laws which shall be necessary and proper for carrying into Execution the foregoing Powers, and all other Powers vested by this Constitution in the Government of the United States, or in any Department or Officer thereof.

Section 9. Powers Denied to Congress

[1]. The Migration or Importation of such Persons as any of the States now existing shall think proper to admit, shall not be prohibited by the Congress prior to the Year one thousand eight hundred and eight, but a Tax or duty may be imposed on such Importation, not exceeding ten dollars for each Person.

[2.] The Privilege of the Writ of Habeas Corpus shall not be suspended, unless when in Cases of Rebellion or Invasion the public Safety may require it.

[3.] No Bill of Attainder or ex post facto Law shall be passed.

[4.] No Capitation, or other direct Tax shall be laid, unless in Proportion to the Census or Enumeration herein before directed to be taken.

[5.] No Tax or Duty shall be laid on Articles exported from any State.

[6.] No Preference shall be given by any Regulation of Commerce or Revenue to the Ports of one State over those of another: nor shall Vessels bound to, or from, one State, be obliged to enter, clear, or pay Duties in another.

What it means

Clauses 15 and 16. The militia is *a body of citizen soldiers*. Congress can call up the militia to put down rebellions or fight foreign invaders. Each state has its own militia, today called the National Guard.

What it means

Clause 18. The final enumerated power is often called the "elastic clause." This clause gives Congress the right to make all laws "necessary and proper" to carry out the powers expressed in the other clauses of Article I. It is called the elastic clause because it lets Congress "stretch" its powers to meet situations the Founders could never have anticipated.

What it means

Clauses 2 and 3. A writ of habeas corpus issued by a judge requires a law official to bring a prisoner to court and show cause for holding the prisoner. A bill of attainder is a bill that punished a person without a jury trial. An "ex post facto" law is one that makes an act a crime after the act has been committed.

What it means

Clause 7. The federal government cannot spend money unless Congress appropriates it, or passes a law allowing it.

[7.] No Money shall be drawn from the Treasury, but in Consequence of Appropriations [*funds set aside for a specific use*] made by Law; and a regular Statement and Account of the Receipts and Expenditures of all public Money shall be published from time to time.

[8.] No Title of Nobility shall be granted by the United States: And no Person holding any Office of Profit or Trust under them, shall, without the Consent of the Congress, accept of any present, Emolument, Office, or Title, of any kind whatever, from any King, Prince, or foreign State.

Section 10. Powers Denied to the States

What it means

Clause 1. The writers of the Constitution did not want states to act like separate nations, so they prohibited states from making treaties or coining money.

[1.] No State shall enter into any Treaty, Alliance, or Confederation; grant Letters of Marque and Reprisal; coin Money; emit Bills of Credit; make any Thing but gold and silver Coin a Tender in Payment of Debts; pass any Bill of Attainder, ex post facto Law, or Law impairing the Obligation of Contracts; or grant any Title of Nobility.

[2.] No State shall, without the Consent of the Congress, lay any Imposts or Duties on Imports or Exports, except what may be absolutely necessary for executing its inspection Laws: and the net Produce of all Duties and Imposts, laid by any State on Imports and Exports, shall be for the Use of the Treasury of the United States; and all such Laws shall be subject to the Revision and Controul of the Congress.

What it means

Clause 3. No state can maintain an army or navy without the consent of Congress. States cannot declare war or make treaties unless an enemy invades or is about to invade.

[3.] No State shall, without the Consent of Congress, lay any Duty of Tonnage, keep Troops, or Ships of War in time of Peace, enter into any Agreement or Compact with another State, or with a foreign Power, or engage in War, unless actually invaded, or in such imminent Danger as will not admit of delay.

Creation and Powers of the Executive Branch

Article II provides for an executive, or law-enforcing, branch of government headed by a president and vice president. Article II explains how these leaders are to be elected and how they can be removed from office. The article also describes some of the president's powers and duties. These include commanding the armed forces, dealing with the leaders of other countries, and appointing certain government officials.

Article II: The Executive Branch

Section 1. President and Vice President

[1.] The executive Power shall be vested in a President of the United States of America. He shall hold his Office during the Term of four Years, and, together with the Vice President, chosen for the same Term, be elected, as follows

[2.] Each State shall appoint, in such Manner as the Legislature thereof may direct, a Number of Electors, equal to the whole Number of Senators and Representatives to which the State may be entitled in the Congress: but no Senator or Representative, or Person holding an Office of Trust or Profit under the United States, shall be appointed an Elector.

[3.] The Electors shall meet in their respective States, and vote by Ballot for two Persons, of whom one at least shall not be an Inhabitant of the same State with themselves. And they shall make a List of all the Persons voted for, and of the Number of Votes for each; which List they shall sign and certify, and transmit sealed to the Seat of the Government of the United States, directed to the President of the Senate. The President of the Senate shall, in the Presence of the Senate and House of Representatives, open all the Certificates, and the Votes shall then be counted. The Person having the greatest Number of Votes shall be the President, if such Number be a Majority of the whole Number of Electors appointed; and if there be more than one who have such Majority, and have an equal Number of Votes, then the House of Representatives shall immediately chuse by Ballot one of them for President; and if no person have a Majority, then from the five highest on the List the said House shall in like Manner chuse the President. But in chusing the President, the Votes shall be taken by States, the Representation from each State having one Vote; A quorum for this Purpose shall consist of a Member or Members from two thirds of the States, and a Majority of all the States shall be necessary to a Choice. In every Case, after the Choice of the President, the Person having the greatest Number of Votes of the Electors shall be the Vice President. But if there should remain two or more who have equal Votes, the Senate shall chuse from them by Ballot the Vice President.

[4.] The Congress may determine the Time of chusing the Electors, and the Day on which they shall give their Votes; which Day shall be the same throughout the United States.

What it means

Article II. The Executive Branch. Article II creates an executive branch to carry out laws passed by Congress. Article II lists the powers and duties of the presidency, describes qualifications for office and procedures for electing the president, and provides for a vice president.

What it means

Clauses 2 and 3. Directs states to choose electors or delegates to the Electoral College, to vote for President. A state's electoral vote is equal to the combined number of senators and representatives. Members of Congress and federal officeholders may not serve as electors. The Twelfth Amendment, added in 1804, changed the method of electing the president stated in Article II, Section 3. The Twelfth Amendment requires that the electors cast separate ballots for president and vice president.

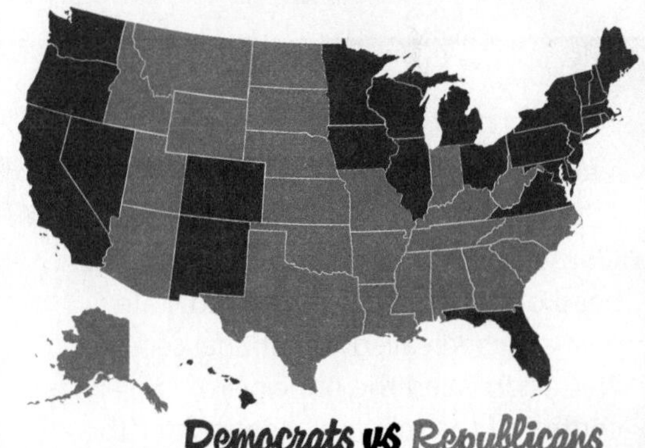

Electoral votes from the 2012 Presidential Election.

© Vector Art Design/Fotolia.com

What it means

Clause 5. The president must be a citizen of the United States by birth, at least 35 years of age, and a resident of the United States for 14 years.

[5.] No Person except a natural born Citizen, or a Citizen of the United States, at the time of the Adoption of this Constitution, shall be eligible to the Office of President; neither shall any Person be eligible to that Office who shall not have attained to the Age of thirty five Years, and been fourteen Years a Resident within the United States.

What it means

Clause 6. If the president dies, resigns, is removed from office by impeachment, or is unable to carry out the duties of the office, the vice president becomes president. The Twenty-fifth Amendment sets procedures for presidential succession.

[6.] In Case of the Removal of the President from Office, or of his Death, Resignation, or Inability to discharge the Powers and Duties of the said Office, the Same shall devolve [*pass to*] on the Vice President, and the Congress may by Law provide for the Case of Removal, Death, Resignation or Inability, both of the President and Vice President, declaring what Officer shall then act as President, and such Officer shall act accordingly, until the Disability be removed, or a President shall be elected.

What it means

Clause 7. Originally, the president's salary was $25,000 per year. The president's current yearly salary is $400,000 plus a $50,000 nontaxable expense account per year. Neither of these has increased since 2001. The president's salary cannot be raised or lowered during his or her time in office.

[7.] The President shall, at stated Times, receive for his Services, a Compensation, which shall neither be encreased nor diminished during the Period for which he shall have been elected, and he shall not receive within that Period any other Emolument from the United States, or any of them.

[8.] Before he enter on the Execution of his Office, he shall take the following Oath or Affirmation:—"I do solemnly swear (or affirm) that I will faithfully execute the Office of President of the United States, and will to the best of my Ability, preserve, protect and defend the Constitution of the United States."

Section 2. Powers of the President

What it means

Clause 1. The president, a civilian, is the head of the armed services and state militias when called to national service. This established the principle of civilian control of the military. Mention of "the principal officer in each of the executive departments" is the only suggestion of the president's cabinet to be found in the Constitution. The cabinet is an advisory body, and its power depends on the president.

[1.] The President shall be Commander in Chief of the Army and Navy of the United States, and of the Militia of the several States, when called into the actual Service of the United States; he may require the Opinion, in writing, of the principal Officer in each of the executive Departments, upon any Subject relating to the Duties of their respective Offices, and he shall have Power to grant Reprieves and Pardons for Offences against the United States, except in Cases of Impeachment.

[2.] He shall have Power, by and with the Advice and Consent of the Senate, to make Treaties, provided two thirds of the Senators present concur; and he shall nominate, and by and with the Advice and Consent of the Senate, shall appoint Ambassadors, other public Ministers and Consuls, Judges of the supreme Court, and all other Officers of the United States, whose Appointments are not herein otherwise provided for, and which shall be established by Law: but the Congress may by Law vest the Appointment of such inferior Officers, as they think proper, in the President alone, in the Courts of Law, or in the Heads of departments.

[3.] The President shall have Power to fill up all Vacancies that may happen during the Recess of the Senate, by granting Commissions that shall expire at the End of their next Session.

What it means

Clause 2. The president has the power to make treaties with other nations. Under the system of checks and balances, all treaties must be approved by the Senate with a two-thirds vote.

The president has the power to appoint ambassadors to foreign countries and to appoint other high officials. The Senate must confirm, or approve, these appointments.

Section 3. Duties of the President

He shall from time to time give to the Congress Information of the State of the Union, and recommend to their Consideration such Measures as he shall judge necessary and expedient; he may, on extraordinary Occasions, convene both Houses, or either of them, and in Case of Disagreement between them, with Respect to the Time of Adjournment, he may adjourn them to such Time as he shall think proper; he shall receive Ambassadors and other public ministers; he shall take Care that the Laws be faithfully executed, and shall Commission all the Officers of the United States.

What it means

Section 3. The president serves as chief executive, or head of the executive branch. The Constitution states the President must "take care that the laws be faithfully executed." One way the president gives orders is through executive orders, which are rules and regulations the government must follow. The president's orders may not violate the Constitution or laws passed by Congress.

Section 4. Impeachment

The President, Vice President and all civil Officers of the United States, shall be removed from Office on Impeachment for, and Conviction of, Treason, Bribery, or other high Crimes and Misdemeanors.

What it means

Section 4. Civil officers include federal judges and members of the Cabinet. High crimes are major crimes, misdemeanors are lesser crimes. The president, vice president, and others can be forced out of office if impeached and found guilty of certain crimes.

Impeachment ticket.
Courtesy of the US Senate/www.senate.gov

Establishing Federal Courts

The judicial branch is the part of government that interprets the laws and sees that they are fairly applied. Article III calls for "one Supreme Court" and such lower courts as Congress deems appropriate.

Article III then lists the powers of the federal courts and describes the kinds of cases they may hear. These include cases involving the Constitution, federal laws and treaties, and disputes between states.

Article III: The Judicial Branch

What it means

Section 1. Federal courts deal mostly with "statute law," or laws passed by Congress, treaties, and cases involving the Constitution itself.

Section 1. Courts, Terms of Office

The judicial Power of the United States, shall be vested in one supreme Court, and in such inferior Courts as the Congress may from time to time ordain and establish. The Judges, both of the supreme and inferior Courts, shall hold their Offices during good Behaviour, and shall, at stated Times, receive for their Services, a Compensation, which shall not be diminished during their Continuance in Office.

What it means

Clause 1. "Jurisdiction" refers to the right of a court to hear a case. Federal courts have jurisdiction (*authority to be the first court to hear a case*) for cases that involve the Constitution, federal laws, treaties, foreign ambassadors and diplomats, naval and maritime laws, disagreements between states or between citizens from different states, and disputes between a state or citizen and a foreign state or citizen.

Section 2. Jurisdiction

[1.] The judicial Power shall extend to all Cases, in Law and Equity, arising under this Constitution, the Laws of the United States, and Treaties made, or which shall be made, under their Authority;—to all Cases affecting Ambassadors, other public Ministers and Consuls;—to all Cases of admiralty and maritime Jurisdiction;—to Controversies to which the United States shall be a Party;—to Controversies between two or more States;—between a State and Citizens of another State;—between Citizens of different States,— between Citizens of the same State claiming Lands under Grants of different States, and between a State, or the Citizens thereof, and foreign States, Citizens or Subjects.

[2.] In all Cases affecting Ambassadors, other public Ministers and Consuls, and those in which a State shall be Party, the supreme Court shall have original Jurisdiction. In all the other Cases before mentioned, the supreme Court shall have appellate jurisdiction [*authority to hear cases that have been appealed from lower courts*], both as to Law and Fact, with such Exceptions, and under such Regulations as the Congress shall make.

[3.] The Trial of all Crimes, except in Cases of Impeachment, shall be by Jury; and such Trial shall be held in the State where the said Crimes shall have been committed; but when not committed within any State, the Trial shall be at such Place or Places as the Congress may by Law have directed.

Section 3. Treason

[1.] Treason [*violation of the allegiance owed by a person to his or her own country; for example, by aiding an enemy*] against the United States, shall consist only in levying War against them, or in adhering to their Enemies, giving them Aid and Comfort. No Person shall be convicted of Treason unless on the Testimony of two Witnesses to the same overt Act, or on confession in open Court.

[2.] The Congress shall have Power to declare the Punishment of Treason, but no Attainder of Treason shall work Corruption of Blood, or Forfeiture except during the Life of the Person attainted.

Article IV: Relations Among the States

Section 1. Full Faith and Credit

Full Faith and Credit shall be given in each State to the public Acts, Records, and judicial Proceedings of every other State. And the Congress may by general Laws prescribe the Manner in which such Acts, Records and Proceedings shall be proved, and the Effect thereof.

What it means

Clause 2. A Court with "original jurisdiction" has the authority to be the first court to hear a case. The Supreme Court has "appellate jurisdiction" and mostly hears cases appealed from lower courts.

What it means

Article IV. Relationships Among the States. Article IV explains the relationship of the states to one another and to the national government. This article requires each state to give citizens of other states the same rights as its own citizens, addresses admitting new states, and guarantees that the national government will protect the states.

What it means

Section 1. Each state must recognize the official acts and records of any other state. For example, each state must recognize marriage certificates issued by another state.

What it means

Clause 2. State governors must return a suspect to another state; this is called extradition, or *the surrender of a suspected criminal or escaped prisoner to another authority*. However, the Supreme Court has ruled that a governor cannot be forced to do so if he or she feels that justice will not be done.

What it means

Clause 3. The Thirteenth Amendment replaced this clause.

What it means

Section 3. Congress has the power to admit new states. It also determines the basic guidelines for applying for statehood. Two states, Maine and West Virginia, were created within the boundaries of another state. In the case of West Virginia, President Lincoln recognized the West Virginia government as the legal government of Virginia during the Civil War. This allowed West Virginia to secede from Virginia without obtaining approval from the Virginia legislature.

What it means

Section 4. In a republic, voters choose representatives to govern them. The federal government must protect the states from foreign invasion and from domestic (internal) disorder, if asked to do so by the state.

Section 2. Privileges and Immunities of Citizens

[1.] The Citizens of each State shall be entitled to all Privileges and Immunities of Citizens in the several States.

[2.] A Person charged in any State with Treason, Felony, or other Crime, who shall flee from Justice, and be found in another State, shall on Demand of the executive Authority of the State from which he fled, be delivered up, to be removed to the State having Jurisdiction of the Crime.

[3.] No Person held to Service of Labour in one State, under the Laws thereof, escaping into another, shall, in Consequence of any Law or Regulation therein, be discharged from such Service or Labour, but shall be delivered up on Claim of the Party to whom such Service or Labour may be due.

Section 3. New States and Territories

[1.] New States may be admitted by the Congress into this Union; but no new State shall be formed or erected within the Jurisdiction of any other State; nor any State be formed by the Junction of two or more States, or Parts of States, without the Consent of the Legislatures of the States concerned as well as of the Congress.

[2.] The Congress shall have Power to dispose of and make all needful Rules and Regulations respecting the Territory or other Property belonging to the United States; and nothing in this Constitution shall be so construed as to Prejudice any Claims of the United States, or of any particular State.

Section 4. Protection Afforded to States by the Nation

The United States shall guarantee to every State in this Union a Republican Form of Government, and shall protect each of them against Invasion; and on Application of the Legislature, or of the Executive (when the Legislature cannot be convened) against domestic Violence.

Article V. Provisions for Amendments

The Congress, whenever two thirds of both Houses shall deem it necessary, shall propose Amendments [*changes*] to this Constitution, or, on the Application of the Legislatures of two thirds of the several States, shall call a Convention for proposing Amendments, which, in either Case, shall be valid to all Intents and Purposes, as Part of this Constitution, when ratified by the Legislatures of three fourths of the several States, or by Conventions in three fourths thereof, as the one or the other Mode of Ratification [*the process by which an amendment is approved*] may be proposed by the Congress; Provided that no Amendment which may be made prior to the Year One thousand eight hundred and eight shall in any Manner affect the first and fourth Clauses in the Ninth Section of the first Article; and that no State, without its Consent, shall be deprived of its equal Suffrage in the Senate.

> ***What it means***
>
> **Article V. Provisions for Amendments.** This article spells out the ways that the Constitution can be amended, or changed. All of the 27 amendments were proposed by a two-thirds vote of both houses of Congress. Only the Twenty-first Amendment was ratified by constitutional conventions of the states. All other amendments have been ratified by state legislatures.

Article VI. National Debts, Supremacy of National Law, Oath

Section 1. Validity of Debts

All Debts contracted and Engagements [*commitments*] entered into, before the Adoption of this Constitution, shall be as valid against the United States under this Constitution, as under the Confederation.

Section 2. Supremacy of National Law

This Constitution, and the Laws of the United States which shall be made in Pursuance thereof; and all Treaties made, or which shall be made, under the Authority of the United States, shall be the supreme Law of the Land; and the Judges in every State shall be bound thereby, any Thing in the Constitution or Laws of any State to the Contrary notwithstanding.

> ***What it means***
>
> **Section 2.** The "supremacy clause" in this section establishes the Constitution, federal laws, and treaties that the Senate has ratified as the supreme, or highest, law of the land. State judges must overturn a state law that conflicts with the Constitution or with federal law.

Section 3. Oaths of Office

The Senators and Representatives before mentioned, and the Members of the several State Legislatures, and all executive and judicial Officers, both of the United States and of the several States, shall be bound by Oath or Affirmation, to support this Constitution; but no religious Test shall ever be required as a Qualification to any Office or public Trust under the United States.

What it means

Article VII. Ratification of the Constitution. Article VII addresses ratification and declares that the Constitution would take effect after it was ratified by nine states.

Article VII. Ratification of the Constitution

The Ratification of the Conventions of nine States, shall be sufficient for the establishment of this Constitution between the States so ratifying the Same.

Done in Convention by the Unanimous Consent of the States present the Seventeenth Day of September in the Year of our Lord one thousand seven hundred and Eighty seven and of the Independence of the United States of America the Twelfth. In witness whereof We have hereunto subscribed our Names,

Signers

George Washington,
President and Deputy from Virginia

New Hampshire
John Langdon
Nicholas Gilman

Massachusetts
Nathaniel Gorham
Rufus King

Connecticut
William Samuel Johnson
Roger Sherman

New York
Alexander Hamilton

New Jersey
William Livingston
David Brearley
William Paterson
Jonathan Dayton

Pennsylvania
Benjamin Franklin
Thomas Mifflin
Robert Morris
George Clymer
Thomas Fitzsimons
Jared Ingersoll
James Wilson
Gouverneur Morris

Delaware
George Read
Gunning Bedford, Jr.
John Dickinson
Richard Bassett
Jacob Broom

Maryland
James McHenry
Daniel of St. Thomas Jennifer
Daniel Carroll

Virginia
John Blair
James Madison, Jr.

North Carolina
William Blount
Richard Dobbs Spaight
Hugh Williamson

South Carolina
John Rutledge
Charles Cotesworth Pinckney
Charles Pinckney
Pierce Butler

Georgia
William Few
Abraham Baldwin

Attest: William Jackson,
Secretary

The Process of Amending the Constitution

Since the Constitution was signed in 1787, it has been amended 27 times. The Bill of Rights, *the addition to the Constitution that consists of the first 10 amendments*, was added in 1791. A number of amendments address entirely different matters, such as improving the way our government works. For example, the Sixteenth Amendment was passed in 1913 to allow Congress to collect an income tax—*a tax on people's earnings*. This is now an important source of money for the government, helping it pay for services.

The Amendment Process

Would it surprise you to know that thousands of amendments to the Constitution have been considered over the years? Only 27 have become law because the framers deliberately made the amendment process difficult. After months of debate and compromise, they knew how delicately balanced the Constitution was. Changing even one small detail could have dramatic effects throughout the government. Therefore, the framers made sure the Constitution could not be altered without the overwhelming support of the people. At the same time, the ability to amend the Constitution is necessary. Constitutional amendments safeguard many of our freedoms. For example, the abolition of slavery and giving women the right to vote were added as amendments. If the Constitution could not have been amended to protect the rights of African Americans, women, and other oppressed groups, it—and our government—might not have survived. Figure 5.3 details the amendment process.

The process for making an amendment to the Constitution, as outlined in Article V, involves two steps: proposal and ratification. An amendment may be proposed in one of two ways.

The first method is by congressional action. Two-thirds of the members of both houses of Congress must approve, or pass, the measure.

The second method is by a national convention requested by two-thirds of the state legislatures. Once a national amendment has been proposed, three-fourths of the states must ratify it. The states have two ways to do this: by a vote of either the state legislature or a special state convention. Only one amendment, the Twenty-first Amendment, has been ratified by means of state conventions. Congress proposed and the state legislatures ratified all others.

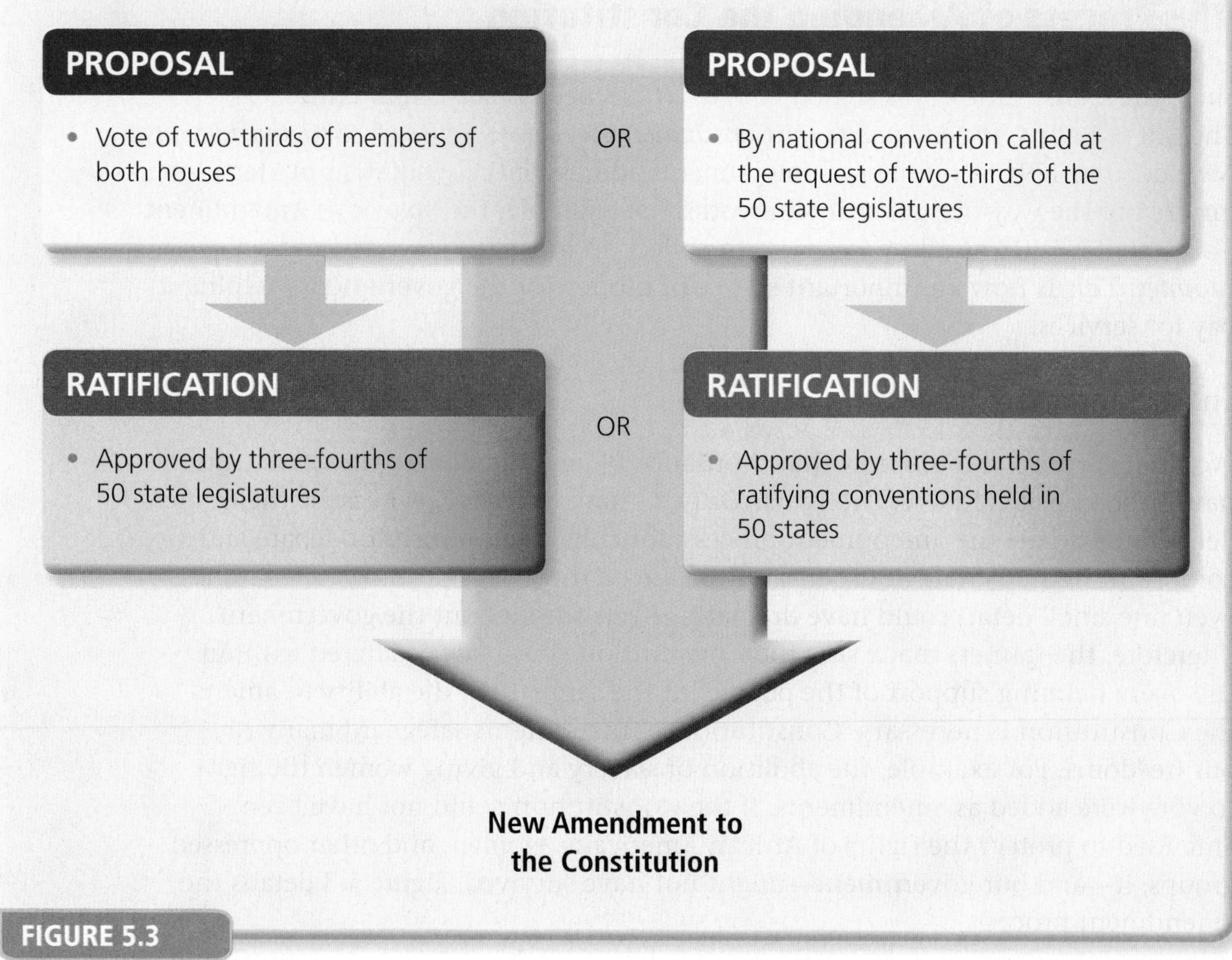
PROPOSAL
Vote of two-thirds of members of both houses
OR
PROPOSAL
By national convention called at the request of two-thirds of the 50 state legislatures
RATIFICATION
Approved by three-fourths of 50 state legislatures
OR
RATIFICATION
Approved by three-fourths of ratifying conventions held in 50 states
New Amendment to the Constitution

FIGURE 5.3

Amending the Constitution

Bill of Rights

The first 10 amendments are known as the Bill of Rights (1791). These amendments limit the powers of government. The amendment freedoms are not absolute, however. They are limited by the rights of other individuals. The numbers in parentheses next to the amendment number is the year of ratification.

Amendments

Amendment I (1791)

Congress shall make no law respecting an establishment of religion, or prohibiting the free exercise thereof; or abridging [*limiting the rights*] the freedom of speech, or of the press; or the right of the people peaceably to assemble, and to petition the Government for a redress of grievances.

> **What it means**
>
> **Amendment I.** Congress cannot set up an established, or official, church or religion for the nation, nor can it forbid the practice of religion. The framers of the Constitution wanted to keep government and religion separate.

Amendment II (1791)

A well-regulated Militia, being necessary to the security of a free State, the right of the people to keep and bear Arms, shall not be infringed.

Amendment III (1791)

No Soldier shall, in time of peace be quartered [*provided living accommodations*] in any house, without the consent of the Owner, nor in time of war, but in a manner to be prescribed by law.

Amendment IV (1791)

The right of the people to be secure in their persons, houses, papers, and effects, against unreasonable searches and seizures, shall not be violated, and no Warrants [*documents that give police particular powers*] shall issue, but upon probable cause [*police must have a reasonable basis to believe a person is linked to a crime*], supported by Oath or affirmation, and particularly describing the place to be searched, and the persons or things to be seized.

Amendment V (1791)

No person shall be held to answer for a capital, or otherwise infamous crime, unless on a presentment or indictment of a Grand Jury, except in cases arising in the land or naval forces, or in the Militia, when in actual service in time of War or public danger; nor shall any person be subject for the same offence to be twice put in jeopardy of life or limb; nor shall be compelled in any criminal case to be a witness against himself, nor be deprived of life, liberty, or property, without due process of law; nor shall private property be taken for public use without just compensation.

> **What it means**
>
> **Amendment V.** This amendment contains important protections for people accused of crimes. One of the protections is that government may not deprive any person of life, liberty, or property without due process of law. This means that the government must follow proper constitutional procedures in trials and in other actions it takes against individuals. Persons cannot be tried twice for the same crime. A person cannot be forced to testify against himself or herself. The government cannot seize private property for public use without paying the owner a fair price.

What it means

Amendment VI. A basic protection is the right to a speedy, public trial. The jury must hear witnesses and evidence on both sides before deciding the guilt or innocence of a person charged with a crime. This amendment also provides that legal counsel must be provided to a defendant. In 1963, the Supreme Court ruled, in Gideon v. Wainwright, that if a defendant cannot afford a lawyer, the government must provide one to defend him or her.

Amendment VI (1791)

In all criminal prosecutions, the accused shall enjoy the right to a speedy and public trial, by an impartial jury of the State and district wherein the crime shall have been committed, which district shall have been previously ascertained by law, and to be informed of the nature and cause of the accusation; to be confronted with the witnesses against him; to have compulsory process for obtaining Witnesses in his favor, and to have the assistance of counsel for his defence.

Amendment VII (1791)

In Suits at common law [*law established by previous court decisions*], where the value in controversy shall exceed twenty dollars, the right of trial by jury shall be preserved, and no fact tried by a jury, shall be otherwise reexamined in any Court of the United States, than according to the rules of common law.

Amendment VIII (1791)

Excessive bail [*money that an accused person provides to the court as a guarantee that he or she will be present for a trial*] shall not be required, nor excessive fines imposed, nor cruel and unusual punishments inflicted.

What it means

Amendment IX. This amendment prevents government from claiming that the only rights people have are those listed in the Bill of Rights.

Amendment IX (1791)

The enumeration in the Constitution, of certain rights, shall not be construed to deny or disparage others retained by the people.

What it means

Amendment X. The final amendment of the Bill of Rights protects the states and the people from an all-powerful federal government. It establishes that powers not given to the national government—or denied to the states—by the Constitution belong to the states or to the people.

Amendment X (1791)

The powers not delegated to the United States by the Constitution, nor prohibited by it to the States, are reserved to the States respectively, or to the people.

Amendment XI (1795)

The Judicial power of the United States shall not be construed to extend to any suit in law or equity, commenced or prosecuted against one of the United States by Citizens of another State, or by Citizens or Subjects of any Foreign State.

Amendment XII (1804)

The electors shall meet in their respective states and vote by ballot for President and Vice President, one of whom, at least, shall not be an inhabitant of the same state with themselves; they shall name in their ballots the person voted for as President, and in distinct ballots the person voted for as Vice President, and they shall make distinct lists of all persons voted for as President, and of all persons voted for as Vice President, and of the number of votes for each, which lists they shall sign and certify, and transmit sealed to the seat of the government of the United States, directed to the President of the Senate;—The President of the Senate shall, in the presence of the Senate and House of Representatives, open all the certificates and the votes shall then be counted;—The person having the greatest number of votes for President, shall be the President, if such number be a majority of the whole number of Electors appointed; and if no person have such majority, then from the persons having the highest numbers not exceeding three on the list of those voted for as President, the House of Representatives shall choose immediately, by ballot, the President.

But in choosing the President, the votes shall be taken by states, the representation from each state having one vote; a quorum for this purpose shall consist of a member or members from two-thirds of the states, and a majority of all the states shall be necessary to a choice. And if the House of Representatives shall not choose a President whenever the right of choice shall devolve upon them, before the fourth day of March next following, then the Vice President shall act as President, as in the case of the death or other constitutional disability of the President. The person having the greatest number of votes as Vice President, shall be the Vice President, if such number be a majority of the whole number of Electors appointed, and if no person have a majority, then from the two highest numbers on the list, the Senate shall choose the Vice President; a quorum for the purpose shall consist of two-thirds of the whole number of Senators, and a majority of the whole number shall be necessary to a choice. But no person constitutionally ineligible to the office of President shall be eligible to that of Vice President of the United States.

What it means

Amendment XI. This amendment limits the jurisdiction of the federal courts. A private citizen from one state cannot sue the government of another state in federal court. However, a citizen can sue a state government in a state court.

What it means

Amendment XII. The Twelfth Amendment corrected a problem that had arisen from Article II, Section 1, Clause 3. This amendment provides for the Electoral College to use separate ballots in voting for president and vice president. If no candidate for president receives a majority of electoral votes, the House of Representatives chooses the president. If no candidate for vice president receives a majority of electoral votes, the Senate elects the vice president.

Amendment XIII (1865)

Section 1

Neither slavery nor involuntary servitude, except as a punishment for crime whereof the party shall have been duly convicted, shall exist within the United States, or any place subject to their jurisdiction.

Section 2

Congress shall have power to enforce this article by appropriate legislation.

> *What it means*
>
> **Amendment XIII.** The Thirteenth Amendment freed all slaves and outlawed slavery. It also forbids involuntary servitude, or labor done against someone's will. However, it does not prevent wardens from making prisoners work.

Amendment XIV (1868)

Section 1

All persons born or naturalized in the United States, and subject to the jurisdiction thereof, are citizens of the United States and of the State wherein they reside.

No State shall make or enforce any law which shall abridge the privileges or immunities of citizens of the United States; nor shall any State deprive any person of life, liberty, or property, without due process of law; nor deny to any person within its jurisdiction the equal protection of the laws.

> *What it means*
>
> **Section 1.** The Fourteenth Amendment originally was intended to protect the legal rights of the freed slaves. Today it protects the rights of citizenship in general by prohibiting a state from depriving any person of life, liberty, or property without "due process of law." In addition, it states that all citizens have the right to equal protection of the law in all states.

Section 2

Representatives shall be apportioned among the several States according to their respective numbers, counting the whole number of persons in each State, excluding Indians not taxed. But when the right to vote at any election for the choice of electors for President and Vice President of the United States, Representatives in Congress, the Executive and Judicial officers of a State, or the members of the Legislature thereof, is denied to any of the male inhabitants of such State, being twenty-one years of age, and citizens of the United States, or in any way abridged, except for participation in rebellion, or other crime, the basis of representation therein shall be reduced in the proportion which the number of such male citizens shall bear to the whole number of male citizens twenty-one years of age in such State.

> *What it means*
>
> **Section 2.** This section reduced the number of members a state had in the House of Representatives if it denied its citizens the right to vote. Later civil rights laws and the Twenty-fourth Amendment guaranteed the vote to African Americans.

Section 3

No person shall be a Senator or Representative in Congress, or elector of President and Vice President, or hold any office, civil or military, under the United States, or under any State, who, having previously taken an oath, as a member of Congress, or as an officer of the United States, or as a member of any State legislature, or as an executive or judicial officer of any State, to support the Constitution of the United States, shall have engaged in insurrection or rebellion against the same, or given aid or comfort to the enemies thereof. But Congress may by a vote of two-thirds of each House, remove such disability.

> *What it means*
>
> **Section 3.** The leaders of the Confederacy were barred from state or federal offices unless Congress agreed to remove this ban. By the end of Reconstruction all but a few Confederate leaders were allowed to return to public life.

Section 4

The validity of the public debt of the United States, authorized by law, including debts incurred for payment of pensions and bounties for service in suppressing insurrection or rebellion, shall not be questioned. But neither the United States nor any State shall assume or pay any debt or obligation incurred in aid of insurrection or rebellion against the United States, or any claim for the loss or emancipation [*freedom from slavery*] of any slave; but all such debts, obligations and claims shall be held illegal and void.

> *What it means*
>
> **Section 4.** The public debt acquired by the federal government during the Civil War was valid and could not be questioned by the South. However, the debts of the Confederacy were declared to be illegal.

Section 5

The Congress shall have power to enforce, by appropriate legislation, the provisions of this article.

Amendment XV (1870)

Section 1

The right of citizens of the United States to vote shall not be denied or abridged by the United States or by any State on account of race, color, or previous condition of servitude.

Section 2

The Congress shall have power to enforce this article by appropriate legislation.

> *What it means*
>
> **Sections 1 and 2.** The Fifteenth Amendment prohibits the government from denying a person's right to vote on the basis of race. Despite the law, many states denied African Americans the right to vote by such means as poll taxes, literacy tests, and white primaries. During the 1950s and 1960s, Congress passed successively stronger laws to end racial discrimination in voting rights.

Amendment XVI (1913)

The Congress shall have power to lay and collect taxes on incomes, from whatever source derived, without apportionment [*dividing into portions*] among the several States and without regard to any census or enumeration.

Internal Revenue Service.

Courtesy of the Internal Revenue Service/ www.irs.gov

Amendment XVII (1913)

What it means

Section 1. The Seventeenth Amendment states that the people, instead of state legislatures, elect United States senators.

Section 1

The Senate of the United States shall be composed of two Senators from each State, elected by the people thereof, for six years; and each Senator shall have one vote. The electors in each State shall have the qualifications requisite for electors of the most numerous branch of the State legislatures.

Section 2

When vacancies [*offices or positions that are unfilled or unoccupied*] happen in the representation of any State in the Senate, the executive authority of such State shall issue writs of election to fill such vacancies: *Provided*, That the legislature of any State may empower the executive thereof to make temporary appointments until the people fill the vacancies by election as the legislature may direct.

Section 3

This amendment shall not be so construed as to affect the election or term of any Senator chosen before it becomes valid as part of the Constitution.

Amendment XVIII (1919)

What it means

Section 1. The Eighteenth Amendment prohibited the production, sale, or transportation of alcoholic beverages in the United States. Prohibition proved to be difficult to enforce. This amendment was later repealed by the Twenty-first Amendment.

Section 1

After one year from ratification of this article, the manufacture, sale, or transportation of intoxicating liquors within, the importation thereof into, or the exportation thereof from the United States and all territory subject to the jurisdiction thereof for beverage purposes is hereby prohibited.

Section 2

The Congress and the several States shall have concurrent power to enforce this article by appropriate legislation.

Section 3

This article shall be inoperative unless it shall have been ratified as an amendment to the Constitution by the legislatures of the several States, as provided in the Constitution, within seven years from the date of the submission hereof to the States by the Congress.

Amendment XIX (1920)

Section 1

The right of citizens of the United States to vote shall not be denied or abridged by the United States or by any State on account of sex.

Section 2

Congress shall have power by appropriate legislation to enforce the provisions of this article.

> *What it means*
>
> **Section 1.** The Nineteenth Amendment guaranteed women suffrage, or *the right to vote*. By then women had already won the right to vote in many state elections, but the amendment put their right to vote in all state and national elections on a constitutional basis.

Amendment XX (1933)

Section 1

The terms of the President and Vice President shall end at noon on the 20th day of January, and the terms of the Senators and Representatives at noon on the 3rd day of January, of the years in which such terms would have ended if this article had not been ratified; and the terms of their successors shall then begin.

> *What it means*
>
> **Section 1.** The Twentieth Amendment sets new dates for Congress to begin its term and for the inauguration of the president and vice president. Under the original Constitution, elected officials who retired or who had been defeated remained in office for several months. For the outgoing president, this period ran from November until March. Such outgoing officials had little influence and accomplished little, and they were called lame ducks because they were so inactive.

Section 2

The Congress shall assemble at least once in every year, and such meeting shall begin at noon on the 3rd day of January, unless they shall by law appoint a different day.

Section 3

If, at the time fixed for the beginning of the term of the President, the President elect shall have died, the Vice President elect shall become President. If a President shall not have been chosen before the time fixed for the beginning of his term, or if the President elect shall have failed to qualify, then the Vice President elect shall act as President until a President shall have qualified; and the Congress may by law provide for the case wherein neither a President elect nor a Vice President elect shall have qualified, declaring who shall then act as President, or the manner in which one who is to act shall be selected, and such person shall act accordingly until a President or Vice President shall have qualified.

> *What it means*
>
> **Section 3.** This section provides that if the president-elect dies before taking office, the vice president-elect becomes president. It also allows Congress to choose a person to act as president if neither the president-elect or the vice president-elect is qualified to take office.

John Tyler was the first vice president to become president when a chief executive died.

Courtesy of the Library of Congress/ www.loc.gov

What it means

Section 1. The Twenty-first Amendment repeals the Eighteenth Amendment. It is the only amendment ever passed to overturn an earlier amendment. It is also the only amendment ratified by special state conventions instead of state legislatures.

Section 4

The Congress may by law provide for the case of the death of any of the persons from whom the House of Representatives may choose a President whenever the right of choice shall have devolved upon them, and for the case of the death of any of the persons from whom the Senate may choose a Vice President whenever the right of choice shall have devolved upon them.

Section 5

Sections 1 and 2 shall take effect on the 15th day of October following the ratification of this article.

Section 6

This article shall be inoperative unless it shall have been ratified as an amendment to the Constitution by the legislatures of three-fourths of the several States within seven years from the date of its submission.

Amendment XXI (1933)

Section 1

The eighteenth article of amendment to the Constitution of the United States is hereby repealed.

Section 2

The transportation or importation into any State, Territory, or possession of the United States for delivery or use therein of intoxicating liquors, in violation of the laws thereof, is hereby prohibited.

Section 3

This article shall be inoperative unless it shall have been ratified as an amendment to the Constitution by conventions in the several States, as provided in the Constitution, within seven years from the date of the submission hereof to the States by the Congress.

Amendment XXII (1951)

Section 1

No person shall be elected to the office of the President more than twice, and no person who had held the office of President, or acted as President, for more than two years of a term to which some other person was elected President shall be elected to the office of the President more than once. But this Article shall not apply to any person holding the office of President when this Article was proposed by the Congress, and shall not prevent any person who may be holding the office of President, or acting as President, during the term within which this article becomes operative from holding the office of President or acting as President during the remainder of such term.

Section 2

This article shall be inoperative unless it shall have been ratified as an amendment to the Constitution by the legislatures of three-fourths of the several States within seven years from the date of its submission to the States by the Congress.

What it means

Section 1. The Twenty-second Amendment limits presidents to a maximum of two elected terms. It was passed largely as a reaction to Franklin D. Roosevelt's election to four terms between 1933 and 1945.

Presidential campaign buttons.
Images © grandeduc/Fotolia.com

Amendment XXIII (1961)

Section 1

The District constituting the seat of Government of the United States shall appoint in such manner as the Congress may direct:

A number of electors of President and Vice President equal to the whole number of Senators and Representatives in Congress to which the District would be entitled if it were a State, but in no event more than the least populous State; they shall be in addition to those appointed by the States, but they shall be considered, for the purposes of the election of President and Vice President, to be electors appointed by a State; and they shall meet in the District and perform such duties as provided by the twelfth article of amendment.

Section 2

The Congress shall have power to enforce this article by appropriate legislation.

What it means

Section 1. The Twenty-third Amendment allows citizens living in Washington, DC to vote for president and vice president, a right previously denied residents of the nation's capital. The District of Columbia now has three presidential electors, the number to which it would be entitled if it were a state.

Amendment XXIV (1964)

What it means

Section 1. The Twenty-fourth Amendment prohibits poll taxes in federal elections. Prior to the passage of this amendment, some states had used such taxes to keep low-income African Americans from voting. In 1966, the Supreme Court banned poll taxes in state elections as well.

Section 1

The right of citizens of the United States to vote in any primary or other election for President or Vice President, for electors for President or Vice President, or for Senator or Representative in Congress, shall not be denied or abridged by the United States or any State by reason of failure to pay any poll tax or other tax.

Section 2

The Congress shall have power to enforce this article by appropriate legislation.

Amendment XXV (1967)

What it means

Section 1. The Twenty-fifth Amendment established a process for the vice president to take over leadership of the nation when a president is disabled. It also set procedures for filling a vacancy in the office of vice president. This amendment was used in 1973, when Vice President Spiro Agnew resigned from office after being charged with accepting bribes. President Richard Nixon then appointed Gerald R. Ford as vice president in accordance with the provisions of the Twenty-fifth Amendment. A year later, President Nixon resigned during the Watergate scandal and Ford became president. President Ford then had to fill the vice presidency, which he had left vacant upon assuming the presidency. He named Nelson A. Rockefeller as vice president. Thus, individuals who had not been elected held both the presidency and the vice presidency.

Section 1

In case of the removal of the President from office or his death or resignation, the Vice President shall become President.

Section 2

Whenever there is a vacancy in the office of the Vice President, the President shall nominate a Vice President who shall take the office upon confirmation by a majority vote of both Houses of Congress.

Section 3

Whenever the President transmits to the President pro tempore of the Senate and the Speaker of the House of Representatives his written declaration that he is unable to discharge the powers and duties of his office, and until he transmits to them a written declaration to the contrary, such powers and duties shall be discharged by the Vice President as Acting President.

Section 4

Whenever the Vice President and a majority of either the principal officers of the executive departments or of such other body as Congress may by law provide, transmit to the President pro tempore of the Senate and the Speaker of the House of Representatives their written declaration that the President is unable to discharge the powers and duties of his office, the Vice President shall immediately assume the power and duties of the office of Acting President.

Vice President Gerald Ford became President Gerald Ford.

Courtesy of the Library of Congress/www.log.gov

Thereafter, when the President transmits to the President pro tempore of the Senate and the Speaker of the House of Representatives his written declaration that no inability exists, he shall resume the powers and duties of his office unless the Vice President and a majority of either the principal officers of the executive department or of such other body as Congress may by law provide, transmit within four days to the President pro tempore of the Senate and the Speaker of the House of Representatives their written declaration that the President is unable to discharge the powers and duties of his office. Thereupon Congress shall decide the issue, assembling within forty-eight hours for that purpose if not in session. If the Congress, within twenty-one days after receipt of the latter written declaration, or, if Congress is not in session, within twenty-one days after Congress is required to assemble, determines by two-thirds vote of both Houses that the President is unable to discharge the powers and duties of his office, the Vice President shall continue to discharge the same as Acting President; otherwise, the President shall resume the power and duties of his office.

What it means

Section 4. This section provides that the vice president and Cabinet may declare the president disabled. The vice president becomes the acting president until the president can return to the duties of the office. If the president, vice president, and Cabinet disagree over the president's abilities, then Congress must decide. A two-thirds majority is required in both houses to show the president is disabled or unable to fulfill the duties of the office. When President Ronald Reagan was shot 70 days after taking office, Vice President George H.W. Bush met with cabinet members and decided not to invoke section 4 of the Twenty-fifth amendment.

Amendment XXVI (1971)

Section 1

The right of citizens of the United States, who are eighteen years of age or older, to vote shall not be denied or abridged by the United States or by any State on account of age.

Section 2

The Congress shall have power to enforce this article by appropriate legislation.

What it means

Section 1. The Twenty-sixth Amendment lowered the voting age in both federal elections to 18. However, the Supreme Court decided that Congress could not set a minimum age for state elections.

What it means

Amendment XXVII. If members of Congress vote themselves a pay increase, it cannot go into effect until after the next congressional election. James Madison offered the amendment in 1789, but it was never adopted. In 1982 Gregory Watson, then a student at the University of Texas, discovered the forgotten amendment while doing research for a school paper. Watson made the amendment's passage his crusade.

Amendment XXVII (1992)

No law, varying the compensation for the services of Senators and Representatives, shall take effect, until an election of representatives shall have intervened.

Joint Session of Congress.
Courtesy of the Library of Congress/www.loc.gov

How the Constitution Is Interpreted

Although the Constitution has been amended only 27 times, there have been many other changes to it. These changes have taken place through interpretation, or *a particular meaning or significance to something*. The framers of the Constitution wrote a general document, so many matters are left open to interpretation.

The Necessary and Proper Clause

Article I of the Constitution lists the powers of Congress. Within it, Congress is given the power "to make all Laws which shall be necessary and proper" to carry out its duties. This "necessary and proper clause" allows Congress to exercise powers that are not specifically listed in the Constitution. These powers are known as "implied powers."

Many Americans, though, do not agree about which laws are "necessary and proper." Some people feel Congress should be allowed to make any laws the Constitution does not specifically forbid. These people believe in a loose interpretation of the Constitution. Others believe in a strict interpretation. They feel Congress should make only the kinds of laws mentioned by the Constitution.

Interpretation Through Court Decisions

The Supreme Court has the final authority on interpreting the Constitution. Over the years, the Supreme Court has interpreted the Constitution in different ways—sometimes strictly, sometimes loosely. With each new interpretation, government policies change. The impact on American life is also felt in some way.

Interpretation Through Congressional and Presidential Actions

Actions taken by Congress and the president have also caused new interpretations of the Constitution. The Constitution allows the House of Representatives to impeach, or accuse, federal officials, while the Senate determines the person's guilt or innocence. Congress has investigated more than 60 people on impeachment charges, however, less than one-third have led to full impeachments.

How has the president interpreted the Constitution? In 1841, William Henry Harrison became the first president to die in office. Vice President John Tyler assumed the powers of the president according to the Constitution. The Constitution, however, was unclear on this matter. Did Tyler automatically become president, or was he merely acting as president until the next election? Tyler went ahead and took the presidential oath. Not until 1967, when the Twenty-fifth Amendment was ratified, was Tyler's action officially part of the Constitution.

Presidents interpret the Constitution in other ways, too. The president makes agreements with other countries without congressional approval. The president may also request legislative action by Congress on certain matters. The Constitution does not direct the president to take these actions.

Interpretation Through Custom

The interpretation of the Constitution has also changed through customs that have developed over time. For example, the Constitution does not mention political parties. Yet, they are a very important part of today's political system. Today, parties help organize the government and conduct elections. The government under the Constitution today is very different from the government set up by the Constitution in 1787. It will probably go through many more changes, too. However, the basic structure and principles of our government—a delicate balance between three branches—will no doubt remain.

Lesson 3 Review

Using complete sentences, answer the following questions on a sheet of paper.

1. When the US Constitution was written, what four areas formed the basis for our democracy?
2. What does the Preamble to the US Constitution establish and declare?
3. What do the seven articles that follow the Preamble explain?
4. What do the first three articles of the Constitution explain?
5. What is a framer of the Constitution?
6. How many amendments have been added to the Constitution?
7. What are the two steps involved for an amendment to the Constitution?
8. What is meant by the term "quartered"?
9. What did the Sixteenth Amendment to the Constitution give to Congress?
10. Although the Constitution has been amended only 27 times, there have been many other changes to it. How have these other changes taken place?
11. Who has the final authority on interpreting the Constitution?
12. When William Henry Harrison died in office, what situation was created that caused the need for the Twenty-fifth Amendment?

APPLYING YOUR LEARNING

13. The Constitution has stood the test of time and the many changes to the leadership of our government over its 225-plus years. Which article or amendment to the Constitution do you think has had the greatest impact on our country? In a short paragraph, explain your answer.

LESSON 4

Interpreting the Bill of Rights and Other Amendments

Quick Write

As American citizens, we have many rights. List some of the rights that are important to you.

"The rights of persons, and the rights of property, are the objects, for the protection of which Government was instituted."

James Madison, Fourth President of the United States and writer of the Bill of Rights

Learn About

- protections of individual freedoms
- protecting the rights of the accused
- protecting other rights
- protecting all Americans

Why We Have the Bill of Rights and Other Amendments

As discussed in the previous lesson about our Constitution, the founders of the United States believed that protecting individual rights and providing for the safety and well-being of citizens were important purposes of government. During the struggle to get states to ratify the Constitution, many representatives criticized it for giving the government too much power. To answer this criticism, the framers agreed to add a Bill of Rights as soon as the new government was established. The Constitution might not have been ratified had the Bill of Rights not been promised. Added in 1791, the 10 amendments in the Bill of Rights place strict limits on how the national government can use its power over the people. The Bill of Rights protects our civil liberties—*the freedoms we have to think and act without government interference or fear of unfair treatment.*

Protections of Individual Freedoms

The Bill of Rights spells out basic rights that are protected under our form of government. These rights fall into four main categories: individual freedoms, rights of people accused of crimes, protecting other rights, and finally, protecting all Americans. The first area we will discuss is our protections of individual freedoms.

In the 20th century, the Bill of Rights has become something it never was in the 18th century. It is, perhaps, the most important single document protecting individual rights. The struggle to extend its protections to all Americans has taken more than 200 hundred years, however, and the struggle continues today.

Vocabulary

- civil liberties
- censorship
- extracurricular
- petition
- slander
- libel
- search warrant
- grand jury
- double jeopardy
- self-incrimination
- testimony
- due process
- eminent domain
- forfeited
- arms
- federalism
- socialism
- Quakers
- temperance
- poll taxes
- discrimination
- segregation
- civil rights
- affirmative action

First Amendment Freedoms (1791)

> *Congress shall make no law respecting an establishment of religion, or prohibiting the free exercise thereof; or abridging the freedom of speech, or of the press; or the right of the people peaceably to assemble, and to petition the Government for a redress of grievances.*

The First Amendment to the Constitution protects five basic freedoms: freedom of religion, freedom of speech, freedom of the press, freedom of assembly, and freedom to petition the government. Sometimes referred to as the freedom of expression, this amendment protects an individual's right to expression of deep convictions.

These civil liberties are the cornerstone of our democracy. They ensure that each of us can develop our own beliefs, express ourselves freely, meet openly with others, and have our views on public matters heard by those who govern (Figure 5.4).

Freedom of Religion

Intolerance of different beliefs in their homelands forced many colonists to come to America in the first place. To safeguard religious freedom, the First Amendment prohibits Congress from establishing an official religion in the United States. It protects the freedom of Americans to practice their faith as they wish or not to practice any religion at all. The government may not favor one religion over another or treat people differently because of their personal beliefs.

The First Amendment says the government may not "establish" religion; this affects public schools. The Supreme Court has struck down teacher-led prayer in public schools because students are impressionable young people and they are a captive audience required by the state to attend school. The Supreme Court often emphasizes that schools be religious-neutral. This means that public schools may neither promote nor restrict religion. They also may not prefer one religion over another.

Freedom of Speech

In some countries, people can be jailed for criticizing the government or voicing unpopular ideas, even if they do so only in private conversations. In the United States, however, the First Amendment guarantees that we can say what is on our minds, in public or in private, without fear of punishment by the government.

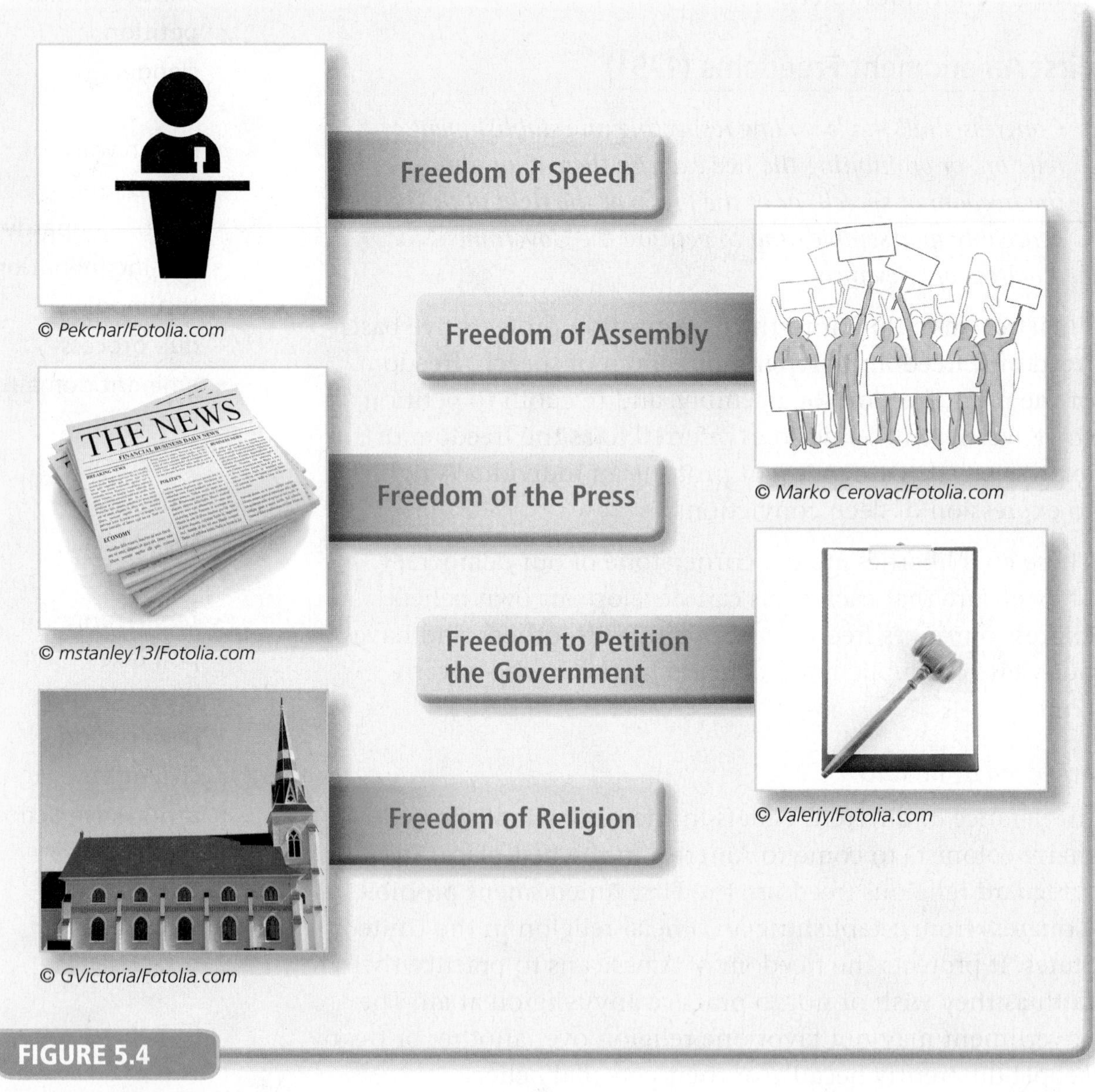

FIGURE 5.4

First Amendment Freedoms

Face-to-face discussions, telephone conversations, lectures, and radio and TV broadcasts are covered by the guarantee of free speech; so are other forms of expression besides the spoken word. As interpreted by the Supreme Court, "speech" can mean Internet communication, art, music, or even clothing.

In 1965, for example, 13-year-old Mary Beth Tinker (*Tinker v. Des Moines Independent School District*) and two other students wore black armbands to school to mourn those who died in the Vietnam War. School authorities suspended them for wearing the armbands, and the teens eventually took their case to the Supreme Court. In its landmark 1969 decision, the Court ruled that the armbands were a form of speech protected by the First Amendment.

The Bill of Rights guards against censorship.

© iQoncept/Fotolia.com

This Supreme Court ruling means that school officials may not silence student expression just because they dislike it. They must reasonably determine, based on evidence, that the student expression would lead to either substantial disruption of the school environment or an invasion of the rights of others. Read more about *Tinker v. Des Moines Independent School District* on page 480.

Freedom of the Press

The First Amendment allows Americans to express themselves in print as well as in speech. When the Bill of Rights was written, "the press" referred to printed publications such as books, newspapers, and magazines. Today the press includes many other sources of media, such as radio, television, social media, and Internet websites (*Reno v. American Civil Liberties Union*, 1997). Freedom of the press ensures that the American people are exposed to a wide variety of viewpoints. The government cannot practice censorship. Censorship includes *banning printed materials or films just because they contain alarming or offensive ideas*. The government also cannot censor information before it is published or broadcast.

School safety is arguably the single most compelling interest of all communities. Therefore, courts have become increasingly respectful of school safety concerns. Within limits, public schools have discretion in enforcing speech codes, especially involving harassment and bullying. Such codes are provided to create a safe environment where all students are comfortable and free to learn.

Freedom of Assembly

The First Amendment protects our right to gather in groups for any reason, so long as the assemblies are peaceful. We have the right to attend meetings, parades, political rallies, and public celebrations. Governments may make rules about when and where such activities can be held, but they cannot ban them.

The Supreme Court has decided that freedom of assembly implies freedom of association. Therefore, the First Amendment also protects our right to form and join social clubs, political parties, labor unions, and other organizations. Even if we never assemble with fellow members, we have the right to belong to such groups.

If schools allow any other extracurricular groups such as Key Club, Interact, Speech, or Debate clubs, they must also allow religious, political, or social awareness clubs on campus. Extracurricular refers to *groups or activities not considered as part of a normal school day or curriculum.*

Thomas Jefferson

© Daniel Watt/Fotolia.com

Thomas Jefferson was an outspoken supporter of Americans' personal freedoms. In a letter to Colonel Edward Carrington, dated January 16, 1787, Jefferson wrote, "[W]ere it left to me to decide whether we should have a government without newspapers, or newspapers without a government, I should not hesitate a moment to prefer the latter." In his lifetime, Jefferson took full advantage of the freedom of the press. He wrote and published dozens of articles and papers to express his views and to encourage his fellow citizens to think and act according to their beliefs.

Freedom to Petition the Government

Finally, the First Amendment guarantees all Americans the right to petition the government. A petition is simply *a formal request*. Often we use the word to refer to a specific kind of document—a brief, written statement signed by hundreds or thousands of people. Even a simple letter or e-mail written by an individual, however, could be considered a petition.

Many early colonists and immigrants throughout history came to the United States so they could freely practice religion.

The right to petition means the right to express one's ideas to the government. If you want to complain about overcrowded schools, for example, or suggest that a skating park be built in your community, you can write to your elected representatives. If enough people express similar views, government leaders may take action.

Limits to First Amendment Freedoms

The Supreme Court has decided that compelling public interests—the safety and security of Americans—may justify limitations on our First Amendment freedoms. Freedom of speech, for example, does not include the right to endanger our government or other Americans. You do not have freedom to provoke a riot or other violent behavior. You are not free to speak or write in a way that immediately leads to criminal activities or efforts to overthrow the government by force.

Citizens should use their civil liberties responsibly, which means they should not interfere with the rights of others. For example, you are free to talk with your friends in the street, but you must not block traffic. You may campaign for causes, but you may not disturb your neighbors with blaring loudspeaker broadcasts. You may criticize government officials, but you may not spread lies that harm a person's reputation.

Spreading such lies is a crime called slander *if the lies are spoken* and libel *if they are printed*.

The First Amendment was never intended to allow Americans to do whatever they please. Unlimited freedom is not possible in a society of many people. The rights of one individual must be balanced against the rights of others and against the rights of the community. When there is a conflict, the rights of the community often come first. Otherwise, the society would break apart.

Tinker v. Des Moines Independent Community School District

Courtesy of United States Courts/www.uscourts.gov

Background of the Case

Division over the war in Vietnam racked the nation during the 1960s. Millions of Americans agreed with the war, while many other millions disagreed. Protests occurred frequently. One night in December 1965, a group of public school students, led by high school sophomores Christopher Eckhardt and John Tinker and eighth grader Mary Beth Tinker, planned their own protest. They decided to wear black armbands to school as silent expressions of mourning for deaths on both sides of the war. As other students joined the armband protest, principals and members of the school board met the growing protest with a ban on armbands—to prevent "disturbing influences."

On December 16, 1965, Christopher, John, and Mary Beth were suspended for wearing their armbands to school. Their parents protested the suspensions in federal courts. They contended the students' First Amendment free speech rights had been violated.

The Decision

On February 24, 1969, the United States Supreme Court, in a 7–2 decision, declared the school suspensions unconstitutional. Justice Abe Fortas, who wrote the majority opinion, first established the students' action was "akin to pure speech." Even though their protest involved no speaking, it deserved "protection under the First Amendment." He wrote, "It can hardly be argued that either students or teachers shed their constitutional rights to freedom of speech or expression at the schoolhouse gate."

Why It Matters

Supporters saluted the decision. Critics predicted harmful consequences. Dissenter Justice Hugo Black suggested the Court's decision was "the beginning of a new revolutionary era or permissiveness in this country fostered by the judiciary." He argued that no one has a complete right to freedom of speech and expression.

Protecting the Rights of the Accused

The First Amendment freedoms you have just read about are among our most important civil liberties. Equally precious, however, is the right to fair legal treatment. This is the subject of several amendments in the Bill of Rights.

Suppose someone accuses you of committing a crime. In some countries, government agents might ransack your home, drag you off to jail, beat you, and hold a trial without even letting you respond to the charges. In the United States, the Fourth, Fifth, Sixth, and Eighth Amendments help prevent such a scenario from occurring.

The Fourth Amendment (1791)

The right of the people to be secure in their persons, houses, papers, and effects, against unreasonable searches and seizures, shall not be violated, and no Warrants shall issue, but upon probable cause, supported by Oath or affirmation, and particularly describing the place to be searched, and the persons or things to be seized.

Searches and Seizures. During the years leading up to the American Revolution, tensions between England and the colonies were very high. The British Parliament, England's legislative body, allowed British officers unlimited search and seizure authority of colonial property. Homes and businesses could be searched without warning.

Are School Lockers Private?

The Fourth Amendment is an important safeguard against "unreasonable searches and seizures." This amendment protects Americans from unlawful searches by the police. However, you, as a student, are not protected in the same way. In the case of *New Jersey v. T.L.O.*, the Supreme Court ruled that the Fourth Amendment's warrant requirement "is unsuited to the school environment." The Constitution includes other amendments that protect the rights of Americans accused of crimes.

© Andres Rodriguez/Fotolia.com

The Fourth Amendment protects Americans "against unreasonable searches and seizures." No soldier, government agent, or police officer can search your home or take your property without good cause.

However, if law enforcement officers believe you have committed a crime, they can ask a judge to issue a search warrant. A search warrant is *a court order allowing law enforcement officers to search a suspect's home or business and take specific items as evidence.*

Judges do not give out search warrants readily. They must be convinced that a search will probably turn up evidence of criminal activity. If warrants were issued frivolously, the Fourth Amendment would give us little sense of security. Any time of the day or night, the police could invade our privacy and confiscate our possessions.

The Fifth Amendment (1791)

No person shall be held to answer for a capital, or otherwise infamous crime, unless on a presentment or indictment of a Grand Jury, except in cases arising in the land or naval forces, or in the Militia, when in actual service in time of War or public danger; nor shall any person be subject for the same offence to be twice put in jeopardy of life or limb; nor shall be compelled in any criminal case to be a witness against himself, nor be deprived of life, liberty, or property, without due process of law; nor shall private property be taken for public use without just compensation.

Rights of the Accused. The Fifth Amendment protects the rights of people accused of crimes. It states that no one can be put on trial for a serious federal crime without an indictment, or formal charge. The charge is made by the grand jury, which is *a group of citizens who make the indictment and review the evidence against the accused.*

A person who is indicted is not necessarily guilty of a crime. An indictment simply indicates the grand jury's belief that an individual may have committed a crime. This provision protects people from being brought to trial hastily and perhaps needlessly.

The Fifth Amendment also protects people from double jeopardy. This means that *people who are accused of a crime and judged not guilty may not be put on trial again for the same crime.*

In addition, the Fifth Amendment protects an accused person's right to remain silent. Throughout history, innocent people have been threatened, tortured, or bullied into confessing to crimes they did not commit. To prevent this, the Fifth Amendment states that people cannot be forced to testify against themselves. This is called protection against self-incrimination, *a speech or action that suggests your own guilt, especially during court testimony.* Testimony is *the evidence that a witness gives in a court of law.* This is why you may hear someone state in a courtroom that they "take the fifth," or you may hear them say "I refuse to answer on the grounds that it may incriminate me" or "make me appear guilty." Figure 5.5 discusses the rights of the accused more.

FIFTH AMENDMENT

- No trial may be held unless a person is formally charged, or indicted by a grand jury.
- A person found not guilty may not be put on trial again for the same crime.
- Accused persons may not be forced to testify against themselves.
- Every person is entitled to due process of law.
- No one may be deprived of their property by the government without compensation.

SIXTH AMENDMENT

- The accused must be informed of the nature of the charges.
- The accused must be allowed a speedy and public trial by an impartial jury.
- If possible, the trial must be held in the area where the crime took place.
- The accused must be permitted to hear and question all witnesses.
- The accused is entitled to a lawyer and to call witnesses for his or her defense.

FIGURE 5.5

Rights of the Accused

The Fifth Amendment goes on to say that no one may be denied life, liberty, or property "without due process of law." Due process means *following established legal procedures*. It also includes the idea that the laws themselves must be reasonable.

Finally, the Fifth Amendment protects citizens' property rights by limiting the government's power of eminent domain. Eminent domain is *the right of the government to take private property—usually land—for public use*. For example, if your home lies in the path of a proposed highway, the government may legally take the land and destroy your house. Under the Fifth Amendment, however, the government must pay you a fair price for the property.

The Sixth Amendment (1791)

In all criminal prosecutions, the accused shall enjoy the right to a speedy and public trial, by an impartial jury of the State and district wherein the crime shall have been committed, which district shall have been previously ascertained by law, and to be informed of the nature and cause of the accusation; to be confronted with the witnesses against him; to have compulsory process for obtaining Witnesses in his favor, and to have the assistance of counsel for his defence.

Criminal Proceedings. The Sixth Amendment gives additional due process rights to people accused of crimes. It requires that they be told the exact nature of the charges against them. It also guarantees them the right to a fair, speedy, public trial by jury, although they may ask to be tried by only a judge instead. If possible, the trial should be held in the same district where the crime took place.

Accused individuals have the right to hear and question all witnesses against them. They must also be permitted to call witnesses in their own defense. Finally, they are entitled to have a lawyer. Since the Sixth Amendment was written, the Supreme Court has ruled that if an accused person cannot afford a lawyer, the government must provide one and pay his or her fees.

The Sixth and Seventh amendments reflect the belief that a trial by jury is important if people have trust and confidence in the law. The work of courts is open to public view and public participation. When people serve as jurors, they help to make sure that their fellow citizens are treated fairly. We'll discuss the Seventh Amendment in more detail later in the lesson.

The Eighth Amendment (1791)

Excessive bail shall not be required, nor excessive fines imposed, nor cruel and unusual punishments inflicted.

Punishment for Crimes. Although the Sixth Amendment guarantees a speedy trial, sometimes months go by before a case can be heard. During that time, the accused may have two choices: stay in jail or remain free by paying bail. If the accused person comes to court for the trial, the bail is returned. If the person fails to appear, the bail is forfeited. Forfeited is *when something is taken away as a penalty for breaking a contract.*

The judge decides how much bail a person must pay, and may deny a request to pay bail. Judges consider various factors, including the type of crime committed, the record of the accused person, the likelihood that he or she will appear in court, and what he or she can afford. The Eighth Amendment, however, forbids "excessive" bail—that is, an amount that is much too high.

John Marshall (1755-1835)

John Marshall, the fourth Chief Justice of the US Supreme Court, was a significant influence in establishing the Supreme Court's role in federal government as a center of power in determining how the Constitution, including the Bill of Rights and other amendments, is interpreted and applied. Marshall was Chief Justice of the United States, serving from February 4, 1801, until his death in 1835. The longest serving Chief Justice in Supreme Court history, Marshall played a significant role in the development of the American legal system, especially in establishing that the courts have the power to strike down laws that violate the Constitution. One of his most memorable quotes is "The Constitution is colorblind, and neither knows nor tolerates classes among citizens."

Courtesy of www.capitol.gov

The Eighth Amendment also forbids excessive fines for people convicted of crimes. In addition, it forbids "cruel and unusual punishments." For many years, Americans have debated what kinds of punishment are cruel and unusual. It is generally agreed that punishment should be in proportion to the crime committed. For example, a sentence of life imprisonment for stealing a loaf of bread would be too harsh. People disagree strongly, however, about whether the death penalty for very serious crimes is cruel and unusual punishment.

Protecting Other Rights

In addition to the First Amendment freedoms and due process guarantees, the Bill of Rights includes other protections for American citizens.

The Second Amendment (1791)

> *A well-regulated Militia, being necessary to the security of a free State, the right of the people to keep and bear Arms, shall not be infringed.*

Right to Possess Firearms. When this amendment was written, the American Revolution was fresh on the minds of citizens. Americans remember the important role that armed militias played in defeating the powerful British armies and gaining independence.

Throughout our history, Americans have debated the exact meaning guaranteed by the Second Amendment. Some argue that it provides only for each state to maintain "a well-regulated militia" by allowing the members of those militias to carry arms, or *weapons equipping a person or army*. When the Second Amendment was written, a militia was a small, local army made up of volunteer soldiers. Militias helped to win America's war with Great Britain.

Other people hold that the Second Amendment guarantees the right of all individual citizens to "keep and bear arms" without the interference of the government. The courts have generally ruled that the government can pass laws to control, but not prevent, the possession of weapons. For example, federal and state laws determine who can be licensed to own firearms.

Lawmakers continue to discuss the extent of our right to bear arms today. They also debate the kinds of gun regulations that may be necessary for public safety.

The Third Amendment (1791)

No Soldier shall, in time of peace be quartered in any house, without the consent of the Owner, nor in time of war, but in a manner to be prescribed by law.

Housing of Troops. One cause of the American Revolution was the colonists' resentment of the law requiring them to house and feed British soldiers. The Third Amendment makes it unlikely that Americans will ever be forced to shelter the military again. The amendment says that, in peacetime, soldiers may not move into private homes without the consent of the homeowner. In times of war, Congress must authorize the practice.

The Seventh Amendment (1791)

In Suits at common law where the value in controversy shall exceed twenty dollars, the right of trial by jury shall be preserved, and no fact tried by a jury, shall be otherwise reexamined in any Court of the United States, than according to the rules of common law.

Civil Trials. The Fifth, Sixth, and Eighth Amendments deal with people's rights in criminal cases. The Seventh Amendment concerns civil cases—lawsuits that involve disagreements between people rather than crimes. If you were disputing a contract, for example, or claiming that a doctor had not treated you properly, you could initiate a civil suit.

The Seventh Amendment permits jury trails in cases where there are conflicts over property or money, as long as the value in dispute is greater than twenty dollars. This is one reason why small claims courts were established. Small claims courts handle private disputes without tying up too many courtrooms. Each state places limits on the dollar amount that can be disputed.

Then Federal District Judge Sonia Sotomayor of New York, now a member of the Supreme Court, issued the ruling that ended the professional baseball players' strike in 1995. The Seventh Amendment states that the players could have settled their case by a jury trial.

Courtesy of the US Supreme Court/www.supremecourt.gov

The Ninth Amendment (1791)

The enumeration in the Constitution, of certain rights, shall not be construed to deny or disparage others retained by the people.

Powers of the People. The men who wrote the Bill of Rights realized that they could not spell out every right of the American people. The Ninth Amendment makes it clear that citizens have other rights beyond those listed in the Constitution. These unwritten rights are just as valuable and may not be taken away.

The right to privacy, for example, is not mentioned in the Constitution. However, the Supreme Court has drawn on the First, Fourth, Fifth, and Ninth Amendments to uphold this right. Because of these rulings, we enjoy privacy in our homes, confidentiality in our medical and financial records, and freedom from government interference in our personal choices regarding friends, families, and careers.

The Tenth Amendment (1791)

The powers not delegated to the United States by the Constitution, nor prohibited by it to the States, are reserved to the States respectively, or to the people.

Powers of the States. The Constitution discusses certain powers of the national and state governments. Many other powers of government—such as the authority to set up schools and license lawyers—are not mentioned at all.

Under the Tenth Amendment, any powers the Constitution does not specifically give to the national government are reserved to the states or to the people. In this way, the Tenth Amendment prevents Congress and the president from becoming too strong. The government of the United States can have only the powers the people give it.

As discussed in the previous lesson, the people who originally supported the Constitution called themselves Federalists. They chose this name to emphasize that the Constitution would create a system of **federalism**, *a form of government in which power is divided between the federal, or national, government and the states.*

Protecting All Americans

The Bill of Rights was passed to safeguard individual liberties. However, the rights guaranteed to all Americans have not always been applied equally and fairly. The Bill of Rights was intended originally to restrain only the national government. For many years, local and state governments were not bound by its terms. As a result, states sometimes used their reserved powers to pass laws that violated civil liberties. In most parts of the country, for example, women and African Americans could not vote to elect representatives in government. Before 1865, many states had laws that sanctioned and approved slavery for African Americans, who were treated as property and had no rights at all.

Gradually, however, the Bill of Rights came to cover all Americans equally and to limit government power at all levels. Additional amendments to the Constitution (Figure 5.6) and court rulings both played a part in this process.

Three amendments were passed after the Civil War ended in 1865 to extend civil liberties to African Americans. The promise of these Civil War amendments, as they are known, was not fulfilled, however, for almost 100 years. Many states were slow to change their customs; some actively resisted. The federal government, including the Supreme Court, often seemed indifferent. Nonetheless, the Civil War amendments signaled a move toward greater equality.

William Lloyd Garrison

Even as a teenager, William Lloyd Garrison's dedication to the abolition of slavery was apparent. As a newspaper apprentice, and later as the owner of his own newspapers, ending slavery was nearly his sole concern. In the first edition of *The Liberator*, published in 1831, Garrison promised his readers, "I am in earnest—I will not equivocate—I will not excuse—I will not retreat a single inch—AND I WILL BE HEARD." Thirty-four years later came proof that Garrison's words had been heard when the Thirteenth Amendment was passed.

Courtesy of the Library of Congress/www.loc.gov

Amendment	Date	Purpose
11	1795	Removed cases in which a state was sued without its consent from the jurisdiction of the federal courts
12	1804	Required presidential electors to vote separately for president and vice president
13	1865	Abolished slavery and authorized Congress to pass legislation implementing its abolition
14	1868	Granted citizenship to all persons born or naturalized in the United States; banned states from denying any person life, liberty, or property without due process of law; and banned states from denying any person equal protection under the laws
15	1870	Guaranteed voting rights to African Americans by outlawing denial of the right to vote on the basis of race, color, or previous condition of servitude
16	1913	Empowered Congress to levy an income tax
17	1913	Provided for the election of US senators by direct popular vote instead of by state legislatures
18	1919	Authorized Congress to prohibit the manufacture, sale, and transportation of liquor
19	1920	Guaranteed the right to vote to women
20	1933	Shortened the time between a presidential election and inauguration by designating January 20 as Inauguration Day; set January 3 as the date for the opening of a new Congress
21	1933	Repealed the Eighteenth Amendment and empowered Congress to regulate the liquor industry
22	1951	Limited presidents to two full terms in office
23	1961	Granted voters in the District of Columbia the right to vote for president and vice president
24	1964	Forbade requiring the payment of a poll tax to vote in a federal election
25	1967	Provided for succession to the office of president in the event of death or incapacity and for filling vacancies in the office of the vice president
26	1971	Guaranteed the right to vote to 18-year-olds
27	1992	Banned Congress from increasing its members' salaries until after the next election

Amendments changing the powers of the national and state governments

Amendments changing the government structure or function

Amendments extending the suffrage and powers of voters

FIGURE 5.6

Constitutional Amendments 11 to 27

The Thirteenth Amendment (1865)

Section 1

Neither slavery nor involuntary servitude, except as a punishment for crime whereof the party shall have been duly convicted, shall exist within the United States, or any place subject to their jurisdiction.

Abolishment of Slavery. The Thirteenth Amendment officially outlawed slavery in the United States and thus freed thousands of African Americans. It also outlawed any sort of forced labor, except as punishment for a crime.

The Constitution now banned slavery. But the struggle of citizenship and voting rights had only just begun for African Americans. Freedom from slavery did not mean equality. For one thing, state governments still held the right to determine who could be a citizen of a state, and many states continued to deny citizenship to African Americans. Additionally, states passed "black codes" that kept African Americans from holding certain jobs, limited their property rights, and restricted them in other ways.

The Fourteenth Amendment (1868)

Section 1

All persons born or naturalized in the United States, and subject to the jurisdiction thereof, are citizens of the United States and of the State wherein they reside. No State shall make or enforce any law which shall abridge the privileges or immunities of citizens of the United States; nor shall any State deprive any person of life, liberty, or property, without due process of law; nor deny to any person within its jurisdiction the equal protection of the laws.

Rights of Citizens. To prevent states from denying citizenship and other rights to African Americans, the Fourteenth Amendment was passed in 1868. It defined a United States citizen as anyone "born or naturalized in the United States," a definition that included most African Americans. The amendment also required every state to grant its citizens "equal protection of the laws." This clause has been extremely important. In recent years, it has been used to benefit women, people with disabilities, and other groups whose rights have not always been protected fairly.

Another element of the Fourteenth Amendment forbids state governments from interfering with the "privileges or immunities of citizens of the United States." Further, state governments may not take an individual's "life, liberty, or property, without due process of law or equal protection of the law." The intent of these provisions was to make the Bill of Rights binding for state governments as well as the federal government. This is called the nationalization of the Bill of Rights.

For many years, however, the Supreme Court ignored this interpretation of the Fourteenth Amendment. Finally, in 1925, the Supreme Court ruled in *Gitlow v. New York* that the Fourteenth Amendment could safeguard free speech and a free press "from impairment by the states." Benjamin Gitlow was a member of the American Socialist party, promoting immediate attempts to bring socialism to America, including the use of violence if needed. Socialism is *a political system in which property and wealth are controlled by the citizens and evenly distributed.*

Since the Gitlow case, the Supreme Court has used the Fourteenth Amendment to apply other rights in the Bill of Rights to the states. This "incorporation" of the Bill of Rights by the Fourteenth Amendment's due process clause means that US citizens in every part of the country have the same basic rights. A string of later cases further extended the reach of the Bill of Rights. By the end of the 1960s, most protections in the Bill of Rights were considered to apply at the state level.

The Fifteenth Amendment (1870)

Section 1

The right of citizens of the United States to vote shall not be denied or abridged by the United States or by any State on account of race, color, or previous condition of servitude.

Right to Vote. The last of the Civil War amendments, the Fifteenth, says that no state may take away a person's voting rights on the basis of race, color, or previous enslavement. The amendment clearly aimed to guarantee suffrage, "the right to vote," to African Americans. Still, many states found ways to keep African Americans away from the polls.

The Fifteenth Amendment protected only men in practice. The various states had the power to decide whether women could vote. Women, regardless of their race, could not vote in most federal or state elections.

The Nineteenth Amendment (1920)

Section 1

The right of citizens of the United States to vote shall not be denied or abridged by the United States or by any State on account of sex.

Women's Right to Vote. Although the Constitution did not guarantee women the right to vote, it did not directly deny them suffrage. As a result, states made their own laws on the matter, using the powers reserved to them under the Tenth Amendment. The territory of Wyoming permitted women to vote in 1869, and several other territories and states did so as well in the years that followed.

However, national support for woman suffrage was slow in coming. Leaders like Susan B. Anthony and Elizabeth Cady Stanton had insisted as early as 1848 that women belonged at the polls. It was not until 1920, however, that the Nineteenth Amendment protected the right of women to vote in all national and state elections.

Susan B. Anthony (1820–1906)

Susan B. Anthony was a prominent women's rights activist in 19th-century America who initiated the women's suffrage movement. She was also active in the anti-slavery movement before the Civil War. Raised in a Quaker family, she spent much of her life working on social causes. Quakers are *a Christian group whose members avoid violence and hold simple religious services*. Her activities were wide-ranging, from the elimination of slavery and the securing of voting rights to women to the temperance movement, which focused on *reducing the sale and use of alcohol*.

Courtesy of the Library of Congress/www.loc.gov

The Twenty-third Amendment (1961)

Section 1

The District constituting the seat of Government of the United States shall appoint in such manner as the Congress may direct:

A number of electors of President and Vice President equal to the whole number of Senators and Representatives in Congress to which the District would be entitled if it were a State, but in no event more than the least populous State; they shall be in addition to those appointed by the States, but they shall be considered, for the purposes of the election of President and Vice President, to be electors appointed by a State; and they shall meet in the District and perform such duties as provided by the twelfth article of amendment.

Presidential Elections for the District of Columbia (Washington, DC). African Americans and women were not the only citizens who were denied voting rights for many years. Residents of our nation's capital, Washington, DC, also fell into this group.

"DC," as you may know, stands for the District of Columbia, an area located between the states of Maryland and Virginia. Because the District is not a state, the people who lived there were not initially allowed to vote in national elections. The Twenty-third Amendment changed that in 1961. The amendment says that residents of the District of Columbia may vote for the president and vice president, just as other Americans do.

The Twenty-fourth Amendment (1964)

Section 1

The right of citizens of the United States to vote in any primary or other election for President or Vice President, for electors for President or Vice President, or for Senator or Representative in Congress, shall not be denied or abridged by the United States or any State by reason of failure to pay any poll tax or other tax.

Right to Vote in Federal Elections (Poll Taxes Banned). Although the Fifteenth Amendment gave African Americans the right to vote, many had trouble exercising this right. One reason was that several Southern states had poll taxes. In other words, poll taxes *required voters to pay a sum of money before casting a ballot.* Because many African Americans could not afford the tax, they could not vote. Poor white families were also unable to vote if they could not pay the poll taxes.

In 1964, the Twenty-fourth Amendment made poll taxes illegal in national elections. Two years later, the Supreme Court ruled that poll taxes were illegal in state elections as well.

Key Events and People in the Struggle for Civil Rights

Despite the advances made after the Civil War, African Americans routinely faced discrimination, or *unfair treatment based on prejudice against a certain group.* Southern states, for example, passed so-called "Jim Crow" laws requiring African Americans and whites to be separated in most public places, such as schools. Later, African Americans had to ride in the back of buses and sit in separate sections of restaurants and theaters. They even had to use separate public restrooms. *The social separation of the races* was known as segregation. African Americans in the North fared better. They could vote freely, and segregation was less noticeable. Even so, prejudice restricted opportunities for many. It would take more than 100 years for African Americans to secure their civil rights—*the rights of full citizenship and equality under the law.*

Through reading and understanding the Constitution and the Bill of Rights, you will not have to depend on others to interpret your rights as an American citizen. When you share your understanding with classmates, friends, and family, you help strengthen your community while exercising your leadership skills.

From the earliest days of American history, many people objected to the treatment of African Americans as "second-class citizens." In 1909, a group of African Americans and white Americans founded the National Association for the Advancement of Colored People (NAACP). The association worked mainly through the courts to challenge laws and customs that denied African Americans their constitutional rights. In 1910, other concerned citizens formed the National Urban League. The Urban League aided the growing numbers of African Americans in cities, helping them find jobs and improve their opportunities to get ahead.

Gradually, these organizations and other groups and individuals built a civil rights movement supported by millions. An important gain came in 1948, when President Harry Truman ordered an end to segregation in our nation's military. A bigger victory was the Supreme Court's decision in *Brown v. Board of Education of Topeka, Kansas* (1954). In the landmark case, NAACP lawyers successfully argued that racial segregation in the public schools was unconstitutional. Segregation violated the Fourteenth Amendment's principle of equal protection under the law.

In the 1950s, Dr. Martin Luther King, Jr. became one of the main leaders of the civil rights movement. A Baptist minister and stirring speaker, Dr. King believed in nonviolent resistance—the peaceful protest of unfair laws. He helped organize marches, boycotts, and demonstrations that opened many people's eyes to the need for change. African American students began staging "sit-ins" at lunch counters that served only whites. White and African American "Freedom Riders" traveled together on buses to protest segregation. In his 1963 "I Have a Dream" speech, King inspired thousands with his hopes for racial equality and harmony. As the civil rights movement gained strength, however, some opposed it with violence. In response to the growing demand for government action, Congress passed the Civil Rights Act of 1964. This far-reaching law prohibited discrimination in public facilities, employment, education, and voter registration. It also banned discrimination not only by race and color, but also by gender, religion, and national origin.

Martin Luther King, Jr.

On August 23, 1963, more than 200,000 people marched in Washington, DC for their rights. On that day, they heard Reverend Martin Luther King, Jr. utter the words:

> "I have a dream that one day this nation will rise up and live out the true meaning of its creed: 'We hold these truths to be self-evident; that all men are created equal.' I have a dream that my four little children will one day live in a nation where they will not be judged by the color of their skin, but by the content of their character."

Courtesy of the Library of Congress/www.loc.gov

Landmark Acts of the Civil Rights Movement

Brown v. Board of Education of Topeka, Kansas, 1954

- Supreme Court rules segregated schools unconstitutional.

Civil Rights Act of 1957

- Congress sets up commission on civil rights and creates a division of civil rights in the Justice Department.

Equal Pay Act of 1963

- Bans wage discrimination based on race, gender, religion, or national origin.

Civil Rights Act of 1964

- Strengthens Fourteenth Amendment protections; bans discrimination in employment, voting, and public accommodations.

Voting Rights Act of 1965

- Empowers federal government to intervene in voter registration discrimination.

Open House Act of 1968

- Prevents people selling or renting homes from using certain forms of discrimination.

Equal Employment Opportunity Act of 1972

- Provides that businesses receiving federal funds must have affirmative action programs to increase number of female and minority employees.

Americans with Disabilities Act of 1990

- Bans discrimination in employment, transportation, public accommodations, and telecommunications against persons with physical or mental disabilities.

Ongoing Challenges

The civil rights laws of the 1960s certainly opened more doors for minorities. African Americans, Hispanic Americans, and other minorities have made significant gains in educational achievement. They increasingly hold professional and managerial jobs and serve in government, yet white Americans still tend to have more opportunities. In the 1970s, the federal government began affirmative action programs to try to make up for past discrimination. Affirmative action programs *encouraged the hiring and promoting of minorities and women in fields that were traditionally closed to them*. Colleges, too, practiced affirmative action to help minorities gain admission.

As planned, affirmative action was supposed to be a short-term policy to make up for past discrimination. From the start, affirmative action was controversial. Critics complained that giving preferential treatment to women and minorities amounted to discrimination against men and whites. Recent court decisions and state laws have curtailed many affirmative action programs.

The Twenty-sixth Amendment (1971)

Section 1

The right of citizens of the United States, who are eighteen years of age or older, to vote shall not be denied or abridged by the United States or by any State on account of age.

Voting Age. Throughout our nation's history, Americans still in their teens have bravely fought for our country. By law, however, they were not old enough to vote for the leaders who sent them into battle. Although the Constitution did not specify a minimum age for voters, most states set the minimum at 21.

That standard finally changed in 1971, a year when many young Americans were fighting in the Vietnam War. The Twenty-sixth Amendment guaranteed the right

Throughout the history of our nation, a number of constitutional amendments related to the voting process have been passed. These amendments have broadened the definition of who has the right to vote. This timeline shows some of the major legislation related to voting rights.

1800 **1825** **1850** **1875**

1804 12th Amendment allows citizens to vote for the President and Vice President separately

© Buyenlarge/Getty Images, Inc.

1870 15th Amendment establishes voting rights for African American men

1878 First proposed amendment giving suffrage to women fails to pass

FIGURE 5.7

Voting in the United States

to vote to citizens 18 and older for all national and state elections. As a result, millions more Americans could now exercise their right to vote.

Figure 5.7 shows how voting rights have been addressed to ensure all eligible voters are guaranteed the right to vote.

The voting rights amendments show the Constitution can be changed in response to new attitudes and conditions in society. The Thirteenth, Fourteenth, and Fifteenth Amendments came about as a result of the Civil War. However, all the other changes in the Constitution were made through mostly peaceful efforts of citizens. The framers of our Constitution could not have possibly seen the future of our government. However, their hard work laid the foundation for a truly remarkable document; in over 225 years, we have only had to add 27 amendments.

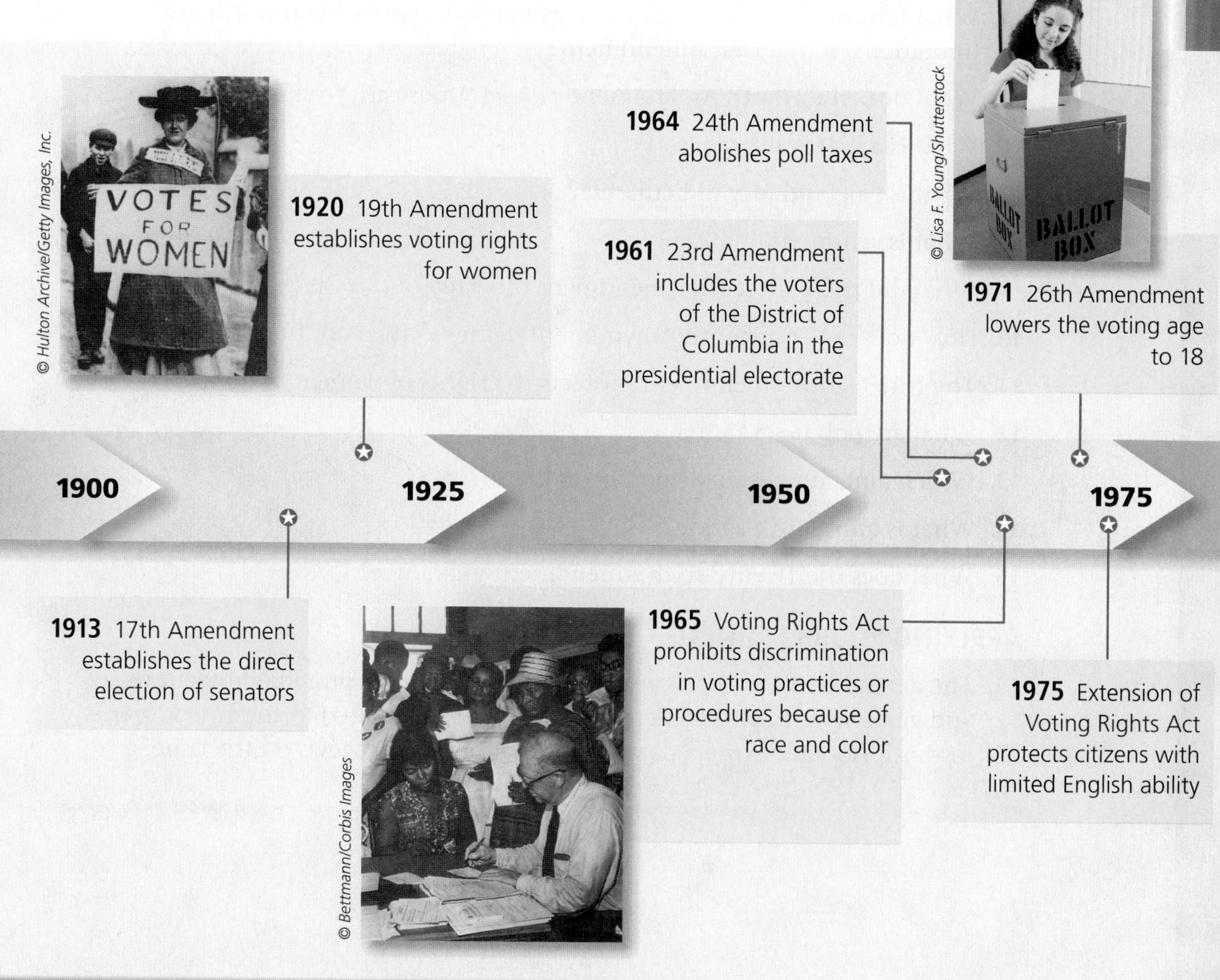

© Hulton Archive/Getty Images, Inc.
VOTES FOR WOMEN
1920 19th Amendment establishes voting rights for women
1964 24th Amendment abolishes poll taxes
1961 23rd Amendment includes the voters of the District of Columbia in the presidential electorate
© Lisa F. Young/Shutterstock
BALLOT BOX
1971 26th Amendment lowers the voting age to 18
1900
1925
1950
1975
1913 17th Amendment establishes the direct election of senators
© Bettmann/Corbis Images
1965 Voting Rights Act prohibits discrimination in voting practices or procedures because of race and color
1975 Extension of Voting Rights Act protects citizens with limited English ability

Voting in the United States, *continued*

Lesson 4 Review

Using complete sentences, answer the following questions on a sheet of paper.

1. The First Amendment protects five basic freedoms of all Americans. List these freedoms.
2. Why did the Supreme Court strike down teacher-led prayer in public schools?
3. What does the freedom of press ensure?
4. What has the Supreme Court listed as public interests when justifying limitations on the First Amendment?
5. What does the Fourth Amendment protect Americans from?
6. What is a search warrant?
7. What is "a grand jury indictment"?
8. What is self-incrimination?
9. What did the Thirteenth Amendment officially outlaw in the United States?
10. How does the Fourteenth Amendment define a citizen of the United States?
11. The Nineteenth Amendment protects the rights of women to do what?
12. What are poll taxes?
13. Which amendment made poll taxes illegal?
14. What is affirmative action?
15. What does the Twenty-sixth Amendment guarantee?

APPLYING YOUR LEARNING

16. The amendments to the Constitution were passed to provide protections and guarantees to all Americans. Select one issue related to the amendments in this lesson and write a paragraph describing your views on the issue.

LESSON 5

US National Government

Quick Write

Make a list of things you know about our US government, including the president, Congress, and the federal court system. As you read, see how many facts from your list you can find in this lesson.

"I believe that truth is the glue that holds government together...our Constitution works; our great Republic is a Government of laws and not of men. Here the people rule."

Gerald R. Ford, 38th President of the United States

Learn About

- the legislative branch
- the executive branch
- the judicial branch

The Legislative Branch

Every year, inside the US Capitol in Washington, DC, 535 American citizens gather to make new laws and address major issues facing our country. These are our elected representatives, the men and women who make up the United States Congress. While the framers intended that no one part of the government dominated the others, they saw the legislative branch, as James Madison put it in the first part of the Constitution, Article I, as "the First Branch of this Government."

Terms of Congress

Each **term**, or *meeting period*, of Congress starts on 3 January of odd-numbered years (unless a different day is appointed), and lasts for two years. Each "new" Congress is given a number to identify its two-year term. For example, the first Congress met in 1789, and the 113th Congress began meeting in 2013.

Each term of Congress is divided into two sessions, or meetings. A typical session of Congress today lasts from January until November or December. Congress may also meet in times of crisis. These are called special sessions.

A joint session occurs when the House and Senate meet together. This usually occurs when the Congress gathers to hear the president's State of the Union address. But a joint session may also be called during times of crisis or major controversy needing resolution.

Congress—A Bicameral Legislature

One of the major conflicts at the Constitutional Convention in 1787 concerned state representation in Congress. While delegates from the smaller states wanted equal representation, delegates from the larger states wanted representation to be based on population. The resulting Great Compromise established Congress as a bicameral legislative body, meaning *a legislative body with two branches*. These two branches are the House of Representatives, based on population, and the Senate, based on the concept of equal representation within each state, but with longer terms for each member.

The American Two-Party Political System

The United States has had, for almost its entire history, two primary political parties. These parties tend to define the basic ways Americans think about important issues needing our action or attention. The two current parties, Democratic and Republican, try to translate the views of the people and create platforms, or *formal declarations of the things for which a group (each party) stands and appeals to the public—especially voters—to support*. Basically, a platform becomes a set of viewpoints on issues that large groups of people may rally behind in order to vote for a candidate within a party who most closely represents their views.

When the voters see either party as not representing them properly, there may be a new political wing, or *group formed as an affiliate or subordinate of a larger organization*, that gains influence within the broader party.

In recent years, for example, the Tea Party has become a wing of the Republican Party. This "party within a party" formed because many Republican supporters felt that there needed to be a more conservative platform within the broader Republican Party. Conservatives are *members who want to preserve the traditional values and customs*.

Vocabulary

- term
- bicameral legislative body
- platforms
- wing
- conservatives
- census
- constituents
- gerrymandering
- incumbents
- majority party
- minority party
- caucus
- pro tempore
- standing committees
- seniority
- resolutions
- special-interest groups
- riders
- filibuster
- cloture
- partisan politics
- voice vote
- standing vote
- roll-call vote
- Electoral College
- electors
- diplomat
- jurisdiction
- exclusive jurisdiction
- concurrent jurisdiction
- district courts
- original jurisdiction

continued on next page

Vocabulary

continued

- appeals courts
- appellate jurisdiction
- circuit
- remand
- opinion
- precedent
- subpoena

There have been other times when third parties, independent of the two major parties, have been formed. Often called the Independent Party in some presidential elections, independents have at times had impact on the election results, but no independent candidate for president has ever won an election.

Historically, there was actually no desire on the part of the framers of the Constitution to have political parties. They sought a united country. But once the Constitution was ratified, it became clear that different views of how our new government should operate existed. Those views became the basis of two "original" political parties—the Federalists and the anti-Federalists.

Two Major Political Parties in the US

Republican Party

Founded 28 Feb 1854

The Republican Party was the successor of other conservative parties that fell through, such as the Federalists and the Whigs. In the beginning, they were against the spread of slavery. They favor higher protective tariffs and minimal government intervention in people's lives. The elephant symbol of the party was born in the imagination of cartoonist Thomas Nast and first appeared in *Harper's Weekly* on 7 November 1874.

© Fotolia365/Fotolia.com

Democratic Party

Founded 1 Feb 1792

Thomas Jefferson was the first leader of what was originally named the "Democratic-Republican" party. In 1828, when Andrew Jackson was running for office, the name was shortened to the Democratic Party and the donkey became the party's symbol. Advocating more rights for the middle class, this party favored states' rights as well as labor unions and laws that gave more power to the people. They wanted as little power as possible in the hands of the federal government.

© Fotolia365/Fotolia.com

There have been times in our nation's history when there has been substantial political unity between our two major parties. World War II was one instance. However, recent decades have split the country into what some call the "Era of Divided Government." You may hear people say that our political parties have become extremely distrustful of each other. In truth, this atmosphere has existed since the late 1960s, when the Civil Rights Act and the Vietnam War dominated the news. The political split between parties has been large from that point on. No one party since 1968 has consistently held the presidency. And usually, Congress has been controlled by the other party than that of the president.

The House of Representatives

The House of Representatives, the larger body of Congress, has 435 voting members. These members are allotted to the states according to population. Article I of the Constitution allows each state at least one seat in the House, no matter how small its population. After each 10-year census, or *population count* taken by the US Census Bureau, Congress adjusts the number of representatives given to each state. See Figure 5.8 to get a view of the changing congressional apportionments throughout history.

Each state is divided into one or more congressional districts, or areas, with one representative elected from each district. State legislatures must draw the boundaries so that the districts include roughly the same number of constituents, or *people represented.* Sometimes states abuse this process by gerrymandering. Gerrymandering is *to divide a state or voting areas into election districts that give one political party an election majority.* For example, if most of a state's representatives are Republican, they might draw the lines so that as many districts as possible have more Republican than Democratic voters. The term *gerrymandering* came from an incident in 1812 when Governor Elbridge Gerry created a new voting district in Andover, Massachusetts. In response, artist Gilbert Stuart drew the outline of the district and added a head, claws, and wings. A newspaper editor named the fictional beast, which resembled a salamander, a "Gerrymander."

In recent years, there has been renewed controversy over gerrymandering. Often referred to as "redistricting" or "reapportionment," some critics view these shifts in voting districts as having allowed one party to gain a more a favorable position to win elections and place more of their party members into the House of Representatives.

Representatives in the House serve two-year terms and may not be well known outside their districts. They usually focus on concerns from within their districts, rather than the state as a whole.

The framers of the Constitution intended to structure the Congress in a way that members of the House of Representatives would be close to the people they represented. In recent years, people within Congressional districts have often become dissatisfied with their representatives, believing they are "too closely tied to special interests in Washington." Some were voted out of office because of this. In the future, you will make voting decisions, so you will want to understand how your interests are represented in Congress.

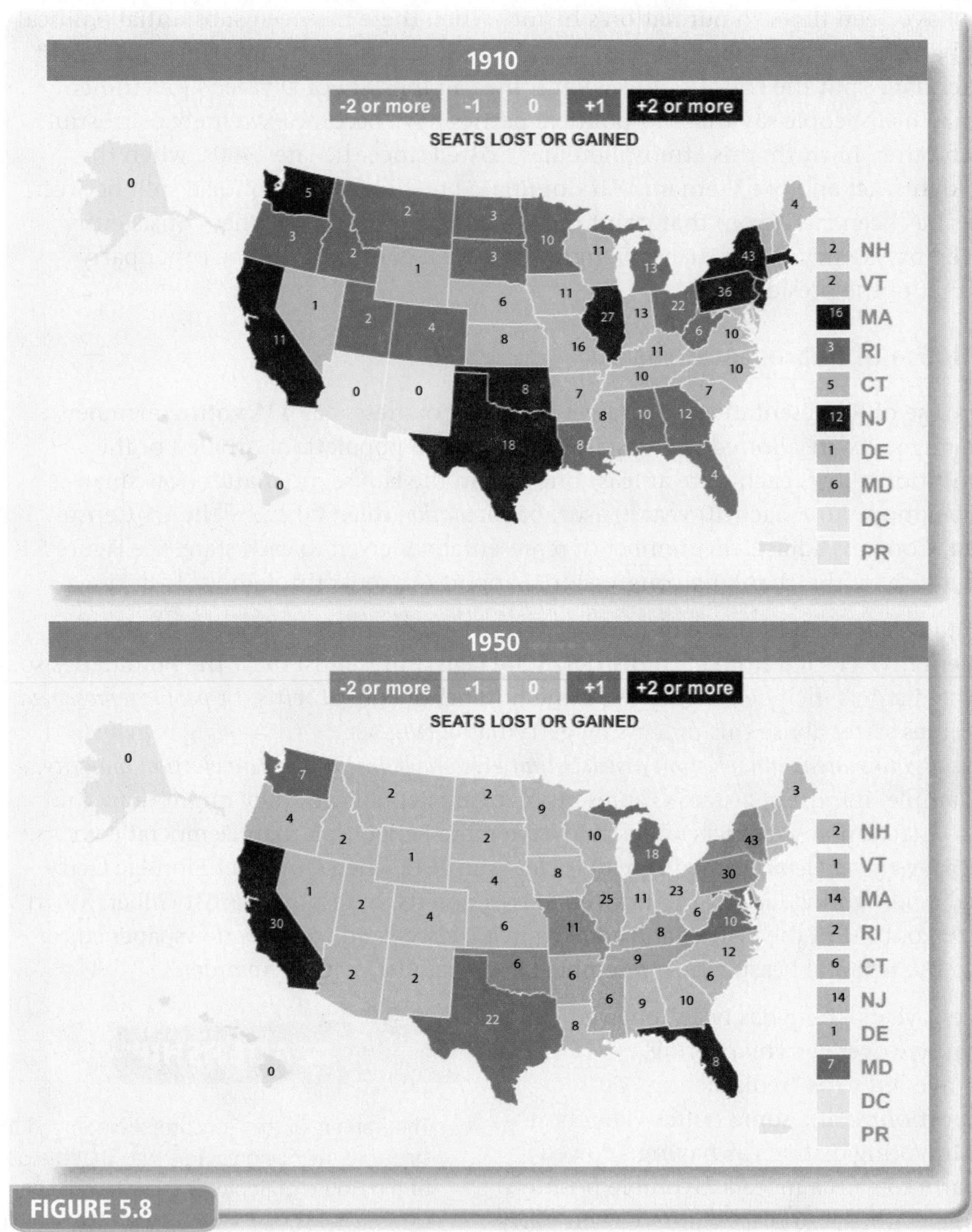

FIGURE 5.8

Congressional Apportionment, Selected Years

Courtesy of the United States Census Bureau/www.census.gov

The Senate

The Senate has 100 members—two from each of the 50 states. Each senator represents his or her entire state rather than a particular district. Senators serve six-year terms, but elections are staggered so that no more than one-third of the senators are up for reelection at any one time. This ensures a certain amount of stability and continuity.

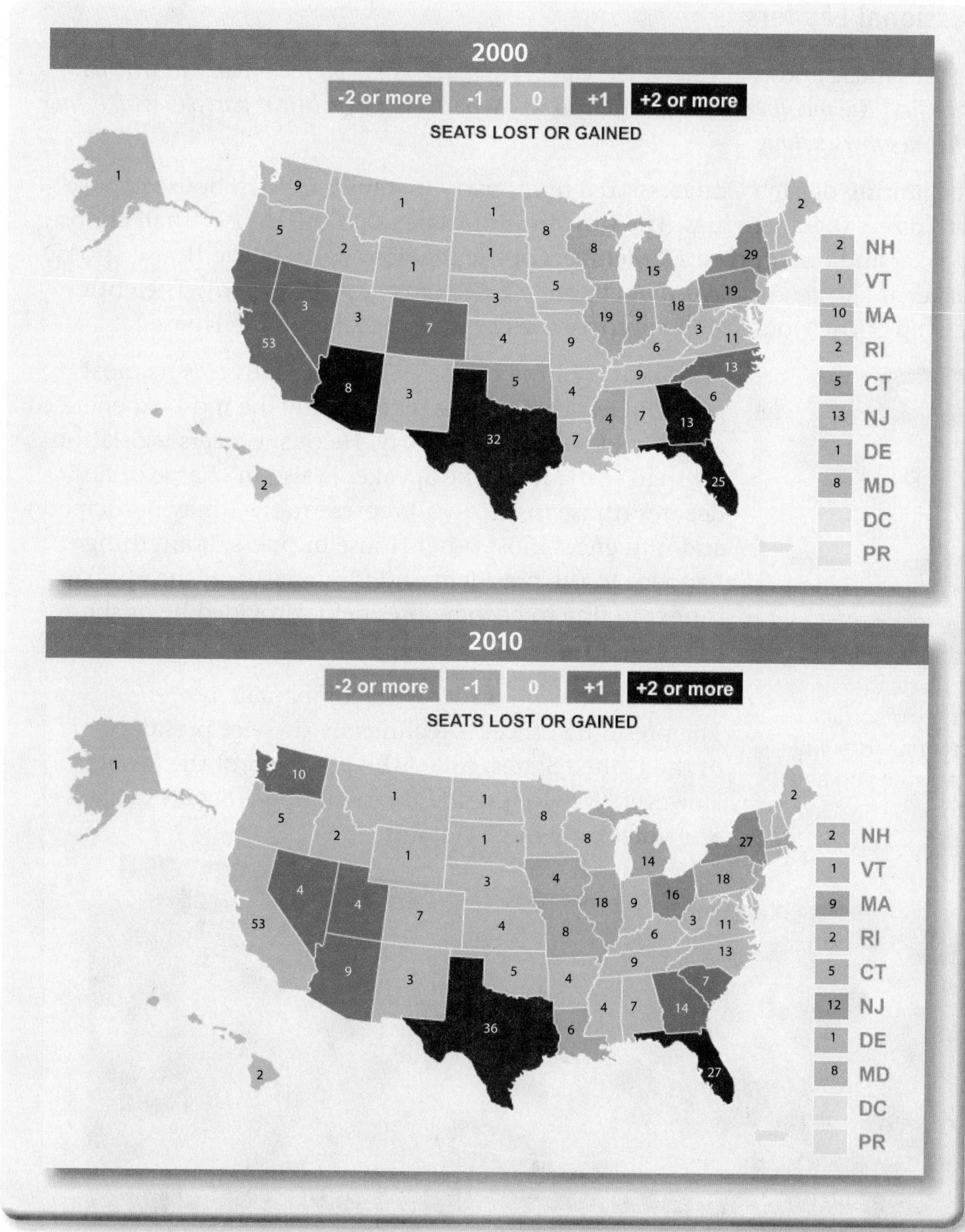

Congressional Apportionment, Selected Years, *continued*

Courtesy of the United States Census Bureau/www.census.gov

Those elected to the House and Senate running for reelection are considered incumbents, meaning *those currently holding a specified office*. The current president up for reelection is also called the incumbent.

Congressional Leaders

In both the House and the Senate, the **majority party** is *the political party to which more than half the members belong*. The **minority party** is *the political party to which the rest of the members belong*.

At the beginning of each Congressional term, party members in each house choose leaders to direct their activities. The Constitution states that the House "shall choose their Speaker and other officers." Members of the majority party of the House choose the Speaker at a **caucus**, or *closed meeting of people from one political party*. The entire membership of the House then approves the choice of Speaker of the House.

> *keys to* **LEADERSHIP**
>
> On a typical day, the Speaker of the House will talk with dozens of members of Congress. Often these talks involve listening to concerns or requests. Former Speaker of the House Thomas P. "Tip" O'Neill once stated, "The world is full of little things you can do for people." In return, the Speaker expects the representatives' support on important issues. As a future leader, your listening skills can be a valuable asset to you and those you will work with.

The Speaker of the House of Representatives is its most powerful leader. The Speaker is usually the most experienced member of the majority party. He or she steers legislation through the House. The Speaker is also in charge of floor debates (those in which all representatives may participate) and influences most other House business. If anything happens to the president and vice president, the Speaker is next in line to become president, provided he or she is legally qualified.

The Senate has no leader with comparable power. The presiding officer is technically the vice president of the United States, called the president of the Senate. However, the vice president rarely attends Senate debates and votes only in case of a tie.

The State of the Union Address is a joint session of Congress.
Courtesy of Amanda Lucidon for the US White House/www.whitehouse.gov

The person who usually acts as chairperson of the Senate is the "president pro tempore" (or "pro tem," for short). Pro tempore means *temporary or for the time being*. This position is typically filled by someone from the majority party and is more ceremonial than influential.

The real leaders in the Senate, and the most powerful players in the House of Representatives, aside from the Speaker, are the floor leaders. Floor leaders try to make sure that the laws Congress passes are in the best interest of their own political party. The majority and minority floor leaders in each house speak for their parties on the issues, push bills along, and try to sway votes. Party "whips" help the floor leaders. They keep track of where party members stand on proposed legislation and round up their colleagues for key votes.

Committees—Little Legislatures

The detailed work of lawmaking is done in committee rather than on the House or Senate floors. So many bills are introduced each year that few of them would be considered if the work were not divided among smaller groups of legislators.

Types of Committees

Each house of Congress has both well-established, ongoing committees and those set up for a specific short-term purpose. The *permanent committees that continue their work from session to session* are called standing committees. The Senate had 16 standing committees as of 2014 and the House had 20, covering areas such as education, veterans affairs, and commerce.

Most standing committees are divided into smaller subcommittees that deal with more specialized issues. For example, the Senate Armed Services Committee has subcommittees on military readiness, personnel, and armament.

In addition to standing committees, both houses of Congress also have select committees that are created to do a special job for a limited period. In 1976, for example, the House formed the Select Committee on Assassinations to investigate the deaths of President John F. Kennedy and Dr. Martin Luther King, Jr. Like all select committees, the House Assassinations Committee disbanded when it finished its work. Sometimes these select committees are also called special committees, but there is no major difference between the two. In 2014, the House had just one select committee, the Permanent Select Committee on Intelligence. The Senate had its own Select Committee on Intelligence. In addition, the Senate had Select Committees on Aging, Ethics, and Indian Affairs.

The House and Senate have also formed four joint committees, which include members of both houses. The Joint Economic Committee reviews economic conditions and recommends improvements in economic policy. Other joint committees focus on federal tax policy, the Library of Congress, and the Government Printing Office. Figure 5.9 shows how House and Senate standing committees, select and special committees, and joint committees are organized.

HOUSE OF REPRESENTATIVES—Standing Committees

- Agriculture
- Appropriations
- Armed Services
- Budget
- Education and the Workforce
- Energy and Commerce
- Financial Service
- Government Reform
- House Administration
- International Relations
- Judiciary
- Resources
- Rules
- Science
- Small Business
- Standards of Official Conduct
- Transportation and Infrastructure
- Veterans Affairs
- Ways and Means

Select and Special Committees

- Intelligence
- Aging
- Ethics
- Intelligence
- Indian Affairs

Joint Committees

- Economic
- Printing
- Taxation
- Library

SENATE—Standing Committees

- Agriculture, Nutrition, and Forestry
- Appropriations
- Armed Services
- Banking, Housing, and Urban Affairs
- Budget
- Commerce, Science, and Transportation
- Energy and Natural Resources
- Environment and Public Works
- Finance
- Foreign Relations
- Governmental Affairs
- Health, Education, Labor, and Pensions
- Judiciary
- Rules and Administration
- Small Business and Entrepreneurship
- Veterans Affairs

KEY

- House Committee
- Senate Committee
- Joint Committee

FIGURE 5.9

Standing Committees

A fourth type of committee is a temporary committee, the conference committee, which helps the House and Senate agree on the details of a proposed law. A conference committee is often called together to work out the differences between amended versions of a single bill initiated by the House or Senate. Other times, both the House and Senate will pass individual bills. The members of the joint conference committee will then debate sections of the two bills and come to an agreeable compromise.

Then, a final version will be passed as a House or Senate bill to be sent to the president for signature. The House and Senate often pass different versions of a Defense Appropriations (money approved) Bill, for example. The two bills are then sent to the joint conference where the differences are hashed out between House and Senate members selected for this committee.

Committee Assignments

When senators and representatives first come to Congress, they try to get assigned to important committees that affect the people who elected them. For example, members of Congress from farm areas might want to serve on agriculture committees. Those with many factories in their districts might be interested in serving on labor committees. Leaders of the political parties make committee assignments. In doing so, they consider members' preferences, expertise, and loyalty to the party.

Another key factor is seniority, or *years of service*. The senators and representatives who have been in Congress longest usually get the preferred committee spots. The longest-serving committee member from the majority party traditionally becomes chairperson. Chairpersons of standing committees are the most powerful members of Congress. These members decide when and if a committee will meet, what bills will be studied, and who will serve on which subcommittees. Some people think the seniority system is a good idea. They say it prevents fights over committee jobs and ensures that chairpersons will have experience. Other people complain that talented people may be overlooked in favor of those who have simply been around for a while. There has been so much criticism of the seniority system over the years that both political parties have moved slightly away from it. The senior majority party member on a committee still usually wins the role of chairperson, but it is no longer guaranteed.

Code Talkers

On 20 November 2013, Congressional Gold Medals, the nation's highest civilian honor, were awarded honoring the service of hundreds of overlooked "code talkers" of WWII from 33 Native American tribes. The obscure languages spoken by Native American tribes could not be understood by the enemy, allowing the code talkers to transmit messages quickly and securely, giving American forces a critical edge.

Courtesy of the US Army/www.army.mil

Types of Bills

It is Congress' job to pass laws that the nation needs. Many elements may go into the final bill, and the process requires patience. One scholar has compared lawmaking to running an obstacle course. More than 10,000 bills are often introduced during each term of Congress, yet only several hundred pass all the hurdles and become law.

Bills generally fall into two categories. Private bills concern individual people or places. They usually deal with people's claims against the government. Public bills apply to the entire nation and involve general matters like taxation, civil rights, or terrorism. They may be debated for months and get much media coverage.

Along with bills, Congress considers different kinds of resolutions, or *formal statements expressing lawmakers' opinions or decisions*. Many resolutions, such as those creating a new congressional committee or permitting a ceremony in the Capitol, do not have the force of law. Joint resolutions passed by both houses of Congress also become laws when signed by the president. Congress uses joint resolutions to propose constitutional amendments, designate money for a special purpose, and correct errors in bills already passed.

From Bill to Law

Every bill starts with an idea. Some of these ideas come from members of Congress or private citizens. Many more ideas begin in the White House. Other bills are suggested by special-interest groups, or *organizations made up of people with some common interest who try to influence government decisions*. Whatever their source, only senators and representatives can introduce bills in Congress. Any bill that involves money must start in the House. Every bill is given a title and a number when it is submitted. For example, during the first session of Congress, the first bill introduced is called S.1 in the Senate and H.R.1 in the House of Representatives. The bill is then sent to the standing committee that seems most qualified to handle it.

Former Senator Kent Conrad, a Democrat from North Dakota, is outspoken about government spending and often spoke before the Senate Budget Committee.
Courtesy of the US Air Force/Minot Air Force Base

Committee Action

Committees receive far more bills than they can process. The committee chair is the main person to decide which bills get ignored and which get studied. Those that merit attention are often researched and reported on by a subcommittee. Public hearings may be held to allow experts and concerned citizens to voice their opinions. People may also submit written statements for or against the bill that go into the hearing's record.

Standing committees have life-and-death power over bills. The committee can:

1. Pass the bill without changes
2. Mark up a bill with changes and suggest that it be passed
3. Replace the original bill with a new alternative
4. Ignore the bill and let it die (which is called "pigeonholing" the bill)
5. Kill the bill outright by majority vote

The full House or Senate can overrule the decisions of its committees, but this rarely happens. When a committee is against a bill, it almost never becomes a law.

Floor Debate

Bills approved in committee are ready for consideration by the full House or Senate. The bills are put on calendars, or schedules, in chronological order as they come out of committees. The Senate usually takes up bills in the order listed. The powerful Rules Committee, however, controls the House schedule. This "traffic cop" can give priority to the bills that are most important. It can also kill a bill by not letting it get to the floor.

When bills do reach the floor of the House or Senate, the members argue their pros and cons. They may also discuss amendments. The House accepts only amendments relevant to the bill. The Senate, however, allows riders—*completely unrelated amendments*—to be tacked onto the bill. Senators include riders to bills that are likely to pass. Sometimes they attach these riders to benefit their constituents.

In the House, the Rules Committee sets the terms for debate. It usually puts time limits on the discussion, for example, to speed up action. The Senate, because it is smaller, has fewer rules. Senators can speak as long as they wish, and they are not even required to address the topic at hand. Now and then they take advantage of this custom to filibuster, or *to attempt to defeat a bill through prolonged debate, sometimes referred to as "talking a bill to death."* In this situation, a member will hold the floor for hour after hour, delaying a vote until the bill's sponsor gives up and withdraws the measure. The Senate can end a filibuster if three-fifths of the members vote for cloture, *a rule under which the Senate may limit consideration of a pending matter to (no more than) 30 additional hours*. Senators rarely resorted to cloture, until recently. In one of the longest debates in our history, over the Civil Rights Act in 1964, the Senate waited out a 74-day filibuster by senators opposed to the legislation. In recent years, the number of clotures imposed by the Senate has increased, partly because of partisan politics, which is *the showing of favoritism to one's own party within Congress*. With that has come a big increase in what some call "parliamentary maneuvering," or actions that stop one political party from passing legislation, or amendments to a bill. Political analysts say that partisan politics can result in fewer compromises and less productivity in the legislative branch. Figure 5.10 shows the entire process of how bills are passed.

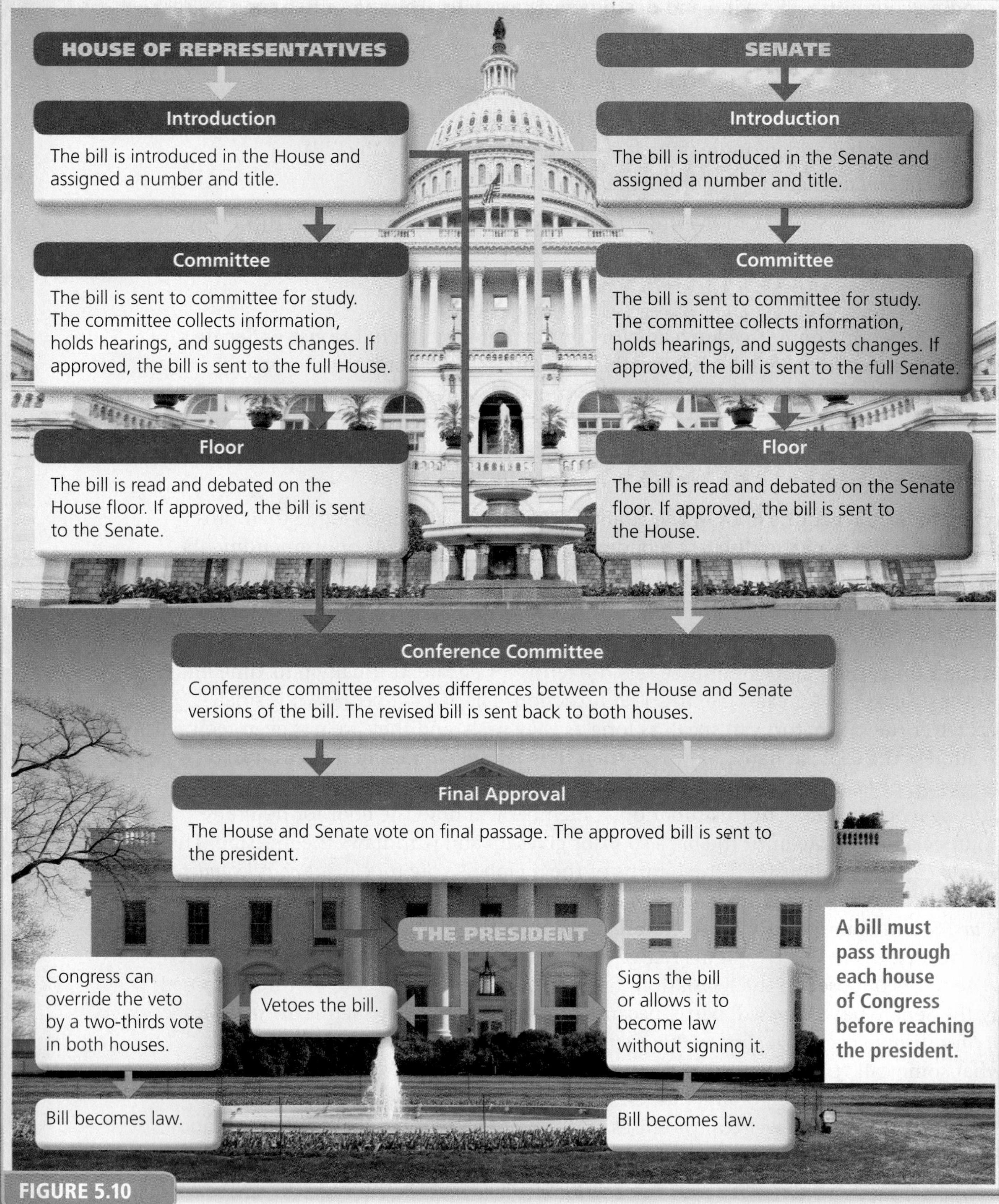

HOUSE OF REPRESENTATIVES
SENATE
Introduction
The bill is introduced in the House and assigned a number and title.
Introduction
The bill is introduced in the Senate and assigned a number and title.
Committee
The bill is sent to committee for study. The committee collects information, holds hearings, and suggests changes. If approved, the bill is sent to the full House.
Committee
The bill is sent to committee for study. The committee collects information, holds hearings, and suggests changes. If approved, the bill is sent to the full Senate.
Floor
The bill is read and debated on the House floor. If approved, the bill is sent to the Senate.
Floor
The bill is read and debated on the Senate floor. If approved, the bill is sent to the House.
Conference Committee
Conference committee resolves differences between the House and Senate versions of the bill. The revised bill is sent back to both houses.
Final Approval
The House and Senate vote on final passage. The approved bill is sent to the president.
THE PRESIDENT
Congress can override the veto by a two-thirds vote in both houses.
Vetoes the bill.
Signs the bill or allows it to become law without signing it.
A bill must pass through each house of Congress before reaching the president.
Bill becomes law.
Bill becomes law.

FIGURE 5.10

How a Bill Becomes Law

© camrocker/Fotolia.com (top); © sic2005/Fotolia.com (bottom)

Voting on a Bill

When members of Congress are ready to vote on a proposed law, they may do so in several ways. In the House and Senate, the simplest is a voice vote, in which *those in favor say "Yea" and those against say "Nay."* If there is no clear distinction between the "yeas" and the "nays," there may be a different method employed. In a standing vote, *those in favor of a bill stand to be counted, and then those against it stand to be counted.* Today the House uses a computerized voting system to produce a permanent record of each representative's vote. In the more tradition-bound Senate, the way most votes are done is by a roll-call vote, in which *members voice their votes in turn as an official records them.*

A simple majority of all members that are present is needed to pass a bill. If a bill passes in one house, it is sent to the other. If either the Senate or the House rejects a bill, it dies. The Constitution requires that the Senate and House pass a bill in identical form before it becomes law. If either house of Congress makes changes in a bill after receiving it from the other house, a conference committee is formed with members from both houses. They meet privately to work out differences between the two versions of the bill. Once they have a revised bill, the House and Senate must either accept it without amendments or completely reject it.

Presidential Action

After both houses of Congress approve a bill, it goes to the president. One of four things may then happen. The president may sign the bill and declare it a new law. As discussed in Chapter 5, Lesson 3, the president may exercise the veto option by refusing to sign the bill. The president may also do nothing. The president is allowed 10 days to review a bill passed by the Congress. If the president has not signed it after 10 days, it becomes law automatically. However, if Congress adjourns during the 10-day period, and the president does not sign the bill, it does not become law. In this case, it is called a "pocket veto" of the bill.

If the president vetoes a bill, Congress has one last chance to save it. As you read earlier, Congress can override the veto with a two-thirds vote of each house. This is not an easy task, though. In recent decades, Congress has managed to overturn only about one out of five regular vetoes.

The Executive Branch

The president heads the executive branch of the United States government. The presidency is the top political job in the country. Because of the power and global influence of the United States, the president is generally considered to hold the most important job in the world. The president also serves as the commander in chief of the US Armed Forces, which you learned as part of Chapter 5, Lesson 3 on the Constitutional powers of the president.

Our country's first president was George Washington. Just as the nation has grown tremendously since that time, so has the office of the presidency.

Qualifications for President

The constitutional requirements for the presidency remain the same as they did when George Washington was president. The US Constitution lists only three rules about who can become president of the United States. A person must be:

1. At least 35 years old
2. A native-born American citizen
3. A resident of the United States for at least 14 years

By law, anyone who meets these qualifications can become president. Of course, someone who hopes to become president must have many more qualifications than those three.

Only in the past few decades has the presidency become a possibility for a wider group of Americans. Until 2008, for example, every American president had been a white male. President Barack Obama was the first African American to be elected. All but one of our presidents have been Protestant Christians. John F. Kennedy became the first Catholic president in 1960. Most presidents had won other elections before running for the nation's highest office. Most have had a college education. Many have been lawyers. Most came from states with large populations.

A woman has yet to be elected president, but that can change. Women are taking many more prominent roles in important elected and appointed offices within our government.

President Harry S. Truman

President Truman.

Courtesy of the Library of Congress/www.loc.gov

"The presidency of the United States carries with it a responsibility so personal as to be without parallel…No one can make decisions for him…Even those closest to him… never know all the reasons why he does certain things and why he comes to certain conclusions. To be President of the United States is to be lonely, very lonely at times of great decisions."

—Harry S. Truman

Electing a President

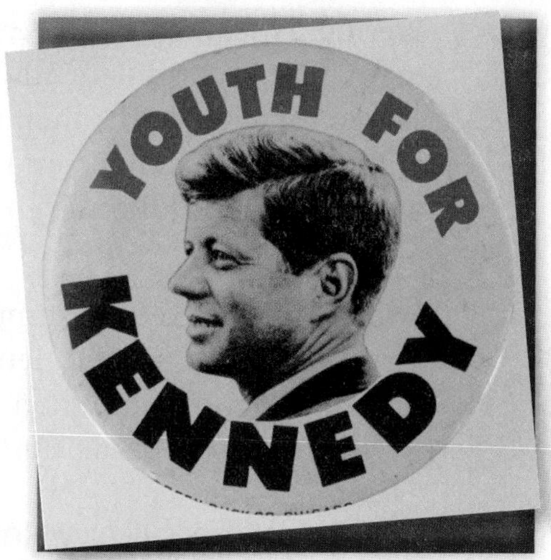

John F. Kennedy became the first Catholic to win the presidency in 1960.
Courtesy of the US National Archives and Records Administration/www.archives.gov

Presidential elections take place every four years in years evenly divisible by the number 4—for example, 1996, 2000, 2004, 2008, and 2012. The Constitution does not provide for direct popular election of the president. Instead, it set up what is called an Electoral College, *an indirect method of election*. The Constitution requires that each state "shall appoint" electors, *those who are chosen to vote for one of the major candidates*. Although the ballot will show the names of the presidential candidates, when people in each state vote for president, their votes are tallied, and the state's electors cast these "pledged" votes for president.

Each state has as many electoral votes as the total number of its US senators and representatives. The Electoral College includes 538 electors (Washington, DC has three electoral votes). This means that the states with large populations have many more electoral votes than less-populated states.

In almost every state, the Electoral College is a "winner-take-all" system. Even if a candidate wins the popular vote by just a tiny majority, that candidate usually gets all of the state's electoral votes.

To be elected president or vice president, a candidate must win at least 270 of the 538 electoral votes. The winner-take-all system makes it difficult for third-party candidates—candidates not from the two major parties—to win electoral votes.

Although the winning presidential candidate is usually announced on the same evening as the popular election, which is in November, the formal election by the Electoral College doesn't take place until December. This is when the electors meet in each state capital to cast their ballots. Congress counts the electoral votes and declares the winner officially as the next president.

Term of Office

Article II, Section 1 of the Constitution requires that before presidents can assume their duties they must take the oath of office. The completion of this 35-word oath ends one president's term and begins the next.

The Oath of Office:

I do solemnly swear (or affirm) that I will faithfully execute the Office of President of the United States, and will to the best of my Ability, preserve, protect and defend the Constitution of the United States.

Presidents serve four-year terms. Originally, the Constitution placed no limits on how many terms a president could serve. The nation's first president, George Washington, served for eight years, then refused to run for a third term. Presidents followed Washington's example, and no president served more than two terms until 1940, when Franklin D. Roosevelt ran for, and won, a third term. In 1944 he then won a fourth term.

Roosevelt's fourth term stimulated a major debate over how long any president should serve. The 22nd Amendment was finally ratified in 1951 to call for limits for each president of not more than two elected terms in office, or a maximum of 10 years if the presidency began during another president's term.

The President's Many Roles

The framers of the Constitution knew the nation needed a leader who could both carry out the laws and represent the nation in meeting leaders of other countries. Through the examples of our first president, George Washington, and presidents that have followed him, the role of president has become more clearly defined over the years. Figure 5.11 summarizes the many roles of the president.

Chief Executive

The president is the head of the executive branch of our government. The Constitution states that the president must "take care that the laws be faithfully executed." To *execute* means to make sure they are carried out. Although Congress makes the laws, it is up to the executive branch to decide how these laws are carried out.

One way the president gives orders is through *executive orders*, which are rules and regulations the government must follow. However, the power of executive orders is limited, as they may not violate the Constitution or laws passed by Congress.

As chief executive, the president also has the power to appoint about 4,000 executive branch officials. Congress is not required to approve all appointments, only key appointments such as Supreme Court justices or cabinet members.

Commander in Chief

The Constitution states, "The President shall be commander in chief of the Army and Navy of the United States." This statement points to the president's important role as the leader of our military. The role was given to the president because the framers wanted to maintain civilian authority of the military.

The president's role as commander in chief has grown dramatically since the days of George Washington. Besides affecting American military service members who are sent to fight on foreign soil, the president's decisions can also alter the lives of other nations and change the course of history. One of the most difficult decisions made by a president was the dropping of the atomic bomb on Japan to end World War II. This action would not have taken place without the president's permission.

© Chip Somodevilla/Getty Images, Inc.

Chief Executive

As leader of the executive branch, the president has many important roles. The president chooses justices for the Supreme Court and other federal courts. Former President Bill Clinton appointed Ruth Bader Ginsburg as a justice to the Supreme Court.

Commander in Chief

In this photo, Franklin Delano Roosevelt (right) meets with Richard Byrd (left), an admiral in the US Navy.

© Imagno/Getty Images, Inc.

Chief Diplomat

Acting as chief diplomat, former President Richard Nixon made a historic trip to the People's Republic of China in 1972. Nixon's visit to China was hailed as a diplomatic triumph during the Cold War.

© Keyston/Getty Images, Inc.

© Bill Pugliano/Getty Images, Inc.

Legislative Chief

One of the president's duties as legislative leader is to give an annual State of the Union address to all Americans. Here, former President George W. Bush delivers his address before officials from all three branches of government.

FIGURE 5.11

Roles of the President

Chief Diplomat

The president is also the head diplomat; he or she is the most important representative of the United States. A **diplomat** is *someone who represents his or her country in dealings with other nations*. The president leads in making foreign policy, plans for guiding our relationships with other nations.

Foreign policy is clearly the president's vision; however, Congress may still set limits. If the president makes a treaty or other formal agreement with another nation, the Senate must approve it. The Senate must also approve any ambassador appointed by the president.

Legislative Chief

Congress makes the laws; however, the president has a good deal of power to influence what those laws will be and how they are enforced. Congress is expected to consider the president's ideas and not act alone in making laws. A powerful tool the president has for influencing Congress to change a bill before it becomes law is to veto it. By vetoing a bill the president is telling Congress that the bill should be changed. Congress can override the veto, but this has only been done 100 times of the 2,500 vetoes in our nation's history.

The Vice President

The vice president is elected with the president through the Electoral College system. The qualifications for the office are the same as those for the presidency. The Constitution gives little authority to the vice president. Article I states that the vice president shall preside over the Senate and vote in that body in case of a tie.

Vice presidents are usually not very visible to the public. Their activities rarely receive front-page newspaper coverage. Yet, if the president dies, is removed from office, becomes seriously ill, or resigns, the vice president becomes president. Nine vice presidents have become president due to the death or resignation of a president. John Adams, our nation's first vice president, described the situation well. He said, "I am Vice President. In this I am nothing, but I may become everything." In that sense, it is important for presidents to choose vice presidents wisely and well.

Presidential Succession

Eight presidents have died while in office. The original wording of the Constitution states that if the president dies or leaves office during his term, the vice president takes on the "powers and duties" of the presidency. Early government officials were not sure what that meant. Should the vice president become president, or should he remain vice president while doing the president's job?

In 1841, Vice President John Tyler settled the question when William Henry Harrison became the first president to die in office. Tyler declared himself president, took the oath of office, moved into the White House, and served out the remainder of Harrison's term.

More than a century later, in 1947, Congress passed the Presidential Succession Act, which indicates the line of succession after the vice president. According to this law, if both the president and vice president die or leave office, the Speaker of the House becomes president. Next in line is the president pro tempore of the Senate, then the secretary of state and other members of the cabinet.

The 25th Amendment

Twenty years later, remaining questions about presidential succession were answered with the adoption of the 25th Amendment to the Constitution, which says that if the president dies or leaves office, the vice president becomes president. The new president then chooses another vice president. Both the Senate and House of Representatives must approve the choice.

This amendment also gives the vice president a role in determining whether a president is disabled and unable to do the job. Should that occur, the vice president would serve as acting president until the president is able to go back to work.

The 25th Amendment has been used only twice. In 1973 Vice President Spiro Agnew resigned, and President Richard Nixon replaced him with Gerald Ford, a representative from Michigan. When Nixon resigned from the presidency in 1974, Ford became the new president and chose Nelson A. Rockefeller to be his vice president.

The Judicial Branch

Federal courts, the highest level being the Supreme Court, make up the third branch of the US government. Courts use the law to settle civil disputes and to decide on the guilt or innocence of people accused of crimes.

A civil dispute can be between two private parties (people, companies, or organizations), between a private party and the government, or between the United States and a state or local government. In each situation, both sides come before a court to present their positions. The court then applies the law to the facts that have been presented and makes a decision in favor of one or the other. The courts also hold criminal trials in which witnesses' present evidence and a jury or a judge delivers a verdict on the guilt or innocence of the accused offender or offenders.

Our legal system is based on an ideal goal to treat every person the same. Under the Constitution, every person accused of breaking the law has the right to have a public trial and a lawyer. If an accused person cannot afford a lawyer, the court will appoint and pay for one. Each person is considered innocent until proven guilty. Each person also has the right to ask for a review of his or her case if, in that person's view, the courts have made a mistake.

The ideal of equal justice is often difficult to achieve. Judges and juries are not free from personal prejudices or the prejudices of their communities. Poor people do not have the money to spend on the best available legal help, unlike wealthy citizens and large companies.

For example, during World War II in the 1940s, the Supreme Court upheld an act of Congress that allowed the relocation of thousands of Japanese Americans to internment camps. The high court claimed such camps were constitutional. Later the United States government would acknowledge the injustice of the camps and apologize. Shortly after, the Supreme Court made its decision in the *Ex parte Mitsuye Endo* case, and many detained Japanese Americans were released and returned home.

Despite some of these examples of weaknesses in the legal system, American courts do try to uphold the ideal of equal justice.

The Mitsuye Endo Case

In 1942, the government dismissed Mitsuye Endo from her civil service job in California and ordered her to a relocation center. Although Endo was a US citizen with a brother serving in the US Army, she and other Japanese Americans were forced into relocation camps during World War II because the government questioned their loyalty. Endo took the matter to the Supreme Court and won her case. The Court ruled 9–0 that Endo "should be given her liberty." Justice William O. Douglas proclaimed that "loyalty is a matter of the heart and mind, not of race, creed or color."

Japanese Americans were locked up in internment camps during World War II.

Courtesy of the Library of Congress/www.loc.gov

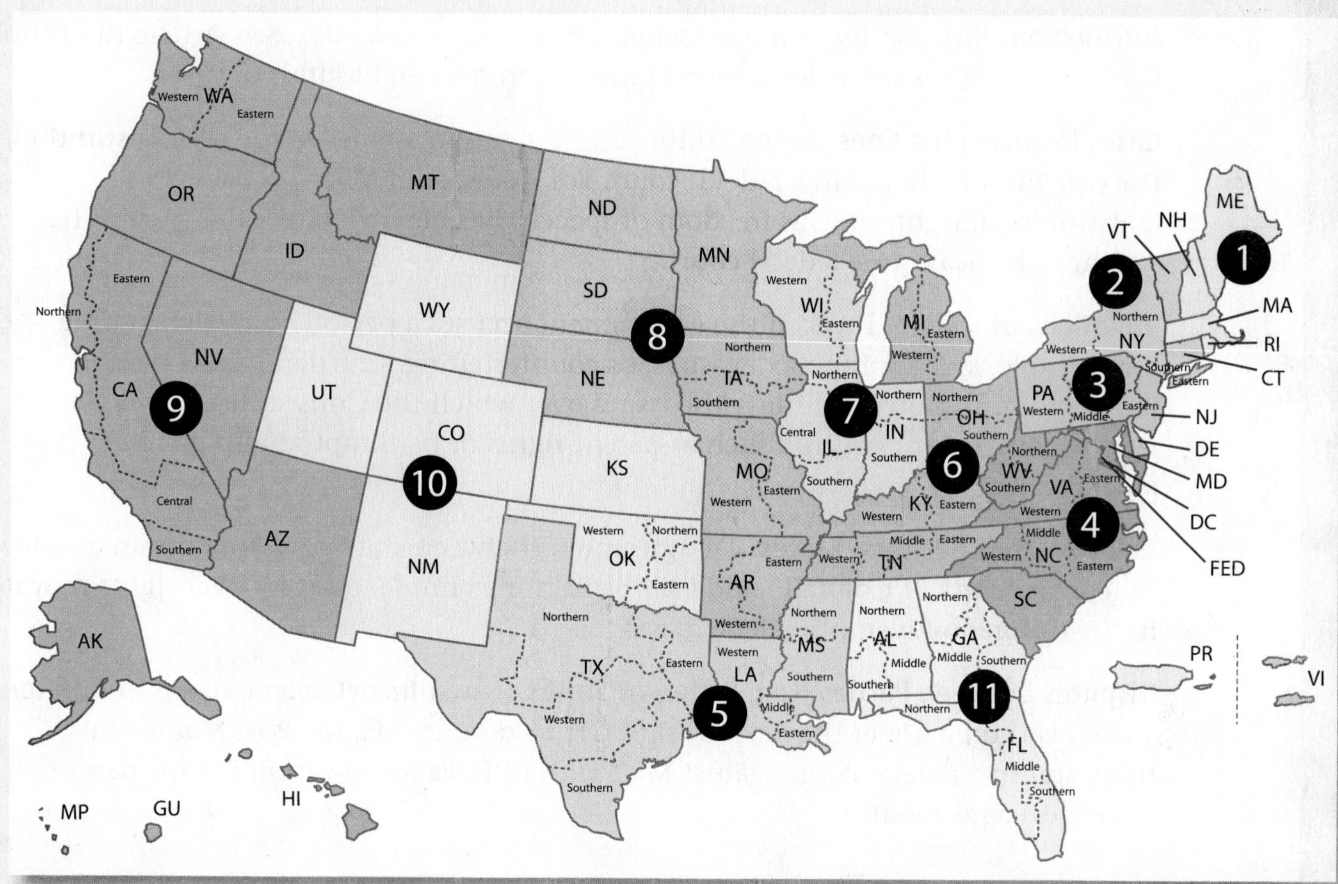

FIGURE 5.12

Federal Judicial Circuits and Districts

Courtesy of the United States Census Bureau/www.census.gov

The Federal Court System

The nation's founders created the federal court system in Article III of the Constitution. This article established a national Supreme Court and gave Congress the power to establish lower federal courts. Figure 5.12 indicates the regions of responsibility and number of federal judicial districts.

Over the years, Congress has created two kinds of lower courts. In 1789, it passed the Judiciary Act, which established federal district courts and circuit courts of appeals. Much later, in 1891, Congress created a system of federal appeals courts. Now the federal court system has three levels—the district courts at the bottom, the appeals courts in the middle, and the Supreme Court at the top. Our federal court system exists alongside 50 separate state court systems. Each state has its own laws and courts, including state-level Supreme Courts. The state courts get their powers from state constitutions and laws.

Cases Heard in Federal Courts

Jurisdiction. Jurisdiction is *a court's authority to hear and decide cases*. Article III of the Constitution gives the federal courts jurisdiction over eight kinds of cases.

Cases Involving the Constitution. If the law in question applies to the US Constitution, the case must be heard in a federal court. For example, if a person believes a constitutional right, such as freedom of speech, has been violated, that person has a right to be heard in a federal court.

Violations of Federal Laws. If the government accuses a person of a federal crime—for example, kidnapping, tax evasion, or counterfeiting—a federal court has jurisdiction. Disputes regarding the issues over which the Constitution gives the federal government control, such as patent rights or bankruptcy, also go to a federal court.

Controversies Between States. Disagreements between state governments are resolved in federal courts. If Colorado and California, for example, disagree over rights to water in the Colorado River, it is a federal case.

Disputes Between Parties from Different States. Lawsuits between citizens of different states also come under the federal courts. For example, Ms. Jones of Maine may bring suit in a federal court against Mr. Smith of Iowa for not fulfilling his part of a business agreement.

Judge Kathleen O'Malley

As her college alumni magazine states, "You won't find many thirteen-year-old girls who dream of being a federal judge." But once Kathleen O'Malley decided on a judicial career as a young teenager, she pursued that dream until she made it reality. O'Malley was appointed to the US Court of Appeals for the Federal Circuit by President Obama in 2010, after serving on the US District Court for the Northern District of Ohio.

Judge O'Malley's journey started when she read the book *Gideon's Trumpet*, the true story of the landmark 1963 US Supreme Court decision in *Gideon v. Wainwright*, which stated that courts have to provide attorneys to defendants unable to afford to them. "I was fascinated with the whole process of how the Supreme Court justices worked," she said, "and how a letter from a poor defendant could spark a massive change in the law."

Judge O'Malley being sworn in as a federal judge.

Courtesy of the US Court of Appeals for the Federal Circuit/www.cafc.uscourts.gov

Suits Involving the Federal Government. The US government may sue someone. For example, the Defense Department might sue a company that was contracted to build missile parts but did not complete the work on time. The suit would be heard in a federal court. Also, private parties can sue the government. For example, if a mail truck hit you, you could sue the US Postal Service for damages; or if the Department of Agriculture failed to pay your company for equipment it ordered, you could sue for your money.

Cases Involving Foreign Governments and Treaties. Any dispute between a foreign government and either the US government or an American private party is heard in a federal court. A treaty case might involve a dispute over the way the State Department interpreted a trade agreement.

Cases Based on Admiralty and Maritime Laws. These laws concern accidents or crimes on the high seas. One recent case involved a dispute over the rights to millions of dollars in sunken treasure recovered from a shipwreck 160 miles off the coast of South Carolina.

Cases Involving US Diplomats. If an American diplomat working in a US embassy is accused of breaking an American law, the case goes to a federal court.

Relation to State Courts

For most of the areas just described, federal courts have exclusive jurisdiction. This means that *only federal courts may hear and decide certain cases.* State courts have jurisdiction over all other matters. Most US court cases involve state law and are tried in state courts.

In a few circumstances, however, a case can be heard in either a state or a federal court. In these instances, there is concurrent jurisdiction, meaning that *federal and state courts share jurisdiction.* Either court may try crimes that violate both state and federal law. Concurrent jurisdiction also applies when citizens of different states are involved in a dispute that involves at least $50,000. In such a case, a person may sue in either a federal court or a state court. The person being sued may insist, however, that the case be tried in a federal court. Such appeals, on occasion, may reach the US Supreme Court.

US District Courts

The federal court system can be illustrated as a pyramid (Figure 5.13). The Supreme Court sits alone above a number of appeals courts, and has a broad base of district courts. Most federal cases are handled in the 94 US district courts. District courts are *the federal courts where trials are held and lawsuits are begun.* Every state has at least one district court, and some states have as many as four.

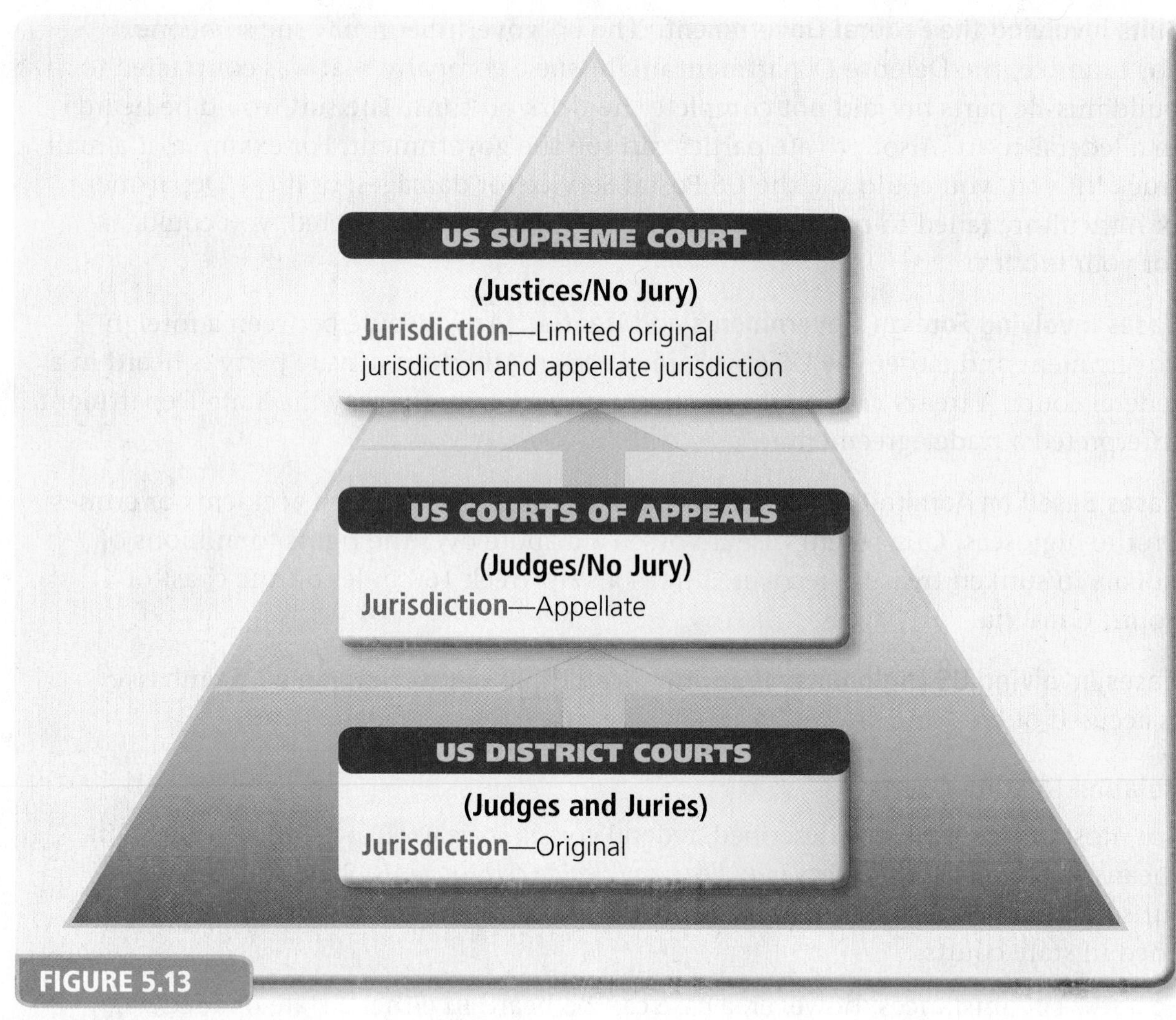

FIGURE 5.13

United States Court System

All federal cases must begin in a district court, because district courts have original jurisdiction, *the authority to hear cases for the first time*. District courts are responsible for determining the facts of a case; they are the trial courts for both criminal and civil federal cases. Thus, in a criminal case, a district court will decide if a person is guilty or innocent based on the evidence presented. District courts are the only federal courts in which witnesses testify and juries hear cases and reach verdicts.

US Courts of Appeals

A large percentage of people who lose their cases in a district court appeal to the next highest level—a US Court of Appeals. These courts are also referred to as federal appeals courts, circuit courts of appeals, or appellate courts. The job of the appeals courts is to *review decisions made in lower district courts*. This is referred to as appellate jurisdiction, or *the authority of a court to hear a case appealed from a lower court*. Lawyers usually appeal when they think the judge in their case applied the law incorrectly, used the wrong procedures, or if new evidence turns up. Appeals courts may also review federal regulatory agency rulings, if the people or groups involved believe the agency acted unfairly.

There are 12 United States courts of appeals. Each one has a circuit, or *a court that covers a particular geographic area*. In addition, a 13th appeals court, the Court of Appeals for the Federal Circuit, has nationwide jurisdiction to hear special cases, such as those involving patent law or international trade.

Making a Decision

Appeals courts do not hold trials. Instead, these courts may decide an appeal in one of three ways: uphold the original decision, reverse that decision, or remand the case. To remand a case means *to send the case back to the lower court to be tried again*. A panel of three or more judges reviews the record of the case being appealed and listens to arguments from lawyers for each side. The judges then meet and make a decision by majority vote.

The judges do not decide the guilt or innocence of a defendant in a criminal case or which side should win in a civil lawsuit. They rule only on whether the defendant's rights have been protected and on whether he or she received a fair trial. In the majority of cases, the decision of the appeals court is final. In some cases, however, lawyers may appeal the decision to the US Supreme Court.

Judge Mary M. Schroeder

Mary M. Schroeder used to be a judge for the Arizona Court of Appeals in Phoenix. Now she is a senior circuit judge of the United States Court of Appeals for the Ninth Circuit. She is the first woman to serve in this post in the Ninth Circuit. This, the largest circuit, comprises the seven westernmost continental states, plus Alaska, Hawaii, and the islands of Guam and the Northern Marianas. Schroeder has come a long way from the days in the 1960s, when she was one of just six women in her law school class. Her role, and that of other female judges, says Schroeder, is "not to feminize the courts but to humanize them."

The Ninth US Circuit Court of Appeals.
Courtesy of US Courts for the Ninth Circuit/www.ca9.uscourts.gov

Announcing the Decision

When an appeals court makes a decision, one judge writes an opinion for the court. The opinion offers a *detailed explanation of the legal thinking behind the court's decision.* The opinion sometimes sets a precedent, or *a model upon which to base decisions on similar cases for all courts and agencies within the district.* A precedent gives guidance to other judges. It does not have the force of law, but it is a very powerful argument to use in court. Judges and courts follow precedents in nearly all cases.

Federal Judges

The chief decision makers in the judicial branch are the federal judges. There are more than 870 judges who preside over the district courts. District courts in high-population areas have more judges because there are more cases to hear. Each appeals court has from 6 to 27 judges. The Supreme Court has 9 justices.

Selection and Tenure of Judges

According to the US Constitution, the president appoints judges, with the approval of the Senate. The Constitution sets forth no particular qualifications for federal judges. Presidents want to appoint judges who share their ideas about politics and justice. Thus, they usually choose people who belong to their political party. Because judges are appointed for life, presidents view their judicial appointments as an opportunity to affect the country after they have left the White House.

When naming judges, presidents usually follow a practice called senatorial courtesy. Under this system, a president submits the name of a candidate for judicial appointment to the senators from the candidate's state before formally submitting it to the entire Senate for approval. If either or both senators object to the candidate, the president will usually withdraw the name and nominate another candidate. The practice of senatorial courtesy usually applies only to the selection of judges to the district courts and other trial courts, not to the selection of judges to courts of appeals or the Supreme Court.

Once appointed, federal judges may have their jobs for life. A judge can be removed from office only through the process of impeachment. The writers of the Constitution gave federal judges this sort of job security because they wanted judges to be able to decide cases free from public or political pressures. Federal judges know their jobs are safe even if they make unpopular decisions.

Other Court Officials

Judges do not work alone. They have help from clerks, secretaries, court reporters, probation officers, and other workers. Each district court has magistrate judges. These officials take care of much of a judge's routine work. They issue court orders, like search and arrest warrants in federal cases. They hear preliminary evidence in a case to determine whether the case should be brought to trial. They also decide whether people who have been arrested should be held in jail or released on bail. Magistrates may also hear minor cases.

Every federal judicial district also has a United States attorney and one or more deputies. The US attorneys are government lawyers who prosecute people accused of breaking federal laws. They look into complaints of crime, prepare formal charges, and then present evidence in court. It is the US attorney's job to represent the United States in civil cases in which the government is involved. US attorneys are appointed to four-year terms by the president, with consent of the Senate. They report to the Attorney General of the United States, who is the head of the Justice Department.

Each federal judicial district also has a United States marshal. Marshals and their staff make arrests, collect fines, and take convicted persons to prison. They protect jurors, keep order in federal courts, and serve legal papers, including subpoenas. A subpoena is *a court order requiring someone to appear in court.* Marshals work for the Department of Justice. The president appoints US marshals with Senate approval.

The United States Supreme Court

The United States Supreme Court is at the top of the federal court system. If you visit the Supreme Court, you will see the words "Equal Justice Under Law" on the face of its marble building that sits behind the Capitol Building in Washington, DC. The Court stands above all other courts in its influence. Its main job is to decide whether laws are allowable under the US Constitution.

The Supreme Court has original jurisdiction in only two instances. It can preside over trials in cases that involve diplomats from foreign countries and in cases in which a state is involved. Otherwise, the Supreme Court hears cases that have come on appeal from lower district courts or from federal regulatory agencies.

Justice Stephen G. Breyer

Stephen G. Breyer received President Bill Clinton's Supreme Court nomination on 14 May 1994. The Senate confirmed Breyer with an 87–9 vote. Breyer has summarized his view of the Court's role in the following way: "It is important that the public, trying to cope with the problems of the nation, state, and local community, understand that the Constitution does not resolve, and was not intended to resolve, society's problems. Rather, the Constitution provides a framework for the creation of democratically determined solutions, which protect each individual's basic liberties…while securing a democratic form of government. We judges cannot insist that Americans participate in that government, but we can make clear that our Constitution depends upon it."

Justice Breyer.
Courtesy of the US Supreme Court/ www.supremecourt.gov

Since 1869, the number of justices serving on the Supreme Court has been nine.

Courtesy of the US Supreme Court/www.supremecourt.gov

The Supreme Court is not required to hear all the cases presented to it. It carefully chooses the cases it hears. It has final authority in any case involving the Constitution, acts of Congress, and treaties with other nations. The decisions of the Court are binding on all lower courts. When the Court refuses to review a case the decision of the lower court remains unchanged.

The Supreme Court Justices

The Supreme Court is made of nine justices; eight associate justices led by a chief justice. Congress sets this number and has the power to change it. The justices are important political decision makers. Their rulings often affect citizens as much as do presidential or congressional decisions.

The main duty of justices is to hear and rule on cases. They choose which cases to hear from among the thousands appealed to the Court each year, then decide the case itself and issue a written explanation for the decision, called the Court's opinion. The chief justice has additional duties, such as presiding over sessions and conferences at which cases are discussed.

Selection of Justices

The president appoints Supreme Court justices, with the consent of the Senate. Presidents are careful to choose nominees who are likely to be approved (the formal term used is "confirmed") by the Senate. When selecting nominees, the president often gets help from the attorney general and other Justice Department officials. The president's decision may also be influenced by the American Bar Association, the largest national organization of attorneys; interest groups, such as labor and civil rights groups; and other Supreme Court justices, who may recommend or support certain candidates. Senators have usually felt that the president should have a fairly free hand in appointing new justices.

Throughout history, though, the Senate has rejected many presidential nominees to the Supreme Court because of doubts about the qualifications or the legal philosophy of the persons nominated.

Backgrounds of the Justices

Supreme Court justices are always lawyers. They have had successful careers practicing or teaching law, serving as judges in lower courts, or holding other public positions prior to appointment. Political support and agreement with the president's ideas are important factors in who is appointed. Of course, once appointed, a justice may make rulings that the president does not like.

Conclusion

Learning about how our national government makes laws and ensures justice for all citizens is the first step to understanding the privileges and responsibilities that all American citizens should be aware of and cherish.

Now, it's up to you to put the traditions and the wellness and citizenship skills you have learned to good use, benefiting yourself and others at home, at school, and in your community.

Continue to build your leadership and social skills as a member of the JROTC. Continue to use your knowledge to live a healthy and productive life through physical activity and good nutrition. And continue to apply good judgment to make safe and ethical decisions. Putting these together, you will be demonstrating the best qualities of a good citizen and a future leader.

Lesson 5 Review

Using complete sentences, answer the following questions on a sheet of paper.

1. How many American citizens are members of the US Congress?
2. What is a bicameral legislative body?
3. Define caucus.
4. Who is the most powerful leader in the House of Representatives?
5. What is the role of the House and Senate floor leader?
6. If a bill involves money, where must it start?
7. What are the five ways standing committees may cause the "life or death" of a bill?
8. What are the three rules listed in the Constitution for someone to become president?
9. Why is the Electoral College a winner-take-all system?
10. As legislative chief, what message is the president sending to Congress when he vetoes a bill?
11. If the vice president becomes president, how is the new vice president selected?
12. What right does the Constitution provide to every person accused of breaking the law?
13. Which article of the US Constitution created the federal court system?
14. Name the three levels of federal court system.
15. Define jurisdiction.
16. Why do all federal cases begin in a district court?
17. What is the job of the US Court of Appeals?
18. Once selected, how long may federal judges hold this position?

APPLYING YOUR LEARNING

19. Based on what you have learned about the House of Representatives and Senate, write a brief paragraph on the role each plays in the legislative branch of our government.

References

CHAPTER 1 Introduction to JROTC Programs

LESSON 1 Organization of the JROTC

John F. Kennedy Inaugural Address, 20 January 1961. Retrieved 1 May 2013 from http://www.jfklibrary.org/Asset-Viewer/BqXIEM9F4024ntFl7SVAjA.aspx

JROTC Historical Dates. Retrieved 20 January 2013 from
http://www.norwich.edu/about/history.html
http://www.au.af.mil/au/holmcenter/AFJROTC/history.asp

Service JROTC Programs. Retrieved 2 February 2013 from
http://www.af.mil/AboutUs/FactSheets.aspx
http://www.cadetcommand.army.mil/jrotc-history.aspx

Retrieved 3 September 2014 from
http://www.njrotc.navy.mil/what_is_njrotc.asp
http://www.marines.mil/Portals/59/Publications/MCO%201533.6E.pdf

Retrieved 8 September 2014 from http://www.mcjrotc.org/
http://chicagojrotc.com/pdf/marine_cadet_handbook.pdf
http://dbhsmcjrotc.com/?page_id=91

Retrieved 6 May 2013 from http://www.usarmyjrotc.com/

Retrieved 10 February 2013 from http://www.gocoastguard.com/
http://www.gocoastguard.com/get-the-answers/faq#Does%20the%20USCG%20have%20a%20JROTC%20program?

JROTC and Community Service. Retrieved 5 Feb 2013 from http://www.beaverpa.us/news/JROTC.pdf

Lines of Responsibility and Authority. Retrieved 10 February 2013 from
http://www.hydeparkcps.org/ourpages/auto/2009/10/27/43464528/JROTC%20Duties%20and%20Responsibilities.pdf
http://www.hydeparkcps.org/ourpages/auto/2009/10/27/43464528/JROTC%20Duties%20and%20Responsibilities.pdf

LESSON 2 The Military Uniform and Appearance Standards

Roman Empire.net website (2008). Retrieved 10 April 2013 from http://www.roman-empire.net/society/soc-dress.html

About.com Classic Literature website (2013). Retrieved 15 March 2013 from http://classiclit.about.com/od/kingmartinluther/a/aa_mlkingjr.htm

LESSON 3 Customs and Courtesies for Junior ROTC

Introduction to the Navy Junior Reserve Officer Training Corps (2008). Boston, MA: Pearson Custom Publishing.

Thinkexist.com website (2013). Retrieved 13 May 2013 from http://thinkexist.com/quotation/to_be_humble_to_superiors_is_duty-to_equals/146119.html

Hand salute, AFMAN 36-2203, Drill and Ceremonies (1996). US Air Force website. Retrieved 3 April 2013 from http://www.mortuary.af.mil/shared/media/document/AFD-110303-025.pdf

Local Customs and Cultural Adjustment. North Carolina State University website. Retrieved 22 March 2013 from http://www.ncsu.edu/ois/research/culturaladjustment.php

Greenwich Mean Time. Retrieved 10 October 2013 from http://www.greenwichmeantime.com

LESSON 4 Attitude, Discipline, and Respect

Cam Suarez-Bitar, *Vince Lombardi's Leadership and the Path to Wisdom*. 16 November 2009. Communications on Sports Business website. Retrieved 10 April 2013 from http://comsportsbiz.wordpress.com/2009/11/16/vince-lombardis-leadership-and-the-path-to-wisdom/

Oprah Winfrey's Leadership Style. StudyMode.com website. Retrieved 12 April 2013 from http://www.studymode.com/essays/Oprah-Winfrey-s-Leadership-Style-953091.html http://www.the-benefits-of-positive-thinking.com/oprah-positive-quotes.html

Jenna Goudreau, *How to Lead Like Oprah*. 22 October 2010. Retrieved 12 April 2013 from http://www.forbes.com/sites/jennagoudreau/2010/10/22/how-to-lead-like-oprah-winfrey-own-rachael-ray-dr-oz-phil/

W. Clement Stone quote. Retrieved 9 April 2013 from http://www.goodreads.com/quotes/tag/attitude?page=3

Introduction to the Navy Junior Reserve Officer Training Corps (2008). Boston, MA: Pearson Custom Publishing.

Leadership Education II: Communication, Awareness and Leadership (2006). Boston, MA: Pearson Custom Publishing.

Victor Parachin, *Laws for Positive Leadership*. The Toastmaster. September 2006. Retrieved 15 Apr 2013 from http://www.toastmasters.org/laws.aspx

Remembering the Titans. Retrieved 20 May 2013 from http://www.cbsnews.com/stories/2000/09/29/earlyshow/saturday/main237291.shtml http://espn.go.com/page2/s/closer/020808.html

LESSON 5 Ethics, Values, and Morals

Air Force Core Values. Retrieved 3 September 2014 from http://www.peterson.af.mil/shared/media/document/AFD-090212-058.pdf

Army Core Values. Retrieved 3 September 2014 from http://www.army.mil/values

Navy and Marine Corps Core Values. Retrieved 3 September 2014 from http://www.navy.mil/navydata/nav_legacy.asp?id=193

Coast Guard Core Values. Retrieved 3 September 2014 from http://www.uscg.mil/hq/cg3/cg3pcx/corevalues.asp

Declaration of Human Rights. Retrieved 3 September 2014 from http://www.un.org/en/documents/udhr/index/html

LESSON 6 Social Etiquette and Dining-In, Dining Out

Military Etiquette. Retrieved 3 September 2014 from http://www.116pvi.org/Documents/MilitaryEtiquette.doc

Text messaging. Emily Post website. Retrieved 3 September 2014 from http://www.emilypost.com/home-and-family-life/133-college-and-beyond/391-text-messaging

CHAPTER 2 Personal Behavior

LESSON 1 Note Taking and Study Skills

Nelson Mandela quotation. Retrieved 1 September 2014 from http://www.un.org/en/globalissues/briefingpapers/efa/quotes.shtml

PQRST method. Retrieved 11 November 2013 from http://www.lintech.org/study-skills/The_PQRST_method.html

LESSON 2 Managing Stress

Andrew Bernstein quotation. Retrieved 27 August 2014 from http://www.brainyquote.com/quotes/authors/a/andrew_bernstein.html

Life Skills: Health (2007). Boston, MA: Pearson Custom Publishing.

Lynch, Elmore, and Morgan, *Choosing Health* (2012). San Francisco, CA: Pearson Education, Inc., publishing as Benjamin Cummings.

Pruitt, Allegrante, and Prothro-Stith, *Prentice Hall Health* (2010). Boston, MA: Pearson Education, Inc.

Fight, flight or freeze response. Retrieved 10 October 2014 from http://www.aacap.org/AACAP/AACAP/Families_and_Youth/Facts_for_Families/Facts_for_Families_Pages/Helping_Teenagers_With_Stress_66.aspx

Retrieved 8 September 2014 from http://www.ncbi.nlm.nih.gov/pmc/articles/PMC2489204/

Retrieved 8 September 2014 from http://youth.anxietybc.com/ask-an-expert/what-is-fight-flight-freeze

Pituitary gland. Retrieved 8 September 2014 from http://www.neurosurgery.pitt.edu/centers-excellence/neurosurgical-oncology/brain-and-brain-tumors/terms-and-definitions

Adrenaline. Retrieved 8 September 2014 from http://www.nlm.nih.gov/medlineplus/ency/article/002219.htm

Stress and illness. Retrieved 8 September 2014 from http://www.sciencedaily.com/releases/2012/04/120402162546.htm

LESSON 3 Making Positive Decisions

Life Skills: Health (2007). Boston, MA: Pearson Custom Publishing.

Lynch, Elmore, and Morgan, *Choosing Health* (2012). San Francisco, CA: Pearson Education, Inc., publishing as Benjamin Cummings.

Pruitt, Allegrante, and Prothro-Stith, *Prentice Hall Health* (2010). Boston, MA: Pearson Education, Inc.

SMART Goal Examples. Studentleadership.com website (2013). Retrieved 20 November 2013 from http://studentleadership.com/smart-goal-examples/

Mottet, Vogl-Bauer and Houser, *Your Personal Communication* (2012). Boston, MA: Pearson Education, Inc.

Goals Setting Skills Test (2011). Retrieved 23 November 2013 from http://psychologytoday.tests.psychtests.com/take_test.php?idRegTest=1601

Effective Communications Skills (n.d.). Retrieved 26 November 2013 from http://only-effective-communication-skills.com/imessages.html/

International Coach Academy website (2012). Retrieved 10 December 2013 from http://www.icoachacademy.com/blog/coaching_niche/parent_and_youth_coaching/renee-erlich-goal-setting-for-children-and-teens/

Making Kids Work On Goals (And Not Just In Soccer). Wall Street Journal website (2014). Retrieved 12 December 2013 from http://online.wsj.com/news/articles/SB10001424052748704758904576188453057819300?mg=reno64-wsj&url=http%3A%2F%2Fonline.wsj.com%2Farticle%2FSB100014240527487047589045761884530578 19300.htm l

12 Things Students Should Never Do on Social Networks (2013). Retrieved 11 December 2013 from http://mashable.com/2012/09/04/students-social-media-warnings/

Safe and Responsible Social Networking. Cyberbullying Research Center website (2014). Retrieved 13 December 2013 from http://cyberbullying.us/

Is Social Media Sabotaging Real Communication? Forbes Magazine website (2012). Retrieved 12 December 2013 from http://www.forbes.com/sites/susantardanico/2012/04/30/is-social-media-sabotaging-real-communication/

LESSON 4 Emotional and Mental Health Care

Life Skills: Health (2007). Boston, MA: Pearson Custom Publishing.

Lynch, Elmore, and Morgan, *Choosing Health* (2012). San Francisco, CA: Pearson Education, Inc., publishing as Benjamin Cummings.

Pruitt, Allegrante, and Prothro-Stith, *Prentice Hall Health* (2010). Boston, MA: Pearson Education, Inc.

Daniel Goleman quote. Retrieved 5 January 2014 from http://www.brainyquote.com/quotes/quotes/d/danielgole285391.html#iUPIXMfrFceKxDFJ.99

Emotional Intelligence. Psychology Today website (2014). Retrieved 6 January 2014 from http://www.psychologytoday.com/basics/emotional-intelligence

John D. Mayer, *What Emotional Intelligence Is and Is Not*. Psychology Today website (2014). Retrieved 6 January 2014 from http://www.psychologytoday.com/blog/the-personality-analyst/200909/what-emotional-intelligence-is-and-is-not

Nonsuicidal Self-Injury Often Begins in Younger Children. American Psychiatric Association website (2014). Retrieved 7 January 2014 from http://alert.psychiatricnews.org/2012/06/nonsuicidal-self-injury-often-begins-in.html

Rates of Nonsuicidal Self-Injury in Youth: Age, Sex, and Behavioral Methods in a Community Sample. Barrocas, Hankin, Young, and Abela. American Academy of Pediatrics website (2013). Retrieved 12 January 2014 from http://pediatrics.aappublications.org/content/early/2012/06/06/peds.2011-2094.abstract

Depressed Adolescents Respond Best to Combination Treatment (2007). National Institutes of Health website. Retrieved 13 January 2014 from http://www.nimh.nih.gov/news/science-news/2007/depressed-adolescents-respond-best-to-combination-treatment.shtml

Suicide. Centers for Disease Control website (2012). Retrieved 13 January 2014 from http://www.cdc.gov/violenceprevention/pdf/suicide-datasheet-a.PDF

Freshman Gage Crispe Dedicated to Suicide Prevention. Denver University website (2012). Retrieved 15 January 2014 from http://www.du.edu/give/news-freshman-gage-crispe-dedicated-to-suicide-prevention.html

National Suicide Prevention Week Information and Media Kit (2014). Retrieved 9 September 2014 from http://www.suicidology.org/Portals/14/docs/MediaKit2014.1.pdf

LESSON 5 Avoiding and Preventing Violence

Pruitt, Allegrante, Prothro-Stith, *Prentice Hall Health* (2010). Boston, MA: Pearson Education, Inc.

Mahatma Ghandi quotation. Retrieved 23 January 2014 from http://www.brainyquote.com/quotes/keywords/non-violence.html#TrMA8M7ZJUvRIcuk.99

Facts and figures on teen violence. Retrieved 24 January 2014 from http://cultureandyouth.org/stats/teen-violence/http://www.cdc.gov/VIOLENCEPREVENTION/youthviolence/stats_at-a_glance/

Gun violence. Retrieved 30 January 2014 from http://usnews.nbcnews.com/_news/2013/01/16/16547690-just-the-facts-gun-violence-in-america?litehttp://www.cdc.gov/VIOLENCEPREVENTION/youthviolence/stats_ at-a_glance/

CHAPTER 3 Be Health Smart

LESSON 1 Your Body Systems

Life Skills: Health (2007). Boston, MA: Pearson Custom Publishing.

Lynch, Elmore, and Morgan, *Choosing Health* (2012). San Francisco, CA: Pearson Education, Inc., publishing as Benjamin Cummings.

Pruitt, Allegrante, Prothro-Stith, *Prentice Hall Health* (2010). Boston, MA: Pearson Education, Inc.

Buddha quotation. Retrieved 8 March 2014 from http://www.brainyquote.com/quotes/topics/topic_health.html

World Health Organization quotation. Retrieved 8 March 2014 from http://www.greatest-inspirational-quotes.com/inspirational-health-quotes.html

Best Bones Forever website. Retrieved 9 March 2014 from http://www.bestbonesforever.gov/parents/foods/dictionary.html

Heart Disease: Exercise for a Healthy Heart. WebMD website. Retrieved 10 March 2014 from http://www.webmd.com/heart-disease/guide/exercise-healthy-heart

USHHS Agency for Healthcare Research and Quality website. Retrieved 10 March 2014 from http://www.ahrq.gov/patients-consumers/prevention/understanding/bodysys/index.html

LESSON 2 Nutrition

Healthy Eating Plan. National Heart, Lung and Blood Institute website. Retrieved 5 January 2014 from http://www.nhlbi.nih.gov/health/educational/lose_wt/eat/calories.htm

Potassium. Retrieved 5 January 2014 from http://www.encyclopedia.com/topic/potassium.aspx

Obesity in America, N. Jay Sorensen, MBA RD. Retrieved 6 January 2014 from http://www.foodandnutrition.com/nutrition/obesity.htm

Physical Activity Guidelines for Americans. President's Council on Fitness, Sports and Nutrition. Retrieved 7 January 2014 from http://www.fitness.gov/be-active/physical-activity-guidelines-for-americans/

How to Understand and Use the Nutrition Facts Label. US Food and Drug Administration website. Retrieved 7 January 2014 from http://www.fda.gov/food/ingredientspackaginglabeling/labelingnutrition/ucm274593.htm

LESSON 3 The Benefits of Physical Activity

Plato quotation. Retrieved 22 February 2014 from http://www.lexiyoga.com/fitness-quotes

Kids need to step up physical activity, report says. Nanci Helmick. USA Today website. Retrieved 24 February 2014 from http://www.usatoday.com/story/news/nation/2013/03/08/kids-physical-activity/1971063/

Physical Activity Facts. US Center for Disease Control and Prevention website. Retrieved 25 February 2014 from http://www.cdc.gov/healthyyouth/physicalactivity/facts.htm

Physical Activity Guidelines for Americans (2008). US Department of Health and Human Services. Washington, DC: US Department of Health and Human Services.

Physical activity, exercise, and physical fitness: definitions and distinctions for health-related research. Caspersen, Powell, and Christenson, 1985. Retrieved 8 February 2014 from http://www.ncbi.nlm.nih.gov/pmc/articles/PMC1424733/

The 5 Components of Physical Fitness. Retrieved 10 February 2014 from http://www.functional-fitness-facts.com/5-components-of-physical-fitness.html

Land of the free, home of the very fat. Vitoria Cavaliere. New York Daily News website. Retrieved 12 February 2014 from http://www.nydailynews.com/life-style/health/land-free-home-fat-report-obesity-surpass-50-percent-mark-states-20-years-article-1.1162227#ixzz2PPlE72ZO

Overweight and Obesity Statisitics. Retrieved 12 February 2014 from http://win.niddk.nih.gov/statistics/#ref2

Effects of Sports on Emotional Health. Daniel Thomas. Retrieved 14 February 2014 from http://healthyliving.azcentral.com/effects-sports-emotional-health-6567.html

Effects of Steroids, Doping and Performance-Enhancing Drugs. USDA website. Retrieved 15 February 2014 from http://www.usada.org/substances/effects-of-performance-enhancing-drugs/

Body Mass Index Formula. Retrieved 15 February 2014 from http://www.epic4health.com/bmiformula.html

Target heart rate. US Center for Disease Control and Prevention website. Retrieved 16 February 2014 from http://www.cdc.gov/physicalactivity/everyone/measuring/heartrate.html

LESSON 4 Understanding Your Body Image

Pruitt, Allegrante, and Prothro-Stith, *Prentice Hall Health* (2010). Boston, MA: Pearson Education, Inc.

Lynch, Elmore, and Morgan, *Choosing Health* (2012). San Francisco, CA: Pearson Education, Inc., publishing as Benjamin Cummings.

Oprah Winfrey quotation. Retrieved 28 February 2014 from http://www.goodreads.com/quotes/tag/body-image

Beware These Empty Calories! WebMD website. Retrieved 2 March 2014 from http://www.webmd.com/diet/features/beware-empty-calories

BMI Calculator. Retrieved 3 March 2014 from
http://www.bmi-calculator.net/bmr-calculator/bmr-formula.php
http://www.bmi-calculator.net/bmr-calculator/harris-benedict-equation/

10 Things You Need to Know About Metabolism. Retrieved 6 March 2014 from http://health.howstuffworks.com/wellness/diet-fitness/weight-loss/10-things-dieters-need-to-know-about-metabolism.htm#p age=2

LESSON 5 First Aid

Clara Barton quotation. Retrieved 12 March 2014 from http://www.brainyquote.com/quotes/authors/c/clara_barton.html

Pruitt, Allegrante, and Prothro-Stith, *Prentice Hall Health* (2010). Boston, MA: Pearson Education, Inc.

Choking Rescue Procedures. Retrieved 12 August 2014 from
http://www.webmd.com/first-aid/tc/choking-rescue-procedure-heimlich-maneuver-overview
http://www.nlm.nih.gov/medlineplus/ency/article/000047.htm

Lyme Disease Transmission. US Center for Disease Control and Prevention website. Retrieved 10 March 2014 from http://www.cdc.gov/lyme/transmission/index.html

Rocky Mountain Spotted Fever. US Center for Disease Control and Prevention website. Retrieved 10 March 2014 from http://www.cdc.gov/rmsf/index.html

CPR. American Red Cross website. Retrieved 13 March 2014 from
http://www.redcross.org/lp/take-a-class
American Heart Association website. Retrieved 13 March 2014 from
http://www.heart.org/HEARTORG/CPRAndECC/CPR_UCM_001118_SubHomePage.jsp
http://www.firstaidweb.com/adult_review.php

First Aid. Mayo Clinic website. Retrieved 14 March 2014 from http://www.mayoclinic.org/first-aid

Automated External Defibrillator. National Heart, Lung and Blood Institute website. Retrieved 15 March 2014 from http://www.nhlbi.nih.gov/health/health-topics/topics/aed/

CHAPTER 4 Making Safe, Drug-Free Decisions

LESSON 1 Medicines and Drugs

Medicines and Drugs. Food and Drug Administration website. Retrieved 2 April 2014 from http://www.fda.gov

Life Skills: Health (2007). Boston, MA: Pearson Custom Publishing.

Lynch, Elmore, and Morgan, *Choosing Health* (2012). San Francisco, CA: Pearson Education, Inc., publishing as Benjamin Cummings.

Pruitt, Allegrante, and Prothro-Stith, *Prentice Hall Health* (2010). Boston, MA: Pearson Education, Inc.

LESSON 2 Tobacco

Life Skills: Health (2007). Boston, MA: Pearson Custom Publishing.

Lynch, Elmore, and Morgan, *Choosing Health* (2012). San Francisco, CA: Pearson Education, Inc., publishing as Benjamin Cummings.

Pruitt, Allegrante, and Prothro-Stith, *Prentice Hall Health* (2010). Boston, MA: Pearson Education, Inc.

History of tobacco. Retrieved 24 April 2014 from http://healthliteracy.worlded.org/docs/tobacco/Unit1/2history_of.html

Master Settlement Agreement. Retrieved 25 April 2014 from http://www.legacyforhealth.org/about/our-history/about-the-master-settlement-agreement

Cigarette smoking statistics. Center for Disease Control website. Retrieved 26 April 2014 from http://www.cdc.gov/tobacco/data_statistics/fact_sheets/adult_data/cig_smoking/
http://www.cdc.gov/tobacco/data_statistics/fact_sheets/tobacco_industry/cigars/#current

Chewing tobacco. Retrieved 26 April 2014 from
http://www.cdc.gov/tobacco/data_statistics/fact_sheets/fast_facts/#use
http://www.bostonglobe.com/sports/2014/03/06/tobacco-chewing-nasty-habit-still-kicking-mlb/nZDZK9LOFDlr0MFj9X1WkO/story.html
http://newyork.cbslocal.com/2012/03/01/by-the-numbers-tony-gwynn-and-smokeless-tobacco-in-baseball/
http://www.cnn.com/2011/11/25/us/baseball-chewing-tobacco-no-more

Retrieved 27 April 2014 from
http://www.cancer.org/cancer/cancercauses/tobaccocancer/smokeless-tobacco
http://www.fda.gov/TobaccoProducts/Labeling/ucm388395.htm
http://www.fda.gov/NewsEvents/Newsroom/PressAnnouncements/ucm394667.htm
http://www.fda.gov/ForConsumers/ConsumerUpdates/ucm392735.htm

E-cigarettes 101. Retrieved 27 April 2014 from http://www.webmd.com/smoking-cessation/features/electronic-cigarettes

Alternate forms of tobacco. Retrieved 30 April 2014 from http://www.cancer.org/cancer/cancercauses/tobaccocancer/questionsaboutsmokingtobaccoandhealth/questions-about-smoking-tobacco-and-health-other-forms-of-smoking

Smoking health costs. Retrieved 29 April 2014 from
http://www.hhs.gov/ash/initiatives/tobacco/
http://www.surgeongeneral.gov/library/reports/preventing-youth-tobacco-use/full-report.pdf
http://www.surgeongeneral.gov/library/reports/preventing-youth-tobacco-use/exec-summary.pdf
http://www.theawl.com/2012/06/pack-of-cigarettes-cost

Teenagers and tobacco. Retrieved 1 May 2014 from
http://therealcost.betobaccofree.hhs.gov/facts/did-you-know/index.html?gclid=CJXuqMfnl74CFcNlOgodgQwAvg
http://www.cancer.org/acs/groups/cid/documents/webcontent/002963-pdf.pdf
http://www.legacyforhealth.org/our-issues/youth-and-young-adult-tobacco-use

Adult smoking. Retrieved 29 April 2014 from
http://www.cdc.gov/mmwr/preview/mmwrhtml/mm6035a5.htm?s_cid=%20mm6035a5.htm_w

Quitting smoking. Retrieved 2 May 2014 from
http://teen.smokefree.gov/
http://www.cancer.gov/cancertopics/factsheet/Tobacco/cessation
http://www.mayoclinic.org/healthy-living/quit-smoking/expert-answers/smoking/faq-20058153

LESSON 3 Alcohol

Marilyn vos Savant quotation. Retrieved 15 May 2014 from
http://www.brainyquote.com/quotes/quotes/m/marilynvos365170.html
Underage Drinking. Retrieved 15 May 2014 from
http://www.niaaa.nih.gov/alcohol-health/special-populations-co-occurring-disorders/underage-drinking
http://pubs.niaaa.nih.gov/publications/arh284/205-212.htm
http://pubs.niaaa.nih.gov/publications/arh283/125-132.htm
http://pubs.niaaa.nih.gov/publications/aa68/aa68.htm

Retrieved 20 May 2014 from http://www.nytimes.com/health/guides/disease/alcoholism/risk-factors.html
http://www.thecoolspot.gov/

Economic Costs of Alcohol Abuse. Retrieved 17 May 2014 from http://www.addict-help.com/alcoholabuse.asp

Toll of Underage Drinking. Retrieved 17 May 2014 from http://www.camy.org/factsheets/sheets/The_Toll_of_Underage_Drinking.html

Study: Music is Just Advertisement for Alcohol Brands. Julie Beck. The Atlantic website. Retrieved 19 May 2014 from http://www.theatlantic.com/health/archive/2014/04/study-music-is-just-advertisement-for-alcohol-brands/360435/

Stages of alcoholism. Retrieved 21 May 2014 from http://www.my-alcoholic-addict.com/stages-of-alcoholism.html

Helping a Family Member or Friend. Retrieved 20 May 2014 from http://ncadd.org/index.php/for-friends-and-family/helping-someone

Date rape. Retrieved 22 May 2014 from http://www.fit.edu/caps/documents/daterape.pdf

LESSON 4 Environmental Health

World Health Organization (WHO). *Preventing disease through healthy environments* (2006). Geneva, Switzerland: WHO.

Youth violence statistics. Retrieved 20 May 2014 from http://www.healthypeople.gov/2020/topicsobjectives2020/overview.aspx?topicid=12

National Geographic website. Retrieved 22 May 2014 from http://ngm.nationalgeographic.com/2010/05/mount-st-helens/blast-zone-animation

11 Surprising Natural Lessons from Mount St. Helens. Retrieved 22 May 2014 from http://www.scientificamerican.com/slideshow/mount-st-helens-lessons/

Health and Environmental Effects of Ozone Layer Depletion. Retrieved 24 May 2014 from http://www.epa.gov/spdpublc/science/effects/index.html

Water pollution. University of Hawaii website. Retrieved 25 May 2014 from http://www.soest.hawaii.edu/GG/ASK/waterpol3.html

Livestock pollution and public health. Retrieved 27 May 2014 from http://www.nrdc.org/water/pollution/ffarms.asp

Light and noise pollution. Retrieved 28 May 2014 from http://education.nationalgeographic.com/education/encyclopedia/pollution/?ar_a=1

Land pollution. Retrieved 28 May 2014 from http://www.britannica.com/EBchecked/topic/329175/land-pollution

E-waste. Retrieved 29 May 2014 from http://www.recycleforce.org/recycling-services/e-waste

CHAPTER 5 The Foundations of United States Citizenship

Thomas Paine quotation. Retrieved 28 August 2014 from http://thinkexist.com/quotation/our_citizenship_in_the_united_states_is_our/322653.html

LESSON 1 The American Flag and Other National Symbols

Ulysses S. Grant quotation. Retrieved 28 August 2014 from http://www.usa-patriotism.com/quotes/potus-03.htm

History of the American flag. Retrieved 1 June 2014 from http://publications.usa.gov/epublications/ourflag/history2.htm

Facts About the Flag of the United States. Retrieved 3 June 2014 from http://www.si.edu/encyclopedia_si/nmah/flag.htm

US Department of Education website. Retrieved 9 September 2014 from http://www2.ed.gov/about/offices/list/os/september11/ssbfacts.html

Star Spangled Banner. Retrieved 9 September 2014 from http://www.smithsonianmag.com/history/the-story-behind-the-star-spangled-banner-149220970/?no-ist

Original Design of the Great Seal of the United States. Retrieved 3 June 2014 from http://www.ourdocuments.gov/doc.php?flash=true&doc=5

The Background and Symbolism of the Air Force Seal. Retrieved 2 June 2014 from http://military.answers.com/air-force/the-background-and-symbolism-of-the-air-force-seal

Air Force Symbol Meaning. Retrieved 2 June 2014 from http://www.trademark.af.mil/factsheets/factsheet.asp?id=13404

Air Force Emblem. Retrieved 2 June 2014 from http://www.trademark.af.mil/logos/afe/index.asp

Army Seal and Emblem. Retrieved 27 August 2014 from http://www.history.army.mil/reference/Heritage/Emblem.htm

Navy Seal. Retrieved 27 August 2014 from http://www.history.navy.mil/faqs/faq43-1.htm

Marine Corps Seal and Emblem. Retrieved 29 August 2014 from
https://www.mcu.usmc.mil/historydivision/Pages/Customs_Traditions/Emblem_Seal.aspx
http://www.milbadges.com/corps/usa/marine
http://www.aviation.marines.mil/Portals/11/Documents/SECNAVINST%205720.44c%5B1%5D.pdf
http://www.hqmc.marines.mil/divpa/Units/MarineCorpsTrademarkLicensingProgram.aspx

Coast Guard Seal and Emblem. Retrieved 29 August 2014 from
http://www.uscg.mil/history/img/logos/USCGShield.png
http://www.uscg.mil/history/articles/Traditions.asp
http://www.uscg.mil/directives/cim/5000-5999/CIM_5200_14A.pdf

The American's Creed. Retrieved 5 June 2014 from
http://www.marshallhall.org/dar/am-creed.html
http://www.usflag.org/american.creed.html
http://www.spangledwithstars.com/national-symbols/american-creed.htm

LESSON 2 Civics

The Collected Works of Abraham Lincoln. Retrieved 29 August 2014 from http://quod.lib.umich.edu/l/lincoln/lincoln2/1:261?rgn=div1;view=fulltext

Almond, et. al. *Comparative Politics Today: A World View* (2008). Boston, MA: Pearson-Longman.

Davis, Ferlund, and Woll. *Civics: Government and Economics in Action* (2009). Boston, MA: Pearson-Prentice Hall.

Tannahill. *Think American Government* (2013). Boston, MA: Pearson Education.

Hometown Security. Department of Homeland Security website. Retrieved June 12 2014 from http://www.dhs.gov/topic/if-you-see-something-say-something

Immigration and Naturalization. Retrieved 13 June 2014 from
http://www.uscis.gov/
http://www.uscis.gov/news/fact-sheets/naturalization-through-military-service-fact-sheet

Oscar Handlin quotation on immigration. Retrieved 29 August 2014 from http://www.journalofamericanhistory.org/issues/972/latino-interchange.html

World Charity Index 2011. Retrieved 29 August 2014 from http://www.huffingtonpost.com/2011/12/19/world-giving-index-us-ran_n_1159562.html

Barack Obama quotation. NBC News website. Retrieved 29 August 2014 from http://www.nbcnews.com/id/31546835/ns/us_news-giving/t/obama-community-service-national-duty

Charitable organizations. Retrieved 5 August 2014 from http://www.nptrust.org/

LESSON 3 The Constitution of the United States

Chief Justice John Marshall quotation. Retrieved 8 August 2014 from http://www2.liu.edu/cwis/cwp/library/exhibits/constitution/quotes.htm

Congressional information. Retrieved 10 August 2014 from http://pressgallery.house.gov/member-data/salaries

American Heritage Dictionary of the English Language, fifth edition (2011). Boston, MA: Houghton, Mifflin, Harcourt Publishing.

LESSON 4 Interpreting the Bill of Rights and Other Amendments

Thomas Jefferson quotation. Retrieved 15 August 2014 from http://www.brainyquote.com/quotes/keywords/bill_of_rights.html#QHgFOqo20zX0iKot.99

Civics: Government and Economics in Action. Pearson Education, Inc. website. Retrieved 10 August 2014 from http://www.phschool.com/webcodes10/index.cfm?area=view&wcprefix=mpk&wcsuffix=1000

Voting. Retrieved 11 August 2014 from http://votesmart.org/

LESSON 5 US National Government

Gerald R. Ford quotation. Retrieved 3 September 2014 from http://www.fordlibrarymuseum.gov/library/speeches/740001.asp

Political Parties. Retrieved 3 September 2014 from http://www.u-s-history.com/pages/h279.html

McClenaghan, William A. *Magruder's American Government* (2007). Boston, MA: Pearson/Prentice-Hall.

Types of Committees. Retrieved 3 September 2014 from
http://www.house.gov/committees
http://clerk.house.gov/committee_info/scsoal.pdf
http://www.senate.gov/artandhistory/history/common/briefing/Committees.htm
http://www.senate.gov/pagelayout/committees/d_three_sections_with_teasers/committees_home.htm

Standing Committees. Retrieved 3 September 2014 from https://beta.congress.gov/committees

Floor Debate. Retrieved 3 September 2014 from
http://www.senate.gov/reference/glossary_term/cloture.htm
http://www.dispatch.com/content/stories/local/2014/06/01/gop-filibusters-dems-fill-the-tree.html

Civics: Government and Economics in Action, Pearson Education, Inc. website. Retrieved 3 September 2014 from http://www.phschool.com/webcodes10/index.cfm?area=view&wcprefix=mpk&wcsuffix=1000

Presidential Action. Retrieved 3 September 2014 from http://www.senate.gov/reference/glossary_term/pocket_veto.htm

The President Has Many Roles. Retrieved 3 September 2014 from http://www.whitehouse.gov/about/inside-white-house

Mary M. Schroeder feature. Retrieved 3 September 2014 from http://www.ca9.uscourts.gov/content/view_seniority_list.php?pk_id=0000000035

Glossary

A

abridging—limiting the rights. (p. 459)
active listening—hearing, thinking about, and responding to the other person's message. (p. 164)
addiction—a physical or psychological need for a drug. (p. 304)
addictive drug—one that is capable of causing a user to develop intense cravings for it. (p. 326)
adjectives—words that describe objects. (p. 127)
adjourn—suspend a session. (p. 444)
adrenaline—the "emergency hormone" that prepares the body to respond to a stressor. (p. 143)
aerobic capacity—the ability of your heart and lungs to supply the muscles of your body with oxygen. (p. 245)
aerobic exercise—rhythmic, nonstop, and moderate to vigorous activity that requires large amounts of oxygen and improves the cardiorespiratory system. (p. 244)
affirmative action—encouraged the hiring and promoting of minorities and women in fields that were traditionally closed to them. (p. 495)
air pollution—a mixture of natural and human-made substances in the air we breathe. (p. 358)
algae—a plantlike organism. (p. 366)
aliens—people who are not citizens. (p. 419)
alcohol—a drug that is produced by a chemical reaction in fruits, vegetables, and grains. (p. 340)
alcoholism—a progressive, chronic disease involving a mental and physical need for alcohol. (p. 347)
allegiance—loyalty or obligation to a person, nation, leader, or cause. (p. 43)
alternatives—other ways of thinking or acting. (p. 353)
alveoli—a cluster of tiny balloon-like air sacs with thin walls. (p. 212)
amendments—changes. (p. 455)
amino acids—small units that make up protein. (p. 226)
ammonia—a poisonous gas with a strong unpleasant smell, mainly used in cleaning products. (p. 326)
amphetamine—a drug that stimulates the central nervous system. (p. 306)
amphibious—capable of being used both on water and on land. (p. 406)
anabolic steroids—drugs that cause muscle tissue to develop at an abnormally fast rate. (p. 258)
anabolism—when energy is created and stored from food. (p. 265)

anaerobic exercise—intense physical activity that requires little oxygen but uses short bursts of energy. (p. 244)

analgesics—medicines that help relieve pain (p. 299)

analogy—a comparison between two situations, processes, etc. that is intended to show that the two are similar. (p. 129)

anorexia nervosa—an eating disorder characterized by self-starvation leading to extreme weight loss. (p. 269)

antibiotics—medicines that reduce or kill harmful bacteria in the body. (p. 299)

antibodies—proteins that attack and kill or disable specific germs that cause disease. (p. 299)

antidepressants—drugs used to prevent or reduce depression. (p. 182)

anxiety disorder—a condition in which intense anxiety or fear keeps a person from functioning normally. (p. 179)

appeals courts—review decisions made in lower district courts. (p. 524)

appellate jurisdiction—authority to hear cases that have been appealed from lower courts. (p. 453)

appetite—the psychological desire for food. (p. 222)

apportionment—dividing into portions. (p. 463)

appropriate weight—the weight that is best for your body. (p. 260)

appropriations—funds set aside for a specific use. (p. 448)

arms—weapons equipping a person or army. (p. 486)

arrhythmias—problems with the internal electrical system (that) can cause abnormal heart rhythms. (p. 291)

assert—state or express positively. (p. 148)

assertive—behaving with confidence and clearly stating your intentions. (p. 166)

Attention Deficit Hyperactivity Disorder (ADHD)—a common childhood disorder that includes symptoms such as not staying focused or paying attention, difficulty controlling behavior, and hyperactivity. (p. 305)

attitude—a state of mind. (p. 59)

auditory nerve—the part of your ear that sends information to your brain. (p. 216)

authenticate—to establish or prove as real or true. (p. 401)

B

bail—money that an accused person provides to the court as a guarantee that he or she will be present for a trial. (p. 460)

Basal Metabolic Rate (BMR)—measures how many calories you burn when you're doing nothing. (p. 266)

basic concepts—the most basic understanding. (p. 120)

bicameral legislative body—a legislative body with two branches. (p. 501)

Bill of Rights—the addition to the Constitution that consists of the first 10 amendments. (p. 457)

bills—drafts of proposed laws. (p. 445)

binge drinking—the consumption of several alcoholic drinks in a very short period of time. (p. 342)

binge eating disorder—the rapid consumption of an excessive amount of food. (p. 271)

biodegradable—capable of being slowly destroyed and broken down into very small parts by natural processes. (p. 375)

bipolar disorder—going from one extreme of feeling upbeat and energetic to feeling desolate and tired for no apparent reason. (p. 180)

blood alcohol concentration (BAC)—the amount of alcohol in a person's bloodstream. (p. 346)

blood pressure—the force of blood on the walls of blood vessels and arteries. (p. 210)

board—a group of persons having managerial, supervisory, and/or advisory powers. (p. 48)

body composition—the ratio of body fat to lean body tissue, such as bone, muscle, and fluid. (p. 261)

body image—the way you see your physical self. (p. 260)

body language—a form of nonverbal communication. (p. 162)

Body Mass Index (BMI)—a measurement that allows you to assess your body size, taking your height and weight into account. (p. 261)

brain stem—connects the cerebrum to the spinal cord. (p. 214)

bronchi—breathing tubes. (p. 212)

budget—a plan for collecting and spending money. (p. 414)

bulimia nervosa—a condition in which a person eats large amounts of food and then tries to purge. (p. 270)

bulk—the distance that the hair projects from the scalp when groomed. (p. 31)

bullying—the use of threats or physical force to intimidate and control another person. (p. 191)

bunting—a lightweight, loosely woven fabric used mainly for flags and festive decorations. (p. 392)

bureaucracies—complex systems with many departments, rules, and people in the chain of command. (p. 427)

bylaw—a rule made by an organization for its members. (p. 415)

---

calories—units of heat that allow us to measure the energy used by the body and the energy that foods supply to the body. (p. 223)

cancer—diseases in which abnormal cells divide out of control and are able to invade other tissues. (p. 329)

carbohydrates—the sugars and starches that provide your body with most of its energy. (p. 226)

carbon monoxide—a colorless, odorless, poisonous gas that is produced when tobacco burns. (p. 327); a gas that has no odor or color. (p. 364)

cardiac muscles—the muscles in the walls of your heart that contract regularly to pump blood throughout your body. (p. 208)

cardiopulmonary resuscitation (CPR)—a first aid procedure that combines rescue breaths with chest compressions to restore breathing and circulation. (p. 289)

cartilage—a strong but flexible material found in some parts of the body such as the joints, nose, and ears. (p. 206)

catabolism—when energy is released for use. (p. 265)

caucus—closed meeting of people from one political party. (p. 506)

cause and effect—the producer and the result. (p. 126)

cells—the smallest independently functioning unit of the human body. (p. 205)

censorship—banning of printed materials or films just because they contain alarming or offensive ideas. (p. 477)

census—population count. (p. 503)

cerebellum—the part of the brain that controls balance and helps coordinate muscular activities, such as walking. (p. 214)

cerebrum—the part of the brain that lets a person read, think, and remember. (p. 214)

chest cavity—includes ribs and muscles that surround your heart and lungs. (p. 213)

cholesterol—a waxy substance used by the body to build cells and hormones, and to protect nerve fibers. (p. 230)

circulatory system—the system that moves blood through the body. (p. 209)

cilia—the tiny hairs in the nose and air passages that help protect the lungs. (p. 327)

circuit—a court that covers a particular geographic area. (p. 525)

citizens—community members who owe loyalty to the government and are entitled to protection from it. (p. 411)

citizenship—the status of a person loyal to a nation, entitled to its rights and protection, while also assuming some responsibilities for service to the nation. (p. 23)

civics—the study of the rights and duties of citizens. (p. 410)

civic responsibilities—legal or social obligations to your community. (p. 410)

civil liberties—the freedoms we have to think and act without government interference or fear of unfair treatment. (p. 474)

civil rights—the rights of full citizenship and equality under the law. (p. 493)

clinical ecology—the science dealing with the harmful effects of human-made and natural materials on humans. (p. 358)

clinical depression—a major mood disorder in which people lose interest in life and can no longer find enjoyment in anything. (p. 181)

chlorofluorocarbons (CFCs)—aerosol sprays and cooling fluids for refrigeration, among other products, give off damaging chemicals. (p. 363)

closed fracture—a break that does not pierce the skin and may be difficult to identify. (p. 279)

clotting—sticking together to form a plug to stop bleeding. (p. 209)

cloture—a rule under which the Senate may limit consideration of a pending matter to no more than 30 additional hours. (p. 511)

club drugs—dangerous, illegal substances available at dance clubs and all-night parties. (p. 410)

cold turkey—stopping all at once. (p. 336)

colonists—those who settled in America from Europe. (p. 382)

coma—a deep state of unconsciousness. (p. 309)

common law—law established by previous court decisions. (p. 460)

community—a group of people united by common government, location, interest, or activity. (p. 410)
comparing and contrasting—to examine two or more people, things, or ideas in order to discover similarities and differences between or among them. (p. 127)
complete proteins—proteins that provide all of the essential amino acids. (p. 227)
comprehension—understanding the meaning of something. (p. 126)
comradeship—companionship. (p. 113)
concurrent jurisdiction—federal and state courts share jurisdiction. (p. 523)
conscience—the awareness of a desire to act properly and the awareness of guilt when improper acts are committed or intended. (p. 86)
consequences—direct results of your actions. (p. 168)
conservation—an effort to preserve and protect the environment by managing natural resources. (p. 376)
conservatives—members who want to maintain traditional values and customs. (p. 501)
constituents—people represented. (p. 503)
constitution—the system of fundamental laws and principles that prescribes the nature, functions, and limits of a government or other institution. (p. 436)
context—the setting for an event, statement, or idea, in terms of which it can be fully understood. (p. 127)
cool-down—a period of low to moderate exercise to prepare your body to end a workout session. (p. 254)
cornea—the transparent membrane that covers the pupil of the eye. (p. 215)
courtesy—polite behavior or gesture; a willingness or generosity to provide what is needed to a person or group. (p. 43)
court-martial—a military or naval court of officers and, occasionally, enlisted personnel appointed by a commander to try offenders under military law. (p. 53)
cross-training—switching between different exercises. (p. 245)
custom—a traditional practice or a usual way of doing something followed by a social group or people; a habitual practice of a person; or, the tradition or body of such practices. (p. 42)
cyberbullying—bullying via email, text or instant messaging, Facebook®, or other social media outlets. (p. 193)

D

decision-making—the process of making a choice or finding a solution. (p. 157)
deforestation—the cutting down and clearing away of trees from forests. (p. 369)
dehydration—an excessive water loss from the body. (p. 256)
democracy—government in which the people rule. (p. 415)
deoxyribonucleic acid (DNA)—the cell's "instruction manual" that controls a cell's normal growth and function. (p. 329)
deport—to expel a person back to their own country. (p. 422)
depressants—substances that slow down the body's functions and reactions. (p. 307)
desolate—the feeling of sadness, depression, and hopelessness. (p. 180)

detoxification—the physical process of freeing the body of an addictive substance. (p. 350)
devolve—pass to. (p. 450)
diabetes—a serious disease in which the body cannot properly control the amount of sugar in your blood because it does not have enough insulin. (p. 218)
diaphragm—a band of muscle tissue beneath your lungs. (p. 213)
diastolic pressure—as the heart relaxes to refill, blood pressure is at the lowest point. (pp. 210–11)
dictatorship—a government controlled by one person or a small group of people. (p. 415)
die—a block of metal used for pressing or cutting something into a shape or pattern. (p. 402)
Dietary Guidelines for Americans—recommendations about food choices for all healthy Americans age 2 and over. (p. 232)
digestion—breaking down food into smaller parts and changing it to a form that cells can use. (p. 217)
dignitary—a person of importance or someone who holds a high office. (p. 93)
Dining-In—a formal dinner for members of the military only. (p. 113)
Dining-Out—a formal dinner to which non-military guests are invited. (p. 113)
diplomat—someone who represents his or her country in dealings with other nations. (p. 518)
direct democracy—a governmental system in which all citizens meet to debate government matters and vote firsthand. (p. 415)
discipline—training expected to produce a specific character or pattern of behavior. (p. 63)
discrimination—unfair treatment based on prejudice against a certain group. (p. 493)
distress—negative stress. (p. 140)
district courts—the federal courts where trials are held and lawsuits are begun. (p. 523)
double jeopardy—people who are accused of a crime and judged not guilty may not be put on trial again for the same crime. (p. 482)
draft—the action by the government of selecting those required to serve in the military. (p. 424)
drugs—substances other than food that change the structure or function of the body or mind. (p. 296)
due process—following established legal procedures. (p. 483)
duties—things we must do. (p. 422)
duties, imposts, and excises—forms of collected taxes on products brought in or sold in the United States. (p. 446)

eardrum—a thin piece of tissue stretched across the ear canal. (p. 216)
eating disorders—extreme and damaging eating behaviors that can lead to sickness and even death. (p. 269)

ecology—the study of how living things and the environment work together and depend on each other. (p. 358)
ecosystem—the interrelationship between living organisms and their environment. (p. 366)
Electoral College—an indirect method of election. (p. 515)
electors—those who are chosen to vote for one of the major candidates. (p. 515)
electrolytes—help to control fluid levels and maintain normal potassium levels in the body. (p. 228)
emancipation—freedom from slavery. (p. 463)
eminent domain—the right of the government to take private property—usually land—for public use. (p. 483)
emoluments—payments for holding office. (p. 445)
emotional intelligence—the ability to accurately sense, assess, and manage your emotions. (p. 172)
emotional needs—needs that affect your feelings and sense of well-being. (p. 177)
emotions—your feelings created in response to thoughts, remarks, and events. (p. 172)
emphysema—a chronic medical disorder of the lungs in which the air sacs are dilated or enlarged and lack flexibility. (p. 330)
endocrine system—the system in charge of many of our body's processes, from cell and tissue growth and repair to reproductive functions and mood regulation. (p. 265)
endorphins—tranquilizing chemicals. (p. 149)
engagements—commitments. (p. 455)
en masse—as a whole group. (p. 64)
ensign—a national flag displayed on ships and aircraft, often with the special insignia of a branch or unit of the armed forces. (p. 384)
enumeration—a census or population count. (p. 442)
environment—the place in which people live and work. (p. 356)
enzyme—a special chemical that breaks down food. (p. 217)
esprit de corps—a common spirit of enthusiasm and devotion to a cause among the members of a group. (p 43)
esophagus—a long tube that connects your mouth and your stomach. (p. 218)
ethanol—a colorless liquid used in alcoholic beverages, gasoline, and cleaning solutions. (p. 340); alcohol made from corn. (p. 375)
ethics—rules of conduct that people should follow. (p. 70)
etiquette—a code of behavior or courtesy based on rules of a polite society. (p. 90)
evaluate—to determine the value of something. (p. 158)
e-waste—hazardous waste generated by the production or disposal of electronic or digital devices. (p. 368)
exclusive jurisdiction—only federal courts may hear and decide certain cases. (p. 523)
excretory system—a system of organs that work to remove waste from the body. (p. 219)
executive or military department—any agency listed under sections 101 and 102 of title 5, United States Code. (p. 391)
exercise—a planned and organized session of physical activity that you do to improve or maintain your physical fitness. (p. 241)

exertion—the act of strenuous exercise or effort. (p. 252)
exhale—breathe out. (p. 213)
extinct—an animal or plant that does not exist anymore. (p. 358)
extort—obtain something by force, threats, or other unfair means. (p. 191)
extracurricular—groups or activities not considered as part of a normal school day or curriculum. (p. 478)
extradition—the surrender of a suspected criminal or escaped prisoner to another country. (p. 454)
eye contact—direct visual contact with another person's eyes. (p. 163)

F

family therapy—counseling that seeks to improve troubled family relationships. (p. 185)
fasting—not eating for long periods. (p. 268)
fats—nutrients that provide energy and perform many functions for your body. (p. 227)
fatigue—the body losing its ability to adapt to a situation when exposed to prolonged periods of stress. (p. 144)
federalism—a form of government in which power is divided between the federal, or national, government and the states. (p. 488)
Federalists—supporters of ratification for the U.S. Constitution. (p. 437)
feedback—a response by the listener to what the speaker has said. (p. 164)
felony—a more serious crime than a misdemeanor that violates federal laws and can lead to severe punishments, such as being sentenced to prison. (p. 310)
fetal alcohol spectrum disorders (FASD)—a range (spectrum) of alcohol-related birth defects that include both physical and mental problems. (p. 347)
fiber—the part of fruits, vegetables, grains, and beans that your body cannot digest. (p. 230)
fight, flight or freeze response—the body and mind's preparation to help us to respond to a tense situation or danger. (p. 141)
filibuster—to attempt to defeat a bill through prolonged debate, sometimes referred to as "talking a bill to death." (p. 511)
first aid—the immediate emergency care given to a sick or injured person before professional medical care can be provided. (p. 274)
flexibility—the ability of your body's joints to move easily through a full range of motion. (p. 247)
foodborne illness—a sickness that results from eating food that is not safe to eat. (p. 235)
forfeited—when something is taken away as penalty for breaking a contract. (p. 484)
foundation—underlying base or support. (p. 61)
fracture—a break in a bone. (p. 279)
framers—the group of delegates who drafted the United States Constitution at the Constitutional Convention of 1787. (p. 441)

G

gang—a group of criminals who associate with one another to take part in criminal or antisocial activity. (p. 195)

gerrymandering—to divide a state or voting areas into election districts that give one political party an election majority. (p. 503)

goal setting—the process of working toward something you want to accomplish. (p. 159)

government—the people and system for exercising authority over a community. (p. 411)

grand jury—a group of citizens who make the indictment and review the evidence against the accused. (p. 482)

greenhouse gas (GHG)—any gas that absorbs infrared radiation in the atmosphere. (p. 369)

Greenwich Mean Time (GMT)—established to aid worldwide navigation and based on the zero degree north/south line running through Greenwich, England. (p. 55)

ground-level ozone—a reactive form of oxygen that emits harmful gases. (p. 359)

groundwater—the water located within the earth that supplies wells and springs. (p. 368)

H

half-staff—the position of the flag when it is one-half the distance between the top and bottom of the staff. (p. 390)

hallucinogens—drugs that distort moods, thoughts, and senses. (p. 312)

halyard—a rope for hoisting and lowering things. (p. 389)

heat cramps—painful, involuntary muscle spasms that usually occur during heavy exercise in hot weather. (p. 284)

heat exhaustion—a condition characterized by faintness, nausea, rapid heartbeat, and hot, red, dry, cold, pale, and clammy skin or heavy sweating. (p. 284)

heatstroke—a serious condition that results from heat exhaustion that remains untreated and the victim continues to overheat. (p. 284)

Heimlich maneuver—a series of abdominal thrusts to force out an obstruction blocking the airway. (p. 285).

hemp—a strong stemmed plant used for making rope; marijuana is made from types of hemp. (p. 309)

hepatitis—a disease that can cause inflammation of the liver and sometimes be fatal. (p. 275)

heraldry—a system of designing and recording of any coats of arms. (p. 401)

homicide—the killing of one human being by another. (p. 190)

Human Immunodeficiency Virus (HIV)—a virus that infects and destroys cells of the immune system. (p. 275)

hunger—the physical need for food. (p. 222)

hydration—providing enough water for somebody or something in order to reestablish or maintain a correct fluid balance. (p. 228)

hydrogen—produced from water and fossil fuels, providing a cleaner alternative. (p. 375)

hydrogen cyanide—an extremely poisonous, colorless liquid or gas with a characteristic smell of almonds. (p. 326)

hypothalamus—sometimes referred to as the "master gland" as it controls important bodily functions such as our temperature and growth during childhood. (p. 143)

I

immigrants—people who leave one country to settle permanently in another country. (p. 420)

immunity privilege—whereby they (Senators and Congressmen) cannot be sued or prosecuted for anything they say in Congress. (p. 444)

impaired—having a condition that reduces physical or mental function. (p. 156)

impeach—to put federal officials accused of wrongdoing on trial, and if necessary remove them from office. (p. 443)

impeachment—the process of removing from office a government official accused of wrongdoing. (p. 442)

income tax—a tax on people's earnings. (p. 457)

incomplete proteins—proteins that lack one or more of the essential amino acids. (p. 227)

incumbents—those currently holding a specified office. (p. 505)

indictment—charging a person with an offense. (p. 443)

inhalants—substances whose fumes are sniffed and inhaled to produce mind-altering sensations. (p. 314)

inhale—breathe in. (p. 213)

insignia—badge or mark of office or honor. (p. 32)

insurrections—rebellions. (p. 446)

instinctive thinking—relates to actions that happen instantly without your thinking consciously about them. (p. 214)

integration—a federal law requiring the equal access to schools, buildings, or organizations regardless of the color of one's skin color or ethnic background. (p. 60)

integrity—a moral compass, the inner voice, the voice of self-control, and the basis for trust. (p. 68); being honest and sincere with ourselves and with others, closely following a consistent code of ethics. (p. 73)

interpersonal communication—the exchange of thoughts, feelings, and beliefs between two or more people. (p. 162)

interpret—to attribute a particular meaning or feeling. (p. 164)

interpretation—a particular meaning or significance to something. (p. 471)

intoxicated—physically and mentally impaired by the use of alcohol. (p. 346)

iris—the part of the eye surrounding the pupil that gives your eye its color. (p. 216)

J

joint—a place in your body where two or more of your bones come together. (p. 205)
jurisdiction—authority to be the first court to hear a case. (p. 452); a court's authority to hear and decide cases. (p. 522)
jury—a group of adult citizens who listen to the evidence in a court case and decide which side is in the right. (p. 424)

L

land pollution—the depositing of solid or liquid waste materials on land or underground in a manner that can contaminate the soil and groundwater. (p. 368)
lead—a metal that occurs naturally within the earth. (p. 367)
learned emotions—emotions not common to all peoples that are expressed according to the culture and environment in which a person grows up. (p. 172)
legislature—elected lawmaking body. (p. 441)
Letters of Marque—letters giving authority to a citizen to outfit an armed ship and use it to attack enemy ships in time of war. (p. 446)
libel—if lies are printed. (p. 479)
ligaments—tough bands of stretchy tissue that hold joints together and keep organs in place. (p. 206)
light pollution—the excess amount of light in the night sky. (p. 371)
lungs—the major breathing organs in your body. (p. 212)

M

mainstream smoke—smoke that a smoker inhales and then exhales. (p. 332)
majority—more than half. (p. 441)
majority party—the political party to which more than half the members belong. (p. 506)
majority rule—when differences of opinion arise, all members of a group, community, or nation will abide by what most people want. (p. 418)
malnutrition—a condition in which the body doesn't get the nutrients it needs to grow and function properly. (p. 263)
manners—socially correct ways of acting as shown in widespread customs. (p. 90)
marrow—a type of tissue that fills in the spaces in bones. (p. 206)
mediation—both sides in a dispute working to reach a peaceful agreement. (p. 198)
medicine—a type of drug we use to treat or prevent disease and other conditions. (p. 296)
medulla—controls the body's automatic activities. (p. 214)
member of Congress—a senator, a representative, a delegate, or the resident commissioner from Puerto Rico. (p. 391)
metabolism—the process by which your body gets energy from food. (p. 242)
metaphor—a word or phrase that means one thing and is used for referring to another thing in order to emphasize their similar qualities. (p. 129)
military time—the 24-hour clock. (p. 54)

militia—a body of citizen soldiers. (p. 447)

minerals—elements needed in small quantities for forming healthy bones and teeth, and for regulating certain body processes. (p. 228)

minority party—the political party to which the rest of the members belong. (p. 506)

misdemeanor—a crime less serious than a felony that results in a less severe punishment. (p. 310)

mixed message—when your words say one thing but your body language says another. (p. 162)

mold—a type of fungus. (p. 364)

monopolize—to take exclusive ownership or control. (p. 103)

mood disorder—a disorder in which a person undergoes changes in mood that seem inappropriate or extreme. (p. 180)

morale—a mental and emotional state of enthusiasm, confidence, and loyalty in team members and followers. (p. 43); a sense of common purpose. (p. 67)

morals—our behavior, right or wrong. (p. 78)

muscle endurance—the ability of a muscle to repeatedly exert a force over a prolonged period. (p. 246)

muscle strength—the most force you can exert or weight you can lift at one time. (p. 246)

muscular system—includes the tissue that connects the bones and other parts of your body, allowing your body to move and to maintain posture. (p. 204)

N

narcolepsy—a condition that causes individuals to suffer frequent, brief, and uncontrollable deep sleep. (p. 306)

narcotics—specific drugs that are obtainable only by prescription and are used to relieve pain. (p. 304)

natural gas—a fossil fuel that is formed in the same way as coal and oil, but provides a cleaner burning fuel. (p. 375)

natural resources—the air, water, land, and living things. (p. 356)

naturalization—the legal process by which citizens from another country can choose to become an American citizen. (p. 419); procedure by which a citizen of a foreign nation becomes a citizen of the United States. (p. 446)

netiquette—the rules for communication using the Internet or electronic devices. (p. 107)

nicotine—an addictive drug found in tobacco leaves and in all tobacco products. (p. 326)

nicotine patch—a medication that allows tobacco users to give up tobacco right away while gradually cutting down on nicotine. (p. 336)

noise pollution—the constant presence of loud, disruptive noises in an area. (p. 371)

non-universal norms—values such as duties specific to one's religion toward which some people may feel a serious personal obligation. (p. 85)

norms—patterns of behavior considered acceptable or proper by a social group. (p. 84)

notehand—something written down using an abbreviated form such as symbols. (p. 121)

nutrient deficiency—a shortage of a necessary nutrient. (p. 224)

nutrients—parts of food that help the body function and grow properly. (p. 205); substances in food that your body needs. (p. 224)

nutrition—the process of using food and its substances to help your body have energy, grow, develop, and work properly. (p. 224)

nutritionist—someone who studies or is an expert in nutrition. (p. 226)

O

obese—having a body weight more than 20 percent greater than recommended for a person of a certain height. (p. 241)

obsession—an emotional state in which something seems so important that you are always thinking about it. (p. 269)

obverse—the front of. (p. 401)

open fracture—a complete break, with one or both sides of the bone piercing the skin. (p. 279)

opinion—a detailed explanation of the legal thinking behind the court's decision. (p. 526)

optic nerve—the nerve that sends the information received by the eye to the brain. (p. 216)

organization—two or more people combining efforts to do a job. (p. 15)

organization chart—a graphic description of positions and lines of authority and responsibility in an organization or unit. (p. 15)

original jurisdiction—the authority to hear cases for the first time. (p. 524)

osteoporosis—a condition marked by bone loss, brittle and fragile bones, bone pain, and increased risk of fractures to bones. (p. 263)

overdose—when you take more than the normal or recommended amount of something, usually a prescribed medicine or illegal drug. (p. 302)

over-the-counter (OTC) medicines—medicines that are safe enough to be taken without a written order from a physician. (p. 297)

overweight—to weigh more than the appropriate weight range for gender, height, age, body frame, and growth pattern. (p. 262)

ozone layer—a protective layer in the atmosphere that absorbs harmful ultraviolet light from the sun. (p. 362)

P

page—a student whose job is to help a member of the Congress. (p. 400)

panic—a feeling of sudden, intense fear. (p. 175)

Parkinson's disease—a progressive nervous disorder where the individual shows symptoms of trembling hands, lifeless face, and a slow, shuffling walk. (p. 306)

particulates—tiny pieces of solid materials such as dust, ash, dirt, and soot that float in the air. (p. 363)

partisan politics—the showing of favoritism to one's own party within Congress. (p. 511)

passage—a short section of a book, article, poem, or music. (p. 436)

patriot—someone who has strong feelings of love, respect, and duty toward their country. (p. 383)

peer mediation—a process in which trained students help other students find fair ways to resolve conflicts and settle their differences. (p. 198)

Percent Daily Value—the percent of the recommended daily amount of a nutrient provided in a serving of food. (p. 236)

peripheral nervous system—a network of nerves outside the central nervous system that connects limbs and organs to the central nervous system. (p. 214)

personality disorders—a variety of psychological conditions that affect a person's ability to get along with others. (p. 180)

pesticides—products that contain chemicals that kill insects, and are also used to control weeds, rodents, mildew, and germs. (p. 367)

petition—a formal request. (p. 479)

pharmaceutical waste—the byproduct of drugs and medicines used by humans and animals. (p. 367)

pharmacist—someone trained and licensed to prepare and sell medicines that a doctor prescribes. (p. 297)

philosophy—the study of people's most fundamental and basic beliefs and how these beliefs are justified. (p. 70)

physical activity—any movements that require your large muscle groups to work. (p. 149); any kind of movement that uses up energy. (p. 241)

physical dependence—a type of addiction in which the body itself (rather than just the mind, as with psychological dependence) feels a direct need for a drug. (p. 314); a type of addiction in which the body feels a direct need for a drug. (p. 331)

physical fitness—the ability to perform moderate to vigorous levels of activity, and to respond to physical demands without excessive fatigue. (p. 241)

place card—a name card for a formal dinner. (p. 102)

platelets—small particles in the blood that help clotting. (p. 209)

platforms—formal declarations of the things for which a group (each party) stands and appeals to the public—especially voters—to support. (p. 501)

political party—a group of individuals with broad common interests who organize to support candidates for office and determine public policy. (p. 418)

pollutants—substances that are harmful to your environment. (p. 356)

pollution—the presence of harmful materials in our soil, water, and air. (p. 357)

poll taxes—required voters to pay a sum of money before casting a ballot. (p. 493)

Preamble—an introduction that states the goals and purposes of the government. (p. 438)

precedent—a model upon which to base decisions on similar cases for all courts and agencies within the district. (p. 526)

prejudice—an unfair opinion or judgment of a particular group of people. (p. 166)

President of the Mess—usually the cadet group/wing commander hosting the Dining-in. (p. 114)

President Pro Tempore—the presiding officer of the Senate who serves when the vice president is absent. (p. 443)

prescription medicines—medicines that can be sold only with a written order by a physician. (p. 297)

preview—to review any notes or other material to help prepare for the day's assignment before you get to class. (p. 121)

primary emotions—common emotions felt and expressed by everyone in all cultures. (p. 172)

probable cause—police must have a reasonable basis to believe a person is linked to a crime. (p. 459)

procrastination—to put off doing something, especially on a regular basis. (p. 154)

professional—one who conforms to a technical or ethical standard of a profession. (p. 67)

proteins—nutrients your body uses to build, repair, and maintain cells and tissues. (p. 226)

pro tempore—temporary or for the time being. (p. 507)

protocol—a code of precedence in rank and status and of correct procedure in ceremonies; a form of etiquette observed in ceremonies; a combination of good manners and common sense that facilitates effective communication. (p. 113)

psychiatrist—a medical doctor who treats mental health problems. (p. 187)

psychological dependence—an addiction in which the mind sends the body a message that it needs more of a drug. (p. 312, 331)

psychologist—a mental health professional who is trained and licensed by the state to provide counseling. (p. 187)

psychology—the study of the mind and of behavior. (p. 70)

psychosomatic response—a physical reaction that results from stress rather than from an injury or illness. (p. 145)

psychotherapist—someone who treats individuals with mental disorders by using intense counseling methods. (p. 182)

public policy—a course of government action to achieve community goals. (p. 414)

pulse (heart rate)—regular beat of your heart. (pp. 210); the regular expansion and contraction of an artery, caused by the heart pumping blood through the body. (p. 247)

Q

Quakers—a Christian group whose members avoid violence and hold simple religious services. (p. 492)

quartered—provided living accommodations. (p. 459)

quorum—minimum number of members that must be present to conduct sessions. (p. 444)

R

radiation—energy that comes from a source and travels through space in the form of waves. (p. 372)
radon—a natural, radioactive gas in the ground. (p. 363)
rape—any kind of unlawful sexual intercourse against a person's will. (p. 199)
ratification—an approval or sanction. (p. 401); the process by which an amendment is approved. (p. 455)
receptor cells—cells that receive information. (p. 217)
recovery—the process of learning to live an alcohol-free life. (p. 349)
recycling—reusing materials instead of buying new ones. (p. 375)
reflexes—automatic responses to something such as heat or pain. (p. 215)
refusal skills—strategies that help you say no, effectively. (p. 165)
relaxation response—the body's action to release tension, such as a decrease in our heart rate and breathing rate, and an increasing sense of well-being. (p. 142)
receiving line—a group of people, including the host and honored guests, who stand in line and individually welcome guests attending a function. (p. 91)
remand—to send the case back to the lower court to be tried again. (p. 525)
representative democracies—citizens choose a smaller group to represent them, make laws, and govern on their behalf. (p. 415)
reprisal—taking by force property or territory belonging to another country or its citizens. (p. 446)
resilience—the ability to adapt to and recover from disappointment, difficulty, or crisis. (p. 175)
resistance—your body adapting to the rush created by alarm and reacting to the stressor. (p. 143)
resolution—a formal expression of the majority at a meeting and usually as a result of a vote. (p. 445)
resolutions—formal statements expressing lawmakers' opinions or decisions. (p. 510)
respiration—breathing in oxygen and breathing out carbon dioxide. (p. 212)
responsibilities—things we should do; these are obligations that we fulfill voluntarily. (p. 422)
retreat—signals the end of the official duty day and also serves as a ceremony for paying respect to the flag. (p. 393)
reveille—the signal for the start of the official duty day. (p. 393)
revenue—income raised by government. (p. 445)
riders—completely unrelated amendments. (p. 511)
RHIP—rank has its privileges. (p. 50)
roll-call vote—members voice their votes in turn as an official records them. (p. 513)
RSVP—you must reply to the hosts to let them know if you can or cannot attend the function to which you've been invited. (p. 104)
rule—drawing a line used to separate columns or create borders. (p. 124)
runoffs—water that drains from land into streams and other water sources. (p. 366)

S

saturated fats—fats that are solid at room temperature. (p. 227)
saliva—a liquid in your mouth. (p. 217)
schizophrenia—a severe mental disorder in which people lose contact with reality. (p. 180); a very serious mental illness in which someone cannot think or behave normally and often experiences delusions. (p. 306)
search warrant—a court order allowing law enforcement officers to search a subject's home or business and take specific items as evidence. (p. 482)
secondhand smoke—air that has been contaminated by tobacco smoke. (p. 332)
sedentary—a lot of sitting and very little exercise. (p. 244)
segregation—the social separation of the races. (p. 493)
selective service system—the agency that keeps records and executes the draft if it is ever needed. (p. 424)
self-incrimination—a speech or action that suggests your own guilt, especially during court testimony. (p. 482)
seniority—years of service. (p. 509)
sense organs—specialized parts of your body that function as receivers of outside information. (p. 215)
sewage—the waste material carried from toilets and drains. (p. 367)
shellfish—ocean creatures that have a hard shell around them; examples are crabs, mussels, and oysters. (p. 366)
shock—a life-threatening condition in which the circulatory system fails to deliver enough blood to vital tissues and organs. (p. 287)
shyness—a feeling of apprehension and anxiety in social situations, especially unfamiliar people and situations. (p. 175)
side effect—any effect of a medicine other than the one intended. (p. 300)
sidestream smoke—smoke given off by the burning end of a cigarette, cigar, or pipe. (p. 332)
skeletal muscles—voluntary muscles. (p. 208)
skeletal system—your body's system of connected bones, or your skeleton. (p. 204)
skin—sense organ for touch. (p. 217)
slander—if lies are spoken. (p. 479)
smog—a brownish haze that forms when the pollutants in the air react to sunlight. (p. 359)
smooth muscles—involuntary muscles. (p. 207)
sobriety—living without alcohol. (p. 350)
socialism—a political system in which property and wealth are controlled by the citizens and evenly distributed. (p. 491)
society—a group of people living together in organized communities with shared laws, traditions, and values. (p. 410)
solar energy—a source of energy that comes directly from the sun. (p. 374)
special-interest groups—organizations made of up people with some common interest who try to influence government decisions. (p. 510)

spice—a term for a variety of mixtures of plant material and chemicals that create mind-altering effects like marijuana. (p. 311)
spinal cord—the major pathway your brain uses to send messages to your body. (p. 214)
spine, or vertebral column—the center of your skeleton. (p. 205)
sports conditioning—regular physical activity or exercise to strengthen and condition muscles for a particular sport. (p. 255)
sprain—a condition in which the ligaments that hold the joints in position are stretched or torn. (p. 278)
standards—widely recognized and expected levels of value or measurement. (p. 22)
standing committees—permanent committees that continue their work from session to session. (p. 507)
standing vote—those in favor of a bill stand to be counted, and then those against it stand to be counted. (p. 513)
stereotyping—having an exaggerated or oversimplified belief about a group of people. (p. 166)
stilted—stiffly or artificially dignified or formal, pompous, or lofty. (p. 107)
stimulants—substances that speed up the body's functions. (p. 305)
street drug—any drug made or sold illegally. (p. 308)
strength—the ability of your muscles to exert a force. (p. 246)
stress—your body's response to change. (p. 140)
stress-management skills—ways to prevent and overcome problems related to stress. (p. 147)
stressor—anything that causes stress. (p. 141)
subpoena—a court order requiring someone to appear in court. (p. 527)
sudden cardiac arrest (SCA)—a condition in which the heart suddenly and unexpectedly stops beating. (p. 291)
suffrage—the right to vote. (p. 465)
suicide—the act of intentionally killing oneself. (p. 182)
sulfur dioxide—a poisonous gas that gets into the air from the burning of fossil fuels. (p. 358)
symbolism—the use of symbols to represent a thing, idea, or quality. (p. 402)
symptom—a bodily reaction that signals an illness or a physical problem. (p. 178)
synthetic—made from artificial materials or substances, not natural ones. (p. 311)
systolic pressure—the maximum pressure placed on your arteries. (p. 210)

T

taboo—a prohibition excluding something from use, approach, or mention. (p. 53)
tar—a dark, thick, sticky liquid that forms when tobacco burns. (p 327)
taste buds—receptors for each kind of taste. (p. 217)
temperance—reducing the sale and use of alcohol. (p. 492)
tendon—a strong set of fibers joining muscle to bone or muscle to muscle. (p. 208)
tendonitis—an inflammation of a tendon. (p. 209)
term—meeting period. (p. 500)

terrorist—someone who seeks to use violence or the fear or threat of violence to send a message or to get what he or she wants. (p. 413)
test anxiety—the excessive worry about doing well on a test. (p. 134)
testimony—the evidence that a witness gives in a court of law. (p. 482)
THC (tetrahydrocannabinol)—the main mind-altering chemical in marijuana. (p. 309)
therapeutic—anything used in the treatment of disease or disorders. (p. 326)
therapy—treatment. (p. 185)
time management—using your time wisely. (p. 152)
tinnitus—a condition in which a ringing, buzzing, whistling, roaring, hissing, or other sound is heard in the ear. (p. 217)
title—a formal name given to a person because of office, grade/rank, hereditary privilege, or as a mark of respect. (p. 51)
tolerance—the ability to accept others' differences and allow them to be who they are without your expressing disapproval. (p. 166); a condition in which a person's body becomes used to the effect of a medicine and needs greater and greater amounts of it in order for it to be effective. (p. 300); respecting and accepting others, regardless of their beliefs, practices, or differences. (p. 426)
tourniquet—a constricting band placed around an arm or leg to control bleeding. (p. 288)
toxins—poisonous substances that cause disease. (p. 368)
trachea, or windpipe—a long tube running from your nose to your chest. (p. 212)
***trans* fats**—artificial fats made when hydrogen gas reacts with oil. (p. 230)
treason—violation of the allegiance owed by a person to his or her own country; for example, by aiding an enemy. (p. 453)
tribunals—courts of law. (p. 446)
triglycerides—the chemical form in which most fat exists in food and the chief form of fat storage in the body. (p. 227)
tsunami—a series of ocean waves caused by sudden displacement of the ocean floor, usually from an earthquake. (p. 372)

U

unbiased—free of favoritism. (p. 71)
underage drinking—when anyone under the minimum legal drinking age of 21 drinks alcohol. (p. 343)
underweight—to weigh less than the appropriate weight range for gender, height, age, body frame, and growth pattern. (p. 262)
uniform—-a distinctive mode of dress. (p. 23)
union—the upper left corner of the flag, representing a group of states that join together. (p. 382)
universal norms—the normal beliefs of people in most cultures. (p. 84)
universal precautions—actions taken to prevent the spread of disease by treating all blood as if it were contaminated. (p. 275)
unsaturated fats—fats that remain liquid at room temperature. (p. 227)

V

vacancies—offices or positions that are unfilled or unoccupied. (p. 464)
vaccines—medicines that prevent a disease from developing. (p. 299)
values—the beliefs, ideals, and standards that guide the way a person lives. (p. 157)
value system—our set of ideals, beliefs, interests, likes, and dislikes that we use every day to make decisions. (p. 76)
ventricular fibrillation (v-fib)—the ventricles (the heart's lower chambers) don't beat normally. (p. 291)
veto—to exercise the right to reject a bill or measure. (p. 445)
victim—someone who is hurt by somebody or something, especially in a crime, accident, or disaster. (p. 200)
villi—tiny, fingerlike projections that absorb the food that has been broken down into chemicals. (p. 218)
violence—any act that causes physical or psychological harm to a person or damage to property. (p. 190)
vitamins—substances needed in small quantities to help regulate body functions. (p. 228)
voice vote—those in favor say "Yea" and those against say, "Nay." (p. 513)
volunteerism—the practice of offering your time and services to others without payment. (p. 428)

W

warm-up—a period of low to moderate exercise to prepare your body for more vigorous activity. (p. 252)
warrants—documents that give police particular powers. (p. 459)
welfare—health, prosperity, and happiness. (p. 427)
wing—group formed as an affiliate or subordinate of a larger organization. (p. 501)
withdrawal—the physical and psychological symptoms that occur when someone stops using an addictive substance. (p. 317)

zero tolerance policy—a policy that makes no exceptions to anybody for any reason. (p. 198)

Index

Note: Page numbers followed by *b* indicate boxed text.

B

C

D

E

F

G

H

I

J

K

L

M

N

Q

R

Q

R

S

T

U

V

W

Y

Z